MATTHEW
COMMENTARY

THE FOUR GOSPELS

The Training
Centre

A companion volume

Matthew Henry's Commentary: The Acts to Revelation

MATTHEW HENRY'S COMMENTARY

THE FOUR GOSPELS

edited and introduced by
David Winter

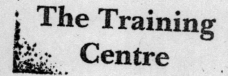

HODDER AND STOUGHTON
LONDON SYDNEY AUCKLAND TORONTO

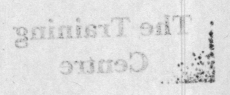

CONTENTS

INTRODUCTION

Why another edition of Matthew Henry's Commentary on the New Testament—and why an abridged one, at that? They are perfectly reasonable questions. It is hard to think of another area of knowledge where a "text book" nearly two hundred years old would be considered worth re-issuing for general use. Yet the undeniable fact is that this monumental work from another age—and another world, almost—has maintained its appeal for the modern reader. In terms of sales, and in terms of genuine affection and spiritual impact, there is probably no Bible commentary to equal it . . . for all that it represents a voice from the distant past.

It is worth asking why this should be so. After all, there are plenty of better commentaries, as commentaries. Since Henry's day much has come to light about biblical manuscripts, about exegesis, and about New Testament Greek. In some of these areas, Matthew Henry is, frankly, an unreliable guide. His style—repetitive and at times irritatingly over-elaborate —is hardly calculated to endear him to the modern reader. And at times he is quite inexcusably prejudiced, not to say bigoted—Baptists and "Papists" get very short shrift, for example.

Yet, having lived with this Commentary for the best part of two years, I have to record that Matthew Henry has done more for my "soul" than any modern Commentary. However intrusive the voice of Henry, the voice of God comes through: and comes through with a force and clarity unequalled in the most minutely researched, meticulously scholarly modern equivalent. The only commentary of modern times which is in any way comparable is William Temple's magnificent devotional commentary on St. John's Gospel. There, too, God speaks, the heart is warmed, the spirit rises.

Matthew Henry's idea of a commentary is rather different from that of most modern theologians. Questions of authorship, textual criticism, historical background, dating and literary sources do not concern him very much. Unlike his successors, he is less concerned with why, when and how. His overriding concern is *what*—what has God said? What does it mean (in general), and what does it mean *to me*? His aim is to help the reader hear the voice of God through the Scriptures, and authorship, text, history and background are only important as they serve that end.

So the effect of reading Matthew Henry is to be directed to the Scriptures themselves, and especially the Scriptures applied to the human condition. Nobody has worked out how many embryonic sermons there are to a page of this Commentary, but no preacher ever came up dry from Henry's well. That alone would be reason enough for keeping it in print.

But why in an abridged version? What is gained by cutting out great swathes of a book that has been such a help to so many? The answer, I think, lies in the different uses to which this work can be put. There are undoubtedly readers who will find the entire work—all the millions of words of it—immensely fascinating and helpful. But for most readers today, the need is for something more precise and streamlined. They want the devotional insights, the flashes of illumination that make a familiar parable, or an obscure verse in Romans, come across with totally new force. They want help in preparing talks and sermons, and help in applying the message of the New Testament to their lives as individuals, and as men and women in society. But they do not want to have to plough through pages of polemic, or illustration piled upon illustration, or lengthy examples drawn from the master-servant relationship in the time of Queen Anne. Much can go with no loss at all to the general reader of today.

So in this edited version the reader will find the essential Matthew Henry, but not all the trimmings. Where he repeated himself—as he often did in covering identical passages in Matthew, Mark and Luke, for instance—it has been removed. Passages of purely antiquarian interest have also gone. So have passages where he argues through problems which are largely irrelevant today—slavery, or the courtesies due to the gentry.

The polemical passages caused some heart-searching, because clearly Matthew Henry felt strongly about some issues which divide Christians, and it is misleading, in a way, to excise his harsh words and sometimes sweeping judgments. On the other hand, religious controversy was conducted in his day with a degree of vituperation and even venom which most of us would regard as sub-Christian today. We are used to a more muted, apologetic style of dissent and have, perhaps, learnt that some things which once seemed of the essence of the Gospel are not in fact so.

In the event, the polemic has, for the most part, been omitted from this edition. With it, necessarily, has gone some valuable material relating to controversies about baptism, the Christian ministry, confirmation, ordination and the papacy. On the other hand, Matthew Henry's positive views on these subjects will be crystal clear to the discerning reader.

What we are left with, in the end, is a work of rare spiritual quality, one of the few books on the Bible which drives the reader all the time back to the scriptural text, and magnifies its message without distorting it. Time and again, and sometimes in the unlikeliest places, Matthew Henry strikes true mystical gold. As often, he puts an uncannily perceptive finger on human frailty and inconsistency. But always the Scripture itself is the source and inspiration. He is a servant of the Word.

THE GOSPEL ACCORDING TO

ST. MATTHEW

We have before us *the Gospel according to St. Matthew*. The penman was by birth a Jew, by calling a publican, till Christ commanded his attendance, and then he left *the receipt of custom*, to follow him, and was one of those that accompanied him *all the time that the Lord Jesus went in and out, beginning from the baptism of John unto the day that he was taken up*, Acts i. 21, 22. He was therefore a competent witness of what he has here recorded. He is said to have written this history about eight years after Christ's ascension.

CHAPTER ONE

THE GENEALOGY (*vv*. 1–17)

In calling Christ *the son of David*, and *the son of Abraham* (*v*. 1), Matthew shows that God is faithful to his promise, and will make good every word that he has spoken; and this, 1. Though the performance be long deferred. Note, Delays of promised mercies, though they exercise our patience, do not weaken God's promise. 2. Though it begin to be despaired of. This *son of David*, and *son of Abraham*, who was to be the glory of his Father's house, was born when the seed of Abraham was a despised people, recently become tributary to the Roman yoke, and when the house of David was buried in obscurity.

Note, God's time for the performance of his promises is when it labours under the greatest improbabilities.

Some particulars we may observe in this genealogy.

1. The line is brought down, not to Mary the mother of our Lord, but to *Joseph the husband of Mary* (*v*. 16); for the Jews always reckoned their genealogies by the males: yet Mary was of the same tribe and family with Joseph, so that, both by his mother and by his supposed father, he was of the house of David; yet his interest in that dignity is derived by Joseph, to whom really according to the flesh he had no relation, to show that the kingdom of the Messiah is not founded in a natural descent from David.

2. The centre in whom all these lines meet is *Jesus, who is called Christ, v*. 16. *Jesus* is called *Christ*, that is, the *Anointed*, the same with the *Hebrew* name *Messiah*. He is called *Messiah the Prince* (Dan. ix. 25), and often God's *Anointed* (Ps. ii. 2). Under this character he was expected: *Art thou the Christ*—the *anointed one?—anointed with the oil of gladness above his fellows*; and from this name of his, which is as ointment poured forth, all his followers are called *Christians*, for they also have *received the anointing*.

THE BIRTH OF JESUS
(*vv.* 18–25)

The mystery of Christ's incarnation is to be adored, not pried into. If we *know not the way of the Spirit* in the formation of common persons, nor *how the bones are formed in the womb of* any one *that is with child* (Eccles. xi. 5), much less do we know how the blessed Jesus was formed in the womb of the blessed virgin. Some circumstances attending the birth of Christ we find here which are not in Luke, though it is more largely recorded there. Here we have:

I. Mary's espousals to Joseph. Mary, the mother of our Lord, *was espoused to Joseph*, not completely married, but contracted. Christ was born of a virgin, but a betrothed virgin, 1. To put respect upon the marriage state, and to recommend it as *honourable among all*, against that doctrine of devils which *forbids to marry*, and places perfection in the single state. Who more highly favoured than Mary was in her espousals? 2. To save the credit of the blessed virgin, which otherwise would have been exposed. 3. That the blessed virgin might have one to be the guide of her youth, the companion of her solitude and travels, a partner in her cares, and a help meet for her.

II. Her pregnancy of the promised seed; *before they came together*, she *was found with child*, which really was *of the Holy Ghost*. The marriage was deferred so long after the contract that she appeared to be *with child* before the time came for the solemnizing of the marriage, though she was contracted before she conceived. Probably, it was after her return from her cousin Elizabeth, with whom she continued *three months* (Luke i. 56), that she was perceived by Joseph to be with child, and did not herself deny it. Note, Those in whom Christ is formed will show it: it will be *found to be* a work of God which he will own. Now we may well imagine, what a perplexity this might justly occasion to the blessed virgin. Yet we do not find that she tormented herself about it; but, being conscious of her own innocence, she kept her mind calm and easy, and committed her cause to *him that judgeth righteously*.

III. Joseph's perplexity, and his care what to do in this case. We may well imagine what a great trouble and disappointment it was to him to find one he had such an opinion of, and value for, come under the suspicion of such a heinous crime.

Observe, 1. The extremity which he studied to avoid. He was *not willing to make her a public example*. He might have done so; for, by the law, a *betrothed virgin*, if she played the harlot, was to be stoned to death, Deut. xxii. 23, 24. How good is it to *think on things*, as Joseph did here! Were there more of deliberation in our censures and judgments, there would be more of mercy and moderation in them.

Some persons of a rigorous temper would blame Joseph for his clemency: but it is here spoken of to his praise; because *he was a just man*, therefore he was not willing to expose her. He was a *religious, good man*; and therefore inclined to be merciful as God is, and to *forgive* as one that was *forgiven*. Note, It becomes us, in many cases, to be gentle towards those that come under suspicion of having offended, to hope the best concerning them, and make the best of that which at first appears bad, in hopes that it may prove better.

2. The expedient he found out for avoiding this extremity. He was *minded to put her away privily*, that is, to give a bill of divorce into her hand before two witnesses, and so to hush up the matter among themselves.

IV. Joseph's discharge from this perplexity by a messenger sent from heaven, *vv*. 20, 21. *While he thought on these things* and knew not what to determine, God graciously directed him what to do, and made him easy. Note, Those who would have direction from God must *think on things* themselves, and consult with themselves. It is the *thoughtful*, not the *unthinking*, whom God will guide. God's comforts most delight the soul *in the multitude* of its perplexed *thoughts*. The message was sent to Joseph by an *angel of the Lord*, probably the same angel that brought to Mary the tidings of the conception—the angel Gabriel. This angel appeared to Joseph *in a dream* when he was asleep, as God sometimes spoke unto the fathers.

1. Joseph is here *directed* to proceed in his intended marriage. *Fear not to take Mary for thy wife*; so it may be read. From whatever cause his fears arose, they were all silenced with this word.

2. He is here *informed* concerning that *holy thing* with which his espoused wife was now pregnant. That which is conceived in her is of a divine original. He is so far from being in danger of sharing in an impurity by marrying her, that he will thereby share in the highest dignity he is capable of. Two things he is told,

(1) That she had conceived *by the power of the Holy Ghost*; not by the power of nature.

(2) That she should bring forth *the Saviour of the world* (*v*. 21). *She shall bring forth a Son*; what he shall be is intimated,

[1] In the name that should be given to her Son: *Thou shalt call his name Jesus, a Saviour*. Jesus is the same name as Joshua, the termination only being changed, for the sake of conforming it to the Greek. Christ is our Joshua; both the *Captain of our salvation*, and the *High Priest of our profession*, and, in both, our Saviour—a Joshua who comes in the stead of Moses, and does that for us which *the law could not do, in that it was weak*.

[2] In the reason of that name: *For he shall save his people from their sins*; not the nation of the Jews only (he came to *his own*, and they *received him not*), but all who were given him by *the Father's choice*, and all who have given themselves to him by *their own*.

V. The fulfilling of the scripture in all this. This evangelist, writing among the Jews, more frequently observes this than any other of the evangelists. Here the Old Testament prophecies had their accomplishment in our Lord Jesus, by which it appears that this was he that should come, and we are to look for no other; for this was he *to whom all the prophets bore witness*.

1. The sign given is that the

Messiah shall be *born of a virgin* (Isa. vii. 14). *A virgin shall conceive*, and, by her, he shall be manifested *in the flesh*. The word *Almah* signifies a *virgin* in the strictest sense, such as Mary professes herself to be (Luke i. 34), *I know not a man*; nor had it been any such wonderful sign as it was intended for, if it had been otherwise. It was intimated from the beginning that the Messiah should be born of a virgin, when it was said that he should be the *seed of the woman*; so the seed of the woman as not to be the seed of any man. Christ was born of a virgin not only because his birth was to be *supernatural*, and altogether extraordinary, but because it was to be *spotless*, and pure, and without any stain of sin.

2. The truth proved by this sign is, that he is the Son of God, and the Mediator between God and man: for *they shall call his name Immanuel*; that is, he shall be *Immanuel*; as when it is said, *He shall be called*, it is meant, he shall be, *the Lord our righteousness*. *Immanuel* signifies *God with us*; a mysterious name, but very precious; God *incarnate* among us, and so God *reconcilable* to us, at peace with us, and taking us into covenant and communion with himself. By the light of *nature*, we see God as a God *above us*; by the light of the *law*, we see him as a God *against us*; but by the light of the gospel, we see him as *Immanuel*, God *with us*, in our own nature, and (which is more) in our interest. Herein the Redeemer *commended his love*. With Christ's name, *Immanuel*, we may compare the name given to the gospel church (Ezek. xlviii. 35).

Jehovah Shammah—The Lord is there; the Lord of hosts is with us.

VI. Joseph's obedience to the divine precept (*v.* 24). *Being raised from sleep* by the impression which the dream made upon him, *he did as the angel of the Lord had bidden him*, though it was contrary to his former sentiments and intentions; *he took unto him his wife*; he did it speedily, without delay, and cheerfully, without dispute; he was not disobedient to the heavenly vision. Extraordinary direction like this we are not now to expect; but God has still ways of making known his mind in doubtful cases, by hints of providence, debates of conscience, and advice of faithful friends; by each of these, applying the general rules of the written word, we should, therefore, in all the steps of our life, particularly the great turns of it, such as this of Joseph's, take direction from God, and we shall find it safe and comfortable to do as he bids us.

VII. The accomplishment of the divine promise (*v.* 25). *She brought forth her first-born* son. The circumstances of it are more largely related, Luke ii. 1, etc.

It is here further observed, 1. That Joseph, though he solemnized the marriage with Mary, his espoused wife, kept at a distance from her while she was with child of this Holy thing; *he knew her not till she had brought him forth*. 2. That Christ was the *first-born*; and so he might be called though his mother had not any other children after him, according to the language of scripture. Nor is it without a mystery that Christ is called her *first-born*, for he is the *first-born of every creature*, that is, the Heir of all things; and he is the *first-born among many brethren*, that in all things he may have the preeminence.

CHAPTER TWO

THE WISE MEN (*vv.* 1–12)

It was a *mark of humiliation* put upon the Lord Jesus that, though he was the *Desire of all nations*, yet his coming into the world was little observed and taken notice of, his birth was obscure and unregarded: herein he emptied himself, and made himself of no reputation.

The first who took notice of Christ after his birth were the shepherds (Luke ii. 15, etc.), who saw and heard glorious things concerning him, and *made them known abroad*, to the amazement of all that heard them, *vv.* 17, 18. After that, Simeon and Anna spoke of him, by the Spirit, to all that were disposed to heed what they said, Luke ii. 38. Now, one would think, these hints should have been taken by the men of Judah and the *inhabitants of Jerusalem*, and they should with both arms have embraced the long-looked-for Messiah; but, for aught that appears, he continued nearly two years after at Bethlehem, and no further notice was taken of him till these wise men came. Observe,

I. When this enquiry was made concerning Christ. It was *in the days of Herod the king*. This Herod was an Edomite, made king of Judea by Augustus and Antonius, the then chief rulers of the Roman state, a man made up of falsehood and cruelty; yet he was complimen-

ted with the title of *Herod the Great*. Christ was born in the 35th year of his reign.

II. Who and what these *wise men* were; they are here called *Magicians*. Some take it in a good sense; the *Magi* among the *Persians* were their philosophers and their priests; nor would they admit any one for their king who had not first been enrolled among the *Magi*; others think they dealt in unlawful arts; the word is used of Simon, the sorcerer (Acts viii. 9, 11), and of Elymas, the sorcerer (Acts xiii. 6), nor does the scripture use it in any other sense. Well, whatever sort of wise men they were before, now they began to be *wise men* indeed when they set themselves to enquire after Christ.

This we are sure of, 1. That they were Gentiles, and not belonging to the commonwealth of Israel. The Jews regarded not Christ, but these Gentiles enquired him out. 2. That they were *scholars*. They dealt in arts, curious arts; good scholars should be good Christians, and *then* they complete their *learning* when they *learn Christ*. 3. That they were *men of the east*, who were noted for their *soothsaying*, Isa. ii. 6. Arabia is called the land of *the east* (Gen. xxv. 6), and the *Arabians* are called *men of the east*, Judg. vi. 3.

III. What induced them to make this enquiry. The birth of Christ was notified to the Jewish shepherds by *an angel*, to the Gentile philosophers by a *star*; to both God spoke in their own language, and in the way they were best acquainted with. Some think that the light which the shepherds saw shining round about them, the night after Christ was born, was the very same which to the wise men, who lived at such a distance, appeared as a star; but this we cannot easily admit, because the same star which they had seen in the *east* they saw a great while after, leading them to the house where Christ lay; it was a candle set up on purpose to guide them to Christ. The idolaters worshipped the stars as the *host of heaven*, especially the *eastern* nations, whence the planets have the names of their idol-gods; we read of a particular *star* they had in veneration, Amos v. 26. Thus the stars that had been misused came to be put to the right use, to lead men to Christ; the gods of the heathen became his servants.

IV. How they prosecuted this enquiry. So impatient were they to be better acquainted with him, that they took a long journey on purpose to enquire after him. Note, Those who truly desire to know Christ, and find him, will not regard pains or perils in seeking after him. *Then shall we know, if we follow on to know the Lord.*

V. How this enquiry was treated at Jerusalem. News of it at last came to court; and *when Herod heard it he was troubled, v. 3.* He could not be a stranger to the prophecies of the *Old Testament*, concerning the Messiah and his kingdom, and the times fixed for his appearing by Daniel's weeks; but, having himself reigned so long and so successfully, he began to hope that those promises would for ever fail, and that his kingdom would be established and perpetuated in spite of them. What a damp therefore must it needs be upon

him, to hear talk of this King being born, now, when the time fixed for his appearing had come!

But though Herod, an Edomite, was troubled, one would have thought Jerusalem should rejoice greatly to hear that her King comes; yet, it seems, *all Jerusalem*, except the few there that *waited for the consolation of Israel, were troubled with* Herod, and were apprehensive of I know not what ill consequences of the birth of this new king, that it would involve them in war, or restrain their lusts; they, for their parts, desired no king but Herod; no, not the Messiah himself.

VI. What assistance they met with in this enquiry from the scribes and the priests, *vv.* 4–6. It was generally known that Christ should be *born at Bethlehem* (John vii. 42); but Herod would have counsel's opinion upon it, and therefore applies himself to the proper persons; and *demands of them* what was the place, according to the scriptures of the Old Testament, *where Christ should be born*? Many a good question is put with an ill design, so was this by Herod.

The priests and scribes agree that the Messiah must be *born in Bethlehem, the city of David,* here called *Bethlehem of Judea,* to distinguish it from another city of the same name in the land of Zebulun, Josh. xix. 15. *Bethlehem* signifies *the house of bread*; the fittest place for him to be born in who is the true manna, *the bread which came down from heaven,* which was *given for the life of the world.* The proof they produce is taken from Mic. v. 2, where it is foretold that though

Bethlehem be little among the thousands of Judah (so it is in *Micah*), no very populous place, yet it shall be found *not the least among the princes of Judah* (so it is here); for Bethlehem's honour lay not, as that of other cities, in the multitude of the people, but in the magnificence of the princes it produced.

VII. The bloody project and design of Herod, occasioned by this enquiry, *vv.* 7, 8.

Now, 1. See how cunningly he laid the project (*vv.* 7, 8). *He privily called the wise men,* to talk with them about this matter. He would not openly own his fears and jealousies; it would be his disgrace to let the wise men know them, and dangerous to let the people know them. Sinners are often tormented with secret fears, which they keep to themselves. Herod learns of the wise men the *time when the star appeared,* that he might take his measures accordingly; and then employs them to enquire further, and bids them bring him an account.

2. See how strangely he was fooled and infatuated in this, that he trusted it with the wise men, and did not choose some other managers, that would have been true to his interests. It was but seven miles from Jerusalem; how easily might he have sent spies to watch the wise men, who might have been as soon there to destroy the child as they to worship him!

VIII. We have here (*vv.* 9–12) the wise men's humble attendance upon this new-born *King of the Jews,* and the honours they paid him.

See how they found out Christ by the same star that they had seen in their own country, *vv.* 9, 10. Observe, 1. How graciously God directed them. By the first appearance of the star they were given to understand where they might enquire for this King, and then it disappeared, and they were left to take the usual methods for such an enquiry. Note, Extraordinary helps are not to be expected where ordinary means are to be had. Well, they had traced the matter as far as they could; they were upon their journey to Bethlehem, but that is a populous town, where shall they find him when they come thither? Here they were at a loss, at their wit's end, but not at their faith's end; they believed that God, who had brought them thither by his word, would not leave them there; nor did he; for, behold, *the star which they saw in the east went before them.* Note, If we go on as far as we can in the way of our duty, God will direct and enable us to do that which of ourselves we cannot do. 2. Observe how joyfully they followed God's direction (*v.* 10). *When they saw the star, they rejoiced with exceeding great joy.* Now they saw they were not deceived, and had not taken this long journey in vain. What a transport of joy these wise men were in upon this sight of the star; none know so well as those who, after a long and melancholy night of temptation and desertion, under the power of a *Spirit of bondage,* at length *receive the spirit of adoption, witnessing with their spirits that they are the children of God;* this is light out of darkness; it is life from the dead.

IX. See how they made their

address to him when they had found him, *v.* 11. We may well imagine their expectations were raised to find this royal babe, though slighted by the nation, yet honourably attended at home; and what a disappointment it was to them when they found a cottage was his palace, and his own poor mother all the retinue he had! However, these wise men were so wise as to see through this veil, and in this despised babe to discern *the glory as of the Only-begotten of the Father*; they did not think themselves balked or baffled in their enquiry; but, as having found the King they sought, they presented themselves first, and then their gifts, to him.

1. They presented themselves to him: *they fell down, and worshipped him.* We do not read that they gave such honour to Herod, though he was in the height of his royal grandeur; but to this babe they gave this honour, not only as to a king (then they would have done the same to Herod), but as to a God.

2. *They presented their gifts to him.* In the eastern nations, when they did homage to their kings, they made them presents; thus the subjection of the kings of Sheba to Christ is spoken of (Ps. lxxii. 10), *They shall bring presents, and offer gifts.* See Isa. lx. 6. Note, With ourselves, we must give up all that we have to Jesus Christ; and if we be sincere in the surrender of ourselves to him, we shall not be unwilling to part with what is dearest to us, and most valuable, to him and for him; nor are our gifts accepted, unless we first present ourselves to him living sacrifices. Some think there was a significancy in their gifts; they offered him *gold*, as a king, paying him tribute, to *Cæsar, the things that are Cæsar's; frankincense*, as God, for they honoured God with the smoke of incense; and *myrrh*, as a Man that should die, for *myrrh* was used in embalming dead bodies.

X. See how they left him when they had made their address to him, *v.* 12. We do not find that the wise men promised to come back to Herod, and, if they had, it must have been with the usual proviso, *If God permit*; God did not permit them, and prevented the mischief Herod designed to the Child Jesus, and the trouble it would have been to the wise men to have been made involuntarily accessory to it. They were *warned not to return to Herod*, nor to Jerusalem. *They departed into their own country another way*, to bring the tidings to their countrymen; but it is strange that we never hear any more of them, and that they or theirs did not afterwards attend *him* in the temple, whom they had worshipped in the cradle. However, the direction they had from God in their return would be a further confirmation of their faith in this Child, as *the Lord from heaven*.

CHRIST IN EGYPT (*vv.* 13–15)

We have here Christ's flight into Egypt to avoid the cruelty of Herod.

Now here observe, I. The command given to Joseph concerning it, *v.* 13. Joseph knew neither the danger the child was in, nor how to escape it; but God, by *an angel*, tells him both *in a dream*, as before he directed him in like manner what to do, *ch*. i. 20. Joseph, before his alliance to Christ, had not been wont to converse with angels as now. Those who are spiritually related to Christ by faith have that communion and correspondence with Heaven which before they were strangers to.

1. Joseph is here told what their danger was: *Herod will seek the young child to destroy him*. Note, God is acquainted with all the cruel projects and purposes of the enemies of his church.

2. He is directed what to do, to escape the danger; *Take the young child, and flee into Egypt*. Thus early must Christ give an example to his own rule (*ch*. x. 23): *When they persecute you in one city, flee to another*. He that came to die for us, when *his hour was not yet come*, fled for his own safety.

This as a trial of the faith of Joseph and Mary. They might be tempted to think, "If this child be the Son of God, as we are told he is, has he no other way to secure himself than by such a mean and inglorious retreat as this?" They had been lately told that he should be *the glory of his people Israel*; and is the land of Israel so soon become too hot for him? But we find not that they made any such objections; their faith, being tried, was found firm.

God intimates the continuance of his care and guidance, when he saith, *Be thou there until I bring thee word*, so that he must expect to hear from God again, and not stir without fresh orders. Thus God will keep his people still in a dependence upon him.

II. Joseph's obedience to this command, *v*. 14. The journey would be inconvenient and perilous both to the young child and to his mother; they were but poorly provided for it, and were likely to meet with cold entertainment in Egypt: yet Joseph *was not disobedient to the heavenly vision*, made no objection, nor was dilatory in his obedience. As soon as he had received his orders, he immediately *arose*, and went away *by night*, the same night, as it should seem, that he received the orders. Note, Those that would make *sure* work of their obedience must make *quick* work of it.

Joseph took the young child and his mother. Some observe, that *the young child* is put first, as the principal person, and Mary is called, not *the wife of Joseph*, but, which was her greater dignity, *the mother of the young child*.

III. The fulfilling of the scripture in all this—that scripture (Hos. xi. 1), *Out of Egypt have I called my son*. Of all the evangelists, Matthew takes most notice of the fulfilling of the scripture in what concerned Christ, because his gospel was first published among the Jews, with whom that would add much strength and lustre to it. Now this word of the prophet undoubtedly referred to the deliverance of Israel out of Egypt, in which God owned them for his son, his first-born (Exod. iv. 22); but it is here applied, by way of analogy, to Christ, the Head of the church. Note, The scripture has many accomplishments, so full and copious is it, and so well ordered in all things. God is every day fulfilling the scripture.

RETURN TO NAZARETH
(*vv.* 16–23)

Here is, I. Herod's resentment of the departure of the wise men, which made him *exceeding wroth*; and he is the more desperate and outrageous for his being disappointed.

II. Herod was now about seventy years old, so that an infant, at this time *under two years old*, was not likely ever to give him any disturbance. Nor was he a man over fond of his own children, or of their preferment, having formerly slain two of his own sons, Alexander and Aristobulus, and his son Antipater after this, but five days before he himself died; so that it was purely to gratify his own brutish lusts of pride and cruelty that he did this. All is fish that comes to his net.

Observe, What large measures he took, 1. As to time; He *slew all from two years old and under*. It is probable that the blessed Jesus was at this time not a year old; yet Herod took in all the infants *under two years old*, that he might be sure not to miss of his prey. He cares not how many heads fall, which he allows to be innocent, provided that escape not which he supposes to be guilty. 2. As to place; He kills all the male children, not only *in Bethlehem*, but *in all the coasts thereof*, in all the villages of that city. This was being *overmuch wicked*, Eccl. vii. 17. But we must look upon this murder of the infants under another character: it was their martyrdom. How early did persecution commence against Christ and his kingdom! *Think ye that he came to send peace on the earth?* No, *but a sword*, such a sword as this, *ch.* x. 34, 35. A passive testimony was hereby given to the Lord Jesus. They shed their blood for him, who afterwards shed his for them. These were the infantry of *the noble army of martyrs*.

III. The fulfilling of the scripture in this (*vv.* 17, 18); *Then was fulfilled* that prophecy (Jer. xxxi. 15), *A voice was heard in Ramah*. See and adore the fullness of the scripture! That prediction was accomplished in Jeremiah's time, when Nebuzaradan, after he had destroyed Jerusalem, brought all his prisoners to Ramah (Jer. xl. 1), and there disposed of them as he pleased, for the sword, or for captivity. Then was the cry *in Ramah heard* to Bethlehem (for those two cities, the one in Judah's lot, and the other in Benjamin's, were not far asunder); but now the prophecy is again fulfilled in the great sorrow that was for the death of these infants. The scripture was fulfilled,

1. In the place of this mourning. The noise of it was heard from Bethlehem to Ramah; for Herod's cruelty extended itself to *all the coasts of Bethlehem*, even into the lot of Benjamin, among the children of Rachel.

2. In the degree of this mourning. It was *lamentation and weeping, and great mourning*; all little enough to express the sense they had of this aggravated calamity. Here was a representation of this world we live in. We hear in it *lamentation, and weeping, and mourning*, and see *the tears of the oppressed*, some upon one account, and some upon an-

other. Our way lies through a *vale of tears*.

IV. We have here (*vv.* 19–23) Christ's return out of Egypt into the *land of Israel* again. Christ was *sent to the lost sheep of the house of Israel*, and therefore to them he must return. Observe,

What it was that made way for his return—the death of Herod, which happened not long after the murder of the infants; some think not above three months. Such quick work did divine vengeance make!

V. The orders given from heaven concerning their return, and Joseph's obedience to those orders, *vv.* 19–21. God had sent Joseph into Egypt, and there he staid till the same that brought him thither ordered him thence. Note, In all our removes, it is good to see our way plain, and God going before us; we should not move either one way or the other without order.

VI. The further direction he had from God, which way to steer, and where to fix in the land of Israel, *vv.* 22, 23. God could have given him these instructions with the former, but God reveals his mind to his people by degrees, to keep them still waiting on him, and expecting to hear further from him. These orders Joseph received *in a dream*, probably, as those before, by the ministration of an angel.

Now the direction given this holy, royal family, is, 1. That it might not settle in Judea, *v.* 22. Joseph might think that Jesus, being *born in Bethlehem*, must be brought up there; yet he is prudently *afraid* for *the young Child*, because *he hears that Archelaus reigns in* Herod's stead, not over all

the kingdom as his father did, but only over Judea, the other provinces being put into other hands. See what a succession of enemies there is to fight against Christ and his church! If one drop off, another presently appears, to keep up the old enmity. But for this reason Joseph must not take the young Child into Judea.

2. That it must settle in Galilee, *v.* 22. There Philip now ruled, who was a mild, quiet, man. Note, The providence of God commonly so orders it, that his people shall not want a quiet retreat from the storm and from the tempest; when one climate becomes hot and scorching, another shall be kept more cool and temperate. Galilee lay far north; Samaria lay between it and Judea; thither they were sent, to Nazareth, a city upon a hill, in the centre of the lot of Zebulun; there the mother of our Lord lived, when she conceived that *holy thing*; and, probably, Joseph lived there too, Luke i. 26, 27. Thither they were sent, and there they were well known, and were among their relations; the most proper place for them to be in. There they continued, and from thence our Saviour was called *Jesus of Nazareth*, which was to *the Jews a stumbling-block*, for, *Can any good thing come* out of *Nazareth*?

In this is said to be fulfilled what was *spoken by the prophets, He shall be called a Nazarene*, which may be looked upon, (1) As a name of honour and dignity, though primarily it signifies no more than *a man of Nazareth*; there is an allusion or mystery in it, speaking Christ to be, [1] The *Man, the Branch*, spoken of, Isaiah xi. 1. The word there is *Netzar*, which signifies either a *branch*, or *the city of Nazareth*; in being denominated from that *city*, he is declared to be that Branch. [2] It speaks him to be the *great Nazarite*; of whom the legal Nazarites were a type and figure (especially Samson, Judg. xiii. 5), and Joseph, who is called a *Nazarite among his brethren* (Gen. xlix. 26). Not that Christ was, *strictly*, *a Nazarite*, for he drank wine, and touched dead bodies; but he was *eminently* so, both as he was singularly holy, and as he was by a solemn designation and dedication set apart to the honour of God in the work of our redemption, as Samson was to save Israel.

CHAPTER THREE

JOHN THE BAPTIST

Matthew says nothing of the conception and birth of John the Baptist, which is largely related by St. Luke, but finds him at full age, as if dropt from the clouds to preach in the wilderness. For above three hundred years the church had been without prophets; those lights had been long put out, that *he* might be the more desired, who was to be the great prophet. After Malachi there was no prophet, nor any pretender to prophecy, till John the Baptist, to whom therefore the prophet Malachi points more directly than any of the Old Testament prophets had done (Mal. iii. 1); *I send my messenger*.

The beginning of the gospel in a wilderness, speaks comfort to the deserts of the Gentile world. Now must the prophecies be fulfilled, *I*

will plant in the wilderness the cedar, Isa. xli. 18, 19. The wilderness shall be *a fruitful field*, Isa. xxxii. 15. And the *desert shall rejoice*, Isa. xxxv. 1, 2. The Septuagint reads, *the deserts of Jordan*, the very wilderness in which John preached.

John came, not fighting, nor disputing, but *preaching* (*v.* 1); for by the foolishness of preaching, Christ's kingdom must be set up.

I. The doctrine he preached was that of repentance (*v.* 2); *Repent ye*. He preached this in *Judea*, among those that were called *Jews*, and made a profession of religion; for even they needed repentance. He preached it, not in Jerusalem, but in the wilderness of Judea, among the plain country people; for even those who think themselves most out of the way of temptation, and furthest from the vanities and vices of the town, cannot wash their hands in innocency, but must do it in repentance. John Baptist's business was to call men to *repent* of their sins; *Bethink yourselves*; "Admit a second *thought*, to correct the errors of the first—an *afterthought*. Consider your ways, *change your minds*; you have thought amiss; *think again*, and *think aright*." Note, True penitents have *other thoughts* of God and Christ, and sin and holiness, and this world and the other, than they have had, and stand otherwise affected toward them. The change of the *mind* produces a change of the *way*. Those who are truly sorry for what they have done amiss, will be careful to do so no more. This repentance is a necessary duty, in obedience to the command of God (Acts xvii. 30); and a necessary preparative and qualification for the comforts of the gospel of Christ.

II. The argument he used to enforce this call was, *For the kingdom of heaven is at hand* (v. 2). It is a *kingdom* of which Christ is the Sovereign, and we must be the willing, loyal subjects of it. It is a kingdom of *heaven*, not of this world, a spiritual kingdom: its original from heaven, its tendency to heaven. John preached this as *at hand*; then it was at the door; to us it is come, by the pouring out of the Spirit, and the full exhibition of the riches of gospel-grace. Now, (1) This is a great *inducement* to us *to repent*. There is nothing like the consideration of divine grace to break the heart, both *for sin* and *from sin*. That is evangelical repentance, that flows from a sight of Christ, from a sense of his love, and the hopes of pardon and forgiveness through him. (2) It is a *great encouragement* to us *to repent*; "Repent, for your sins shall be pardoned upon your repentance. Return to God in a way of duty, and he will, through Christ, return to you in a way of mercy.'

1. As the *voice of one crying in the wilderness* (v. 3). John owned it himself (John i. 23); *I am the voice*, and that is all, God is the Speaker, who makes known his mind by John, as a man does by his voice. The word of God must be received as such (1 Thes. ii. 13); what else is Paul, and what is Apollos, but the voice!

2. As one whose business it was to *prepare the way of the Lord, and to make his paths straight*; so it was said of him before he was born, that he should *make ready a people prepared for the Lord* (Luke i. 17), as Christ's harbinger and forerunner: he was such a one as intimated the nature of Christ's kingdom, for he came not in the gaudy dress of a herald at arms, but in the homely one of a hermit. Officers are sent before great men to clear the way; so John prepares the way of the Lord. Note, There is a great deal to be done, to make way for Christ into a soul, to *bow the heart* for the reception of the Son of David (2 Sam. xix. 14); and nothing is more needful, in order to this, than the discovery of sin, and a conviction of the insufficiency of our own righteousness.

They, who expected the Messiah as a temporal prince, would think that his forerunner must come in great pomp and splendour; but it proves quite contrary; he shall be *great in the sight of the Lord*, but mean in the eye of the world; to intimate that the glory of Christ's kingdom was to be spiritual, and the subjects of it such as ordinarily were either *found* by *it*, or *made* by it, poor and despised, who derived their honours, pleasures, and riches, from another world.

1. His *dress* was plain. This same John had *his raiment of camel's hair, and a leathern girdle about his loins*; he did not go in *long clothing*, as the *scribes*, or *soft clothing*, as the courtiers, but in the clothing of a country husbandman; for he lived in a country place, and suited his *habit* to his *habitation*. Note, It is good for us to accommodate ourselves to the place and condition which God, in his providence, has put us in.

2. His *diet* was plain; his *meat*

was *locusts* and *wild honey*; not as if he never ate anything else; but these he frequently fed upon, and made many meals of them, when he retired into solitary places, and continued long there for contemplation. He was so entirely taken up with spiritual things, that he could seldom find time for a set meal.

Then went out to him Jerusalem, and all Judea (v. 5). Great multitudes came to him from the city, and from all parts of the country; some of all sorts, men and women, young and old, rich and poor, Pharisees and publicans; they *went out to him*, as soon as they heard of his preaching the *kingdom of heaven*, that they might hear what they heard so much of. This was an evidence that it was now a time of great expectation; it was generally thought that the *kingdom of God* would presently *appear* (Luke xix. 11), and therefore, when John showed himself to Israel, lived and preached in this way, so very different from the Scribes and Pharisees, they were ready to say of him, that he was *the Christ* (Luke iii. 15); and this occasioned such a confluence of people about him. It appears later that of the many who came to John's Baptism, there were few who adhered to it; witness the cold reception Christ had in Judea, and about Jerusalem.

Those who received his doctrine, and submitted to his discipline, were *baptized of him in Jordan* (v. 6), thereby professing their repentance, and their belief that the kingdom of the Messiah was at hand. 1. They testified their repentance by *confessing their sins*; a general confession, it is probable, they made to John that they were *sinners*, that they were polluted by sin, and needed cleansing; but to God they made a confession of particular sins, for he is the party offended. The Jews had been taught to *justify* themselves; but John teaches them to *accuse* themselves, and not to rest, as they used to do, in the general confession of sin made for all Israel, once a year, upon the day of atonement. 2. The benefits of the *kingdom of heaven*, now *at hand*, were thereupon sealed to them by baptism. He washed them with water, in token of this—that from all their iniquities God would *cleanse them*. It was usual with the Jews to baptize those whom they admitted proselytes to their religion, especially those who were only *Proselytes of the gate*, and were not circumcised, as the *Proselytes of righteousness* were. The *ceremonial law* consisted in *divers washings or baptisms* (Heb. ix. 10); but John's baptism refers to the remedial law, the law of repentance and faith. He is said to baptize them in Jordan, that river which was famous for Israel's passage through it, and Naaman's cure; yet it is probable that John did not baptize in that river at first, but that afterward, when the people who came to his baptism were numerous, he removed to Jordan. By baptism he obliged them to live a holy life, according to the profession they took upon themselves.

The doctrine John preached was that of repentance, in consideration of the *kingdom of heaven* being *at hand*. Application is the life of preaching, so it was of John's preaching.

Observe, 1. To whom he applied it; to the Pharisees and Sadducees that came to his baptism, *v.* 7. To others he thought it enough to say, *Repent, for the kingdom of heaven is at hand*; but when he saw these Pharisees and Sadducees come about him, he found it necessary to explain himself, and deal more closely. These were two of the three noted sects among the Jews at that time, the third was that of the Essenes, whom we never read of in the gospels, for they affected retirement, and declined busying themselves in public affairs. The Pharisees were zealots for the ceremonies, for the power of the church, and the traditions of the elders; the Sadducees ran into the other extreme, and were little better than deists, denying the existence of spirits and a future state. 2. What the application was. It is directed to their consciences. Though his education was private, he was not bashful when he appeared in public, nor did he fear the face of man, for he was full of the Holy Ghost, and of power.

He begins harshly, calls them not Rabbi, gives them not the titles, much less the applauses, they had been used to. 1. The *title* he gives them is, *O generation of vipers* (*v.* 7). Christ gave them the same title; *ch.* xii. 34; xxiii. 33. The *alarm* he gives them is, *Who has warned you to flee from the wrath to come?* This intimates that they were in danger of the wrath to come; and that their case was so nearly desperate, and their hearts so hardened in sin (the Pharisees by their parade of religion, and the Sadducees by their arguments against religion)

that it was next to a miracle to effect anything hopeful among them.

"*Bring forth therefore fruits meet for repentance*" (*v.* 8). "*Therefore*, because you are *warned to flee from the wrath to come*, let the terrors of the Lord persuade you to a holy life."

Here is a word of caution, not to trust to their external privileges, so as with them to shift off these calls to repentance (*v.* 9); *Think not to say within yourselves, We have Abraham to our father*. Note, There is a great deal which carnal hearts are apt to say within themselves, to put by the convincing, commanding power of the word of God, which ministers should labour to meet with and anticipate; vain thoughts which lodge within those who are called to *wash their hearts*, Jer. iv. 14.

Their pretence was; "*We have Abraham to our father*; we are not sinners of the Gentiles; it is fit indeed that *they* should be called to repent; but we are Jews, a holy nation, a peculiar people, what is this to us?"

How foolish and groundless this pretence was; they thought that being the seed of Abraham, they were the only people God had in the world, and therefore that, if they were cut off, he would be at a loss for a church; but John shows them the folly of this conceit; *I say unto you* (whatever you say within yourselves), that *God is able of these stones to raise up children unto Abraham*. He was now baptizing in Jordan at Bethabara (John i. 28), *the house of passage*, where the children of *Israel passed over*; and there were the twelve stones, one for each tribe, which Joshua set up for a memorial, Josh. iv. 20. It is not unlikely that he pointed to those stones, which God could raise to be, more than in representation, the *twelve tribes of Israel*.

Here is a word of terror to the careless and secure Pharisees and Sadducees, and other Jews, that knew not the signs of the times, nor the day of their visitation, *v*. 10. "Now look about you, now that *the kingdom of God is at hand*, and be made sensible."

"How strict and short your trial is; *Now the axe is carried before you*, now it is *laid to the root of the tree*, now you are upon *your good behaviour*, and are to be so but a *while*; now you are marked for ruin, and cannot avoid it but by a speedy and sincere repentance. Now you must expect that God will make quicker work with you by his judgments than he did formerly, and that they will *begin at the house of God*: where God allows more means, he allows less time."

With the warning, a word of instruction concerning Jesus Christ, in whom all John's preaching centred. Christ's ministers preach, not themselves, but him. Here is,

1. The dignity and pre-eminence of Christ above John. See how meanly he speaks of himself, that he might magnify Christ (*v*. 11); "*I indeed baptize you with water*, that is the utmost I can do." But *he that comes after me is mightier than I*. Though John had much power, for he came in the *spirit and power of Elias*, Christ had more; though John was truly great, great in the sight of the Lord (not a greater was

born of woman), yet he thinks himself unworthy to be in the meanest place of attendance upon Christ, *whose shoes I am not worthy to bear*.

When it was prophesied that John should be sent as Christ's forerunner (Mal. iii. i, 2), it immediately follows, *The Lord, whom ye seek, shall suddenly come*, and shall *sit as a refiner, v*. 3. And after the coming of Elijah, *the day comes that shall burn as an oven* (Mal. iv. 1), to which the Baptist seems here to refer. Christ will come to make a distinction,

(1) By the powerful working of his grace; *He shall baptize you*, that is, some of you, *with the Holy Ghost and with fire*. Note, [1] It is Christ's prerogative to baptize *with the Holy Ghost*. This he did in the extraordinary gifts of the Spirit conferred upon the apostles, to which Christ himself applies these words of John, Acts i. 5. This he does in the graces and comforts of the Spirit given to them that ask him, Luke xi. 13; John vii. 38, 39; See Acts xi. 16. [2] They who are baptized with the Holy Ghost are baptized as *with fire*; the seven spirits of God appear as *seven lamps of fire*, Rev. iv. 5. Is fire enlightening? So the Spirit is a Spirit of illumination. Is it warming? And do not their hearts burn within them? Is it consuming? And does not the Spirit of judgment, as a *Spirit of burning*, consume the dross of their corruptions? Does fire make all it seizes like itself? And does it move upwards? So does the Spirit make the soul holy like itself, and its tendency is heaven-ward. Christ says *I am come to send fire*, Luke xii. 49.

(2) By the final determinations of his judgment (*v.* 12); *Whose fan is in his hand.* His ability to distinguish, as the eternal wisdom of the Father, who sees all by a true light, and his authority to distinguish, as the Person to whom all judgment is committed, is the *fan* that is *in his hand,* Jer. xv. 7.

THE BAPTISM OF JESUS

Our Lord Jesus, from his childhood till now, when he was almost thirty years of age, had lain hid in Galilee, as it were, buried alive; but now, after a long and dark night, behold, *the Sun of righteousness* rises in glory.

Now in this story of Christ's baptism we may observe,

1. How hardly John was persuaded to admit of it, *vv.* 14, 15. It was an instance of Christ's great humility, that he would offer himself *to be baptized of John*; that he *who knew no sin* would submit to the baptism of repentance. Note, As soon as ever Christ began to preach, he preached humility, preached it by his example, preached it to all, especially to young ministers. Christ was designed for the highest honours, yet in his first step he thus abases himself. Note, Those who would rise high must begin low. Now here we have,

1. The objection that John made against baptizing Jesus, *v.* 14. *John forbade him,* as Peter did, when Christ went about to wash his feet, John xiii. 6, 8. Note, Christ's gracious condescensions are so surprising, as to appear at first incredible to the strongest believers.

(1) John thinks it necessary that he should be baptized of Christ; *I have need to be baptized of thee* with the baptism of the Holy Ghost, as of fire, for that was Christ's baptism, *v.* 11.

(2) He therefore thinks it very preposterous and absurd, that Christ should be baptized by him; *Comest thou to me?* Does the holy Jesus, that is separated from sinners, come to be baptized by a sinner, as a sinner, and among sinners? How can this be?

2. The overruling of this objection (*v.* 15); *Jesus said, Suffer it to be so now.* Christ accepted his humility, but not his refusal; he will have the thing done; and it is fit that Christ should take his own method, though we do not understand it, nor can give a reason for it. See,

(1) How Christ insists upon it; It must *be so now.* He does not deny that *John had need to be baptized of* him, yet he will now be *baptized of John. Let it be yet so; suffer it to be so now.* Note, Every thing is beautiful in its season. But why *now*? Why yet? [1] Christ is *now* in a state of humiliation: he has emptied himself, and *made himself of no reputation.* [2] John's baptism is now in reputation, it is that by which God is now doing his work; that is the present dispensation, and therefore Jesus will now be baptized with water; but his baptizing with the Holy Ghost is reserved for hereafter, *many days hence,* Acts i. 5. [3] it must *be so now,* because now is the time for Christ's appearing in public, and this will be a fair opportunity for it, See John i. 31–34.

(2) The reason he gives for it;

Thus it becomes us to fulfil all righteousness. Our Lord Jesus looked upon it as a thing well becoming him, *to fulfil all righteousness*, that is (as Dr. Whitby explains it), to own every divine institution, and to show his readiness to comply with all God's righteous precepts. *Thus it becomes* him to justify God, and approve his wisdom, in sending John to prepare his way by the baptism of repentance. *Thus it becomes us* to countenance and encourage every thing that is good, by pattern as well as precept. Thus Jesus began *first to do, and then to teach*; and his ministers must take the same method. Thus *Christ filled up the righteousness of the ceremonial law*, which consisted in divers washings; thus he recommended the gospel-ordinance of baptism to his church, put honour upon it, and showed what virtue he designed to put into it.

With the will of Christ, and this reason for it, John was entirely satisfied, and *then he suffered him*. The same modesty which made him at first decline the honour Christ offered him, now made him do the service Christ enjoined him.

How solemnly Heaven was pleased to grace the baptism of Christ with a special display of glory (*vv.* 16, 17); *Jesus when he was baptized, went up straightway out of the water*. Others that were baptized stayed to *confess their sins* (*v.* 6); but Christ, having no sins to confess, *went up* immediately *out of the water*; so we read it, but not right: for it is *from the water*; from the brink of the river, to which he went down to be washed with water, that is, to have his head or face washed (John xiii. 9). *He went up straightway*, as one that entered upon his work with the utmost cheerfulness and resolution; he would lose no time. *How was he straightened till it was accomplished!*

Now, when he was coming *up out of the water*, and all the company had their eye upon him,

1. *Lo! the heavens were opened unto him*, so as to discover something above and beyond the starry firmament, at least, to him.

2. *He saw the Spirit of God descending like a dove*, or *as a dove, and* coming or *lighting upon him*. Christ saw it (Mark i. 10), and John saw it (John i. 33, 34), and it is probable that all the standers-by saw it; for this was intended to be his public inauguration.

(1) *The Spirit of God descended, and lighted on him.* In the beginning of the old world, *the Spirit of God moved upon the face of the waters* (Gen. i. 2), hovered as a bird upon the nest. So here, in the beginning of this new world, Christ, as God, needed not to receive the Holy Ghost, but it was foretold that *the Spirit of the Lord should rest upon him* (Isa. xi. 2; lxi. 1), and here he did so.

(2) He *descended on him like a dove*; whether it was a real, living dove, or, as was usual in visions, the representation or similitude of a dove, is uncertain. Of all fowl none was so significant as the dove. [1] The Spirit of Christ is a dove-like spirit; not like *a silly dove, without heart* (Hos. vii. 11), but like an innocent dove, without gall. [2] The dove was the only fowl that was offered in sacrifice (Lev. i. 14),

18

and Christ by the Spirit, *the eternal Spirit, offered himself without spot to God.* [3] The tidings of the decrease of Noah's flood were brought by a dove, with an olive-leaf in her mouth; fitly therefore are the glad tidings of peace with God brought by the Spirit as *a dove.* It speaks God's *good will towards men*; that his thoughts towards us are *thoughts of good, and not of evil.*

3. To explain and complete this solemnity, *there came a voice from heaven*, which, we have reason to think, was heard by all that were present.

(1) See here how God owns our Lord Jesus; *This is my beloved Son.* Observe, [1] The relation he stood in to him; He *is my Son.* Jesus Christ is the Son of God, *by eternal generation*, as he was *begotten of the Father before all worlds* (Col. i. 15; Heb. i. 3); and by supernatural conception; he was *therefore* called *the Son of God*, because he *was conceived by the power of the Holy Ghost* (Luke i. 35); yet this is not all; he is the Son of God by special designation to the work and office of the world's Redeemer. [2] The affection the Father had for him; He *is my beloved Son*; his dear Son, *the Son of his love* (Col. i. 13); he had lain in his bosom from all eternity (John i. 18), had been *always his delight* (Prov. viii. 30), but particularly as Mediator, and in undertaking the work of man's salvation, he was his *beloved Son.* He is *my Elect, in whom my soul delights.* See Isa. xlii. 1. Because he consented to the covenant of redemption, and delighted to do that *will of God, therefore the Father loved him.* John x. 17; iii. 35.

(2) See here how ready he is to own us in him: He *is my beloved Son*, not only *with* whom, but *in* whom, I am well pleased. He is pleased with all that are in him, and are united to him by faith. Hitherto God had been displeased with the children of men, but now his anger is turned away, and he has made us *accepted in the Beloved*, Eph. i. 6.

CHAPTER FOUR
TEMPTATION OF JESUS

Concerning Christ's temptation, observe,

I. The time when it happened: *Then*; there is an emphasis laid upon that. Immediately after *the heavens were opened* to him, and *the Spirit descended on him*, and he was declared to be the Son of God, and the Saviour of the world, the next news we hear of him is, he is *tempted*; for *then* he is best able to grapple with the temptation.

Then, when he was newly come from a solemn ordinance, when he was baptized, *then* he was *tempted.* Note, After we have been admitted into communion with God, we must expect to be set upon by Satan. The enriched soul must double its guard. *Then*, when he began to show himself publicly to Israel, *then* he was *tempted*, so as he never had been while he lived in privacy.

II. The place where it was; *in the wilderness*; probably in the great wilderness of *Sinai*, where Moses and Elijah *fasted forty days*, for no part of *the wilderness* of Judea was so abandoned to wild beasts as this is said to have been, Mark i. 13. Christ withdrew into the wilderness, 1. To gain advantage to himself. Retirement gives an opportunity for meditation and communion with God; even they who are called to the most active life must yet have their contemplative hours, and must find time to be alone with God. Those are not fit to speak of the things of God in public to others, who have not first conversed with those things in secret by themselves. 2. To give advantage to the tempter, that he might have a readier access to him than he could have had in company. Those who, under pretence of sanctity and devotion, retire into dens and deserts, find that they are not out of reach of their spiritual enemies, and that there they lack the benefit of the communion of saints. Christ retired, (1) That Satan might have leave to do his worst. To make his victory the more illustrious, he gave the enemy sun and wind on his side, and yet baffled him. (2) That he might have an opportunity to do his best himself, that he might be exalted in his own strength; for so it was written, *I have trod the wine-press alone*, and of the people there was none with me. Christ entered the lists without a second.

III. The preparatives for it, which were two.

1. He was directed to the combat; he did not wilfully thrust himself upon it, but he *was led up of the Spirit to be tempted of the Devil.*

Now Christ's temptation is, (1) An instance of his own condescension and humiliation, because he would humble himself, *in all things to be made like unto his brethren*; thus he *gave his back to the smiters*. (2) An occasion of Satan's confusion. There is no conquest without a combat. Christ was tempted, that he might overcome the tempter. Satan tempted the first Adam, and triumphed over him; but he shall not always triumph, the second Adam shall overcome him and *lead captivity captive*. (3) Matter of comfort to all the saints. In the temptation of Christ it appears that our enemy is subtle, spiteful, and very daring in his temptations; but it also appears that he is not invincible. Though he is *a strong man armed*, yet the Captain of our salvation is *stronger than he*.

2. He was dieted for the combat, as wrestlers, who are *temperate in all things* (1 Cor. ix. 25); but Christ beyond any other, for he *fasted forty days and forty nights*, in compliance with the type and example of Moses the great lawgiver, and of Elias, the great reformer, of the Old Testament. Christ did not need to fast for mortification (he had no corrupt desires to be subdued); yet he *fasted*, (1) That herein he might humble himself, and might seem as one abandoned, *whom no man seeketh after*. (2) That he might give Satan both occasion and advantage against him; and so make his victory over him the more illustrious. (3) That he might sanctify and recommend fasting to us, when God in his providence calls to it, or when we are reduced to straits, and are destitute of daily food, or when it is requisite for the keeping under of the body, or the

quickening of prayer, those excellent preparatives for temptation.

IV. The temptations themselves (*vv.* 3–10). That which Satan aimed at, in all his temptations, was, to bring him to *sin against God*, and so to render him for ever incapable of being a Sacrifice for the sin of others. Now, whatever the colours were, that which he aimed at was, to bring him, 1. To despair of his Father's goodness. 2. To presume upon his Father's power. 3. To alienate his Father's honour, by giving it to Satan. In the two former, that which he tempted him *to*, seemed innocent, and therein appeared the subtlety of the tempter; in the last, that which he tempted him *with*, seemed desirable. The two former are artful temptations, which there was need of great wisdom to discern; the last was a strong temptation, which there was need of great resolution to resist; yet he was baffled in them all.

1. Christ began to be hungry, and therefore the motion seemed very proper, to turn *stones* into *bread* for his necessary support. Note, It is one of the wiles of Satan to take advantage of our outward condition, in that to plant the battery of his temptations. [2] Christ was newly declared to be *the Son of God*, and here the Devil tempts him to doubt of that; *If thou be the Son of God.*

"If God were thy Father, he would not see thee starve, for *all the beasts of the forest are his*, Ps. l. 10, 12. It is true there *was a voice from heaven, This is my beloved Son*, but surely it was delusion, and thou wast imposed upon by it; for either

God is not thy Father, or he is a very unkind one." But see how unreasonable this suggestion was, and how easily answered. If Christ seemed to be a mere Man now, because he was hungry, why was he not confessed to be more than a Man, even the *Son of God*, when for *forty days he fasted*, and was not hungry?

Secondly, "Thou hast now an opportunity to show that thou art *the Son of God. If thou* art *the Son of God*, prove it by this, *command that these stones*" (a heap of which, probably, lay now before him) "*be made bread, v.* 3. John Baptist said but the other day, that God *can out of stones raise up children to Abraham*, a divine power therefore can, no doubt, out of stones, make bread for those children; if therefore thou hast that power, exert it now in a time of need for thyself."

See how this temptation was resisted and overcome.

[1] Christ refused to comply with it. He would not *command these stones to be made bread*; not because he could not; his power, which soon after this turned *water into wine*, could have turned *stones* into *bread*; but he would not. And why would he not? *First*, That looked like questioning the truth of the voice he heard from heaven, or putting that upon a new trial which was already settled. *Secondly*, That looked like distrusting his Father's care of him, or limiting him to one particular way of providing for him. *Thirdly*, That looked like setting up for himself; or, *Fourthly*, That looked like gratifying Satan, by doing a thing at his motion.

[2] He was ready to reply to it

(*v.* 4); *He answered and said, It is written.* This is observable, that Christ answered and baffled all the temptations of Satan with, *It is written.* He is himself the eternal Word, and could have produced the mind of God without having recourse to the writings of Moses; but he put honour upon the scripture, and, to set us an example, he appealed to what was written in the law; and he says this to Satan, taking it for granted that he knew well enough what was written.

This answer, as all the rest, is taken out of the book of *Deuteronomy*, which signifies *the second law*, and in which there is very little ceremonial; the Levitical sacrifices and purifications could not drive away Satan, though of divine institution, but moral precepts and evangelical promises, mixed with faith, are *mighty, through God*, for the vanquishing of Satan. This is here quoted from Deut. viii. 3, where the reason given why God fed the Israelites with manna is, because he would teach them that *man shall not live by bread alone.* This Christ applies to his own case.

2. He tempted him to presume upon his Father's power and protection.

Now in this second attempt we may observe,

(1) What the temptation was, and how it was managed. In general, finding Christ so confident of his Father's care of him, in point of nourishment, he endeavours to draw him to presume upon that care in point of safety.

Now in this temptation we may observe,

[1] How he made way for it. He took Christ, not by force and against his will, but moved him to go, and went along with him, to Jerusalem. Intending to solicit Christ to an ostentation of his own power, and a vain-glorious presumption upon God's providence, he fixes him on a public place in Jerusalem, a populous city, and *the joy of the whole earth*; in the temple, one of the wonders of the world, continually gazed upon with admiration by some one or other. There he might make himself remarkable, and be taken notice of by every body, and prove himself the Son of God; not, as he was urged in the former temptation, in the obscurities of a wilderness, but before multitudes, upon the most eminent stage of action.

[2] How he moved it; "*If thou be the Son of God*, now show thyself to the world, and prove thyself to be so; *cast thyself down*, and then," *First*, "Thou wilt be admired, as *under the special protection of heaven.*" *Secondly*, "Thou wilt be received, as coming *with a special commission from heaven.* All Jerusalem will see and acknowledge, not only that thou art more than a man, but that thou art that *Messenger*, that *Angel of the covenant*, that should *suddenly come to the temple* (Mal. iii. 1), and from thence descend into the streets of the holy city; and thus the work of convincing the Jews will be cut short, and soon done."

[3] How he backed this motion with a scripture; *For it is written, He shall give his angels charge concerning thee.* The devil would persuade Christ to *throw himself down*, hoping that he would be his

own murderer, and that there would be an end of him and his undertaking, which he looked upon with a jealous eye; to encourage him to do it, he tells him, that there was no danger, that the good angels would protect him, for so was the promise (Ps. xci. 11), *He shall give his angels charge over thee*. In this quotation,

First, There was *something right*. It is true, there is such a promise of the ministration of the angels, for the protection of the saints.

Secondly, There was a great deal *wrong in it*; and perhaps the devil had a particular spite against this promise, and perverted it, because it often stood in his way, and baffled his mischievous designs against the saints. See here, 1. How he *misquoted* it; and that was *bad*. The promise is, They shall *keep thee*; but how? *In all thy ways*; not otherwise; if we go *out of our way*, out of the way of our duty, we forfeit the promise, and put ourselves out of God's protection. If Christ had *cast himself down*, he had been *out of his way*, for he had no call so to expose himself. 2. How he *misapplied* it; and that was *worse*. Scripture is abused when it is pressed to patronize sin; and when men thus wrest it to their own temptation, they do it to *their own destruction*, 2 Pet. iii. 16. This promise is firm, and stands good; but the devil made an ill use of it, when he used it as an encouragement to presume upon the divine care.

(2) How Christ overcame this temptation; he resisted and overcame it, as he did the former, with, *It is written*. The devil's *abusing* of scripture did not prevent Christ

from using it, but he immediately urges, Deut. vi. 16, *Thou shalt not tempt the Lord thy God*. Satan said, *It is written*; Christ says, *It is written*; not that one scripture contradicts another. God is one, and his word one, and he in one mind, but that is a promise, this is a precept, and therefore that is to be explained and applied by this; for scripture is the best interpreter of scripture; and they who prophesy, who expound scripture, must do it according to the proportion of faith (Rom. xii. 6), consistently with practical godliness.

If Christ should *cast himself down*, it would be the tempting of God, [1] As it would be *requiring a further confirmation* of that which was so well confirmed. [2] As it would be *requiring a special preservation* of him, in doing that which he had no call to. If we expect that because God has promised not to forsake us, therefore he should follow us out of the way of our duty; that because he has promised to supply our wants, therefore he should humour us, and please our fancies; that because he has promised to keep us, we may wilfully thrust ourselves into danger, and may expect the desired end, without using the appointed means; this is presumption, this is tempting God.

3. He tempted him to the most *black and horrid idolatry*, with the offer of the *kingdoms of the world, and the glory of them*.

In this temptation, we may observe,

[1] What he *showed him—all the kingdoms of the world*. In order to this, he took him to an *exceeding high mountain*; in hopes of prevail-

ing, as Balak with Balaam, he changed his ground. Hence observe, concerning *Satan's temptations*, that, *First*, They often *come in at the eye*, which is blinded to the things it should see, and dazzled with the vanities it should be turned from. The first sin began in the eye, Gen. iii. 6. We have therefore need to make a covenant with our eyes, and to pray that God would *turn them away from beholding vanity*. *Secondly*, That temptations commonly take rise from the world, and the things of it. The *lust of the flesh*, and of *the eye*, with the *pride of life*, are the topics from which the devil fetches most of his arguments. *Thirdly*, That it is a *great cheat* which the devil puts upon poor souls, in his temptations. He deceives, and so destroys; he imposes upon men with shadows and false colours; shows the world and the glory of it, and hides from men's eyes the sin and sorrow and death which stain the pride of all this glory, the cares and calamities which attend great possessions, and the thorns which crowns themselves are lined with. *Fourthly*, That the *glory of the world* is the most *charming* temptation to the *unthinking* and *unwary*, and that by which men are most imposed upon.

[2] What he *said to him* (*v.* 9); *All these things will I give thee, if thou wilt fall down and worship me*. See, *First*, How *vain the promise* was. *All these things will I give thee*. He seems to take it for granted, that in the former temptations he had in part gained his point, and proved that Christ was not the *Son of God*, because he had not given him those evidences of it which he demanded;

so that here he looks upon him as a mere man. The fallacy of this promise lies in that, *All this will I give thee*. And what was *all that*? It was but a map, a picture, a mere fantasy, that had nothing in it real or solid, and this he would give him; a goodly prize! Yet such are Satan's offers. The *nations of the earth* had been, long before, promised to the Messiah; if he be *the Son of God*, they belong to him; Satan pretends now to be a good angel, probably one of those that were set over kingdoms, and to have received a commission to deliver possession to him according to promise.

Secondly, How *vile* the *condition* was; *If thou will fall down, and worship me*. Note, The devil is fond of being worshipped. All the worship which the heathen performed to their gods, was directed to the devil (Deut. xxxii. 17), who is therefore called the *god of this world*, 2 Cor. iv. 4; 1 Cor. x. 20. What temptation could be more hideous, more black?

4. See how Christ warded off the thrust, baffled the assault, and came off a conqueror. He rejected the proposal,

[1] With *abhorrence* and *detestation*; *Get thee hence, Satan*. The two former temptations had something of colour, which would admit of a consideration, but this was so gross as not to bear a parley; it appears abominable at the first sight, and therefore is immediately rejected. Some temptations have their wickedness written in their forehead, they are open before-hand; they are not to be disputed with, but rejected; "*Get thee hence,*

Satan. Away with it, I cannot bear the thought of it!" Note, It is good to be *peremptory* in resisting temptation, and to *stop our ears* to Satan's charms.

[2] With an argument fetched from scripture. The argument is very suitable, and exactly to the purpose, taken from Deut. vi. 13, and x. 20. *Thou shalt worship the Lord thy God, and him only shalt thou serve.* Christ does not dispute whether he were an angel of light, as he pretended, or not; but though he were, yet he must not be worshipped, because that is an honour due to God only. Our Saviour has recourse to the fundamental law in this case, which is indispensable, and universally obligatory. Religious worship is due to God only, and must not be given to any creature; it is a flower of the crown which cannot be alienated, a branch of God's glory which he will not give to another, and which he would not give to his own Son, by obliging all men to *honour the Son, even as they honour the Father,* if he had not been God, *equal to him,* and *one with him.*

V. We have here the end and issue of this combat, *v.* 11. Though the children of God may be exercised with many and great temptations, yet God will not suffer them to be tempted above the strength which either they have, or he will put into them, 1 Cor. x. 13. It is but for a season that they are in heaviness, through manifold temptations.

Now the issue was glorious, and much to Christ's honour: for,

1. The devil was baffled, and quitted the field; *Then the devil*

leaveth him, forced to do so by the power that went along with that word of command, *Get thee hence, Satan.* He made a shameful and inglorious retreat, and came off with disgrace.

2. The holy angels came and attended upon our victorious Redeemer; *Behold, angels came and ministered unto him.* They came in a visible appearance, as the devil had done in the temptation. It is worth taking notice of: (1) That as there is a world of wicked, malicious spirits that fight against Christ and his church, and all particular believers, so there is a world of holy, blessed spirits engaged and employed for them. In reference to our *war with devils,* we may take abundance of comfort from our *communion with angels.* (2) That Christ's victories are the angels' triumphs. (3) That the angels ministered to the Lord Jesus, not only food, but whatever else he wanted after this great fatigue. See how the instances of Christ's condescension and humiliation are balanced with tokens of his glory.

Lastly, Christ, having been thus signalized and made great in the invisible world by the voice of the Father, the descent of the Spirit, his victory over devils, and his dominion over angels, was doubtless qualified to appear in the visible world as the Mediator between God and man; for *consider how great this man was!*

PREACHING IN GALILEE
(vv. 12–17)

We have here an account of Christ's preaching in the synagogues of Galilee, for he came into

25

the world to be a Preacher; the great salvation which he wrought out, he himself began to publish (Heb. ii. 3) to show how much his heart *was* upon it, and ours *should* be.

I. The time; *When Jesus had heard that John was cast into prison,* then he *went into Galilee,* v. 12. Note, The cry of the saints' sufferings comes up into the ears of the Lord Jesus. If John be cast into prison, Jesus hears it, takes cognizance of it, and steers his course accordingly: *he remembers the bonds* and afflictions that abide his people. Observe, 1. Christ did *not* go into the country, *till he heard of* John's imprisonment; for he must have time given him to *prepare the way of the Lord,* before the Lord himself appear. Providence wisely ordered it, that John should be *eclipsed* before Christ *shone forth*; otherwise the minds of people would have been distracted between the two; one would have said, *I am of John,* and another, *I am of Jesus.* John must be Christ's harbinger, but not his rival.

II. The place where he preached; in Galilee, a remote part of the country, that lay furthest from Jerusalem, and was there looked upon with contempt, as rude and boorish. The inhabitants of that country were reckoned stout men, fit for soldiers, but not polite men, or fit for scholars. Thither Christ went, there he set up the standard of his gospel; and in this, as in other things, he humbled himself. Observe,

1. The particular city he chose for his residence; not Nazareth, where he had been bred up; no, he left Nazareth; but he *came and dwelt in Capernaum,* which was a city of Galilee, but many miles distant from Nazareth, a great city and of much resort. Capernaum is glad of Nazareth's leavings. If Christ's own countrymen be not gathered, yet he will be glorious. "And thou, Capernaum, hast now a day of it; thou art now lifted up to heaven; be wise for thyself, and know the time of thy visitation."

2. The prophecy that was fulfilled in this, *vv.* 14–16. It is quoted from Isa. ix. 1, 2, but with some variation. The punishment of the Jewish nation for rejecting the gospel should be sorer than either (see Isa. viii. 21, 22); for those captivated places had some reviving in their bondage, and saw a great light again, *ch.* ix. 2. This is Isaiah's sense; but the Scripture has many fulfillings; and the evangelist here takes only the latter clause, which speaks of the return of the light of liberty and prosperity to those countries that had been in the darkness of captivity, and applies it to the appearing of the gospel among them.

III. The text he preached upon (v. 17): *From that time,* that is, from the time of his coming into Galilee, into the land of Zebulun and Naphtali, from that time, he began to preach. He had been preaching, before this, in Judea, and had made and baptized many disciples (John iv. 1); but his preaching was not so public and constant as now it began to be. The work of the ministry is so great and awful, that it is fit to be entered upon by steps and gradual advances.

The subject which Christ dwelt upon now in his preaching (and it was indeed the sum and substance of all his preaching), was the very same that John had preached upon (*ch*. iii. 2); *Repent, for the kingdom of heaven is at hand*; for the gospel is the same for substance under various dispensations; the commands the same, and the reasons to enforce them the same; an *angel from heaven* dares not preach any other gospel (Gal. i. 8), and will preach this, for it is the *everlasting gospel. Fear God, and,* by repentance, *give honour to him,* Rev. xiv. 6, 7. *Repent, for the kingdom of heaven is at hand.* [1] This he preached *first* upon; he began with this. As John prepared Christ's way, so Christ prepared his own, and made way for the further discoveries he designed, with the doctrine of repentance. [2] This he preached *often* upon; wherever he went, this was his subject, and neither he nor his followers ever reckoned it worn threadbare, as those would have done, that have *itching ears*, and are fond of novelty and variety more than that which is truly edifying. Note, That which has been preached and heard before, may yet very profitably be preached and heard again; but then it should be preached and heard better, and with new affections; what Paul had said before, he said again, *weeping*, Phil. iii. 1, 18. [3] This he preached as gospel; "Repent, review your ways, and return to yourselves." Note, The doctrine of repentance is right gospel-doctrine. Not only the austere Baptist, who was looked upon as a melancholy, morose man, but the sweet and gracious Jesus, whose lips dropped as a honey-comb, preached repentance; for it is an unspeakable privilege that room is left for repentance. [4] The reason is still the same; The *kingdom of heaven is at hand*; for it was not reckoned to be fully come, till the pouring out of the Spirit after Christ's ascension.

FOUR DISCIPLES CALLED
(*vv*. 18–22)

When Christ began to preach, he began to *gather disciples*, who should now be the *hearers*, and hereafter the *preachers*, of his doctrine, who should now be witnesses *of* his miracles, and hereafter *concerning* them. Now, in these verses, we have an account of the first disciples that he called into fellowship with himself.

And this was an instance, 1. Of *effectual calling* to Christ. In all his preaching he gave a common call to all the country, but in this he gave a special and particular call to those that were given him by the Father. 2. It was an instance of *ordination*, and appointment to the work of the ministry. When Christ, as a Teacher, set up his great school, one of his first works was to appoint ushers, or under masters, to be employed in the work of instruction. Now he began to give gifts unto men, to put the treasure into earthen vessels. It was an early instance of his care for his church.

Now we may observe here,

I. *Where* they were called—by the *sea of Galilee*, where Jesus was walking, Capernaum being situated near that sea. Galilee was a remote part of the nation, the inhabitants were less cultivated and refined, their very language was broad and uncouth to the curious, their *speech betrayed them.* They who were picked up at the sea of Galilee, had not the advantages and improvements, no, not of the more polished Galileans; yet thither Christ went, to call his apostles that were to be the prime ministers of state in his kingdom, for he *chooses the foolish things of the world, to confound the wise.*

II. *Who* they were. We have an account of the call of two pairs of brothers in these verses—Peter and Andrew, James and John; the two former, and, probably, the two latter also, had had acquaintance with Christ before (John i. 40, 41), but were not till now called into a close and constant attendance upon him. We may observe concerning them,

1. That they were *brothers.* Note, It is a blessed thing, when they who are *kinsmen according to the flesh* (as the apostle speaks, Rom. ix. 3), are brought together into a spiritual alliance to Jesus Christ.

2. That they were *fishers.* Being fishers, (1) They were *poor men*: if they had had estates, or any considerable stock in trade, they would not have made fishing their trade, however they might have made it their recreation. (2) They were *unlearned men.* Note, Christ sometimes chooses to endow those with the gifts of grace who have least to show of the gifts of nature. (3) They were *men of business*, who had been bred up to labour. Note, Diligence in an honest calling is pleasing to Christ, and no hindrance to a holy life. (4) They were men that were

accustomed to *hardships* and hazards. Note, Those who have learned to bear hardships, and to run hazards, are best prepared for the fellowship and discipleship of Jesus Christ. Good soldiers of Christ must endure hardness.

III. *What they were doing.* Peter and Andrew were then using their nets, they were fishing; and James and John were *mending their nets*, which was an instance of their industry and good husbandry.

IV. *What the call was* (v. 19): *Follow me, and I will make you fishers of men.* They had followed Christ before, as ordinary disciples (John i. 37), but so they might follow Christ, and follow their calling too; therefore they were called to a more close and constant attendance, and must leave their calling. Note, Even they who have been called to follow Christ, have need to be called to follow on, and to follow nearer, especially when they are designed for the work of the ministry. Observe,

1. What Christ intended them for; *I will make you fishers of men*; this alludes to their former calling. Note, (1) Ministers are *fishers of men*, not to destroy them, but to save them, by bringing them into another element. They must fish, not for wrath, wealth, honour, and preferment, to gain them to themselves, but for souls, to gain them to Christ. *They watch for your souls* (Heb. xiii. 17), *and seek not yours, but you,* 2 Cor. xii. 14, 16. (2) It is Jesus Christ that makes them so; *I will make you fishers of men.* It is he that qualifies men for this work, calls them to it, authorizes them in it, and gives them success in it;

gives them commission to fish for souls, and wisdom to win them. Those ministers are likely to have comfort in their work, who are thus made by Jesus Christ.

2. What they must do to achieve this; *Follow me*. They must separate themselves to a diligent attendance on him, and set themselves to a humble imitation of him; must follow him as their Leader. Note, (1) Those whom Christ employs in any service for him, must first be fitted and qualified for it. (2) Those who would *preach Christ*, must first *learn* Christ, and learn of him.

V. What was the *success* of this call. Peter and Andrew *straightway left their nets* (*v.* 20); and James and John *immediately left the ship and their father* (*v.* 22); *and they* all *followed him*. Note, Those who would follow Christ aright, must *leave all* to follow him. Now,

1. This instance of the power of the Lord Jesus gives us good encouragement to depend upon the sufficiency of his grace. How strong and effectual is his word! *He speaks, and it is done*.

2. This instance of the pliableness of the disciples, gives us a good example of obedience to the command of Christ. Being called, they obeyed, and, like Abraham, *went out not knowing whither they went*, but knowing very well whom they followed.

THE GREAT PHYSICIAN
(*vv.* 23–25)

See here, I. What an industrious preacher Christ was; He *went about all Galilee, teaching in their synagogues, and preaching the gospel of the kingdom. The kingdom of*

heaven, that is, of grace and glory, is emphatically *the kingdom, the kingdom* that was now to come; that kingdom which shall survive, as it doth surpass, all the kingdoms of the earth. *The gospel* is the charter of that kingdom, containing the King's coronation oath, by which he has graciously obliged himself to pardon, protect, and save the subjects of that kingdom; it contains also their oath of allegiance, by which they oblige themselves to observe his statutes and seek his honour; this is *the gospel of the kingdom*; this Christ was himself the Preacher of, that our faith in it might be confirmed.

II. What a powerful physician Christ was; he *went about* not only *teaching*, but *healing*, and both with his word. *He sent his word, and healed them*. Now observe,

1. What diseases he cured—all without exception. He *healed all manner of sickness, and all manner of disease*.

None was too bad, none too hard, for Christ to heal with a word's speaking.

2. What patients he had. See here, what flocking there was to him from all parts; great multitudes of people came, not only *from Galilee* and the country about, but even *from Jerusalem* and *from Judea*, which lay a great way off; for *his fame* went throughout all *Syria*, not only among all the people of the Jews, but among the neighbouring nations.

Christ both *taught and healed*. They who came for cures, met with instruction concerning *the things that belonged to their peace*. It is well if any thing will bring people to Christ; and they who come to him will find more in him than they expected.

Now concerning the cures which Christ wrought, let us, once for all, observe the *miracle*, the *mercy*, and the *mystery*, of them.

(1) The *miracle* of them. They were wrought in such a manner, as plainly spake them to be the immediate products of a divine and supernatural power, and they were God's seal to his commission. He appeals to these as credentials, *ch.* xi. 4, 5; John v. 36. It was expected that the Messiah should work miracles (John vii. 31); miracles of this nature (Isa. xxxv. 5, 6); and we have this indisputable proof of his being the Messiah; never was there any man that did thus; and therefore his healing and his preaching generally went together, for the former confirmed the latter; thus here he *began to* do *and to* teach, Acts i. 1.

(2) The *mercy* of them. The miracles that Moses wrought, to prove his mission, were most of them plagues and judgments, to intimate the terror of that dispensation, though from God; but the miracles that Christ wrought, were most of them cures, and all of them (except the cursing of the barren fig-tree) blessings and favours; for the gospel dispensation is founded, and built up in love, and grace, and sweetness.

(3) The *mystery* of them. Christ, by curing *bodily diseases*, intended to show, that his great errand into the world was to cure *spiritual maladies*. He is the *Sun of righteousness*, that *arises with* this *healing under his wings*. As the Converter of

sinners, he is the *Physician of souls*, and has taught us to call him so, *ch.* ix. 12, 13. Sin is the *sickness*, *disease*, and *torment* of the soul; Christ *came to take away sin*, and so to heal these.

CHAPTER FIVE

THE SERMON ON THE MOUNT: THE PREACHER, THE PEOPLE
(*vv.* 1, 2)

We have here a general account of this sermon.

I. *The Preacher* was our Lord Jesus, the Prince of preachers, the great Prophet of his church, who *came into the world*, to be *the Light of the world*. His text was, *Repent, for the kingdom of heaven is at hand*. This is a sermon on the former part of that text, showing what it is to *repent*; it is to reform, both in judgment and practice; and he here tells us wherein, in answer to that question (Mal. iii. 7), *Wherein shall we return?* He afterward preached upon the latter part of the text, when, in various parables, he showed what the kingdom of heaven is like, *ch.* xiii.

II. *The place* was a mountain in Galilee. As in other things, so in this, our Lord Jesus was but ill accommodated; he had no convenient place to preach in, any more than *to lay his head* on. By which Christ would intimate that there is no such distinguishing holiness of places now, under the gospel, as there was under the law; but that it is *the will of God that men should pray* and preach *every where*, any where, provided it be decent and convenient.

III. *The hearers* were *his disciples*, who *came unto him*; came at his call, as appears by comparing Mark iii. 13, Luke vi. 13. To them he directed his speech, because they followed him for love and learning, while others attended him only for cures. *He taught them*, because they were willing to be *taught* (*the meek will he teach his way*); because they would *understand* what he taught, which to others was foolishness; and because they were to teach others; and it was therefore requisite that they should have a clear and distinct knowledge of these things themselves. But though this discourse was directed to the disciples, it was in the hearing of *the multitude*; for it is said (*ch. vii.* 28), *The people were astonished*. No bounds were set about *this mountain*, to keep the people off, as were about *mount Sinai* (Exod. xix. 12); for, through Christ, we have access to God, not only to speak to him, but to hear from him. Nay, he had an eye to *the multitude*, in preaching this sermon. When the fame of his miracles had brought a vast crowd together, he took the opportunity of so great a confluence of people, to instruct them.

IV. *The solemnity* of his sermon is intimated in that word, *when he was set*. Christ preached many times occasionally, and by interlocutory discourses; but this was a set sermon, when he had placed himself so as to be best heard. He sat down as a Judge or Lawgiver.

THE BEATITUDES (*vv.* 3–12)

Christ begins his sermon with blessings, for *he came into the world to bless us* (Acts iii. 26). The Old Testament ended with a curse (Mal. iv. 6), the gospel begins with a blessing; for *hereunto are we called, that we should inherit the blessing*. Each of the blessings Christ here pronounces has a double intention: 1. To show who they are that are to be accounted truly happy, and what their characters are. 2. What that is wherein true happiness consists, in the promises made to persons of certain characters, the performance of which will make them happy, Now,

1. This is designed to rectify the ruinous mistakes of a blind and carnal world. The general opinion is, *Blessed are they* that are rich, and great, and honourable in the world. Now our Lord Jesus comes to correct this fundamental error, to advance a new hypothesis, and to give us quite another notion of blessedness and blessed people, which, however paradoxical it may appear to those who are prejudiced, yet is in itself, and appears to be to all who are savingly enlightened, a rule and doctrine of eternal truth and certainty, by which we must shortly be judged.

2. It is designed to remove the discouragements of the weak and poor who receive the gospel, by assuring them that his gospel did not make only those happy that were eminent in gifts, graces, comforts, and usefulness.

3. It is designed to invite souls to Christ, and to make way for his law into their hearts. Christ pronounced these blessings, not at the end of his sermon, to dismiss the people, but at the beginning of it, to prepare them for what he had further to say to them.

Our Saviour here gives us eight characters of blessed people; which represent to us the principal graces of a Christian. On each of them a present blessing is pronounced; *Blessed are* they; and to each a future blessedness is promised, which is variously expressed, so as to suit the nature of the grace or duty recommended.

Do we ask then who are happy? It is answered,

I. *The poor in spirit* are happy, *v.* 3. There is a poor-spiritedness that is so far from making men blessed that it is a sin and a snare—cowardice and base fear, and a willing subjection to the lusts of men. But this poverty of spirit is a gracious disposition of soul, by which we are emptied of self, in order to our being filled with Jesus Christ. To be *poor in spirit* is, 1. To be contentedly poor, willing to be empty of worldly wealth, if God orders that to be our lot. 2. It is to be humble and lowly in our own eyes. To be *poor in spirit*, is to think meanly of ourselves, of what we are, and have, and do; the poor are often taken in the Old Testament for the humble and self-denying, as opposed to those that are at ease, and the proud; it is to be as little children in our opinion of ourselves, weak, foolish, and insignificant, *ch.* xviii. 4; xix. 14. It is to look with a holy contempt upon ourselves, to value others and undervalue ourselves in comparison of them. It is to be willing to make ourselves cheap, and mean, and little, to do good; to *become all things to all men*. It is to acknowledge that God is great, and we are mean; that he is holy and we are sinful; that he is

all and we are nothing, less than nothing, worse than nothing; and to humble ourselves before him, and under his mighty hand. 3. It is to come off from all confidence in our own righteousness and strength, that we may depend only upon the merit of Christ for our justification, and the spirit and grace of Christ for our sanctification.

Now, (1) This poverty in spirit is put first among the Christian graces. The philosophers did not reckon humility among their moral virtues, but Christ puts it first.

(2) They are *blessed*. Now they are so, in this world. God looks graciously upon them. They are his little ones, and have their angels. To them he gives more grace; they live the most comfortable lives, and are easy to themselves and all about them, and nothing comes amiss to them; while high spirits are always uneasy.

(3) *Theirs is the kingdom of heaven.* The kingdom of *grace* is composed of such; they only are fit to be members of Christ's church, which is called *the congregation of the poor* (Ps. lxxiv. 19); the kingdom of *glory* is prepared for them.

II. *They that mourn* are happy (*v.* 4); *Blessed are they that mourn.* This is another strange blessing, and fitly follows the former. The poor are accustomed to mourn, the graciously poor mourn graciously. We are apt to think, Blessed are the *merry*; but Christ, who was himself a great mourner, says, Blessed are the *mourners*. There is a sinful mourning, which is an enemy to blessedness—*the sorrow of the world*. There is a natural mourning, which may prove a friend to blessedness, by the grace of God working with it, and sanctifying the afflictions to us, for which we mourn. But there is a gracious mourning, which qualifies for blessedness. 1. A penitential mourning for our own sins; this is *godly sorrow*, a sorrow according to God; sorrow for sin, with an eye to Christ, Zech. xii. 10. 2. A sympathizing mourning for the afflictions of others; the mourning of those who *weep with them that weep*, are sorrowful *for the solemn assemblies, for the desolations of Zion* (Zeph. iii. 18; Ps. cxxxvii. 1), especially who look with compassion on perishing souls, and *weep over* them, as Christ *over Jerusalem.*

Now these gracious mourners, (1) *Are blessed*, for they are like the Lord Jesus, who *was a man of sorrows*, and of whom we never read that he laughed, but often that he wept. (2) *They shall be comforted.* Though perhaps they are not immediately comforted, yet plentiful provision is made for their comfort; light is sown for them; and in heaven, it is certain, *they shall be comforted*, as Lazarus, Luke xvi. 25.

III. *The meek* are happy (*v.* 5); *Blessed are the meek.* The meek are those who quietly submit themselves to God, to his word and to his rod, who follow his directions, and comply with his designs, and are *gentle towards all men* (Tit. iii. 2); who can bear provocation without being inflamed by it; are either silent, or return a soft answer; who can be cool when others are hot; and in their patience keep possession of their own souls, when they can scarcely keep possession of any thing else.

They are the meek, who are rarely and hardly provoked, but quickly and easily pacified; and who would rather forgive twenty injuries than revenge one, having the rule of their own spirits.

These meek ones are here represented as happy, even in this world. 1. They are *blessed*, for they are like the blessed Jesus, in that wherein particularly they are to learn of him, *ch.* xi. 29. They are *blessed*, for they have the most comfortable, undisturbed enjoyment of themselves, their friends, their God; they are fit for any relation, any condition, any company; fit to live, and fit to die. 2. *They shall inherit the earth*; it is quoted from Ps. xxxvii. 11, and it is almost the only express temporal promise in all the New Testament. Meekness, however ridiculed and run down, has a real tendency to promote our health, wealth, comfort, and safety, even in this world. *The meek* and quiet are observed to live the most easy lives, compared with the froward and turbulent.

IV. *They that hunger and thirst after righteousness* are happy, *v.* 6. 1. *Righteousness* is here put for all spiritual blessings. See Ps. xxiv. 5; *ch.* vi. 33. They are purchased for us by *the righteousness of Christ*; conveyed and secured by the imputation of that righteousness to us; and confirmed by the faithfulness of God. 2. These we must *hunger and thirst after*. We must truly and really desire them, as one who is hungry and thirsty desires meat and drink. *Hunger and thirst* are appetites that return frequently, and call for fresh satisfactions; so these holy desires rest not in any thing attained, but are carried out toward renewed pardons, and daily fresh supplies of grace.

Those who thus *hunger and thirst* after spiritual blessings, *are blessed* in those desires, and *shall be filled* with those blessings.

V. The *merciful* are happy, *v.* 7. This, like the rest, is a paradox; for the merciful are not taken to be the wisest, nor are likely to be the richest; yet Christ pronounces them *blessed*. Those are the *merciful*, who are piously and charitably inclined to pity, help, and succour persons in misery. We must not only bear our own afflictions patiently, but we must, by Christian sympathy, partake of the afflictions of our brethren; pity must be shown (Job vi. 14), and *bowels of mercy put on* (Col. iii. 12).

Now, as to the merciful, 1. They are *blessed*; so it was said in the Old Testament; *Blessed is he that considers the poor*, Ps. xli. 1. Herein they resemble God, whose goodness is his glory; in being *merciful as he is merciful*, we are, in our measure, *perfect as he is perfect*. One of the purest and most refined delights in this world, is that of *doing good*. In this word, *Blessed are the merciful*, is included that saying of Christ, which otherwise we find not in the gospels, *It is more blessed to give than to receive*, Acts xx. 35. 2. *They shall obtain mercy*; mercy *with men*, when they need it; *he that watereth, shall be watered also himself* (we know not how soon we may stand in need of kindness, and therefore should be kind); but especially mercy *with God*, for *with the merciful he will show himself merciful*, Ps. xviii. 25.

VI. The *pure in heart* are happy (*v.* 8); *Blessed are the pure in heart, for they shall see God*. This is the most comprehensive of all the beatitudes; here holiness and happiness are fully described and put together.

1. Here is the most *comprehensive character* of the blessed; they are the *pure in heart*. Note, True religion consists in heart-purity. Those who are inwardly pure, show themselves to be under the power of *pure and undefiled* religion. True Christianity lies in the heart, in the *purity of the heart*; the *washing* of that *from wickedness*, Jer. iv. 14. We must lift up to God, not only clean hands, but a pure heart, Ps. xxiv. 4, 5; 1 Tim. i. 5. *Create in me such a clean heart, O God!*

2. Here is the most *comprehensive comfort* of the blessed; They shall see God. Note, (1) It is the perfection of the soul's happiness to *see God; seeing him*, as we may by faith in our present state, is a *heaven upon earth*; and seeing him as we shall in the future state, is the *heaven of heaven*. (2) The happiness of seeing God is promised to those, and those only, who are *pure in heart*. None but the *pure* are capable of *seeing* God, nor would it be a felicity to the impure. What pleasure could an unsanctified soul take in the vision of a holy God? As *he* cannot endure to look upon their iniquity, so *they* cannot endure to look upon his purity.

VII. The *peace-makers* are happy, *v.* 9. The wisdom that is from above is first *pure*, and then *peaceable*; the blessed ones are *pure* toward God, and *peaceable* toward men; for with reference to both, conscience must be kept *void of offence*. The *making of peace* is sometimes a *thankless office*, and it is the lot of him who parts a fray, to have *blows on both sides*; yet it is a good office, and we must be forward to it. Some think that this is intended especially as a lesson for ministers, who should do all they can to reconcile those who are at variance, and to promote Christian love among those under their charge.

Now, (1) Such persons are *blessed*; for they have the satisfaction of *enjoying themselves*, by keeping the peace, and of being truly serviceable to others, by disposing them to peace. They are working together with Christ, who came into the world to *slay all enmities*, and to proclaim *peace on earth*. (2) *They shall be called the children of God*; it will be an evidence to themselves that they are so; God will own them as such, and herein they will resemble him. The children of this world love to fish in troubled waters, but the children of God are the peacemakers, the *quiet in the land*.

VIII. Those who are *persecuted for righteousness' sake*, are happy. This is the greatest paradox of all, and peculiar to Christianity; and therefore it is put last, and more largely insisted upon than any of the rest, *vv.* 10–12. Observe here,

1. The case of suffering saints described; and it is a hard case, and a very piteous one.

(1) They are persecuted, hunted, pursued, run down, as dangerous beasts are, that are sought for to be destroyed. Christ has told us that it would be so with the Christian church, and we are not to think it

strange, 1 John iii. 13. He has left us an example.

(2) They are *reviled, and have all manner of evil said against them falsely*. Nicknames, and names of reproach, are fastened upon them, upon particular persons; sometimes to make them despicable, that they may be trampled upon; sometimes to make them formidable, that they may be powerfully assailed.

(3) All this is *for righteousness' sake* (v. 10); *for my sake*, v. 11. If for *righteousness' sake*, then for *Christ's sake*, for he is closely interested in the work of righteousness. This precludes those from this blessedness who suffer *justly*, and are evil spoken of *truly* for their real crimes; let such be ashamed and confounded, it is part of their punishment; it is not the suffering, but the cause, that makes the martyr.

2. The comforts of suffering saints laid down.

(1) They *are blessed*; for they now, in their life-time, receive *their evil things* (Luke xvi. 25), and receive them upon a good account. They are *blessed*, for it is an honour to them (Acts v. 41); it is an opportunity of glorifying Christ, of doing good, and of experiencing special comforts and visits of grace and tokens of his presence, 2 Cor. i. 5; Dan. iii. 25; Rom. viii. 29.

(2) They shall be *recompensed*; Theirs is *the kingdom of heaven*. They have at present a sure title to it, and sweet foretastes of it; and shall ere long be in possession of it.

(3) *"So persecuted they the prophets that were before you, v."* 12. They were *before you* in excellency,

above what you are yet arrived at;
they were *before you* in time, that
they might be examples to you of
suffering affliction and *of patience*,
James v. 10. They were in like
manner persecuted and abused; and
can you expect to go to heaven in a
way by yourselves? That grace
which was *sufficient for them*, to
carry them through their sufferings,
shall not be *deficient to you*.

(4) Therefore *rejoice and be
exceeding glad*, *v.* 12. It is not
enough to be patient and content
under these sufferings as under
common afflictions, and not to
render railing for railing; but we
must rejoice, because the honour
and dignity, the pleasure and
advantage, of suffering for Christ,
are much more considerable than
the pain or shame of it.

SALT AND LIGHT (*vv.* 13–16)

Christ had lately called his disciples,
and told them that they should be
fishers of men; here he tells them
further what he designed them to be
—*the salt of the earth*, and *lights of
the world*, that they might be indeed
what it was expected they should
be.

I. *Ye are the salt of the earth.*
What could they do in so large a
province as *the whole earth*?
Nothing, if they were to work by
force of arms and dint of sword;
but, being to work silently as salt,
one handful of that salt would
diffuse its savour far and wide;
would go a great way, and work
insensibly and irresistibly as leaven,
ch. xiii. 33. The doctrine of the
gospel is as *salt*; it is penetrating,
buick, and *powerful* (Heb. iv. 12); it
reaches *the heart*, Acts ii. 37. It is

cleansing, it is relishing, and preserves from putrefaction.

If Christians be such as they
should be they are *as good salt*,
white, and small, and broken into
many grains, but very useful and
necessary. If they be not, they are
as *salt* that has *lost its savour*. If
you, who should season others, are
yourselves unsavoury, void of
spiritual life, relish, and vigour; if a
Christian be so, especially if a
minister be so, his condition is very
sad; for *Wherewith shall it be
salted?* Salt is a remedy for *unsavoury meat*, but there is no
remedy for *unsavoury salt*. Christianity will give a man a relish; but
if a man can take up and continue
the profession of it, and yet remain
flat and foolish, and graceless and
insipid, no other doctrine, no other
means, can be applied, to make him
savoury. If Christianity do not do
it, nothing will.

II. *Ye are the light of the world*,
v. 14. Christ calls himself *the Light
of the world* (John viii. 12), and
Christians are *workers together
with him*, and have some of his
honour put upon them.

This similitude is here explained
in two things:

1. As *the lights of the world*, they
are illustrious and conspicuous,
and have many eyes upon them. A
city that is *set on a hill cannot be hid*.
The disciples of Christ, especially
those who are forward and zealous
in his service, become remarkable,
and are taken notice of as beacons.

2. As the *lights of the world*, they
are intended to illuminate and give
light to others (*v.* 15), and therefore, (1) They shall be *set up* as
lights. Christ having lighted these

candles, they shall not be put under a bushel, not confined always, as they are now, to the cities of Galilee, or the lost sheep of the house of Israel, but they shall be sent into all the world. (2) They must *shine* as lights, [1] By their *good preaching*. The knowledge they have, they must communicate for the good of others; not put it *under a bushel*, but spread it. [2] By their *good living*. They must be *burning and shining lights* (John v. 35); must evidence, in their whole manner of life, that they are indeed the followers of Christ, James iii. 13.

See here, *First*, *How* our light must shine. We must do good works *that may be seen* to the edification of others, but not *that they may be seen* to our own ostentation.

Secondly, For what *end* our light must shine—"That those who see your good works may be brought, not to glorify *you* (which was the thing the Pharisees aimed at, and it spoiled all their performances), but to *glorify your Father which is in heaven*." Note, The glory of God is the great thing we must aim at in every thing we do in religion, 1 Pet. iv. 11. The sight of our *good works* will do this, by furnishing them, 1. With *matter for praise*. "Let them see *your good works*, that they may see the power of God's grace in you, and may thank him for it, and give him the glory of it, who has given such power unto men." 2. With *motives to piety*. "Let them see your good works, that they may be convinced of the truth and excellency of the Christian religion, may be provoked by a holy emulation to imitate your good works, and so may glorify God."

THE OLD AND THE NEW LAW (*vv*. 17–32)

Those to whom Christ preached, and for whose use he gave these instructions to his disciples, were such as in their religion had an eye, 1. To the *scriptures* of the *Old Testament* as their *rule*, and therein Christ here shows them they were in the right: 2. To the scribes and Pharisees as their *example*, and therein Christ here shows them they were in the wrong; for,

I. The rule which Christ came to establish exactly agreed with the scriptures of the *Old Testament*, here called *the law* and *the prophets*.

1. He protests against the thought of cancelling and weakening the *Old Testament*; *Think not that I am come to destroy the law and the prophets*. The Saviour of souls is the *destroyer* of nothing but the *works of the devil*, of nothing that comes from God, much less of those excellent dictates which we have from Moses and the prophets. No, he came to *fulfil* them. That is, [1] To obey the commands of the law, for he was *made under the law*, Gal. iv. 4. He in all respects yielded obedience to the law, honoured his parents, sanctified the sabbath, prayed, gave alms, and did that which never any one else did, obeyed perfectly, and never broke the law in any thing. [2] To make good the promises of the law, and the predictions of the prophets, which all bore witness to him. [3] To answer the types of the law; thus (as Bishop Tillotson expresses it), he did not make *void*, but made

good, the ceremonial law, and manifested himself to be the Substance of all those shadows. [4] To fill up the defects of it, and so to complete and perfect it.

2. He asserts the perpetuity of it. "*Verily I say unto you*, I, the *Amen*, the faithful Witness, solemnly declare it, that *till heaven and earth pass*, when time shall be no more, and the unchangeable state of recompences shall supersede all laws, *one jot, or one tittle*, the least and most minute circumstance, *shall in no wise pass from the law till all be fulfilled*."

3. He gives it in charge to his disciples, carefully to preserve the law, and shows them the danger of the neglect and contempt of it (*v.* 19). It is a dangerous thing, in doctrine or practice, to dis-annul the least of God's commands; to break them, that is, to go about either to *contract the extent*, or *weaken the obligation* of them; whoever does so, will find it is at his peril. It is impudence enough to break the command, but it is a greater degree of it to teach men so (*v.* 19). This plainly refers to those who at this time sat in Moses' seat, and by their comments corrupted and perverted the text.

II. The righteousness which Christ came to establish by this rule, must exceed that of the scribes and Pharisees, *v.* 20. This was strange doctrine to those who looked upon the scribes and Pharisees as having arrived at the highest pitch of religion. The scribes were the most noted teachers of the law, and the Pharisees the most celebrated professors of it, and they both sat in Moses' chair

(*ch.* xxiii. 2). It was therefore a great surprise to hear that they must be better than they, or they should not go to heaven; and therefore Christ here avers it with solemnity; *I say unto you*, It is so. We must do more than they, and better than they, or we shall come short of heaven. They were *partial in the law*, and laid most stress upon the ritual part of it; but we must be *universal*, and not think it enough to give the priest his tithe, but must give God our hearts. They minded only the *outside*, but we must make conscience of *inside* godliness. They aimed at the *praise* and *applause of men*, but we must aim at *acceptance with God*: they were *proud* of what they did in religion, and trusted to it as *a righteousness*; but we, when we have done all, must *deny ourselves*, and say, We are *unprofitable servants*, and trust only to the *righteousness of Christ*; and thus we may go beyond the scribes and Pharisees.

THE SIXTH COMMANDMENT

Christ having laid down these principles, that Moses and the prophets were still to be their rulers, but that the scribes and Pharisees were to be no longer their rulers, proceeds to expound the law in some particular instances, and to vindicate it from the corrupt glosses which those expositors had put upon it. He adds nothing new, only limits and restrains some permissions which had been abused: and as to the precepts, shows the breadth, strictness, and spiritual nature of them. In these verses (*vv.* 21–26), he explains the law of the sixth commandment, according to the true intent and full extent of it.

Here is the *command itself* laid down (v. 21); *We have heard it*, and remember it. *Killing* is here forbidden, killing ourselves, killing any other, directly or indirectly, or being any way accessory to it. The law of God, the God of life, is a hedge of protection about our lives. It was one of the precepts of Noah, Gen. ix. 5, 6.

Here is the exposition of this command which the Jewish teachers contented themselves with; their comment upon it was, *Whosoever shall kill, shall be in danger of the judgment*. This was all they had to say upon it, that wilful murderers were liable to the sword of justice, and casual ones to the judgment of the city of refuge. Now this gloss of theirs upon this commandment was faulty, for it intimated, 1. That the law of the sixth commandment was only external, and forbade no more than the act of murder, and laid no restraint upon the inward lusts, from which *wars and fightings come.* This was indeed *the fundamental error* of the Jewish teachers, that the divine law prohibited only the sinful act, not the sinful thought. Another mistake of theirs was, that this law was merely *political* and *municipal*, given for them, and intended as a directory for their courts, and no more; as if they only were the people, and the wisdom of the law must die with them.

And here is the exposition which Christ gave of this commandment. Christ tells them that *rash anger is heart-murder* (v. 22); *Whosoever is angry with his brother without a*

cause, breaks the sixth commandment. Anger is a natural passion; there are cases in which it is lawful and laudable; but it is then *sinful*, when we are angry without cause.

2. He tells them, that giving opprobrious language to our brother is tongue-murder, calling him, *Raca*, and, *Thou fool.* When this is done with mildness and for a good end, to convince others of their vanity and folly, it is not sinful. Thus James says, *O vain man*; and Paul, *Thou fool*; and Christ himself, *O fools, and slow of heart*. But when it proceeds from anger and malice within, it is the smoke of that fire which is kindled from hell, and falls under the same character.

He tells them, that how light soever they made of these sins, they would certainly be reckoned for; he *that is angry with his brother shall be in danger of the judgment* and anger of God; he that calls him *Raca*, *shall be in danger of the council*, of being punished by the Sanhedrim for reviling an Israelite; *but whosoever saith*, *Thou fool*, thou profane person, thou child of hell, *shall be in danger of hell-fire*, to which he condemns his brother; so the learned Dr. Whitby.

From all this it is here inferred, that we ought carefully to preserve Christian love and peace with all our brethren, and that if at any time a breach happens, we should labour for a reconciliation, by confessing our fault, humbling ourselves to our brother, begging his pardon, and making restitution, or offering satisfaction for wrong done in word or deed, according as the nature of the thing is; and that we should do this quickly.

THE SEVENTH COMMANDMENT

We have (in *vv.* 27–32) an exposition of the seventh commandment, given us by the same hand that made the law, and therefore was fittest to be the interpreter of it: it is the law against uncleanness, which fitly follows upon the former; *that* laid a restraint upon sinful passions, *this* upon sinful appetites, both which ought always to be under the government of reason and conscience, and if indulged, are equally pernicious.

The command is here laid down (*v.* 27), *Thou shalt not commit adultery*; which includes a prohibition of all other acts of uncleanness, and the desire of them: but the Pharisees, in their expositions of this command, made it to extend no further than the act of adultery, suggesting, that if the iniquity was only *regarded in the heart*, and went no further, God could not hear it, would not regard it (Ps. lxvi. 18), and therefore they thought it enough to be able to say that they were *no adulterers*, Luke xviii. 11.

But we are here taught, that there is such a thing as *heart-adultery*, adulterous thoughts and dispositions, which never proceed to the act of adultery or fornication; and perhaps the defilement which these give to the soul, that is here so clearly asserted, was not only included in the seventh commandment, but was signified and intended in many of those ceremonial pollutions under the law, for which they were to *wash their clothes, and bathe their flesh in water. Whosoever looketh on a woman to lust after her,* has committed adultery with her in his heart, *v.* 28.

Such looks are so very dangerous and destructive to the soul, that it is better to lose the eye and the hand that thus offend than to give way to the sin, and perish eternally in it (*vv.* 29, 30).

There are some sins from which we need to be *saved with fear*, particularly *fleshly lusts*, which are such *natural brute beasts* as cannot be checked, but by being frightened; cannot be kept from a forbidden tree, but by *cherubim, with a flaming sword.*

Men's divorcing their wives upon dislike, or for any other cause except adultery, however tolerated and practised among the Jews, was a violation of the seventh commandment, as it opened a door to adultery, *vv.* 31, 32. Here observe,

(1) How the matter now stood with reference to divorce. *It hath been said* (he does not say as before, *It hath been said by them of old time*, because this was not a precept, as those were, though the Pharisees were willing so to understand it (*ch.* xix. 7), but only a permission), "*Whosoever shall put away his wife, let him give her a bill of divorce*". Thus the law had prevented rash and hasty divorces; and perhaps at first, when writing was not so common among the Jews, that made divorces rare things; but in process of time they became very common, and this direction how to do it, when there was just cause for it, was construed into a permission of it for any cause, *ch.* xix. 3.

(2) How this matter was rectified and amended by our Saviour. He

reduced the ordinance of marriage to its primitive institution: *They two shall be one flesh*, not to be easily separated, and therefore divorce is not to be allowed, except in case of adultery, which breaks the marriage covenant; but he that puts away his wife upon any other pretence, *causeth her to commit adultery*, and him also that shall marry her when she is thus divorced. Note, Those who lead others into temptation to sin, or leave them in it, or expose them to it, make themselves guilty of their sin, and will be accountable for it. This is one way of being *partaker with adulterers*, Ps. l. 18.

THE THIRD COMMANDMENT
(*vv.* 33–37)

We have here an exposition of the third commandment, which we are the more concerned rightly to understand, because it is particularly said, that *God will not hold him guiltless*, however he may hold himself, who breaks this commandment, by *taking the name of the Lord God in vain*. Now as to this command.

I. It is agreed on all hands that it forbids perjury, forswearing, and the violation of oaths and vows, *v.* 33. This was said to them of old time, and is the true intent and meaning of the third commandment. *Thou shall not* use, or *take up, the name of God* (as we do by an oath) *in vain*, or *unto vanity*, or *a lie*.

II. It is here added, that the commandment does not only forbid false swearing, but all rash, unnecessary swearing: *Swear not at all*, *v.* 34; Compare Jam. v. 12. Not that all swearing is sinful; so far

from that, if rightly done, it is a part of religious worship, and we in it *give unto God the glory due to his name*. See Deut. vi. 13; x. 20; Isa. xlv. 23; Jer. iv. 2. We find Paul confirming what he said by such solemnities (2 Cor. i. 23), when there was a necessity for it. In swearing, we pawn the truth of something known, to confirm the truth of something doubtful or unknown; we appeal to a greater knowledge, to a higher court, and imprecate the vengeance of a righteous Judge, if we swear deceitfully.

Now the mind of Christ in this matter is,

1. That we must *not swear at all*, but when we are duly called to it, and justice or charity to our brother, or respect to the commonwealth, make it necessary for *the end of strife* (Heb. vi. 16).

2. That we must not swear lightly and irreverently, in common discourse: it is a very great sin to make a ludicrous appeal to the glorious Majesty of heaven, which, being a sacred thing, ought always to be very serious.

3. That we must in a special manner avoid promissory oaths, of which Christ more particularly speaks here, for they are oaths that are to be performed. The influence of an affirmative oath immediately ceases, when we have faithfully discovered the truth, and the whole truth; but a promissory oath binds so long, and may be so many ways broken, by the surprise as well as strength of a temptation, that it is not to be used but upon great necessity.

4. That we must not swear by

any creature. It should seem there were some, who, in civility (as they thought) to the name of God, would not make use of that in swearing, but would swear *by heaven* or *earth*, *&c.* This Christ forbids here (*v.* 34), and shows that there is nothing we can swear by, but it is some way or other related to God, who is the Fountain of all beings, and therefore that it is as dangerous to swear by them, as it is to swear by God himself.

5. That therefore in all our communications we must content ourselves with, *Yea, yea,* and *Nay, nay, v.* 37. In ordinary discourse, if we affirm a thing, let us only say, *Yea,* it is so; and, if need be, to evidence our assurance of a thing, we may double it, and say, *Yea, yea,* indeed it is so: *Verily, verily,* was our Saviour's *yea, yea.* So if we deny a thing, let it suffice to say, No; or if it be requisite, to repeat the denial, and say, No, no; and if our fidelity be known, that will suffice to gain us credit; and if it be questioned, to back what we say with swearing and cursing, is but to render it more suspicious.

THE LAW OF RETALIATION
(*vv.* 38–42)

In these verses the law of retaliation is expounded, and in a manner repealed. Observe,

I. What the *Old Testament permission* was, in case of injury. It was not a command, that every one should of necessity require such satisfaction; but they might lawfully insist upon it, if they pleased; *an eye for an eye, and a tooth for a tooth.* This we find, Exod. xxi. 24; Lev. xxiv. 20; Deut. xix. 21.

But some of the Jewish teachers, who were not the most compassionate men in the world, insisted upon it as necessary that such revenge should be taken, even by private persons themselves, and that there was no room left for remission, or the acceptance of satisfaction.

II. What the *New Testament precept* is, as to the complainant himself, his duty is, to *forgive the injury* as done to himself, and no further to insist upon the punishment of it than is necessary to the public good: and this precept is consonant to the meekness of Christ, and the gentleness of his yoke.

Two things Christ teaches us here:

1. We must not be revengeful (*v.* 39); *I say unto you, that ye resist not evil;*—the evil person that is injurious to you. Yet this does not repeal the law of self-preservation, and the care we are to take of our families; we may *avoid evil,* and may *resist* it, so far as is necessary to our own security; but we must not *render evil for evil,* must not bear a grudge, nor avenge ourselves, nor study to be even with those that have treated us unkindly, but we must go beyond them by forgiving them, Prov. xx. 22; xxiv. 29; xxv. 21, 22. Rom. xii. 17.

Three things our Saviour specifies, to show that Christians must patiently yield to those who bear hard upon them, rather than contend; and these include others.

(1) A blow on the cheek, which is an injury to me in my body; "*Whosoever shall smite thee on thy right cheek,* which is not only a

hurt, but an affront and indignity (2 Cor. xi. 20), if a man in anger or scorn thus abuse thee, "*turn to him the other cheek.*" Though this may perhaps, with some base spirits, expose us to the like affront another time, and so it is, in effect, to *turn the other cheek*, yet let not that disturb us, but let us trust God and his providence to protect us in the way of our duty. Perhaps, the forgiving of one injury may prevent another, when the avenging of it would but draw on another; some will be overcome by submission, who by resistance would but be the more exasperated, Prov. xxv. 22.

(2) The loss of a coat, which is a wrong to me in my estate (*v.* 40); *If any man will sue thee at the law, and take away thy coat.* It is a hard case. Though judges be just and circumspect, yet it is possible for bad men who make no conscience of oaths and forgeries, by course of law to force off the coat from a man's back. *Marvel not at the matter* (Eccl. v. 8), but, in such a case, rather than go to law by way of revenge, rather than exhibit a cross bill, or stand out to the utmost, in defence of that which is thy undoubted right, *let him* even take *thy cloak also.*

(3) The going a mile by constraint, which is a wrong to me in my liberty (*v.* 41); "*Whosoever shall compel thee to go a mile*, to run an errand for him, or to wait upon him, grudge not at it, but *go with him two miles* rather than fall out with him:" say not, "I would do it, if I were not compelled to it, but I hate to be forced;" rather say, "Therefore I will do it, for otherwise there will be a quarrel;" and it

is better to serve him, than to serve thy own lusts of pride and revenge.

The sum of all is, that Christians must not be litigious; small injuries must be submitted to, and no notice taken of them; and if the injury be such as requires us to seek reparation, it must be for a good end, and without thought of revenge: though we must not invite injuries, yet we must meet them cheerfully in the way of duty, and make the best of them.

2. We must be charitable and beneficent (*v.* 42); must not only do no hurt to our neighbours, but labour to do them all the good we can. What God says to us, we should be ready to say to our poor brethren, *Ask, and it shall be given you.*

THE LAW OF LOVE
(*vv.* 43–48)

We have here, lastly, an exposition of that great fundamental law, *Thou shalt love thy neighbour*, which was the fulfilling of the law.

I. See here how this law was corrupted by the comments of the Jewish teachers, *v.* 43. God said, *Thou shalt love thy neighbour*; and by *neighbour* they understood those only of their own country, nation, and religion; and those only that they were pleased to look upon as their friends: yet this was not the worst; from this command, *Thou shalt love thy neighbour*, they were willing to infer what God never designed; *Thou shalt hate thine enemy*; and they looked upon whom they pleased as their enemies, thus making void the great command of God by their traditions, though there were express laws to the contrary, Exod. xxiii. 4, 5; Deut. xxiii. 7.

II. See how it is cleared by the command of the Lord Jesus, who teaches us another lesson: "*But I say unto you, I,* who come to be the great Peace-Maker, the general Reconciler, who loved you when you were strangers and enemies, *I say, Love your enemies,*" *v.* 44. We are here told,

1. That we must *speak* well of them: *Bless them that curse you.* They, in whose tongues is *the law of kindness,* can give good words to those who give bad words to them.

2. That we must *do* well to them: "*Do good to them that hate you,* and that will be a better proof of love than good words. Be ready to do them all the real kindness that you can, and glad of an opportunity to do it, in their bodies, estates, names, families; and especially to do good to their souls."

3. We must *pray for them*: *Pray for them that despitefully use you, and persecute you.* We must pray that God will forgive them, that they may never fare the worse for any thing they have done against us, and that he would make them to be at peace with us; and this is one way of making them so.

Two reasons are here given to enforce this command (which sounds so harsh) of *loving our enemies.* We must do it,

[1] That we may be *like God our Father*; "that ye may be, may approve yourselves to be, *the children of your Father which is in heaven.*" Can we write after a better copy? It is a copy in which love to the worst of enemies is reconciled to, and consistent with, infinite purity and holiness.

[2] That we may herein *do more than others,* vv. 46, 47. *First, Publicans love their friends.* Nature inclines them to it; interest directs them to it. The publicans were men of no good fame, yet they were grateful to such as had helped them to their places, and courteous to those they had a dependence upon; and shall we be no better than they? In doing this we serve ourselves and consult our own advantage; and what reward can we expect for that, unless a regard to God, and a sense of duty, carry us further than our natural inclination and worldly interest? *Secondly,* We must therefore love our enemies, that we may exceed them. If we must go beyond scribes and Pharisees, much more beyond publicans. Note, Christianity is something more than humanity. We *know* more than others; we *talk* more of the things of God than others; we *profess,* and have *promised,* more than others; God has done more for us, and therefore justly expects more from us than from others; the glory of God is more concerned in us than in others; but *what do we more than others?* In this especially we must do more than others, that while every one will render *good for good,* we must render *good for evil*; and this will speak a nobler principle, and is consonant to a higher rule, than the most of men act by.

Lastly, Our Saviour concludes this subject with this exhortation (*v.* 48), *Be ye therefore perfect, as your Father which is in heaven is perfect.* Which may be understood,

1. In general, including all those things wherein we must be *followers of God as dear children*. Or, 2. In this particular before mentioned, of *doing good to our enemies*; see Luke vi. 36. It is God's perfection to *forgive injuries* and to *entertain strangers*, and to do good to the evil and unthankful, and it will be ours to be like him.

CHAPTER SIX
DOING ALMS (*vv.* 1–4)

As we must do better than the scribes and Pharisees in avoiding heart-sins, heart-adultery, and heart-murder, so likewise in maintaining and keeping up heart-religion, doing what we do from an inward, vital principle, that we may be approved of God, not that we may be applauded of men; that is, we must watch against hypocrisy, which was the leaven of the Pharisees, as well as against their doctrine, Luke xii. 1. *Almsgiving, prayer*, and *fasting*, are three great Christian duties—the three foundations of the law, say the Arabians: by them we do homage and service to God with our three principal interests; by *prayer* with our *souls*, by *fasting* with our *bodies*, by *alms-giving* with our *estates*.

Now in these verses we are cautioned against hypocrisy in giving alms.

Two things are here supposed,

I. The *giving of alms* is a great duty, and a duty which all the disciples of Christ, according to their ability, must abound in.

II. That it is such a duty as has a great reward attending it, which is lost if it be done in hypocrisy.

This being supposed, observe now,

1. What was the *practice of the hypocrites* about this duty. They did it indeed, but not from any principle of obedience to God, or love to man, but in pride and vain-glory. Not that it is unlawful to give alms *when men see us*; we may do it, we must do it, but not *that men may see us*; we should rather choose those objects of charity that are less observed. The hypocrites, if they gave alms at their own houses, *sounded a trumpet*, under pretence of calling the poor together to be served, but really to proclaim their charity, and to have that taken notice of and made the subject of discourse.

Now the judgment that Christ passes upon this is very observable; *Verily I say unto you, they have their reward*. At first view this seems a promise—If they have their reward they have enough, but two words in it make it a threatening.

(1) It is a reward, but it is *their* reward; not the reward which God promises to them that do good, but the reward which they promise themselves, and a poor reward it is.

(2) It is a reward, but it is a *present reward*, they *have* it; and there is none reserved for them in the future state.

2. What is the *precept of our Lord Jesus* about it, *vv.* 3, 4. He that was himself such an example of humility, pressed it upon his disciples, as absolutely necessary to the acceptance of their performances. "*Let not thy left hand know what thy right hand doeth* when thou givest alms." It is intimated,

(1) That we must not let *others* know what we do; no, not those that stand *at our left hand*, that are very near us. (2) That we must not observe it too much *ourselves*: the left hand is a part of ourselves; we must not within ourselves take notice too much of the good we do, must not applaud and admire ourselves.

3. What is the *promise to those who are thus sincere and humble* in their alms-giving. Let *thine alms be in secret*, and then *thy Father who seeth in secret* will observe them. But this is not all; not only the observation and praise, but the recompence is of God, *himself shall reward thee openly*. Observe how emphatically it is expressed; *himself shall reward*, he will himself be the Rewarder, Heb. xi. 6. If the work be not open, the reward shall, and that is better.

PRAYING (*vv.* 5–8)

In *prayer* we have more immediately to do with God than in *giving alms*, and therefore are yet more concerned to be *sincere*, which is what we are here directed to. *When thou prayest* (*v.* 5). It is taken for granted that all the disciples of Christ *pray*.

Now there were two great faults they were guilty of in prayer, against each of which we are here cautioned—vain-glory (*vv.* 5, 6); and vain repetitions, *vv.* 7, 8.

I. We must not be *proud* and *vain-glorious* in prayer, nor aim at the praise of men. In all their exercises of devotion, it was plain, the chief thing they aimed at was to be commended by their neigh-

bours, and thereby to make an interest for themselves.

The *product* of all this is—*they have their reward*; they have all the recompence they must ever expect from God for their service, and a poor recompence it is. What will it avail us to have the good word of our fellow-servants, if our Master do not say, *Well done?*

What is the *will of Jesus Christ* in opposition to this? Humility and sincerity are the two great lessons that Christ teaches us.

Observe, (1) The directions here given about it.

[1] Instead of praying in *the synagogues* and in the *corners of the streets, enter into thy closet*, into some place of privacy and retirement.

[2] Instead of doing it to be *seen of men, pray to thy Father who is in secret; to me, even to me*, Zech. vii. 5, 6. By *secret* prayer we give God the glory of his universal presence (Acts xvii. 24), and may take to ourselves the comfort of it.

(2) The encouragements here given us to it.

[1] Thy Father *seeth in secret*; his eye is upon thee to accept thee, when the eye of no man is upon thee to applaud thee.

[2] He *will reward thee openly*; they have their reward that do it openly, and you shall not lose yours for doing it in secret. It is called a *reward*, but it is *of grace*, not *of debt*; what merit can there be in begging? The Pharisees had their reward *before all the town*, and it was a *mere flash and shadow*; true Christians shall have theirs *before all the world*, angels and men, and it shall be a *weight of glory*.

II. We must not *use vain repetitions* in prayer, *vv.* 7, 8. Now observe,

1. What the *fault* is that is here reproved and condemned; it is making a mere lip-labour of the duty of prayer, the service of the tongue, when it is not the service of the soul. This is expressed here by two phrases, (1) *Vain repetitions*—tautology, idle babbling over the same words again and again to no purpose. It is not all repetition in prayer that is here condemned, but vain repetitions. Christ himself prayed, saying the same words (*ch.* xxvi. 44), out of a more than ordinary fervour and zeal, Luke xxii. 44. But the superstitious rehearsing of a tale of words, or the barren and dry going over of the same things again and again, merely to drill out the prayer to such a length, and to make a show of affection when really there is none; these are the vain repetitions here condemned. (2) *Much speaking*, an affectation of prolixity in prayer, either out of pride or superstition, or an opinion that God needs either to be informed or argued with by us, or out of mere folly and impertinence, because men love to *hear themselves talk*. Not that all long prayers are forbidden; Christ prayed all night, Luke vi. 12. But merely to prolong the prayer, as if that would make it more pleasing or more prevailing with God, is that which is here condemned; it is not much *praying* that is condemned; no, we are bid to *pray always*, but much *speaking*.

2. What reasons are given against this.

(1) This is the way of the heathen, *as the heathen do*; and it ill becomes Christians to worship their God as the Gentiles worship theirs.

(2) "It need not be your way, *for your Father* in heaven *knoweth what things ye have need of before ye ask him.*" Consider, [1] The God we pray to is our Father by creation, by covenant; and therefore our addresses to him should be easy, natural, and unaffected; children do not use to make long speeches to their parents when they want anything. [2] He is a Father that knows our case and knows our wants better than we do ourselves. We need not be long, nor use many words in representing our case; God knows it better than we can tell him, only he will know it *from us* (*what will ye that I should do unto you?*).

THE LORD'S PRAYER
(*vv.* 9–15)

When Christ had condemned what was amiss, he directs to do better; for his are reproofs of instruction. Because we know not what to pray for as we ought, he here helps our infirmities, by putting words into our mouths; *after this manner therefore pray ye, v.* 9. Not that we are tied up to the use of this form only, or of this always, as if this were necessary to the consecrating of our other prayers; we are here bid to pray after this manner, with these words, or to this effect.

The Lord's prayer (as indeed every prayer) is a letter sent from earth to heaven. Here is the inscription of the letter, the person to whom it is directed, *our Father*; the place where, *in heaven*; the contents of it in several errands of request; the close, *for thine is the kingdom*; the seal, *Amen*; and if you will, the date too, *this day*.

Plainly thus: there are three parts of the prayer.

I. *The preface, Our Father who art in heaven.* Before we come to our business, there must be a solemn address to him with whom our business lies; *Our Father*.

1. We must address ourselves to him as *our Father*, and must call him so. He is a common Father to all mankind by creation, Mal. ii. 10; Acts xvii. 28. He is in a special manner a Father to the saints, by adoption and regeneration (Eph. i. 5; Gal. iv. 6); and an unspeakable privilege it is.

2. As our Father *in heaven*: so in heaven as to be every where else, for the heaven cannot contain him; yet so in heaven as there to manifest his glory, for it is his throne (Ps. ciii. 19), and it is to believers a throne of grace: thitherward we must direct our prayers, for Christ the Mediator is now in heaven, Heb. viii. 1.

II. *The petitions*, and those are six; the three first relating more immediately to God and his honour, the three last to our own concerns, both temporal and spiritual.

1. *Hallowed be thy name.* It is the same word that in other places is translated *sanctified*. In these words, (1) We give glory to God; it may be taken not as a petition, but as an adoration. We must begin our prayers with praising God, and it is very fit he should be first served, and that we should give glory to God, before we expect to receive

mercy and grace from him. (2) We fix our end, and it is the right end to be aimed at, and ought to be our chief and ultimate end in all our petitions, that God may be glorified; all our other requests must be in subordination to this, and in pursuance of it.

2. *Thy kingdom come.* This petition has plainly a reference to the doctrine which Christ preached at this time, which John Baptist had preached before, and which he afterwards sent his apostles out to preach—*the kingdom of heaven is at hand*. What God has promised we must pray for; for promises are given, not to supersede, but to quicken and encourage prayer; and when the accomplishment of a promise is near and at the door, when the kingdom of heaven is at hand, we should then pray for it the more earnestly.

3. *Thy will be done in earth as it is in heaven.* We pray that God's kingdom being come, we and others may be brought into obedience to all the laws and ordinances of it. We make Christ but a titular Prince, if we call him King, and do not do his will: having prayed that he may rule us, we pray that we may in every thing be ruled by him, and that it may *be done on earth*, in this place of our trial and probation (where our work must be done, or it never will be done), *as it is done in heaven*, that place of rest and joy.

4. *Give us this day our daily bread.* Because our natural being is necessary to our spiritual well-being in this world, therefore, after the things of God's glory, kingdom, and will, we pray for the

necessary supports and comforts of this present life, which are the gifts of God, and must be asked of him, —*Bread for the day approaching*, for all the remainder of our lives.

Every word here has a lesson in it: (1) We ask for *bread*; that teaches us sobriety and temperance; we ask for *bread*, not dainties, not superfluities; that which is wholesome, though it be not nice. (2) We ask for *our* bread; that teaches us honesty and industry: we do not ask for the bread out of other people's mouths, not *the bread of deceit* (Prov. xx. 17), not *the bread of idleness* (Prov. xxxi. 27), but the bread honestly gotten. (3) We ask for our *daily* bread; which teaches us not to *take thought for the morrow* (*v.* 34), but constantly to depend upon divine Providence, as those that live from hand to mouth. (4) We beg of God to *give* it us, not sell it us, nor lend it us, but *give* it. The greatest of men must be beholden to the mercy of God for their *daily bread*, (5) We pray, "Give it to *us*; not to me only, but to others in common with me." This teaches us charity, and a compassionate concern for the poor and needy. It intimates also, that we ought to pray with our families; we and our households eat together, and therefore ought to pray together. (6) We pray that God would give it us *this day*: as duly as the day comes, we must pray to our heavenly Father, and reckon we could as well go a day without meat, as without prayer.

5. *And forgive us our debts, as we forgive our debtors.* This is connected with the former; *and forgive*, intimating, that unless our sins be pardoned, we can have no comfort in life, or the supports of it. Here we have,

(1) A petition; *Father in heaven forgive us our debts*, our debts to thee. Note, [1] Our sins are our debts. A debtor is liable to process, so are we; a malefactor is a debtor to the law, so are we. [2] Our heart's desire and prayer to our heavenly Father every day should be, that he would *forgive us our debts*; that the obligation to punishment may be cancelled and vacated, that we may *not come into condemnation*.

(2) An argument to enforce this petition; *as we forgive our debtors*. This is not a plea of merit, but a plea of grace. Note, Those that come to God for the forgiveness of their sins against him, must make conscience of forgiving those who have offended them, else they curse themselves when they say the Lord's prayer.

6. *And lead us not into temptation, but deliver us from evil.* This petition is expressed,

(1) Negatively: *Lead us not into temptation.* Having prayed that the guilt of sin may be removed, we pray, as is fit, that we may never return again to folly, that we may not be tempted to it. It is not as if God tempted any to sin; but, "Lord, do not let Satan loose upon us; chain up that *roaring lion*, for he is subtle and spiteful; Lord, do not leave us to ourselves (Ps. xix. 13), for we are very weak."

(2) Positively: *But deliver us from evil; from the evil one*, the devil, the tempter; "keep us, that either we may not be assaulted by him, or

49

we may not be overcome by those assaults".

III. The conclusion: *For thine is the kingdom, and the power and the glory, for ever. Amen.* Some refer this to David's doxology, 1 Chron. xxix. 11. *Thine, O Lord, is the greatness.* It is,

1. A form of plea to enforce the foregoing petitions. It is our duty to plead with God in prayer, to fill our mouth with arguments (Job xxiii. 4) not to move God, but to affect ourselves; to encourage our faith, to excite our fervency, and to evidence both.

2. It is a form of praise and thanksgiving. The best pleading with God is praising of him; it is the way to obtain further mercy, as it qualifies us to receive it. Observe, how full this doxology is, *The kingdom, and the power and the glory*, it is all thine.

Most of the petitions in the Lord's prayer had been commonly used by the Jews in their devotions, or words to the same effect: but that clause in the fifth petition, *As we forgive our debtors*, was perfectly new, and therefore our Saviour here shows for what reason he added it. God, in forgiving us, has a peculiar respect to our forgiving those that have injured us; and therefore, when we pray for pardon, we must mention our making conscience of that duty, not only to remind ourselves of it, but to bind ourselves to it. See that parable, *ch.* xviii. 23–35. Selfish nature is loth to comply with this, and therefore it is here inculcated, *vv.* 14, 15.

1. In a promise. *If ye forgive, your heavenly Father will also for-give*. Not as if this were the only condition required; there must be repentance and faith, and new obedience; but as where other graces are in truth, there will be this, so this will be a good evidence of the sincerity of our other graces.

2. In a threatening. "*But if you forgive not* those that have injured you, that is a bad sign you have not the other requisite conditions, but are altogether unqualified for pardon: and therefore *your Father*, whom you call Father, and who, as a father, offers you his grace upon reasonable terms, will nevertheless *not forgive you*.

FASTING (*vv.* 16–18)

We are here cautioned against hypocrisy in fasting, as before in almsgiving, and in prayer.

I. It is here supposed that religious fasting is a duty required of the disciples of Christ, when God, in his providence, calls to it. It is a laudable practice, and we have reason to lament that it is so generally neglected among Christians. Anna was much in fasting, Luke ii. 37. Cornelius fasted and prayed, Acts x. 30. The primitive Christians were much in it, see Acts xiii. 3; xiv. 23. Private fasting is supposed, 1 Cor. vii. 5. It is an act of self-denial, and mortification of the flesh, a holy revenge upon ourselves, and humiliation under the hand of God.

II. We are cautioned not to do this *as the hypocrites* did it, lest we lose the reward of it; and the more difficulty attends the duty, the greater loss it is to lose the reward of it.

Now, 1. The *hypocrites* pretended

fasting, when there was nothing of that contrition or humiliation of soul in them, which is the life and soul of the duty.

2. They proclaimed their fasting, and managed it so that all who saw them might take notice that it was a fasting-day with them. Note, It is sad that men, who have, in some measure, mastered their pleasure, which is sensual wickedness, should be ruined by their pride, which is spiritual wickedness, and no less dangerous. Here also *they have their reward*, that praise and applause of men which they court and covet so much; *they have* it, and it is their all.

III. We are directed how to manage a private fast; we must keep it private, *vv.* 17, 18. "And while thou deniest thyself thy bodily refreshments, do it so as that it may not be taken notice of, no, not by those that are nearest to thee; look pleasant, *anoint thine head and wash thy face*, as thou dost on ordinary days, on purpose to conceal thy devotion; and thou shalt be no loser in the praise of it at last; for though it be not of men, it shall be of God." Fasting is the humbling of the soul (Ps. xxxv. 13), that is the inside of the duty; let that therefore be thy principal care, and as to the outside of it, covet not to let it be seen.

TREASURE (*vv.* 19–24)

We must take heed of hypocrisy and worldly-mindedness, in the choice we make of our treasure, our end, and our masters.

I. In choosing the *treasure* we *lay up*. Something or other every man has which he makes his *treasure*,

his portion, which his heart is upon, to which he carries all he can get, and which he depends upon for futurity. Now Christ designs not to deprive us of our treasure, but to direct us in the choice of it; and here we have,

1. A *good caution* against making *the things that are seen*, that *are temporal*, our best things, and placing our happiness in them. *Lay not up for yourselves treasures upon earth*.

2. Here is a *good reason* given why we should not look upon anything *on earth* as our *treasure*, because it is liable to loss and decay: (1) From corruption within. That which is treasure *upon earth moth and rust do corrupt*. Note, Worldly riches have in themselves a principle of corruption and decay; they wither of themselves, and *make themselves wings*. (2) From violence without. *Thieves break through and steal*. Every hand of violence will be aiming at the house where *treasure* is laid up; nor can anything be laid up so safe, but we may be spoiled of it. It is folly to make that our *treasure* which we may so easily be robbed of.

3. *Good counsel*, to make the joys and glories of the other world, those *things not seen* that *are eternal*, our best things, and to place our happiness in them. *Lay up for yourselves treasures in heaven*. It is a great encouragement to us to *lay up* our *treasure in heaven*, that there it is safe; it will not decay of itself, no *moth* nor *rust* will *corrupt* it; nor can we be by force or fraud deprived of it; *thieves do not break through and steal*. It is a happiness above and beyond the changes and

chances of time, *an inheritance incorruptible.*

4. A *good reason* why we should thus choose, and an evidence that we have done so (*v.* 21), *Where your treasure is,* on earth or in heaven, *there will your heart be.* The *heart* follows the *treasure,* as the needle follows the loadstone, or the sun-flower the sun.

This direction about laying up our *treasure,* may very fitly be applied to the foregoing caution, of not doing what we do in religion *to be seen of men.* Our *treasure* is our alms, prayers, and fastings, and the reward of them; if we have done these only to gain the applause of men, we have *laid up this treasure on earth,* have lodged it in the hands of men, and must never expect to hear any further of it. But if we have prayed and fasted and given alms in truth and up-rightness, with an eye to God and to his acceptance, and have approved ourselves to him therein, we have laid up that treasure *in heaven.*

II. We must take heed of hypocrisy and worldly-mindedness in choosing the *end we look at.* Our concern as to this is represented by two sorts of eyes which men have, a *single eye* and an *evil eye, vv.* 22, 23.

1. *The eye,* that is, *the heart* (so some) if that *be single, free and bountiful* (so the word is frequently rendered, as Rom. xii. 8; 2 Cor. viii. 2, ix. 11. 13; Jam. i. 5, and we read of a *bountiful eye,* Prov. xxii. 9) will direct the man to Christian actions, his whole life *will be full of light,* full of the evidences and instances of true Christianity, that *pure religion and*

undefiled before God and the Father (Jam. i. 27), *full of light,* of good works, which are our *light shining before men;* but *if the heart be evil,* covetous, and hard, and envious, griping and grudging (such a temper of mind is often expressed by an *evil eye, ch.* xx. 15; Mark vii. 22; Prov. xxiii. 6, 7), *the body will be full of darkness,* the whole way of life will be heathenish and unchristian.

2. *The eye,* that is, *the under-standing* (so some); the practical judgment, the conscience, which is to the other faculties of the soul, as *the eye* is to the *body,* to guide and direct their motions; now *if this eye be single,* if it make a true and right judgment, it will rightly guide the affections and actions, which will all be *full of the light* of grace and comfort; *but if this be evil* and corrupt, and instead of leading the inferior powers, is led, and bribed, and biassed by them, if this be erroneous and misinformed, the heart and life must needs be *full of darkness,* and the whole way of life corrupt.

3. *The eye,* that is, *the aims* and *intentions;* by *the eye* we set our end before us, the mark we shoot at, the place we go to, we keep that in view, and direct our motion accord-ingly; in every thing we do in religion, there is something or other that we have in our *eye;* now *if our eye be single,* if we aim honestly, fix right ends, and move rightly towards them, if we aim purely and only at the glory of God, seek his honour and favour, and direct all entirely to him, then *the eye is single. But if this eye be evil,* if, instead of aiming only at the

glory of God, and our acceptance with him, we look aside at the applause of men, and while we profess to honour God, contrive to honour ourselves, and seek our own things under colour of *seeking the things of Christ*, this spoils all, and the foundations being thus out of course, there can be nothing but *confusion and every evil work* in the superstructure.

III. We must take heed of hypocrisy and worldly-mindedness in choosing the master we serve, *v.* 24. *No man can serve two masters.* Serving *two masters* is contrary to *the single eye*; for *the eye* will be to the master's hand, Ps. cxxiii. 1, 2. Our Lord Jesus here exposes the cheat which those put upon their own souls, who think to divide between God and the world, to have a *treasure on earth*, and a *treasure in heaven* too, to please God and please men too. Why not? says the hypocrite; it is good to have two strings to one's bow. No, says Christ, this will not do; it is but a supposition that *gain is godliness*, 1 Tim. vi. 5. Here is,

1. A general maxim laid down; it is likely it was a proverb among the Jews, *No man can serve two masters*, much less two gods; for their commands will some time or other cross or contradict one another, and their occasions interfere.

2. The application of it to the business in hand. *Ye cannot serve God and Mammon. Mammon* is a Syriac word, that signifies gain; so that whatever in this world is, or is accounted by us to be, *gain* (Phil. iii. 7), is *mammon*. He does not say, We *must* not or we *should* not, but we *cannot serve God and Mammon*;

we *cannot* love both (1 John ii. 15; Jam. iv. 4); or hold to both, or hold by both in observance, obedience, attendance, trust, and dependence, for they are contrary, the one to the other.

PRIORITIES (*vv.* 25–34)

There is scarcely any one sin against which our Lord Jesus more largely and earnestly warns his disciples, or against which he arms them with more variety of arguments, than the sin of disquieting, distracting, distrustful cares about the things of this life, which are a bad sign that both the *treasure* and the heart are *on the earth*; and therefore he thus largely insists upon it. Here is,

I. The prohibition laid down. It is the repeated command of the Lord Jesus to his disciples, that they should not divide and pull in pieces their own minds with care about the world.

But the *thought* here forbidden is, 1. A disquieting, tormenting *thought*, which hurries the mind hither and thither, and hangs it in suspense; which disturbs our joy in God, and is a damp upon our hope in him; which breaks the sleep, and hinders our enjoyment of ourselves, of our friends, and of what God has given us. 2. A distrustful, unbelieving *thought*. God has promised to provide for those that are his all things needful for life as well as godliness, *the life that now is*, food and a covering: not dainties, but necessaries. Observe the cautions here,

(1) *Take no thought for your life.* Life is our greatest concern for this world; *All that a man has will he*

give for his life; yet take no thought about it. [1] Not about the *continuance* of it; refer it to God to *lengthen* or *shorten* it as he pleases; *my times are in thy hand*, and they are in a good hand. [2] Not about the *comforts* of this life; refer it to God to embitter or sweeten it as he pleases.

(2) *Take no thought for the morrow*, for the time to come. Be not solicitous for the future, how you shall live next year, or when you are old, or what you shall leave behind you. As we must not *boast of* tomorrow, so we must not *care for* tomorrow, or the events of it.

II. The reasons and arguments to enforce this prohibition. Consider then,

1. *Is not the life more than meat, and the body than raiment? v.* 25. Yes, no doubt it is; so he says who had reason to understand the true value of present things, for he made them, he supports them, and supports us by them; and the thing speaks for itself. Note, (1) Our *life* is a greater blessing than our *livelihood*. Food and raiment are in order to life, and the *end* is more noble and excellent than the *means*. (2) This is an encouragement to us to trust God for *food* and *raiment*, and so to ease ourselves of all perplexing cares about them. God has given us life, and given us the body; it was an act of power, it was an act of favour, it was done without our care: what cannot he do for us, who did that?—what will he not? If we take care about our souls and eternity, which are more than the body, and its life, we may leave it to God to provide for us food and raiment, which are less.

2. *Behold the fowls of the air*, and *consider the lilies of the field.* Here is an argument taken from God's common providence toward the inferior creatures, and their dependence, according to their capacities, upon that providence. A fine pass fallen man has come to, that he must be sent to school to the *fowls of the air*, and that they must *teach him!* Job xii. 7, 8.

(1) Look upon the *fowls*, and learn to trust God *for food* (*v.* 26), and disquiet not yourselves with thoughts *what you shall eat*.

(2) Look upon the *lilies*, and learn to trust God for *raiment*. That is another part of our care, *what we shall put on.* Now to ease us of this care, let us *consider the lilies of the field*; not only *look upon* them (every eye does that with pleasure), but *consider* them.

3. *Which of you*, the wisest, the strongest of you, *by taking thought, can add one cubit to his stature?* (*v.* 27), to *his age*, so some; but the measure of a cubit denotes it to be meant of the stature, and the age at longest is but a span, Ps. xxxix. 5. Let us consider, (1) We did not arrive at the stature we are of by our own care and thought, but by the providence of God. Now he that made our bodies, and made them of such a size, surely will take care to provide for them. (2) We cannot alter the stature we are of, if we would: what a foolish and ridiculous thing would it be for a man of low stature to perplex himself, to break his sleep, and beat his brains, about it, and to be continually taking thought how he might be a cubit higher; when, after all, he knows he cannot effect it, and

therefore he had better be content and take it as it is! Now as we do in reference to our bodily stature, so we should do in reference to our worldly estate. [1] We should not covet an abundance of the wealth of this world. [2] We must reconcile ourselves to our state, as we do to our stature; we must set the conveniences against the inconveniences, and so make a virtue of necessity: what cannot be remedied must be made the best of.

4. *After all these things do the Gentiles seek*, v. 32. Thoughtfulness about the world is a *heathenish* sin, and unbecoming *Christians*. The *Gentiles* seek *these things*, because they know not *better things*; they are eager for this world, because they are strangers to a better; they seek these things with care and anxiety, because they are *without God in the world*, and understand not his providence.

5. *Your heavenly Father knows ye have need of all these things*; these necessary things, food and raiment; he knows our wants better than we do ourselves; though he be in heaven, and his children on earth, he observes what the least and poorest of them has occasion for (Rev. ii. 9), *I know thy poverty*. Therefore, we should ease ourselves of the burden of care, by casting it upon God, because it is he *that careth for us* (1 Pet. v. 7), and what needs all this ado? If he care, why should we care?

6. *Seek first the kingdom of God, and his righteousness, and all these things shall be added unto you*, v. 33. Here is a double argument against the sin of *thoughtfulness; take no thought* for your life, the life of the body. Thoughtfulness for our souls is the most effectual cure of thoughtfulness for the world. Observe here,

[1] The great duty required: it is the sum and substance of our whole duty: "*Seek first the kingdom of God*; mind religion as your great and principal concern." Now observe, *First*, The object of this seeking; *The kingdom of God, and his righteousness*; we must mind heaven as our end, and holiness as our way. "Seek the comforts of the kingdom of grace and glory as your felicity, aim at the *kingdom of heaven*; press towards it; give diligence to make it sure; resolve not to take up short of it; seek for this glory honour, and immortality; prefer heaven and heavenly blessings far before earth and earthly delights." We make nothing of our religion, if we do not make heaven of it. And with the *happiness* of this kingdom, seek the *righteousness* of it; *God's righteousness*, the righteousness which he requires to be wrought *in* us, and wrought *by* us, such as exceeds that of the scribes and Pharisees; we must *follow peace and holiness*, Heb. xii. 14. *Secondly*, The order of it. *Seek first the kingdom of God*. Let your care for your souls and another world take place of all other cares: and let all the concerns of this life be made subordinate to those of the life to come: we must seek the things of Christ more than our own things; and if ever they come in competition, we must remember to which we are to give the preference.

[2] The gracious promise annexed; *all these things*, the necessary supports of life, *shall be added unto*

you; shall be *given over and above*; so it is in the margin. You shall have what you seek, the *kingdom of God and his righteousness*, for never any sought *in vain*, that sought *in earnest*; and besides that, you shall have food and raiment, by way of overplus.

7. *The morrow shall take thought for the things of itself: sufficient unto the day is the evil thereof, v.* 34. We must not perplex ourselves inordinately about future events, because every day brings along with it its own burden of cares and grievances. So that we are here told,

(1) That *thoughtfulness* for the morrow is *needless*; *Let the morrow take thought for the things of itself.* If wants and troubles be renewed with the day, there are aids and provisions renewed likewise; *compassions*, that are *new every morning*, Lam. iii. 22, 23. The meaning is, let us *mind present duty*, and then *leave events to God*; do the *work of the day in its day*, and then let *tomorrow bring its work along with it.*

(2) That thoughtfulness for the morrow is one of those *foolish and hurtful lusts*, which those that will be rich fall into, and one of the *many sorrows*, wherewith they *pierce themselves through. Sufficient unto the day is the evil thereof.* What a folly is it to take that trouble upon ourselves this day by care and fear, which belongs to another day, and will be never the lighter when it comes? Let us not pull that upon ourselves all together at once, which Providence has wisely ordered to be borne by parcels.

CHAPTER SEVEN

CENSURE AND REPROOF
(*vv.* 1–6)

Our Saviour is here directing us how to conduct ourselves in reference to the faults of others.

I. A caution *against judging, vv.* 1, 2. Now observe,

1. The prohibition; *Judge not.* We must judge ourselves, and judge of our own acts, but we must not judge our brother. We must not sit in the judgment-seat, to make our word a law to every body. We must not make the worst of people, nor infer such invidious things from their words and actions as they will not bear. We must not judge uncharitably, unmercifully, nor with a spirit of revenge, and a desire to do mischief. We must not judge of a man's state by a single act, nor of what he is in himself by what he is to us, because in our own cause we are apt to be partial. We must not judge the hearts of others, nor their intentions, for it is God's prerogative to try the heart, and we must not step into his throne; nor must we judge of their eternal state. Counsel him, and help him, but do not judge him.

2. The reason to enforce this prohibition. *That ye be not judged.* This intimates, (1) That if we presume to judge others, we may expect to be ourselves judged. (2) That if we be modest and charitable in our censures of others, and decline judging them, and judge ourselves rather, *we shall not be judged of the Lord.* As God will forgive those that forgive their brethren; so he will not judge those

that will not judge their brethren; the *merciful shall find mercy*.

The judging of those that judge others is according to the law of retaliation; *With what judgment ye judge, ye shall be judged, v.* 2. What would become of us, if God should be as exact and severe in judging us, as we are in judging our brethren; if he should weigh us in the same balance?

II. Some cautions *about reproving*. Now observe here,

1. It is not everyone who is fit to reprove. Those who are themselves guilty of the same faults of which they accuse others, or of worse, bring shame upon themselves, and are not likely to do good to those whom they reprove, *vv.* 3-5. Here is,

(1) A just reproof to the censorious, who quarrel with their brother for small faults, while they allow themselves in great ones. Note, [1] There are degrees in sin: some sins are comparatively but as *motes*, others as *beams*; some as a *gnat*, others as a *camel*: not that there is any sin little, for there is no little God to sin against: if it be a *mote* (or *splinter*, for so it might better be read), it is in the eye; if a *gnat*, it is in the throat; both painful and perilous, and we cannot be easy or well till they are got out. [2] Our own sins ought to appear greater to us than the same sins in others: that which charity teaches us to call but a *splinter in our brother's eye*, true repentance and godly sorrow will teach us to call a *beam in our own*. [3] There are many that have *beams in their own eyes*, and yet do not consider it. They are under the guilt and dominion of very great

sins, and yet are not aware of it, but justify themselves, as if they needed no repentance nor reformation. [4] It is common for those who are most sinful themselves, and least sensible of it, to be most forward and free in judging and censuring others: the Pharisees, who were most haughty in justifying themselves, were most scornful in condemning others. But, [5] Men's being so severe upon the faults of others, while they are indulgent of their own, is a mark of hypocrisy. *Thou hypocrite, v.* 5. [6] The consideration of what is amiss in ourselves, though it ought not to keep us from administering friendly reproof, ought to keep us from magisterial censuring, and to make us very candid and charitable in judging others.

(2) Here is a good rule for reprovers, *v.* 5. Go in the right method, *first cast the beam out of thine own eye*. A man's *of*fence will never be his *de*fence: but I must first reform myself, that I may thereby help to reform my brother, and may qualify myself to reprove him.

2. It is not everyone who is fit to be reproved; *Give not that which is holy unto the dogs, v.* 6. This may be considered, either, (1) As a rule to the disciples in preaching the gospel; not that they must not preach it to any who were wicked and profane. (Christ himself preached to publicans and sinners), but the reference is to such as they found obstinate after the gospel was preached to them, such as blasphemed it, and persecuted the preachers of it; let them not spend much time among such, for it would

be lost labour, but let them turn to others, Acts xiii. 41. So Dr. Whitby. Or, (2) As a rule to all in giving reproof. Our zeal against sin must be guided by discretion, and we must not go about to give instructions, counsels, and rebukes, much less comforts, to hardened scorners, to whom it will certainly do no good, but who will be exasperated and enraged at us. See here what is the evidence of men's being *dogs* and *swine*. Those are to be reckoned such, who *hate reproofs* and reprovers, and fly in the face of those who, in kindness to their souls, show them their sin and danger. These sin against the remedy; who shall heal and help those that will not be healed and helped?

ASKING ARIGHT (*vv.* 7–11)

Our Saviour, in the foregoing chapter, had spoken of prayer as a commanded duty, by which God is honoured, and which, if done aright, shall be rewarded; here he speaks of it as the appointed means of obtaining what we need, especially grace to obey the precepts he had given, some of which are so displeasing to flesh and blood.

I. Here is a precept in three words to the same purport, *Ask, Seek, Knock* (*v.* 7); that is, in one word, "Pray; pray often, pray with sincerity and seriousness; pray, and pray again; make conscience of prayer, and be constant in it; make a business of prayer, and be earnest in it. *Ask,* as a beggar asks alms." Those that would be rich in grace, must betake themselves to the poor trade of begging, and they shall find it a thriving trade. *Seek* as for a thing of value that we have lost, or as the merchantman that *seeks goodly pearls. Seek by prayer,* Dan. ix. 3. *Knock,* as he that desires to enter into the house knocks at the door." We would be admitted to converse with God, would be taken into his love, and favour, and kingdom; sin has shut and barred the door against us; by prayer, we knock; *Lord, Lord, open to us.*

II. Here is a promise annexed: *our labour* in prayer, if indeed we do labour in it, *shall not be in vain.* Now here,

1. The promise is made, and made so as exactly to answer the precept, *v.* 7. God will meet those that attend on him; *Ask, and it shall be given you. Seek,* and *ye shall find,* and then you do not lose your labour; God is himself *found of those that seek* him, and if we find him we have enough. "*Knock, and it shall be opened*; the door of mercy and grace shall no longer be shut against you as enemies and intruders, but opened to you as friends and children."

2. It is repeated, *v.* 8. It is to the same purport, yet with some addition. (1) It is made to extend to all that pray aright; "Not only you my disciples shall receive what you pray for, but *every one that asketh, receiveth,* whether Jew or Gentile, young or old, rich or poor, high or low, master or servant, learned or unlearned, they are all alike welcome to *the throne of grace,* if they come in faith: *for God is no respecter of persons.* (2) It is made so as to amount to a grant, in words of the present tense, which

is more than a promise for the future. *Every one that asketh*, not only *shall* receive, but *receiveth*. Christ hereby puts his *fiat* to the petition; and he having all power, that is enough.

3. It is illustrated, by a similitude taken from earthly parents, and their innate readiness to give their children what they ask. Christ appeals to his hearers, *What man is there of you*, though never so morose and ill-humoured, *whom if his son ask bread, will he give him a stone?* vv. 9, 10. Whence he infers (*v.* 11), *If ye then, being evil*, yet grant your children's requests, *much more will your heavenly Father give you the good things you ask*. Now this is of use,

(1) To *direct* our prayers and expectations. [1] We must come to God, as children to a *Father in heaven*, with reverence and confidence. [2] We must come to him for *good things*, for those he *gives to them that ask him*; which teaches us to refer ourselves to him; we know not what is good for ourselves (Eccl. vi. 12), but he knows what is good for us, we must therefore leave it with him; *Father, thy will be done*.

(2) To *encourage* our prayers and expectations. We may hope that we shall not be denied and disappointed. The world often gives *stones for bread*, and *serpents for fish*, but God never does; nay, we shall be heard and answered, for children are by their parents.

THE WAY TO LIFE
(*vv.* 12–14)

Our Lord Jesus here presses upon us that righteousness towards men which is an essential branch of true religion, and that religion towards God which is an essential branch of universal righteousness.

I. We must make righteousness our rule, and be ruled by it, *v.* 12. *Therefore*, lay this down for your principle, to do as you would be done by. Now here we have,

1. The rule of justice laid down; *Whatsoever ye would that men should do to you, do you even so to them*. This is grounded upon that great commandment, *Thou shalt love thy neighbour as thyself*. (1) We must do that to our neighbour which we ourselves acknowledge to be fit and reasonable. (2) We must put other people upon the level with ourselves, and reckon we are as much obliged to them, as they to us. (3) We must, in our dealings with men, suppose ourselves in the same particular case and circumstances with those we have to do with, and deal accordingly. If I were making such a one's bargain, labouring under such a one's infirmity and affliction, how should I desire and expect to be treated?

2. A reason given to enforce this rule; *This is the law and the prophets*. It is the summary of that second great commandment, which is one of the two, *on which hang all the law and the prophets*, ch. xxii. 40. We have not this in so many words, either in *the law* or *the prophets*, but it is the concurring language of the whole. All that is there said concerning our duty towards our neighbour (and that is no little) may be reduced to this rule.

II. We must make religion our business, and be intent upon it; we must be strict and circumspect in our conversation, which is here represented to us as entering in at a *strait gate*, and walking on in a *narrow way*, vv. 13, 14. Observe here,

1. The account that is given of the bad way of sin, and the good way of holiness. There are but two ways, right and wrong, good and evil; the way to heaven, and the way to hell; in the one of which we are all of us walking: no middle place hereafter, no middle way now.

Here is, (1) An account given us of the way of sin and sinners; both what is the best, and what is the worst of it.

[1] That which allures multitudes into it, and keeps them in it; *the gate is wide, and the way broad*, and there are many travellers in that way. You may go in at this gate with all your lusts about you; it gives no check to your appetites, to your passions. It is a *broad way*, for there is nothing to hedge in those that walk in it, but they wander endlessly; a *broad way*, for there are many paths in it; there is choice of sinful ways, contrary to each other, but all paths in this *broad way*. *Secondly*, "You will have abundance of company in that way: *many there be that go in* at this gate, and walk in this way." If we *follow the multitude*, it will be *to do evil*: if we go with the crowd, it will be the wrong way.

[2] That which should affright us all from it is, that it *leads to destruction*. Death, eternal death, is at the end of it (and the way of sin tends to it),—everlasting *destruction from the presence of the Lord*. Whether it be the high way of open profaneness, or the back way of close hypocrisy, if it be a way of sin, it will be our ruin, if we repent not.

(2) Here is an account given us of the way of holiness.

[1] What there is in it that frightens many from it.

First, That *the gate is strait*. Conversion and regeneration are *the gate*, by which we enter into this way, in which we begin a life of faith and serious godliness; out of a state of sin into a state of grace we must pass, by the new birth, John iii. 3, 5. This is a *strait gate*, hard to find, and hard to get through; like a passage between two rocks, 1 Sam. xiv. 4. There must be *a new heart, and a new spirit*, and *old things must pass away*.

Secondly, That *the way is narrow*. We are not in heaven as soon as we have got through *the strait gate*, not in Canaan as soon as we have got through the Red Sea; no, we must go through a wilderness, must travel a *narrow way*, must endure hardness, must wrestle and be in an agony, must watch in all things, and walk with care and circumspection.

Thirdly, The *gate* being so *strait and the way so narrow*, it is not strange that there are but *few that find it*, and choose it. Many pass it by, through carelessness. Others look upon it, but shun it; they like not to be so limited and restrained. Those that are going to heaven are but few, compared to those that are going to hell; a remnant, a little flock.

[2] Let us see what there is in this way, which, notwithstanding this, should invite us all to it; it *leads to life*, to present comfort in the favour of God, which is the life of

the soul; to eternal bliss, the hope of which, at the end of our way, should reconcile us to all the difficulties and inconveniences of the road.

2. The great concern and duty of every one of us, in consideration of all this; *Enter ye in at the strait gate.* The matter is fairly stated; life and death, good and evil, are set before us; both the ways, and both the ends: now let the matter be taken entire, and considered impartially, and then choose you this day which you will walk in. It is true, we can neither go in, nor go on, without the assistance of divine grace; but it is as true, that grace is freely offered, and shall not be wanting to those that seek it, and submit to it. Conversion is hard work, but it is needful, and, blessed be God, it is not impossible if we strive, Luke xiii. 24.

FALSE PROPHETS
(*vv.* 15–20)

We have here a caution against *false prophets*, to take heed that we be not deceived and imposed upon by them.

They are false teachers and *false prophets*, 1. Who produce false commissions, who pretend to have immediate warrant and direction from God to set up for *prophets*, and to be divinely inspired, when they are not so. Here is,

I. A good reason for this caution, *Beware of* them, for they are *wolves in sheep's clothing, v.* 15.

1. We have need to be very cautious, because their pretences are very fair and plausible, and such as will deceive us, if we be not upon our guard. They pretend to be sheep, and outwardly appear so innocent, harmless, meek, useful' and all that is good, as to be excelled by none. They and their errors are gilded with the specious pretences of sanctity and devotion· Satan turns himself *into an angel of light,* 2 Cor. xi. 13, 14.

2. Because under these pretensions their designs are very malicious and mischievous; *inwardly they are ravening wolves.* Every *hypocrite* is a *goat* in sheep's clothing; but a *false prophet* is a *wolf* in sheep's clothing; not only not a sheep, but the worst enemy the sheep has, that comes not but to tear and devour, to *scatter the sheep* (John x. 12), to drive them from God, and from one another, into crooked paths.

II. Here is a good rule to go by in this caution; we must *prove all things* (1 Thess. v. 21), *try the spirits* (1 John iv. 1), and here we have a touchstone; *ye shall know them by their fruits,* 16–20. Observe,

1. The illustration of this comparison, of the fruit's being the discovery of the tree. You cannot always distinguish them by their bark and leaves, nor by the spreading of their boughs, but *by their fruits ye shall know them.* An apple may be stuck, or a bunch of grapes may hang, upon a thorn; so may a good truth, a good word or action, be found in a bad man, but you may be sure it never grew there.

2. The application of this to the false prophets.

(1) By way of terror and threatening (*v.* 19); *Every tree that brings not forth good fruit is hewn down.* This very saying John the Baptist had used, *ch.* iii. 10. God will deal with them as men deal with dry

trees that cumber the ground. Compare this with Ezek. xxxi. 12, 13; Dan. iv. 14; John xv. 6.

(2) By way of trial; *By their fruits ye shall know them.*

[1] *By the fruits* of their persons, their words and actions, and the course of their conversation. If you would know whether they be right or not, observe how they live; their works will testify for them or against them.

[2] *By the fruits* of their doctrine. What do they tend to? What affections and practices will they lead those into, that embrace them? If *the doctrine be of God*, it will tend to promote serious piety, humility, charity, holiness, and love, with other Christian graces; but if, on the contrary, the doctrines these prophets preach have a manifest tendency to make people proud, worldly, and contentious, to make them loose and careless, unjust or uncharitable, factious or disturbers of the public peace; if it indulge carnal liberty, and take people off from governing themselves and their families by the strict rules of *the narrow way*, we may conclude, that *this persuasion comes not of him that calleth us*, Gal. v. 8.

TRUE AND FALSE
(*vv.* 21–29)

We have here the conclusion of this long and excellent sermon, the scope of which is to show the indispensable necessity of obedience to the commands of Christ.

I. He shows, by a plain remonstrance, that an outward profession of religion, however remarkable, will not bring us to heaven, unless there be a correspondent way of life, *vv.* 21–23. Observe here,

1. Christ's law laid down, *v.* 21. *Not every one that saith, Lord, Lord, shall enter into the kingdom of heaven, into the kingdom of* grace and glory. Christ here shows,

(1) That it will not suffice to say, *Lord, Lord.* This is not to take us off from saying, *Lord, Lord*; from praying, and being earnest in prayer, from professing Christ's name, and being bold in professing it, but from resting in these, in the *form of godliness*, without *the power.*

(2) That it is necessary to our happiness that we *do the will of* Christ, which is indeed *the will of* his *Father in heaven.*

2. The hypocrite's plea against the strictness of this law, offering other things in lieu of obedience, *v.* 22. They put in their plea with great importunity, *Lord, Lord*; and with great confidence, appealing to Christ concerning it; *Lord,* dost not thou know, (1) That *we have prophesied in thy name*? Note, A man may be a preacher, may have gifts for the ministry, and an external call to it, and perhaps some success in it, and yet be a wicked man; may help others to heaven, and yet come short himself. (2) That *in thy name we have cast out devils*? A man might *cast devils out* of others, and yet have a devil, nay, and be a devil himself. (3) That *in thy name we have done many wonderful works.* There may be a faith of miracles, where there is no justifying faith; none of that *faith which works by love* and obedience.

3. The rejection of this plea as

frivolous. The same that is the Law-Maker (*v.* 21) is here the Judge according to that law (*v.* 23), and he will overrule the plea, will overrule it publicly; he *will profess to them* with all possible solemnity, as sentence is passed by the Judge, *I never knew you*, and therefore *depart from me, ye that work iniquity.*—Observe, (1) Why, and upon what ground, he rejects them and their plea—because they were *workers of iniquity.* (2) How it is expressed; *I never knew you;* "I never owned you as my servants, no, not when you *prophesied in* my *name*, when you were in the height of your profession, and were most extolled." This intimates, that if he had ever known them, as *the Lord knows them that are his*, had ever owned them and loved them as his, he would have known them, and owned them, and *loved them, to the end*; but he *never* did *know* them, for he always knew them to be hypocrites, and rotten at heart, as he did Judas; therefore, says he, *depart from me.*

II. He shows, by a parable, that hearing these sayings of Christ will not make us happy, if we do not make conscience of doing them; but that if we hear them and do them, we are *blessed in our deed*, *vv.* 24–27.

1. The hearers of Christ's word are here divided into two sorts; some that hear, and do what they hear; others that hear and do not.

(1) Some that *hear his sayings and do them*: blessed be God that there are any such, though comparatively few. To hear Christ is not barely to give him the hearing, but to obey him. Observe, It is not enough to *hear* Christ's *sayings*, and understand them, *hear* them, and remember them, *hear* them, and talk of them, repeat them, dispute for them; but we must *hear, and do* them. *This do, and thou shalt live.* Those only *that hear, and do*, are *blessed* (Luke xi. 28; John xiii. 17), and are akin to Christ, *ch.* xii. 50.

(2) There are others who *hear* Christ's *sayings and do them not*; their religion rests in bare hearing, and goes no further. Those who only *hear* Christ's *sayings, and do them not*, sit down in the midway to heaven, and that will never bring them to their journey's end.

2. These two sorts of hearers are here represented in their true characters, and the state of their case, under the comparison of two builders; one was *wise*, and *built upon a rock*, and his building stood in a storm; the other *foolish*, and *built upon the sand*, and his building fell.

III. In the two last verses, we are told what impressions Christ's discourse made upon the hearers. It was an excellent sermon; and it is probable that he said more than is here recorded; and doubtless the delivery of it from the mouth of him, into whose lips grace was poured, did mightily set it off. Now, 1. *They were astonished at his doctrine*; it is to be feared that few of them were brought by it to follow him: but for the present, they were filled with wonder. Note, It is possible for people to admire good preaching, and yet to remain in ignorance and unbelief; to be astonished, and yet not sanctified. 2. The reason was because he taught them *as one having authority, and not as the scribes*. The scribes pretended to as much authority as any teachers whatsoever, and were supported by all the external advantages that could be obtained, but their preaching was mean, and flat, and jejune: they spake as those that were not themselves masters of what they preached: the word did not come from them with any life or force; they delivered it as a schoolboy says his lesson; but Christ delivered his discourse, as a judge gives his charge. He did indeed, *dominari in conscionibus— deliver his discourses with a tone of authority*; his lessons were laws; his word a word of command. Christ, upon the mountain, showed more true authority, than the scribes in Moses's seat. Thus when Christ teaches by his Spirit in the soul, he teaches with authority. He says, *Let there be light, and there is light*.

CHAPTER EIGHT

THE LEPER CLEANSED

(*vv*. 1–4)

The first verse refers to the close of the foregoing sermon: the people that heard him were *astonished at his doctrine*; and the effect was, that *when he came down from the mountain, great multitudes followed him*. It is pleasing to see people so well affected to Christ, as to think they can never hear enough of him; so well affected to the best things, as thus to flock after good preaching, and to *follow the Lamb* whithersoever he goes.

In these verses we have an account of Christ's *cleansing a leper*. It should seem, by comparing Mark i. 40, and Luke v. 12, that this passage, though placed, by St. Matthew, after the sermon on the mount, because he would give account of his doctrine first, and then of his miracles, happened some time before; but that is not at all material. This is fitly recorded with the first of Christ's miracles, 1. Because the leprosy was looked upon, among the Jews, as a particular mark of God's displeasure: hence we find Miriam, Gehazi, and Uzziah, smitten with leprosy for some one particular sin; and therefore Christ, to show that he came to turn away the wrath of God, by taking away sin, began with the cure of a leper. 2. Because this disease, as it was supposed to come immediately from the hand of God, so also it was supposed to be removed immediately by his hand, and therefore it was not attempted to be cured by physicians, but was put under the inspection of the priests, the Lord's ministers, who waited to see what God would do. The law discovered sin (for by the law is the knowledge of sin), and pronounced sinners unclean; it shut them up (Gal. iii. 23), as the priest did the ᵒleper, but could go no further; it could not *make the comers thereunto perfect*. But Christ takes away sin; cleanses us from it, and so *perfecteth for ever them that are sanctified*. Now here we have,

I. The leper's address to Christ: *Lord, if thou wilt, thou canst make me clean*. The cleansing of him may be considered,

1. As a temporal mercy; a mercy to the body, delivering it from a disease, which, though it did not threaten life, embittered it.

2. As a typical mercy. Sin is the leprosy of the soul; it shuts us out from communion with God, to which that we may be restored, it is necessary that we be cleansed from this leprosy, and this ought to be our great concern.

II. Christ's answer to this address, which was very kind, *v.* 3.

1. *He put forth his hand and touched him.* There was a ceremonial pollution contracted by the touch of a leper; but Christ would show, that when he conversed with sinners, he was in no danger of being infected by them, for the prince of this world had nothing in him. If we touch pitch, we are defiled; but Christ was *separate from sinners*, even when he lived among them.

2. He said, *I will, be thou clean.* He did not say, as Elisha to Naaman, *Go, wash in Jordan*; did not put him upon a tedious, troublesome, chargeable course of physic, but spake the word and healed him. (1) Here is a word of kindness, *I will*; I am as willing to help thee, as thou art to be helped. Note, They who by faith apply themselves to Christ for mercy and grace, may be sure that he is willing, freely willing, to give them the mercy and grace they come to him for. (2) A word of power, *Be thou clean.* Both a power of authority, and a power of energy, are exerted in this word. Christ heals by a word of command to us; *Be thou clean*; "Be willing to be clean, and use the means; cleanse thyself from all filthiness;" but there goes along with this a word of command concerning us, a word that does the work; *I will that thou be clean.*

Such a word as this is necessary to the cure, and effectual for it; and the Almighty grace which speaks it, shall not be wanting to those who truly desire it.

III. The happy change hereby wrought: *Immediately his leprosy was cleansed.* Nature works gradually, but the God of nature works immediately; he speaks, it is done; and yet he works effectually; he *commands, and it stands fast.*

IV. The after-directions Christ gave him. It is fit that they who are cured by Christ should ever after be ruled by him.

1. *See thou tell no man*; "Tell no man till thou hast shown thyself to the priest, and he has pronounced thee clean; and so thou hast a legal proof, both that thou wast before a leper, and art now thoroughly cleansed." Christ would have his miracles to appear in their full light and evidence, and not to be published till they could appear so.

2. *Go show thyself to the priest*, according to the law, Lev. xiv. 2. Christ took care to have the law observed, lest he should give offence, and to show that he will have order kept up, and good discipline and respect paid to those that are in office.

3. *Offer the gift that Moses commanded*, in token of thankfulness to God, and recompence to the priest for his pains; and this *for a testimony unto them.*

THE CENTURION'S SERVANT
(*vv.* 5–13)

We have here an account of Christ's curing the centurion's servant of a palsy. This was done at Capernaum, where Christ now dwelt, *ch.*

iv. 13. Christ went about doing good, and came home to do good too; every place he came to was the better for him.

The persons Christ had now to do with were,

1. A *centurion*; he was a supplicant, a Gentile, a Roman, an officer of the army; probably commander-in-chief of that part of the Roman army which was quartered at Capernaum, and kept garrison there. (1) Though he was a soldier (and a little piety commonly goes a great way with men of that profession), yet he was a godly man; he was eminently so. Note, God has his remnant among all sorts of people. (2) Though he was a Roman soldier, and his very dwelling among the Jews was a badge of their subjection to the Roman yoke, yet Christ, who was *King of the Jews*, favoured him; and therein has taught us to do good to our enemies, and not needlessly to interest ourselves in national enmities. (3) Though he was a Gentile, yet Christ countenanced him. Now good old Simeon's word began to be fulfilled, that he should be *a light to lighten the Gentiles*, as well as *the glory of his people Israel*.

2. *The centurion's servant*; he was the patient. In this also it appears, that there is no respect of persons with God; for *in Christ Jesus*, as there is *neither circumcision nor uncircumcision*, so there is *neither bond nor free*. He is as ready to heal the poorest servant, as the richest master; for himself *took upon him the form of a servant*, to show his regard to the meanest.

Now in the story of the cure of this servant, we may observe an intercourse or interchanging of graces, very remarkable between Christ and the centurion. See here,

I. The grace of the centurion working towards Christ. Observe,

1. His affectionate address to Jesus Christ, which speaks,

(1) A pious regard to our great Master, as one able and willing to succour and relieve poor petitioners. He came to him *beseeching him*, not as Naaman the Syrian (a centurion too) came to Elisha, demanding a cure, taking state, and standing upon points of honour; but with cap in hand as a humble suitor.

(2) A charitable regard to his poor servant. We read of many that came to Christ for their children, but this is the only instance of one that came to him for a servant: *Lord, my servant lieth at home sick*. The centurion's servants were very dutiful to him (*v.* 9), and here we see what made them so; he was very kind to them, and that made them the more cheerfully obedient to him. Observe, How pathetically he represents his servant's case as very sad; he is *sick of the palsy*, a disease which commonly makes the patient senseless of pain, but this person was *grievously tormented*; being young, nature was strong to struggle with the stroke, which made it painful.

2. Observe his great humility and self-abasement: *Lord, I am not worthy that thou shouldst come under my roof* (*v.* 8), which speaks mean thoughts of himself, and high thoughts of our Lord Jesus. He does not say, "My servant is not worthy that thou shouldst come into his chamber, because it is in

the garret;" But *I am not worthy that thou shouldst come into my house*. The centurion was a great man, yet he owned his unworthiness before God.

3. Observe his great faith. The more humility the more faith; the more diffident we are of ourselves, the stronger will be our confidence in Jesus Christ. He had an assurance of faith not only that Christ could cure his servant, but,

(1) That he could cure him at a distance. There needed not any physical contact, as in natural operations, nor any application to the part affected; but the cure, he believed, might be wrought, without bringing the physician and patient together.

(2) That he could cure him with a *word*, not send him a medicine, much less a charm; but *speak the word only*, and I do not question but *my servant shall be healed*. With men, saying and doing are two things; but not so with Christ, who is therefore the *Arm of the Lord*, because he is the *eternal Word*.

The centurion's faith in the power of Christ he here illustrates by the dominion he had, as a centurion, over his soldiers, as a master over his servants; he says to one, *Go, and he goes*, &c. Thus could Christ speak, and it is done; such a power had he over all bodily diseases. Now, [1] Such servants we all should be to God: we must go and come at his bidding, according to the directions of his word, and the disposals of his providence; run where he sends us, return when he remands us, and do what he appoints. *What saith my Lord unto his servant?* When his will crosses our own, his must take place, and our own be set aside. [2] Such servants bodily diseases are to Christ. They seize us when he sends them; they leave us when he calls them back; they have that effect upon us, upon our bodies, upon our souls, that he orders. It is a matter of comfort to all that belong to Christ, for whose good his power is exerted and engaged, that every disease has his commission, executes his command, is under his control, and is made to serve the intentions of his grace. They need not fear sickness, nor what it can do, who see it in the hand of so good a Friend.

II. Here is the grace of Christ appearing towards this centurion; for to the gracious he will show himself gracious.

1. He complies with his address at the first word. He did but tell him his servant's case, and was going on to beg a cure, when Christ prevented him, with this good word, and comfortable word, *I will come and heal him* (v. 7).

2. He commends his faith, and takes occasion from it to speak a kind word of the poor Gentiles, *vv*. 10–12. See what great things a strong but self-denying faith can obtain from Jesus Christ, even of general and public concern.

PETER'S MOTHER-IN-LAW
(*vv*. 14–17)

Here we have,

I. A particular account of the cure of *Peter's wife's mother*, who was ill *of a fever*; in which observe,

1. The *case*, which was nothing extraordinary; fevers are the most common illnesses; but, the

patient being a near relation of Peter's, it is recorded as an instance of Christ's peculiar care of, and kindness to, the families of his disciples.

2. The *cure, v.* 15. (1) How it was *effected; He touched her hand*; not to know the disease, as the physicians do, by the pulse, but to heal it. This was an intimation of his kindness and tenderness; he is *himself touched with the feeling of our infirmities*; it likewise shows the way of spiritual healing, by the exerting of the power of Christ with his word, and the application of Christ to ourselves.

II. Here is a general account of the many cures that Christ wrought. This cure of Peter's mother-in-law brought him abundance of patients. "He healed such a one; why not me? Such a one's friend, why not mine?" Now we are here told,

1. What he did, *v.* 16. (1) *He cast out devils; cast out the* evil *spirits with his word.* (2) *He healed all that were sick;* all without exception, though the patient was ever so mean, and the case ever so bad.

2. How the scripture was herein fulfilled, *v.* 17. The accomplishment of the Old-Testament prophecies was the great thing Christ had in his eye, and the great proof of his being the Messiah: among other things, it was written of him (Isa. liii. 4), *Surely he hath borne our griefs, and carried our sorrows*: it is referred to, 1 Pet. ii. 24, and there it is construed, *he hath borne our sins*; here it is referred to, and is construed, *he hath borne our sicknesses*; our sins make our sicknesses our griefs; Christ bore away sin by the merit of his death, and bore away sickness

by the miracles of his life; nay, though those miracles are ceased, we may say, that *he bore our sicknesses* then, *when he bore our sins in his own body upon the tree*; for sin is both the cause and the sting of sickness.

TWO DISCIPLES
(*vv.* 18–22)

Here is Christ's communication with two, who, upon his remove to *the other side*, were loth to stay behind, and had a mind to follow him, not as others, who were his followers at large, but to come into close discipleship, which the most were shy of; for it carried such a face of strictness as they could not like, nor be well reconciled to; but here is an account of two who seemed desirous to come into communion, and yet were not right; which is here given as a specimen of the hindrances by which many are kept from closing with Christ, and cleaving to him; and a warning to us, to set out in following Christ, so as that we may not come short; to lay such a foundation, as that our building may stand.

1. Here is one that was *too hasty in promising*; and he was *a certain scribe* (*v.* 19), a scholar, a learned man, one of those who studied and expounded the law. Now observe,

(1) How he expressed his forwardness; *Master, I will follow thee, whithersoever thou goest.* I know not how any man could have spoken better. Now we should think ourselves sure of such a man as this; and yet it appears, by Christ's answer, that his resolution was rash, his ends low and carnal. Note, There are many resolutions

for religion, produced by some sudden pangs of conviction, and taken up without due consideration, that prove abortive, and come to nothing: soon ripe, soon rotten.

(2) How Christ tried his forwardness, whether it were sincere or not, *v.* 20. He let him know that this *Son of man,* whom he is so eager to follow, *has not where to lay his head, v.* 20.

It is strange that such a declaration should be made on this occasion. When a scribe offered to follow Christ, one would think he would have encouraged him, and said, *Come, and I will take care of thee;* one scribe might be capable of doing him more credit and service than twelve disciples: but Christ saw his heart, and answered to the thoughts of that, and therein teaches us all how to come to Christ. *First,* The scribe's resolve seems to have been sudden; and Christ would have us, when we take upon us a profession of religion, to *sit down and count the cost* (Luke xiv. 28), to do it intelligently, and with consideration, and choose the way of godliness, not because we know no other, but because we know no better. *Secondly,* His resolve seems to have been from a worldly, covetous principle. He saw what abundance of cures Christ wrought, and concluded that he had large fees, and would get an estate quickly, and therefore he would follow him in hopes of growing rich with him; but Christ rectifies his mistake, and tells him, he was so far from growing rich, that he had not a place to *lay his head on;* and that if he follow him, he cannot expect to fare better than he fared.

2. Here is another that was too *slow in performing.* Delay in execution is as bad, on the one hand, as precipitancy in resolution is on the other hand; when we have taken time to consider, and then have determined, let it never be said, we left that to be done to-morrow, which we could do today. Now observe here,

(1) The excuse that this disciple made, to defer an immediate attendance on Christ (*v.* 21); "*Lord, suffer me first to go and bury my father.*" His father (some think) was now sick, or dying, or dead; others think, he was only aged, and not likely in a course of nature, to continue long; and he desired leave to attend upon him in his sickness, at his death, and to his grave, and then he would be at Christ's service. This seemed a reasonable request, and yet it was not right. He had not the zeal he should have had for the work, and therefore pleaded this, because it seemed a plausible plea.

(2) Christ's disallowing of this excuse (*v.* 22). His excuse is laid aside as insufficient; *Let the dead bury their dead.* It is a proverbial expression; "Let one dead man bury another: rather let them lie unburied, than that the service of Christ should be neglected. *Let the dead* spiritually *bury the dead* corporally; let worldly offices be left to worldly people; do not thou encumber thyself with them. Burying the dead, and especially a dead father, is a good work, but it is not thy work at this time: it may be done as well by others, that are not called and qualified, as thou art, to be employed for Christ; thou hast

something else to do, and must not defer that."

STORM ON THE LAKE
(vv. 23–27)

Now observe here,

I. The peril and perplexity of the disciples in this voyage; and in this appeared the truth of what Christ had just now said, that those who follow him must count upon difficulties, v. 20.

1. *There arose a very great storm*, v. 24. Christ could have prevented this storm, and have ordered them a pleasant passage, but that would not have been so much for his glory and the confirmation of their faith as their deliverance was: this storm was *for their sakes*, as John xi. 4. The church is *tossed with tempests* (Isa. liv. 11); it is only the upper region that enjoys a perpetual calm, this lower one is ever and anon disturbed and disturbing.

2. Jesus Christ *was asleep in this storm*. We never read of Christ's sleeping but at this time; he was in watchings often, and continued all night in prayer to God: this was a sleep, not of security, like Jonah's in a storm, but of holy serenity, and dependence upon his Father. He slept at this time, to try the faith of his disciples, whether they could trust him when he seemed to slight them. He slept not so much with a desire to be refreshed, as with a design to be awaked.

3. The poor disciples, though used to the sea, were in a great fright, and in their fear *came to* their Master, v. 25. Whither else should they go? It was well they had him so near them. They *awoke him* with

their prayers; *Lord, save us, we perish*.

II. The power and grace of Jesus Christ put forth for their succour: then the Lord Jesus awaked, as one refreshed, Ps. lxxviii. 65. Christ may sleep when his church is in a storm, but he will not outsleep himself: the time, the set time to favour his distressed church, will come, Ps. cii. 13.

1. He rebuked the disciples (v. 26); *Why are ye fearful, O ye of little faith?* He does not chide them for disturbing him with their prayers, but for disturbing themselves with their fears. Christ reproved them first, and then delivered them; this is his method, to prepare us for a mercy, and then to give it us.

2. *He rebukes the wind*; the former he did as the God of *grace*, and the Sovereign of the heart, who can do what he pleases *in* us; this he did as the God of *nature*, the Sovereign of the world, who can do what he pleases *for* us. It is the same *power that stills the noise of the sea*, and the tumult of fear, Ps. lxv. 7.

CASTING OUT DEVILS
(vv. 28–34)

The scope of this chapter is to show the divine power of Christ, by the instances of his dominion over bodily diseases, which to us are irresistible; over winds and waves, which to us are yet more uncontrollable; and lastly, over devils, which to us are most formidable of all. Christ has not only all *power in heaven and earth* and all deep places, but has the keys of hell too.

Now, besides the general instance which this gives us of Christ's power over Satan, and his design against him to disarm and dispossess him, we have here especially discovered to us the way and manner of evil spirits in their enmity to man. Observe, concerning this legion of devils, What work they made where they *were*, and where they *went*.

I. What work they made where they *were*; which appears in the miserable condition of these two that were possessed by them ; and some think, these two were man and wife, because the other Evangelists speak but of one.

1. They dwelt among *the tombs*; thence they came when they met Christ. The devil having *the power of death*, not as judge, but as executioner, he delighted to converse among the trophies of his victory, the dead bodies of men; but there, where he thought himself in the greatest triumph and elevation, as afterwards in Golgotha, the place of a skull, did Christ conquer and subdue him.

2. They were *exceeding fierce*; not only ungovernable themselves, but mischievous to others, frightening many, having hurt some; *so that no man durst pass that way*.

3. They bid defiance to Jesus Christ, and disclaimed all interest in him, *v. 29*. It is an instance of the power of God over the devils, that, notwithstanding the mischief they studied to do *by* and *to* these poor creatures, yet they could not keep them from meeting Jesus Christ, who ordered the matter so as to meet them. It was his overpowering hand that dragged these unclean spirits into his presence, which they dreaded more than any thing else: his chains could hold them, when

the chains that men made for them could not. But being brought before him, they protested against his jurisdiction, and broke out into a rage, *What have we to do with thee, Jesus, thou Son of God?*

II. Let us now see what work they made where they *went*, when they were turned out of the men possessed, and that was into *a herd of swine*, which *was a good way off, v.* 30. These Gadarenes, though living on the other side Jordan, were Jews. What had they to do with *swine*, which by the law were unclean, and not to be eaten nor touched? Probably, lying in the outskirts of the land, there were many Gentiles among them, to whom this *herd of swine* belonged: or they kept them to be sold, or bartered, to the Romans, with whom they had now great dealings, and who were admirers of *swine's* flesh. Now observe,

1. How the devils seized the *swine*. Though they were *a good way off*, and, one would think, out of danger, yet the devils had an eye upon them, to do them a mischief: for they *go up and down, seeking to devour*, seeking an opportunity; and they seek not long but they find.

2. *Whither they hurried them*, when they had seized them. They were not bid to *save their lives*, and, therefore, they were made to *run violently down a steep place into the sea*, where they all perished, to the number of about *two thousand*, Mark v. 13. Note, The possession which the devil gets is for destruction. Thus the devil hurries people to sin, hurries them to that which they have resolved against, and which they know will be shame and

grief to them: with what a force doth the evil spirit *work in the children of disobedience*, when by so many foolish and hurtful lusts they are brought to act in direct contradiction, not only to religion, but to right reason, and their interest in this world!

3. *What effect this had upon the owners*. The report of it was soon brought them by the swine-herds, who seemed to be more concerned for the loss of the swine than anything else, for they went not to tell *what was befallen to the possessed of the devils*, till the swine were lost, *v.* 33. Christ went not *into the city*, but the news of his being there did, by which he was willing to feel how their pulse beat, and what influence it had upon them, and then act accordingly.

Now, (1) Their curiosity brought them out to see Jesus. The *whole city came out to meet him*, that they might be able to say, they had seen a man who did such wonderful works. Thus many go out, in profession, to meet Christ for company, that have no real affection for him, nor desire to know him.

(2) Their covetousness made them *willing to be rid of him*. Instead of inviting him into their city, or bringing their sick to him to be healed, they desired him *to depart out of their coasts*, as if they had borrowed the words of the devils, *What have we to do with thee, Jesus thou Son of God?* And now the devils had what they aimed at in drowning the swine; *they* did it, and then made the people believe that *Christ* had done it, and so prejudiced them against him. He seduced our first parents, by possessing them with hard thoughts of God, and kept the Gadarenes from Christ, by suggesting that he came into their country to destroy their cattle, and that he would do more hurt than good; for though he had cured two men, yet he had drowned two thousand swine. Thus the devil sows tares in God's field, does mischief in the Christian church, and then lays the blame upon Christianity, and incenses men against that.

CHAPTER NINE

THE PARALYSED MAN
(*vv.* 1–8)

The first words of this chapter oblige us to look back to the close of that which precedes it, where we find the Gadarenes so resenting the loss of their swine, that they were disgusted with Christ's company, and besought him to *depart out of their coasts*. Now here it follows, *He entered into a ship, and passed over*. They bid him begone, and he took them at their word, and we never read that he came into their coasts again.

He came *into his own city, Capernaum*, the principal place of his residence at present (Mark ii. 1), and therefore called *his own city*. At Capernaum all the circumstances recorded in this chapter happened, and are, therefore put, together here, though, in the harmony of the evangelists, other events intervened. When the Gadarenes desired Christ to depart, they of Capernaum received him. If Christ be affronted by some, there are others in whom he will be glorious; if one will not, another will.

Now the first occurrence, after Christ's return to Capernaum, as recorded in these verses, was the cure of the man sick of the palsy. In which we may observe,

I. The *faith of his friends* in bringing him to Christ. *Jesus saw their faith*, the faith of the paralytic himself, as well as of them that brought him; Jesus saw the habit of faith, though his disability, perhaps, impaired his intellect, and obstructed the actings of it. Now their faith was, 1. A strong faith; they firmly believed that Jesus Christ both could and would heal him; else they would not have brought the sick man to him so publicly, and through so much difficulty. 2. A humble faith; though the sick man was unable to stir a step, they would not ask Christ to make him a visit, but brought him to attend on Christ. It is fitter that we should wait on Christ, than he on us. 3. An active faith; in the belief of Christ's power and goodness, they brought the sick man to him, *lying on a bed*, which could not be done without a deal of pains. Note, a strong faith regards no obstacles in pressing after Christ.

II. The *favour of Christ*, in what he said to him; *Son, be of good cheer, thy sins be forgiven thee.* Christ bids him *be of good cheer*; and then cures him. He would have those to whom he deals his gifts, to be cheerful in seeking him, and in trusting in him; to be of good courage. 3. A good reason for that encouragement; *Thy sins are forgiven thee.* Now this may be considered, (1) as an introduction

to the cure of his bodily disability; "Thy sins are *pardoned*, and therefore thou shalt be healed." Or, (2) As a reason of the command to *be of good cheer*, whether he were cured of his disease or not; "Though I should not heal thee, wilt thou not say thou hast not sought in vain, if I assure thee that *thy sins are pardoned*; and wilt thou not look upon that as a sufficient ground of comfort, though thou shouldst continue *sick of the palsy*?" Note, They who, through grace, have some evidence of the forgiveness of their sins, have reason to be of good cheer, whatever outward troubles or afflictions they are under; see Isa. xxxiii. 24.

III. The *cavil of the scribes* at that which Christ said (*v.* 3); They *said within themselves, This man blasphemeth*. See how the greatest instance of heaven's power and grace is branded with the blackest note of hell's enmity; Christ's pardoning sin is termed blasphemy; nor had it been less, if he had not had commission from God for it.

IV. The conviction which Christ gave them of the unreasonableness of this cavil, before he proceeded.

1. He *charged them with it*. Though they did but say it within themselves, he *knew their thoughts*.

2. He *argued them out of it*, *vv.* 5, 6. Where observe,

(1) How he *asserts* his authority in the *kingdom of grace*. He undertakes to make out, that the *Son of man*, the Mediator, has *power on earth to forgive sins*; for *therefore* the Father has *committed all judgment to the Son*, and has given him this authority, *because he is the Son of man*, John v. 22, 27. If he has

power to give eternal life, as he certainly has (John xvii. 2), he must have power to forgive sin; for guilt is a bar that must be removed, or we can never get to heaven. What an encouragement is this to poor sinners to repent, that the power of pardoning sin is put into the hands of the *Son of man*, who is bone of our bone! And if he had this *power on earth*, much more now that he is exalted to the Father's right hand, to give *repentance and remission of sins*, and so to be both *a Prince and a Saviour*, Acts v. 31.

(2) How he *proves* it, by his power in the kingdom of nature; his power to cure diseases. Is it not as easy to say, *Thy sins are forgiven thee*, as to say, *Arise and walk?* He that can cure the disease, can, in like manner, forgive the sin. Now, [1] This is a general argument to prove that Christ had a divine mission. His miracles, especially his miraculous cures, confirm what he said of himself, that he was the Son of God; the *power* that appeared in his cures proved him *sent of God*; and the *pity* that appeared in them proved him sent of God *to heal and save*. The God of truth would not set his seal to a lie. [2] It had a particular cogency in this case. The palsy was but a symptom of the disease of sin; now he made it to appear, that he could effectually cure the original disease, by the immediate removal of that symptom; so close a connection was there between the sin and the sickness He that had power to remove the punishment, no doubt, had power to remit the sin.

V. The immediate cure of the sick man. Christ turned from disputing with them, and spake healing to him. The most necessary arguings must not divert us from doing the good that our *hand finds to do*. He saith to *the sick of the palsy, Arise, take up thy bed, and go to thine house*; and a healing, quickening, strengthening power accompanied this word (*v.* 7): *he arose and departed to his house*.

VI. The impression which this made upon the multitude (*v.* 8); they *marvelled*, and *glorified God*. Though few of this multitude were so convinced, as to be brought to believe in Christ, and to follow him, yet they admired him, not as God, or the Son of God, but as a *man* to whom God *had given such power*.

MATTHEW CALLED
(*vv.* 9–13)

In these verses we have an account of the grace and favour of Christ to poor publicans, particularly to Matthew. What he did to the bodies of people was to make way for a kind design upon their souls. Now observe here,

I. The call of Matthew, the penman of this gospel. Mark and Luke call him Levi; it was ordinary for the same person to have two names. Some think Christ gave him the name of Matthew when he called him to be an apostle; as Simon, he surnamed Peter. Matthew signifies, *the gift of God*. Ministers are God's gifts to the church; their ministry, and their ability for it, are God's gifts to them. Now observe the posture that Christ's call found Matthew in. He was *sitting at the receipt of custom*, for he was a publican, Luke v. 27. He was a custom-house officer at the port of

Capernaum, or an exciseman, or collector of the land-tax. It was a calling of ill fame among serious people; because it was attended with so much corruption and temptation, and there were so few in that business that were honest men. Matthew himself owns what he was before his conversion, as does St. Paul (1 Tim. i. 13), that the grace of Christ in calling him might be the more magnified, and to show, that God has his remnant among all sorts of people. None can justify themselves in their unbelief, by their calling in the world; for there is no *sinful* calling, but some have been saved *out of it*, and no *lawful calling*, but some have been saved *in it*.

We do not find that Matthew looked after Christ, or had any inclination to follow him, though some of his kindred were already disciples of Christ, but Christ came to him with the blessings of his goodness. He is found of those that seek him not. Christ *spoke first*; we have not chosen him, but he hath chosen us. He said, *Follow me*; and the same divine, almighty power accompanied this word to convert Matthew, which attended that word (*v.* 6), *Arise and walk*, to cure the man sick of the palsy.

II. Christ's converse with publicans and sinners upon this occasion; Christ called Matthew, to introduce himself into an acquaintance with the people of that profession. *Jesus sat at meat in the house, v.* 10.

Now observe, 1. When Matthew invited Christ, he invited his disciples to *come along with him.* Note, They that welcome Christ, must welcome all that are his, for his sake, and let them have a room in their hearts. 2. He invited many publicans and sinners to *meet him.* This was the chief thing Matthew aimed at in this treat, that he might have an opportunity of bringing his old associates acquainted with Christ. He knew by experience what their temptations were, and pitied them; knew by experience what the grace of Christ could do, and would not despair concerning them.

III. The displeasure of the Pharisees at this, *v.* 11. They cavilled at it; *why eateth your Master with publicans and sinners?*

IV. The defence that Christ made for himself and his disciples, in justification of their converse with publicans and sinners. Two things he urges in his defence,

1. The need of the publicans, which called aloud for his help, and therefore justified him in conversing with them for their good. It was the extreme necessity of poor, lost sinners, that brought Christ from the pure regions above, to these impure ones; and the same was it, that brought him into this company which was thought impure. Now,

(1) He proves the need of the publicans: *they that be whole need not a physician, but they that are sick.* The publicans are sick, and they need one to help and heal them, which the Pharisees think they do not.

(2) He proves, that their need did sufficiently justify his conduct, in conversing familiarly with them, and that he ought not to be blamed for it; for that necessity made it *an act of charity.* This he proves

(*v.* 13) by a passage quoted out of Hos. vi. 6, *I will have mercy and not sacrifice.*

2. He urges the nature and end of his own commission. He must keep to his orders, and prosecute that for which he was appointed to be the great Teacher; now, says he, "*I am not come to call the righteous, but sinners to repentance,* and therefore must converse with publicans." Observe, (1) What his errand was; it was to *call to repentance.* This was his first text (*ch.* iv. 17), and it was the tendency of all his sermons. (2) With whom his errand lay; not with *the righteous,* but with *sinners.* That is, [1] If the children of men had not been *sinners,* there had been no occasion for Christ's coming among them. He is the Saviour, not of man as *man,* but of man as *fallen.* [2] Therefore his *greatest business* lies with the *greatest sinners;* the more dangerous the sick man's case is, the more occasion there is for the physician's help. Christ came into the world to *save sinners,* but especially *the chief* (1 Tim. i. 15); to call not those so much, who, though sinners, are comparatively righteous, but the worst of sinners. [3] The more aware any sinners are of their sinfulness, the more welcome will Christ and his gospel be to them; is desired, not to those who would rather have his room; to them Christ will come, for to them he will be welcome.

NEW AND OLD WINE
(*vv.* 14–17)

The objections which were made against Christ and his disciples gave occasion to some of the most profitable of his discourses. Observe,

I. The objection which the disciples of John made against Christ's disciples, for not fasting so often as they did; which they are charged with, as another instance of the looseness of their profession, besides that of eating with publicans and sinners; and it is therefore suggested to them, that they should change that profession for another more strict.

1. How they boasted of their own fasting. *We and the Pharisees fast often.* The disciples of John *fasted often,* partly in compliance with their master's practice, for he came *neither eating nor drinking* (*ch.* xi. 18); and people are apt to imitate their leaders, though not always from the same inward principle; partly in compliance with their master's doctrine of repentance. Now they come to Christ to tell him that they *fasted often,* at least they thought it often.

2. How they blamed Christ's disciples for not fasting so often as they did. *Thy disciples fast not.* They could not but know, that Christ had instructed his disciples to keep their fasts private, and to manage themselves so as that they might not *appear unto men to fast;* and, therefore, it was very uncharitable in them to conclude they did *not fast,* because they did not proclaim their fasts. Note, We must not judge of people's religion by that which falls under the eye and observation of the world.

3. How they brought this complaint to Christ. Note, If Christ's disciples, either by omission or commission, give offence, Christ

himself will be sure to hear of it, and be reflected upon for it. *O, Jesus, are these thy Christians?* Therefore, as we tender the honour of Christ, we are concerned to conduct ourselves well. Observe, The quarrel with Christ was brought to the disciples (*v.* 11), the quarrel with the disciples was brought to Christ (*v.* 14), this is the way of sowing discord and killing love, to set people against ministers, ministers against people, and one friend against another.

II. The apology which Christ made for his disciples in this matter. When they had nothing to say for themselves, he had something ready to say for them.
But thou shalt answer, Lord, for me.
                              Herbert.
Two things Christ pleads in defence of their *not fasting*.

1. That it was not a season proper for that duty (*v.* 15): *Can the children of the bride-chamber mourn, as long as the bridegroom is with them?* Observe, Christ's answer is so framed, as that it might sufficiently justify the practice of his own disciples, and yet not condemn the institution of John, or the practice of his disciples.

Now his argument is taken from the common usage of joy and rejoicing during the continuance of marriage solemnities; when all instances of melancholy and sorrow are looked upon as improper and absurd, as it was at Samson's wedding, Judges xiv. 17. The disciples of Christ had *the bridegroom with them*, which the disciples of John had not; their master was now cast into prison, and lay there in continual danger

of his life, and therefore it was seasonable for them to *fast often*. Such a day would come upon the disciples of Christ, when the bridegroom should be taken from them, when they should be deprived of his bodily presence, and *then should they fast*.

2. That they had not strength sufficient for that duty. This is set forth in two similitudes, one of putting *new cloth into an old garment*, which does but pull the old to pieces (*v.* 16); the other of putting *new wine into old bottles*, which does but burst the bottles, *v.* 17. Christ's disciples were not able to bear these severe exercises so well as those of John and of the Pharisees, who led an austere life. Christ's disciples, being taken immediately from their callings, had not been used to such religious austerities, and were unfit for them, and would by them be rather unfitted for their other work.

JAIRUS'S DAUGHTER
(*vv.* 18–26)

We have here two passages of history put together; that of the raising of Jairus's daughter to life, and that of the curing of the woman that had *the bloody issue*, as he was going to Jairus's house, which is introduced in a parenthesis, in the midst of the other. Here is,

I. The ruler's address to Christ, *v.* 18. *A certain ruler*, a ruler of the synagogue, *came and worshipped him. Have any of the rulers believed on him?* Yes, here was one, a church ruler, whose faith condemned the unbelief of the rest of the rulers. This ruler had a little daughter, of twelve years old, just dead, and this breach made upon his family comforts was the occasion of his coming to Christ. Now observe,

1. His humility in this address to Christ. He came with his errand to Christ himself, and did not send his servant.

2. His faith in this address; "*My daughter is even now dead*", and though any other physician would come too late, yet Christ comes not too late; he is a Physician after death, for he is *the resurrection and the life*; "*O come* then, *and lay thy hand upon her, and she shall live.*"

II. The readiness of Christ to comply with his address, *v.* 19. *Jesus* immediately *arose*, left his company, *and followed him*; he was not only willing to grant him what he desired, in raising his daughter to life, but to gratify him so far as to come to his house to do it.

III. The healing of the poor woman's bloody issue. I call her a poor woman, not only because her case was piteous, but because, though she had had something in the world, she had *spent it all upon physicians*, for the cure of her trouble, and was no better. This *woman was diseased with a constant issue of blood twelve years* (*v.* 20); a disease, which was not only weakening and wasting, and under which the body must needs languish; but which also rendered her ceremonially unclean, and shut her *out from the courts of the Lord's house*; but it did not cut her off from approaching to Christ. Observe,

1. The woman's great faith in Christ, and in his power. Her disease was of such a nature, that her modesty would not suffer her to speak openly to Christ for a cure, as others did, but by a peculiar impulse of the Spirit of faith, she believed him to have such an overflowing fulness of healing virtue, that the very *touch of his garment* would be her cure.

2. Christ's great favour to this woman. He did not suspend (as he might have done) his healing influences, but suffered this bashful patient to steal a cure unknown to anyone else, though she could not think to do it unknown to him. He *turned about* to see for her (*v.* 22), and soon discovered her. Now here,

(1) He *puts gladness into her heart*, by that word, *Daughter, be of good comfort*. She feared being chidden for coming clandestinely, but she is encouraged.

(2) He puts honour upon her faith. That grace of all others gives most honour to Christ, and therefore he puts most honour upon it; *Thy faith has made thee whole.* Thus *by faith she obtained a good report.* And as of all graces Christ puts the greatest honour on faith, so of all believers he puts the greatest honour upon those that are most humble; as here on this woman, who had more faith than she thought she had.

IV. The posture in which he found the ruler's house, *v.* 23. — He *saw the people and the minstrels*, or musicians, *making a noise.* The house was in a hurry: such work does death make, when it comes into a family; and, perhaps, the necessary cares that arise at such a time, when our dead is to be decently buried out of our sight, give some useful diversion to that grief which is apt to prevail and play the tyrant. The people in the neighbourhood came together to condole on account of the loss, to comfort the parents, to prepare for, and attend on, the funeral, which the Jews were not wont to defer long. The musicians were among them, according to the custom of the Gentiles, with their doleful, melancholy tunes, to increase the grief, and stir up the lamentations of those that attended on this occasion. Notice is taken of this, to show that the girl was really dead, in the undoubted apprehension of all about her.

V. The rebuke that Christ gave to this hurry and noise, *v.* 24. He said, *Give place.* He gives a good reason why they should not thus disquiet themselves and one another; *The maid is not dead but sleepeth.* 1. This was eminently true of this maid, that was immediately to be raised to life; she was really dead, but not so to Christ, who knew within himself what he would do, and could do, and who had determined to make her death but as a sleep.

Now could it be thought that such a comfortable word as this, from the mouth of our Lord Jesus, should be ridiculed as it was? *They laughed him to scorn.* These people lived in Capernaum, knew Christ's character, that he never spake a rash or foolish word; they knew how many mighty works he had done; so that if they did not understand what he meant by this, they might at least have been silent in expectation of the issue.

VI. The raising of the damsel to life by the power of Christ, *v.* 25.

Christ went in and *took her by the hand*, as it were to awake her, and to help her up, prosecuting his own metaphor of her being asleep. He *took her by the hand, and the maid arose.* So easily, so effectually was the miracle wrought; not by prayer, as Elijah did (1 Kings xvii. 21), and Elisha (2 Kings iv. 33), but by a touch. They did it as servants, he as a Son, as a God, *to whom belong the issues from death.* Note, Jesus Christ is the Lord of souls, he commands them forth, and commands them back, when and as he pleases. Dead souls are not raised to spiritual life, unless Christ *take them by the hand*: it is done in the *day of his power.* He helps us up, or we lie still.

VII. The general notice that was taken of this miracle, though it was wrought privately; *v.* 26, *the fame thereof went abroad into all that land*: it was the common subject of discourse.

TWO BLIND MEN
(*vv.* 27–34)

In these verses we have an account of two more miracles wrought together by our Saviour.

I. The giving of sight to two blind men, *vv.* 27–31. Christ is the Fountain of light as well as life; and as, by raising the dead, he showed himself to be the same that at first *breathed into man the breath of life*, so, by giving sight to the blind, he showed himself to be the same that at first *commanded the light to shine out of darkness.* Observe,

1. The importunate address of the blind men to Christ. Observe,

(1) The title which these blind men gave to Christ; *Thou Son of David, have mercy on us.* The promise made to David, that of his loins the Messiah should come, was well known, and the Messiah was therefore commonly called *the Son of David.* At this time there was a general expectation of his appearing; these blind men know, and own, and proclaim it in the streets of Capernaum, that he is come, and that this is he. They could not see him and his miracles, but *faith comes by hearing.*

(2) Their petition, *Have mercy on us.* It was foretold that the *Son of David* should be *merciful* (Ps. lxxii. 12, 13), and in him *shines the tender mercy of our God,* Luke i. 78.

(3) Their importunity in this request; they *followed him, crying.* It seems, he did not take notice of them at first, for he would try their faith, which he knew to be strong; would quicken their prayers, and make his cures the more valued, when they did not always come at the first word. Christ would not heal them publicly in the streets, for this was a cure he would have kept private (*v.* 30), but *when he came into the house,* they *followed him* thither, and *came to him.* Note, Christ's doors are always open to believing and importunate petitioners; it seemed rude in them to rush into the house after him, when he desired to retire; but, such is the tenderness of our Lord Jesus, that they were not more bold than welcome.

2. The confession of faith, which Christ drew from them upon this occasion. When they came to him for mercy, he asked them, *Believe ye that I am able to do this?* Note, Faith is the great condition of Christ's favours. They who would receive the *mercy* of Christ, must firmly believe the *power* of Christ. What we would have him do for us, we must be fully assured that he is *able to do.*

To this question they give an immediate answer, without hesitation: they said, *Yea, Lord.*

3. The cure that Christ wrought on them; *he touched their eyes, v.* 29. This he did to encourage their faith, which, by his delay, he had tried, and to show that he gives sight to blind souls by the operations of his grace accompanying the word, *anointing the eyes with eye-salve*: and he put the cure upon their faith, *According to your faith be it unto you.* This speaks, (1) His knowledge of the sincerity of their faith, and his acceptance and approbation of it. (2) His insisting upon their faith as necessary; "If you believe, take what you come for." Note, They who apply themselves to Jesus Christ, shall be dealt with *according to their faith*; not according to their *fancies*, nor according to their *profession*, but *according to their faith.*

4. The charge he gave them to keep it private (*v.* 30), *See that no man know it.* He gave them this charge, (1) To set us an example of that humility and lowliness of mind, which he would have us to learn of him. (2) Some think that Christ, in keeping it private, showed his displeasure against the people of Capernaum, who had seen so many miracles, and yet believed not.

(3) He did it in discretion, for his own preservation; because the more he was proclaimed, the more jealous would the rulers of the Jews be of his growing interest among the people. (4) Dr. Whitby gives another reason, which is very considerable, why Christ sometimes concealed his miracles, and afterwards forbid the publishing of his transfiguration; because he would not indulge that pernicious conceit which obtained among the Jews, that their Messiah should be a temporal prince, and so give occasion to the people to attempt the setting up of his kingdom, by tumults and seditions, as they offered to do, John vi. 15. And he observes, that the miracles which Christ wrought among the Gentiles and the Gadarenes, were ordered to be published, because with them there was not that danger.

But honour is like the shadow, which, as it flees from those that follow it, so it follows those that flee from it (v. 31); *They spread abroad his fame.*

II. The healing of a *dumb man*, that was *possessed with a devil*. And here observe,

1. His case, which was very sad. He was under the power of the devil in this particular instance, that he was disabled from speaking, v. 32.

2. His cure, which was very sudden (v. 33), *When the devil was cast out, the dumb spake*. Note, Christ's cures strike at the root, and remove the effect by taking away the cause; they open the lips, by breaking Satan's power in the soul.

3. The consequences of this cure.

(1) *The multitudes marvelled*; and well they might; though *few believed, many wondered.*

(2) *The Pharisees* blasphemed, v. 34. When they could not gainsay the convincing evidence of these miracles, they fathered them upon the devil, as if they had been wrought by compact and collusion: *he casteth out devils* (say they) by *the prince of the devils* — a suggestion horrid beyond expression.

THE SCATTERED SHEEP
(vv. 35–38)

Here is a preface, or introduction, to the account in the following chapter, of his sending forth his apostles. *He* took notice of *the multitude* (v. 36); not only of the crowds that *followed him*, but of the vast numbers of people with whom (as he passed along) he observed the country to be replenished; he noticed what nests of souls the towns and cities were, and how thick of inhabitants; what abundance of people there were in every synagogue, and what places of concourse the openings of the gates were: so very populous was that nation now grown; and it was the effect of God's blessing on Abraham. Seeing this,

1. He pitied them, and was concerned for them (v. 36); *He was moved with compassion on them*; not upon a temporal account, as he pitied the blind, and lame, and sick; but upon a spiritual account; he was concerned to see them ignorant and careless, and ready to perish for lack of vision. The most Christian compassion is compassion to souls; it is most Christ-like. See what moved this pity. (1)

They fainted; they were destitute, vexed, wearied. *They strayed*, so some; were loosed one from another; *The staff of bands was broken*, Zech. xi. 14. They wanted help for their souls, and had none at hand that was good for anything. (2) *They were scattered abroad, as sheep having no shepherd*. That expression is borrowed from 1 Kings xxii. 17, and it sets forth the sad condition of those that are destitute of faithful guides to go before them in the things of God.

He excited his disciples to pray for them. His pity put him upon devising means for the good of these people. It appears (Luke vi. 12, 13) that upon this occasion, before he sent out his apostles, he did himself spend a great deal of time in prayer. Note, Those we pity we should pray for. Having spoken to God for them he turns to his disciples, and tells them,

(1) How the case stood; *The harvest truly is plenteous, but the labourers are few*. People desired good preaching, but there were few good preachers. There was a great deal of work to be done, and a great deal of good likely to be done, but there wanted hands to do it. [1] It was an encouragement, that *the harvest* was so *plenteous*. [2] It was a pity when it was so that *the labourers* should be so *few*; loiterers many, but *labourers* very *few*.

(2) What was their duty in this case (*v.* 38); *Pray ye therefore the Lord of the harvest*. When things look discouraging, we should pray more, and then we should complain and fear less. Note, [1] God is *the Lord of the harvest; my Father is the Husbandman*, John xv. 1. It is

the vineyard of the Lord of hosts, Isa. v. 7. It is for him and to him, and to his service and honour, that *the harvest* is gathered in. [2] Ministers are and should be *labourers* in God's *harvest*; the ministry is a *work* and must be attended to accordingly; it is *harvest-work*, which is needful work; work that requires every thing to be done in its season, and diligence to do it thoroughly; but it is pleasant work; they *reap in joy*. [3] It is God's work to *send forth labourers*; Christ makes ministers (Eph. iv. 11); the office is of his appointing, the qualifications of his working, the call of his giving. [4] All that love Christ and souls, should show it by their earnest prayers to God, especially when *the harvest is plenteous, that he would send forth* more skilful, faithful, wise, and industrious *labourers into his harvest*.

CHAPTER TEN

THE DISCIPLES (*vv.* 1–4)

Here we are told, I. Who they were that Christ ordained to be his apostles or ambassadors; they were his disciples, *v.* 1. He had called them some time before to be disciples, his immediate followers and constant attendants, and he then told them that they should be made fishers of men, which promise he now performed. Note, Christ commonly confers honours and graces by degrees; the light of both, like that of the morning, *shines more and more*.

II. What the commission was that he gave them.

1. He *called them to him, v.* 1. He had called them to come *after* him

before; now he calls them to come *to* him, admits them to a greater familiarity, and will not have them to keep at such a distance as they had hitherto observed. They that *humble themselves* shall thus be *exalted*. It is observable, that when the disciples were to be *instructed*, they *came unto* him of their own accord, *ch.* v. 1. But now they were to be *ordained*, he *called them*.

2. He *gave them power, authority* in his name, to command men to obedience, and for the confirmation of that authority, to command devils too into a subjection. Note, The design of the gospel was to *conquer the devil* and to *cure the world*. These preachers were sent out destitute of all external advantages to recommend them; they had no wealth, nor learning, nor titles of honour, and they made a very mean figure; it was therefore requisite that they should have some extraordinary power to advance them above the scribes.

He gave them power to *heal all manner of sickness*. He authorized them to work miracles for the confirmation of their doctrine, to prove that it was of God; and they were to work useful miracles for the illustration of it, to prove that it is not only faithful, but well *worthy of all acceptation*; that the design of the gospel is to heal and save.

III. The number and names of those that were commissioned; they are made apostles, that is, messengers. An angel, and an apostle, both signify the same thing—one *sent on an errand*, an ambassador. All faithful ministers are sent of Christ, but they that were first, and immediately, sent by him, are eminently called *apostles*, the prime ministers of state in his kingdom. Yet this was but the infancy of their office; it was when Christ *ascended on high* that he *gave some apostles*, Eph. iv. 11. Christ himself is called an apostle (Heb. iii. 1), for he was *sent by the Father*, and so sent them, John xx. 21. The prophets were called God's messengers.

There are some of these twelve apostles, of whom we know no more, from the scripture, than their names; as Bartholomew, and Simon the Canaanite; and yet they were faithful servants to Christ and his church. Note, all the good ministers of Christ are not alike famous, nor their actions alike celebrated.

They are named by couples; for at first they were sent forth *two and two*, because *two are better than one*; they would be serviceable to each other, and the more serviceable jointly to Christ and souls.

Judas Iscariot is always named last, and with that black brand upon his name, *who also betrayed him*; which intimates that from the first, Christ knew what a wretch he was, that he had a devil, and would prove a traitor; yet Christ took him among the apostles, that it might not be a surprise and discouragement to his church, if, at any time, the vilest scandals should break out in the best societies.

THEIR INSTRUCTIONS
(*vv.* 5–15)

We have here the instructions that Christ gave to his disciples, when he gave them their commission. Observe,

I. The people to whom he sent them. These ambassadors are directed what places to go to.

1. Not to the Gentiles nor the Samaritans. They must not *go into the way of the Gentiles*, nor into any road out of the land of Israel, whatever temptations they might have. The Gentiles must not have the gospel brought them, till the Jews have first refused it. As to the Samaritans, who were the posterity of that mongrel people that the king of Assyria planted about Samaria, their country lay between Judea and Galilee, so that they could not avoid *going into the way* of the Samaritans, but they must *not enter into any of their cities*. Christ had declined manifesting himself to the Gentiles or Samaritans, and therefore the apostles must not preach to them. If the gospel be hid from any place, Christ thereby hides himself from that place. This restraint was upon them only in their first mission, afterwards they were appointed to go *into all the world*, and teach *all nations*.

2. But *to the lost sheep of the house of Israel*. To them Christ appropriated his own ministry (*ch.* xv. 24), for he was a *minister of the circumcision* (Rom. xv. 8): and, therefore, to them the apostles, who were but his attendants and agents, must be confined. The first offer of salvation must be made to the Jews, Acts iii. 26.

II. The preaching work which he appointed them. He did not send them forth without an errand; no, *As ye go, preach, v.* 7. They were to be itinerant preachers: wherever they come they must proclaim the beginning of the gospel, saying, *The kingdom of heaven is at hand.* Not that they must say nothing else, but this must be their text; on this subject they must enlarge: let people know, that the kingdom of the Messiah, who is the Lord from heaven, is now to be set up according to the scriptures; from whence it follows, that men must *repent* of their sins and forsake them, that they might be admitted to the privileges of that kingdom.

III. The power he gave them to work miracles for the confirmation of their doctrine, *v.* 8. When he sent them to preach the same doctrine that he had preached, he empowered them to confirm it, by the same divine seals, which could never be set to a lie. This is not necessary now the kingdom of God is come; to call for miracles now is to lay again the foundation when the building is reared. The point being settled, and the doctrine of Christ sufficiently attested, by the miracles which Christ and his apostles wrought, it is tempting God to ask for more signs. They are directed here,

1. To use their power in doing good: not "Go and remove mountains," or "fetch fire from heaven," but, *Heal the sick, cleanse the lepers*.

2. In *doing good freely; Freely ye have received, freely give*. Those that had power to heal all diseases, had an opportunity to enrich themselves; who would not purchase such easy certain cures at any rate? Therefore they are cautioned not to make a gain of the power they had to work miracles: they must cure *gratis*, further to exemplify the nature and complexion of the

gospel kingdom, which is made up, not only of grace, but of free grace.

IV. The provision that must be made for them in this expedition.

1. They must make no provision for it themselves, *vv.* 9, 10. *Provide neither gold nor silver.* Christ would teach them, (1) To act *under the conduct of human prudence.* They were now to make but a short excursion, and were soon to return to their Master, and to their headquarters again, and, therefore, why should they burden themselves with that which they would have no occasion for? (2) To act in *dependence upon Divine Providence.* They must be taught to live, without *taking thought for life, ch.* vi. 25, &c. Those whom he employs, as they are taken under special protection, so they are entitled to special provisions. Christ's hired servants shall have *bread enough and to spare*; while we abide faithful to God and our duty, and are in care to do our work well, we may cast all our other care upon God.

2. They might expect that those to whom they were sent would *provide for them* what was necessary, *v.* 10. The *workman is worthy of his meat.* They must not expect to be fed by miracles, as Elijah was: but they might depend upon God to incline the hearts of those they went among, to be kind to them, and provide for them.

V. The proceedings they were to observe in dealing with any place, *vv.* 11–15.

1. They are here directed how to conduct themselves toward those that were *strangers to them*; How to do,

(1) In *strange towns and cities*:

when you come to a town, *enquire who* in it *is worthy.* [1] It is supposed that there were some such in every place, as were better disposed than others to receive the gospel, and the preachers of it; though it was a time of general corruption and apostasy. [2] They must enquire out such; not enquire for the best inns; public houses were no proper places for them that neither took money with them (*v.* 9), nor expected to receive any (*v.* 8); but they must look out for accommodations in private houses, with those that would entertain them well, and expect no other recompence for it but a prophet's reward, an apostle's reward, their praying and preaching. [3] In the house of those they found worthy, they must continue; which intimates that they were to make so short a stay at each town, that they needed not change their lodging, but whatever house providence brought them to at first, there they must continue till they left that town.

(2) In strange houses. When they had found the house of one they thought worthy, they must at their entrance salute it.

When they had saluted the family after a godly sort, they must, by the return, judge concerning the family, and proceed accordingly. If *the house be worthy, let your peace come* and rest *upon it; if not, let it return to you, v.* 13. It seems then, that after they had enquired for the *most worthy* (*v.* 11), it was possible they might light upon those that were unworthy.

The case is put (*v.* 14) of those that *would not receive them, nor hear their words.* The apostles might think, that now they had such a doctrine to preach, and such a power to work miracles for the confirmation of it, no doubt but they should be universally entertained and made welcome: they are, therefore, told before, that there would be those that would slight them, and put contempt on them and their message. Note, The best and most powerful preachers of the gospel must expect to meet with some, that will not so much as give them the hearing, nor show them any token of respect.

Now in this case we have here,

(1) The directions given to the apostles what to do. They must *depart out of that house or city*. At their departure they must *shake off the dust of their feet*.

(2) The *doom passed* upon such *wilful recusants*, *v*. 15. It shall be *more tolerable, in the day of judgment, for the land of* Sodom, as wicked a place as it was.

COUNSEL AND COMFORT
(*vv*. 16–42)

All these verses relate to the sufferings of Christ's ministers in their work, which they are here taught to expect, and prepare for; they are directed also how to bear them, and how to go on with their work in the midst of them.

I. We have here predictions of trouble: which the disciples should meet with in their work: Christ foresaw *their* sufferings as well as his own, and yet will have them go on, as he went on himself; and he foretold them, not only that the troubles might not be a surprise to them, and so a shock to their faith, but that, being the accomplishment

of a prediction, they might be a confirmation to their faith.

He tells them what they should suffer, and from whom.

1. *What they should suffer*; hard things to be sure; for, *Behold, I send you forth as sheep in the midst of wolves*, *v*. 16. And what may a flock of poor, helpless, unguarded sheep expect, in the midst of a herd of ravenous wolves, but to be worried and torn? Note, Wicked men are like wolves, in whose nature it is to devour and destroy. God's people, and especially his ministers, are like sheep among them, of a contrary nature and disposition, exposed to them, and commonly an easy prey to them.

(1) They must expect to be hated, *v*. 22. *Ye shall be hated for my name's sake*; that is the root of all the rest, and a bitter root it is.

(2) They must expect to be apprehended and arraigned as malefactors. They must look for trouble, not only from inferior magistrates in the councils, but from governors and kings, the supreme magistrates. We find this often fulfilled in the *acts of the apostles*.

(3) They must expect to be put to death (*v*. 21); *They shall deliver them to death*, to death in state, with pomp and solemnity, when it shows itself most as *the king of terrors*. They were put to death as criminals, so the enemies meant it, but really as sacrifices (Phil. ii. 17; 2 Tim. iv. 6); as burnt offerings, sacrifices of acknowledgment to the honour of God, and in his truth and cause.

(4) They must expect, in the midst of these sufferings, to be

branded with the most odious and ignominious names and characters that could be. The blackest of all the ill characters they give them is here stated; they call them Beelzebub, the name of the prince of the devils, *v.* 25.

(5) These sufferings are here represented by a sword and division, *vv.* 34, 35. *Think not that I am come to send peace,* temporal peace and outward prosperity; they thought Christ came to give all his followers wealth and power in the world; "no," says Christ, "I did not come with a view to give them *peace*; *peace* in heaven they may be sure of, but not *peace* on earth." Christ came to give us *peace* with God, *peace* in our consciences, *peace* with our brethren, but *in the world ye shall have tribulation.*

These hard things Christ's disciples must suffer,

(1) From men (*v.* 17). The nature of man, if it be not sanctified, is the worst nature in the world next to that of devils. *They are men,* and therefore subordinate, dependent, dying creatures; *they are men,* but *they are but men* (Ps. ix. 20), and *who art thou, that thou shouldst be afraid of a man that shall die?* Isa. li. 12.

(2) From professing men, men that *have a form of godliness,* and make a show of religion. *They will scourge you in their synagogues,* their places of meeting for the worship of God, and for the exercise of their church-discipline: so that they looked upon the scourging of Christ's ministers to be a branch of their religion.

(3) From great men, and men in authority. The Jews did not only scourge them, which was the utmost their remaining power extended to, but when they could go no further themselves, they delivered them up to the Roman powers, as they did Christ, John xviii. 30. *Ye shall be brought before governors and kings* (*v.* 18), who, having more power, are in a capacity of doing the more mischief. *Governors and kings* receive their power from Christ (Prov. viii. 15), and should be his servants, and his church's protectors and nursing-fathers, but they often use their power against him, and are rebels to Christ, and oppressors of his church. *The kings of the earth* set themselves against his kingdom, Ps. ii. 1, 2; Acts iv. 25, 26.

(4) From all men (*v.* 22). *Ye shall be hated of all men,* of all wicked men, and these are the generality of men, *for the whole world lies in wickedness.* As far as the apostasy from God goes, so far the enmity against the saints goes; sometimes it appears more general than at other times, but there is something of this poison lurking in the hearts of all *the children of disobedience.*

(5) From those of their own kindred. *The brother shall deliver up the brother to death,* *v.* 21. In general, *a man's foes shall be they of his own household* (*v.* 36). They who should be his friends will be incensed against him for embracing Christianity, and especially for adhering to it when it comes to be persecuted, and will join with his persecutors against him. Note, The strongest bonds of relative love and duty have often been broken through, by an enmity against Christ and his doctrine.

II. With these predictions of trouble, we have here prescriptions of counsels and comforts for a time of trial. Let us gather up what he says,

1. By way of counsel and direction in several things.

(1) *Be ye wise as serpents, v.* 16. The disciples of Christ are hated and persecuted as *serpents*, and their ruin is sought, and, therefore, they need the *serpent's* wisdom.

(2) *Be ye harmless as doves.* It must be the continual care of all Christ's disciples, to be innocent and inoffensive in word and deed, especially in consideration of the enemies they are in the midst of. We have need of a *dove-like* spirit, when we are beset with birds of prey, that we may neither provoke them nor be provoked by them.

(3) *Beware of men, v.* 17. Ever since our Master was betrayed with a kiss, by one of his own disciples, we have need to *beware of men, of false brethren*.

(4) *Take no thought how or what ye shall speak, v.* 19. The disciples of Christ must be more thoughtful how to *do* well than how to *speak* well; how to *keep* their integrity than how to *vindicate* it.

(5) *When they persecute you in this city, flee to another, v.* 23. He that flies may fight again. It is no inglorious thing for Christ's soldiers to quit their ground, provided they do not quit their colours: they may go out of the way of *danger*, though they must not go out of the way of *duty*.

(6) *Fear them not (v.* 26), because *they can but kill the body (v.* 28). Note, it is the duty and interest of Christ's disciples, not to fear the greatest of their adversaries. They who truly fear God, need not fear man; and they who are afraid of the least sin, need not be afraid of the greatest trouble.

Fear him who is able to destroy both soul and body in hell. Note, First, *Hell* is the destruction both of *soul and body*; not of the *being* of either, but the *well-*being of both; it is the ruin of the whole man; if the soul be lost, the body is lost too. Secondly, This destruction comes from the power of God: he *is able to destroy*; it is a destruction from his *glorious power* (2 Thess. i. 9); *he will* in it *make his power known*; not only his authority to sentence, but his ability to execute the sentence, Rom. ix. 22.

(7) *What I tell you in darkness, that speak ye in light (v.* 27). The particular instructions which he gave his disciples after his resurrection, concerning *the things pertaining to the kingdom of God*, were whispered in the ear (Acts i. 3), for then *he never showed himself openly.* But they must deliver their embassy publicly, *in the light*, and *upon the house-tops*; for the doctrine of the gospel is what all are concerned in (Prov. i. 20, 21; viii. 2, 3), therefore *he that hath ears to hear, let him hear*.

2. By way of comfort and encouragement.

(1) Here is one word peculiar to their present mission, *v.* 23. *Ye shall not have gone over the cities of Israel, till the Son of man be come.* They were to preach that *the kingdom of the Son of man*, the Messiah, was *at hand*; they were to pray, *Thy kingdom come*: now they should *not have gone over all the cities of*

Israel, thus praying and thus preaching, before that kingdom should come, in the exaltation of Christ, and the pouring out of the Spirit.

(2) Here are many words that relate to their work in general, and the troubles they were to meet with in it; and *they are good words and comfortable words*.

[1] That their sufferings were *for a testimony against them and the Gentiles*, v. 18. God's people, and especially God's ministers, are his witnesses (Isa. xliii. 10), not only in their *doing* work, but in their *suffering* work. Hence they are called martyrs — *witnesses* for Christ, that his truths are of undoubted certainty and value; and, being witnesses for him, they are witnesses against those who oppose him and his gospel.

[2] That upon all occasions they should have God's special presence with them, and the immediate assistance of his Holy Spirit, particularly when they should be called out to bear their testimony *before governors and kings; it shall be given you* (said Christ) *in that same hour what ye shall speak*. They cannot but come off well, who have such an advocate; to whom God says, as he did to Moses (Exod. iv. 12), *Go, and I will be with thy mouth, and with thy heart*.

[3] That *he that endures to the end shall be saved*, v. 22. Here it is very comfortable to consider, First, that there will be an *end* of these troubles; they may last long, but will not last always. Christ comforted himself with this, and so may his followers; *The things concerning me have an end*, Luke xxii. 37.

Secondly, That while they continue, they may be *endured*; as they are not *eternal*, so they are not *intolerable*; they may be borne, and borne *to the end*, because the sufferers shall be borne up under them, in everlasting arms.

[4] That whatever hard usage the disciples of Christ meet with, it is no more than what their Master met with before (vv. 24, 25). *The disciple is not above his master*. Let us not think it strange, if they who hated him hate his followers, for his sake; nor think it hard if they who are shortly to be made *like him in glory*, be now made *like him in sufferings*. Christ began in the *bitter cup*, let us be willing to pledge him; his bearing the cross made it easy for us.

[5] That *there is nothing covered that shall not be revealed*, v. 26. We understand this, First, Of the revealing of the gospel to all the world. The *ends of the earth must see this salvation*. Or, Secondly, Of the clearing up of the innocency of Christ's suffering servants, that are called Beelzebub; their true character is now invidiously disguised with false colours, but however their innocency and excellency are now *covered*, they *shall be revealed*: sometimes it is in a great measure done in this world, when the righteousness of the saints is made, by subsequent events, to *shine forth as the light*: however, it will be done at the great day, when their glory shall be manifested to all the world, angels and men, to whom they are now *made spectacles*, 1 Cor. iv. 9.

[6] That the providence of God is in a special manner conversant about the saints, in their suffering,

vv. 29–31. It is good to have recourse to our first principles, and particularly to the doctrine of God's universal providence, extending itself to all the creatures, and all their actions, even the smallest and most minute. The light of nature teaches us this, and it is comfortable to all men, but especially to all good men, who can in faith call this God their Father, and for whom he has a tender concern. He that feeds the sparrows, will not starve the saints. *Fear ye not, therefore, v.* 31. There is enough in the doctrine of God's providence to silence all the fears of God's people: *Ye are of more value than many sparrows.*

But the very hairs of your head are all numbered. This is a proverbial expression, denoting the account which God takes and keeps of all the concernments of his people, even of those that are most minute, and least regarded. If God numbers their hairs, much more does he number their heads, and take care of their lives, their comforts, their souls. It intimates, that God takes more care of them, than they do of themselves.

The foundation of their discipleship was laid in such a temper and disposition, as would make sufferings very light and easy to them; and it was upon the condition of a preparedness for suffering, that Christ took them to be his followers, *vv.* 37–39. He told them at first, that they were *not worthy of* him, if they were not willing to part with all for him. If religion be worth *any* thing, it is worth *every* thing: and, therefore, all who believe the truth of it, will soon come up to the price of it; and they who make it their

business and bliss, will make everything else to yield to it.

Our nearest and dearest relations; *father or mother, son or daughter.* Between these relations, because there is little room left for envy, there is commonly more room for love, and, therefore, these are instanced, as relations which are most likely to affect us. Children must love their parents, and parents must love their children; but if they love them better than Christ, they are unworthy of him.

Secondly, our ease and safety. We must *take up our cross* and *follow him,* else we are *not worthy* of him. They who would *follow Christ,* must expect *their cross* and *take it up.*

Thirdly, life itself, *v.* 39. *He that findeth his life shall lose it*; he that thinks he has found it when he has saved it, and kept it, by denying Christ, *shall lose it* in an eternal death; but *he that loseth his life for Christ's sake,* that will part with it rather than deny Christ, *shall find it,* to his unspeakable advantage, an eternal life. They are best prepared for the life to come, that sit most loose to this present life.

He that receiveth me, receiveth him that sent me. Not only Christ takes it as done to himself, but through Christ God does so too. By entertaining Christ's ministers, they entertain not *angels unawares,* but Christ, nay, and God himself, and *unawares* too, as appears, *ch.* xxv. 37. *When saw we thee an hungered?*

That though the kindness done to Christ's disciples be never so small, yet if there be occasion for it, and ability to do no more, it shall be accepted, though it be *but a cup of cold water given to one of these little ones,* v. 42. They are *little ones,* poor and weak, and often stand in need of refreshment, and glad of the least. The extremity may be such, that a *cup of cold water* may be a great favour. Note, Kindnesses shown to Christ's disciples are valued in Christ's books, not according to the cost of the gift, but according to the love and affection of the giver.

That kindness to Christ's disciples which he will accept, must be done with an eye to Christ, and for his sake. A prophet must be received *in the name of a prophet,* and a *righteous man* in the name of a *righteous man,* and one of those *little ones* in *the name of a disciple*; not because they are learned, nor witty, nor because they are our relations or neighbours, but because they are righteous, and so bear Christ's image; because they are prophets and disciples, and so are sent on Christ's errand.

CHAPTER ELEVEN

A MESSAGE FOR JOHN
(vv. 1–6)

Now John Baptist, hearing of Christ's works, sent two of his disciples to him; and what passed between them and him we have here an account of. Here is,

I. The question they had to propose to him: *Art thou he that should come, or do we look for another?* This was a serious and important question; *Art thou the Messiah promised, or not? Art thou the Christ? Tell us.* 1. It is taken for granted that the Messiah should come. 2. They intimate, that if this

be not *he,* they would *look for another.* Note, We must not be weary of looking for him that is to come, nor ever say, we will no more expect him till we come to enjoy him. 3. They intimate likewise, that if they be convinced that this is he, they will not be sceptics, they will be satisfied, and will look *for no other.* 4. They therefore ask, *Art thou he?* John had said for his part, *I am not the Christ,* John i. 20. Now, (1) Some think that John sent this question for his own satisfaction. It is true he had borne a noble testimony to Christ; he had declared him to be the *Son of God* (John i. 34), the Lamb of God (v. 29), and he that *should baptize with the Holy Ghost* (v. 33), and *sent of God* (John iii. 34), which were great things. But he desired to be further and more fully assured, that he was the Messiah that had been so long promised and expected. (2) John's doubt might arise from his own present circumstances. He was a prisoner, and might be tempted to think, if Jesus be indeed the Messiah, whence is it that I, his friend and forerunner, am brought into this trouble, and am left to be so long in it. It was perhaps a shock to his faith in Christ. Note, [1] Where there is true faith, yet there may be a mixture of unbelief. The best are not always alike strong. [2] Troubles for Christ, especially when they continue long unrelieved, are such trials of faith as sometimes prove too hard to be borne up against. [3] The remaining unbelief of good men may sometimes, in an hour of temptation, strike at the root, and call in question the most fundamental truths which were thought to be well settled. *Will the Lord cast off for ever?* But, (3) Others think that John sent his disciples to Christ with this question, not so much for his own satisfaction as for theirs. Now, [1] They were weak in knowledge, and wavering in their faith, and needed instruction and confirmation. Now John would have their mistakes rectified, and wished them to be as well satisfied as he himself was. [2] John was all along industrious to turn over his disciples to Christ. Perhaps he foresaw his death approaching, and therefore would bring his disciples to be better acquainted with Christ, under whose guardianship he must leave them.

II. Here is Christ's answer to this question, *vv.* 4–6. It was not so direct and express, as when he said, *I that speak unto thee am he*; but it was a real answer, an answer in fact.

1. He points them to what they heard and saw, which they must tell John, that he might from thence take occasion the more fully to instruct and convince them out of their own mouths. Go and tell him *what you hear and see*. Note, Our senses may and ought to be appealed to in those things that are their proper objects.

(1) *What you see* of the *power of Christ's miracles*. They are to be considered, [1] As the *acts of a divine power*. None but the God of nature could thus overrule and outdo the power of nature. It is particularly spoken of as God's prerogative to *open the eyes of the blind*, Ps. cxlvi. 8. Miracles are therefore the broad seal of heaven, and the doctrine they are affixed

to must be of God, for his power will never contradict his truth; nor can it be imagined that he should set his seal to a lie; and they leave no room to doubt that he was sent of God, and that his doctrine was his that *sent him*. [2] As the *accomplishment of a divine prediction*. It was foretold (Isa. xxxv. 5, 6), that our God should come, and that then *the eyes of the blind should be opened*. Now if the works of Christ agree with the words of the prophet, as it is plain they do, then no doubt but this is our God whom we have waited for, who shall *come with a recompence*; this is he who is so much wanted.

(2) Tell him *what you hear* of the *preaching of his gospel*, which accompanies his miracles. Faith, though confirmed by seeing, comes by hearing. Note, It is a proof of Christ's divine mission that his doctrine is gospel indeed; good news to those who are truly humbled in sorrow for their sins, and truly humble in the denial of self.

2. He pronounces a *blessing* on those that *were not offended in him*, *v.* 6. So clear are these evidences of Christ's mission, that they who are not wilfully prejudiced against him, and scandalized in him (so the word is), cannot but receive his doctrine, and so be *blessed in him*.

JOHN HONOURED
(*vv.* 7–15)

Concerning this commendation of John, observe.

I. That Christ spoke thus honourably of John, not in the hearing of John's disciples, but *as they departed*, just after they were gone,

Luke vii. 24. He would not so much as seem to flatter John, nor have these praises of him reported to him.

II. That what Christ said concerning John, was intended not only for his praise, but for the people's profit, to revive the remembrance of John's ministry, which had been well attended, but which was now (as other such things used to be) strangely forgotten: they did for a season, and but *for a season, rejoice in his light*, John v. 35.

III. Let us see what the commendation of John was. They know not what answer to make to Christ's question; well, says Christ, "I will tell you what a man John the Baptist was."

1. "He was a firm, resolute man, and not *a reed shaken with the wind*; *you* have been so in your thoughts of him, but *he* was not so. He was not wavering in his principles, nor uneven in his conversation; but was remarkable for his steadiness and constant consistency with himself."

2. He was a *self-denying* man, and *mortified* to this world. "Was he a man *clothed in soft raiment*? If so, you would not have gone *into the wilderness* to see him, but to the *court*. You went to see one that had *his raiment of camel's hair*, and a *leathern girdle about his loins*; his mien and habit showed that he was dead to all the pomps of the world and the pleasures of sense; his clothing agreed with the *wilderness* he lived in, and the doctrine he preached there, that of repentance.

3. His greatest commendation of all was his office and ministry, which was more his honour than any personal endowments or quali-

fications could be; and therefore this is most enlarged upon in a full encomium.

(1) He was *a prophet*, yea, and *more than a prophet* (v. 9); so he said of him who was the great Prophet, to whom all the prophets bear witness. John said of himself, he was not *that prophet*, that great prophet, the Messiah himself; and now Christ (a very competent Judge) says of him, that he was *more than a prophet*. He owned himself inferior to Christ, and Christ owned him superior to all other prophets. They *saw Christ's day* at a distance, and their vision was yet for a great while to come; but John saw the day dawn, he saw the sun rise, and told the people of the Messiah, as one that stood among them. They spake of Christ, but he pointed to him; they said, *A virgin shall conceive*: he said, *Behold the Lamb of God!*

(2) He was the same that was predicted to be Christ's forerunner (v. 10); *This is he of whom it is written*. He was prophesied of by the other prophets, and therefore was greater than they. Malachi prophesied concerning John, *Behold, I send my messenger before thy face*. That which advanced John above the *Old-Testament* prophets was, that he went immediately before Christ. Note, The nearer any are to Christ, the more truly honourable they are.

(3) There *was not a greater born of women* than John the Baptist, v. 11. Christ knew how to value persons according to the degrees of their worth, and he prefers John before all that went before him, before all that were *born of women*

by ordinary generation. Of all that God had raised up and called to any service in his church, John is the most eminent, even beyond Moses himself; for he began to preach the gospel doctrine of remission of sins to those who are truly penitent; and he had more signal revelations from heaven than any of them had; for he *saw heaven opened*, and the *Holy Ghost descend*.

Yet this high encomium of John has a surprising limitation, *notwithstanding, he that is least in the kingdom of heaven is greater than he*. [1] In the kingdom *of glory*. John was a *great* and *good* man, but he was yet in a state of infirmity and imperfection, and therefore came short of glorified saints, and the *spirits of just men made perfect*. [2] By the *kingdom of heaven* here, is rather to be understood the *kingdom of grace*, the gospel dispensation in the perfection of its power and purity. John came to the dawning of the gospel-day, and therein excelled the foregoing prophets, but he was taken off before the noon of that day, before the rending of the veil, before Christ's death and resurrection, and the pouring out of the Spirit; so that the least of the apostles and evangelists, having greater discoveries made to them, and being employed in a greater embassy, is *greater than John*.

(4) The great commendation of John the Baptist was, that God owned his ministry, and made it wonderfully successful for the breaking of the ice, and the preparing of people for the *kingdom of heaven. From the days of* the first appearing of *John the Baptist*, until now (which was not much above two years), a great deal of good was done; so quick was the motion when it came near to Christ the Centre.

(5) The ministry of John was the *beginning of the gospel*, as it is reckoned, Mark i. 1; Acts i. 22. This is shown here in two things:

[1] In John the Old Testament dispensation began to die, *v*. 13. So long that ministration continued in full force and virtue, but then it began to decline. The law was given by Moses long ago, and there had been no prophets for three hundred years before John, and yet they are both said to *prophecy until John*, because the law was still observed, and Moses and the prophets still read. Their prophecies of a Christ to come became out of date, when John said, *He is come*.

[2] In him the New-Testament day began to dawn; for (*v*. 14) *This is Elias, that was for to come*. John was as the loop that coupled the two Testaments. The concluding prophecy of the Old Testament was, *Behold, I will send you Elijah*, Mal. iv. 5, 6. Those words prophesied until John, and then, being turned into a history, they ceased to prophesy. First, Christ speaks of it as a great truth, that John the Baptist is the Elias of the New Testament; one that should come in the spirit and power of Elias (Luke i. 17), like him in temper and conversation, that should press repentance with terrors, and especially as it is in the prophecy, that should *turn the hearts of the fathers to the children*. Secondly, He speaks of it as a truth, which would

not be easily apprehended by those whose expectations fastened upon the temporal kingdom of the Messiah, and introductions to it agreeable. Christ suspects the welcome of it, *if ye will receive it.* Christ is a Saviour, and John an Elias, to those who will receive the truth concerning them.

Lastly, Our Lord Jesus closes this discourse with a solemn demand of attention (*v.* 15): *He that hath ears to hear, let him hear*; which intimates, that those things were dark and hard to be understood, but of great concern and consequence, and therefore well deserved it.

WORDS OF WARNING
(*vv.* 16–24)

Christ was going on in the praise of John the Baptist and his ministry, but here stops on a sudden, and turns that to the reproach of those who enjoyed both that, and the ministry of Christ and his apostles too, in vain. As to that generation, we may observe to whom he *compares them* (*vv.* 16–19), and as to the particular places he instances in, we may observe with whom he *compares them, vv.* 20–24.

I. As to that *generation*, the body of the Jewish people at that time. There were many indeed that pressed into the kingdom of heaven; but the generality continued in unbelief and obstinacy.

This our Lord Jesus here sets forth in a parable, yet speaks as if he were at a loss to find out a similitude proper to represent this, *Whereunto shall I liken this generation?* The similitude is taken from

some common custom among the Jewish children at their play, who, as is usual with children, imitated the fashions of grown people at their marriages and funerals, *rejoicing* and *lamenting*; but being all a jest, it made no impression; no more did the ministry either of John the Baptist or of Christ upon that generation. He especially reflects on the scribes and Pharisees, who had a proud conceit of themselves; therefore to humble them he compares them to children, and their behaviour to children's play.

In the explanation of the parable is set forth the different temper of John's ministry and of Christ's, who were the two great lights of that generation.

(1) On the one hand, John came *mourning to them, neither eating nor drinking*; not conversing familiarly with people, nor ordinarily eating in company, but alone, in his cell in the wilderness, where *his meat was locusts and wild honey.*

(2) On the other hand, *the Son of man came eating and drinking*, and so he *piped unto them.* Christ conversed familiarly with all sorts of people, not affecting any peculiar strictness or austerity; he was affable and easy of access, not shy of any company, was often at feasts, both with Pharisees and publicans, to try if this would win upon those who were not wrought upon by John's reservedness: those who were not awed by John's frowns, would be allured by Christ's smiles; from whom St. Paul learned to become *all things to all men*, 1 Cor. ix. 22. Now our Lord Jesus, by his freedom, did not at all condemn John, any more than

John did condemn him, though their deportment was so very different.

The various methods which God takes for the conversion of sinners, are with many fruitless and ineffectual: "*Ye have not danced, ye have not lamented*; you have not been suitably affected either with the one or with the other." If people will be neither bound by laws, nor invited by promises, nor frightened by threatenings, will neither be awakened by the *greatest* things, nor allured by the *sweetest* things, nor startled by the most *terrible* things, nor be made sensible by the *plainest* things; if they will hearken to the voice neither of scripture, nor reason, nor experience, nor providence, nor conscience, nor interest, what more can be done? The cause of this great unfruitfulness and perverseness of people under the means of grace, is that they are *like children sitting in the markets*; they are foolish as children. *The market-place they sit in* is to some a place of idleness (*ch.* xx. 3); to others a place of worldly business (Jam. iv. 13); to all a place of noise or diversion; so that if you ask the reason why people get so little good by the means of grace, you will find it is because they are slothful and trifling, and do not love to take pains; or because their heads, and hands, and hearts are full of the world, the cares of which *choke the word*, and choke their souls at last (Ezek. xxxiii. 31; Amos viii. 5); and they study to divert their own thoughts from every thing that is serious. Thus *in the markets* they are, and there they *sit*; in these things their hearts rest, and by them they resolve to abide.

Though the means of grace be thus slighted and abused by many, by the most, yet there is a remnant that through grace do improve them, and answer the designs of them, to the glory of God, and the good of their own souls. *But wisdom is justified of her children.* Christ is *Wisdom*; in him *are hid treasures of wisdom*; the saints are the *children God has given* him, Heb. ii. 13. The gospel is *wisdom*, it is *the wisdom from above*: true believers are begotten again by it, and born from above too: they are wise *children*, wise for themselves, and their true interests; not *like the foolish children that sat in the markets*.

II. As to the particular *places* in which Christ was most conversant. What he said in general of that *generation*, he applied in particular to those *places*, to affect them. *Then began he to upbraid them, v.* 20. Now observe,

1. The sin charged upon them: that *they repented not*. Note, Wilful impenitency is the great damning sin of multitudes that enjoy the gospel, and which (more than any other) sinners will be upbraided with to eternity. The great doctrine that both John the Baptist, and Christ, and the apostles preached, was repentance; the great thing designed, both in the *piping* and in the *mourning*, was to prevail with people to change their minds and ways, to leave their sins and turn to God; and this they would not be brought to.

2. The aggravation of the sin; they were *the cities in which most of*

his mighty works were done; for thereabouts his principal residence had been for some time. By Christ's *mighty works* they should have been prevailed with, not only to receive his doctrine, but to obey his law; the curing of bodily diseases should have been the healing of their souls, but it had not that effect. Christ came *into the world to bless us*; but if that blessing be slighted, he has woes in reserve, and his woes are of all others the most terrible. These two cities were situate upon *the sea of Galilee*, the former on the east side, and the latter on the west, rich and populous places; Bethsaida was lately advanced to a city by Philip the tetrarch; out of it Christ took at least three of his apostles: thus highly were these places favoured! Yet because they *knew not the day of their visitation*, they fell under these woes, which stuck so close to them, that soon after this they decayed, and dwindled into mean, obscure villages. So fatally does sin ruin cities, and so certainly does the word of Christ take place!

Capernaum is here condemned with an emphasis (*v.* 23), "*And thou, Capernaum*, hold up thy hand, and hear thy doom."

We have here Capernaum's doom,

[1] Put absolutely; Thou *which art exalted to heaven shalt be brought down to hell*. Note, Those who enjoy the gospel in power and purity, are thereby *exalted to heaven*; they have therein a great honour for the present, and a great advantage for eternity; they are lifted up toward *heaven*; but if, notwithstanding, they still *cleave to the*

earth, they may thank themselves that they are not lifted up *into heaven*.

[2] We have it here put in comparison with the doom of Sodom— a place more remarkable, both for sin and ruin, than perhaps any other; and yet Christ here tells us,

First, That Capernaum's means would have saved Sodom. If these miracles had been done among the Sodomites, as bad as they were, they would have repented, and *their city would have remained unto this day* a monument of sparing mercy, as now it is of destroying justice, Jude 7.

Secondly, That Sodom's ruin will therefore be less at the great day than Capernaum's. Sodom will have many things to answer for, but not the sin of neglecting Christ, as Capernaum will.

COME UNTO ME (*vv.* 25–30)

I. Christ here returns thanks to God for his favour to those *babes* who had the mysteries of the gospel *revealed to them* (*vv.* 25, 26).

Now in this thanksgiving of Christ, we may observe,

1. The titles he gives to God; *O Father, Lord of heaven and earth*. When we come to God as a Father, we must withal remember, that he is *Lord of heaven and earth*; which obliges us to come to him with reverence, as to the sovereign Lord of all, and yet with confidence, as one able to do for us whatever we need or can desire; to defend us from all evil and to supply us with all good.

2. The thing he gives thanks for: *Because thou hast hid these things from the wise and prudent, and yet*

revealed them to babes. These things; he does not say what things, but means the great things of the gospel, *the things that belong to our peace*, Luke xix. 42.

The great things of the everlasting gospel have been and are hid from many that were *wise and prudent*, that were eminent for learning and worldly policy; some of the greatest scholars and the greatest statesmen have been the greatest strangers to gospel mysteries.

While *the wise and prudent men* of the world are in the dark about gospel mysteries, even the *babes in Christ* have the sanctifying saving knowledge of them: *Thou hast revealed them unto babes.* Such the disciples of Christ were; men of mean birth and education; no scholars, no artists, no politicians unlearned and ignorant men, Acts iv. 13.

3. This difference between *the prudent* and the *babes* is of God's own making. [1] It is he that has *hid these things from the wise and prudent.* God is not the Author of their ignorance and error, but he leaves them to themselves, and their sin becomes their punishment, and the Lord is righteous in it. See John xii. 39, 40; Rom. xi. 7, 8; Acts xxviii. 26, 27. Had they honoured God with the wisdom and prudence they had, he would have given them the knowledge of these better things; but because they served their lusts with them, he has *hid their hearts from this understanding*. [2] It is he that has *revealed them unto babes.* Things revealed belong to our children (Deut. xxix. 29), and to them he *gives an understanding* to

receive these things, and the impressions of them. Thus *he resists the proud*, and *gives grace to the humble*, Jam. iv. 6.

This way of dispensing divine grace is to be acknowledged by us, as it was by our Lord Jesus, with all thankfulness. We must thank God, [1] That *these things* are *revealed*; the mystery hid from ages and generations is manifested; that they are *revealed*, not to a few, but to be published to all the world. [2] That they are *revealed to babes*; that the meek and humble are beautified with this salvation; and this honour put upon those whom the world pours contempt upon. [3] It magnifies the mercy to them, that *these things* are *hid from the wise and prudent*: distinguishing favours are most obliging.

II. Christ here makes a gracious offer of the benefits of the gospel to all, and these are the things which are *revealed to babes*, *v.* 25, &c.

Two things he here lays before us, *v.* 27.

[1] His commission from the Father: *All things are delivered unto me of my Father.* Christ, as God, is equal in power and glory with the Father; but as Mediator he receives his power and glory from the Father; has *all judgment committed to him*.

(2) His intimacy with the Father: *No man knoweth the Son but the Father, Neither knoweth any man the Father save the Son.* This gives us a further satisfaction, and an abundant one. It must therefore be a great encouragement to us to be assured, that they understood one another very well in this affair; that the Father knew the Son, and the

Son knew the Father, and both perfectly (a mutual consciousness we may call it, between the Father and the Son), so that there could be no mistake in the settling of this matter.

After so solemn a preface, we may well expect something very great; and it is *a faithful saying*, and well *worthy of all acceptation*; *words whereby we may be saved*. We are here invited to Christ as our Priest, Prince, and Prophet, to be saved, and, in order to that, to be ruled and taught by him.

(1) We must come to Jesus Christ as our Rest, and repose ourselves in him (*v.* 28), *Come unto me all ye that labour*. Observe, [1] The character of the persons invited; *all that labour, and are heavy laden*. This is a word in season to him that is weary, Isa. l. 4. Those who complain of the burden of the ceremonial law, which was an intolerable yoke, and was made much more so by the tradition of the elders (Luke xi. 46), let them come to Christ, and they shall be made easy; he came to free his church from this yoke, to cancel the imposition of those carnal ordinances, and to introduce a purer and more spiritual way of worship; but it is rather to be understood of the burden of sin, both the guilt and the power of it.

[2] The invitation itself: *Come unto me*. That glorious display of Christ's greatness which we had (*v.* 27), as Lord of all, might frighten us from him, but see here how he holds out *the golden sceptre*, that we may touch the top of it and may live. *Come* and *cast that burden upon* him, under which thou art

heavy laden. This is the gospel call, *The Spirit saith, Come*; and *the bride saith, Come*; *Let him that is athirst come; Whoever will, let him come*.

[3] The blessing promised to those that do come: *I will give you rest*. Note, Jesus Christ will give assured rest to those weary souls, that by a lively faith come to him for it; *rest* from the terror of sin, in a well-grounded peace of conscience; *rest* from the power of sin, in a regular order of the soul, and its due government of itself; a *rest* in God, and a complacency of soul, in his love. Ps. xi. 6, 7. This is that *rest which remains for the people of God* (Heb. iv. 9), begun in grace, and perfected in glory.

(2) We must come to Jesus Christ as our Ruler, and submit ourselves to him (*v.* 29). *Take my yoke upon you*. This must go along with the former, for Christ is exalted to be both a *Prince and a Saviour*, a *Priest upon his throne*. The *rest* he promises is a release from the drudgery of sin, not from the service of God, but an obligation to the duty we owe to him.

Now this is the hardest part of our lesson, and therefore it is qualified (*v.* 30). *My yoke is easy and my burden is light*; you need not be afraid of it.

[1] The *yoke* of Christ's commands is an *easy yoke*; not only *easy*, but gracious, so the word signifies; it is sweet and pleasant; there is nothing in it to gall the yielding neck, nothing to hurt us, but, on the contrary, much to refresh us. It is a *yoke* that is lined with love. Such is the nature of all Christ's commands, so reasonable

in themselves, so profitable to us, and all summed up in one word, and that a sweet word, love.

[2] The *burden* of Christ's cross is a *light burden*, very *light*: afflictions from Christ, which befall us as men; afflictions for Christ, which befall us as Christians; the latter are especially meant. This *burden* in itself is *not joyous, but grievous*; yet as it is Christ's, it is *light*. As afflictions abound, and are prolonged, consolations abound, and are prolonged too.

(3) We must come to Jesus Christ as our Teacher, and set ourselves to learn of him, *v.* 29. Some make the following words, *for I am meek and lowly in heart*, to be the particular lesson we are required to learn from the example of Christ. We must learn of him to be *meek* and *lowly*, and must mortify our pride and passion, which render us so unlike to him. We must so *learn of Christ* as to *learn Christ* (Eph. iv. 20), for he is both Teacher and Lesson, Guide and Way, and All in All.

Two reasons are given why we must *learn of Christ*.

[1] *I am meek and lowly in heart*, and therefore fit to teach you.

First, He is *meek*, and can have *compassion on the ignorant*, whom others would be in a passion with. Secondly, *He is lowly in heart*. He condescends to teach poor scholars, to teach novices; he chose disciples, not from the court, nor the schools, but from the seaside. This humility and meekness, as it qualifies him to be a Teacher, so it will be the best qualification of those who are to be taught by him; *for the meek will he guide in judgment*, Ps. xxv. 9.

[2] *You shall find rest to your souls*. The way of duty is the way of rest. The *understanding* finds *rest* in the *knowledge of* God and Jesus Christ, and is there abundantly satisfied, finding *that* wisdom in the gospel which has been sought for in vain throughout the whole creation, Job xxviii. 12. The truths Christ teaches are such as we may venture our souls upon. The affections find rest in the love of God and Jesus Christ, and meet with that in them which gives them an abundant satisfaction; quietness and assurance for ever.

CHAPTER TWELVE

LORD OF THE SABBATH
(*vv.* 1–13)

The Jewish teachers had corrupted many of the commandments, by interpreting them more loosely than they were intended; a mistake which Christ discovered and rectified (*ch.* v.) in his sermon on the mount: but concerning the fourth commandment, they had erred in the other extreme, and interpreted it too strictly.

Christ's industrious explanation of the fourth commandment, intimates its perpetual obligation to the religious observation of *one day in seven*, as a *holy sabbath*. He would not expound a law that was immediately to expire, but doubtless intended hereby to settle a point which would be of use to his church in all ages; and so it is to teach us, that our Christian sabbath, though under the direction of the fourth commandment, is not under the injunctions of the Jewish elders.

It is usual to settle the meaning of

a law by judgments given upon cases that happen in fact, and in like manner is the meaning of this law settled. Here are two passages of story put together for this purpose, happening at some distance of time from each other, and of a different nature, but both answering this intention.

I. Christ, by justifying his disciples in plucking the ears of corn on the sabbath-day, shows that *works of necessity* are *lawful* on that day.

(1) He justifies them by precedents, which were allowed to be good by the Pharisees themselves.

[1] He urges an ancient instance of David, who in a case of necessity did that which otherwise he ought not to have done (*vv.* 3, 4).

[2] He urges a daily instance of the priests, which they likewise *read in the law*, and according to which was the constant usage, *v.* 5. *The priests in the temple* did a great deal of servile work on the sabbath day; and yet it was never reckoned any transgression of the fourth commandment, because the temple-service required and justified it.

(2) He justifies them by arguments, three cogent ones.

[1] *In this place is one greater than the temple, v.* 6.

[2] *God will have mercy and not sacrifice, v.* 7. Ceremonial duties must give way to moral, and the natural, royal law of love and self-preservation must take place of ritual observances. This is quoted from Hos. vi. 6.

[3] *The Son of man is Lord even of the sabbath day, v.* 8. That law, as all the rest, is put into the hand of Christ, to be altered, enforced, or

dispensed with, as he sees good. It was by *the Son* that God *made the world*, and by him he instituted the sabbath in innocency; by him he gave the ten commandments at mount Sinai, and as Mediator he is entrusted with the institution of ordinances, and to make what changes he thought fit; and particularly, as being *Lord of the sabbath*, he was authorized to make such an alteration of that day, as that it should become the Lord's day, the Lord Christ's day.

Christ having thus silenced the Pharisees, and got clear of them (*v.* 9), *departed*, and *went into their synagogue*, the synagogue of these Pharisees, in which they presided, and toward which he was going, when they picked this quarrel with him.

II. Christ, by *healing the man that had the withered hand on the sabbath day*, shows that works of mercy are lawful and proper to be done on that day. The work of necessity was done by the disciples, and justified by him; the work of mercy was done by himself; the works of mercy were his works of necessity; it was his *meat and drink* to *do good. I must preach*, says he, Luke iv. 43. This cure is recorded for the sake of the time when it was wrought, on the sabbath.

CHRIST'S HUMILITY
(*vv.* 14–21)

As in the midst of Christ's greatest humiliations, there were proofs of his dignity, so in the midst of his greatest honours, he gave proofs of his humility; and when the mighty works he did gave him an opportunity of making a figure, yet he made it appear that *he emptied himself*, and *made himself of no reputation*. Here we have,

I. The cursed malice of the Pharisees against Christ (*v.* 14); being enraged at the convincing evidence of his miracles, they *went out, and held a council against him, how they might destroy him*.

II. Christ's absconding upon this occasion, and the privacy he chose, to decline, not his work, but his danger; because *his hour was not yet come* (*v.* 15), *he withdrew himself from thence*.

Christ studied to reconcile usefulness and privacy; he *healed them all*, and yet (*v.* 16), *charged them that they should not make him known*; which may be looked upon, 1. As an act of prudence; it was not so much the miracles themselves, as the public discourse concerning them, that enraged the Pharisees (*vv.* 23, 24); therefore Christ, though he would not omit doing good, yet would do it with as little noise as possible, to avoid offence to them and peril to himself. 2. It may be looked upon as an act of righteous judgment upon the Pharisees, who were unworthy to hear of any more of his miracles, having made so light of those they had seen. By shutting their eyes against the light, they had forfeited the benefit of it. 3. As an act of humility and self-denial. Christ would have his disciples to be the reverse of those who did all their works *to be seen of men*.

III. The fulfilling of the scriptures in all this, *v.* 17. Christ retired into privacy and obscurity, that though he was eclipsed, the word of God might be fulfilled, and so illustrated

and glorified, which was the thing his heart was upon. The scripture here said to be fulfilled is Isa. xlii. 1–4, which is quoted at large, *vv.* 18–21. The scope of it is to show how mild and quiet, and yet how successful, our Lord Jesus should be in his undertaking; instances of both which we have in the foregoing passages.

CONQUEST OF SATAN
(*vv.* 22–37)

In these verses we have,

I. Christ's glorious conquest of Satan, in the gracious cure of one who, by the divine permission, was under his power, and in his possession, *v.* 22. Here observe,

1. The man's case was very sad; he was *possessed with a devil*. More cases of this kind occurred in Christ's time than usual, that Christ's power might be the more magnified, and his purpose the more manifested, in opposing and dispossessing Satan; and that it might the more evidently appear, that he *came to destroy the works of the devil*. This poor man that was possessed was blind and dumb; a miserable case! he could neither see to help himself, nor speak to others to help him.

2. His cure was very strange, and the more so, because sudden; *he healed him*. Note, Christ's mercy is directly opposite to Satan's malice; his favours, to the devil's mischiefs. When Satan's power is broken in the soul, the eyes are opened to see God's glory, and the lips opened to speak his praise.

II. The conviction which this gave to the people, to *all the people*: they *were amazed*. Christ had wrought divers miracles of this kind before; but his works are not the less wonderful, nor the less to be wondered at, for their being often repeated. They inferred from it, "*Is not this the Son of David?* The Messiah promised, that was to spring from the loins of David? Is not this he that should come?" We may take this, 1. As an *enquiring* question; they asked, *Is not this the Son of David?* But they did not stay for an answer: the impressions were cogent, but they were transient. Or, 2. as an *affirming* question; *Is not this the Son of David?* "Yes, certainly it is, it can be no other; such miracles as these plainly evince that the kingdom of the Messiah is now setting up." And they were the people, the vulgar sort of the spectators, that drew this inference from Christ's miracles. So plain and easy was the way made to this great truth of Christ being the Messiah and Saviour of the world, that the common people could not miss it; the *wayfaring men, though fools, could not err therein.* See Isa. xxxv. 8.

III. The blasphemous cavil of the Pharisees, *v.* 24. The Pharisees were a sort of men that pretended to more knowledge in, and zeal for, the divine law, than other people; yet they were the most inveterate enemies to Christ and his doctrine. And when they heard the people say, *Is not this the Son of David?* they were extremely irritated, more at that than at the miracle itself; this made them jealous of our Lord Jesus, and apprehensive, that as *his* interest in the people's esteem increased, *theirs* must of course be eclipsed and diminished. They said, "*This fellow does not cast out devils, but by Beelzebub the prince of the devils*, and therefore is not the Son of David." Observe,

1. How scornfully they speak of Christ, *this fellow*; as if that precious name of his, which is *as ointment poured forth*, were not worthy to be taken into their lips.

2. How blasphemously they speak of his miracles; they could not deny the matter of fact; it was as plain as the sun, that devils were cast out by the word of Christ; nor could they deny that it was an extraordinary thing, and supernatural. Being thus forced to grant the premises, they had no other way to avoid the conclusion, that *this is the Son of David*, than by suggesting that *Christ cast out devils by Beelzebub*; that there was a compact between Christ and the devil. No surmise could be more palpably false and vile than this; that he, who is Truth itself, should be in combination with the father of lies, to cheat the world. This was the last refuge, or subterfuge rather, of an obstinate infidelity, that was resolved to stand it out against the clearest conviction.

IV. Christ's reply to this base insinuation, *vv.* 25–30. Here are three arguments by which he demonstrates the unreasonableness of this suggestion.

1. It would be very strange, and highly improbable, that Satan should be cast out by such a compact, because then Satan's *kingdom would be divided against itself*; which, considering his subtlety, is not a thing to be imagined, *vv.* 25, 26.

(1) Here is a known rule laid down, that in all societies a common ruin is the consequence of mutual quarrels: *Every kingdom divided against itself is brought to desolation.*

(2) The application of it to the case in hand (*v.* 26), *If Satan cast out Satan*; if the prince of the devils should be at variance with the inferior devils, the whole kingdom and interest would soon be broken. *The works of the devil*, as a rebel against God, and a tyrant over the souls of men, were destroyed by Christ; and therefore it was the most absurd thing imaginable, to think that Beelzebub should at all countenance such a design, or come into it: if he should fall in with Christ, *how should then his kingdom stand?*

2. It was not at all strange, or improbable, that devils should be cast out by the Spirit of God; for,

(1) *How* otherwise *do your children cast them out?* There were those among the Jews who, by invocation of the name of the most high God, or the God of Abraham, Isaac, and Jacob, did sometimes cast out devils. Josephus speaks of some of his time that did it; we read of *Jewish exorcists* (Acts xix. 13), and of some that *in Christ's name cast out devils*, though they did not follow him (Mark ix. 38), or were not faithful to him, *ch.* vii. 22. These the Pharisees condemned not, but imputed what they did to the Spirit of God, and valued themselves and their nation upon it. It was therefore merely from spite and envy to Christ, that they would own that others cast out devils by the Spirit of God, but suggest that

he did it by compact with Beelzebub.

(2) This casting out of devils was a certain token and indication of the approach and appearance of the kingdom of God (*v.* 28); "But if it be indeed that *I cast out devils by the Spirit of God*, as certainly I do, then you must conclude, that though you are unwilling to receive it, yet the kingdom of the Messiah is now about to be set up among you." Other miracles that Christ wrought proved him *sent of God*, but this proved him sent of God to destroy the devil's kingdom and his works.

3. The comparing of Christ's miracles, particularly this of casting out devils, with his doctrine, and the design and tendency of his holy religion, evidenced that he was so far from being in league with Satan, that he was at open enmity and hostility against him (*v.* 29); *How can one enter into a strong man's house, and plunder his goods*, and carry them away, *except he first bind the strong man? And then he* may do what he pleases with his goods. The world, that sat in darkness, and lay in wickedness, was in Satan's possession, and under his power, as a house in the possession and under the power of a strong man; so is every unregenerate soul; there Satan resides, there he rules. Now, (1) The design of Christ's gospel was to spoil the devil's house, which, as a strong man, he kept in the world; *to turn the people from darkness to light*, from sin to holiness, from this world to a better, *from the power of Satan unto God* (Acts xxvi. 18); to alter the property of souls. (2)

Pursuant to this design, he bound the strong man, when he cast out unclean spirits by his word: thus he wrested the *sword* out of the devil's hand, that he might wrest the *sceptre* out of it. The doctrine of Christ teaches us how to construe his miracles, and when he showed how easily and effectually he could cast the devil out of people's bodies, he encouraged all believers to hope that, whatever power Satan might usurp and exercise in the souls of men, Christ by his grace would break it: he will spoil him, for it appears that he can bind him.

4. It is here intimated, that this holy war, which Christ was carrying on with vigour against the devil and his kingdom, was such as would not admit of a neutrality (*v.* 30), *He that is not with me is against me.* In the little differences that may arise between the disciples of Christ among themselves, we are taught to lessen the matters in variance, and to seek peace, by accounting those who *are not against us, to be with us* (Luke ix. 50); but in the great quarrel between Christ and the devil, no peace is to be sought, nor any such favourable construction to be made of any indifference in the matter; he that is not hearty *for* Christ, will be reckoned with as really *against* him: he that is cold in the cause, is looked upon as an enemy.

V. Here is a discourse of Christ's upon this occasion, concerning tongue-sins; *Wherefore I say unto you.* He seems to turn from the Pharisees to the people, from disputing to instructing; and from the sin of the Pharisees he warns the people concerning three sorts of

tongue-sins; for others' harms are admonitions to us.

1. Blasphemous words against the Holy Ghost are the worst kind of tongue-sins, and unpardonable, *vv.* 31, 32.

(1) Here is a gracious assurance of the pardon of all sin upon gospel terms: this Christ says to us, and it is a comfortable saying, that the greatness of sin shall be no bar to our acceptance with God, if we truly repent and believe the gospel: *All manner of sin and blasphemy shall be forgiven unto men.*

(2) Here is an exception of *the blasphemy against the Holy Ghost,* which is here declared to be the only unpardonable sin. See here,

[1] What this sin is; it is *speaking against the Holy Ghost.* See what malignity there is in tongue-sins, when the only unpardonable sin is so. *But Jesus knew their thoughts, v.* 25. It is not all speaking against the person or essence of the Holy Ghost, or some of his more private operations, or merely the resisting of his internal working in the sinner himself, that is here meant; for *who then should be saved?* This blasphemy is excepted, not for any defect of mercy in God or merit in Christ, but because it inevitably leaves the sinner in infidelity and impenitency. We have reason to think that none are guilty of this sin, who believe that Christ is *the Son of God,* and sincerely desire to have part in his merit and mercy: and those who fear they have committed this sin, give a good sign that they have not.

[2] What the sentence is that is passed upon it; *It shall not be forgiven, neither in this world, nor in*

the world to come. As in the then present state of the Jewish church, there was no sacrifice of expiation for *the soul that sinned presumptuously*; so neither under the dispensation of gospel grace, which is often in scripture called *the world to come*, shall there be any pardon to *such as tread underfoot the blood of the covenant, and do despite to the Spirit of grace*: there is no cure for a sin so directly against the remedy. It was a rule in our old law, No sanctuary for sacrilege. Or, *It shall be forgiven neither now*, in the sinner's own conscience, *nor in the great day*, when the pardon shall be published. Or, this is a sin that exposes the sinner both to temporal and eternal punishment, both to present wrath and *the wrath to come*.

2. Christ speaks here concerning other wicked words, the products of corruption reigning in the heart, and breaking out thence, *vv.* 33–35.

(1) The heart is the *root*, the language is the *fruit* (*v.* 33); if the nature of the tree be good, it will bring forth fruit accordingly. Where grace is the reigning principle in the heart, the language will be the language of Canaan; and, on the contrary, whatever lust reigns in the heart it will break out.

(2) The heart is the *fountain*, the words are the streams (*v.* 34); *Out of the abundance of the heart the mouth speaks*, as the streams are the overflowings of the spring.

(3) The heart is the *treasury*, the words are the things brought out of that treasury (*v.* 35); and from hence men's characters may be drawn, and may be judged of.

[1] It is the character of a *good*

man, that he has a *good treasure in his heart*, and from thence *brings forth good things*, as there is occasion. Graces, comforts, experiences, good knowledge, good affections, good resolutions, these are a *good treasure in the heart*; the word of God hidden there, the law of God written there, divine truths dwelling and ruling there, are a treasure there, valuable and suitable, kept safe and kept secret, as the stores of the good householder, but ready for use upon all occasions.

[2] It is the character of *an evil man*, that he has an *evil treasure in his heart*, and out of it *bringeth forth evil things*. Lusts and corruptions dwelling and reigning in the heart are an evil treasure, out of which the sinner brings forth bad words and actions, to the dishonour of God, and the hurt of others. See Gen. vi. 5, 12; Matt. xv. 18–20; Jam. i. 15. But *treasures of wickedness* (Prov. x. 2) will be *treasures of wrath*.

3. Christ speaks here concerning *idle words*, and shows what evil there is in them (*vv.* 36, 37); much more is there in such wicked words as the Pharisees spoke. It concerns us to think much of the day of judgment, that *that* may be a check upon our tongues; and let us consider,

(1) How particular the account will be of tongue-sins in that day: even *for every idle word*, or discourse, *that men speak, they shall give account*. This intimates, [1] That God takes notice of every word we say, even that which we ourselves do not notice. See Psalm cxxxix. 4. *Not a word in my tongue*

but thou knowest it: though spoken without regard or design, God takes cognizance of it. [2] That vain, idle, impertinent talk is displeasing to God, which tends not to any good purpose, is not good to any use of edifying; it is the product of a vain and trifling heart. [3] We must shortly account for these idle words; they will be produced in evidence against us, to prove us unprofitable servants, that have not improved the faculties of reason and speech, which are part of the talents we are entrusted with.

(2) How strict the judgment will be upon that account (*v*. 37); *By thy words thou shalt be justified or condemned*; a common rule in men's judgments, and here applied to God's.

A WICKED GENERATION
(*vv*. 38–45)

It is probable that these Pharisees with whom Christ is here in discourse were not the same that cavilled at him (*v*. 24), and would not credit the signs he gave; but another set of them, who saw that there was no reason to discredit them, but would not content themselves with the signs he gave, nor admit the evidence of them, unless he would give them such further proof as they should demand. Here is,

1. Their address to him, *v*. 38. They compliment him with the title of *Master*, pretending respect for him, when they intended to abuse him; all are not indeed Christ's servants, who call him *Master*. Their request is, *We would see a sign from thee*. It was highly reasonable that they should see a

sign, that he should by miracles prove his divine mission: see Exod. iv. 8, 9. He came to take down a model of religion that was set up by miracles, and therefore it was requisite he should produce the same credentials; but it was highly unreasonable to demand a sign now, when he had given so many signs already, that did abundantly prove him *sent of God*.

II. His answer to this address, this insolent demand.

1. He condemns the demand, as the language of *an evil and adulterous generation*, *v*. 39. He fastens the charge, not only on *the scribes and Pharisees*, but the whole nation of the Jews; they were all like their leaders, a seed and succession of evil-doers: they were an evil generation indeed, that not only hardened themselves against the conviction of Christ's miracles, but set themselves to abuse him, and put contempt on his miracles.

2. He refuses to give them any other sign than he has already given them, but *that of the prophet Jonas*.

Justly might Christ have said, They shall never see another miracle: but see his wonderful goodness; (1) They shall have the same signs still repeated, for their further benefit, and more abundant conviction. (2) They shall have one sign of a different kind from all these, and that is, *the resurrection of Christ from the dead by his own power*, called here *the sign of the prophet Jonas*; this was yet reserved for their conviction, and was intended to be the great proof of Christ's being the Messiah; for by that he was *declared to be the Son of God with power*, Rom. i. 4.

Now this sign of the prophet Jonas he further explains here: (*v.* 40). *As Jonas was three days and three nights in the whale's belly*, and then came out again safe and well, thus Christ shall be so long in the grave, and then shall rise again.

3. Christ takes this occasion to represent the sad character and condition of that generation in which he lived, a generation that would not be reformed, and therefore could not but be ruined; and he gives them their character, as it would stand in the day of judgment, under the full discoveries and final sentences of that day. Persons and things now appear under false colours; characters and conditions are here changeable: if therefore we would make a right estimate, we must take our measures from the last judgment; things are really, what they are eternally.

Now Christ represents the people of the Jews,

(1) As a generation that would be condemned by *the men of Nineveh*, whose *repenting at the preaching of Jonas* would *rise up in judgment* against them, *v.* 41. Christ's resurrection will be the sign of the prophet Jonas to them: but it will not have so happy an effect upon them, as that of Jonas had upon the Ninevites, for they were by it brought to such a repentance as prevented their ruin; but the Jews will be hardened in an unbelief that shall hasten their ruin; and in the day of judgment, the repentance of the Ninevites will be mentioned as an aggravation of the sin, and consequently the condemnation of those to whom Christ preached then, and of those to whom Christ is preached now; for this reason, because Christ is greater than Jonah.

(2) As a generation that would be condemned by the queen of the south, the queen of Sheba, *v.* 42. The Ninevites would shame them for not repenting, the queen of Sheba for not believing in Christ. She came from a far country to hear the wisdom of Solomon; yet people will not be persuaded to come and hear the wisdom of Christ, though he is in every thing greater than Solomon.

(3) As a generation that were resolved to continue in the possession, and under the power, of Satan, notwithstanding all the methods that were used to dispossess him and rescue them. They are compared to one out of whom the devil is gone, but returns with double force, *vv.* 43–45. The devil is here called *the unclean spirit*, for he has lost all his purity, and delights in and promotes all manner of impurity among men. Now,

[1] The parable represents his possessing men's bodies: Christ having lately cast out a devil, and they having said *he had a devil*, gave occasion to show how much they were under the power of Satan. This is a further proof that Christ did not cast out devils by compact with the devil, for then he would soon have returned again; but Christ's ejectment of him was final, and such as barred a re-entry: we find him charging the evil spirit to *go out, and enter no more*, Mark ix. 25.

[2] The application of the parable makes it to represent the case of the body of the Jewish church and

nation: *So shall it be with this wicked generation,* that now resist, and will finally reject, the gospel of Christ. The devil, who by the labours of Christ and his disciples had been cast out of many of the Jews, sought for rest among the heathen, from whose persons and temples the Christians would everywhere expel him: so Dr. Whitby: or finding nowhere else in the heathen world such pleasant, desirable habitations, to his satisfaction, as here in the heart of the Jews: so Dr. Hammond: he shall therefore enter again into them, for Christ had not found admission among them, and they, by their prodigious wickedness and obstinate unbelief, were still more ready than ever to receive him; and then he shall take a durable possession here, and the state of this people is likely to be more desperately damnable (so Dr. Hammond) than it was before Christ came among them, or would have been if Satan had never been cast out.

The body of that nation is here represented, *First,* As an apostate people. After the captivity in Babylon, they began to reform, left their idols, and appeared with some face of religion; but they soon corrupted themselves again: though they never relapsed into idolatry, they fell into all manner of impiety and profaneness, grew worse and worse, and added to all the rest of their wickedness a wilful contempt of, and opposition to, Christ and his gospel. *Secondly,* As a people marked for ruin. A new commission was passing the seals against that hypocritical nation, the people of God's wrath (like that,

Isa. x. 6), and their destruction by the Romans was likely to be greater than any other, as their sins had been more flagrant: then it was *that wrath came upon them to the uttermost,* 1 Thess. ii. 15, 16.

MOTHER AND BROTHERS
(*vv.* 46-50)

Observe, I. How Christ was interrupted in his preaching by *his mother and his brethren,* that *stood without, desiring to speak with him* (*vv.* 46, 47); which desire of theirs was conveyed to him through the crowd.

1. He was as yet talking to the people. Note, Christ's preaching was talking; it was plain, easy, and familiar, and suited to their capacity and case. What Christ had delivered had been cavilled at, and yet he went on.

2. His mother and brethren stood outside desiring to speak with him, when they should have been standing inside, desiring to hear him. They had the advantage of his daily converse in private, and therefore were less mindful to attend upon his public preaching.

3. They not only would not hear him themselves, but they interrupted others that *heard him gladly.* The devil was a sworn enemy to our Saviour's preaching. He had sought to baffle his discourse by the unreasonable cavils of the scribes and Pharisees, and when he could not gain his point that way, he endeavoured to break it off by the unseasonable visits of relations.

II. How he resented this interruption, *vv.* 48-50.

1. He would not hearken to it; he was so intent upon his work, that

no natural or civil respects should take him off from it. *Who is my mother and who are my brethren?* Not that natural affection is to be put off, or that, under pretence of religion, we may be disrespectful to parents, or unkind to other relations; but *every thing is beautiful in its season*, and the less duty must stand by, while the greater is done. When our regard to our relations comes in competition with the service of God, and the improving of an opportunity to *do good*, in such a case, we must *say to our Father, I have not seen him*, as Levi did, Deut. xxxiii. 9.

2. He took that occasion to prefer his disciples, who were his spiritual kindred, before his natural relations as such: which was a good reason why he would not leave preaching to speak with his brethren. He would rather be profiting his disciples, than pleasing his relations. Observe,

(1) The description of Christ's disciples. They are such as *do the will of his Father*; not only hear it, and know it, and talk of it, but *do it*; for doing the will of God is the best preparative for discipleship (John vii. 17), and the best proof of it (*ch*. vii. 21); *that* denominates us his disciples indeed. Christ does not say, "Whosoever shall do my will," for he came not to seek or do his own will distinct from his Father's: his will and his Father's are the same; but he refers us to his Father's will, because now in his present state and work he referred himself to it, John vi. 38.

(2) The dignity of Christ's disciples: *The same is my brother, and sister, and mother*. His disciples, that had left all to follow him, and embraced his doctrine, were dearer to him than any that were akin to him according to the flesh. They had preferred Christ before their relations; they *left their father* (*ch*. iv. 22; x. 37); and now to make them amends, and to show that there was no love lost, he preferred them before his relations.

CHAPTER THIRTEEN

PREACHING IN PARABLES
(vv. 1–23)

We have here Christ preaching, and may observe,

1. *When* Christ preached this sermon; it was the same day that he preached the sermon in the foregoing chapter: so unwearied was he in doing good, and working the works of him that sent him.

2. *To whom* he preached; there were *great multitudes gathered together to him*, and they were the auditors; we do not find that any of the scribes or Pharisees were present. They were willing to hear him when he preached in the synagogue (*ch*. xii. 9, 14), but they thought it below them to hear a sermon by the sea-side, though Christ himself was the preacher: and truly he had better have their room than their company, for now they were absent, he went on quietly and without contradiction.

3. *Where* he preached this sermon.

(1) His meeting-place was the sea-side. He went out of the house (because there was no room for the audience) into the open air. As he had not a house of his own to live in, so he had not a chapel of his

110

own to preach in. By this he teaches us in the external circumstances of worship not to covet that which is stately, but to make the best of the conveniences which God in his providence allots to us.

(2) His pulpit was a ship; not like Ezra's pulpit, that was *made for the purpose* (Neh. viii. 4); but converted to this use for want of a better. No place amiss for such a Preacher, whose presence dignified and consecrated any place: let not those who preach Christ be ashamed, though they have mean and inconvenient places to preach in.

4. *What* and *how* he preached. (1) *He spake many things unto them.* Many more it is likely than are here recorded, but all excellent and necessary things, things that belong to our peace, things pertaining to the kingdom of heaven. (2) What he spake was in parables. A parable sometimes signifies any wise, weighty saying that is instructive; but here in the gospels it generally signifies a continued similitude or comparison, by which spiritual or heavenly things were described in language borrowed from the things of this life. Now,

I. We have here the general reason why Christ taught in parables. The disciples were a little surprised at it, for hitherto, in his preaching, he had not much used them, and therefore they ask, *Why speakest thou to them in parables?*

1. This reason is laid down (*v.* 11): *Because it is given unto you to know the mysteries of the kingdom of heaven, but to them it is not given.* That is, (1) The disciples had knowledge, but the people had not.

You know already something of these mysteries, and need not in this familiar way to be instructed; but the people are ignorant, are yet but babes, and must be taught as such by plain similitudes, being yet incapable of receiving instruction in any other way: for though they have eyes, they know not how to use them; so some. Or, (2) The disciples were well inclined to the knowledge of gospel mysteries, and would search into the parables, and by them would be led into a more intimate acquaintance with those mysteries; but the carnal hearers that rested in bare hearing, and would not be at the pains to look further, nor to ask the meaning of the parables, would be never the wiser, and so would justly suffer for their remissness. A parable is a shell that keeps good fruit *for* the diligent, but keeps it *from* the slothful.

2. This reason is further illustrated by the rule God observes in dispensing his gifts; he bestows them on those who improve them, but takes them away from those who bury them.

(1) Here is a promise to him that has true grace, pursuant to the election of grace, and uses what he has; he shall have more abundance: God's favours are earnests of further favours; where he lays the foundation, he will build upon it.

(2) Here is a threatening to him that has not, that has no desire of grace, that makes no right use of the gifts and graces he has: has no root, no solid principle; that has, but uses not what he has; from him shall be *taken away* that which he has or seems to have.

3. This reason is particularly explained, with reference to the two sorts of people Christ had to do with.

(1) Some were willingly ignorant; and such were amused by the parables (*v.* 13); *because they seeing, see not*. They had shut their eyes against the clear light of Christ's plainer preaching, and therefore were noiw left in the dark.

Now n this the scripture would be fulfilled, *vv.* 14, 15. It is quoted from Isa. vi. 9, 10. The evangelical prophet that spoke most plainly of gospel grace, foretold the contempt of it, and the consequences of that contempt. Here is,

First. A description of sinners' wilful blindness and hardness, which is their sin. *This people's heart is waxed gross*; it is *fattened*, so the word is; which denotes both sensuality and senselessness (Ps. cxix. 70).

Secondly. A description of that judicial blindness, which is the just punishment of this. To hear God's word, and see his providences, and yet not to understand and perceive his will, either in the one or in the other, is the greatest sin and the greatest judgment that can be.

Thirdly, The woeful effect and consequence of this; *Lest at any time they should see.* They will not see because they will not turn; and God says that they shall not see, because they shall not turn: *Lest they should be converted, and I should heal them.*

Note, 1. That seeing, hearing, and understanding, are necessary to conversion; for God, in working grace, deals with men as men, as rational agents; he draws with the cords of a man, changes the heart by opening the eyes, and turns *from the power of Satan unto God*, by turning first *from darkness to light*, Acts xxvi. 18. 2. All those who are truly converted to God, shall certainly be healed by him. "If they be converted I shall heal them, I shall save them": so that if sinners perish, it is not to be imputed to God, but to themselves; they foolishly expected to be healed, without being converted. 3. It is just with God to deny his grace to those who have long and often refused the proposals of it, and resisted the power of it.

(2) Others were effectually called to be the disciples of Christ, and were truly desirous to be taught of him; and they were instructed, and made to improve greatly in knowledge, by these parables, especially when they were expounded; and by them the things of God were made more plain and easy, more intelligible and familiar, and more apt to be remembered (*vv.* 16, 17). *Your eyes see, your ears hear.* Now this Christ speaks of,

[1] As a blessing; "*Blessed are your eyes for they see, and your ears for they hear*; it is your happiness, and it is a happiness for which you are indebted to the peculiar favour and blessing of God." It is a promised blessing, that in the days of the Messiah *the eyes of them that see shall not be dim*, Isa. xxxii. 3. The eyes of the meanest believer that knows experimentally the grace of Christ, are more blessed than those of the greatest scholars, the greatest masters in experimental philosophy, that are strangers to God; who, like the other gods they serve, *have eyes, and see not*.

[2] As a transcendent blessing, desired by, but not granted to, many prophets and righteous men, *v.* 17. Though they were the favourites of Heaven, with whom God's secret was, yet they have not seen the things which they desired to see, because God had determined not to bring them to light yet; and his favours shall not anticipate his counsels. There was then, as there is still, a *glory to be revealed*; something in reserve, *that they without us should not be made perfect*, Heb. xi. 40. *Thirdly*, For the exciting of our thankfulness, and the quickening of our diligence. It is good for us to see that our improvements be proportionable to our advantages.

II. We have, in these verses, one of the parables which our Saviour put forth; it is that of the *sower and the seed*; both the parable itself, and the explanation of it.

The parable of the sower is plain enough, *vv.* 3–9. The exposition of it we have from Christ himself, who knew best what was his own meaning.

Let us therefore compare the parable and the exposition.

(1) The seed sown is the word of God, here called *the word of the kingdom* (*v.* 19). The gospel comes *from* that kingdom, and conducts *to* that kingdom; the word of the gospel is the word of the kingdom; it is the word of the King, and where that is, *there is power*; it is a law, by which we must be ruled and governed. This word is the seed sown, which seems a dead, dry thing, but all the product is virtually in it. It is *incorruptible seed* (1 Pet. i. 23); it is the gospel that

brings forth fruit in souls, Col. i. 5, 6.

(2) The sower that scatters the seed is our Lord Jesus Christ, either by himself, or by his ministers; see *v.* 37. The people are God's husbandry, his tillage, so the word is; and ministers are *labourers together with God*, 1 Cor. iii. 9.

(3) The ground in which this seed is sown is the hearts of the children of men, which are differently qualified and disposed, and accordingly the success of the word is different.

Now observe the characters of these four sorts of ground.

[1] The highway ground, *vv.* 4–19. They had pathways through their cornfields (*ch.* xii. 1), and the seed that fell on them never entered, and so the birds picked it up.

Observe, *First*, What kind of hearers are compared to *the highway ground*; such as *hear the word and understand it not*; and it is their own fault that they do not. They take no heed to it, take no hold of it; they do not come with any design to get good, as the highway was never intended to be sown.

Secondly, How they come to be unprofitable hearers. The *wicked one*, that is, the devil, *cometh and catcheth away that which was sown.* —Such mindless, careless, trifling hearers are an easy prey to Satan; who, as he is the great murderer of souls, so he is the great thief of sermons, and will be sure to rob us of the word, if we take not care to keep it.

[2] The *stony ground. Some fell upon stony places* (*vv.* 5, 6), which

represents the case of hearers that go further than the former, who receive some good impressions of the word, but they are not lasting, *vv*. 20, 21.

First, How far they went. 1. They *hear the word*; they turn neither their backs upon it, nor a deaf ear to it. Note, Hearing the word, though ever so frequently, ever so gravely, if we rest in that, will never bring us to heaven. 2. They are *quick in hearing*, swift to hear, he is ready to receive it, *forthwith it sprung up* (*v*. 5), it sooner appeared above ground than that which was sown in the good soil. Note, Hypocrites often get the start of true Christians in the shows of profession, and are often too hot to hold. He *receiveth it straightway*, without trying it; swallows it without chewing, and then there can never be a good digestion. Those are most likely to *hold fast that which is good*, that *prove all things*, 1 Thess. v. 21. 3. They receive it with joy. Note, There are many that are very glad to hear a good sermon, that yet do not profit by it. 4. They *endure for awhile*, like a violent motion, which continues as long as the impression of the force remains, but ceases when that has spent itself.

Secondly, How they fell away, so that no fruit was brought to perfection; no more than the corn, that having no depth of earth from which to draw moisture, is scorched and withered by the heat of the sun. And the reason is,

1. They have *no root in themselves*, no settled, fixed principles in their judgments, no firm resolution in their wills, nor any rooted habits

in their affections: nothing firm that will be either the sap or the strength of their profession.

2. Times of trial come, and then they come to nothing. *When tribulation and persecution arise because of the word, he is offended*; it is a stumbling-block in his way which he cannot get over, and so he flies off, and this is all his profession comes to.

[3] The thorny ground, *Some fell among thorns; and the thorns sprung up*, which intimates that they did not appear, or but little, when the corn was sown, but afterwards they proved choking to it, *v*. 7. This went further than the former, for it had root; and it represents the condition of those who do not quite cast off their profession, and yet come short of any saving benefit by it; the good they gain by the word, being insensibly overcome and overborne by the things of this world. Prosperity destroys the word in the heart, as much as persecution does; and more dangerously, because more silently: the stones spoiled the root, the thorns spoil the fruit.

Now what are these choking thorns?

First, The cares of this world. Care for another world would quicken the springing of this seed, but care for this world chokes it. Note, Worldly cares are great hindrances to our profiting by the word of God, and our proficiency in religion. They eat up that vigour of soul which should be spent in divine things; divert us from duty, distract us in duty, and do us most mischief of all afterwards; quenching the sparks of good affections, and bursting the cords of good resolutions; those who *are careful and cumbered about many things,* commonly neglect *the one thing needful.*

Secondly, The deceitfulness of riches. Observe, It is not so much riches, as *the deceitfulness of riches,* that does the mischief: now they cannot be said to be deceitful to us unless we put our confidence in them, and raise our expectations from them, and then it is that they choke the good seed.

[4] The good ground (*v.* 18); *Others fell into good ground,* and it is pity but that good seed should always meet with good soil, and then there is no loss; such are *good hearers of the word, v.* 23.

Now that which distinguished this good ground from the rest, was in one word, fruitfulness. By *this* true Christians are distinguished from hypocrites, that they *bring forth the fruits of righteousness; so shall ye be my disciples,* John xv. 8. He does not say that this good ground has no stones in it, or no thorns; but there were none that prevailed to hinder its fruitfulness. Saints, in this world, are not perfectly free from the remains of sin; but happily freed from the reign of it.

The hearers represented by the good ground are,

First, Intelligent hearers; they *hear the word and understand it;* they understand not only the sense and meaning of the word, but their own concern in it; they understand it as a man of business understands his business. God in his word deals with men as men, in a rational way, and gains possession of the will and

affections by opening the understanding.

Secondly, Fruitful hearers, which is an evidence of their good understanding: which *also beareth fruit.* Fruit is to every seed its own body, a substantial product in the heart and life, agreeable to the seed of the word received.

Thirdly, Not all alike fruitful; *some a hundred-fold, some sixty, some thirty.* Note, Among fruitful Christians, some are more fruitful than others: where there is true grace, yet there are degrees of it; some are of greater attainments in knowledge and holiness than others; all Christ's scholars are not in the same form. But if the ground be good, and the fruit right, the heart honest, and the life of a piece with it, those who bring forth but thirty-fold shall be graciously accepted of God, and it will be fruit abounding to their account, for *we are under grace, and not under the law.*

Lastly, He closes the parable with a solemn call to attention (*v.* 9), *Who hath ears to hear, let him hear.*

THE TARES (*vv.* 24–43)

In these verses, we have, I. Another reason given why Christ preached by parables, *vv.* 34, 35. *All these things he spoke in parables,* because the time was not yet come for the more clear and plain discoveries of the mysteries of the kingdom. Christ, to keep the people attending and expecting, preached in *parables, and without a parable spake he not unto them;* namely, at this time and in this sermon. Here is, 1. The matter of Christ's preaching; he preached *things which had been kept secret from the foundation of the world*. The mystery of the gospel had been *hid in God*, in his councils and decrees, *from the beginning of the world*. Eph. iii. 9. Compare Rom. xvi. 25; 1 Cor. ii. 7; Col. i. 26.

2. The manner of Christ's preaching; he preached by parables; wise sayings, but figurative, and which help to engage attention and a diligent search.

II. The parable of the *tares*, and the exposition of it; they must be taken together, for the exposition explains the parable and the parable illustrates the exposition.

Observe, 1. The disciples' request to their Master to have this parable expounded to them (*v*. 36); *Jesus sent the multitude away*; and it is to be feared many of them went away no wiser than they came; they had heard a sound of words, and that was all.

2. The exposition Christ gave of the parable, in answer to their request; so ready is Christ to answer such desires of his disciples. Now the drift of the parable is, to represent to us the present and future state of the kingdom of heaven, the gospel church: Christ's care of it, the devil's enmity against it, the mixture that there is in it of good and bad in this world, and the separation between them in the other world. Note, The visible church is the kingdom of heaven; though there be many hypocrites in it, Christ rules in it as a King; and there is a remnant in it, that are the subjects and heirs of heaven.

Let us go over the particulars of the exposition of the parable.

(1) *He that sows the good seed is the Son of man*. Jesus Christ is the Lord of the field, *the Lord of the harvest*, the Sower of good seed.

(2) *The field is the world*; the world of mankind, a large field, capable of bringing forth good fruit; the more is it to be lamented that it brings forth so much bad fruit: the world here is the visible church, scattered all the world over, not confined to one nation.

(3) *The good seed are the children of the kingdom*, true saints. They are, [1] The *children of the kingdom*; not in profession only, as the Jews were (*ch*. viii. 12), but in sincerity; Jews inwardly, Israelites indeed, incorporated in faith and obedience to Jesus Christ the great King of the church. [2] They are the good seed, precious as seed, Ps. cxxvi. 6. The seed is that from which fruit is expected; what fruit of honour and service God has from this world he has from the saints, whom he has *sown unto himself in the earth*, Hos. ii. 23.

(4) *The tares are the children of the wicked one*. Here is the character of sinners, hypocrites, and all profane and wicked people. They are tares in the field of this world; they do no good, they do hurt; unprofitable in themselves, and hurtful to *the good seed*, both by temptation and persecution: they are weeds in the garden, have the same rain, and sunshine, and soil, with the good plants, but are good for nothing: the *tares are among the wheat*. Note, God has so ordered it, that good and bad should be mixed together in this world, that the good may be exercised, the bad left inexcusable,

and a difference made between earth and heaven.

(5) *The enemy that sowed the tares is the devil*; a sworn enemy to Christ and all that is good, to the glory of the good God, and the comfort and happiness of all good men. He is an enemy to the field of the world, which he endeavours to make his own, by sowing his tares in it.

Now concerning the sowing of the tares, observe in the parable,

[1] That they were sown *while men slept*. Magistrates slept, who by their power, ministers slept, who by their preaching, should have prevented this mischief. Note, Satan watches all opportunities, and lays hold of all advantages, to propagate vice and profaneness. The prejudice he does to particular persons is when reason and conscience sleep, when they are off their guard; we have therefore need to *be sober, and vigilant*.

[2] The enemy, when he had sown the tares, *went his way* (*v.* 25), that it might not be known who did it. Note, When Satan is doing the greatest mischief, he studies most to conceal himself.

[3] The tares appeared not till *the blade sprung up, and brought forth fruit*, *v.* 26. There is a great deal of secret wickedness in the hearts of men, which is long hid under the cloak of a plausible profession, but breaks out at last.

[4] The servants, when they were aware of it, complained to their master (*v.* 27); *Sir, didst thou not sow good seed in thy field?* No doubt he did; whatever is amiss in the church, we are sure it is not of Christ: considering the seed which Christ sows, we may well ask, with wonder, *Whence* should *these tares come?*

[5] The Master was soon aware whence it was (*v.* 28); *An enemy has done this*. He does not lay the blame upon the servants; they could not help it, but had done what was in their power to prevent it. Note, The ministers of Christ, that are faithful and diligent, shall not be judged of Christ, and therefore should not be reproached by men, for the mixture of bad with good, hypocrites with the sincere, in the field of the church.

[6] The servants were very forward to have these tares rooted up. "*Wilt thou that we go* and do it presently?" Note, The over-hasty and inconsiderate zeal of Christ's servants, before they have consulted with their Master, is sometimes ready, with the hazard of the church, to root out all that they presume to be tares.

[7] The Master very wisely prevented this (*v.* 29); *Nay, lest while ye gather up the tares, ye root up also the wheat with them.* Note, It is not possible for any man infallibly to distinguish between tares and wheat, but he may be mistaken; and therefore such is the wisdom and grace of Christ, that he will rather permit the tares, than any way endanger the wheat.

(6) *The harvest is the end of the world*, *v.* 39. At the end of the world, there will be a great harvest-day, a day of judgment; at harvest all is ripe and ready to be cut down: both good and bad are ripe at the great-day, Rev. vi. 11. It is *the harvest of the earth*, Rev. xiv. 15.

117

At harvest the reapers cut down all before them; not a field, not a corner, is left behind; so at the great day all must be judged (Rev. xx. 12, 13); God has *set a harvest* (Hos. vi. 11), and it shall not fail, (Gen. viii. 22). At harvest every man reaps as he sowed; every man's ground, and seed, and skill, and industry, will be manifested: see Gal. vi. 7, 8.

(7) *The reapers are the angels:* they shall be employed, in the great day, in executing Christ's righteous sentences, both of approbation and condemnation, as ministers of his justice, *ch.* xxv. 31.

(8) Hell-torments are the *fire*, into which the *tares* shall then be cast, and in which they shall be burned.

[1] The tares will then be gathered out: *The reapers* (whose primary work it is to gather in the corn) shall be charged first to *gather out the tares*. Note, Though good and bad are together in this world undistinguished, yet at the great day they shall be parted; no tares shall then be among the wheat; no sinners among the saints.

[2] They will then be *bound in bundles*, *v.* 30. Sinners of the same sort will be bundled together in the great day: a bundle of atheists, a bundle of epicures, a bundle of persecutors, and a great bundle of hypocrites.

[3] They will *be cast into a furnace of fire*; such will be the end of wicked, mischievous people, that are in the church as *tares in the field*; they are fit for nothing but fire; to it they shall go, it is the fittest place for them.

(9) Heaven is the *barn* into

which all God's wheat shall be gathered in that harvest-day.

In the explanation of the parable, this is gloriously represented (*v.* 43); *Then shall the righteous shine forth as the sun in the kingdom of their Father*. Here they are obscure and hidden (Col. iii. 3), their beauty is eclipsed by their poverty, and the meanness of their outward condition; their own weaknesses and infirmities, and the reproach and disgrace cast upon them, cloud them; but then they shall shine forth as the sun from behind a dark cloud; at death they shall shine forth to themselves; at the great day they will shine forth publicly before all the world.

Our Saviour concludes, as before, with a demand of attention; *Who hath ears to hear, let him hear*. These are things which it is our happiness to hear of, and our duty to hearken to.

III. Here is the parable of the *grain of mustard-seed*, *vv.* 31, 32. The scope of this parable is to show, that the beginnings of the gospel *would be small, but that its latter end would greatly increase*.

Now concerning the work of the gospel, observe.

1. That it is commonly very weak and small at first, *like a grain of mustard-seed, which is one of the least of all seeds*.

2. That yet it is growing and coming on. *A grain of mustard-seed* is small, but, however, it is seed, and has in it a disposition to grow. Grace will be getting ground, shining more and more, Prov. iv. 18.

3. That it will at last come to a great degree of strength and usefulness; *when it is grown to* some

118

maturity, *it becomes a tree*, much larger in those countries than in ours. The church, like the *vine brought out of Egypt*, has taken root, and *filled the earth*, (Ps. lxxx. 9–11).

IV. Here is the parable of the *leaven, v.* 33. The scope of this is much the same with that of the foregoing parable, to show that the gospel should prevail and be successful by degrees, but silently and insensibly; the preaching of the gospel is like leaven, and works like leaven in the hearts of those who receive it.

The leaven hid in the dough, works there, it ferments; *the word is quick and powerful*, Heb. iv. 12. The leaven works speedily, so does the word, and yet gradually. Hide but the leaven in the dough, and all the world cannot hinder it from communicating its taste and relish to it, and yet none sees how it is done, but by degrees *the whole is leavened*.

(1) Thus it was in the world. The apostles, by their preaching, hid a handful of leaven in the great mass of mankind, and it had a strange effect; it put the world into a ferment, and in a sense turned it *upside down* (Acts xvii. 6).

(2) Thus it is in the heart. When the gospel comes into the soul, [1] It works a change, not in the substance; the dough is the same, but in the quality; it makes us to savour otherwise than we have done, and other things to savour with us otherwise than they used to do, Rom. viii. 5. [2] It works a universal change; it diffuses itself into all the powers and faculties of the soul, and alters the property

even of the members of the body, Rom. vi. 13. [3] This change is such as makes the soul to partake of the nature of the word, as the dough does of the leaven.

FOUR PARABLES (*vv.* 44–52)

We have four short parables in these verses.

I. That of the *treasure hid in the field*. Hitherto he had compared *the kingdom of heaven* to small things, because its beginning was small; but, lest any should thence take occasion to think meanly of it, in this parable and the next he represents it as of great value in itself, and of great advantage to those who embrace it, and are willing to come up to its terms; it is here likened *to a treasure hid in the field*, which, if we will, we may make our own.

II. That of *the pearl of price* (*vv.* 45, 46), which is to the same purport with the former, of the treasure.

Jesus Christ is a *Pearl of great price*, a Jewel of inestimable value, which will make those who have it rich, truly rich, rich toward God; in having him, we have enough to make us happy here and for ever.

A true Christian is a spiritual *merchant*, that seeks and finds this pearl of price; that does not take up with any thing short of an interest in Christ, and, as one that is resolved to be spiritually rich, trades high: *He went and bought that pearl*; did not only bid for it, but purchased it. What will it avail us to know Christ, if we do not know him as ours, *made to us wisdom*? (1 Cor. i. 30.)

Those who would have a saving

interest in Christ, must be willing to part with all for him, leave all to follow him. A man may buy gold too dear, but not this pearl of price.

III. That of the *net cast into the sea*, *vv.* 47–49.

1. Here is the parable itself. Where note, (1) The world is a vast sea. (2) The preaching of the gospel is the casting of a net into this sea, to catch something out of it, for his glory who has the sovereignty of the sea. Ministers are *fishers of men*, employed in casting and drawing this net. (3) This net gathers of every kind, as large dragnets do. In the visible church there is a deal of trash and rubbish, dirt and weeds and vermin, as well as fish. (4) There is a time coming when this net will be full, and drawn to the shore; a set time when the gospel shall have fulfilled that for which it was sent, and we are sure it shall not return void, Isa. lv. 10, 11. (5) When the net is full and drawn to the shore, there shall be a separation between the good and bad that were gathered in it. Hypocrites and true Christians shall then be parted; the good shall be gathered into vessels, as valuable, and therefore to be carefully kept, but the bad shall be cast away, as vile and unprofitable; and miserable is the condition of those who are cast away in that day.

2. Here is the explanation of the latter part of the parable, the former is obvious and plain enough: we see gathered in the visible church, *some of every kind*: but the latter part refers to that which is yet to come, and is therefore more particularly explained, *vv.* 49, 50.

So shall it be at the end of the world; then, and not till then, will the dividing, discovering day be. We must not look for the net full of all good fish; the vessels will be so, but in the net they are mixed. See here, (1) The distinguishing of the wicked from the righteous. The angels of heaven shall come forth to do that which the angels of the churches could never do; they shall *sever the wicked from among the just.* (2) The doom of the wicked when they are thus severed. They shall be *cast into the furnace.*

IV. Here is the parable of the *good householder*, which is intended to rivet all the rest.

1. The occasion of it was the good proficiency which the disciples had made in learning, and their profiting by this sermon in particular.

2. The scope of the parable itself was to give his approbation and commendation of their proficiency.

(1) He commends them as *scribes instructed unto the kingdom of heaven.* They were now learning that they might teach, and the teachers among the Jews were the scribes.

(2) He compares them to a good householder, who *brings forth out of his treasure things new and old*; fruits of last year's growth and this year's gathering, abundance and variety, for the entertainment of his friends, Cant. vii. 13. Christ himself received that he might give; so must we, and we shall have more. In bringing forth, things new and old do best together; old truths, but new methods and expressions, especially new affections.

PROPHET AT HOME
(*vv.* 53–58)

We have here Christ in his own country. He went about doing good, yet left not any place till he had finished his testimony there at that time. His own countrymen had rejected him once, yet he came to them again. His treatment this time was much the same as before, scornful and spiteful. Observe,

I. How they expressed their contempt of him. When he *taught them in their synagogue, they were astonished*; not that they were taken with his preaching, or admired his doctrine in itself, but only that it should be his; looking upon him as unlikely to be such a teacher. Two things they upbraided him with.

1. His want of academical education. Thus they turned that against him which was really for him; for if they had not been wilfully blind, they must have concluded him to be divinely assisted and commissioned, who without the help of education gave such proofs of extraordinary wisdom and power.

2. The meanness and poverty of his relations, *vv.* 55, 56.

(1) They upbraid him with his father. *Is not this the carpenter's son?* Yes, it is true he was reputed so: and what harm in that? No disparagement to him to be the son of an honest tradesman.

(2) They upbraid him with his mother; and what quarrel have they with her? Why, truly, *his mother is called Mary*, and that was a very common name, and they all knew her, and knew her to be an ordinary person; and this is turned to his reproach, as if men had nothing to be valued by but foreign extraction, noble birth, or splendid titles; poor things to measure worth by.

(3) They upbraid him with his brethren, whose names they knew, and had them ready enough to serve this turn; James, and Joses, and Simon, and Judas, good men but poor men, and therefore despised; and Christ for their sakes.

(4) His sisters too are all with us; they should therefore have loved him and respected him the more, because he was one of themselves, but therefore they despised him.

II. See how he resented this contempt, *vv.* 57, 58.

1. It did not trouble his heart. It appears he was not much concerned at it; he *despised the shame*, Heb. xii. 2.

2. It did for the present (to speak with reverence), in effect, tie his hands: *He did not many mighty works there, because of their unbelief.* Note, Unbelief is the great obstruction to Christ's favours.

CHAPTER FOURTEEN

THE DEATH OF JOHN (*vv.* 1–12)

We have here the story of John's martyrdom. Observe,

I. The occasion of relating this story here, *vv.* 1, 2. Here is,

1. The account brought to Herod of the miracles which Christ wrought. Herod the tetrarch or chief governor of Galilee *heard of the fame of Jesus*. Christ's disciples were now sent abroad to preach, and to work miracles in his name,

and this spread the fame of him more than ever; which was an indication of the spreading of the gospel by their means after his ascension.

2. The construction he puts upon this (*v.* 2); *He said to his servants* that told him of the fame of Jesus, as sure as we are here, *this is John the Baptist; he is risen from the dead.* Observe here concerning Herod.

(1) How he was disappointed in what he intended by beheading John. He thought if he could get that troublesome fellow out of the way, he might go on in his sins, undisturbed and uncontrolled; yet no sooner is that effected, than he hears of Jesus and his disciples preaching the same pure doctrine that John preached; and, which is more, even the disciples confirming it by miracles in their Master's name.

(2) How he was filled with causeless fears, merely from the guilt of his own conscience.

(3) How, notwithstanding this, he was hardened in his wickedness; for though he was convinced that John was a prophet, and one owned of God, yet he does not express the least remorse or sorrow for his sin in putting him to death. The devils believe and tremble, but they never believe and repent.

II. The story itself of the imprisonment and martyrdom of John. As the first Old-Testament saint, so the first New-Testament minister, died a martyr. And if Christ's forerunner was thus treated, let not his followers expect to be caressed by the world. Observe here,

1. John's faithfulness in reproving Herod, *vv.* 3, 4.

The particular sin he reproved him for was, marrying his brother Philip's wife, not his widow (that had not been so criminal), but his wife. Philip was now living, and Herod inveigled his wife from him, and kept her for his own. Here was a complication of wickedness, adultery, incest, besides the wrong done to Philip, who had had a child by this woman. See Ps. l. 20. For this sin John reproved him; not by tacit and oblique allusions, but in plain terms. *It is not lawful for thee to have her.*

2. The imprisonment of John for his faithfulness, *v.* 3. Faithful reproofs, if they do not profit, usually provoke; if they do not do good, they are resented as affronts, and they that will not bow to the reproof, will fly in the face of the reprover and hate him.

3. The restraint that Herod lay under from further venting of his rage against John, *v.* 5.

(1) He would have put him to death. Perhaps that was not intended at first when he imprisoned him, but his revenge by degrees boiled up to that height.

(2) That which hindered him was his *fear of the multitude, because they counted John as a prophet.* It was not because he feared God (if the fear of God had been before his eyes he would not have imprisoned him), nor because he feared John, though formerly he had had a reverence for him (his lusts had overcome that), but because he feared the people; he was afraid for himself, his own safety, and the safety of

his government, his abuse of which he knew had already rendered him odious to the people, whose resentments being so far heated already would be apt, upon such a provocation as the putting of a prophet to death, to break out into a flame.

4. The contrivance of bringing John to his death.

Herodias laid the plot; her implacable revenge thirsted after John's blood, and would be satisfied with nothing less. Herodias contrived how to bring about the murder of John so artificially as to save Herod's credit, and so to pacify the people. Here we have,

(1) The humouring of Herod by the damsel's dancing upon a birth-day.

(2) The rash and foolish promise which Herod made to this wanton girl, to give her whatsoever she would ask: and this promise confirmed with an oath, *v.* 7.

(3) The bloody demand the young lady made of John the Baptist's head, *v.* 8. She was before instructed of her mother.

(4) Herod's grant of this demand (*v.* 9); *The king was sorry*, at least took on him to be so, but, *for the oath's sake, he commanded it to be given her.*

Thus was that voice silenced, that burning and shining light extinguished; thus did that prophet, that Elias, of the New Testament, fall a sacrifice to the resentments of an imperious, whorish woman. Thus did he, who was great in the sight of the Lord, *die as a fool dieth, his hands were bound, and his feet put into fetters; and as a man falleth before wicked men*, so he

fell, a true martyr to all intents and purposes: dying, though not for the profession of his faith, yet for the performance of his duty. However, though his work was soon done, *it was done and his testimony finished*, for till then none of God's witnesses are slain. And God brought this good out of it, that hereby his disciples, who while he lived, though in prison, kept close to him, now after his death heartily closed with Jesus Christ.

The disciples *buried the body*, and brought the news in tears to our Lord Jesus. The disciples of John had fasted often while their master was in prison, their *bridegroom was taken away from them*, and they prayed earnestly for his deliverance, as the church did for Peter's, Acts xii. 5. They had free access to him in prison, which was a comfort to them, but they wished to see him at liberty, that he might preach to others; but now on a sudden all their hopes are dashed. Disciples weep and lament, when the world rejoices.

FEEDING FIVE THOUSAND
(*vv.* 13–21)

This passage of story, concerning Christ's feeding *five thousand men with five loaves and two fishes*, is recorded by all the four Evangelists, which very few, if any, of Christ's miracles are: this intimates that there is something in it worthy of special remark. Observe,

I. The great resort of people to Christ, when he was retired *into a desert place, v.* 13. He withdrew into privacy when he heard, not of John's death, but of the thoughts

Herod had concerning him, that he was *John the Baptist risen from the dead*, and therefore so feared by Herod as to be hated; he departed further off, to get out of Herod's jurisdiction.

II. The tender compassion of our Lord Jesus towards those who thus followed him, *v.* 14. He did not only pity them, but he helped them; many of them were *sick, and he, in compassion to them, healed them*; for he came into the world to be the great Healer. After awhile, they were all hungry, *and he, in compassion to them, fed them*.

III. The motion which the disciples made for the dismissing of the congregation, and Christ's setting aside the motion. 1. The *evening* drawing on, the disciples moved it to Christ to send the multitude away; they thought there was a good day's work done, and it was time to disperse. See how loth Christ is to part with those who are resolved to cleave to him! *They need not depart*; nor will Christ put his willing followers upon a needless expense, but will make their attendance cheap to them.

But if they be hungry, they have need to depart, for that is a necessity which has no law, therefore *give you them to eat*.

IV. The slender provision that was made for this great multitude; and here we must compare the number of invited guests with the bill of fare.

1. The number of the guests was *five thousand of men, besides women and children*; and it is probable the women and children

might be as many a*, the men, if not more.

2. The bill of fare was very disproportionable to the number of the guests, but *five loaves and two fishes*. This provision the disciples carried about with them for the use of the family, now they *were retired into the desert*. Christ could have fed them by miracle, but to set us an example of providing for those of our own households, he will have their own camp victualled in an ordinary way.

V. The liberal distribution of this provision among the multitude (*vv.* 18, 19); *Bring them hither to me*. Note, The way to have our creature-comforts, comforts indeed to us, is to bring them to Christ; for every thing is sanctified by his word, and by prayer to him: that is likely to prosper and do well with us, which we put into the hands of our Lord Jesus, that he may dispose of it as he pleases, and that we may take it back from his hand, and then it will be doubly sweet to us. What we give in charity, we should bring to Christ first, that he may graciously accept it from us, and graciously bless it to those to whom it is given; this is *doing it as the Lord*.

VI. The plentiful satisfaction of all the guests with this provision. Though the disproportion was so great, yet there was enough and to spare.

1. There was enough: *They did all eat, and were filled*. Note, Those whom Christ feeds, he fills; so runs the promise (Ps. xxxvii, 19), *They shall be satisfied*.

2. There was to spare; *They took up of the fragments that remained,*

twelve baskets full, one basket for each apostle: thus what they gave they had again, and a great deal more with it. This was to manifest and magnify the miracle, and to show that the provision Christ makes for those who are his is not bare and scanty, but rich and plenteous; *bread enough, and to spare* (Luke xv. 17), an overflowing fulness.

It is the same divine power, though exerted in an ordinary way, which multiplies *the seed sown in the ground* every year, and makes *the earth yield her increase*; so that what was brought out by handfuls, is brought home in sheaves. *This is the Lord's doing*; it is *by Christ* that all natural things consist, and *by the word of his power* that they are upheld.

WALKING ON THE SEA
(vv. 22–33)

We have here the story of another miracle which Christ wrought for the relief of his friends and followers, his *walking upon the water to his disciples*. In the foregoing miracle he acted as the Lord of nature, improving its powers for the supply of those who were in want; in this, he acted as the Lord of nature, correcting and controlling its powers for the succour of those who were in danger and distress. Observe,

I. Christ's dismissing of his disciples and *the multitude*, after he had fed them miraculously. He *constrained his disciples to get into a ship, and to go before him unto the other side*, v. 22. St. John gives a particular reason for the hasty breaking up of this assembly,

because the people were so affected with the miracle of the loaves, that they were about *to take him by force, and make him a King* (John vi. 15); to avoid which, he immediately scattered the people, sent away the disciples, lest they should join with them, and he himself withdrew, John vi. 15.

II. Christ's retirement hereupon (v. 23); *He went up into a mountain apart to pray*. Observe here,

1. That he was alone; *he went apart into a solitary place, and was there all alone.* Though he had so much work to do with others, yet he chose sometimes to be alone, to set us an example.

2. That he was alone at prayer; that was his business in this solitude, to pray. Though Christ, as God, was Lord of all, and was prayed to, yet Christ, as Man, had *the form of a servant*, of a beggar, and prayed.

3. That he was long alone. *The night* came on, and it was a stormy, tempestuous night, yet he continued *instant in prayer*.

III. The condition that the poor disciples were in at this time: *Their ship was now in the midst of the sea, tossed with waves*, v. 24. We may observe here,

1. That they were got into the midst of the sea when the storm rose. We may have fair weather at the beginning of our voyage, and yet meet with storms before we arrive at the port we are bound for. Therefore *let not him that girdeth on the harness boast as he that puts it off*, but after a long calm expect some storm or other.

2. The disciples were now where Christ sent them, and yet met with

this storm. Note, It is no new thing for Christ's disciples to meet with storms in the way of their duty, and to be sent to sea then when their Master foresees a storm; but let them not take it unkindly; what he does they *know not now, but they shall know hereafter*, that Christ designs hereby to manifest himself with the more wonderful grace to them and for them.

3. It was a great discouragement to them now that they had not Christ with them, as they had formerly when they were in a storm. Thus Christ used his disciples first to less difficulties, and then to greater, and so trains them up by degrees to live *by faith, and not by sense*.

4. Though *the wind was contrary*, and they were tossed with waves, yet being ordered by their Master *to the other side*, they did not tack about and come back again, but made the best of their way forward.

IV. Christ's approach to them in this condition (*v.* 25); and in this we have an instance,

1. Of his goodness, that he went unto them, as one that took cognizance of their case, and was under a concern about them, as a father about his children.

2. Of his power, that he *went unto them, walking on the sea*. This is a great instance of Christ's sovereign dominion over all the creatures; they are all under his feet, and at his command; they forget their natures, and change the qualities that we call essential. We need not enquire how this was done, whether by condensing the surface of the water, or by sus-

pending the gravitation of his body, which was transfigured as he pleased; it is sufficient that it proves his divine power, for it is God's prerogative to *tread upon the waves of the sea* (Job ix. 8), as it is *to ride upon the wings of the wind*.

V. Here is an account of what passed between Christ and his distressed friends upon his approach.

1. Between him and all the disciples. We are here told,

(1) How their fears were raised (*v.* 26); *When they saw him walking on the sea, they were troubled, saying, It is a spirit*; *It is an apparition*; so it might much better be rendered. It seems, the existence and appearance of spirits were generally believed in by all except the Sadducees, whose doctrine Christ had warned his disciples against; yet, doubtless, many supposed apparitions have been merely the creatures of men's own fear and fancy. These disciples said, *It is a spirit*; when they should have said, *It is the Lord*; it can be no other.

(2) How these fears were silenced, *v.* 27. He straightway relieved them, by showing them their mistake; when they were wrestling *with the waves*, he delayed his succour for some time; but he hastened his succour against their fright, as much the more dangerous; he straightway laid that storm with his word, *Be of good cheer*; *it is I*; *be not afraid*.

[1] He rectified their mistake, by making himself known to them; *It is I*.

[2] He encouraged them against their fright; *It is I*, and therefore,

First, Be of good cheer. If Christ's disciples be not cheerful in a storm, it is their own fault, he would have them so. *Secondly, Be not afraid*; 1. "Be not afraid of me, now that you know it is I; surely you will not fear, for you know I mean you no hurt."

2. Between him and Peter, *vv.* 28-31, where observe,

(1) Peter's courage, and Christ's countenancing that.

[1] It was very bold in Peter, that he would venture to come to Christ *upon the water* (*v.* 28); *Lord, if it be thou, bid me come unto thee.*

[2] It was very kind and condescending in Christ, that he was pleased to own him in it, *v.* 29. He might have condemned the proposal as foolish and rash; nay, and as proud and assuming; "Shall Peter pretend to do as his Master does?" But Christ knew that it came from a sincere and zealous affection to him, and graciously accepted of it.

First, He bid him *come.* When the Pharisees asked a sign, they had not only a repulse, but a reproof, for it, because they did it with a design to tempt Christ; when Peter asked a sign, he had it, because he did it with a resolution to trust Christ.

Secondly, He bore him out when he did come; *Peter walked upon the water.*

He walked upon the water, not for diversion or ostentation, but to go to Jesus; and in that he was thus wonderfully borne up.

(2) Here is Peter's cowardice, and Christ's reproving him and succouring him. Christ bid him come, not only that he might walk upon the water, and so know Christ's power, but that he might sink, and so know his own weakness; for as he would encourage his faith, so he would check his confidence, and make him ashamed of it. Observe then,

[1] Peter's great fear (*v.* 30); He *was afraid.* The strongest faith and the greatest courage have a mixture of fear.

Here is, *First,* The cause of this fear; *He saw the wind boisterous.* While Peter kept his eye fixed upon Christ, and upon his word and power, he *walked upon the water* well enough; but when he took notice withal of the danger he was in, and observed how *the floods lift up their waves,* then he feared. Note, Looking at difficulties with an eye of sense more than at precepts and promises with an eye of faith is at the bottom of all our inordinate fears, both as to public and personal concerns.

Secondly, The effect of this fear; *He began to sink.* While faith kept up, he kept above water: but when faith staggered, *he began to sink.* Note, The sinking of our spirits is owing to the weakness of our faith; we are upheld (but it is as we are saved) *through faith* (1 Pet. i. 5); and therefore, when our *souls are cast down and disquieted,* the sovereign remedy is, *to hope in God,* Ps. xliii. 5.

Thirdly, The remedy he had recourse to in this distress, the old, tried, approved remedy, and that was prayer: he cried, *Lord, save me.*

[2] Christ's great favour to Peter, in this fright. Though there was a

mixture of presumption with Peter's faith in his first adventure, and of unbelief with his faith in his after-fainting, yet Christ did not cast him off; for,

First, He saved him; *he answered him with the saving strength of his right hand* (Ps. xx. 6), for immediately *he stretched forth his hand, and caught him.*

Secondly, He rebuked him; for as many as he loves and saves, he reproves and chides; *O thou of little faith, wherefore didst thou doubt?*

VI. The *ceasing of the storm, v. 32*. When Christ was come into the ship, they were presently at the shore. Christ *walked upon the water* till he came to the ship, and then went into that, when he could as easily have walked to the shore; but when ordinary means are to be had, miracles are not to be expected.

When they were come into the ship, immediately the storm ceased, for it had done its work, its trying work. When Christ comes into a soul, he makes winds and storms to cease there, and commands peace. Welcome Christ, and *the noise of her waves will soon be quelled*. The way to be still is, to know that he is God, that he is the *Lord with us.*

VII. The adoration paid to Christ hereupon (*v.* 33); *They that were in the ship came and worshipped him, and said, Of a truth, thou art the Son of God.*

WHOLESALE MIRACLES
(*vv.* 34–36)

We have here an account of miracles by wholesale, which Christ wrought on the other side of the water, in the land of Gennesaret. Whithersoever Christ went, he was doing good. Gennesaret was a tract of land that lay between Bethsaida and Capernaum, and either gave the name to, or took the name from, this sea, which is called (Luke v. 1) *The lake of Gennesaret*; it signifies the valley of branches. Observe here,

1. How *the men of that place* were brought to Christ; they *had knowledge of him.*

They *had knowledge of him*, that is, of his being among them, and that he would be but awhile among them. It is better to know that there *is* a prophet among us than that there *has been* one, Ezek. ii. 5.

2. How they brought others to Christ, by giving notice to their neighbours of Christ's being come into those parts; *They sent out into all that country.* Note, those that have got the knowledge of Christ themselves, should do all they can to bring others acquainted with him too.

3. What their business was with Christ; not only, perhaps not chiefly, if at all, to be taught, but to have their sick healed; *They brought unto him all that were diseased.* If love to Christ and his doctrine will not bring them to him, yet self-love would. Did we but rightly seek our own things, the things of our own peace and welfare, we should seek the things of Christ.

4. How they made their application to him; *They besought him that they might only touch the hem of his garment, v.* 36. They applied

themselves to him, (1) With great importunity; they besought him. (2) With great humility; they came to him as those that were sensible of their distance, humbly beseeching him to help them; and their desiring to touch the hem of his garment, intimates that they thought themselves unworthy that he should take any particular notice of them, that he should so much as speak to their case, much less touch them for their cure; but they will look upon it as a great favour, if he will give them leave to *touch the hem of his garment*. (3) With great assurance of the all-sufficiency of his power, not doubting but that they should be healed, even by touching the hem of his garment. It was in this country and neighbourhood that the woman with the bloody issue was cured by *touching the hem of his garment*, and was commended for her faith (*ch.* ix. 20–22); and thence, probably, they took occasion to ask this.

When we mix faith with the word, apply it to ourselves, depend upon it, and submit to its influences and commands, then we touch the hem of Christ's garment. It is but thus touching, and we are made whole. On such easy terms are spiritual cures offered by him, that he may truly be said to heal *freely*; so that if our souls die of their wounds, it is not owing to our Physician, it is not for want of skill or will in him; but it is purely owing to ourselves. He *could* have healed us, he *would* have healed us, but we *would not be healed*; so that our blood will lie upon our own heads.

CHAPTER FIFTEEN

HYPOCRITES (*vv.* 1–9)

Evil manners, we say, beget good laws. The intemperate heat of the Jewish teachers for the support of their hierarchy, occasioned many excellent discourses of our Saviour's for the settling of the truth, as here.

I. Here is the cavil of the scribes and Pharisees at Christ's disciples, for *eating with unwashen hands*.

Observe, 1. What was the *tradition of the elders*—That people should often wash their hands, and always at meat. This they placed a great deal of religion in, supposing that the meat they touched with unwashen hands would be defiling to them. The Pharisees practised this themselves, and with a great deal of strictness imposed it upon others, not under civil penalties, but as matter of conscience, and making it a sin against God if they did not do it.

2. What was the transgression of this tradition or injunction by the disciples; it seems, they did not wash their hands when they ate bread. The custom was innocent enough, and had a decency in its civil use. But when it came to be practised and imposed as a religious rite and ceremony, and such a stress laid upon it, the disciples, though weak in knowledge, yet were so well taught as not to comply with it, or observe it; no not when the scribes and Pharisees had their eye upon them.

3. What was the complaint of the scribes and Pharisees against them. They quarrel with Christ

about it, supposing that he allowed them in it, as he did, no doubt, by his own example; "*Why do thy disciples transgress* the canons of the church? And why dost thou suffer them to do it?" It was well that the complaint was made to Christ; for the disciples themselves, though they knew their duty in this case, were perhaps not so well able to give a reason for what they did as were to be wished.

II. Here is Christ's answer to this cavil, and his justification of the disciples in that which was charged upon them as a transgression.

Two ways Christ replies upon them;

1. By way of recrimination, *vv.* 3–6. They were spying motes in the eyes of his disciples, but Christ shows them a beam in their own.

(1) The charge in general is, *You transgress the commandment of God by your tradition.* They called it the *tradition of the elders*, laying stress upon the antiquity of the usage, and the authority of them that imposed it, as the church of Rome does upon fathers and councils; but Christ calls it *their* tradition.

(2) The proof of this charge is in a particular instance, that of their transgressing the fifth commandment.

[1] Let us see what the command of God is (*v.* 4), what the precept, and what the sanction of the law is.

The precept is, *Honour thy father and thy mother.* Our Saviour here supposes it to mean the duty of children's maintaining their parents, and ministering to their wants, if there be occasion,

and being every way serviceable to their comfort. *Honour widows,* that is, maintain them, 1 Tim. v. 3.

The sanction of this law in the fifth commandment, is, a promise, *that thy days may be long*; but our Saviour waives that, lest any should thence infer it to be only a thing commendable and profitable, and insists upon the penalty annexed to the breach of this commandment in another scripture, which denotes the duty to be highly and indispensably necessary; *He that curseth father or mother, let him die the death*: this law we have, Exod. xxi. 17.

[2] Let us see what was the contradiction which the tradition of the elders gave to this command. It was not direct and downright, but implicit; their casuists gave them such rules as furnished them with an easy evasion from the obligation of this command, *vv.* 5, 6. You hear what God saith, *but ye say* so and so.

First, What their tradition was; That a man could not in any case bestow his worldly estate better than to give it to the priests, and devote it to the service of the temple: and that when any thing was so devoted, it was not only unlawful to alienate it, but all other obligations, though ever so just and sacred, were thereby superseded, and a man was thereby discharged from them.

Secondly, How they allowed the application of this to the case of children. When their parents' necessities called for their assistance, they pleaded, that all they could spare from themselves and their children, they had devoted to the

130

treasury of the temple; *It is a gift, by whatsoever thou mightest be profited by me,* and therefore their parents must expect nothing from them.

2. The other part of Christ's answer is by way of reprehension; and that which he here charges them with, is hypocrisy; *Ye hypocrites, v.* 7.

Now Christ fetches his reproof from Isa. xxix. 13. *Well did Esaias prophesy of you.* Isaiah spoke it of the men of that generation to which he prophesied, yet Christ applies it to these scribes and Pharisees. Isaiah prophesied not of them only, but of all other hypocrites, against whom that word of his is still levelled, and stands in force. The prophecies of scripture are every day in the fulfilling.

This prophecy exactly deciphers a hypocritical nation, Isa. ix. 17; x. 6. Here is,

(1) The description of hypocrites, in two things.

[1] In their own performances of religious worship, *v.* 8, when they *draw nigh to God with their mouth, and honour him with their lips, their heart is far from him.*

[2] In their prescriptions to others. This is an instance of their hypocrisy, that *they teach for doctrines the commandments of men.* The Jews paid the same respect to oral tradition that they did to the word of God. When men's inventions are tacked to God's institutions, and imposed accordingly, this is hypocrisy, a mere human religion.

(2) The doom of hypocrites; it is put in a little compass; *In vain*

do they worship me. Their worship does not attain the end for which it was appointed; it will neither please God, nor profit themselves. If it be not *in spirit,* it is not *in truth,* and so it is all nothing.

INNER DEFILEMENT
(*vv.* 10–20)

Christ having proved that the disciples, in eating with unwashen hands, were not to be blamed, as transgressing the traditions and injunctions of the elders, comes here to show that they were not to be blamed, as having done any thing that was in itself evil. In the former part of his discourse he overturned the authority of the law, and in this the reason of it. Observe,

I. The solemn introduction to this discourse (*v.* 10); *He called the multitude.*

II. The truth itself laid down (*v.* 11), in two propositions.

1. *Not that which goes into the mouth defileth the man.* It is not the kind or quality of our food, not the condition of our hands, that affects the soul with any moral pollution or defilement. *The kingdom of God is not meat and drink,* Rom. xiv. 17. That defiles the man, by which guilt is contracted before God, and the man is rendered offensive to him, and disfitted for communion with him; now what we eat, if we do not eat unreasonably and immoderately, does not this; for *to the pure all things are pure,* Tit. i. 15.

2. *But that which comes out of the mouth, this defiles a man.* We are polluted, not by the meat we

eat with unwashen hands, but by the words we speak from an unsanctified heart. It is not the disciples that defile themselves with what they eat, but the Pharisees that defile themselves with what they speak spitefully and censoriously of them.

III. The offence that was taken at this truth and the account brought to Christ of that offence (*v.* 12).

1. It was not strange that the Pharisees should be offended at this plain truth, for they were men made up of error and enmity, mistake and malice.

2. The disciples thought it strange that their Master should say that which he knew would give so much offence. But he knew what he said, and to whom he said it, and what would be the effect of it; and would teach us, that though in indifferent things we must be tender of giving offence, yet we must not, for fear of that, evade any truth or duty.

IV. The doom passed upon the Pharisees and their corrupt traditions. Two things Christ here foretells concerning them.

1. The rooting out of them and their traditions (*v.* 13): *Every plant which my heavenly Father hath not planted, shall be rooted up.* Not only the corrupt opinions and superstitious practices of the Pharisees, but their sect, and way, and constitution, were plants not of God's planting. Those plants that are not of God's planting, shall not be of his protecting, but shall undoubtedly be rooted up. What is not of God shall not stand, Acts v. 38.

2. The ruin of them; and their followers, who had their persons and principles in admiration, *v.* 14. Where,

(1) Christ bids his disciples *let them alone.* "Have no converse with them or concern for them; neither court their favour, nor dread their displeasure." The case of those sinners is sad indeed, whom Christ orders his ministers to let alone.

(2) He gives them two reasons for it. *Let them alone*; for,

[1] They are proud and ignorant; two bad qualities that often meet, and render a man incurable in his folly, Prov. xxvi. 12. *They are blind leaders of the blind.* They are grossly ignorant in the things of God, and strangers to the spiritual nature of the divine law; and yet so proud, that they think they see better and further than any, and therefore undertake to be leaders of others, to show others the way to heaven, when they themselves know not one step of the way.

[2] They are posting to destruction, and will shortly be plunged into it; *Both shall fall into the ditch.* This must needs be the end of it, if both be so blind, and yet both so bold, venturing forward, and yet not aware of danger. Both will be involved in the general desolation coming upon the Jews, and both drowned in eternal destruction and perdition. The blind leaders and the blind followers will perish together.

V. Instruction given to the disciples concerning the truth Christ had laid down, *v.* 10.

Here is, 1. Their desire to be better instructed in this matter

132

(v. 15); in this request as in many others, Peter was their speaker; the rest, it is probable, putting him on to speak, or intimating their concurrence; *Declare unto us this parable.* What Christ said was plain, but, because it agreed not with the notions they had imbibed, though they would not contradict it, yet they call it a parable, and cannot understand it.

2. The reproof Christ gave them for their weakness and ignorance (v. 16); *Are ye also yet without understanding?* As many as Christ loves and teaches, he thus rebukes.

3. The explanation Christ gave them of this doctrine of pollutions. Though he chided them for their dullness, he did not cast them off, but pitied them, and taught them, as Luke xxiv. 25–27. He here shows us,

(1) What little danger we are in of pollution from that which *entereth in at the mouth*, v. 17. What there is of dregs and defilement in our meat, nature (or rather the God of nature) has provided a way to clear us of it; *it goes in at the belly, and is cast out into the draught*, and nothing remains to us but pure nourishment.

(2) What great danger we are in of pollution from that which *proceeds out of the mouth* (v. 18), out of the abundance of the heart: compare *ch.* xii. 34. Now here we have,

[1] The corrupt fountain of that which proceeds out of the mouth; it comes from the heart; that is the spring and source of all sin, Jer. viii. 7. It is the heart that is so desperately wicked (Jer. xvii. 9);

for there is no sin in word or deed, which was not first in the heart.

[2] Some of the corrupt streams which flow from this fountain, specified; though they do not all *come out of the mouth*, yet they all come out of the man, and are the fruits of that wickedness which is in the heart, and is wrought there, Ps. lviii. 2.

First, Evil thoughts, sins against all the commandments. These are the first-born of the corrupt nature, the beginning of its strength, and do most resemble it. Carnal fancies and imaginations are evil thoughts, wickedness in the contrivance, wicked plots, purposes, and devices of mischief to others, Mic. ii. 1.

Secondly, Murders, sins against the sixth commandment; these come from a malice in the heart against our brother's life, or a contempt of it.

Thirdly, Adulteries and *fornications*, sins against the seventh commandment; these come from the wanton, unclean, carnal heart; and the lust that reigns there, is conceived there, and brings forth these sins, Jam. i. 15. There is adultery in the head first, and then in the act, *ch.* v. 28.

Fourthly, Thefts, sins against the eighth commandment; cheats, wrongs, robberies, and all injurious contracts; the fountain of all these is in the heart, that is it that is *exercised in these covetous practices* (2 Pet. ii. 14), that is set upon riches, Ps. lxii .10. *Achan coveted, and then took*, Joshua vii. 20, 21.

Fifthly, False witness, against the ninth commandment; this comes from a complication of falsehood and covetousness, or falsehood and malice in the heart.

Sixthly, *Blasphemies*, speaking evil of God, against the third commandment; speaking evil of our neighbour, against the ninth commandment; these come from a contempt and disesteem of both in the heart; thence *the blasphemy against the Holy Ghost* proceeds (*ch.* xii. 31, 32); these are the overflowing of the gall within.

Now *these are the things which defile a man*, *v.* 20. The mind and conscience are defiled by sin, and that makes everything else so, Tit. i. 15.

These therefore are the things we must carefully avoid, and all approaches toward them, and not lay stress upon the washing of the hands.

A DAUGHTER HEALED
(*vv.* 21–28)

We have here that famous story of Christ's *casting the devil out of the woman of Canaan's daughter*.

I. *Jesus went thence*. Note, Justly is the light taken from those that either play by it, or rebel against it.

II. When he went thence, he *departed into the coasts of Tyre and Sidon*; not to those cities (they were excluded from any share in *Christ's mighty works*, *ch.* xi. 21, 22), but into that part of the land of Israel which lay that way. Here it was, that this miracle was wrought, in the story of which we may observe.

1. The address of the woman of Canaan to Christ, *v.* 22. She was a Gentile, *a stranger to the commonwealth of Israel*; probably one of the posterity of those accursed nations that were devoted by that word, *Cursed be Canaan*.

Her address was very importunate, she *cried* to Christ, as one in earnest; cried, as being at some distance from him, not daring to approach too near, being a Canaanite, lest she should give offence. In her address,

(1) She relates her misery; *My daugher is grievously vexed with a devil*. There were degrees of that misery, and this was the worst sort. It was a common case at that time, and very calamitous.

(2) She requests for mercy; *Have mercy on me, O Lord, thou Son of David*. In calling him *Lord, the Son of David*, she owns him to be the Messiah: that is the great thing which faith should fasten upon, and fetch comfort from.

Her petition is, *Have mercy on me*. She does not limit Christ to this or that particular instance of mercy, but mercy, mercy is the thing she begs: she pleads not merit, but depends upon mercy; *Have mercy upon me*.

2. The discouragement she met with in this address; in all the story of Christ's ministry we do not meet with the like. He was wont to countenance and encourage all that came to him, and either *to answer before they called*, or *to hear while they were yet speaking*; but here was one otherwise treated: and what could be the reason of it? (1) Some think that Christ showed himself backward to gratify this poor woman, because he would not give offence to the Jews, by being as free and as forward in his favour to the Gentiles as to them. Or rather,

(2) Christ treated her thus, to try her; he knows what is in the heart, knew the strength of her faith, and how well able she was, by his grace, to break through such discouragements; he *therefore* met her with them, *that the trial of her faith might be found unto praise, and honour, and glory*, 1 Pet. i. 6, 7.

Observe the particular discouragements given her:

[1] When she cried after him, *he answered her not a word*, v. 23. But Christ knew what he did, and *therefore* did not answer, that she might be the more earnest in prayer.

[2] When the disciples spake a good word for her, he gave a reason why he refused her, which was yet more discouraging.

First, It was some little relief, that the disciples interposed on her behalf; they said, *Send her away, for she crieth after us.* Continued importunity may be uneasy to men, even to good men; but Christ loves to be cried after.

Secondly, Christ's answer to the disciples quite dashed her expectations; "*I am not sent, but to the lost sheep of the house of Israel.*" He doth not only not answer her, but he argues against her, and stops her mouth with a reason. It is true, she is a *lost sheep*, and hath as much need of his care as any, but she is not *of the house of Israel*, to whom he was first sent (Acts iii. 26), and therefore not immediately interested in it, and entitled to it.

Thirdly, When she continued her importunity, he insisted upon the unfitness of the thing, and gave her not only a repulse, but a

seeming reproach too (*v.* 26); *It is not meet to take the children's bread and to cast it to dogs.* This seems to cut her off from all hope, and might have driven her to despair, if she had not had a very strong faith indeed. Gospel grace and miraculous cures (the appurtenances of it), were children's bread; they belonged to them *to whom pertained the adoption* (Róm. ix. 4). The Gentiles were looked upon by the Jews with great contempt, were called and counted *dogs*; and, in comparison with the house of Israel, who were so dignified and privileged, Christ here seems to allow it, and therefore thinks it not meet that the Gentiles should share in the favours bestowed on the Jews. But see how the tables are turned; after the bringing of the Gentiles into the church, the Jewish zealots for the law are called *dogs*, Phil. iii. 2.

Now this Christ urges against this woman of Canaan; "How can she expect to eat of the children's bread, who is not of the family?" Note, 1. Those whom Christ intends most signally to honour, he first humbles and lays low in a sense of their own meanness and unworthiness. We must first see ourselves to be as dogs, *less than the least of all God's mercies*, before we are fit to be dignified and privileged with them. 2. Christ delights to exercise great faith with great trials, and sometimes reserves the sharpest for the last, that, *being tried, we may come forth like gold.*

3. Here is the strength of her faith and resolution, in breaking

through all these discouragements.

She breaks through all these discouragements.

(1) With a holy earnestness of desire in prosecuting her petition. This appeared upon the former repulse (*v.* 25); *Then came she, and worshipped him, saying, Lord, help me.* [1] She continued to pray. What Christ said, silenced the disciples; you hear no more of them; they took the answer, but the woman did not. [2] She improved in prayer. Instead of blaming Christ, or charging him with unkindness, she seems rather to suspect herself, and lay the fault upon herself. She fears lest, in her first address, she had not been humble and reverent enough, and therefore now *she came, and worshipped him,* and paid him more respect than she had done; or she fears that she had not been earnest enough, and therefore now she cries, *Lord, help me.* [3] She waives the question, whether she was of those to whom Christ was sent or no; she will not argue that with him, though perhaps she might have claimed some kindred to the house of Israel; but, "Whether an Israelite or no, I come to the Son of David for mercy, and *I will not let him go, except he bless me.*" [4] Her prayer is very short, but comprehensive and fervent, *Lord, help me.* Take this, *First,* As lamenting her case; "If the Messiah be sent only to the house of Israel, the *Lord help me,* what will become of me and mine." Or, *Secondly,* As begging grace to assist her in this hour of temptation. She found it hard to keep up her faith when it

was thus frowned upon, and therefore prays, "*Lord, help me*; Lord, strengthen my faith now; *Lord, let they right hand uphold me,* while my soul is *following hard after thee,*" Ps. lxiii. 8. Or, *Thirdly,* As enforcing her original request, "*Lord, help me*; Lord, give me what I come for." She believed that Christ could and would help her, though she was not of the house of Israel; else she would have dropt her petition. Still she keeps up good thoughts of Christ, and will not quit her hold.

(2) With a holy skilfulness of faith, suggesting a very surprising plea. Christ had placed the Jews with the children, *as olive-plants round about* God's *table,* and had put the Gentiles with the dogs, under the table; and she doth not deny the aptness of the similitude. *Truth, Lord; yet the dogs eat of the crumbs.* Now, here,

[1] Her acknowledgment was very humble: *Truth, Lord.* Note, You cannot speak so meanly and slightly of a humble believer, but he is ready to speak as meanly and slightly of himself.

[2] Her improvement of this into a plea was very ingenious; *Yet the dogs eat of the crumbs.* It was by a singular acumen, and spiritual quickness and sagacity, that she discerned matter of argument in that which looked like a slight.

Her plea is, *Yet the dogs eat of the crumbs.* We poor Gentiles cannot expect the stated ministry and miracles of the Son of David, that belongs to the Jews; but they begin now to be weary of their meat, and to play with it, they find fault with it, and crumble it away; surely then some of the broken meat may fall to a poor Gentile. Observe here,

First, Her humility and necessity made her glad of crumbs.

Secondly, Her faith encouraged her to expect these crumbs. Why should it not be at Christ's table as at a great man's, where the dogs are fed as sure as the children?

4. The happy issue and success of all this. She came off with credit and comfort from this struggle; and, though a Canaanite, approved herself a true daughter of Israel, who, *like a prince, had power with God, and prevailed.*

(1) He commended her faith. *O woman, great is thy faith.*

(2) He cured her daughter; *"Be it unto thee even as thou wilt:* I can deny thee nothing, take what thou camest for."

The event was answerable to the word of Christ; *Her daughter was made whole from that very hour;* from thenceforward was never vexed with the devil any more; the mother's faith prevailed for the daughter's cure. Though the patient was at a distance, that was no hindrance to the efficacy of Christ's word. *He spake, and it was done.*

FOUR THOUSAND FED
(*vv.* 29–39)

Here is, I. A general account of Christ's cures, his curing by wholesale. The tokens of Christ's power and goodness are neither scarce nor scanty; for there is in him an overflowing fulness.

Now, (1) Such was the goodness

of Christ, that he admitted all sorts of people; the poor as well as the rich are welcome to Christ, and with him there is room enough for all comers. He never complained of crowds or throngs of seekers, or looked with contempt upon the vulgar, the *herd,* as they are called; for the souls of peasants are as precious with him as the souls of princes.

Such was the power of Christ, that he healed all sorts of diseases; those that came to him, brought their sick relations and friends along with them, and *cast them down at Jesus' feet, v.* 30. Whatever our case is, the only way to find ease and relief, is, to lay it at Christ's feet, to spread it before him, and refer it to his cognizance, and then submit it to him, and refer it to his disposal.

Here were *lame, blind, dumb, maimed, and many others,* brought to Christ. See what work sin has made! It has turned the world into an hospital: what various diseases are human bodies subject to! See what work the Saviour makes! He conquers those hosts of enemies to mankind.

II. Here is a particular account of his feeding *four thousand men* with *seven loaves, and a few little fishes,* as he had lately fed *five thousand with five loaves.* The guests indeed were now not quite so many as then, and the provision a little more; which does not intimate that Christ's arm was shortened, but that he wrought his miracles as the occasion required, and not for ostentation, and therefore he suited them to the occasion: both then and now he took as many as were to be fed, and made use of all that was at hand to feed them with. When once the utmost powers of nature are exceeded, we must say, *This is the finger of God*; and it is neither here nor there how far they are outdone; so that this is no less a miracle than the former.

SIGNS OF THE TIMES (*vv.* 1–4)

We have here Christ's discourse with the Pharisees and Sadducees.

I. Their demand, and the design of it.

1. The demand was of a sign from heaven; this they desired him to show them; pretending they were very willing to be satisfied and convinced, when really they were far from being so, but sought excuses from an obstinate infidelity. That which they pretended to desire was,

(1) Some other sign than what they had yet had. They had great plenty of signs; every miracle Christ wrought was a sign, for *no man could do what he did unless God were with him*. But this will not serve, they must have a sign of their own choosing; they despised those signs which relieved the necessity of the sick and sorrowful, and insisted upon some sign which would gratify the curiosity of the proud.

(2) It must be a sign from heaven. They would have such miracles to prove his commission, as were wrought at the giving of the law upon mount Sinai: thunder, and lightning, and the voice of words, were the sign from heaven they required.

2. The design was to tempt him; not to be taught by him, but to ensnare him. If he should show them a sign from heaven, they would attribute it to a confederacy with the *prince of the power of the air*; if he should not, as they supposed he would not, they would have that to say for themselves, *why they did not believe on him*.

II. Christ's reply to this demand: In his answer,

1. He condemns their overlooking of the signs they had, *vv.* 2, 3. They were seeking for the signs of the kingdom of God, when it was already among them.

To expose this, he observes to them,

(1) Their skilfulness and sagacity in other things, particularly in natural prognostications of the weather.

(2) Their sottishness and stupidity in the concerns of their souls; *Can ye not discern the signs of the times?*

[1] "Do you not see that the Messiah is come?" The sceptre was departed from Judah, Daniel's weeks were just expiring, and yet they regarded not. The miracles Christ wrought, and the gathering of the people to him, were plain indications that the *kingdom of heaven was at hand*, that this was *the day of their visitation*.

[2] "Do you not foresee your own ruin coming for rejecting him? You will not entertain the gospel of peace, and can you not evidently discern that hereby you pull an inevitable destruction upon your own heads?"

2. He refuses to give them any other sign (*v.* 4), as he had done before in the same words, *ch.* xii. 39. Those that persist in the same iniquities, must expect to meet with the same reproofs.

This discourse broke off abruptly; *he left them and departed.* Christ will not tarry long with those that tempt him, but justly withdraws from those that are disposed to quarrel with him. He left them as irreclaimable; *Let them alone.* He left them to themselves, left them in the hand of their own counsels; *so he gave them up to their own hearts' lust.*

EVIL LEAVEN (*vv.* 5–12)

We have here Christ's discourse with his disciples concerning bread, in which, as in many other discourses, he speaks to them of spiritual things under a similitude, and they misunderstand him of carnal things. The occasion of it was, their forgetting to victual their ship, and to take along with them provisions for their family on the other side the water.

1. Here is the caution Christ gave them, to *beware of the leaven of the Pharisees.* He had now been discoursing with the Pharisees and Sadducees, and saw them to be men of such a spirit, that it was necessary to caution his disciples to have nothing to do with them. Disciples are in most danger from hypocrites; against those that are openly vicious they stand upon their guard, but against Pharisees, who are great pretenders to devotion, and Sadducees, who pretend to a free and impartial search after truth, they commonly lie unguarded: and therefore the caution is doubled, *Take heed, and beware.*

The corrupt principles and practices of the Pharisees and Sadducees are compared to leaven; they were souring, and swelling, and spreading, like leaven; they fermented wherever they came.

II. Their mistake concerning this caution, *v.* 7. They thought Christ hereby upbraided them with their improvidence and forgetfulness, that they were so busy attending to his discourse with the Pharisees, that *therefore* they forgot their private concerns.

III. The reproof Christ gave them for this.

1. He reproves their distrust of his ability and readiness to supply them in this strait (*v.* 8); "*O ye of little faith*, why are ye in such perplexity because ye have *taken no bread*, that ye can mind nothing else, that ye think your Master is as full of it as you, and apply everything he saith to that?" See how easily Christ forgave his disciples' carelessness, though it was in such a material point as taking bread; and do likewise. But that which he chides them for is their little faith.

(1) He would have them to depend upon him for supply, though it were in a wilderness, and not to disquiet themselves with anxious thoughts about it.

(2) He is displeased at their solicitude in this matter. The weakness and shiftlessness of good people in their worldly affairs is that for which men are apt to condemn them; but it is not such an offence to Christ as their

inordinate care and anxiety about those things.

(3) The aggravation of their distrust was the experience they had so lately had of the power and goodness of Christ in providing for them, *vv.* 9, 10. Though they had no bread with them, they had him with them who could provide bread for them. If they had not the cistern, they had the Fountain. *Do ye not yet understand, neither remember?*

2. He reproves their misunderstanding of the caution he gave them (*v.* 11); *How is it that you do not understand?* Note, Christ's disciples may well be ashamed of the slowness and dullness of their apprehensions in divine things; especially when they have long enjoyed the means of grace; *I spake it not unto you concerning bread.* He took it ill, (1) That they should think him as thoughtful about bread as they were; whereas his *meat and drink were to do his Father's will.* (2) That they should be so little acquainted with his way of preaching, as to take that literally which he spoke by way of parable; and should thus make themselves like the multitude, who, when Christ spoke to them in parables, seeing, saw not, and hearing, heard not, *ch.* xiii. 13.

IV. The rectifying of the mistake by this reproof (*v.* 12); *Then understood they* what he meant. He did not tell them expressly what he meant, but repeated what he had said, that they should beware of the leaven; and so obliged them, by comparing this with his other discourses, to arrive at the sense of it in their own thoughts. Thus

Christ teaches by the Spirit of wisdom in the heart, opening the understanding to the Spirit of revelation in the word.

PETER'S CONFESSION
(*vv.* 13–20)

We have here a private conference which Christ had with his disciples concerning himself. It was in the coasts of Cesarea Philippi, the utmost borders of the land of Canaan northward; there in that remote corner, perhaps, there was less flocking after him than in other places, which gave him leisure for this private conversation with his disciples.

Christ is here catechising his disciples.

I. He enquires what the opinions of others were concerning him; *Who do men say that I, the Son of man, am?*

1. He calls himself the *Son of man*; which may be taken either, (1) As a title common to him with others. He was called, and justly, *the Son of God*, for so he was (Luke i. 35); but he called himself the Son of man; for he is really and truly "Man, made of a woman." Or, (2) As a title peculiar to him as Mediator. He is made known, in Daniel's vision, as the *Son of man*, Dan. vii. 13. I am the Messiah, that Son of man that was promised. But,

2. He enquires what people's sentiments were concerning him: "*Who do men say that I am? The Son of Man?*" (So I think it might better be read). "Do they own me for the Messiah?"

3. To this question the disciples

gave him an answer (*v.* 14), *Some say, thou art John the Baptist, &c.* There were some that said, he was the *Son of David* (*ch.* xii. 23), and the great Prophet, John vi. 14. The disciples, however, do not mention that opinion, but only such opinions as were wide of the truth, which they had gathered up from their countrymen.

II. He enquires what *their* thoughts were concerning him; "*But who say ye that I am? v.* 15. Ye tell me what other people say of me; can ye say better?" 1. The disciples had themselves been better taught than others; had, by their intimacy with Christ, greater advantages of getting knowledge than others had. 2. The disciples were trained up to teach others, and therefore it was highly requisite that they should understand the truth themselves: "Ye that are to preach the gospel of the kingdom, what are your notions of him that sent you?" Note, Ministers must be examined before they be sent forth, especially what their sentiments are of Christ, and who they say that he is; for how can they be owned as ministers of Christ, that are either ignorant or erroneous concerning Christ? This is a question we should every one of us be frequently putting to ourselves, "*Who* do we say, *what* kind of one do we say, that *the Lord Jesus is*? Is he precious to us? Is he in our eyes the chief of ten thousand? Is he the Beloved of our souls?" It is well or ill with us, according as our thoughts are right or wrong concerning Jesus Christ.

Well, this is the question; now let us observe,

(1) Peter's answer to this question, *v.* 16. To the former question concerning the opinion others had of Christ, several of the disciples answered, according as they had heard people talk; but to this Peter answers in the name of all the rest, they all consenting to it, and concurring in it.

Peter's answer is short, but it is full, and true, and to the purpose; *Thou art the Christ, the Son of the living God.* Here is a confession of the Christian faith, addressed to Christ, and so made an act of devotion. Here is a confession of the true God as the living God, in opposition to dumb and dead idols, and of *Jesus Christ, whom he hath sent,* whom to know is *life eternal.* This is the conclusion of the whole matter.

[1] The people called him *a Prophet, that Prophet* (John vi. 14); but the disciples own him to be the Christ, the anointed One; the great Prophet, Priest, and King of the church; the true Messiah promised to the fathers, and depended on by them as *He that shall come.* It was a great thing to believe this concerning one whose outward appearance was so contrary to the general idea the Jews had of the Messiah.

[2] He called himself the *Son of Man*; but they owned him to be *the Son of the living God.* The *people's* notion of him was, that he was the ghost of a dead man, Elias or Jeremias; but *they* know and believe him to be *the Son of the living God,* who has life in himself, and has given to his Son

to have life in himself, and to be the *Life of the world*.

(2) Christ's approbation of his answer (*vv.* 17–19); in which Peter is replied to, both as a believer and as an apostle.

[1] As a believer, *v.* 17. Christ shows himself well pleased with Peter's confession, that it was so clear and express, without *ifs* or *ands*, as we say. But,

First, Peter had the happiness of it; *Blessed art thou, Simon Bar-jona*. He reminds him of his rise and original, the meanness of his parentage, the obscurity of his extraction; he was *Bar-jonas—The son of a dove*; so some. Let him remember *the rock out of which he was hewn*, that he may see he was not born to this dignity, but preferred to it by the divine favour; it was free grace that made him to differ. Having reminded him of this, he makes him sensible of his great happiness as a believer; *Blessed art thou. Blessed are your eyes*, *ch.* xiii. 16. All happiness attends the right knowledge of Christ.

Secondly, God must have the glory of it; "*For flesh and blood have not revealed it to thee.* Thou hadst this neither by the invention of thy own wit and reason, nor by the instruction and information of others; this light sprang neither from nature nor from education, but from my Father who is in heaven." Note, 1. The Christian religion is a revealed religion, has its rise in heaven; it is a religion from above, given by inspiration of God, not the learning of philosophers, nor the politics of statesmen. 2. Saving faith is the gift of God,

and, wherever it is, is wrought by him, as the Father of our Lord Jesus Christ, for his sake, and upon the score of his mediation, Phil. i. 29. *Therefore* thou art blessed, because *my Father has revealed it to thee*.

[2] Christ replies to him as an apostle or minister, *vv.* 18, 19. Peter, in the name of the church, had confessed Christ, and to him therefore the promise intended for the church is directed.

Upon occasion of this great confession made of Christ, which is the church's homage and allegiance, he signed and published this royal, this divine charter, by which that body politic is incorporated.

Now the purport of this charter is,

First, To establish the being of the church; *I say also unto thee*. It is Christ that makes the grant, he who is the church's Head, and Ruler, to whom all judgment is committed, and from whom all power is derived; he who makes it pursuant to the authority received from the Father, and his undertaking for the salvation of the elect. The grant is put into Peter's hand; "I say it to *thee*." The Old Testament promises relating to the church were given immediately to particular persons, eminent for faith and holiness, as to Abraham and David; which yet gave no supremacy to them, much less to any of their successors; so the New-Testament charter is here delivered to Peter as an agent, but to the use and behoof of the church in all ages, according to the purposes therein specified and contained. Now it is here promised,

1. That Christ would build his church upon a rock. This body politic is incorporated by the style and title of *Christ's church*. It is a number of the children of men called out of the world, and set apart from it, and dedicated to Christ.

(1) The Builder and Maker of the church is Christ himself; *I will build it*. By the working of his Spirit with the preaching of his word he adds souls to his church, and so builds it up with living stones, 1 Pet. ii. 5.

(2) The foundation on which it is built, *this Rock*. Let the architect do his part ever so well, if the foundation be rotten, the building will not stand; let us therefore see what the foundation is, and it must be meant of Christ, for *other foundation can no man lay*. See Isa. xxviii. 16.

[1] The church is built upon a *rock*; a firm, strong, and lasting foundation, which time will not waste, nor will it sink under the weight of the building.

[2] It is built upon *this* rock; thou art *Peter*, which signifies *a stone* or *rock*; Christ gave him that name when he first called him (John i. 42), and here he confirms it. From the mention of this significant name, occasion is taken for this metaphor of *building upon a rock*.

First, Some by this rock understand Peter himself as an apostle, the chief, though not the prince, of the twelve, senior among them, but not superior over them. The church is built upon the foundation of the apostles, Eph. ii. 20. The first stones of that building were laid in and by their ministry; hence their names are said to be *written in the foundations* of the new Jerusalem, Rev. xxi. 14. Now Peter being that apostle by whose hand the first stones of the church were laid, both in Jewish converts (Acts ii), and in the Gentile converts (Acts x.), he might in some sense be said to be the rock on which it was built. *Cephas* was one that seemed to be a pillar, Gal. ii. 9. But it sounds very harsh, to call a man that only lays the first stone of a building, which is a transient act, the foundation on which it is built, which is an abiding thing.

Secondly, Others, by this *rock*, understand *Christ*; "*Thou art Peter*, thou hast the name of a *stone*, but *upon this rock*, pointing to himself, *I will build my church.*" Perhaps he laid his hand on his breast, as when he said, *Destroy this temple* (John ii. 19), when he *spoke of the temple of his body*. But this must be explained by those many scriptures which speak of Christ as the only Foundation of the church; see 1 Cor. iii. 11; 1 Pet. ii. 6. Christ is both its Founder and its Foundation; he draws souls, and draws them to himself; to him, they are united, and on him they rest and have a constant dependence.

Thirdly, Others by this *rock* understand this confession which Peter made of Christ, and this comes all to one with understanding it of Christ himself. It was a good confession which Peter witnessed, *Thou art the Christ, the Son of the living God*; the rest concurred with him in it. "Now," saith Christ, "this is that great truth *upon which I will build my church.*" 1. Take away this truth itself, and the universal church falls to the ground. If Christ be not the Son of God, Christianity is a cheat, and the church is a mere chimera; *our preaching is vain, your faith is vain, and you are yet in your sins,* 1 Cor. xv. 14–17. If Jesus be not the Christ, those that own him are not of the church, but deceivers and deceived. 2. Take away the faith and confession of this truth from any particular church, and it ceases to be a part of Christ's church, and relapses to the state and character of infidelity.

2. Christ here promises to preserve and secure his church, when it is built; *The gates of hell shall not prevail against it*; neither against this truth, nor against the church which is built upon it.

(1) This implies that the church has enemies that fight against it, and endeavour its ruin and overthrow, here represented by *the gates of hell, that is,* the city of hell; (which is directly opposite to this heavenly city, this *city of the living God*), the devil's interest among the children of men. These fight against the church by opposing gospel truths, corrupting gospel ordinances, persecuting good ministers and good Christians; drawing or driving, persuading by craft or forcing by cruelty, to that which is inconsistent with the purity of religion; this is the design of the gates of hell, to root out the name of Christianity (Ps. lxxxiii. 4), *to devour the man-child* (Rev. xii. 9), to raze this city to the ground.

(2) This assures us that the enemies of the church shall not gain their point. While the world stands, Christ will have a church in it, in which his truths and ordinances shall be owned and kept up, in spite of all the opposition of the powers of darkness; *They shall not prevail against it,* Ps. cxxix. 1, 2.

Secondly, The other part of this charter is, to settle the order and government of the church, *v.* 19. When a city or society is incorporated, officers are appointed and empowered to act for the common good. A city without government is a chaos. Now this constituting of the government of the church, is here expressed by the delivering of the keys, and, with them, a power to bind and loose. This is not to be understood of any peculiar power that Peter was invested with, as if he were sole door-keeper of the kingdom of heaven, and had that key of David which belongs only to the Son of David; no, this invests all the apostles and their successors with a ministerial power to guide and govern the church of Christ, as it exists in particular congregations or churches, according to the rules of the gospel.

Now, 1. The power here delegated is a spiritual power; it is a power *pertaining to the kingdom of heaven,* that is, to the church, that part of it which is militant here on earth, to the gospel dispensation.

2. It is the *power* of the keys that is given, alluding to the custom of investing men with authority in such a place, by delivering to them the keys of the place.

3. It is a power to *bind and loose,*

that is (following the metaphor of the keys), to shut and open.

4. It is a power which Christ has promised to own the due administration of; he will ratify the sentences of his stewards with his own approbation; *It shall be bound in heaven, and loosed in heaven*: not that Christ hath hereby obliged himself to confirm all church-censures, right or wrong; but such as are duly passed according to the word, such are sealed in heaven; that is, the word of the gospel, in the mouth of faithful ministers, is to be looked upon, not as the word of man, but as the word of God, and to be received accordingly, 1 Thes. ii. 13; John xii. 20.

Now *the keys of the kingdom of heaven are*,

(1) The key of *doctrine*, called the key of *knowledge*. Now the apostles had an extraordinary power of this kind; some things forbidden by the law of Moses were now to be allowed, as the eating of such and such meats; some things allowed there were now to be forbidden, as divorce; and the apostles were empowered to declare this to the world, and men might take it upon their words. When Peter was first taught himself, and then taught others, *to call nothing common or unclean*, this power was exercised. There is also an ordinary power hereby conveyed to all ministers, to preach the gospel as appointed officers; to tell people, in God's name, and according to the scriptures, *what is good, and what the Lord requires of them*: and they who *declare the whole counsel*

of God, use these keys well, Acts xx. 27.

(2) The key of *discipline*, which is but the application of the former to particular persons, upon a right estimate of their characters and actions. It is not legislative power that is hereby conferred, but judicial; the judge doth not make the law, but only declares what is law, and upon an impartial enquiry into the merits of the cause, gives sentence accordingly. Such is *the power of the keys*, wherever it is lodged, with reference to church-membership and the privileges thereof.

Lastly, Here is the charge which Christ gave his disciples, to keep this private for the present (*v.* 20); *They must tell no man that he was Jesus the Christ*. What they had professed to him, they must not yet publish to the world, for several reasons; 1. Because this was the time of preparation for his kingdom: the great thing now preached, was, that *the kingdom of heaven was at hand*. 2. Christ would have his Messiahship proved by his works, and would rather *they* should testify of him than that his *disciples* should, because their testimony was but as his own, which he insisted not on. See John v. 31, 34.

PETER REBUKED (*vv.* 21–23)

We have here Christ's discourse with his disciples concerning his own sufferings; in which observe,

I. Christ's foretelling of his sufferings. Now he *began* to do it, and from this time he frequently spake of them.

From that time, when they had

made that full confession of Christ, that he was the Son of God, then he began to show them this. When he found them knowing in one truth, he taught them another; *for to him that has, shall be given.* Now observe,

1. What he foretold concerning his sufferings, the particulars and circumstances of them, and all surprising.

(1) The place where he should suffer. He must go to Jerusalem, the head city, the holy city, and suffer there. Though he lived most of his time in Galilee, he must die at Jerusalem; there all the sacrifices were offered, there therefore *he* must die, *who is the great sacrifice.*

(2) The persons by whom he should suffer; *the elders, and chief priests, and scribes;* these made up the great sanhedrim, which sat at Jerusalem, and was had in veneration by the people. Those that should have been most forward in owning and admiring Christ, were the most bitter in persecuting him.

(3) What he should suffer; *he must suffer many things, and be killed.*

(4) What should be the happy issue of all his sufferings; he shall *be raised again the third day.* As the prophets, so Christ himself, when he testified beforehand his sufferings, testified withal the glory that should follow, 1 Pet. i. 11. His rising again the third day proved him to be the Son of God, notwithstanding his sufferings; and therefore he mentions that, to keep up their faith.

2. Why he foretold his sufferings.

(1) To show that they were the product of an eternal counsel and consent; were agreed upon between the Father and the Son from eternity; *Thus it behoved Christ to suffer.* The matter was settled in *the determinate counsel and foreknowledge,* in pursuance of his own voluntary susception and undertaking for our salvation; his sufferings were no surprise to him, did not come upon him as a snare, but he had a distinct and certain foresight of them, which greatly magnifies his love, John xviii. 4. (2) To rectify the mistakes which his disciples had imbibed concerning the external pomp and power of his kingdom. Believing him to be the Messiah, they counted upon nothing but dignity and authority in the world; but here Christ reads them another lesson, tells them of the cross and sufferings. Those that follow Christ must be dealt plainly with, and warned not to expect great things in this world. (3) It was to prepare them for the share, at least, of sorrow and fear, which they must have in his sufferings.

II. The offence which Peter took at this, he said, *Be it far from thee, Lord:* probably he spake the sense of the rest of the disciples, as before, for he was chief speaker. *He took him, and began to rebuke him.*

1. It did not become Peter to contradict his Master, or take upon him to advise him; he might have wished, *that, if it were possible, this cup might pass away,* without saying so peremptorily, *This shall not be,* when Christ had said, *It must be.*

2. It savoured much of fleshly

wisdom, for him to appear so warmly against suffering, and to startle thus at the offence of the cross. It is the corrupt part of us, that is thus solicitous to sleep in a whole skin. We are apt to look upon sufferings as they relate to this present life, to which they are uneasy; but there are other rules to measure them by, which, if duly observed, will enable us cheerfully to bear them, Rom. viii. 18.

III. Christ's displeasure against Peter for this suggestion of his, *v.* 23. We do not read of any thing said or done by any of his disciples, at any time, that he resented so much as this, though they often offended.

Observe, 1. How he expressed his displeasure: He turned upon Peter, and (we may suppose) with a frown said, *Get thee behind me, Satan.* Just now, he had said, *Blessed art thou, Simon,* and had even laid him in his bosom; but here, *Get thee behind me, Satan*; and there was cause for both. Note, A good man may by a surprise of temptation soon grow very unlike himself. He answered him as he did Satan himself, *ch.* iv. 10.

2. What was the ground of this displeasure; why did Christ thus resent a motion that seemed not only harmless, but kind? Two reasons are given:

(1) *Thou art an offence to me— Thou art my hindrance* (so it may be read); "thou standest in my way." Christ was hastening on in the work of our salvation, and his heart was so much upon it, that he took it ill to be hindered, or

tempted to start back from the hardest and most discouraging part of his undertaking. Peter was not so sharply reproved for disowning and denying his Master in his sufferings as he was for dissuading him from them; though that was the defect, this the excess, of kindness.

(2) *Thou savourest not the things that are of God, but those that are of men.* Note, [1] *The things that are of God,* that is, the concerns of his will and glory, often clash and interfere with *the things that are of men,* that is, with our own wealth, pleasure, and reputation. [2] Those that inordinately fear, and industriously decline suffering for Christ, when they are called to it, savour more of the things of man than of the things of God; they relish those things more themselves, and make it appear to others that they do so.

LAW OF DISCIPLESHIP
(*vv.* 24–28)

Christ, having shown his disciples that *he* must suffer, and that he was ready and willing to suffer, here shows them that *they* must suffer too, and must be ready and willing. It is a weighty discourse that we have in these verses.

I. Here is the law of discipleship laid down, and the terms fixed, upon which we may have the honour and benefit of it, *v.* 24. He said this to his disciples, not only that they might instruct others concerning it, but that by this rule they might examine their own sincerity. Observe,

1. What it is to be a disciple of Christ; it is to come after him.

When Christ called his disciples, this was the word of command, *Follow me*. A true disciple of Christ is one that doth follow him in duty, and shall follow him to glory.

2. What are the great things required of those that will be Christ's disciples; *If any man will come—If any man be willing* to come. It denotes a deliberate choice, and cheerfulness and resolution in that choice. Many are disciples more by chance or the will of others than by any act of their own will; but Christ will have his people volunteers, Ps. cx. 3.

Now what are these terms?

(1) *Let him deny himself*. Peter had advised Christ to spare himself, and would be ready, in the like case, to take the advice; but Christ tells them all, they must be so far from *sparing* themselves, that they must *deny* themselves. Herein they must come after Christ, for his birth, and life, and death, were all a continued act of self-denial, a self-emptying, Phil. ii. 7, 8. If self-denial be a hard lesson, and against the grain to flesh and blood, it is no more than what our Master learned and practised before us and for us, both for our redemption and for our instruction; and *the servant is not above his lord*.

(2) *Let him take up his cross*. The cross is here put for all sufferings, as men or Christians; providential afflictions, persecutions for righteousness' sake, every trouble that befals us, either for doing well or for not doing ill. The troubles of Christians are fitly called *crosses*, in allusion to the death of the cross, which Christ was obedient to; and it should reconcile us to troubles, and take off the terror of them, that they are what we bear in common with Christ, and such as he hath borne before us. That which we have to do, is, not only to bear the cross (that a stock, or a stone, or a stick may do), not only to be silent under it, but we must *take up* the cross, must improve it to some good advantage. We should not say, "This is an evil, and I must bear it, because I cannot help it;" but, "This is an evil, and I will bear it, because it shall work for my good." When we *rejoice in our afflictions, and glory in them*, then we take up the cross. This fitly follows upon denying ourselves; for he that will not deny himself the pleasures of sin, and the advantages of this world for Christ, when it comes to the push, will never have the heart to take up his cross.

(2) *Let him follow me*, in this particular of taking up the cross. Suffering saints must look unto Jesus, and take from him both direction and encouragement in suffering. Do we bear the cross? We therein follow Christ, who bears it *before* us, bears it *for* us, and so bears it *from* us.

II. Self-denial, and patient suffering, are hard lessons, which will never be learned if we consult with flesh and blood; let us therefore consult with our Lord Jesus, and see what advice he gives us; and here he gives us,

1. Some considerations proper to engage us to these duties of self-denial and suffering for Christ. Consider,

(1) The weight of that eternity which depends upon our present choice (*v.* 25); *Whosoever will save his life*, by denying Christ, *shall lose it; and whosoever* is content to *lose his life*, for owning Christ, *shall find it*. Here are *life and death, good and evil, the blessing and the curse, set before us*. Observe,

[1] The misery that attends the most plausible apostasy. *Whosoever will save his life* in this world, if it be by sin, he *shall lose it* in another; he that forsakes Christ, to preserve a temporal life and avoid a temporal death, will certainly come short of eternal life, and will be hurt of the second death, and eternally held by it.

[2] The advantage that attends the most perilous and expensive constancy; *Whosoever will lose his life for Christ's sake* in this world, *shall find it* in a better, infinitely to his advantage. The loss of other comforts, for Christ, may possibly be made up in this world (Mark x. 30); the loss of life cannot, but it shall be made up in the other world, in an eternal life; the believing prospect of which hath been the great support of suffering saints in all ages. An assurance of the life they should find, in lieu of the life they hazarded, hath enabled them to triumph over death in all its terrors; to go smiling to a scaffold, and stand singing at a stake, and to call the utmost instances of their enemies' rage but *a light affliction*.

[3] The worth of the soul which lies at stake, and the worthlessness of the world in comparison of it (*v.* 26). *What is a man profited, if he gain the whole world and lose his own soul?* The same word which is translated *his life* (*v.* 25), for the *soul* is the *life*, Gen. ii. 7. This alludes to that common principle, that, whatever a man gets, if he lose his life, it will do him no good, he cannot enjoy his gains. But it looks higher, and speaks of the soul as immortal, and a loss of it beyond death, which cannot be compensated by the gain of the whole world. Here is *the whole world* set in the scale against *one soul*, and *Tekel* written upon it; it is weighed in the balance, and found too light to weigh it down. This is Christ's judgment upon the matter, and he is a competent Judge; he had reason to know the price of *souls*, for he redeemed them; nor would he under-rate the world, for he made it.

What shall a man give in exchange for his soul? Note, If once the soul be lost, it is lost for ever. There is no *counter-price*, that can be paid, or will be accepted. Therefore it is good to be wise in time, and do well for ourselves.

2. Here are some considerations proper to encourage us in self-denial and suffering for Christ.

(1) The assurance we have of Christ's glory, at his second coming to judge the world, *v.* 27. If we look to the end of all these things, the period of the world, and the posture of souls then, we shall thence form a very different idea of the present state of things. If we see things as they *will* appear then, we shall see them as they *should* appear now.

The great encouragement to steadfastness in religion is taken from the second coming of Christ, considering it.

(2) The near approach of his kingdom in this world, *v.* 28. It was so near, that there were some attending him who should live to see it. As Simeon was assured that he should not see death till he had seen the Lord's Christ come in the flesh; so some here are assured that they shall not taste death (death is a sensible thing, its terrors are seen, its bitterness is tasted) till they had seen the Lord's Christ coming in his kingdom. At the end of time, he shall come in his Father's glory; but now, in the fulness of time, he was to come in his own kingdom, his mediatorial kingdom. Some little specimen was given of his glory a few days after this, in his transfiguration (*ch.* xvii. 1); then he tried his robes. But this points at Christ's coming by the pouring out of his Spirit, the planting of the gospel church, the destruction of Jerusalem, and the taking away of the place and nation of the Jews, who were the most bitter enemies to Christianity. Here was *the Son of man coming in his kingdom.* Many then present lived to see it, particularly John, who lived till after the destruction of Jerusalem, and saw Christianity planted in the world. Let *this* encourage the followers of Christ to suffer for him.

CHAPTER SEVENTEEN
THE TRANSFIGURATION
(*vv.* 1–13)

We have here the story of Christ's transfiguration; he had said that the *Son of man should* shortly *come in his kingdom,* with which promise all the three evangelists industriously connect this story; as if Christ's transfiguration were intended for a specimen and an earnest of the kingdom of Christ, and of that light and love of his, which therein appears to his select and sanctified ones. Peter speaks of this as *the power and coming of our Lord Jesus* (2 Pet. i. 16); because it was an emanation of his power, and a previous notice of his coming, which was fitly introduced by such prefaces.

Now concerning Christ's transfiguration, observe,

I. The circumstances of it, which are here noted, *v.* 1.

1. The time; *six days* after he had the solemn conference with his disciples, *ch.* xvi. 21. St. Luke saith, *It was about eight days after,* six whole days intervening, and this the eighth day, that day seven-night.

2. The place; it was *on the top of a high mountain apart.* Christ chose a mountain, (1) As a secret place. Christ chose a retired place to be transfigured in, because his appearing publicly in his glory was not agreeable to his present state; and thus he would show his humility, and teach us that privacy much befriends our communion with God.

3. The witnesses of it. He took with him Peter and James and John. (1) He took three, a competent number to testify what they should see; for *out of the mouth of two or three witnesses shall every word be established.* (2) He took these three because they were the

chief of his disciples, the first three of the worthies of the Son of David; probably they excelled in gifts and graces; they were Christ's favourites, singled out to be the witnesses of his retirements. They were present when he raised the damsel to life, Mark v. 37. They were afterward to be the witnesses of his agony, and this was to prepare them for that.

II. The manner of it (v. 2); *He was transfigured before them*. The substance of his body remained the same, but the accidents and appearances of it were greatly altered; he was not turned into a spirit, but his body, which had appeared in weakness and dishonour, now appeared in power and glory. *He was transfigured, he was metamorphosed*. Christ was both God and man; but, in the days of his flesh, he took on him the *form of a servant*—Phil. ii. 7. He drew a veil over the glory of his godhead; but now, in his transfiguration, he put by that veil, appeared in the form of God (Phil. ii. 6), and gave his disciples a glimpse of his glory, which could not but change his form.

The great truth which we declare, is, that *God is Light* (1 John i. 5), *dwells in light* (1 Tim. vi. 16), *covers himself with light*, Ps. civ. 2. And therefore when Christ would appear in the *form of God*, he appeared *in light*, the most glorious of all visible beings, the first-born of the creation, and most nearly resembling the eternal Parent. Christ is *the Light*; while he was in the world, he *shined in darkness*, and therefore *the world knew him not* (John i. 5, 10); but, at this time, that Light shined out of the darkness.

Now his transfiguration appeared in two things:

1. *His face did shine as the sun*. The face is the principal part of the body, by which we are known; therefore such a brightness was put on Christ's face, that face which afterward *he hid not from shame and spitting*. It shone as the sun when he goes forth in his strength, so clear, so bright; for he is the Sun of righteousness, the Light of the world. The face of Moses shone but as the moon, with a borrowed reflected light, but Christ's shone as the sun, with an innate inherent light, which was the more sensibly glorious, because it suddenly broke out, as it were, from behind a black cloud.

2. *His raiment was white as the light*. All his body was altered, as his face was; so that beams of light, darting from every part through his clothes, made them white and glittering. The shining of the face of Moses was so weak, that it could easily be concealed by a thin veil; but such was the glory of Christ's body, that his clothes were enlightened by it.

III. The companions of it. He will come, at last, *with ten thousands of his saints*; and, as a specimen of that, there now *appeared unto them Moses and Elias talking with him*, v. 3. Observe, 1. There were glorified saints attending him, that, when there were *three to bear record on earth*, Peter, James, and John, there might be some to bear record from heaven too. 2. These two were Moses and Elias, men very eminent in their day. In them the law and the prophets honoured Christ, and bore testimony to him. Moses and Elias appeared to the disciples; they saw them, and heard them talk, and, either by their discourse or by information from Christ, they knew them to be Moses and Elias; glorified saints shall know one another in heaven.

IV. The great pleasure and satisfaction that the disciples took in the sight of Christ's glory. Peter, as usual, spoke for the rest; *Lord, it is good for us to be here*. Peter here expresses,

1. The delight they had in this converse; *Lord, it is good to be here*. This intimates a thankful acknowledgment of his kindness in admitting them to this favour.

2. The desire they had of the continuance of it; *Let us make here three tabernacles*. There was in this, as in many other of Peter's sayings, a mixture of weakness and of goodwill, more zeal than discretion.

(1) Here was a zeal for this converse with heavenly things, a laudable complacency in the sight they had of Christ's glory.

It argued great respect for his Master and the heavenly guests, with some commendable forgetfulness of himself and his fellow-disciples, that he would have tabernacles for Christ, and Moses, and Elias, but none for himself. He would be content to lie in the open air, on the cold ground, in such good company.

(2) Yet in this zeal he betrayed a great deal of weakness and ignorance. What need had Moses and Elias of tabernacles? They

belonged to that blessed world, *where they hunger no more, nor doth the sun light upon them*. Christ had lately foretold his sufferings, and bidden his disciples expect the like; Peter forgets this, or, to prevent it, will needs be building tabernacles in the mount of glory, out of the way of trouble.

Yet it is some excuse for the incongruity of Peter's proposal, not only that *he knew not what he said* (Luke ix. 33), but also that he submitted the proposal to the wisdom of Christ; *If thou wilt, let us make tabernacles*.

Now to this which Peter said, there was no reply made; the disappearing of the glory would soon answer it. They that promise themselves great things on this earth will soon be undeceived by their own experience.

V. The glorious testimony which God the Father gave to our Lord Jesus, in which *he received from him honour and glory* (2 Pet. i. 17), when *there came this voice from the excellent glory*.

Now concerning this testimony from heaven to Christ, observe.

1. How it came, and in what manner it was introduced.

(1) There was a cloud. We find often in the Old Testament, that a cloud was the visible token of God's presence; he came down upon mount Sinai in a cloud (Exod. xix. 9), and so to Moses, Exod. xxxiv. 5; Numb. xi. 25. He took possession of the tabernacle in a cloud, and afterwards of the temple; where Christ was in his glory, the temple was, and there God showed himself present.

(2) It was a bright cloud. Under

152

the law it was commonly a thick and dark cloud that God made the token of his presence; he came down upon mount Sinai in a thick cloud (Exod. xix. 16), and said he would *dwell in thick darkness*; see 1 Kings viii. 12. But *we are now come, not to the mount that was covered in blackness and darkness* (Heb. xii. 18), but to the mount that is crowned with a bright cloud.

(3) It overshadowed them. This cloud was intended to break the force of that great light which otherwise would have overcome the disciples, and have been intolerable; it was like the veil which Moses put upon his face when it shone. God, in manifesting himself to his people, considers their frame.

(4) *There came a voice out of the cloud*, and it was the voice of God, who now, as of old, *spake in the cloudy pillar*, Ps. xcix. 7. This voice came from the excellent glory (2 Pet. i. 17), the glory which excelleth, in comparison of which the former had no glory; though the excellent glory was clouded, yet thence came a voice, for *faith comes by hearing*.

2. What this testimony from heaven was; *This is my beloved Son, hear ye him*. Here we have,

(1) The great gospel mystery revealed; *This is my beloved Son, in whom I am well pleased*. This was the very same that was spoken from heaven at his baptism (*ch*. iii. 17); and it was the best news that ever came from heaven to earth since man sinned. Moses and Elias were sometimes instruments of reconciliation between

God and Israel; Moses was a great intercessor, and Elias a great reformer; but in Christ God is reconciling the world; his intercession is more prevalent than that of Moses, and his reformation more effectual than that of Elias.

This repetition of the same voice that came from heaven at his baptism was no vain repetition; but, like the doubling of Pharaoh's dream, was to show the thing was established. What God hath thus spoken once, yea twice, no doubt he will stand to, and he expects we should take notice of it.

(2) The great gospel duty required, and it is the condition of our benefit by Christ; *Hear ye him*. God is well pleased with none in Christ but those that hear him. It is not enough to give him the hearing (what will that avail us?) but we must hear him and believe him, as the great Prophet and Teacher; hear him, and be ruled by him, as the great Prince and Lawgiver; hear him, and heed him.

Moses and Elias were now with him; the law and the prophets; hitherto it was said, *Hear them*, Luke xvi. 29. The disciples were ready to equal them with Christ, when they must have tabernacles for them as well as for him. They had been talking with Christ, and probably the disciples were very desirous to know what they said, and to hear something more from them; No, saith God, *hear him*, and that is enough; him, and not Moses and Elias, who were present, and whose silence gave consent to this voice; they had nothing to say to the contrary;

whatever interest they had in the world as prophets, they were willing to see it all transferred to Christ, that in *all things he might have the pre-eminence*.

VI. The fright which the disciples were put into by this voice, and the encouragement Christ gave them.

1. The disciples *fell on their faces, and were sore afraid*. Ever since man sinned, and heard God's voice in the garden, extraordinary appearances of God have ever been terrible to man, who, knowing he has no reason to expect any good, has been afraid to hear any thing immediately from God.

2. Christ graciously raised them up with abundance of tenderness. Observe here, (1) What he did; *he came, and touched them*. His approaches banished their fears; and when they apprehended that they were apprehended of Christ, there needed no more to make them easy. (2) What he said; *Arise, and be not afraid*. Considering what they had seen and heard, they had more reason to rejoice than to fear, and yet, it seems, they needed this caution. Observe, After they had an express command from heaven to hear Christ, the first word they had from him was, *Be not afraid*, hear that.

VII. The disappearing of the vision (*v.* 8); *They* lift up themselves, and then *lift up their eyes*, and *saw no man, save Jesus only*. Note, Christ will tarry with us when Moses and Elias are gone. The *prophets do not live for ever* (Zech. i. 5), and we see the period of our ministers' conversation; but

Jesus Christ is the same yesterday, to-day, and for ever, Heb. xiii. 7, 8.

VIII. The discourse between Christ and his disciples as they came down from the mountain, *vv.* 9–13.

Here is, (1) The charge that Christ gave the disciples to keep the vision very private for the present (*v.* 9); *Tell it to no man till the Son of man is risen*. If they had proclaimed it, the credibility of it would have been shocked by his sufferings, which were now hastening on. But let the publication of it be adjourned till after his resurrection, and then that and his subsequent glory will be a great confirmation of it.

(2) An objection which the disciples made against something Christ had said (*v.* 10); *"Why then say the scribes that Elias must first come?* If Elias make so short a stay, and is gone so suddenly, and we must say nothing of him; why have we been taught our of the law to expect his public appearance in the world immediately before the setting up of the Messiah's kingdom? Must the coming of Elias be a secret, which everybody looks for?" Or thus; "If the resurrection of the Messiah, and with it the beginning of his kingdom, be at hand, what becomes of that glorious preface and introduction to it, which we expect in the coming of Elias?"

(3) The solving of this objection. [1] Christ allows the prediction (*v.* 11); *"Elias truly shall first come, and restore all things*; so far you are in the right."

[2] He asserts the accomplishment. The scribes say true, that

154

Elias shall come; but I say unto you, what the scribes could not say, that *Elias is come*, *v.* 12. Note, God's promises are often fulfilled, and men perceive it not, but enquire, *Where is the promise?* when it is already performed. *Elias is come, and they knew him not*; they knew him not to be the Elias promised, the forerunner of the Messiah. But it is no wonder that the morning star was not observed, when he who is the Sun itself, was *in the world, and the world knew him not.*

Because they knew him not, *they have done to him whatsoever they listed*; if they had known, they would not have crucified Christ, or beheaded John. 1 Cor. ii. 8. They ridiculed John, persecuted him, and at last put him to death; which was Herod's doing, but is here charged upon the whole generation of unbelieving Jews, and particularly the scribes, who, though they could not prosecute John themselves, were pleased with what Herod did. He adds, *Likewise also shall the Son of man suffer of them.*

(4) The disciples' satisfaction in Christ's reply to their objection (*v.* 13); *They understood that he spake unto them of John the Baptist.* He did not name John, but gives them such a description of him as would put them in mind of what he had said to them formerly concerning him; *This is Elias.*

THE LUNATIC BOY
(*vv.* 14–21)

We have here the miraculous cure of a child that was lunatic and vexed with a devil. Observe,

I. A melancholy representation of the case of this child, made to Christ by the afflicted father. This was immediately upon his coming down from the mountain where he was transfigured.

Two things the father of the child complains of.

1. The distress of his child (*v.* 15); *Lord, have mercy on my son.* Now, (1) The nature of this child's disease was very sad; *He was lunatic and sore vexed.* A lunatic is properly one whose distemper lies in the brain, and returns with the change of the moon. The devil, by the divine permission, either caused this distemper, or at least concurred with it, to heighten and aggravate it. (2) The effects of the disease were very deplorable; *He oft falls into the fire, and into the water.* If the force of the disease made him to fall, the malice of the devil made him to fall into the fire or water; so mischievous is he where he gains possession and power in any soul. He *seeks to devour*, 1 Pet. v. 8.

2. The disappointment of his expectation from the disciples (*v.* 16); *I brought him to thy disciples, and they could not cure him.* Christ gave his disciples power to cast out devils (*ch.* x. 1, 8), and therein they were successful (Luke x. 17); yet at this time they failed in the operation, though there were nine of them together, and before a great multitude. Christ permitted this, (1) To keep them humble, and to show their dependence upon him, that without him they could do nothing. (2) To glorify himself and his own power.

II. The rebukes that Christ gave to the people first, and then to the devil.

1. He chid those about him (*v.* 17); *O faithless and perverse generation!* This is not spoken to the disciples, but to the people, and perhaps especially to the scribes, who are mentioned in Mark ix. 14, and who, as it should seem, insulted over the disciples, because they had now met with a case that was too hard for them.

Two things he upbraids them with. (1) His presence with them so long; "*How long shall I be with you?* Will you always need my bodily presence, and never come to such maturity as to be fit to be left, the people to the conduct of the disciples, and the disciples to the conduct of the Spirit and of their commission? Must the child be always carried, and will it never learn to go alone?" (2) His patience with them so long; *How long shall I suffer you?* Note, [1] The faithlessness and perverseness of those who enjoy the means of grace are a great grief to the Lord Jesus. Thus did he suffer the manners of Israel of old, Acts xiii. 18. [2] The longer Christ has borne with a perverse and faithless people, the more he is displeased with their perverseness and unbelief; and he is God, and not man, else he would not suffer so long, nor bear so much, as he doth.

2. He cured the child, and set him to rights again. He called, *Bring him hither to me.* Note, When all other helps and succours fail, we are welcome to Christ, and may be confident in him and in his power and goodness.

See here an emblem of Christ's undertaking as our Redeemer.

(1) He breaks the power of Satan (*v.* 18); *Jesus rebuked the devil*, as one having authority, who could back with force his word of command.

(2) He redresses the grievances of the children of men; *The child was cured from that very hour.* It was an immediate cure, and a perfect one.

III. Christ's discourse with his disciples hereupon.

1. They ask the reason why they could not cast out the devil at this time (*v.* 19); *They came to Jesus apart.*

2. Christ gives them two reasons why they failed.

(1) It was *because of their unbelief, v.* 20. When he spake to the father of the child and to the people, he charged it upon their unbelief; when he spake to his disciples, he charged it upon theirs; for the truth was, there were faults on both sides. Though they had faith, yet that faith was weak and ineffectual.

Our Lord Jesus takes this occasion to show them the power of faith, that they might not be defective in that, another time, as they were now; *If ye have faith as a grain of mustard-seed*, ye shall do wonders, *v.* 20. Some make the comparison to refer to the quality of the mustard-seed, which is, when bruised, sharp and penetrating; "If you have an active growing faith, not dead, flat, or insipid, you will not be baffled thus." But it rather refers to the quantity; "If you had but a grain of true faith, though so little that it were like that which is the least of all seeds, you would do wonders." Faith in general is a firm assent to, a compliance with, and a confidence in, all divine revelation. The faith here required, is that which had for its object that particular revelation by which Christ gave his disciples power to work miracles in his name, for the confirmation of the doctrine they preached. It was a faith in this revelation that they were defective in; either doubting the validity of their commission, or fearing that it expired with their first mission, and was not to continue when they were returning to their Master; or that it was some way or other forfeited or withdrawn.

It is good for us to be diffident of ourselves and of our own strength; but it is displeasing to Christ, when we distrust any power derived from him or granted by him.

If you have ever so little of this faith in sincerity, if you truly rely upon the powers committed to you, *ye shall say to this mountain, Remove.* This is a proverbial expression, denoting that which follows, and no more, *Nothing shall be impossible to you.*

(2) Because there was something in the kind of the malady, which rendered the cure more than ordinarily difficult (*v.* 21); "*This kind goes not out but by prayer and fasting.* This possession, which works by a falling-sickness, or this kind of devils that are thus furious, is not cast out ordinarily but by great acts of devotion, and therein ye were defective." Fasting and prayer are proper means for the bringing down of Satan's power against us, and the fetching in of divine power to our assistance. Fasting is of use to put an edge upon prayer; it is an evidence and instance of humiliation which is necessary in prayer, and is a means of mortifying some corrupt habits, and of disposing the body to serve the soul in prayer.

A PROPHECY (*vv.* 22, 23)

Christ here foretells his own sufferings; he began to do it before (*ch.* xvi. 21); and, finding that it was to his disciples a hard saying, he saw it necessary to repeat it. There are some things which *God speaketh once, yea twice, and yet man perceiveth it not.* Observe here,

1. What he foretold concerning himself—that he should be betrayed and killed. He perfectly knew, before, all things that should come to him, and yet undertook the work of our redemption, which greatly commends his love; nay, his clear foresight of them was a kind of ante-passion, had not his love to man made all easy to him.

2. How the disciples received this; *They were exceedingly sorry.* Herein appeared their love to their Master's person, but with all their ignorance and mistake concerning his undertaking. Peter indeed durst not say any thing against it, as he had done before (*ch.* xvi. 22), having then been severely chidden for it; but he, and the rest of them, greatly lamented it, as it would be their own loss, their Master's grief, and the sin and ruin of them that did it.

PAYING TRIBUTE (*vv.* 24–27)

We have here an account of Christ's paying tribute.

I. Observe how it was demanded, *v.* 24. Christ was now at Capernaum, his headquarters, where he mostly resided; he did not keep from thence, to decline being called upon for his dues, but he rather came thither, to be ready to pay them.

1. The tribute demanded was not any civil payment to the Roman powers, that was strictly exacted by the publicans, but the church-duties, the half shekel, about fifteen pence, which were required from every person for the service of the temple, and the defraying of the expenses of the worship there; it is called *a ransom for the soul*, Exod. xxx. 12, &c. This was not so strictly exacted now as sometimes it had been, especially not in Galilee.

2. The demand was very modest; the collectors stood in such awe of Christ, because of his mighty works, that they durst not speak to him about it, but applied themselves to Peter, whose house was in Capernaum, and probably in his house Christ lodged; he therefore was fittest to be spoken to as the housekeeper, and they presumed he knew his Master's mind. Their question is, *Doth not your master pay tribute?* Some think that they sought an occasion against him, designing, if he refused, to represent him as disaffected to the temple-service, and his followers as lawless people, that would pay *neither toll, tribute, nor custom*, Ezra. iv. 13. It should rather seem, they asked this with respect, intimating, that if he had any privilege to exempt him from this payment, they would not insist upon it.

Peter presently passed his word for his Master; "*Yes*, certainly; my *Master pays tribute*; it is his principle and practice; you need not fear moving it to him."

II. How it was disputed (*v.* 25), not with the collectors themselves, lest they should be irritated, but with Peter, that he might be satisfied in the reason why Christ paid tribute, and might not mistake about it. He brought the collectors into the house; but Christ anticipated him, to give him a proof of his omniscience, and that no thought can be withholden from him. The disciples of Christ are never attacked without his knowledge.

Now, 1. He appeals to the way of the kings of the earth, which is, to take tribute of strangers, of the subjects of their kingdom, or foreigners that deal with them, but not of their own children that are of their families; there is such a community of goods between parents and children, and a joint-interest in what they have, that it would be absurd for the parents to levy taxes upon the children, or demand any thing from them; it is like one hand taxing the other.

2. He applies this to himself; *Then are the children free.* Christ is the Son of God, and Heir of all things; the temple is his temple (Mal. iii. 1), his Father's house (John ii. 16), in it *he is faithful as a Son in his own house* (Heb. iii. 6), and therefore not obliged to pay this tax for the service of the temple.

III. How it was paid, notwithstanding, *v.* 27.

1. For what reason Christ waived his privilege, and paid this tribute, though he was entitled to an exemption—*Lest we should offend them*. Few knew, as Peter did, that he was *the Son of God*; and it would have been a diminution to the honour of that great truth, which was yet a secret, to advance it now, to serve such a purpose as this. Therefore Christ drops that argument, and considers, that if he should refuse this payment, it would increase people's prejudice against him and his doctrine, and alienate their affections from him, and therefore he resolves to pay it.

2. What course he took for the payment of this tax; he furnished himself with money for it out of the mouth of a fish (*v.* 27), wherein appears,

(1) The poverty of Christ; he had not fifteen pence at command to pay his tax with, though he cured so many that were diseased; it seems, he did all gratis; *for our sakes he became poor*, 2 Cor. viii. 9.

(2) The power of Christ, in fetching money out of a fish's mouth for this purpose. Whether his omnipotence put it there, or his omniscience knew that it was there, it comes all to one; it was an evidence of his divinity, and that he is Lord of hosts.

CHAPTER EIGHTEEN

A LESSON IN HUMILITY
(*vv.* 1–6)

As there never was a greater pattern of humility, so there never was a greater preacher of it, than Christ; he took all occasions to command it, to commend it, to his disciples and followers.

I. The occasion of this discourse concerning humility was an unbecoming contest among the disciples for precedency; they *came to him, saying*, among themselves (for they were ashamed to ask him, Mark ix. 34), *Who is the greatest in the kingdom of heaven?*

1. They suppose that all who have a place in that kingdom are great, for it is a kingdom of priests.

2. They suppose that there are degrees in this greatness. All the saints are honourable, but not all alike so; *one star differs from another star in glory*.

3. They suppose it must be some of them, that must be prime ministers of state. To whom should King Jesus delight to do honour, but to them who had left all for him, and were now his companions in patience and tribulation?

4. They strive who it should be, each having some pretence or other to it.

II. The discourse itself, which is a just rebuke to the question, *Who shall be greatest?*

Christ here teacheth them to be humble.

1. By a sign (*v.* 2); *He called a little child to him, and set him in the midst of them*. Christ often taught by signs or sensible representations (comparisons to the eye), as the prophets of old.

2. By a sermon upon this sign; in which he shows them and us,

(1) The necessity of humility, *v.* 3. His preface is solemn, and

commands both attention and assent; *Verily I say unto you, I, the Amen, the faithful Witness,* say it, *Except ye be converted, and become as little children, ye shall not enter into the kingdom of heaven.* Here observe,

[1] What it is that he requires and insists upon.

First, "You must be converted, you must be of another mind, and in another frame and temper, must have other thoughts, both of yourselves and of the kingdom of heaven, before you be fit for a place in it. The pride, ambition, and affectation of honour and dominion, which appear in you, must be repented of, mortified, and reformed, and you must come to yourselves." *Secondly,* You must *become as little children.* Note, Converting grace makes us like little children, not foolish as children (1 Cor. xiv. 20), nor fickle (Eph. iv. 14), nor playful (*ch.* xi. 16); but, *as children,* we must *desire the sincere milk of the word* (1 Pet. ii. 2); as children, we must be anxious for nothing, but leave it to our heavenly Father to care for us (*ch.* vi. 31); we must, as children, be harmless and inoffensive, and void of malice (1 Cor. xiv. 20), governable, and under command (Gal. iv. 2); and (which is here chiefly intended) we must be humble as little children, who have no great aims at great places, or projects to raise themselves in the world; they *exercise not themselves in things too high for them*; and we should in like manner, *behave, and quiet ourselves,* Ps, cxxxi. 1, 2.

[2] What stress he lays upon

this; Without this, *you shall not enter into the kingdom of heaven.* Note, Disciples of Christ have need to be kept in awe by threatenings, that they may fear *lest they seem to come short,* Heb. iv. 1. The disciples, when they put that question (*v.* 1), thought themselves sure of the kingdom of heaven; but Christ awakens them to be jealous of themselves. They were ambitious of being *greatest in the kingdom of heaven*; Christ tells them, that, except they came to a better temper, they should never come thither.

(2) He shows the honour and advancement that attend humility (*v.* 4), thus furnishing a direct but surprising answer to their question. He that humbles himself as a little child, though he may fear that hereby he will render himself contemptible, as men of timid minds, who thereby throw themselves out of the way of preferment, yet *the same is greatest in the kingdom of heaven.*

(3) The special care Christ takes for those that are humble; he espouses their cause, protects them, interests himself in their concerns, and will see that they are not wronged, without being righted.

Those that thus humble themselves will be afraid,

[1] That nobody will receive them; but (*v.* 5), *Whoso shall receive one such little child in my name, receiveth me.* Whatever kindnesses are done to such, Christ takes as done to himself.

[2] They will be afraid that every body will abuse them; the basest men delight to trample upon the humble. This objection

he obviates (*v.* 6), where he warns all people, as they will answer it at their utmost peril, not to offer any injury to one of Christ's little ones. This word makes a wall of fire about them; he that touches them, touches the apple of God's eye.

HOW SCANDALS COME
(*vv.* 7–14)

Our Saviour here speaks of offences, or scandals,

I. In general, *v.* 7. Having mentioned the offending of little ones, he takes occasion to speak more generally of offences. Now, concerning offences, Christ here tells them,

(1) That they were certain things; *It must needs be, that offences come.* When we are sure there is danger, we should be the better armed.

(2) That they would be woeful things, and the consequence of them fatal. Here is a double woe annexed to offences:

[1] A woe to the careless and unguarded, to whom the offence is given; *Woe to the world because of offences.* The obstructions and oppositions given to faith and holiness in all places are the bane and plague of mankind, and the ruin of thousands. This present world is an evil world, it is so full of offences, of sins, and snares, and sorrows; a dangerous road we travel, full of stumbling-blocks, precipices, and false guides. Woe to the world.

[2] A woe to the wicked, who wilfully give the offence; *But woe to that man by whom the offence comes.* Though it must needs be,

that the offence will come, that will be no excuse for the offenders.

II. In particular, Christ here speaks of offences given,

1. By us to ourselves, which is expressed by our hand or foot offending us; in such a case, it must be *cut off, vv.* 8, 9. This Christ had said before (*ch.* v. 29, 30), where it especially refers to seventh-commandment sins; here it is taken more generally. Now observe,

(1) What it is that is here enjoined. We must part with an *eye*, or a *hand*, or a *foot*, that is, that, whatever it is, which is dear to us, when it proves unavoidably an occasion of sin to us. We must think nothing too dear to part with, for the keeping of a good conscience.

(2) Upon what inducement this is required; *It is better for thee to enter into life maimed, than, having two hands, to be cast into hell.* The argument is taken from the future state, from heaven and hell; thence are fetched the most cogent dissuasives from sin. If the right hand of the old man be cut off, and its right eye plucked out, its chief policies blasted and powers broken, it is well; but there is still an eye and a hand remaining, with which it will struggle. They that are Christ's have nailed the flesh to the cross, but it is not yet dead; its life is prolonged, but its *dominion taken away* (Dan. vii. 12), and the deadly wound given it, that shall not be healed.

1. Concerning offences given by us to others, especially Christ's little ones, which we are here

charged to take heed of, pursuant to what he had said, *v.* 6. Observe,

(1) The caution itself; *Take heed that ye despise not one of these little ones.* This is spoken to the disciples. As Christ will be displeased with the enemies of his church, if they wrong any of the members of it, even the least, so he will be displeased with the great ones of the church, if they despise the little ones of it.

[1] We must not despise them, not think meanly of them, as lambs despised, Job xii. 5. We must not impose upon the consciences of others, nor bring them into subjection to our humours, as they do who say to men's souls, *Bow down, that we may go over.* There is a respect owing to the conscience of every man who appears to be conscientious.

[2] We must take heed that we do not despise them; we must be afraid of the sin, and be very cautious what we say and do, lest we should through inadvertency give offence to Christ's little ones, lest we put contempt upon them, without being aware of it.

(2) The reasons to enforce the caution. We must not look upon these little ones as contemptible, because really they are considerable. To prove that the little ones which believe in Christ are worthy to be respected, consider,

[1] The ministration of the good angels about them; *In heaven their angels always behold the face of my Father.* This Christ saith to us, and we may take it upon *his* word, who came from heaven to let us know what is done there by the world of angels.

[2] The gracious design of Christ concerning them (*v.* 11); *For the Son of man is come to save that which was lost.* This is a reason, *First,* Why the little ones' angels have such a charge concerning them, and attend upon them; it is in pursuance of Christ's design to save them. *Secondly,* Why they are not to be despised; because Christ came to save them, to save them that are lost, the little ones that are lost in their own eyes (Isa. lxvi. 3), that are at a loss within themselves. This is a good reason why the least and weakest believers should not be despised or offended. If Christ put such a value upon them, let us not undervalue them.

[3] The tender regard which our heavenly Father has to these little ones, and his concern for their welfare. This is illustrated by a comparison, *vv.* 12–14. Observe the gradation of the argument; the angels of God are their servants, the Son of God is their Saviour, and, to complete their honour, God himself is their Friend. *None shall pluck them out of my Father's hand,* John x. 28.

Here is, *First,* The comparison, *vv.* 12, 13. The owner that had lost one sheep out of a hundred, does not slight it, but diligently enquires after it, is greatly pleased when he has found it, and has in that a sensible and affecting joy, more than in the ninety and nine that wandered not. The fear he was in of losing that one, and the surprise of finding it, add to the joy. Now this is applicable, 1. To the state of fallen man in general; he is strayed like a lost sheep, the angels that stood were as the ninety-nine that never went astray; wandering man is sought upon the mountains, which Christ, in great fatigue, traversed in pursuit of him, and he is found; which is matter of joy. Greater joy there is in heaven for returning sinners than for remaining angels. 2. To particular believers, who are offended and put out of their way by the stumbling-blocks that are laid in their way, or the wiles of those who seduce them out of the way. Now though but one of a hundred should hereby be driven off, as sheep easily are, yet that one shall be looked after with a great deal of care, the return of it welcomed with a great deal of pleasure; and therefore the wrong done to it, no doubt, will be reckoned for with a great deal of displeasure. If there be joy in heaven for the finding of one of these little ones, there is wrath in heaven for the offending of them.

Secondly, The application of this comparison (*v.* 14); *It is not the will of your Father, that one of these little ones should perish.* More is implied than is expressed. It is not his will that any should perish, but, 1. It is his will, that these little ones should be saved; it is the will of his design and delight: he has designed it, and set his heart upon it, and he will effect it; it is the will of his precept, that all should do what they can to further it, and nothing to hinder it. 2. This care extends itself to every particular member of the flock, even the meanest. We think if but *one* or *two* be

offended and ensnared, it is no great matter, we need not mind it; but God's thoughts of love and tenderness are above ours. 3. It is intimated that those who do any thing by which any of these little ones are brought into danger of perishing, contradict the will of God, and highly provoke him.

Observe, Christ called God, *v.* 19, *my Father which is in heaven*; he calls him, *v.* 14, *your Father which is in heaven*; intimating that he is not ashamed to call his poor disciples *brethren*; for have not he and they one Father? *I ascend to my Father and your Father* (John xx. 17); therefore ours because his.

HEARING COMPLAINTS
(*vv.* 15-20)

Christ, having cautioned his disciples not to give offence, comes next to direct them what they must do in case of offences given them.

I. Let us apply it to the quarrels that happen, upon any account, among Christians. If thy brother trespass against thee, by grieving thy soul (1 Cor. viii. 12), by affronting thee, or putting contempt or abuse upon thee; if he blemish thy good name by false reports or tale-bearing; if he encroach on thy rights, or be any way injurious to thee in thy estate; if he be guilty of any of those trespasses that are specified, Lev. vi. 2, 3; if he transgress the laws of justice, charity, or relative duties; these are trespasses against us, and often happen among Christ's disciples, and sometimes, for want of prudence, are of very mischievous consequence. Now observe what is the rule prescribed in this case,

1. *Go, and tell him his fault between thee and him alone.* Let this be compared with, and explained by, Lev. xix. 17, *Thou shalt not hate thy brother in thy heart.* This agrees with Prov. xxv. 8, 9, "*Go not forth hastily to strive,* but *debate thy cause with thy neighbour himself,* argue it calmly and amicably; and *if he shall hear thee,* well and good, *thou hast gained thy brother,* there is an end of the controversy, and it is a happy end; let no more be said of it, but let the falling out of friends be the renewing of friendship."

2. "*If he will not hear thee,* if he will not own himself in a fault, nor come to an agreement, yet do not despair, but try what he will say to it, if thou take *one or two more,* not only to be witnesses of what passes, but to reason the case further with him; he will be the more likely to hearken to them because they are disinterested; and if reason will rule him, the word of reason in the mouth of two or three witnesses will be better spoken to him and more regarded by him, and perhaps it will influence him to acknowledge his error, and to say, *I repent.*"

3. "If *he shall neglect to hear them,* and will not refer the matter to their arbitration, then *tell it to the church,* to the ministers, elders, or other officers, or the most considerable persons in the congregation you belong to, make them the referees to accommodate the matter, and do not presently appeal to the magistrate, or fetch a writ for him."

4. "If he will not *hear the church,* will not stand to their award, but persists in the wrong he has done thee, and proceeds to do thee further wrong, *let him be to thee as a heathen man, and a publican*; take the benefit of the law against him, but let that always be the last remedy."

II. Let us apply it to scandalous sins, which are an offence to the little ones, of bad example to those that are weak and pliable, and of great grief to those that are weak and timorous. Now let us see,

(1) What is the case supposed? *If thy brother trespass against thee.* [1] "The offender is a brother, one that is in Christian communion, that is baptized." Note, Church discipline is for church members. *Them that are without God judges,* 1 Cor. v. 12, 13. When any trespass is done against us, it is good to remember that the trespasser is a brother, which furnishes us with a qualifying consideration. [2] "The offence is a trespass against thee; if thy brother sin against thee (so the word is), if he do anything which is offensive to thee as a Christian."

(2) What is to be done in this case. We have here,

[1] The rules prescribed, *vv.* 15–17. Proceed in this method:

First, "*Go and tell him his fault between thee and him alone.* Do not stay till he comes to thee, but go to him, as the physician visits the patient, and the shepherd goes after the lost sheep."

"Tell him his fault, argue the case with him" (so the word signifies); "and do it with reason and argument, not with passion." Christian reproof is an ordinance of Christ for the bringing of sinners to repentance, and must be managed as an ordinance. "Let the reproof be private, between thee and him alone; that it may appear you seek not his reproach, but his repentance."

"If he shall hear thee"—that is, "heed thee—if he be wrought upon by the reproof, it is well, *thou hast gained thy brother*; thou hast helped to save him from sin and ruin, and it will be thy credit and comfort," Jam. v. 19, 20.

Secondly, If that doth not prevail, *then take with thee one or two more, v. 16.*

"Take with thee one or two more; 1. To assist thee; they may speak some pertinent convincing word which thou didst not think of, and may manage the matter with more prudence than thou didst." 2. "To affect him; he will be the more likely to be humbled for his fault, when he sees it witnessed against by *two or three*." Deut. xix. 15. 3. "To be witnesses of his conduct, in case the matter should afterward be brought before the church."

Thirdly, If he neglect to hear them, and will not be humbled, *then tell it to the church, v. 17.* The church must receive the complaints of the offended, and rebuke the sins of the offenders, and judge between them, after an impartial enquiry made into the merits of the cause.

Fourthly, "If he neglect to hear the church, if he slight the admonition, and will neither be ashamed of his faults, nor amend them, *let him be unto thee as a heathen man and a publican*; let him be cast out of the communion of the church, secluded from special ordinances, degraded from the dignity of a church member, let him be put under disgrace, and let the members of the society be warned to withdraw from him, that he may be ashamed of his sin, and they may not be infected by it, or made chargeable with it." Christ has appointed this method for the vindicating of the church's honour, the preserving of its purity, and the conviction and reformation of those that are scandalous. But when by this he is humbled and reclaimed, he must be welcomed into communion again, and all shall be well.

[2] Here is a warrant signed for the ratification of all the church's proceedings according to these rules, *v.* 18. What was said before to Peter is here said to all the disciples, and in them to all the faithful office-bearers in the church, to the world's end. While ministers preach the word of Christ faithfully, and in their government of the church strictly adhere to his laws they may be assured that he will own them, and stand by them, and will ratify what they say and do, so that it shall be taken as said and done by himself.

Now it is a great honour which Christ here puts upon the church, that he will condescend not only to take cognizance of their sentences, but to confirm them; and in the following verses we have two things laid down as the ground of this.

(1) God's readiness to answer the church's prayers (*v. 19*); *If two of you shall agree* harmoniously, *touching anything that they shall ask, it shall be done for them.* Apply this,

[1] In general, to all the requests of the faithful praying seed of Jacob; they shall not *seek God's face in vain.* Many promises we have in scripture of a gracious answer to the prayers of faith, but this gives a particular encouragement to joint-prayer; "the requests which two of you agree in, much more which many agree in."

[2] In particular, to those requests that are put up to God about binding and loosing; to which this promise seems more especially to refer. Observe, *First,* That the power of church discipline is not here lodged in the hand of a single person, but two, at least, are supposed to be concerned in it. *Secondly,* It is good to see those who have the management of church discipline, agreeing in it. Heats and animosities, among those whose work it is to remove offences, will be the greatest offence of all. *Thirdly,* Prayer must evermore go along with church discipline. Pass no sentence, which you cannot in faith ask God to confirm.

(2) The presence of Christ in the assemblies of Christians, *v.* 20. Every believer has the presence of Christ with him; but the promise here refers to the meetings where two or three are gathered in his name, not only for discipline, but for religious worship, or any act of Christian communion. Assemblies of Christians for holy purposes are hereby appointed, directed, and encouraged.

[1] They are hereby appointed; the church of Christ in the world exists most visibly in religious assemblies; it is the will of Christ that these should be set up, and kept up, for the honour of God, the edification of men, and the preserving of a face of religion upon the world.

[2] They are hereby directed to gather together in Christ's name. In the exercise of church discipline, they must *come together in the name of Christ,* 1 Cor. v. 4. That name gives to what they do an authority on earth, and an acceptableness in heaven.

[3] They are hereby encouraged with an assurance of the presence of Christ; *There am I in the midst of them.* By his common presence he is in all places, as God; but this is a promise of his special presence. Where his saints are, his sanctuary is, and there he will dwell; it is his rest (Ps. cxxxii. 14), it is his walk (Rev. ii. 1); he is in the midst of them, to quicken and strengthen them, to refresh and comfort them, as the sun in the midst of the universe. He is in the midst of them, that is, in their hearts; it is a spiritual presence, the presence of Christ's Spirit with their spirits, that is here intended.

And though there be but two or three, the smallest number that can be, yet, if Christ make one among them, who is the principal one, their meeting is as honourable and comfortable as if they were two or three thousand.

PERSONAL WRONGS
(*vv*. 1–35)

This part of the discourse concerning offences is certainly to be understood of personal wrongs, which it is in our power to forgive. Now observe,

I. Peter's question concerning this matter (*v.* 21); *Lord, how oft shall my brother trespass against me, and I forgive him?* Will it suffice to do it *seven times*?

1. He takes it for granted that he must forgive; Christ had before taught his disciples this lesson (*ch*. vi. 14, 15), and Peter has not forgotten it.

2. He thinks it a great matter to forgive till seven times; he means not *seven times a day*, as Christ said (Luke xvii. 4), but seven times in his life; supposing that if a man had any way abused him seven times, though he were ever so desirous to be reconciled, he might then abandon his society, and have no more to do with him. Perhaps Peter had an eye to Prov. xxiv. 16. *A just man falleth seven times*; or to the mention of *three transgressions*, and *four*, which God would no more pass by, Amos ii. 1.

II. Christ's direct answer to Peter's question; *I say unto thee, Until seven times* (he never intended to set up any such bounds), but, *Until seventy times seven*; a certain number for an indefinite one, but a great one. God multiplies his pardons, and so should we, Ps. lxxviii. 38, 40. It intimates that we should make it our constant practice to forgive injuries, and should accustom ourselves to it till it becomes habitual.

III. A further discourse of our Saviour's, by way of parable, to show the necessity of forgiving the injuries that are done to us. The parable is a comment upon the fifth petition of the Lord's prayer, *Forgive us our trespasses, as we forgive them that trespass against us.*

There are three things in the parable.

1. The master's wonderful clemency to his servant who was indebted to him; he forgave him ten thousand talents, out of pure compassion to him, *vv*. 23–27. Where observe,

(1) Every sin we commit is a debt to God; not like a debt to an equal, contracted by buying or borrowing, but to a superior; like a debt to a prince when a recognizance is forfeited, or a penalty incurred by a breach of the law or a breach of the peace; like the debt of a servant to his master, by withholding his service, wasting his lord's goods, breaking his indentures, and incurring the penalty. We are all debtors; we owe satisfaction, and are liable to the process of the law.

(2) There is an account kept of these debts, and we must shortly be reckoned with for them.

(3) The debt of sin is a very great debt; and some are more in debt, by reason of sin, than others. When he *began to reckon*, one of the first defaulters appeared to owe *ten thousand talents*. There is no evading the enquiries of divine justice; your sin will be sure to find you out.

(4) The debt of sin is so great,

that we are not able to pay it; *He had not to pay*. Sinners are insolvent debtors; the scripture, *which concludeth all under sin*, is a statute of bankruptcy against us all.

(5) If God should deal with us in strict justice; we should be condemned as insolvent debtors, and God might exact the debt by glorifying himself in our utter ruin.

(6) Convinced sinners cannot but humble themselves before God, and pray for mercy. *The servant*, under this charge, and this doom, *fell down* at the feet of his royal master, *and worshipped him*; or, as some copies read it, *he besought him*; his address was very submissive and very importunate; *Have patience with me, and I will pay thee all, v.* 26. This servant doth not deny the debt, nor seek evasions, nor go about to abscond.

But, [1] He begs time; *Have patience with me*. Patience and forbearance are a great favour, but it is folly to think that these alone will save us; reprieves are not pardons.

[2] He promises payment; *Have patience* awhile, *and I will pay thee all.* He that *had nothing to pay* with (*v.* 25) fancied he could pay *all*. See how close pride sticks, even to awakened sinners; they are convinced, but not humbled.

(7) The God of infinite mercy is very ready, out of pure compassion, to forgive the sins of those that humble themselves before him (*v.* 27); *The lord of that servant*, when he might justly have ruined him, mercifully released him; and, since he could not be

satisfied by the payment of the debt, he would be glorified by the pardon of it. The servant's prayer was, *Have patience with me*; the master's grant is a discharge in full.

2. The servant's unreasonable severity toward his fellow-servant, notwithstanding his lord's clemency toward him, *vv.* 28–30.

See here, (1) How small the debt was, how very small, compared with the *ten thousand talents* which his lord forgave him; *He owed him a hundred pence*, about three pounds and half a crown of our money. Note, Offences done to men are nothing to those which are committed against God.

(2) How severe the demand was; *He laid hands on him, and took him by the throat.*

(3) How submissive the debtor was; *His fellow servant*, though his equal, yet knowing how much he lay at his mercy, *fell down at his feet*, and humbled himself to him for this trifling debt, as much as he did to his lord for that great debt; for *the borrower is servant to the lender*, Prov. xxii. 7. The poor man's request is, *Have patience with me*; he honestly confesses the debt, and puts not his creditor to the charge of proving it, only begs time.

(4) How implacable and furious the creditor was (*v.* 30); *He would not have patience with him*, would not hearken to his fair promise, but without mercy *cast him into prison.*

(5) How much concerned the rest of the servants were; *They were very sorry* (*v.* 31), sorry for the creditor's cruelty, and for the

debtor's calamity. Note, The sins and sufferings of our fellow-servants should be matter of grief and trouble to us.

(6) How notice of it was brought to the master; *They came, and told their lord*. They durst not reprove their fellow-servant for it, he was so unreasonable and outrageous; but they went to their lord, and besought him to appear for the oppressed against the oppressor.

3. The master's just resentment of the cruelty his servant was guilty of. Now observe here,

(1) How he reproved his servant's cruelty (*vv.* 32, 33); *O thou wicked servant*. Note, Unmercifulness is wickedness, it is great wickedness. [1] He upbraids him with the mercy he had found with his master; *I forgave thee all that debt*. Those that will use God's favours, shall never be upbraided with them, but those that abuse them, may expect it, *ch.* xi. 20. [2] He thence shows him the obligation he was under to be merciful to his fellow-servant; *Shouldst not thou also have had compassion on thy fellow-servant, even as I had pity on thee?* Note, It is justly expected, that such as have received mercy, should show mercy. He shows him, *First*, That he should have been more compassionate to the distress of his fellow servant, because he had himself experienced the same distress. *Secondly*, That he should have been more conformable to the example of his master's tenderness, having himself experienced it, so much to his advantage.

(2) How he revoked his pardon

and cancelled the acquittance, so that the judgment against him revived (*v.* 34); *He delivered him to the tormentors, till he should pay all that was due unto him*. See how the punishment answers the sin; he that would not forgive shall not be forgiven; *He delivered him to the tormentors*; the utmost he could do to his fellow servant was but to cast him into prison, but he was himself delivered to the tormentors.

Lastly, Here is the application of the whole parable (*v.* 35); *So likewise shall my heavenly Father do also unto you*. The title Christ here gives to God was made use of, *v.* 19, in a comfortable promise; *It shall be done for them of my Father which is in heaven*; here it is made use of in a terrible threatening. If God's governing be fatherly, it follows thence, that it is righteous, but it does not therefore follow that it is not rigorous, or that under his government we must not be kept in awe by the fear of the divine wrath. When we pray to God as *our Father in heaven*, we are taught to ask for the *forgiveness of sins, as we forgive our debtors*. Observe here,

1. The duty of forgiving; we must *from our hearts* forgive.

2. The danger of not forgiving; *So shall your heavenly Father do*. (1) This is not intended to teach us that God reverses his pardons to any, but that he denies them to those that are unqualified for them, according to the tenour of the gospel. (2) This is intended to teach us, that *they shall have judgment without mercy, that have*

showed no mercy, Jam. ii. 13. It is indispensably necessary to pardon and peace, that we not only *do justly*, but *love mercy*.

CHAPTER NINETEEN

DIVORCE (*vv*. 1–12)

We have here the law of Christ in the case of divorce, occasioned, as some other declarations of his will, by a dispute with *the Pharisees*. Observe here,

I. The case proposed by the Pharisees (*v*. 3); *Is it lawful for a man to put away his wife?* This they asked, tempting him, not desiring to be taught by him. Some time ago, he had, in Galilee, declared his mind in this matter, against that which was the common practice (*ch*. v. 31, 32); and if he would, in like manner, declare himself now against divorce, they would make use of it for the prejudicing and incensing of the people of this country against him, who would look with a jealous eye upon one that attempted to cut them short in a liberty they were fond of.

Their question is, *Whether a man may put away his wife for every cause*. That it might be done for some cause, even for that of fornication, was granted; but may it be done, as now it commonly was done, by the looser sort of people, for every cause; for any cause that a man shall think fit to assign, though ever so frivolous; upon every dislike or displeasure?

II. Christ's answer to this question; though it was proposed to tempt him, yet, being a case of conscience, and a weighty one, he gave a full answer to it, not a direct one, but an effectual one; laying down such principles as undeniably prove that such arbitrary divorces as were then in use, which made the matrimonial bond so very precarious, were by no means lawful. Christ himself would not give the rule without a reason, nor lay down his judgment without scripture proof to support it. Now his argument is this; "If husband and wife are by the will and appointment of God joined together in the strictest and closest union, then they are not to be lightly, and upon every occasion, separated; if the knot be sacred, it cannot be easily untied." Now, to prove that there is such a union between man and wife, he urges three things.

1. The creation of Adam and Eve. *Ye have read* (but have not considered) *that he which made them at the beginning, made them male and female*, Gen. i. 27; v. 2. *He made them male and female*, one female for one male; so that Adam could not divorce his wife, and take another, for there was no other to take. It likewise intimated an inseparable union between them; Eve was a rib out of Adam's side, so that he could not put her away, but he must put away a piece of himself, and contradict the manifest indications of her creation.

2. The fundamental law of marriage, which is, that *a man shall leave father and mother, and shall cleave to his wife*, v. 5. The relation between husband and wife is nearer than that between parents and children; now, if the

filial relation may not easily be violated, much less may the marriage union be broken. See here the power of a divine institution, that the result of it is a union stronger than that which results from the highest obligations of nature.

3. The nature of the marriage contract; it is a union of persons; *They twain shall be one flesh,* so that (*v.* 6) *they are no more twain, but one flesh.* A man's children are pieces of himself, but his wife is himself. They two shall be one, therefore there must be but one wife, for God made but one Eve for one Adam, Mal. ii. 15.

From hence he infers, *What God hath joined together, let not man put asunder.* Note (1) Husband and wife are of God's joining together; *he hath yoked them together,* so the word is, and it is very significant. God himself instituted the relation between husband and wife in the state of innocence. Marriage and the sabbath are the most ancient of divine ordinances. Though marriage be not peculiar to the church, but common to the world, yet, being stamped with a divine institution, and here ratified by our Lord Jesus, it ought to be managed *after a godly sort, and sanctified by the word of God, and prayer.* It is a general rule that man must not go about to *put asunder what God hath joined together.*

III. An objection started by the Pharisees against this; an objection not destitute of colour and plausibility (*v.* 7); "*Why did Moses command to give a writing of divorcement,* in case a man did put away his wife?"

IV. Christ's answer to this objection, in which,

1. He rectifies their mistake concerning the law of Moses; they called it a *command,* Christ calls it but a *permission,* a *toleration.*

But Christ tells them there was a reason for this toleration, not at all to their credit; *It was because of the hardness of your hearts,* that you were permitted to *put away your wives.* Moses complained of the people of Israel in his time, that *their hearts were hardened* (Deut. ix. 6; xxxi. 27), hardened against God; this is here meant of their being hardened against their relations; they were generally violent and outrageous, which way soever they took, both in their appetites and in their passions; and therefore if they had not been allowed to put away their wives, when they had conceived a dislike of them, they would have used them cruelly, would have beaten and abused them, and perhaps have murdered them.

2. He reduces them to the original institution; *But from the beginning it was not so.* Truth was from the beginning; we must therefore enquire for *the good old way* (Jer. vi. 16), and must reform, not by later patterns, but by ancient rules.

3. He settles the point by an express law; *I say unto you* (*v.* 9); and it agrees with what he said before (*ch.* v. 32); there it was said in preaching, here in dispute, but it is the same, for Christ is constant to himself. Now, in both these places,

(1) He allows divorce, in case of

adultery; the reason of the law against divorce being this, *They two shall be one flesh.* If the wife play the harlot, and make herself one flesh with an adulterer, the reason of the law ceases, and so does the law. By the law of Moses adultery was punished with death, Deut. xxii. 22. Now our Saviour mitigates the rigour of that, and appoints divorce to be the penalty.

(2) He disallows it in all other cases; *Whosoever puts away his wife, except for fornication, and marries another, commits adultery.* This is a direct answer to their query, that it is not lawful. In this, as in other things, gospel times are *times of reformation*, Heb. ix. 10. The law of Christ tends to reinstate man in his primitive integrity; the law of love, conjugal love, is no new commandment, but was from the beginning.

V. Here is a suggestion of the disciples against this law of Christ (v. 10); *If the case of the man be so with his wife, it is better not to marry.* It seems, the disciples themselves were loth to give up the liberty of divorce, thinking it a good expedient for preserving comfort in the married state; and therefore, like sullen children, if they have not what they would have, they will throw away what they have.

VI. Christ's answer to this suggestion (vv. 11, 12), in which,

1. He allows it good for some not to marry; *He that is able to receive it, let him receive it.* Christ allowed what the disciples said, *It is good not to marry*; not as an objection against the prohibition of divorce, as they intended it, but as giving them a rule (perhaps no less unpleasing to them), that they who have the gift of continence, and are not under any necessity of marrying, do best if they continue single (1 Cor. vii. 1); for they that are unmarried have opportunity, if they have but a heart, to care more *for the things of the Lord, how they may please the Lord* (1 Cor. vii. 32–34), being less encumbered with the cares of this life, and having a greater vacancy of thought and time to mind better things. The increase of grace is better than the increase of the family, and fellowship with the Father and with his Son Jesus Christ is to be preferred before any other fellowship.

2. He disallows it, as utterly mischievous, to forbid marriage, because *all men cannot receive this saying*; indeed few can, and therefore the crosses of the married state must be borne, rather than that men should run themselves into temptation, to avoid them; *better marry than burn.*

Christ here speaks of a twofold unaptness to marriage.

(1) That which is a calamity by the providence of God; such as those labour under who are born eunuchs, or made so by men, who, being incapable of answering one great end of marriage, ought not to marry.

(2) That which is a virtue by the grace of God; such is theirs who *have made themselves eunuchs for the kingdom of heaven's sake.* This is meant of an unaptness for marriage, not in body (which some, through mistake of this scripture,

have foolishly and wickedly brought upon themselves), but in mind. Those have thus made themselves eunuchs who have attained a holy indifference to all the delights of the married state, have a fixed resolution, in the strength of God's grace, wholly to abstain from them; and by fasting, and other instances of mortification, have subdued all desires toward them.

Now, [1] This affection to the single state must be given of God; for none can receive it, *save they to whom it is given.*

[2] The single state must be chosen for the kingdom of heaven's sake. Note, That condition is best for us, and to be chosen and stuck to accordingly, which is best for our souls, and tends most to the preparing of us for, and the preserving of us to, the kingdom of heaven.

CHILDREN WELCOME
(*vv.* 13–15)

We have here the welcome which Christ gave to some little children that were brought to him. Observe,

I. The faith of those that brought them. How many they were, that were brought, we are not told; but they were so little as to be taken up in arms, a year old, it may be, or two at most.

They desired that he would put his hands on them, and pray. Imposition of hands was a ceremony used especially in paternal blessings; Jacob used it when he blessed and adopted the sons of Joseph, Gen. xlviii. 14. It intimates something of love and familiarity

mixed with power and authority, and bespeaks an efficacy in the blessing. Whom Christ prays for in heaven, he *puts his hand upon* by his Spirit. Note, (1) Little children may be brought to Christ as needing, and being capable of receiving, blessings from him, and having an interest in his intercession. (2) Therefore they should be brought to him. We cannot do better for our children than to commit them to the Lord Jesus, to be wrought upon, and prayed for, by him. We can but beg a blessing for them, it is Christ only that can command the blessing.

II. The fault of the disciples in rebuking them. They discountenanced the address as vain and frivolous, and reproved them that made it as impertinent and troublesome.

III. The favour of our Lord Jesus. See how he carried it here.

1. He rebuked the disciples (*v.* 14); *Suffer little children, and forbid them not*; and he rectifies the mistake they went upon, *Of such is the kingdom of heaven.* Note, (1) The children of believing parents belong to the kingdom of heaven, and are members of the visible church. (2) That for this reason they are welcome to Christ, who is ready to entertain those who, when they cannot come themselves, are brought to him.

2. *He received the little children,* and did as he was desired; *he laid his hands on them,* that is, *he blessed them.* The strongest believer lives not so much by apprehending Christ as by being apprehended of him (Phil. iii. 12), not so much by knowing God as by

being known of him (Gal. iv. 9); and this the least child is capable of. If they cannot stretch out their hands to Christ, yet he can lay his hands on them, and so make them his own, and own them for his own.

THE RICH RULER (*vv.* 16–22)

Here is an account of what passed between Christ and a hopeful young gentleman that addressed himself to him upon a serious errand; he is said to be a *young man* (*v.* 20); and I called him a *gentleman*, not only because he had great possessions, but because he was a ruler (Luke xviii. 18), a magistrate, a justice of peace in his country; it is probable that he had abilities beyond his years, else his youth would have debarred him from the magistracy.

Now concerning this young gentleman, we are told how fair he bid for heaven and came short.

I. How fair he bid for heaven, and how kindly and tenderly Christ treated him, in favour to good beginnings. Here is,

1. The gentleman's serious address to Jesus Christ (*v.* 16); *Good Master, what good thing shall I do, that I may have eternal life?* Not a better question could be asked, nor more gravely.

(1) He gives Christ an honourable title, *Good Master*. It signifies not a ruling, but a teaching Master. His calling him *Master*, bespeaks his submissiveness, and willingness to be taught; and *good Master*, his affection and peculiar respect to the Teacher, like that of Nicodemus, *Thou art a Teacher come from God*.

(2) He comes to him upon an errand of importance (none could be more so), and he came not to tempt him, but sincerely desiring to be taught by him. His question is, *What good thing shall I do, that I may have eternal life?* By this it appears, [1] That he had a firm belief of eternal life; he was no Sadducee. [2] That he was concerned to make it sure to himself that he should live eternally, and was desirous of that life more than of any of the delights of this life. [3] That he was sensible something must be done, some good thing, for the attainment of this happiness. [4] That he was, or at least thought himself, willing to do what was to be done for the obtaining of this eternal life.

2. The encouragement that Jesus Christ gave to this address. It is not his manner to send any away without an answer, that come to him on such an errand, for nothing pleases him more, *v.* 17. In his answer,

(1) He tenderly assists his faith; for, doubtless, he did not mean it for a reproof, when he said, *Why callest thou me good?* But he would seem to find that faith in what he said, when he called him *good Master*, which the gentleman perhaps was not conscious to himself of; he intended no more than to own and honour him as a good man, but Christ would lead him to own and honour him as a good God; for *there is none good but one, that is God*.

(2) He plainly directs his practice, in answer to his question. He started that thought of his being good, and therefore God, but did

not stay upon it, lest he should seem to divert from, and so to drop, the main question, as many do in needless disputes and strifes of words. Now Christ's answer is, in short, this, *If thou wilt enter into life, keep the commandments.*

[1] The end proposed is, entering into life. The young man, in his question, spoke of eternal life. Christ, in his answer, speaks of *life*; to teach us, that eternal life is the only true life. He desired to know how he might *have* eternal life; Christ tells him how he might *enter into it*: we *have* it by the merit of Christ, a mystery which was not as yet fully revealed, and therefore Christ waives that; but the way of *entering into it*, is, by obedience, and Christ directs us in that. By the former we *make* our title, by this, as by our evidence, we *prove* it; it is *by adding to faith virtue*, that an *entrance* (the word here used) is *ministered to us into the everlasting kingdom*, 2 Pet. i. 5, 11.

[2] The way prescribed is, keeping the commandments. Note, Keeping the commandments of God, according as they are revealed and made known to us, is the only way to life and salvation; and sincerity herein is accepted through Christ as our gospel perfection, provision being made of pardon, upon repentance, wherein we come short.

[3] At his further instance and request, he mentions some particular commandments which he must keep (*vv.* 18, 19); *The young man saith unto him, Which?* In answer to this, Christ specifies several, especially the commandments of the second table; not as if the first were of less account, but, 1. Because they that now sat in Moses's seat, either wholly neglected, or greatly corrupted, these precepts in their preaching. 2. Because he would teach him, and us all, that moral honesty is a necessary branch of true Christianity, and to be minded accordingly.

II. See here how he came short, though he bid thus fair, and wherein he failed; he failed by two things.

1. By pride, and a vain conceit of his own merit and strength; this is the ruin of thousands, who keep themselves miserable by fancying themselves happy. When Christ told him what commandments he must keep, he answered very scornfully, *All these things have I kept from my youth up, v.* 20.

It was commendable also, that he desired to know further what his duty was; *What lack I yet?* He was convinced that he wanted something to fill up his works before God, and was therefore desirous to know it, because, if he was not mistaken in himself, he was willing to do it. Having not yet attained, he thus seemed to press forward. And he applied himself to Christ, whose doctrine was supposed to improve and perfect the Mosaic institution. He desired to know what were the peculiar precepts of his religion, that he might have all that was in them to polish and accomplish him. Who could bid fairer?

But, (2) Even in this that he said, he discovered his ignorance and folly. [1] Taking the law in its spiritual sense, as Christ expounded it, no doubt, in many things he had offended against all these commands. Had he been acquainted with the extent and spiritual meaning of the law, instead of saying, *All these have I kept; what lack I yet?* he would have said, with shame and sorrow, "All these have I broken, what shall I do to get my sins pardoned?" [2] Take it how you will, what he said savoured of pride and vainglory, and had in it too much of that boasting which is excluded by the law of faith (Rom. iii. 27), and which excludes from justification, Luke xviii. 11, 14.

2. He came short by an inordinate love of the world, and his enjoyments in it. This was the fatal rock on which he split. Observe,

(1) How he was tried in this matter (*v.* 21); *Jesus said unto him, If thou wilt be perfect, go and sell that thou hast.* Christ waived the matter of his boasted obedience to the law, and let that drop, because this would be a more effectual way of discovering him than a dispute of the extent of the law. What Christ said to him, he thus far said to us all, that, if we would approve ourselves Christians indeed, and would be found at last the heirs of eternal life, we must do these two things:

[1] We must practically prefer the heavenly treasures before all the wealth and riches in this world. That glory must have the preeminence in our judgment and esteem before this glory. Now, as an evidence of this, *First,* We must dispose of what we have in this world, for the honour of God, and

in his service: "*Sell that thou hast, and give to the poor.* If the occasions of charity be very pressing, sell thy possessions that thou mayest have to give to them that need; as the first Christians did, with an eye to this precept, Acts iv. 34." A gracious contempt of the world, and compassion of the poor and afflicted ones in it, are in all a necessary condition of salvation.

Christ knew that covetousness was the sin that did most easily beset this young man, that, though what he had he had got honestly, yet he could not cheerfully part with it, and by this he discovered his insincerity. *Secondly,* We must depend upon what we hope for in the other world as an abundant recompence for all we have left, or lost, or laid out, for God in this world; *Thou shalt have treasure in heaven.* We must, in the way of chargeable duty, trust God for a happiness out of sight, which will make us rich amends for all our expenses in God's service.

[2] We must devote ourselves entirely to the conduct and government of our Lord Jesus; *Come, and follow me.* To sell all, and give to the poor, will not serve, unless we come, and follow Christ. If I give all my goods to feed the poor, and have not love, it profits me nothing. Well, on these terms, and on no lower, is salvation to be had; and they are very easy and reasonable terms, and will appear so to those who are brought to be glad of it upon any terms.

(2) See how he was discovered. This touched him in a tender part (*v.* 22); *When he heard that*

saying, he went away sorrowful, for he had great possessions.

[1] He was a rich man, and loved his riches, and therefore went away. He did not like eternal life upon these terms. Note, *First*, Those who have much in the world are in the greatest temptation to love it, and to set their hearts upon it. *Secondly*, The reigning love of this world keeps many from Christ, who seem to have some good desires toward him.

Yet something of honesty there was in it, that, when he did not like the terms, he went away, and would not pretend to that, which he could not find in his heart to come up to the strictness of; since he could not be a complete Christian, he would not be a hypocrite.

[2] Yet he was a thinking man, and well-inclined, and therefore *went away sorrowful*. He had a leaning toward Christ, and was loth to part with him. Thus this man's wealth was *vexation of spirit* to him, then when it was his temptation. What then would the sorrow be afterward, when his possessions would be gone, and all hopes of eternal life gone too?

THE EYE OF THE NEEDLE
(*vv.* 23–30)

We have here Christ's discourse with his disciples upon occasion of the rich man's breaking with Christ.

I. Christ took occasion from thence to show the difficulty of the salvation of rich people, *vv.* 23–26.

1. That it is a very hard thing for a rich man to get to heaven, such a rich man as this here.

Now, (1) This is vehemently asserted by our Saviour, *vv.* 23, 24. He said this to his disciples, who were poor, and had but little in the world, to reconcile them to their condition with this, that the less they had of worldly wealth, the less hindrance they had in the way to heaven. This saying is ratified, *v.* 23. *Verily I say unto you.* He that has reason to know what the way to heaven is, for he has laid it open, he tells us that this is one of the greatest difficulties in that way. It is repeated, *v.* 24. *Again I say unto you.* Thus he speaks once, yea, twice, that which man is loth to perceive and more loth to believe.

[1] He saith that it is a hard thing for a rich man to be a good Christian, and to be saved; to enter into the kingdom of heaven, either here or hereafter. Rich people have a great account to make up for their estates, their interest, their time, and their opportunities of doing and getting good, above others. It must be a great measure of divine grace that will enable a man to break through these difficulties.

[2] He saith that the conversion and salvation of a rich man is so extremely difficult, that *it is easier for a camel to go through the eye of a needle, v.* 24. This is a proverbial expression, denoting a difficulty altogether unconquerable by the art and power of man; nothing less than the almighty grace of God will enable a rich man to get over this difficulty. *First*, The way to heaven is very

fitly compared to a *needle's eye*, which is hard to hit and hard to get through. *Secondly*, A rich man is fitly compared to a *camel*, a beast of burden, for he has riches, as a camel has his load, he carries it, but it is another's, he has it from others, spends it for others, and must shortly leave it to others.

(2) This truth is very much wondered at, and scarcely credited by the disciples (*v.* 25); *They were exceedingly amazed, saying, Who then can be saved?* Many surprising truths Christ told them, which they were astonished at, and knew not what to make of; this was one, but their weakness was the cause of their wonder. Since so many are rich, and have great possessions, and so many more would be rich, and are well affected to great possessions; who can be saved? If riches are a hindrance to rich people, are not pride and luxury incident to those that are not rich, and as dangerous to them? and who then can get to heaven? This is a good reason why rich people should strive against the stream.

2. That, though it be hard, yet it is not impossible, for the rich to be saved (*v.* 26); *Jesus beheld them,* turned and looked wistfully upon his disciples, to shame them out of their fond conceit of the advantages rich people had in spiritual things. He beheld them as men that had got over this difficulty, and were in a fair way for heaven, and the more so because poor in this world; *and he said unto them, with men this is impossible, but with God all things are possible.* This is a great truth in general, that God is able to do that which quite exceeds all created

power; that nothing is too hard for God, Gen. xviii. 14; Numb. xi. 23. When men are at a loss, God is not, for his power is infinite and irresistible; but this truth is here applied, (1) To the salvation of any. *Who can be saved?* say the disciples. None, saith Christ, by any created power. *With men this is impossible:* the wisdom of man would soon be nonplussed in contriving, and the power of man baffled in effecting, the salvation of a soul. But *with God all things are possible.* (2) To the salvation of rich people especially; it is impossible with men that such should be saved, but with God even this is possible; not that rich people should be saved *in* their worldliness, but that they should be saved *from* it.

II. Peter took occasion from hence to enquire what *they* should get by it, who had come up to these terms, upon which this young man broke with Christ, and had left all to follow him, *vv.* 27, &c. We have here the disciples' expectations from Christ, and his promises to them.

1. We have their expectations from Christ; Peter, in the name of the rest, signifies that they depended upon him for something considerable in lieu of what they had left for him; *Behold, we have forsaken all, and have followed thee; what shall we have therefore?* Christ had promised the young man, that, if he would sell all, and come and follow him, he should *have treasure in heaven*; now Peter desires to know,

(1) Whether they had sufficiently come up to those terms: they had not sold all (for they had many of

them wives and families to provide for), but they had *forsaken all*; they had not given it to the poor, but they had renounced it as far as it might be any way a hindrance to them in serving Christ.

(2) Whether therefore they might expect *that treasure* which the young man shall have if he will sell all. "Lord," saith Peter, "shall *we* have it, who have left all?"

2. We have here Christ's promises to them, and to all others that tread in the steps of their faith and obedience.

(1) To his immediate followers, *v.* 28. They had signalized their respect to him, as the first that followed him, and to them he promises not only *treasure*, but *honour*, in heaven; and here they have a grant or patent for it from him who is the fountain of honour in that kingdom; *Ye which have followed me in the regeneration shall sit upon twelve thrones.*

[1] The *preamble* to the patent, or the *consideration* of the grant, which, as usual, is a recital of their services; "You have followed me in the regeneration, and therefore this will I do for you." The time of Christ's appearing in this world was a time of regeneration, of reformation (Heb. ix. 10), when old things began to pass away, and all things to look new. The disciples had followed Christ when the church was yet in the embryo state, when few did; and therefore on them he will put particular marks of honour.

[2] The *date* of their honour, which fixes the time when it should commence; not immediately from the day of the date of *these presents*, no, they must continue a while in obscurity, as they were. But *when the Son of man shall sit in the throne of his glory*; and to this some refer that, *in the regeneration*; "You who now have followed me, shall, in the regeneration, be thus dignified." Christ's second coming will be a regeneration, when there shall be *new heavens, and a new earth, and the restitution of all things.* All that partake of the regeneration in grace (John iii. 3) shall partake of the regeneration in glory; for as grace is the first resurrection (Rev. xx. 6), so glory is the second regeneration.

[3] The honour itself hereby granted; *Ye also shall sit upon twelve thrones, judging the twelve tribes of Israel.*

The general intendment of this promise is, to show the glory and dignity reserved for the saints in heaven, which will be an abundant recompence for the disgrace they suffered here in Christ's cause. There are higher degrees of glory for those that have done and suffered most. The apostles in this world were hurried and tossed, there they shall sit down at rest and ease; here *bonds, and afflictions, and deaths, did abide them*, but there they *shall sit on thrones of glory*; here they were dragged to the bar, there they shall be advanced to the bench; here the twelve tribes of Israel trampled upon them, there they shall tremble before them. And will not this be recompence enough to make up all their losses and expenses for Christ? Luke xxii. 29.

[4] The ratification of this grant; it is firm, it is inviolably immutably sure; for Christ hath said, "*Verily I say unto you, I the Amen, the*

faithful Witness, who am empowered to make this grant, I have said it, and it cannot be disannulled."

(2) Here is a promise to all others that should in like manner leave all to follow Christ. It was not peculiar to the apostles, to be thus preferred, but *this honour have all his saints*. Christ will take care they shall none of them lose by him (*v.* 29); *Every one that has forsaken* anything for Christ, *shall receive*.

CHAPTER TWENTY

THE VINEYARD (*vv.* 1–16)

This parable of the labourers in the vineyard is intended,

I. To represent to us *the kingdom of heaven* (*v.* 1), that is, the way and method of the gospel dispensation.

II. In particular, to represent to us that concerning the kingdom of heaven, which he had said in the close of the foregoing chapter, that *many that are first shall be last, and the last, first*; with which this parable is connected; that truth, having in it a seeming contradiction, needed further explanation.

Nothing was more a mystery in the gospel dispensation than the rejection of the Jews and the calling in of the Gentiles; so the apostle speaks of it (Eph. iii. 3–6); that the Gentiles should be fellow-heirs: nor was any thing more provoking to the Jews than the intimation of it. Now this seems to be the principal scope of this parable, to show that the Jews should be first called into the vineyard, and many of them should come at the call; but, at length, the gospel should be preached to the Gentiles, and they

should receive it, and be admitted to equal privileges and advantages with the Jews; should be *fellow-citizens with the saints*, which the Jews, even those of them that believed, would be very much disgusted at, but without reason.

But the parable may be applied more generally, and shows us, 1. That God is debtor to no man; a great truth, which the contents in our Bible give as the scope of this parable. 2. That many who begin last, and promise little in religion, sometimes, by the blessing of God, arrive at greater attainments in knowledge, grace, and usefulness, than others whose entrance was more early, and who promised fairer. Thus *many that are last, shall be first*. Some make it a caution to the disciples, who had boasted of their timely and zealous embracing of Christ; they had left all to follow him; but let them look to it, that they keep up their zeal; let them press forward and persevere; else their good beginnings will avail them little; they that seemed to be *first*, would be *last*. Sometimes those that are converted later in their lives, outstrip those that are converted earlier. Paul was *as one born out of due time, yet came not behind the chiefest of the apostles*, and outdid those that were in Christ before him. Something of affinity there is between this parable and that of the prodigal son, where he that returned from his wandering, was as dear to his father as he was, that never went astray; *first and last alike*. 3. That *the recompence of reward* will be given to the saints, not according to the time of their conversion, but according to the preparations for it by grace in this world; not according to the seniority (as Gen. xliii. 33), but *according to the measure of the stature of the fulness of Christ.* Christ had promised the apostles, who followed him *in the regeneration,* at the beginning of the gospel dispensation, great glory (*ch.* xix. 38); but he now tells them that those who are in like manner faithful to him, even in the latter end of the world, shall have the same reward, shall *sit with Christ on his throne,* as well as the apostles, Rev. ii. 26–iii. 21. Sufferers for Christ in the latter days, shall have the same reward with the martyrs and confessors of the primitive times, though they are more celebrated; and faithful ministers now, the same with the first fathers.

Here is the application of the parable (*v.* 16), in that observation which occasioned it (*ch.* xix. 30); *So the first shall be last, and the last first.* There were many that followed Christ now in the regeneration, when the gospel kingdom was first set up, and these Jewish converts seemed to have got the start of others; but Christ, to obviate and silence their boasting, here tells them,

1. That they might possibly be outstripped by their successors in profession, and, though they were before others in profession, might be found inferior to them in knowledge, grace, and holiness. The Gentile church, which was as yet unborn, the Gentile world, which as yet stood *idle in the market-place,* would produce greater numbers of eminent, useful Christians, than were found among the Jews. More and more excellent shall be *the children of the desolate than those of the married wife,* Isa. liv. 1. Who knows but that the church, in its old age, may be more fat and flourishing than ever, to show that the Lord is upright? Though primitive Christianity had more of the purity and power of that holy religion than is to be found in the degenerate age wherein we live, yet what *labourers* may be *sent into the vineyard in the eleventh hour of the* church's *day,* in the Philadelphian period, and what plentiful effusions of the Spirit may then be, above what has been yet, who can tell?

2. That they had reason to fear, lest they themselves should be found hypocrites at last; for *many are called but few chosen.* This is applied to the Jews (*ch.* xxii. 14); it was so then, it is too true still; many are called with a common call, that are not chosen with a saving choice. All that are chosen from eternity, are effectually called, *in the fulness of time* (Rom. viii. 30), so that in making our effectual calling sure we *make sure our election* (2 Pet. i. 10); but it is not so as to the outward call; *many are called,* and yet refuse (Prov. i. 24), nay, as they are called *to* God, so they go *from* him (Hos. xi. 2, 7), by which it appears that they were not chosen, for *the election will obtain,* Rom. xi. 7. Note, There are but few *chosen* Christians, in comparison with the many that are only *called* Christians; it therefore highly concerns us to build our hope for heaven upon the rock of an eternal choice, and not upon the sand of an external call; and we should fear

lest we be found but seeming Christians, and so should really come short; nay, lest we be found blemished Christians, and so should *seem to come short*, Heb. iv. 1.

AMBITION CORRECTED
(*vv.* 17–28)

This is the third time that Christ gave his disciples notice of his approaching sufferings; he was now going up to Jerusalem to celebrate the passover, and to offer up himself the great Passover; both must be done at Jerusalem: there *the passover must be kept* (Deut. xii. 5), and there a prophet must perish, because there the great sanhedrim sat, who were judges in that case, Luke xiii. 33.

There follows the request of the two disciples to Christ, and the rectifying of the mistake upon which that was grounded, *vv.* 20–23. The sons of Zebedee were James and John, two of the first three of Christ's disciples; Peter and they were his favourites; John was the disciple whom Jesus loved; yet none were so often reproved as they; whom Christ loves best he reproves most, Rev. iii. 19.

I. Here is the ambitious address they made to Christ—that they might sit, the one on his right hand, and the other on his left, in his kingdom, *vv.* 20, 21. It was a great degree of faith, that they were confident of his kingdom, though now he appeared in meanness; but a great degree of ignorance, that they still expected a temporal kingdom, with worldly pomp and power, when Christ had so often told them

of sufferings and self-denial. Now observe,

1. There was policy in the management of this address, that they put their mother on to present it, that it might be looked upon as her request, and not theirs. Though proud people think well of themselves, they would not be thought to do so, and therefore affect nothing more than *a show of humility* (Col. ii. 18), and others must be put on to court that honour for them, which they are ashamed to court for themselves.

2. There was pride at the bottom of it, a proud conceit of their own merit, a proud contempt of their brethren, and a proud desire of honour and preferment; pride is a sin that most easily besets us, and which it is hard to get clear of. It is a holy ambition to strive to excel others in grace and holiness; but it is a sinful ambition to covet to exceed others in pomp and grandeur.

II. Christ's answer to this address (*vv.* 22, 23), directed not to the mother, but to the sons that set her on. Christ's answer is very mild; they were overtaken in the fault of ambition, but Christ *restored them with the spirit of meekness*. Observe,

1. How he reproved the ignorance and error of their petition; *Ye know not what ye ask.* (1) They were much in the dark concerning the kingdom they had their eye upon; they dreamed of a temporal kingdom, whereas Christ's kingdom is not of this world. They knew not what it was to sit on his right hand, and on his left; they talked of it as blind men do of colours. (2) They were much in the dark concerning

the way to that kingdom. *They know not what they ask*, who ask for the end, but overlook the means, and so put asunder what God has joined together. The disciples thought, when they had left what little *all* they had for Christ, and had gone about the country awhile preaching the gospel of the kingdom, all their service and sufferings were over, and it was now time to ask, *What shall we have?* As if nothing were now to be looked for but crowns and garlands; whereas there were far greater hardships and difficulties before them than they had yet met with. They imagined their warfare was accomplished when it was scarcely begun.

2. How he repressed the vanity and ambition of their request.

(1) He leads them to the thoughts of their sufferings, which they were not so mindful of as they ought to have been.

Observe, [1] How fairly he puts the matter to them, concerning these difficulties (*v.* 22); "You would stand candidates for the first post of honour in the kingdom; but *are you able to drink of the cup that I shall drink of?* You talk of what great things you must have when you have done your work; but are you able to hold out to the end of it? Put the matter seriously to yourselves. These same two disciples once knew not what manner of spirit they were of, when they were disturbed with anger, Luke ix. 55; and now they were not aware what was amiss in their spirits when they were lifted up with ambition. Christ sees that pride in us which we discern not in ourselves.

Note, *First*, That to suffer for

Christ is *to drink of a cup*, and *to be baptized with a baptism*. In this description of sufferings, 1. It is true, that affliction doth abound. It is supposed to be a bitter cup, that is drunk of, wormwood and gall, those waters of a full cup, that are wrung out to God's people (Ps. lxxiii. 10); a cup of trembling indeed, but not of fire and brimstone, the portion of the cup of wicked men, Ps. xi. 6. It is supposed to be a baptism, a washing with the waters of affliction; some are dipped in them, the waters compass them about even to the soul (Jonah ii. 5); others have but a sprinkling of them; both are baptisms, some are overwhelmed in them, as in a deluge, others ill wet, as in a sharp shower. But, 2. Even in this, *consolation doth more abound*. It is but a cup, not an ocean; it is but a draught, bitter perhaps, but we shall see the bottom of it; it is a cup in the hand of a Father (John xviii. 11); and it is full of mixture, Ps. lxxv. 8. It is but a baptism; if dipped, that is the worst of it, not drowned; perplexed, but not in despair.

Secondly, It is to drink of the same cup that Christ drank of, and to be baptized with the same baptism that he was baptized with. Christ is beforehand with us in suffering, and in that as in other things left us an example.

Thirdly, It is good for us to be often putting it to ourselves, whether we are able to drink of this cup, and to be baptized with this baptism. We must expect suffering, and not look upon it as a hard thing to suffer well and as becomes us. Are we able to suffer cheerfully, and in the worst of times still to hold fast our integrity? The truth is, Religion, if it be worth any thing, is worth every thing; but it is worth little, if it be not worth suffering for. Now let us sit down, and count the cost of dying for Christ rather than denying him, and ask, Can we take him upon these terms?

[2] See how boldly they engage for themselves; they said, *We are able*, in hopes of sitting on his right hand, and on his left; but at the same time they fondly hoped that they should never be tried. As before they knew not what they asked, so now they knew not what they answered. *We are able*; they would have done well to put in, "*Lord, by thy strength*, and *in thy grace, we are able*, otherwise we are not." But the same that was Peter's temptation, to be confident of his own sufficiency, and presume upon his own strength, was here the temptation of James and John; and it is a sin we are all prone to. They knew not what Christ's cup was, nor what his baptism, and therefore they were thus bold in promising for themselves. But those are commonly most confident, that are least acquainted with the cross.

[3] See how plainly and positively their sufferings are here foretold (v. 23); *Ye shall drink of my cup*. Sufferings foreseen will be the more easily borne, especially if looked upon under a right notion, as drinking of his cup, and being baptized with his baptism. Christ began in suffering for us, and expects we should pledge him, in suffering for him. Christ will have us know the worst, that we may make the best of our way to heaven; *Ye shall drink*; that is, ye shall suffer. James drank the bloody cup first of all the apostles, Acts xii. 2. John, though at last he died in his bed, if we may credit the ecclesiastical historians, yet often drank of this bitter cup, as when he was banished into the isle of Patmos (Rev. i. 9), and when (as they say) at Ephesus he was put into a cauldron of boiling oil, but was miraculously preserved. He was, as the rest of the apostles, in deaths often. He took the cup, offered himself to the baptism, and it was accepted.

(2) He leaves them in the dark about the degrees of their glory. To carry them cheerfully through their sufferings, it was enough to be assured that they should have *a place in his kingdom*. The lowest seat in heaven is an abundant recompence for the greatest sufferings on earth. But as to the preferments there, it was not fit there should be any intimation given for whom they were intended; for the infirmity of their present state could not bear such a discovery with any evenness; "*To sit on my right hand and on my left is not mine to give*, and therefore it is not for you to ask it or to know it; *but it shall be given to them for whom it is prepared of my Father*."

III. Here are the reproof and instruction which Christ gave to the other ten disciples for their displeasure at the request of James and John. He had much to bear with in them all, they were so weak in knowledge and grace, yet he bore their manners.

1. The fret that the ten disciples were in (v. 24). *They were moved*

with indignation against the two brethren; not because they were desirous to be preferred, which was their sin, and for which Christ was displeased with them, but because they were desirous to be preferred *before them*, which was a reflection upon them.

2. The check that Christ gave them, which was very gentle, rather by way of instruction what they should be, than by way of reprehension for what they were.

He called them unto him, which intimates great tenderness and familiarity. What he had to say concerned both the two disciples and the ten, and therefore he will have them all together. And he tells them, that, whereas they were asking which of them should have dominion in a temporal kingdom, there was really no such dominion reserved for any of them. For,

(1) They must not be *like the princes of the Gentiles*. Principality doth no more become ministers than Gentilism doth Christians.

Observe, [1] What is the way of the princes of the Gentiles (*v.* 25); to *exercise dominion and authority* over their subjects, and (if they can but win the upper hand with a strong hand) over one another too.

[2] What is the will of Christ concerning his apostles and ministers, in this matter.

First, "*It shall not be so among you.* The constitution of the spiritual kingdom is quite different from this. You are to teach the subjects of this kingdom, to instruct and beseech them, to counsel and comfort them, to take pains with them, and suffer with them, not to exercise dominion or

authority over them; you are not to *lord it over God's heritage* (1 Pet. v. 3), but to labour in it."

Secondly, How then shall it be among the disciples of Christ? Something of greatness among them Christ himself had intimated, and here he explains it; "*He that will be great among you*, that *will be chief*, that would really be so, and would be found to be so at last, *let him be your minister, your servant*," *vv.* 26, 27. Here observe, 1. That it is the duty of Christ's disciples to serve one another, for mutual edification. This includes both humility and usefulness. 2. It is the dignity of Christ's disciples faithfully to discharge this duty. The way to be great and chief is to be humble and serviceable.

(2) They must be like the Master himself; and it is very fit that they should, that, while they were in the world, they should be as he was when he was in the world; for to both the present state is a state of humiliation, the crown and glory were reserved for both in the future state. Let them consider that the *Son of man came not to be ministered to, but to minister, and to give his life a ransom for many*, *v.* 28. Our Lord Jesus here sets himself before his disciples as a pattern of those two things before recommended, humility, and usefulness.

[1] Never was there such an example of humility and condescension as there was in the life of Christ, who came not to be *ministered unto, but to minister.*

[2] Never was there such an example of beneficence and usefulness as there was in the death of Christ, who *gave his life a ransom*

for many. He lived as a servant, and went about doing good; but he died as a sacrifice, and in that he did the greatest good of all.

Now this is a good reason why we should not strive for precedency, because the cross is our banner, and our Master's death is our life. It is a good reason why we should study to do good, and, in consideration of the love of Christ in dying for us, not hesitate *to lay down our lives for the brethren*, 1 John iii. 16. Ministers should be more forward than others to serve and suffer for the good of souls, as blessed Paul was, Acts xx. 24; Phil. ii. 17. The nearer we are all concerned in, and the more we are advantaged by, the humility and humiliation of Christ, the more ready and careful we should be to imitate it.

TWO BLIND MEN
(*vv.* 29–34)

We have here an account of the cure of two poor blind beggars; in which we may observe,

I. Their address to Christ, *vv.* 29, 30. And in this,

1. The circumstances of it are observable. It was as Christ and his disciples departed from Jericho; of that devoted place, which was rebuilt under a curse, Christ took his leave with this blessing, for he received gifts even for the rebellious. It was in the presence of *a great multitude that followed him*; Christ had a numerous, though not a pompous, attendance, and did good to them, though he did not take state to himself. Two blind men concurred in their request; for joint-prayer is pleasing to Christ,

ch. xviii. 19. These joint-sufferers were joint-suitors; being companions in the same tribulation, they were partners in the same supplication.

When they heard that Jesus passed by, they asked no further questions, who were with him, or whether he was in haste, but immediately *cried out*. Note, It is good to improve the present opportunity, to make the best of the price now in the hand, because, if once let slip, it may never return; these blind men did so, and did wisely; for we do not find that Christ ever came to Jericho again. *Now is the accepted time*.

2. The address itself is more observable; *Have mercy on us, O Lord, thou Son of David*, repeated again, *v.* 31. Four things are recommended to us for an example in this address; for, though the eye of the body was dark, the eye of the mind was enlightened concerning truth, duty, and interest.

(1) Here is an example of importunity in prayer. They cried out as men in earnest; men in want are earnest, of course.

(2) Of humility in prayer; in that word, *Have mercy on us*, not specifying the favour, or prescribing what, much less pleading merit, but casting themselves upon, and referring themselves cheerfully to, the Mediator's mercy, in what way he pleases; "Only have mercy." This is that which our hearts must be upon, when we come to *the throne of grace, that we may find mercy*, Heb. iv. 16; Ps. cxxx. 7.

(3) Of faith in prayer; in the title they gave to Christ, which was in the nature of a plea; *O Lord, thou*

Son of David; they confess that *Jesus Christ is Lord*, and therefore had authority to command deliverance for them. Surely it was by the Holy Ghost that they called Christ *Lord*, 1 Cor. xii. 3.

(4) Of perseverance in prayer, notwithstanding discouragement. *The multitude rebuked them*, as noisy, clamorous, and impertinent, and bid them *hold their peace*, and not disturb the Master, who perhaps at first himself seemed not to regard them. In following Christ with our prayers, we must expect to meet with hindrances and manifold discouragements from within and from without, something or other that bids us hold our peace. Such rebukes are permitted, that faith and fervency, patience and perseverance, may be tried.

II. The answer of Christ to this address of theirs. The multitude rebuked them; but Christ encouraged them.

1. *He stood still, and called them, v.* 32. He was now going up to Jerusalem, and was straitened till his work there was accomplished; and yet he stood still to cure these blind men.

2. He enquired further into their case; *What will ye that I shall do unto you?* This implies, (1) A very fair offer; "Here I am; let me know what you would have, and you shall have it." What would we more? He is able to do for us, and as willing as he is able; *Ask, and it shall be given you.* (2) A condition annexed to this offer, which is a very easy and reasonable one—that they should tell him what they would have him do for them. One would think this a strange question, anyone might tell

what they would have. Christ knew well enough; but he would know it from them, whether they begged only for an alms, as from a common person, or for a cure, as from the Messiah.

They soon made known their request to him, such a one as they never made to anyone else; *Lord, that our eyes may be opened.*

3. He cured them; when he encouraged them to seek him, he did not say, *Seek in vain*. What he did was an instance,

(1) Of his pity; *He had compassion on them*. Misery is the object of mercy. They that are poor and blind are *wretched and miserable* (Rev. iii. 17), and the objects of compassion. It was the tender mercy of our God, that gave light and sight to them that sat in darkness, Luke i. 78, 79.

(2) Of his power; *He that formed the eye, can he not heal it?* Yes, he can, he did, he did it easily, he touched their eyes; he did it effectually, *Immediately their eyes received sight*. Thus he not only proved that he was sent of God, but showed on what errand he was sent —to give sight to those that are spiritually blind, *to turn them from darkness to light.*

Lastly, These blind men, when they had received sight, *followed him*. Note, None follow Christ blindfold. He first by his grace opens men's eyes, and so draws their hearts after him.

CHAPTER TWENTY-ONE

PALM SUNDAY (*vv.* 1–11)

All the four evangelists take notice of this passage of Christ's *riding in triumph into Jerusalem,* five days before his death. The passover was on the fourteenth day of the month, and this was the tenth; on which day the law appointed that the paschal lamb should be taken up (Exod. xii. 3), and set apart for that service; on that day therefore Christ our Passover, who was to be sacrificed for us, was publicly showed. So that this was the prelude to his passion. He had lodged at Bethany, a village not far from Jerusalem, for some time; at a supper there the night before Mary had *anointed his feet,* John xii. 3. But, as is usual with ambassadors, he deferred his public entry till some time after his arrival.

Now here we have,

I. The provision that was made for this solemnity; and it was very poor and ordinary, and such as bespoke his *kingdom* to be *not this world.* But in this public appearance,

1. The preparation was sudden and offhand. For his glory in the other world, and ours with him, preparation was made before the foundation of the world, for that was the glory his heart was upon; his glory in this world he was dead to, and therefore, though he had it in prospect, did not forecast for it, but took what came next.

2. It was very mean. He sent only for an ass and her colt, *v.* 2. Yet some think that he had herein an eye to the custom in Israel for the judges to ride upon white asses (Judg. v. 10), and their sons on ass-colts, Judg. xii. 14. And Christ would thus enter, not as a Conqueror, but as the Judge of Israel, *who for judgment came into this world.*

3. It was not his own, but borrowed. Though he had not a house of his own, yet, one would think, like some wayfaring men that live upon their friends, he might have had an ass of his own, to carry him about; but for our sakes he became in all respects poor, 2 Cor. viii. 9.

The disciples who were sent to borrow this ass are directed to say, *The Lord has need of him.* In the borrowing of this ass,

(1) We have an instance of Christ's knowledge. Though the thing was altogether contingent, yet Christ could tell his disciples where they should find an ass tied, and a colt with her. His omniscience extends itself to the meanest of his creatures; asses and their colts, and their being bound or loosed.

(2) We have an instance of his power over the spirits of men. The hearts of the meanest subjects, as well as of kings, *are in the hand of the Lord. If any man say aught to you, ye shall say, The Lord hath need of him.*

(3) We have an example of justice and honesty, in not using the ass, though for so small a piece of service as riding the length of a street or two, without the owner's consent.

II. The prediction that was fulfilled in this, *vv.* 4, 5. Our Lord Jesus, in all that he did and suffered, had very much his eye upon this, *That the scriptures might be fulfilled.* This particularly which was written of him, Zech. ix. 9, where it ushers in a large prediction of the kingdom of the Messiah, *Tell ye the daughter of Sion, Behold, thy*

King cometh, must be accomplished. Now observe here,

1. How the coming of Christ is foretold; *Tell ye the daughter of Sion*, the church, the holy mountain, *Behold, thy King cometh unto thee.*

2. How his coming is described. When a king comes, something great and magnificent is expected, especially when he comes to take possession of his kingdom. The King, the Lord of hosts, was seen *upon a throne, high and lifted up* (Isa. vi. 1); but there is nothing of that here; *Behold, he cometh to thee, meek, and sitting upon an ass.* When Christ would appear in his glory, it is in his meekness, not in his majesty.

(1) His temper is very mild. He comes not in wrath to take vengeance, but in mercy to work salvation.

(2) As an evidence of this, his appearance is very mean, sitting upon an ass, a creature made not for state, but service, not for battles, but for burdens; slow in its motions, but sure, and safe, and constant. The foretelling of this so long before, and the care taken that it should be exactly fulfilled, intimate it to have a peculiar significancy, for the encouragement of poor souls to apply themselves to Christ.

III. The procession itself, which was answerable to the preparation, both being destitute of worldly pomp, and yet both accompanied with a spiritual power.

Observe, 1. His equipage; *The disciples did as Jesus commanded them* (*v.* 6); they went to fetch the ass and the colt, not doubting but

to find them, and to find the owner willing to lend them.

2. His retinue; there was nothing in this stately or magnificent. Sion's King comes to Sion, and the daughter of Sion was told of his coming long before; yet he is not attended by the gentlemen of the country, nor met by the magistrates of the city in their formalities as one might have expected; he should have had the keys of the city presented to him, and should have been conducted with all possible convenience to *the thrones of judgment, the thrones of the house of David*; but here is nothing of all this; yet he has his attendants, *a very great multitude*; they were only the common people, the mob (the *rabble* we should have been apt to call them), that graced the solemnity of Christ's triumph, and none but such.

Now, concerning this great multitude, we are here told,

(1) What they did; according to the best of their capacity, they studied to do honour to Christ. [1] *They spread their garments in the way*, that he might ride upon them. When Jehu was proclaimed king, the captains put their garments under him, in token of their subjection to him. [2] *Others cut down branches from the trees, and strewed them in the way*, as they used to do at the feast of tabernacles, in token of liberty, victory, and joy; for the mystery of that feast is particularly spoken of as belonging to gospel times, Zech, xiv. 16.

(2) What they said; *They that went before, and they that followed*, were in the same tune; both those

that gave notice of his coming, and those that attended him with their applauses, *cried, saying, Hosanna to the Son of David, v.* 9. When they carried branches about at the feast of tabernacles, they were wont to cry *Hosanna*, and from thence to call their bundles of branches their *hosannas. Hosanna* signifies, *Save now, we beseech thee*; referring to Ps. cxviii. 25, 26, where the Messiah is prophesied of as the *Head-stone of the corner, though the builders refused him*; and all his loyal subjects are brought in triumphing with him, and attending him with hearty good wishes to the prosperity of all his enterprises. *Hosanna to the Son of David* is, "This we do in honour of the Son of David."

3. We have here his entertainment in Jerusalem (*v.* 10); *When he was come into Jerusalem, all the city was moved*; every one took notice of him.

Upon this commotion we are further told,

(1) What the citizens said; *Who is this?* [1] They were, it seems, ignorant concerning Christ. Though he was *the Glory of his people Israel*, yet *Israel knew him not*; though he had distinguished himself by the many miracles he wrought among them, yet *the daughters of Jerusalem* knew him not *from another beloved*, Cant. v. 9. The Holy One unknown in the holy city! [2] Yet they were inquisitive concerning him. Who is this that is thus cried up, and comes with so much observation? *Who is this King of glory*, that demands admission into our hearts? Ps. xxiv. 8; Isa. lxiii. 1.

(2) How the multitude answered them; *This is Jesus, v.* 11. The multitude were better acquainted with Christ than the great ones. *The voice of the people*, is sometimes *the voice of God*. Now, in the account they give of him, [1] They were right in calling him *the Prophet, that great Prophet.* [2] Yet they missed it, in saying he was *of Nazareth*; and it helped to confirm some in their prejudices against him.

CLEANSING THE TEMPLE
(*vv.* 12–17)

When Christ came into Jerusalem, he did not go up to the court or the palace, though he came in as a King, but *into the temple*; for his kingdom is spiritual, and *not of this world*; it is in holy things that he rules, in the temple of God that he exercises authority. Now, what did he do there?

I. Thence he drove the buyers and sellers. Abuses must first be purged out, and the plants not of God's planting be plucked up, before that which is right can be established. The great Redeemer appears as a great Reformer, that turns away ungodliness, Rom. xi. 26. Here we are told,

1. What he did (*v.* 12); *He cast out all them that sold and bought*; he had done this once before (John ii. 14, 15), but there was occasion to do it again.

(1) The abuse was, buying and selling, and changing money, in the temple. Note, Lawful things, ill timed and ill placed, may become sinful things. That which was decent enough in another place, and not only lawful, but laudable,

on another day, *defiles the sanctuary*, and *profanes the sabbath*.

(2) The purging out of this abuse. Christ *cast them out that sold*. He did it before *with a scourge of small cords* (John ii. 15); now he did it with a look, with a frown, with a word of command. This was the only act of regal authority and coercive power that Christ did in the days of his flesh; he began with it, John ii. and here ended with it.

2. What he said, to justify himself, and to convict them (*v.* 13); *It is written*. Note, In the reformation of the church, the eye must be upon the scripture, and that must be adhered to as the rule, the pattern in the mount; and we must go no further than we can justify ourselves with, *It is written*.

(1) He shows, from a scripture prophecy, what the temple should be, and was designed to be; *My house shall be called the house of prayer*; which is quoted from Isa. lvi. 7.

(2) He shows, from a scripture reproof, how they had abused the temple, and perverted the intention of it; *Ye have made it a den of thieves*. This is quoted from Jer. vii. 11, *Is this house become a den of robbers in your eyes?* The priests lived, and lived plentifully, upon the altar; but, not content with that, they found other ways and means to squeeze money out of the people; and therefore Christ here calls them *thieves*, for they exacted that which did not belong to them.

II. There, in the temple, *he healed the blind and the lame*, *v.* 14. When he had driven the buyers and sellers out of the temple, he invited the blind and lame into it; for *he fills the hungry with good things, but the rich he sends empty away*.

There also he silenced the offence which the chief priests and scribes took at the acclamations with which he was attended, *vv.* 15, 16. They that should have been most forward to give him honour, were his worst enemies.

1. They were inwardly vexed at the wonderful things that he did; they could not deny them to be true miracles, and therefore were cut to the heart with indignation at them, as Acts iv. 16; 33.

2. They openly quarrelled at the children's hosannas; they thought that hereby an honour was given him, which did not belong to him, and that it looked like ostentation.

Just now we had Christ preferring the blind and the lame before the buyers and sellers; now here we have him (*v.* 16), taking part with the children against priests and scribes.

Observe, (1) The children were in the temple, perhaps playing there; no wonder, when the rulers make it a *market-place*, that the children make it a place of pastime; but we are willing to hope that many of them were worshipping there.

(2) They were there *crying Hosanna to the Son of David*. This they learned from those that were grown up. Note, *Hosanna to the Son of David* well becomes the mouths of little children, who should learn young the language of Canaan.

(3) Our Lord Jesus not only allowed it, but was very well pleased with it, and quoted a scripture which was fulfilled in it (Ps. viii. 2), or, at least, may be accommodated to it; *Out of the*

mouth of babes and sucklings thou has perfected praise.

Lastly, Christ, having thus silenced them, forsook them, *v.* 17. *He left them*, in prudence, lest they should now have seized him before his hour was come; in justice, because they had forfeited the favour of his presence.

THE BARREN FIG TREE
(*vv.* 19–22)

(1) This cursing of the barren fig-tree, represents the state of hypocrites in general; and so it teaches us, [1] That the fruit of fig-trees may justly be expected from those that have the leaves. Christ looks for the power of religion from those that make profession of it; the favour of it from those that have the show of it; grapes from the vineyard that is planted in a fruitful hill: he hungers after it, his soul *desires the first ripe fruits.* [2] Christ's just expectations from flourishing professors are often frustrated and disappointed; he comes to many, seeking fruit, and finds leaves only, and he discovers it. Many have a name to live, and are not alive indeed; dote on the form of godliness, and yet deny the power of it. [3] The sin of barrenness is justly punished with the curse and plague of barrenness; *Let no fruit grow on thee henceforward for ever.* As one of the chiefest blessings, and which was the first, is, *Be fruitful*; so one of the saddest curses is, *Be no more fruitful.* Thus the sin of hypocrites is made their punishment; they *would* not do good, and therefore they *shall* do none; he that is fruitless, let him be fruitless still,

and lose his honour and comfort. [4] A false and hypocritical profession commonly withers in this world, and it is the effect of Christ's curse; the fig-tree that had no fruit, soon lost its leaves.

(2) It represents the state of the nation and people of the Jews in particular; they were a fig-tree planted in Christ's way, as a church. Now observe, [1] The disappointment they gave to our Lord Jesus. He came among them, expecting to find some fruit, something that would be pleasing to him; he hungered after it; not that he *desired a gift*, he needed it not, *but fruit that might abound to a good account.* But his expectations were frustrated; he found nothing but leaves; they called *Abraham their father, but did not do the works of Abraham*; they professed themselves expectants of the promised Messiah, but, when he came, they did not receive and entertain him. [2] The doom he passed upon them, *that never any fruit should grow upon them*, or be gathered from them, as a church or as a people, *from henceforward for ever.*

2. See the *power* of Christ.

(1) The disciples admired the effect of Christ's curse (*v.* 20); *They marvelled*; no power could do it but his, *who spake, and it was done.* They marvelled at the suddenness of the thing; *How soon is the fig-tree withered away!*

(2) Christ empowered them by faith to do the like (*vv.* 21, 22); as he said (John xiv. 12), *Greater works than these shall ye do.*

Observe, [1] The description of this wonder-working faith; *If ye have faith, and doubt not.* Note,

Doubting of the power and promise of God is the great thing that spoils the efficacy and success of faith.

[2] The power and prevalence of it expressed figuratively; *If ye shall say to this mountain*, meaning the mount of Olives, *Be thou removed, it shall be done.* This is a proverbial expression; intimating that we are to believe that nothing is impossible with God, and therefore that what he has promised shall certainly be performed, though to us it seem impossible.

[3] The way and means of exercising this faith, and of doing that which is to be done by it; *All things whatsoever ye shall ask in prayer, believing, ye shall receive.* Faith is the soul, prayer is the body; both together make a complete man for any service.

THE BAPTISM OF JOHN
(vv. 23–27)

Our Lord Jesus (like St. Paul after him) preached his gospel *with much contention*; his first appearance was in a dispute with *the doctors in the temple, when he was twelve years old*; and here, just before he died, we have him engaged in controversy. Observe,

I. As soon as he came into Jerusalem, he went to the temple, though he had been affronted there the day before, was there in the midst of enemies and in the mouth of danger.

II. In the temple he was teaching; he had called it *a house of prayer* (*v.* 13), and here we have him preaching there.

III. When Christ was teaching the people, the priests and elders came upon him, and challenged

him to produce his orders; the hand of Satan was in this, to hinder him in his work.

Now, in this dispute with them, we may observe,

1. How he was assaulted by their insolent demand; *By what authority doest thou these things, and who gave thee this authority?* Had they duly considered his miracles, and the power by which he wrought them, they needed not to have asked this question; but they must have something to say for the shelter of an obstinate infidelity. Christ had often said it, and proved it beyond contradiction, and Nicodemus, a master in Israel, had owned it, that he was *a teacher sent of God* (John iii. 2); yet, at this time of day, when that point had been so fully cleared and settled, they come to him with this question.

2. How he answered this demand with another, which would help them to answer it themselves (*vv.* 24, 25); *I also will ask you one thing.* He declined giving them a direct answer, lest they should take advantage against him; but answers them with a question.

Now this question is concerning John's baptism, here put for his whole ministry, preaching as well as baptizing; "Was this *from heaven, or of men?* One of the two it must be; either what he did was of his own head, or he was sent of God to do it." This question was not at all shuffling, to evade theirs; but,

(1) If they answered this question, it would answer theirs: should they say, against their consciences, that John's baptism was of men, yet it would be easy to answer, *John did no miracle* (John x. 41),

Christ did many; but should they say, as they could not but own, that John's baptism was from heaven (which was supposed in the questions sent him, John i. 21, *Art thou Elias, or that prophet?*) then their demand was answered, for he bare testimony to Christ.

(2) If they refused to answer it, that would be a good reason why he should not offer proofs of his authority to men that were obstinately prejudiced against the strongest conviction; it was but to cast pearls before swine.

3. How they were hereby baffled and run aground; they knew the truth, but would not own it, and so were taken in the snare they laid for our Lord Jesus. Observe,

(1) How *they reasoned with themselves*, not concerning the merits of the cause, what proofs there were of the divine original of John's baptism; no, their care was, how to make their part good against Christ.

(2) How they replied to our Saviour, and so dropped the question. They fairly confessed *We cannot tell*; that is, "We will not; *We never knew.*" The more shame for them, while they pretended to be leaders of the people, and by their office were obliged to take cognizance of such things; when they would not confess their knowledge, they were constrained to confess their ignorance. And observe, by the way, when they said, *We cannot tell*, they told a lie, for they knew that John's baptism was of God.

Thus Christ avoided the snare they laid for him, and justified himself in refusing to gratify them;

Neither tell I you by what authority I do these things. If they be so wicked and base as either not to believe, or not to confess, that the baptism of John was from heaven (though it obliged to repentance, that great duty, and sealed the kingdom of God at hand, that great promise), they were not fit to be discoursed with concerning Christ's authority; for men of such a disposition could not be convinced of the truth, nay, they could not but be provoked by it, and therefore *he that is thus ignorant, let him be ignorant still.*

TWO SONS (*vv.* 28–32)

In these verses, we have the parable of the *two sons* sent to work in the vineyard, the scope of which is to show that they who knew not John's baptism to be of God, were shamed even by the publicans and harlots, who knew it, and owned it. Here is,

I. The parable itself, which represents two sorts of persons; some that prove better than they promise, represented by the first of those sons; others that promise better than they prove, represented by the second.

1. They had both one and the same father, which signifies that God is a common Father to all mankind.

2. They had both the same command given them; *Son, go work today in my vineyard.* It is the command of a Father, which carries with it both authority and affection.

3. Their conduct was very different.

(1) One of the sons did better than he said, proved better than he

promised. His answer was bad, but his actions were good.

Note, There are many who in the beginning are wicked and wilful, and very unpromising, who afterward repent and mend, and come to something. Observe, When he repented, he went; that was the *fruit meet for repentance*. The only evidence of our repentance for our former resistance, is, immediately to comply, and set to work; and then what is past, shall be pardoned, and all shall be well.

(2) The other son said better than he did, promised better than he proved; his answer was good but his actions bad.

Many· with their mouth show much love, but their heart goes another way. They had a good mind to be religious, but they met with something to be done, that was too hard, or something to be parted with, that was too dear, and so their purposes are to no purpose. Buds and blossoms are not fruit.

II. A general appeal upon the parable; *Whether of them twain did the will of his father?* v. 31. They both had their faults, but the question is, Which was the better of the two, and the less faulty? And it was soon resolved; the first, because his actions were better than his words, and his latter end than his beginning.

III. A particular application of it to the matter in hand, vv. 31, 32. The primary scope of the parable is, to show how the publicans and harlots, who never talked of the Messiah and his kingdom, yet entertained the doctrine, and submitted to the discipline, of John the Baptist, his forerunner, when the priests and elders, who were big with expectations of the Messiah, and seemed very ready to go into his measures, slighted John the Baptist, and ran counter to the designs of his mission. But it has a further reach; the Gentiles were *sometimes disobedient*, had been long so, children of disobedience, like the elder son (Tit. iii. 3, 4); yet, when the gospel was preached to them, they became obedient to the faith; whereas the Jews who said, *I go, sir*, promised fair (Exod. xxiv. 7; Josh. xxiv. 24); yet went not; they did but flatter God with their mouth, Ps. lxxviii. 36.

THE WICKED HUSBANDMEN
(vv. 33–46)

This parable plainly sets forth the sin and ruin of the Jewish nation; they and their leaders are the husbandmen here; and what is spoken for conviction to them, is spoken for caution to all that enjoy the privileges of the visible church, not to be high-minded, but fear.

I. We have here the privileges of the Jewish church, represented by the letting out of a vineyard to the husbandmen; they were as tenants holding by, from, and under, God the great Householder.

II. God's expectation of rent from these husbandmen, v. 34. It was a reasonable expectation; for *who plants a vineyard, and eats not of the fruit thereof?* Note, From those that enjoy church-privileges, both ministers and people, God looks for fruit accordingly. He did not demand more than they could make of it, but some fruit of that which he himself planted—an observance of the laws and statutes he gave them. What could have been done more reasonable? Israel was an empty vine, nay it was become the degenerate plant of a strange vine, and brought forth wild grapes.

III. The husbandmen's baseness in abusing the messengers that were sent to them.

1. When he sent them his servants, they abused them, though they represented the master himself, and spoke in his name. See here what hath all along been the lot of God's faithful messengers, more or less; (1) To suffer; *so persecuted they the prophets*, who were hated with a cruel hatred. (2) It has been their lot to suffer from their Master's own tenants; they were the husbandmen that treated them thus, the chief priests and elders that *sat in Moses's chair*, that professed religion and relation to God; these were the most bitter enemies of the Lord's prophets, that cast them out, and killed them, and said, *Let the Lord be glorified*, Isa. lxvi. 5. See Jer. xx. 1, 2; xxvi. 11.

Now see, [1] How God persevered in his goodness to them. He sent other servants, more than the first; though the first sped not, but were abused. He had sent them John the Baptist, and him they had beheaded; and yet he sent them his disciples, to prepare his way. O the riches of the patience and forbearance of God, in keeping up in his church a despised, persecuted ministry! [2] How they persisted in their wickedness. They *did unto them likewise*. One sin makes way for another of the same kind.

2. At length, he sent them his Son; we have seen God's goodness in sending, and their badness in abusing, the servants; but in the latter instance both these exceed themselves.

(1) Never did grace appear more gracious than in *sending the Son*. This was done *last of all*. Note, All the prophets were harbingers and forerunners to Christ. He was sent last; for if nothing else would work upon them, surely this would; it was therefore reserved for the *last expedient. Surely they will reverence my Son*, and therefore I will send him.

(2) Never did sin appear more sinful than in the abusing of him, which was now to be done in two or three days. Observe,

[1] How it was plotted (*v.* 38); *When they saw the Son:* when he came, whom the people owned and followed as the Messiah, who would either have the rent paid, or distrain for it; this touched their copyhold, and they were resolved to make one bold push for it, and to preserve their wealth and grandeur by taking *him* out of the way, who was the only hindrance of it, and rival with them. *This is the heir, come, let us kill him.*

[2] How this plot was executed, *v.* 39. While they were so set upon killing him, in pursuance of their design to secure their own pomp and power, and while he was so set upon dying, in pursuance of his design to subdue Satan, and save his chosen, no wonder if they soon *caught him, and slew him*, when his hour was come.

IV. Here is their doom read out of their own mouths, *vv.* 40, 41. He puts it to them, *When the Lord of the vineyard cometh, what will he do unto these husbandmen?*

1. Our Saviour, in his question, supposes that *the lord of the vineyard will come*, and reckon with them. God is the Lord of the vineyard; the property is his, and he will make *them* know it, who now *lord it over his heritage*, as if it were all their own. The Lord of the vineyard will come. Persecutors say in their hearts, He *delays his coming*, he *doth not see*, he *will not require*; but they shall find, though he bear long with them, he will not bear always.

2. They, in their answer, suppose that it will be a terrible reckoning; the crime appearing so very black, you may be sure.

(1) That he will *miserably destroy those wicked men*; it is destruction that is their doom. This was fulfilled upon the Jews, in that miserable destruction which was brought upon them by the Romans, and was completed about forty years after this; an unparalleled ruin, attended with all the most dismal aggravating circumstances. It will be fulfilled upon all that tread in the steps of their wickedness; hell is everlasting destruction, and it will be the most miserable destruction to them of all others, that have enjoyed the greatest share of church privileges, and have not improved them.

(2) That he will *let out his vineyard to other husbandmen*. The Jews imagined that no doubt *they were the people*, and wisdom and holiness must *die with them*; and if they were cut off, what would God do for a church in the world? But when God makes use of any to bear up his name, it is not because he

needs them, nor is he at all beholden to them.

V. The further illustration and application of this by Christ himself, telling them, in effect, that they had rightly judged.

1. He illustrates it by referring to a scripture fulfilled in this (*v.* 42); *Did ye never read in the scriptures?* The scripture he quotes is Ps. cxviii. 22, 23, the same context out of which the children fetched their hosannas. The same word yields matter of praise and comfort to Christ's friends and followers, which speaks conviction and terror to his enemies. Such a two-edged sword is the word of God. That scripture, the *Stone which the builders refused is become the headstone of the corner*, illustrates the preceding parable, especially that part of it which refers to Christ.

(1) The builders' rejecting of the stone is the same with the husbandmen's abusing of the son that was sent to them. The chief priests and the elders were the builders, had the oversight of the Jewish church, which was God's building: and they would not allow Christ a place in their building, would not admit his doctrine or laws into their constitution; they threw him aside as a despised broken vessel, a stone that would serve only for a stepping-stone, to be trampled upon.

(2) The advancing of this stone to be the head of the corner is the same with *letting out the vineyard to other husbandmen*. He who was rejected by the Jews was embraced by the Gentiles; and to that church where there is no difference of circumcision or uncircumcision, *Christ is all, and in all*. His authority

over the gospel church, and influence upon it, his ruling it as the Head, and uniting it as the Cornerstone, are the great tokens of his exhaltation.

(3) The hand of God was in all this; *This is the Lord's doing.* Even the rejecting of him by the Jewish builders was by the determinate counsel and foreknowledge of God; he permitted and overruled it; much more was his advancement to the Head of the corner; his right hand and his holy arm brought it about; it was God himself that *highly exalted him,* and gave him *a name above every name; and it is marvellous in our eyes.*

2. He applies it to them, and application is the life of preaching.

(1) He applies the sentence which they had passed (*v.* 41), and turns it upon themselves; not the former part of it, concerning the miserable destruction of the husbandmen (he could not bear to speak of that), but the latter part, of *letting out the vineyard to others*; because though it looked black upon the Jews, it spoke good to the Gentiles.

(2) He applies the scripture which he had quoted (*v.* 42), to their terror, *v.* 44. This *Stone,* which the *builders refused, is set for the fall of many in Israel*; and we have here the doom of two sorts of people, for whose fall it proves that Christ is set.

[1] Some, through ignorance, stumble at Christ in his estate of humiliation; when this Stone lies on the earth, where the builders threw it, they, through their blindness and carelessness, fall on it, fall over it, and *they shall be broken.*

[2] Others, through malice, oppose Christ, and bid defiance to him in his estate of exaltation, when this Stone is advanced to the head of the corner; and on them *it shall fall,* for they pull it on their own heads, as the Jews did by that challenge, *His blood be upon us and upon our children,* and *it will grind them to powder.*

Lastly, The entertainment which this discourse of Christ met with among the chief priests and elders, that heard his parables.

1. *They perceived that he spake of them* (*v.* 45), and that in what they said (*v.* 41) they had but read their own doom.

2. *They sought to lay hands on him.* Note, When those who hear the reproofs of the word, perceive that it speaks of them, if it do not do them a great deal of good, it will certainly do them a great deal of hurt.

3. They durst not do it, *for fear of the multitude, who took him for a prophet,* though not for the Messiah; this served to keep the Pharisees in awe. The fear of the people restrained them from speaking ill of John (*v.* 26), and here from doing ill to Christ.

CHAPTER TWENTY-TWO

THE WEDDING FEAST
(*vv.* 1–14)

We have here the parable of the guests invited to *the wedding-feast.* In this it is said (*v.* 1), *Jesus answered,* not to what his opposers *said* (for they were put to silence), but to what they *thought,* when they were wishing for an opportunity to *lay hands on him,* ch. xxi. 46.

I. Gospel preparations are here

represented by a feast which a king made *at the marriage of his son*; such is *the kingdom of heaven*, such the provision made for precious souls, in and by the new covenant. The *King* is God, *a great King, King of kings*. Now,

1. Here is *a marriage made for his son*. Christ is the Bridegroom, the church is the bride; the gospel-day is *the day of his espousals*, Cant. iii. 11.

2. Here is *a dinner prepared for this marriage, v.* 4. All the privileges of church-membership, and all the blessings of the new covenant, pardon of sin, the favour of God, peace of conscience, the promises of the gospel, and all the riches contained in them, access to the throne of grace, the comforts of the Spirit, and a well-grounded hope of eternal life. These are the preparations for this feast, a heaven upon earth now, and a heaven in heaven shortly.

II. Gospel calls and offers are represented by an invitation to this feast. Those that make a feast will have guests to grace the feast with. God's guests are the children of men. *Lord, what is man*, that he should be thus dignified! *The guests* that were first invited were the Jews; wherever the gospel is preached, this invitation is given; ministers are the *servants* that are sent to invite, Prov. ix. 4, 5.

Now, 1. The guests *are called, bidden* to the wedding. All that are within hearing of the joyful sound of the gospel, to them is the word of this invitation sent.

2. The guests are called upon; for in the gospel there are not only gracious proposals made, but gracious persuasives. *We persuade men, we beseech them in Christ's stead*, 2 Cor. v. 11, 20. One would think it had been enough to give men an intimation that they had leave to come, and should be welcome; but, because *the natural man discerns not*, and therefore desires not, *the things of the Spirit of God*, we are pressed to accept the call by the most powerful inducements, *drawn with the cords of a man, and all the bonds of love*.

III. The cold treatment which the gospel of Christ often meets with among the children of men, represented by the cold treatment that this message met with and the hot treatment that the messengers met with, in both which the king himself and the royal bridegroom are affronted. This reflects primarily upon the Jews, who rejected the counsel of God against themselves; but it looks further, to the contempt that would, by many in all ages, be put upon, and the opposition that would be given to, the gospel of Christ.

1. The message was basely slighted (*v.* 3); *They would not come*. Note, Making light of Christ, and of the great salvation wrought out by him, is the damning sin of the world. *They were careless*.

And the reason why *they made light of the marriage feast* was, because they had other things that they minded more, and had more mind to; *they went their ways, one to his farm, and another to his merchandise*. Note, The business and profit of worldly employments prove to many a great hindrance in closing with Christ: none turn their back on the feast, but with some plausible excuse or other, Luke xiv. 18.

2. The messengers were basely abused; *The remnant*, or the rest of them, that is, those who did not go to the *farms*, or *merchandise*, were neither husbandmen nor tradesmen, but ecclesiastics, *the scribes, and Pharisees, and chief priests*; these were the persecutors, these *took the servants, and treated them spitefully, and slew them.* The prophets and John the Baptist had been thus abused already, and the apostles and ministers of Christ must count upon the same.

IV. The utter ruin that was coming upon the Jewish church and nation is here represented by the revenge which the king, in wrath, took on these insolent recusants (*v.* 7); *He was wroth.* Now observe here,

1. What was the crying sin that brought the ruin; it was their being *murderers.* He does not say, he destroyed those *despisers of his call*, but *those murderers of his servants*; as if God were more jealous for the lives of his ministers than for the honour of his gospel.

2. What was the ruin itself, that was coming? *He sent forth his armies.* The Roman armies were his armies, of his raising, of his sending against the people of his wrath; and he *gave them a charge to tread them down*, Isa. x. 6. This points out very plainly the destruction of the Jews, and the burning of Jerusalem, by the Romans, forty years after this.

V. The replenishing of the church again, by the bringing in of the Gentiles, is here represented by the furnishing of the feast with guests *out of the high-ways, vv.* 8–10.

Here is, 1. The complaint of the master of the feast concerning those that were first bidden (*v.* 8), *The wedding is ready*, the covenant of grace ready to be sealed, a church ready to be founded; *but they which were bidden*, that is, the Jews, *to whom pertained the covenant and the promises*, by which they were of old invited to the *feast of fat things*, they *were not worthy*, they were utterly unworthy, and, by their contempt of Christ, had forfeited all the privileges they were invited to.

2. The commission he gave to the servants, to invite other guests. The inhabitants of the *city* (*v.* 7) had refused; *Go into the high-ways* then; into *the way of the Gentiles*, which at first they were to decline, *ch.* x. 5. Thus by the fall of the Jews salvation is come to the Gentiles, Rom. xi. 11, 12; Eph. iii. 8.

3. The success of this second invitation; if some will not come, others will (*v.* 10); *They gathered together all, as many as they found.* The servants obeyed their orders.

Now the guests that were gathered were, [1] A multitude, *all, as many as they found*; so many, that the guest-chamber was filled. The sealed ones of the Jews were numbered, but those of other nations *were without number, a very great multitude*, Rev. vii. 9. See Isa. lx. 4, 8. [2] A mixed multitude, *both bad and good*; some that before their conversion were sober and well-inclined, as the devout Greeks (Acts xvii. 4), and Cornelius; others that had run to an excess of riot, as the Corinthians (1 Cor. vi. 11).

VI. The case of hypocrites, who are *in* the church, but not *of* it, who have a name to live, but are not alive indeed, is represented by *the guest that had not on a wedding garment*; one of the bad that were gathered in. Concerning this hypocrite observe,

1. His discovery, how he was found out, *v.* 11.

(1) *The king came in to see the guests*, to bid those welcome who came prepared, and to turn those out who came otherwise.

Observe, This hypocrite was never discovered to be without *a wedding garment*, till *the king himself came in to see the guests*. Note, It is God's prerogative to know who are sound at heart in their profession, and who are not.

(2) As soon as he came in, he presently espied the hypocrite; *He saw there a man which had not on a wedding garment.*

2. His trial (*v.* 12); and here we may observe,

(1) How he was arraigned (*v.* 12); *Friend, how camest thou in hither, not having a wedding garment?* A startling question to one that was priding himself in the place he securely possessed at the feast. *Friend!* That was a cutting word; a seeming friend, a pretended friend, a friend in profession, under manifold ties and obligations to be a friend. Note, There are many in the church who are false friends to Jesus Christ, who say that they love him, while their hearts are not with him. *How camest thou in hither?* He does not chide the servants for letting him in (the wedding garment is an inward thing, ministers must go according to that which falls within their cognizance); but he checks his presumption in crowding in, when

he knew that his heart was not upright.

(2) How he was convicted; *he was speechless: he was muzzled* (so the word is used, 1 Cor. ix. 9); the man stood mute, upon his arraignment, being convicted and condemned by his own conscience. They who live within the church, and die without Christ, will not have one word to say for themselves in the judgment of the great day, they will be without excuse.

3. His sentence (*v.* 13); *Bind him hand and foot*, &c.

Lastly, The parable is concluded with that remarkable saying which we had before (*ch.* xx. 16), *Many are called, but few are chosen, v.* 14. Of the many that are called to the wedding feast, if you set aside all those as unchosen that make light of it, and avowedly prefer other things before it; if then you set aside all that make a profession of religion, but the temper of whose spirits and the tenour of whose conversation are a constant contradiction to it; if you set aside all the profane, and all the hypocritical, you will find that they are few, very few, that are chosen; many called to the wedding feast, but few chosen to the wedding garment, that is, to *salvation, by sanctification of the Spirit.* This *is the strait gate, and narrow way*, which *few find*.

TRIBUTE TO CÆSAR
(*vv.* 15–22)

In these verses, we have him attacked by the Pharisees and Herodians with a question about paying tribute to Cæsar. Observe,

I. What the design was, which they proposed to themselves; *They took counsel to entangle him in his talk.*

1. *They took counsel.* It was foretold concerning him, that *the rulers* would *take counsel against him* (Ps. ii. 2); and *so persecuted they the prophets. Come, and let us devise devices against Jeremiah.* See Jer. xviii. 18; xx. 10.

2. That which they aimed at was *to entangle him in his talk.* They saw him free and bold in speaking his mind, and hoped by that, if they could bring him to some nice and tender point, to get an advantage against him.

II. The question which they put to him pursuant to this design, *vv.* 16, 17. Observe,

1. The persons they employed; they did not go themselves, lest the design should be suspected and Christ should stand the more upon his guard; but they sent their disciples, who would look less like tempters, and more like learners.

With them they sent the Herodians, a party among the Jews, who were for a cheerful and entire subjection to the Roman emperor, and to Herod his deputy; and who made it their business to reconcile people to that government, and pressed all to pay their tribute.

2. The preface, with which they were plausibly to introduce the question; it was highly complimentary to our Saviour (*v.* 16); *Master, we know that thou art true, and teachest the way of God in truth.* Note, It is a common thing for the most spiteful projects to be covered with the most specious pretences.

3. The proposal of the case; *What thinkest thou? Is it lawful to give tribute to Cæsar, or not?*

This implies a further question; Has Cæsar a right to demand it?

Now the question was, Whether it was lawful to pay these taxes voluntarily, or, Whether they should not insist upon the ancient liberty of their nation, and rather suffer themselves to be distrained upon? The ground of the doubt was, that they *were Abraham's seed*, and should not by consent be *in bondage to any man*, John viii. 33. God had given them a law, that they should not *set a stranger over them*. Did not that imply, that they were not to yield any willing subjection to any prince, state, or potentate, that was not of their own nation and religion? This was an old mistake, arising from that *pride* and that *haughty spirit* which bring *destruction and a fall*.

However, by this question they hoped to entangle Christ, and, which way soever he resolved it, to expose him to the fury either of the jealous Jews, or of the jealous Romans; they were ready to triumph, as Pharaoh did over Israel, that *the wilderness had shut him in*, and his doctrine would be concluded either injurious to the rights of the church, or hurtful to kings and provinces.

III. The breaking of this snare by the wisdom of the Lord Jesus.

1. He discovered it (*v.* 18); *He perceived their wickedness*; for, *surely in vain is the net spread in the sight of any bird*, Prov. i. 17. A temptation perceived is half conquered, for our greatest danger lies from snakes under the green grass; *and he said, Why tempt ye me, ye hypocrites?*

2. He evaded it; his convicting

them of hypocrisy might have served for an answer: but our Lord Jesus gave a full answer to their question, and introduced it by an argument sufficient to support it, so as to lay down a rule for his church in this matter, and yet to avoid giving offence, and to break the snare.

(1) He forced them, ere they were aware, to confess Cæsar's authority over them, *vv.* 19, 20. *Show me the tribute-money.* He had none of his own to convince them by; it should seem, he had not so much as one piece of money about him, for for our sakes he emptied himself, and became poor. They presently *brought him a penny*, a Roman penny in silver, in value about sevenpence half-penny of our money, the most common piece then in use: it was stamped with the emperor's image and super-scription, which was the warrant of the public faith for the value of the pieces so stamped; a method agreed on by most nations, for the more easy circulation of money with satisfaction. The coining of money has always been looked upon as a branch of the prerogative, a flower of the crown, a royalty belonging to the sovereign powers; and the admitting of that as the good and lawful money of a country is an implicit submission to those powers, and an owning of them in money matters.

Christ asked them, *Whose image is this?* They owned it to be Cæsar's, and thereby convicted those of falsehood who said, *We were never in bondage to any*; and confirmed what afterward they said, *We have no king but Cæsar.*

It is a rule in the Jewish Talmud, that "he is the king of the country whose coin is current in the country." Some think that the super-scription upon this coin was a memorandum of the conquest of Judea by the Romans, *anno post captum Judæam—the year after that event*; and that they admitted that too.

(2) From thence he inferred the lawfulness of paying tribute to Cæsar (*v.* 21); *Render therefore to Cæsar the things that are Cæsar's*; not, "*Give* it him" (as they ex-pressed it, *v.* 17), but, "*Render* it; Return," or "Restore it." Now by this answer,

[1] No offence was given. It was much to the honour of Christ and his doctrine, that he did not inter-pose as a Judge or a Divider in matters of this nature, but left them as he found them, for *his kingdom is not of this world*; and in this he hath given an example to his ministers, who deal in sacred things, not to meddle with disputes about things secular, not to wade far into controversies relating to them, but to leave that to those whose proper business it is.

[2] His adversaries were re-proved. *First*, Some of them would have had him make it unlawful to give tribute to Cæsar, that they might have a pretence to save their money. Thus many excuse them-selves from that which they must do, by arguing whether they may do it or no. *Secondly*, They all withheld from God his dues, and are reproved for that: while they were vainly contending about their civil liberties, they had lost the life and power of religion, and

needed to be put in mind of their duty to God, with that to Cæsar.

[3] His disciples were instructed, and standing rules left to the church.

First, That the Christian religion is no enemy to civil government, but a friend to it. Christ's kingdom doth not clash or interfere with the kingdoms of the earth, in any thing that pertains to their jurisdiction. By Christ kings reign.

Secondly, It is the duty of subjects to render to magistrates that which, according to the laws of their country, is their due.

Thirdly, When we render to Cæsar the things that are Cæsar's, we must remember withal to render to God the things that are God's. If our purses be Cæsar's, our consciences are God's; he hath said, *My son, give me thy heart*: he must have the innermost and uppermost place there; we must render to God that which is his due, out of our time and out of our estates; from them he must have his share as well as Cæsar his; and if Cæsar's commands interfere with God's *we must obey God rather than men*.

Lastly, Observe how they were nonplussed by this answer; they *marvelled, and left him, and went their way, v.* 22. They admired his sagacity in discovering and evading a snare which they thought so craftily laid.

MARRIAGES AND HEAVEN
(*vv.* 23–33)

We have here Christ's dispute with the Sadducees concerning the resurrection; it was the same day on which he was attacked by the Pharisees about paying tribute. Observe here,

I. The opposition which the Sadducees made to a very great truth of religion; they say, *There is no resurrection*, as there are some fools who say, *There is no God*. These heretics were called *Sadducees* from one Sadoc, a disciple of Antigonus Sochæus, who flourished about two hundred and eighty-four years before our Saviour's birth. As the Pharisees and Essenes seemed to follow Plato and Pythagoras, so the Sadducees were much of the genius of the Epicureans; they denied the resurrection, they said, There is no future state, no life after this; that, when the body dies, the soul is annihilated, and dies with it; that there is no state of rewards or punishments in the other world; no judgment to come in heaven or hell. They maintained, that, except God, there is no spirit (Acts xxiii. 8), nothing but matter and motion. They would not own the divine inspiration of the prophets, nor any revelation from heaven, but what God himself spoke upon mount Sinai. Now the doctrine of Christ carried that great truth of the resurrection and a future state much further than it had yet been revealed, and therefore the Sadducees in a particular manner set themselves against it. The Pharisees and Sadducees were contrary to each other, and yet confederates against Christ.

II. The objection they made against the truth, which was taken from a supposed case of a woman that had seven husbands successively; now they take it for granted, that, if there be a resurrection, it must be a return to such a state as this we are now in, and to the same circumstances, like the imaginary Platonic year; and if so, it is an invincible absurdity for this woman in the future state to have seven husbands, or else an insuperable difficulty which of them should have her, he whom she had first, or he whom she had last, or he whom she loved best, or he whom she lived longest with.

1. They suggest the law of Moses in this matter (*v.* 24), that the next of kin should marry the widow of him that died childless (Deut. xxv. 5); we have it practised, Ruth iv. 5.

2. They put a case upon this statute, which, whether it were a *case in fact* or only a *moot case*, is not at all material; if it had not really occurred, yet possibly it might. It was of seven brothers, who married the same woman, *vv.* 25–27.

3. They propose a doubt upon this case (*v.* 28); "*In the resurrection, whose wife shall she be of the seven?* You cannot tell whose; and therefore we must conclude *there is no resurrection.*"

III. Christ's answer to this objection; by reproving their ignorance, and rectifying their mistake, he shows the objection to be fallacious and unconcluding.

1. He reproves their ignorance (*v.* 29); *Ye do err, not knowing.* Note, Ignorance is the cause of error; those that are in the dark, miss their way. Now observe,

(1) *They know not the power of God;* which would lead men to infer that there *may be* a resurrection and a future state. God is omnipotent, and can do what he will; and then no room is left for doubting but that he will do what he has promised; and, if so, *why should it be thought a thing incredible with you that God should raise the dead?* Acts xxvi. 8. His power far exceeds the power of nature.

(2) *They know not the scriptures,* which decidedly affirm that there shall be a resurrection and a future state.

2. He rectifies their mistake, and (*v.* 30) corrects those gross ideas which they had of the resurrection and a future state, and fixes these doctrines upon a true and lasting basis. Concerning that state, observe,

(1) It is not like the state we are now in upon earth; *They neither marry, nor are given in marriage.* In our present state marriage is necessary; it was instituted in innocency; whatever intermission or neglect there has been of other institutions, this was never laid aside, nor will be till the end of time. But, in the resurrection, there is no occasion for marriage; whether in glorified bodies there will be any distinction of sexes some too curiously dispute (the ancients are divided in their opinions about it); but, whether there will be a distinction or no, it is certain that there will be no conjunction; where God will be *all in all,* there needs no other *meet-help;* the body will be *spiritual,* and there will be in it no carnal desires to be gratified. The joys of that state are pure and spiritual, and arise from the marriage of all of them to the Lamb, not of any of them to one another.

(2) It is like the state angels are now in, in heaven; *They are as the angels of God in heaven*; they *are* so, that is, undoubtedly they shall be so. The bodies of the saints shall be raised incorruptible and glorious, like the uncompounded vehicles of those pure and holy spirits (1 Cor. xv. 42, &c.), swift and strong, like them.

IV. Christ's argument to confirm this great truth of the resurrection and a future state; the matters being of great concern, he did not think it enough (as in some other disputes) to discover the fallacy and sophistry of the objections, but backed the truth with a solid argument. Now observe,

1. Whence he fetched his argument—from the scripture; that is the great magazine or armoury whence we may be furnished with spiritual weapons, offensive and defensive.

2. What his argument was (*v.* 32); *I am the God of Abraham*. This was not an express proof, *in so many words*; and yet it was really a conclusive argument.

Now the drift of the argument is to prove,

(1) That there is a future state, another life after this, in which the righteous shall be truly and constantly happy. This is proved from what God said; *I am the God of Abraham*.

[1] For God to be any one's God supposes some very extraordinary privilege and happiness; unless we know fully what God is, we could not comprehend the riches of that word, *I will be to thee a God*, that is, a Benefactor like myself.

[2] It is manifest that these good men had no such extraordinary happiness, in *this* life, as might look any thing like the accomplishment of so great a word as that. If no happiness had been reserved for these great and good men on the other side death, that melancholy word of poor Jacob's, when he was old (Gen. xlvii. 9), *Few and evil have the days of the years of my life been*, would have been an eternal reproach to the wisdom, goodness, and faithfulness, of that God who had so often called himself *the God of Jacob*.

[3] Therefore there must certainly be a future state, in which, as God will ever live to be eternally rewarding, so Abraham, Isaac, and Jacob, will ever live to be eternally rewarded.

(2) That the soul is immortal, and the body shall rise again, to be united; if the former point be gained, these will follow; but they are likewise proved by considering the time when God spoke this; it was to Moses at the bush, long after Abraham, Isaac, and Jacob, were dead and buried; and yet God saith, not, "*I was*," or "*have been*," but, *I am the God of Abraham*. Now *God is not the God of the dead, but of the living*. He is a living God, and communicates vital influences to those to whom he is a God. If, when Abraham died, there had been an end of him, there had been an end likewise of God's relation to him as his God; but at that time, when God spoke to Moses, he was the God of Abraham, and therefore Abraham must be then alive; which proves the immortality of the soul in a state of bliss; and that, by consequence, infers the resurrec-

tion of the body; for there is such an inclination in the human soul to its body, as would make a final and eternal separation inconsistent with the bliss of those that have God for *their God*. The Sadducees' notion was, that the union between body and soul is so close, that, when the body dies, the soul dies with it. Now, upon the same hypothesis, if the soul lives, as it certainly does, the body must some time or other live with it.

Lastly, We have the issue of this dispute. The Sadducees were *put to silence* (*v.* 34), and so put to shame. But the multitude *were astonished at his doctrine, v.* 33.

THE GREAT
COMMANDMENT
(*vv.* 34–40)

Here is a discourse which Christ had with a Pharisee-lawyer, about the great commandment of the law.

This lawyer *asked him a question, tempting him*; not with any design to ensnare him, as appears by St. Mark's relation of the story, where we find that this was he to whom Christ said, *Thou art not far from the kingdom of God*, Mark xii. 34, but only to see what he would say, and to draw on discourse with him, to satisfy his own and his friends' curiosity.

I. The question was, *Master, which is the greatest commandment of the law?* A needless question, when all the things of God's law are great things (Hos. viii. 12).

II. The design was to try him, or tempt him; to try, not so much his knowledge as his judgment. It was a question disputed among the critics in the law. Some would have the law of circumcision to be the great commandment, others the law of the sabbath, others the law of sacrifices, according as they each stood affected, and spent their zeal; now they would try what Christ said to this question, hoping to incense the people against him, if he should not answer according to the vulgar opinion; and if he should magnify one commandment, they would reflect on him as vilifying the rest.

III. Christ's answer to this question. Now Christ recommends to us those as the great commandments, not which are so exclusive of others, but which are *therefore* great because inclusive of others. Observe,

1. Which these great commandments are (*vv.* 37–39); not the judicial laws, those could not be the greatest now that the people of the Jews, to whom they pertained, were so little; not the ceremonial laws, those could not be the greatest, now that they were waxen old, and were ready to vanish away; nor any particular moral precept; but the love of God and our neighbour, which are the spring and foundation of all the rest, which (these being supposed) will follow of course.

All the law is fulfilled in one word, and that is, *love*. See Rom. xiii. 10. All obedience begins in the affections, and nothing in religion is done right, that is not done there first. Love is the leading affection, which gives law, and gives ground, to the rest; and therefore that, as the main fort, is to be first secured and garrisoned for God. Man is a creature cut out for love; thus therefore is the law written in the heart, that it is a *law of love*. Love is a short and sweet word; and, if that be *the fulfilling of the law*, surely the yoke of the command is very easy. Love is the rest and satisfaction of the soul; if we walk in this good old way, we shall find rest.

2. Observe what the weight and greatness of these commandments is (v. 40); *On these two commandments hang all the law and the prophets*; that is, This is the sum and substance of all those precepts relating to practical religion which were written in men's hearts by nature, revived by Moses, and backed and enforced by the preaching and writing of the prophets. All hang upon the law of love; take away this, and all falls to the ground, and comes to nothing.

SON OF DAVID (vv. 41–46)

Many questions the Pharisees had asked Christ, by which, though they thought to pose him, they did but *ex*pose themselves; but now let him ask them a question; and he will do it when they are gathered together, v. 41. Now here,

I. Christ proposes a question to them, which they could easily answer; it was a question in their own catechism; "*What think ye of Christ? Whose Son is he?* Whose Son do you expect the Messiah to be, who was promised to the fathers?" This they could easily answer, *The Son of David*.

What think ye of Christ? They had put questions to him, one after another, out of the law; but he comes and puts a question to them upon the promise.

II. He starts a difficulty upon their answer, which they could not so easily solve, vv. 43–45. The objection Christ raised was, *If Christ be David's son, how then doth David, in spirit, call him Lord?* He did not hereby design to ensnare them, as they did him, but to instruct them in a truth they were loth to believe—that the expected Messiah is God.

1. It is easy to see that David calls Christ *Lord*, and this in spirit being divinely inspired, and actuated therein by a spirit of prophecy; for it was *the Spirit of the Lord that spoke by him*, 2 Sam. xxiii. 1, 2. David was one of those *holy men that spoke as* they were *moved by the Holy Ghost*, especially in calling Christ *Lord*; for it was then, as it is still (1 Cor. xii. 3), that *no man can say that Jesus is the Lord, but by the Holy Ghost*. Now, to prove that David, in spirit, called Christ *Lord*, he quotes Ps. cx. 1, which psalm the scribes themselves understood of Christ; of him, it is certain, the prophet there speaks, of him and of no other man; and it is a prophetical summary of the doctrine of Christ, it describes him executing the offices of a Prophet, Priest, and King, both in his humiliation and also in his exaltation.

Christ quotes the whole verse, which shows the Redeemer in his exaltation; (1) *Sitting at the right hand of God*. His sitting denotes both rest and rule; his sitting at God's right hand denotes superlative honour and sovereign power. See in what great words this is expressed (Heb. viii. 1); *He is set on the right hand of the throne of the*

Majesty. See Phil. ii. 9; Eph. i. 20. He did not take this honour to himself, but was entitled to it by covenant with his Father, and invested in it by commission from him, and here is that commission. (2) Subduing his enemies. There he shall sit, till they be all made either his friends or his footstool.

But that which this verse is quoted for is, that David calls the Messiah *his Lord; the Lord,* Jehovah, *said unto my Lord.* This intimates to us, that in expounding scripture we must take notice of, and improve, not only that which is the main scope and sense of a verse, but of the words and phrases, by which the Spirit chooses to express that sense, which have often a very useful and instructive significance. Here is a good note from that word, *My Lord.*

2. It is not so easy for those who believe not the Godhead of the Messiah, to clear this from an absurdity, if Christ be David's son. It is incongruous for the father to speak of his son, the predecessor of his successor, as his *Lord.* We must hold this fast, that he is David's Lord, and by that explain his being David's son. The seeming differences of scripture, as here, may not only be accommodated, but contribute to the beauty and harmony of the whole.

III. We have here the success of this gentle trial which Christ made of the Pharisees' knowledge, in two things.

1. It puzzled them (*v.* 46); *No man was able to answer him a word.* Either it was their ignorance that they did not know, or their impiety that they would not own, the

Messiah to be God; which truth was the only key to unlock this difficulty.

2. It silenced them, and all others that sought occasion against him; *Neither durst any man, from that day forth, ask him any more* such captious, tempting, ensnaring *questions.*

CHAPTER TWENTY-THREE

WOE, SCRIBES AND PHARISEES (*vv.* 1–33)

We find not Christ, in all his preaching, so severe upon any sort of people as upon these *scribes and Pharisees*; for the truth is, nothing is more directly opposite to the spirit of the gospel than the temper and practice of that generation of men, who were made up of pride, worldliness, and tyranny, under a cloak and pretence of religion; yet these were the idols and darlings of the people, who thought, if but two men went to heaven, one would be a Pharisee.

Now, in this discourse,

I. Christ allows their office as expositors of the law; *The scribes and Pharisees sit in Moses's seat* (*v.* 2), as public teachers and interpreters of the law; and, the law of Moses being the municipal law of their state, they were as judges, or a bench of justices; teaching and judging seem to be equivalent, comparing 2 Chron. xvii. 7, 9, with 2 Chron. xix. 5, 6, 8.

Hence he infers (*v.* 3), "*Whatsoever they bid you observe, that observe and do.* As far as they *sit in Moses's seat*, that is, read and preach the law that was given by Moses" (which, as yet, continued in full force, power, and virtue), "and judge according to that law, so far you must hearken to them, as remembrancers to you of the written word."

II. He condemns the men. He had ordered the multitude to do as they taught; but here he annexeth a caution not to do as they did, to beware of their leaven; *Do not ye after their works.* Their traditions were their works, were their idols, the works of their fancy. Or, "Do not according to their example."

Our Saviour here, and in the following verses, specifies diverse particulars of their works, wherein we must not imitate them. In general, they are charged with hypocrisy, dissimulation, or double-dealing in religion; a crime which cannot be enquired of at men's bar, because we can only judge according to outward appearance; but God, who searcheth the heart, can convict of hypocrisy; and nothing is more displeasing to him, for he desireth truth.

He cautions his disciples against being like them; they must not do after their works; "But be not ye called so, for ye shall not be of such a spirit," *v.* 8, &c.

Here is, [1] A prohibition of pride. They are here forbidden,

First, To challenge titles of honour and dominion to themselves, *vv.* 8–10. It is repeated twice; *Be not called Rabbi, neither be ye called Master* or *Guide*: not that it is unlawful to give civil respect to *those that are over us in the Lord*, nay, it is an instance of the honour and esteem which it is our duty to show them; but, 1. Christ's ministers must not affect the name of *Rabbi* or *Master*, by way of distinction from other people; it is not agreeable to the simplicity of the gospel, for them to covet or accept the honour which they have that are in kings' palaces. 2. They must not assume the authority and dominion implied in those names; they must not be magisterial, nor domineer over their brethren, or over God's heritage, as if they had dominion over the faith of Christians.

(1) *One is your Master, even Christ, v.* 8, and again, *v.* 10. Note, [1] Christ is our Master, our Teacher, our Guide. Mr. George Herbert, when he named the name of *Christ*, usually added, *My Master.* [2] Christ only is our Master, ministers are but ushers in the school.

(2) *All ye are brethren.* Ministers are brethren not only to one another, but to the people; and therefore it ill becomes them to be masters, when there are none for them to master it over but their brethren.

Secondly, They are forbidden to ascribe such titles to others (*v.* 9); "*Call no man your father upon the earth*; constitute no man the father of your religion, that is, the founder, author, director, and governor, of it."

The reason given is, *One is your Father, who is in heaven.* God is our Father, and is All in all in our religion.

[2] Here is a precept of humility and mutual subjection (*v.* 11); *He that is greatest among you shall be your servant*; not only call himself so, but he shall be so. Take it as a promise; "*He* shall be accounted

greatest, and stand highest in the favour of God, that is most submissive and serviceable": or as a precept; "He that is advanced to any place of dignity, trust, and honour, in the church, *let him be your servant*."

[3] Here is a good reason for all this, *v*. 12. Consider,

First, The punishment intended for the proud; *Whosoever shall exalt himself shall be abased*.

Secondly, The preferment intended for the humble; *He that shall humble himself shall be exalted*.

The gospel has its woes as well as the law, and gospel curses are of all curses the heaviest. These woes (*vv*. 13–16) are the more remarkable, not only because of the authority, but because of the meekness and gentleness, of him that denounced them.

This is here the burden of the song, and it is a heavy burden; *Woe unto you, scribes and Pharisees, hypocrites*.

Now each of these woes against the scribes and Pharisees has a reason annexed to it, containing a separate crime charged upon them, proving their hypocrisy, and justifying the judgment of Christ upon them; for his woes, his curses, are never causeless.

(1) They were sworn enemies to the gospel of Christ, and consequently to the salvation of the souls of men (*v*. 13); *They shut up the kingdom of heaven against men*, that is, they did all they could to keep people from believing in Christ, and so entering into his kingdom.

1. They would not go in themselves; *Have any of the rulers*, or *of the Pharisees, believed on him?* John vii. 48. No; they were too proud to stoop to his meanness, too formal to be reconciled to his plainness; they did not like a religion which insisted so much on humility, self-denial, contempt of the world, and spiritual worship. Repentance was the door of admission into this kingdom, and nothing could be more disagreeable to the Pharisees, who justified and admired themselves, than to repent, that is, to accuse and abase and abhor themselves; therefore they *went not in themselves*; but that was not all.

2. They would not *suffer them that were entering to go in*. It is bad to keep away from Christ ourselves, but it is worse to keep others from him; yet that is commonly the way of hypocrites: they do not love that any should go beyond them in religion, or be better than they.

(2) They made religion and the form of godliness a cloak and stalking-horse to their covetous practices and desires, *v*. 14. Observe here,

1. What their wicked practices were; they *devoured widows' houses*, either by quartering themselves and their attendants upon them for entertainment, which must be of the best for men of their figure; or by insinuating themselves into their affections, and so getting to be the trustees of their estates, which they could make an easy prey of; for who could presume to call such as they were to an account? The thing they aimed at was to enrich themselves; and, this being their chief and highest end, all considerations of justice and equity were laid

aside, and even widows' houses were sacrificed to this.

2. What was the cloak with which they covered this wicked practice; *For a pretence they made long prayers*; very long indeed, if it be true which some of the Jewish writers tell us, that they spent three hours at a time in the formalities of meditation and prayer, and did it thrice every day, which is more than an upright soul, that makes a conscience of being inward with God in the duty, dares pretend ordinarily to do; but to the Pharisees it was easy enough, who never made a business of the duty, and always made a trade of the outside of it. Note, It is no new thing for the show and form of godliness to be made a cloak to the greatest enormities. But dissembled piety, however it passeth now, will be reckoned for as double iniquity, *in the day when God shall judge the secrets of men.*

3. The doom passed upon them for this; *Therefore ye shall receive the greater damnation.* Note, (1) There are degrees of damnation; there are some whose sin is more inexcusable, *and whose ruin will therefore be more intolerable.* (2) The pretences of religion, with which hypocrites disguise or excuse their sin now, will aggravate their condemnation shortly.

(3) While they were such enemies to the conversion of souls to Christianity, they were very industrious in the perversion of them to their faction. They shut up the kingdom of heaven against those that would turn to Christ, but at the same time *compassed sea and land to make proselytes* to themselves, *v.* 15.

(4) Their seeking their own worldly gain and honour more than God's glory put them upon coining false and unwarrantable distinctions, with which they led the people into dangerous mistakes, particularly in the matter of oaths; which, as an evidence of a universal sense of religion, have been by all nations accounted sacred (*v.* 16); *Ye blind guides.*

Now, to prove their blindness, he specifies the matter of swearing, and shows what corrupt casuists they were.

1. He lays down the doctrine they taught.

[1] They allowed swearing by creatures provided they were consecrated to the service of God, and stood in any special relation to him. They allowed swearing by the temple and the altar, though they were the work of men's hands, intended to be the servants of God's honour, not sharers in it. An oath is an appeal to God, to his omniscience and justice; and to make this appeal to any creature is to put that creature in the place of God. See Deut. vi. 13.

[2] They distinguished between an oath by *the temple* and an oath by the *gold of the temple*; an oath by *the altar* and an oath by *the gift upon the altar*; making the latter binding, but not the former. Here was a double wickedness; *First*, That there were some oaths which they dispensed with, and made light of, and reckoned a man was not bound by to assert the truth, or perform a promise. They ought not to have sworn by the temple or the altar; but, when they had so sworn, they were taken in

the words of their mouth. That doctrine cannot be of the God of truth which gives countenance to the breach of faith in any case whatsoever. Oaths are edge-tools and are not to be jested with. *Secondly,* That they preferred the gold before the temple, and the gift before the altar, to encourage people to bring gifts to the altar, and gold to the treasures of the temple, which they hoped to be gainers by.

2. He shows the folly and absurdity of this distinction (*vv.* 17–19); *Ye fools, and blind.* It was in the way of a necessary reproof, not an angry reproach, that Christ called them *fools.*

To convict them of folly, he appeals to themselves, *Whether is greater, the gold* (the golden vessels and ornaments, or the gold in the treasury), *or the temple that sanctifies the gold; the gift, or the altar that sanctifies the gift?* The temple and altar were dedicated to God fixedly, the gold and gift but secondarily. Christ is our altar (Heb. xiii. 10), our temple (John ii. 21); for it is he that sanctifies all our gifts, and puts an acceptableness in them, 1 Pet. ii. 5.

3. He rectifies the mistake (*vv.* 20–22), by reducing all the oaths they had invented to the true intent of an oath, which is, By the name of the Lord: so that though an oath by the temple, or the altar, or heaven, be formally bad, yet it is binding.

(5) They were very strict and precise in the smaller matters of the law, but as careless and loose in the weightier matters, *vv.* 23, 24. They were *partial in the law* (Mal. ii. 9),

would pick and choose their duty, according as they were interested or stood affected. The partiality of the scribes and Pharisees appears here, in two instances.

1. They observed smaller duties, but omitted greater; they were very exact in paying tithes, till it came to *mint, anise,* and *cummin,* their exactness in tithing of which would not cost them much, but would be cried up, and they should buy reputation cheap.

But that which Christ here condemns them for, is, that they *omitted the weightier matters of the law, judgment, mercy, and faith*; and their niceness in paying tithes, was, if not to atone before God, yet at least to excuse and palliate to men the omission of those. All the things of God's law are weighty, but those are most weighty, which are most expressive of inward holiness in the heart; the instances of self-denial, contempt of the world, and resignation to God, in which lies the life of religion. Judgment and mercy toward men, and faith toward God, are the weightier matters of the law, the *good things* which the *Lord our God requires* (Mic. vi. 8); to do justly, and love mercy, and humble ourselves by faith to walk with God. This is the obedience which is better than sacrifice or tithe; judgment is preferred before sacrifice, Isa. i. 11.

2. They avoided lesser sins, but committed greater (*v.* 24); *Ye blind guides*; so he had called them before (*v.* 16), for their corrupt teaching; here he calls them so for their corrupt living, for their example was leading as well as their doctrine; and in this also they

213

were blind and partial; they *strained at a gnat, and swallowed a camel*. In their doctrine they strained at gnats, warned people against every the least violation of the tradition of the elders. But they made no difficulty of those sins which, in comparison with them, were as a camel to a gnat; when they devoured widows' houses, they did indeed *swallow a camel*.

It is not the scrupling of a little sin that Christ here reproves; if it be a sin, though but a gnat, it must be strained at, but the doing of that, and then swallowing a camel. In the smaller matters of the law to be superstitious, and to be profane in the greater, is the hypocrisy here condemned.

(6) They were all for the outside, and not at all for the inside, of religion. They were more desirous and solicitous to appear pious to men than to approve themselves so toward God. This is illustrated by two similitudes.

1. They are compared to a vessel that is clean washed on the outside, but all dirt within, *vv.* 25, 26.

2. They are compared to *whited sepulchres*, *vv.* 27, 28.

(1) They were fair outside, like sepulchres, *which appear beautiful outward*. Now the righteousness of the scribes and Pharisees was like the ornaments of a grave, or the dressing up of a dead body, only for show. The top of their ambition was to *appear righteous before men*, and to be applauded and had in admiration by them. But,

(2) They were *foul* within, like sepulchres, *full of dead men's bones, and all uncleanness*: so vile are our bodies, when the soul has deserted

them! Thus were they full of hypocrisy and iniquity. Hypocrisy is the worst iniquity of all other.

(7) They pretended a deal of kindness for the memory of the prophets that were dead and gone, while they hated and persecuted those that were present with them. This is put last, because it was the blackest part of their character. God is jealous for his honour in his laws and ordinances, and resents it if they be profaned and abused; but he has often expressed an equal jealousy for his honour in his prophets and ministers, and resents it worse if they be wronged and persecuted: and therefore, when our Lord Jesus comes to this head, he speaks more fully than upon any of the other (*vv.* 29–37); for he that toucheth his ministers, *toucheth his Anointed,* and toucheth the *apple of his eye*.

THE BLIND FOLLOWERS
(*vv.* 34–39)

We have left the blind leaders fallen into the ditch, under Christ's sentence, into the damnation of hell; let us see what will become of the blind followers, of the body of the Jewish church, and particularly Jerusalem.

I. Jesus Christ designs yet to try them with the means of grace; *I send unto you prophets, and wise men, and scribes*. The connection is strange; "*You are a generation of vipers*, not likely to *escape the damnation of hell*"; one would think it should follow, "Therefore you shall never have a prophet sent to you any more"; but no, "*Therefore I will send unto you prophets*, to see if you will yet at length be wrought upon, or else to leave you inexcusable, and to justify God in your ruin." It is therefore ushered in with a note of admiration, behold!

II. He foresees and foretells the ill usage that his messengers would meet with among them; "*Some of them ye shall kill and crucify*, and yet I will send them." Christ knows beforehand how ill his servants will be treated, and yet sends them, and appoints them their measure of sufferings; yet he loves them nevertheless for his thus exposing them, for he designs to glorify himself by their sufferings, and them after them; he will counterbalance them, though not prevent them. Observe,

1. The cruelty of these persecutors; *Ye shall kill and crucify them.* It is no less than the blood, the life-blood, that they thirst after; their lust is not satisfied with any thing short of their destruction, Exod. xv. 9.

2. Their unwearied industry; *Ye shall persecute them from city to city.* As the apostles went from city to city, to preach the gospel, the Jews dodged them, and haunted them, and stirred up persecution against them, Acts xiv. 19; xvii. 13.

3. The pretence of religion in this; they scourged them in their synagogues, their places of worship, where they kept their ecclesiastical courts; so that they did it as a piece of service to the church; cast them out, and said, *Let the Lord be glorified*, Isa. lxvi. 5; John xvi. 2.

III. He imputes the sin of their fathers to them, because they imitated it; *That upon you may come all the righteous blood shed upon the earth*, vv. 35, 36. Though God bear long with a persecuting generation, he will not bear always; and patience abused, turns into the greatest wrath.

Observe, 1. The extent of this imputation; it takes in *all the righteous blood shed upon the earth*, that is, the blood shed for righteousness' sake, which has all been laid up in God's treasury, and not a drop of it lost, for *it is precious*, Ps. lxxii. 14.

2. The effect of it; *All these things shall come*; all the guilt of this blood, all the punishment of it, it shall *all come upon this generation.* The destruction shall be so dreadful, as if God had once for all arraigned them for all the righteous blood shed in the world. It shall *come upon this generation*; which intimates, that it shall come quickly; some here shall live to see it.

IV. He laments the wickedness of Jerusalem, and justly upbraids them with the many kind offers he had made them, *v.* 37. See with what concern he speaks of that city; *O Jerusalem, Jerusalem!* The repetition is emphatical, and bespeaks abundance of commiseration. A day or two before Christ had wept over Jerusalem, now he sighed and groaned over it. Jerusalem, *the vision of peace* (so it signifies), must now be the seat of war and confusion.

1. She persecuted God's messengers; *Thou that killest the prophets, and stonest them that are sent unto thee.* This sin is especially charged upon Jerusalem; because there the Sanhedrim, or great council, sat, who took cognizance of church matters, and therefore a prophet

could not perish but in Jerusalem, Luke xiii. 33.

2. She refused and rejected Christ, and gospel offers. The former was a sin *without* remedy, this *against* the remedy.

V. He reads Jerusalem's doom (*vv.* 38, 39); *Therefore behold your house is left unto you desolate*. Both the city and the temple, God's house and their own, all shall be laid waste. But it is especially meant of the temple, which they boasted of, and trusted to; that holy mountain because of which they were so haughty.

1. Their house shall be *deserted*; *It is left unto you*. Christ was now departing from the temple, and never came into it again, but by this word abandoned it to ruin.

2. It shall be *desolate*; *It is left unto you desolate*; it is left *a wilderness*. (1) It was immediately, when Christ left it, in the eyes of all that understood themselves, a very dismal melancholy place. (2) It was, not long after, destroyed and ruined, and *not one stone left upon another*. The lot of Jerusalem's enemies will now become Jerusalem's lot, *to be made of a city a heap, of a defenced city a ruin* (Isa. xxv. 2), *a lofty city laid low, even to the ground*, Isa. xxvi. 5. The temple, that holy and beautiful house, became desolate. When God goes out, all enemies break in.

Lastly, Here is the final farewell that Christ took of them and their temple; *Ye shall not see me henceforth, till ye shall say, Blessed is he that cometh*. This bespeaks,

1. His departure from them. The time was at hand, when *he should leave the world, to go to his Father*,

and be seen no more. *After his resurrection, he was seen only by a few chosen witnesses*, and they saw him not long, but he soon removed to the invisible world, and there will be *till the time of the restitution of all things*, when his welcome at his first coming will be repeated with loud acclamations; *Blessed is he that cometh in the name of the Lord*. Christ will not be seen again till he *come in the clouds, and every eye shall see him* (Rev. i. 7); and then, even they, who, when time was, rejected and pierced him, will be glad to come in among his adorers.

2. Their continued blindness and obstinacy; *Ye shall not see me*, that is, not see me to be the Messiah (for otherwise they did see him upon the cross), not see the light of the truth concerning me, nor *the things that belong to your peace, till ye shall say, Blessed is he that cometh*. They will never be convinced, till Christ's second coming convince them, when it will be too late to make an interest in him, and nothing will remain *but a fearful looking for of judgment*.

CHAPTER TWENTY-FOUR

WHAT IS THE SIGN?
(*vv.* 1–3)

Here is,

I. Christ's quitting *the temple*, and his public work there. He had said, in the close of the foregoing chapter, *Your house is left unto you desolate*; and here he made his words good; *He went out, and departed from the temple*.

II. His private discourse with his disciples; he left the temple, but he did not leave the twelve, who were the seed of the gospel church, which the casting off of the Jews was the enriching of. When he left the temple, his disciples left it too, and came to him. Observe,

1. *His disciples came to him, to show him the buildings of the temple.* They showed Christ these things, and desired him to take notice of them, either,

(1) As being greatly pleased with them themselves, and expecting he should be so too.

Or, (2) As grieving that this house should be left desolate; they showed him the buildings, as if they would move him to reverse the sentence; "Lord, let not this holy and beautiful house, where our fathers praised thee, be made a desolation."

2. Christ, hereupon, foretells the utter ruin and destruction that were coming upon this place, *v.* 2. *See ye not all these things?* They would have Christ look upon them, and be as much in love with them as they were; he would have them look upon them, and be as dead to them as he was. There is such a sight of these things as will do us good; so to see them as to see through them and see to the end of them.

Christ, instead of reversing the decree, ratifies it; *Verily, I say unto you, there shall not be left one stone upon another.*

3. The disciples, not disputing either the truth or the equity of this sentence, nor doubting of the accomplishment of it, enquire more particularly of the time when it should come to pass, and the signs of its approach, *v.* 3.

[1] Some think, these questions do all point at one and the same thing—the destruction of the temple, and the period of the Jewish church and nation, which Christ had himself spoken of as his coming (*ch.* xvi. 28), and which would be the consummation of the age (for so it may be read), the finishing of that dispensation. Or, they thought the destruction of the temple must needs be the end of the world. If that house be laid waste, the world cannot stand; for the Rabbin used to say that the house of the sanctuary was one of the seven things for the sake of which the world was made; and they think, if so, the world will not survive the temple.

[2] Others think their question, *When shall these things be?* refers to the destruction of Jerusalem, and the other two to the end of the world; or Christ's coming may refer to his setting up his gospel kingdom, and the end of the world to the day of judgment. I rather incline to think that their question looked no further than the event Christ now foretold; but it appears by other passages, that they had very confused thoughts of future events; so that perhaps it is not possible to put any certain construction upon this question of theirs.

But Christ, in his answer, though he does not expressly rectify the mistakes of his disciples (that must be done by the pouring out of the Spirit), yet looks further than their question, and instructs his church, not only concerning the great events of that age, the destruction of Jerusalem, but concerning his second coming at the end of time,

217

which here he insensibly slides into a discourse of, and of that it is plain he speaks in the next chapter, which is a continuation of this sermon.

THE LAST DAYS (*vv.* 4–31)

The disciples had asked concerning the times, *When shall these things be?* Christ gives them no answer to that, after what number of days and years his prediction should be accomplished, for *it is not for us to know the times* (Acts i. 7); but they had asked, *What shall be the sign?* That question he answers fully, for we are concerned to *understand the signs of the times, ch.* xvi. 3. Now the prophecy primarily respects the events near at hand—the destruction of Jerusalem, the period of the Jewish church and state, the calling of the Gentiles, and the setting up of Christ's kingdom in the world; but this prophecy also under the type of Jerusalem's destruction, looks as far forward as the general judgment.

I. Christ here foretells the going forth of deceivers; he begins with a caution, *Take heed that no man deceive you.*

Three times in this discourse he mentions the appearing of *false prophets*, which was, 1. A presage of Jerusalem's ruin. Justly were they who killed the true prophets, left to be ensnared by false prophets; and they who crucified the true Messiah, left to be deceived and broken by false Christs and pretended Messiahs. 2. It was a trial to the disciples of Christ, and therefore agreeable to their state of probation, *that they which are perfect, may be made manifest.*

Now concerning these deceivers, observe here,

(1) The pretences they should come under. Satan acts most mischievously, when he appears as an angel of light: the colour of the greatest good is often the cover of the greatest evil.

(2) The proof they should offer for the making good of these pretences; *They shall show great signs and wonders* (*v.* 24), not true miracles, those are a divine seal, and with those the doctrine of Christ stands confirmed. But these were *lying wonders* (2 Thess. ii. 9), wrought by Satan (God permitting him), who is *the prince of the power of the air.*

(3) The success they should have in these attempts,

[1] *They shall deceive many* (*v.* 5), and again, *v.* 11. Note, The devil and his instruments may prevail far in deceiving poor souls; few find the strait gate, but many are drawn into the broad way; many will be imposed upon by their signs and wonders, and many drawn in by the hopes of deliverance from their oppressions. Note, Neither miracles nor multitudes are certain signs of a true church; for *all the world wonders after the beast,* Rev. xiii. 3.

[2] *They shall deceive, if it were possible, the very elect, v.* 24. This bespeaks, *First,* The strength of the delusion. *Secondly,* The safety of the elect in the midst of this danger, which is taken for granted in that parenthesis, *If it were possible,* plainly implying that it is not possible, for they are *kept by the power of God,* that *the purpose of God, according to the election, may stand.*

(4) The repeated cautions which our Saviour gives to his disciples to stand upon their guard against them; *therefore* he gave them warning, that they might watch (*v.* 25); *Behold, I have told you before.*

[1] We must not believe those who say, *Lo, here is Christ*; or, *Lo, he is there, v.* 23. We believe that the true Christ is at the right hand of God, and that his spiritual presence is *where two or three are gathered together in his name.*

[2] We must not go forth after those that say, *He is in the desert,* or, *He is in the secret chambers, v.* 26. We must not hearken to every empiric and pretender, nor follow every one that puts up the finger to point us to a new Christ, and a new gospel.

II. He foretells wars and great commotions among the nations, *vv.* 6, 7. From the time that the Jews rejected Christ, and he *left their house desolate, the sword did never depart from their house, the sword of the Lord* was never quiet, because he had given it a charge against a hypocritical nation and the people of his wrath, and by it brought ruin upon them.

Here is, 1. A prediction of the event of the day; You will now shortly *hear of wars, and rumours of wars.* See what comes of refusing the gospel! Those that will not hear the messengers of peace, shall be made to hear the messengers of war.

2. A prescription of the duty of the day; *See that ye be not troubled.* Is it possible to hear such sad news, and not be troubled? Yet, where the heart is fixed, trusting in God, it is kept in peace, and is not afraid, no not of the evil tidings of wars, and rumours of wars; no not the noise of *Arm, arm.*

We must not be troubled, for two reasons.

(1) Because we are bid to expect this: the Jews must be punished, ruin must be brought upon them; by this the justice of God and the honour of the Redeemer must be asserted; and therefore *all those things must come to pass*; the word is gone out of God's mouth, and it shall be accomplished in its season.

(2) Because we are still to expect worse; *The end is not yet*; the end of time is not, and, while time lasts, we must expect trouble, and that the end of one affliction will be but the beginning of another; or, "The end of these troubles is not yet; there must be more judgments than one made use of to bring down the Jewish power. Therefore be not troubled, do not give way to fear and trouble, sink not under the present burden, but rather gather in all the strength and spirit you have, to encounter what is yet before you.

III. He foretells other judgments more immediately sent of God— *famines, pestilences, and earthquakes.* Beside war (and that is enough), there shall be,

1. *Famine,* signified by the *black horse* under the *third seal,* Rev. vi. 5, 6.

2. *Pestilences,* signified by the *pale horse, and death upon him,* and *the grave at his heels,* under the *fourth seal,* Rev. vi. 7, 8. This destroys without distinction, and in a little time lays heaps upon heaps.

3. *Earthquakes in divers places,* or from place to place, pursuing those that flee from them, as they did

from the earthquake *in the days of Uzziah*, Zech. xiv. 5. When we look forward to the eternity of misery that is before the obstinate refusers of Christ and his gospel, we may truly say, concerning the greatest temporal judgments, "They are but the beginning of sorrows; bad as things are with them, there are worse behind."

IV. He foretells the persecution of his own people and ministers, and a general apostasy and decay in religion thereupon, *vv.* 9, 10, 12. Observe,

1. The *cross* itself foretold, *v.* 9. Christ had told his disciples, when he first sent them out, what hard things they should suffer; but they had hitherto experienced little of it, and therefore he reminds them again, that the less they had suffered, the more there was behind to be filled up, Col. i. 24.

(1) They shall be *afflicted* with bonds and imprisonments, *cruel mockings and scourgings*, as blessed Paul (2 Cor. xi. 23–25); not killed outright, but *killed all the day long, in deaths often*, killed so as to feel themselves die, *made a spectacle to the world*, 1 Cor. iv. 9, 11.

(2) They shall be *killed*; so cruel are the church's enemies, that nothing less will satisfy them than the blood of the saints, which they thirst after, suck, and shed, like water.

(3) They shall be *hated of all nations for Christ's name sake*, as he had told them before, *ch.* x. 22. The world was generally leavened with enmity and malignity to Christians.

2. *The offence of the cross, vv.* 10–12. Satan thus carries on his interest by force of arms, though

Christ, at length, will bring glory to himself out of the sufferings of his people and ministers. Three ill effects of persecution are here foretold.

(1) The *apostasy* of some. When the profession of Christianity begins to cost men dear, *then shall many be offended*, shall first fall out with, and then fall off from, their profession.

(2) The *malignity* of others. When persecution is in fashion, envy, enmity, and malice, are strangely diffused into the minds of men by contagion: and charity, tenderness, and moderation, are looked upon as singularities, which make a man like a speckled bird. Then *they shall betray one another*.

(3) The general *declining* and *cooling* of most, *v.* 12. In seducing times, when false prophets arise, in persecuting times, when the saints are hated, expect these two things,

[1] The *abounding* of iniquity; though the world always lies in wickedness, yet there are some times in which it may be said, that *iniquity doth* in a special manner abound.

[2] The *abating* of love; this is the consequence of the former; *Because iniquity shall abound, the love of many shall wax cold.* It is too common for professors of religion to grow cool in their profession, when the wicked are hot in their wickedness; as the church of Ephesus in bad times *left her first love*, Rev. ii. 2–4.

3. Comfort administered in reference to this offence of the cross, for the support of the Lord's people under it (*v.* 13); *He that endures to*

the end, shall be saved. Perseverance wins the crown, through free grace, and shall wear it. *They shall be saved*: perhaps they may be delivered out of their troubles, and comfortably survive them in this world; but it is eternal salvation that is here intended. They that endure to the end of their days, shall then receive the end of their faith and hope, *even the salvation of their souls*, 1 Pet. i. 9; Rom. ii. 7; Rev. iii. 20. The crown of glory will make amends for all; and a believing regard to that will enable us to choose rather to die at a stake with the persecuted, than to live in a palace with the persecutors.

V. He foretells the preaching of the gospel in all the world (*v.* 14); *This gospel shall be preached, and then shall the end come*. Observe here, 1. It is called *the gospel of the kingdom*, because it reveals the kingdom of grace, which leads to the kingdom of glory; sets up Christ's kingdom in this world; and secures ours in the other world. 2. This gospel, sooner or later, is to be preached in all the world, to every creature, and all nations are to be discipled by it; for in it Christ is to be *Salvation to the ends of the earth*; for this end the gift of tongues was *the first-fruits of the Spirit*. 3. The gospel is preached *for a witness to all nations*, that is, a faithful declaration of the mind and will of God concerning the duty which God requires from man, and the recompence which man may expect from God. It is a *record* (1 John v. 11), it is a *witness*, for those who believe, that they shall be saved, and against those who persist in unbelief, that they shall be damned. See Mark xvi. 16. But how does this come in here?

(1) It is intimated that the gospel should be, if not heard, yet at least heard of, throughout the then known world, before the destruction of Jerusalem; that the Old-Testament church should not be quite dissolved till the New Testament was pretty well settled, had got considerable footing, and began to make some figure. Better is the face of a corrupt degenerate church than none at all. Within forty years after Christ's death, the *sound* of the gospel was *gone forth to the ends of the earth*, Rom. x. 18. St. Paul *fully preached the gospel from Jerusalem, and round about unto Illyricum*; and the other apostles were not idle. The persecuting of the saints at Jerusalem helped to disperse them, so that they *went every where, preaching the word*, Acts viii. 1–4. And when the tidings of the Redeemer are sent over all parts of the world, then shall come the end of the Jewish state. Thus, that which they thought to prevent, by putting Christ to death, they thereby procured; all men *believed on him, and the Romans came, and took away their place and nation*, John xi. 48. Paul speaks of the gospel being *come to all the world, and preached to every creature*, Col. i. 6–23.

(2) It is likewise intimated that even in times of temptation, trouble, and persecution, the gospel of the kingdom shall be preached and propagated, and shall force its way through the greatest opposition.

(3) That which seems chiefly intended here, is, that the end of the

world shall be *then*, and not till then, when the gospel has done its work in the world. The gospel shall be preached, and that work carried on, when you are dead; so that all nations, first or last, shall have either the enjoyment, or the refusal, of the gospel; and *then cometh the end*, when the kingdom *shall be delivered up to God, even the Father*. The world shall stand as long as any of God's chosen ones remain uncalled; but, when they are all gathered in, it will be set on fire immediately.

VI. He foretells more particularly the ruin that was coming upon the people of the Jews, their city, temple, and nation, *vv.* 15, &c.

1. The Romans *setting up the abomination of desolation in the holy place*, *v.* 15. Now, (1) Some understand by this an image, or statue, set up in the temple by some of the Roman governors, which was very offensive to the Jews, provoked them to rebel, and so brought the desolation upon them. (2) Others choose to expound it by the parallel place (Luke xxi. 20), *when ye shall see Jerusalem compassed with armies*. Jerusalem was the holy city, Canaan the holy land, the Mount Moriah, which lay about Jerusalem, for its nearness to the temple was, they thought, in a particular manner holy ground; on the country lying round about Jerusalem the Roman army was encamped, that was the abomination that made desolate.

2. The means of preservation which thinking men should betake themselves to (*vv.* 16, 20); *Then let them which are in Judea, flee*. Then conclude there is no other way to help yourselves than by flying for the same.

Now those to whom Christ said this immediately, did not live to see this dismal day, none of all the twelve but John only; they needed not to be hidden in the mountains (Christ hid them in heaven), but they left the direction to their successors in profession, who pursued it, and it was of use to them; for when the Christians in Jerusalem and Judea saw the ruin coming on, they all retired to a town called *Pella*, on the other side Jordan, where they were safe; so that of the many thousands that perished in the destruction of Jerusalem, there was not so much as one Christian. See *Euseb. Eccl. Hist.* lib. 3, cap. 5. Thus *the prudent man foresees the evil, and hides himself*, Prov. xxii. 3; Heb. xi. 7. This warning was not kept private. St. Matthew's gospel was published long before that destruction, so that others might have taken the advantage of it; but their perishing through their unbelief of this, was a figure of their eternal perishing through their unbelief of the warnings Christ gave concerning the wrath to come.

3. The greatness of the troubles which should immediately ensue (*v.* 21).

It was a desolation unparalleled, such as *was not since the beginning of the world, nor ever shall be*. Many a city and kingdom has been made desolate, but never any with a desolation like this.

It was a desolation which, if it should continue long, would be intolerable, so that *no flesh should be saved*, *v.* 22. He doth not say, "No *soul* shall be saved," for the destruction of the flesh may be for *the saving of the spirit in the day of the Lord Jesus*; but temporal lives will be sacrificed so profusely, that one would think, if it last awhile, it would make a full end.

But here is one word of comfort in the midst of all this terror—that *for the elects' sake these days shall be shortened*, not made shorter than what God had determined (for *that which is determined, shall be poured upon the desolate*, Dan. ix. 27), but shorter than what he might have decreed, if he had dealt with them according to their sins; shorter than what the enemy designed, who would have cut all off, if God who made use of them to serve his own purpose, had not set bounds to their wrath; shorter than one who judged by human probabilities would have imagined.

And now comes in the repeated caution, which was opened before, to take heed of being ensnared by false Christs, and false prophets (*vv.* 23, &c.), who would promise them deliverance, as the lying prophets in Jeremiah's time (Jer. xiv. 13; xxiii. 16, 17; xxvii. 16; xxviii. 2), but would delude them. Times of great trouble are times of great temptation, and therefore we have need to double our guard then. If they shall say, *Here is a Christ, or there is one*, that shall deliver us from the Romans, do not heed them, it is all but talk; such a deliverance is not to be expected, and therefore not such a deliverer.

VII. He foretells the sudden spreading of the gospel in the world, about the time of these great events (*vv.* 27, 28); *As the lightning comes out of the east, so shall the coming of the Son of man be.*

1. It seems primarily to be meant of his coming to set up his spiritual kingdom in the world; where the gospel came in its light and power, there the Son of man came, and in a way quite contrary to the fashion of the seducers and false Christs, who came creeping *in the desert*, or the *secret chambers* (2 Tim. iii. 6); whereas Christ comes not with such a *spirit of fear*, but *of power, and of love, and of a sound mind.*

2. Some understand these verses of the coming of the Son of man *to destroy Jerusalem*, Mal. iii. 1, 2, 5. So much was there of an extraordinary display of divine power and justice in that event, that it is called *the coming of Christ*.

Now here are two things intimated concerning it.

(1) That to the most it would be as unexpected as a flash of lightning, which indeed gives warning of the clap of thunder which follows, but is itself surprising. The seducers say, *Lo, here is Christ* to deliver us; or there is one, a creature of their own fancies; but ere they are aware, the wrath of the Lamb, the true Christ, will arrest them, and they shall not escape.

(2) That it might be as justly expected as that the eagle should fly to the carcases; though they put far from them the evil day, yet the desolation will come as certainly as the birds of prey to a dead carcase, that lies exposed in the open field.

3. It is very applicable to the day of judgment, the coming of our Lord Jesus Christ in that day, and *our gathering together unto him*, 2 Thess. ii. 1. Now see here,

(1) How he shall come; *as the lightning*. He shall *come in the clouds*, as the lightning doth, and *every eye shall see him*, as they say it is natural for all living creatures to turn their faces towards the lightning, Rev. i. 7. Christ will appear to all the world, from one end of heaven to the other; nor shall any thing be hid from the light and heat of that day.

(2) How the saints shall be gathered to him; as the eagles are to the carcase by natural instinct, and with the greatest swiftness and alacrity imaginable. Saints, when they shall be fetched to glory, will be carried as on eagles' wings (Exod. xix. 4), as on angels' wings.

VIII. He foretells his second coming at the *end of time*, *vv*. 29-31. *The sun shall be darkened*, &c.

1. Some think this is to be understood only of the destruction of Jerusalem and the Jewish nation.

2. It seems rather to refer to Christ's second coming. The destruction of the particular enemies of the church was typical of the complete conquest of them all; and therefore what will be done really at the great day, may be applied metaphorically to those destructions: but still we must attend to the principal scope of them; and while we are all agreed to expect Christ's second coming, what need is there to put such strained constructions as some do, upon these verses, which speak of it so clearly, and so agreeably to other scriptures, especially when Christ is here answering an enquiry concerning his coming at the end of the world, which Christ was never shy of speaking of to his disciples?

The only objection against this, is, that it is said to be *immediately after the tribulation of those days*; but as to that, (1) It is usual in the prophetical style to speak of things great and certain as near and just at hand, only to express the greatness and certainty of them. (2) *A thousand years are* in God's sight *but as one day*, 2 Pet. iii. 8. It is there urged, with reference to this very thing, and so it might be said to be immediately after.

Now concerning Christ's second coming, it is here foretold,

[1] That there shall be then a great and amazing change of the creatures, and particularly the *heavenly bodies* (*v*. 29). *The sun shall be darkened, and the moon shall not give her light*. The moon shines with a borrowed light, and therefore if the sun, from whom she borrows her light, is turned into darkness, she must fail of course, and become bankrupt. *The stars shall fall*; and shall lose their light, and disappear, and be as if they were fallen; and *the powers of heaven shall be shaken*.

[2] That *then shall appear the sign of the Son of man in heaven* (*v*. 30), the Son of man himself, as it follows here, *They shall see the Son of man coming in the clouds*. At his first coming, he was *set for a Sign that should be spoken against* (Luke ii. 34), but at his second coming, a sign that should be admired. It will certainly be such a clear convincing sign as will dash infidelity quite out of countenance, and fill their faces with shame, who said, *Where is the promise of his coming?*

[3] That *then all the tribes of the earth shall mourn*, *v*. 30. See Rev. i.

7. *All the kindreds of the earth shall then wail because of him*; some of all the tribes and kindreds of the earth shall mourn; for the greater part will tremble at his approach, while the chosen remnant, one of a family and two of a tribe, shall lift up their heads with joy, knowing that their redemption draws nigh, and their Redeemer.

[4] That *then they shall see the Son of man coming in the clouds of heaven, with power and great glory.*

[5] That *he shall send his angels with a great sound of a trumpet, v.* 31. By the law, trumpets were to be sounded for the calling of assemblies (Numb. x. 2), in praising God (Ps. lxxxi. 3), in offering sacrifices (Numb. x. 10), and in proclaiming the year of jubilee, Lev. xxv. 9. Very fitly therefore shall there be the sound of a trumpet at the last day, when the general assembly shall be called, when the praises of God shall be gloriously celebrated, when sinners shall fall as sacrifices to divine justice, and when the saints shall enter upon their eternal jubilee.

[6] That *they shall gather together his elect from the four winds*. The elect of God are scattered abroad (John xi. 52), there are some in all places, in all nations (Rev. vii. 9); but when that great gathering day comes, there shall not one of them be missing; distance of place shall keep none out of heaven, if distance of affection do not. *Undique ad cælos tantundem est viæ— Heaven is equally accessible from every place.* See *ch.* viii. 11; Isa. xliii. 6; xlix. 12.

We have here the practical application of the foregoing pre-

diction; in general, we must expect and prepare for the events here foretold.

I. We must expect them; "*Now learn a parable of the fig-tree, vv.* 32, 33. The parable of the fig-tree is no more than this, that its budding and blossoming are a presage of summer; for as the *stork* in the heaven, so the trees of the field, *know their appointed time.* The beginning of the working of second causes assures us of the progress and perfection of it. Thus when God begins to fulfil prophecies, he will make an end. There is a certain series in the works of providence, as there is in the works of nature.

Now touching the events foretold here, which we are to expect,

1. Christ here assures us of the certainty of them (*v.* 35); *Heaven and earth shall pass away*; they continue this day indeed, according to God's ordinance, but they shall not continue for ever (Ps. cii. 25, 26; 2 Pet. iii. 10); *but my words shall not pass away.* Note, The word of Christ is more sure and lasting than heaven and earth. *Hath he spoken? And shall he not do it?*

2. He here instructs us as to the time of them, *vv.* 34, 36.

(1) As to *these things*, the wars, seductions, and persecutions, here foretold, and especially the ruin of the Jewish nation; "*This generation shall not pass away, till all these things be fulfilled* (*v.* 34); there are those now alive, that shall see Jerusalem destroyed, and the Jewish church brought to an end."

(2) But as to *that day and hour* which will put a period to time, *that knoweth no man, v.* 36. There-

fore take heed of confounding these two, as *they* did, who, from the words of Christ and the apostles' letters, inferred that *the day of Christ was at hand*, 2 Thess. ii. 2. No, it was not; *this generation*, and many another, *shall pass*, before *that day and hour* come. Note, [1] There is a certain day and hour fixed for the judgment to come; it is called *the day of the Lord*, because so unalterably fixed. [2] That day and hour are a great secret. *No man knows it*; not the wisest by their sagacity, not the best by any divine discovery. This is one of those *secret things* which *belong to the Lord our God.*

II. To this end we must expect these events, that we may prepare for them, *vv.* 37–41. In these verses we have such an idea given us of the judgment day, as may serve to startle and awaken us, that we may not sleep as others do.

It will be a surprising day, and a separating day.

1. It will be a surprising day, as the deluge was to the old world, *vv.* 37–39. That which he here intends to describe, is, the posture of the world at the coming of the Son of man; besides his first coming, to save, he has other comings to judge. He saith (John ix. 39), *For judgment I am come*; and for judgment he will come; for all judgment is committed to him, both that of the word, and that of the sword.

2. It will be a separating day (*vv.* 40, 41); *Then shall two be in the field.* Two ways this may be applied.

(1) We may apply it to the success of the gospel, especially at the first preaching of it; it divided the world; *some believed the things which were spoken*, and were taken to Christ; *others believed not*, and were left to perish in their unbelief.

(2) We may apply it to the second coming of Jesus Christ, and the separation which will be made in that day. He had said before (*v.* 31), that the elect will be *gathered together*. Christ will come unlooked for, will find people busy at their usual occupations, *in the field*, *at the mill*; and then, according as they are vessels of mercy prepared for glory, or vessels of wrath prepared for ruin, accordingly it will be with them; the one taken *to meet the Lord and his angels in the air, to be for ever with him and them*; the other left to the devil and his angels, who, when Christ has gathered out his own, will sweep up the residue.

III. Here is a general exhortation to us, *to watch, and be ready* against that day comes, enforced by divers weighty considerations, *v.* 42, &c. Observe,

1. The duty required; *Watch, and be ready*, *vv.* 42, 44.

(1) *Watch therefore*, *v.* 42. Note, It is the great duty and interest of all the disciples of Christ to watch, to be awake and keep awake, that they may mind their business. As a sinful state or way is compared to *sleep*, senseless and inactive (1 Thess. v. 6), so a gracious state or way is compared to *watching* and *waking.*

(2) *Be ye also ready*. We wake in vain, if we do not get ready. It is not enough to *look* for such things; but we must therefore *give diligence*, 2 Pet. iii. 11, 14.

2. The reasons to induce us to this watchfulness and diligent pre-

paration for that day; which are two.

(1) Because the time of our Lord's coming is very uncertain. This is the reason immediately annexed to the double exhortation (*vv.* 42, 44); and it is illustrated by a comparison, *v.* 43. If the master of a house had notice that a thief would come such a night, and such a watch of the night (for they divided the night into four watches, allowing three hours to each), and would make an attempt upon his house, though it were the midnight-watch, when he was most sleepy, yet he would be up, and listen to every noise in every corner, and be ready to give him a warm reception. Now, though we know not *just when* our Lord will come, yet, knowing that he *will* come, and come quickly, and without any other warning that what he hath given in his word, it concerns us to watch always.

(2) Because the issue of our Lord's coming will be very happy and comfortable to those that shall be found ready, but very dismal and dreadful to those that shall not, *v.* 45, &c. This is represented by the different state of good and bad servants, when their lord comes to reckon with them. It is likely to be well or ill with us to eternity, according as we are found ready or unready at that day; for Christ comes *to render to every man according to his works.* Now this parable, with which the chapter closes, is applicable to all Christians, who are in profession and obligation God's servants; but it seems especially intended as a warning to ministers; for the servant spoken of is a *steward.*

CHAPTER TWENTY-FIVE

THE TEN VIRGINS
(*vv.* 1–13)

I. That in general which is to be illustrated is, *the kingdom of heaven*, the state of things under the gospel, the external kingdom of Christ, and the administration and success of it. The professors of Christianity shall then be likened to these ten virgins, and shall be thus distinguished.

II. That by which it is illustrated, is, a marriage solemnity. It was a custom sometimes used among the Jews on that occasion, that the bridegroom came, attended with his friends, late in the night, to the house of the bride, where she expected him, attended with her bride-maids; who, upon notice given of the bridegroom's approach, were to go out with lamps in their hands, to light him into the house with ceremony and formality, in order to the celebrating of the nuptials with great mirth. And some think that on these occasions they had usually *ten virgins*; for the Jews never held a synagogue, circumcised, kept the passover, or contracted marriage, but ten persons at least were present. Boaz, when he married Ruth, had *ten witnesses*, Ruth iv. 2. Now in this parable,

1. The *Bridegroom* is our Lord Jesus Christ; he is so represented in the 45th Psalm, Solomon's Song, and often in the New Testament.

2. The virgins are the professors of religion, members of the church; but here represented as *her companions* (Ps. xlv. 14), as elsewhere her *children* (Isa. liv. 1), her *ornaments*, Isa. xlix. 18.

3. The office of these virgins is to meet the bridegroom, which is as much their happiness as their duty. They come to wait *upon* the bridegroom when he appears, and in the mean time to wait *for* him. See here the nature of Christianity. As Christians, we profess ourselves to be, (1) Attendants upon Christ, to do him honour, as the glorious Bridegroom, to be to him for a name and a praise, especially then when he shall come to be glorified in his saints. We must follow him as honorary servants do their masters, John xii. 26. Hold up the name, and hold forth the praise of the exalted Jesus; this is our business. (2) Expectants of Christ, and of his second coming. As Christians, we profess, not only to believe and look for, but to love and long for, the appearing of Christ, and to act in our whole conversation with a regard to it. The second coming of Christ is the centre in which all the lines of our religion meet, and to which the whole of the divine life hath a constant reference and tendency.

4. Their chief concern is to have lights in their hands, when they attend the bridegroom, thus to do him honour and do him service. Note, Christians are children of light. The gospel is light, and they who receive it must not only be enlightened by it themselves, but must *shine as lights*, must *hold it forth*, Phil. ii. 15, 16. This in general.

Now concerning these ten virgins, we may observe,

(1) Their different character, with the proof and evidence of it.

[1] Their character was, that *five were wise, and five foolish* (*v.* 2); and *wisdom excelleth folly, as far as light excelleth darkness*; so saith Solomon, a competent judge, Eccl. ii. 13. Sincere Christians are the *wise* virgins, and hypocrites the *foolish ones*, as in another parable they are represented by wise and foolish builders.

[2] The evidence of this character was in the very thing which they were to attend to; by that they are judged of.

First, It was the folly of the foolish virgins, that they *took their lamps, and took no oil with them*, *v.* 3. They had just oil enough to make their lamps burn for the present, to make a show with, as if they intended to meet the bridegroom; but no cruse or bottle of oil with them if the bridegroom tarried; thus hypocrites,

1. They have no principle within. They have a lamp of profession in their hands, but have not in their hearts that stock of sound knowledge, rooted dispositions, and settled resolutions, which is necessary to carry them through the services and trials of the present state.

2. They have no prospect of, nor make provision for, what is to come. They took lamps for a present show, but not oil for after use.

Secondly, It was the wisdom of the wise virgins, that *they took oil in their vessels with their lamps*, *v.* 4. They had a good principle within, which would maintain and keep up their profession. 1. The heart is the vessel, which it is our wisdom to get furnished. 2. Grace is the *oil* which we must have in this *vessel*; in the tabernacle there was constant provision made of *oil for the light,* Exod. xxxv. 14. Our light must shine before men in good works, but this cannot be, or not long, unless there be a fixed active principle in the heart, of faith in Christ, and love to God and our brethren.

(2) Their common fault, during the bridegroom's delay; *They all slumbered and slept, v.* 5. Observe here,

[1] The bridegroom tarried, that is, he did not come out so soon as they expected. But though Christ tarry past *our* time, he will not tarry past the *due* time.

[2] While he tarried, those that waited for him, grew careless, and forgot what they were attending; *They all slumbered and slept;* as if they had given over looking for him; for *when the Son of man cometh,* he will *not find faith,* Luke xviii. 8.

(3) The surprising summons given them, to attend the bridegroom (*v.* 6); *At midnight there was a cry made, Behold, the bridegroom cometh.*

(4) The address they all made to answer this summons (*v.* 7); *They all arose, and trimmed their lamps,* snuffed them and supplied them with oil, and went about with all expedition to put themselves in a posture to receive the bridegroom. Now, [1] This, in the wise virgins, bespeaks an actual preparation for the Bridegroom's coming. [2] In the foolish virgins, it denotes a vain confidence, and conceit of the goodness of their state, and their readiness for another world.

(5) The distress which the foolish virgins were in, for want of *oil, vv.*

8, 9. This bespeaks, [1] The apprehensions which some hypocrites have of the misery of their state, even on this side death, when God opens their eyes to see their folly, and themselves perishing *with a lie in their right hand.* Or, however, [2] The real misery of their state on the other side death, and in the judgment; how far their fair, but false, profession of religion will be from availing them any thing in the great day; see what comes of it.

First, Their lamps are gone out. The lamps of hypocrites often go out in this life; when they who have begun in the spirit, end in the flesh, and the hypocrisy breaks out in an open apostasy, 2 Pet. ii. 20.

Secondly, They wanted oil to supply them when they were going out. Note, Those that take up short of true grace, will certainly find the want of it one time or other. An external profession well humoured may carry a man far, but it will not carry him through; it may light him along this world, but the damps of the valley of the shadow of death will put it out.

Thirdly, They would gladly be beholden to the wise virgins for a supply out of their vessels; *Give us of your oil.* Note, The day is coming, when carnal hypocrites would gladly be found in the condition of true Christians. God would have given them oil, had they asked in time; but there is no buying when the market is over, no bidding when the inch of candle is dropped.

Fourthly, They were denied a share in their companions' oil. It is a sad presage of a repulse with God, when they were thus repulsed by good people. *The wise answered, Not so*; that peremptory denial is not in the original, but supplied by the translators: these wise virgins would rather give a reason without a positive refusal, than (as many do) give a positive refusal without a reason. They were well inclined to help their neighbours in distress; but, We must not, we cannot, we dare not, do it, *lest there be not enough for us and you*; charity begins at home; but *go, and buy for yourselves*. Note, 1. Those that would be saved, must have grace of their own. 2. Those that have most grace, have none to spare; all we have, is little enough for ourselves to appear before God in.

(6) The coming of the bridegroom, and the issue of all this different character of the wise and foolish virgins. See what came of it.

[1] *While they went out to buy, the bridegroom came*. Note, With regard to those that put off their great work to the last, it is a thousand to one, that they have not time to do it then. Getting grace is a work of time, and cannot be done in a hurry.

[2] *They that were ready, went in with him to the marriage.*

[3] *The door was shut*, as is usual when all the company is come, that are to be admitted. The door was shut, *First*, To secure those that were within; that, being now made *pillars in the house of our God, they may go no more out*, Rev. iii. 12. *Secondly*, To exclude those that were out. The state of saints and sinners will then be unalterably fixed, and those that are shut out then, will be shut out for ever.

[4] The foolish virgins came when it was *too late* (v. 11); *Afterward came also the other virgins*.

[5] They were *rejected*, as Esau was (v. 12); *I know you not*. Note, We are all concerned to *seek the Lord while he may be found*; for there is a time coming when he will not be found.

Lastly, Here is a practical inference drawn from this parable (v. 13); *Watch therefore*. We had it before (*ch. xxiv.* 42), and here it is repeated as the most needful caution.

THE PARABLE OF THE TALENTS (*vv.* 14–30)

We have here the parable of the *talents* committed to three servants; this implies that we are in a state of work and business, as the former implies that we are in a state of expectancy.

In this parable, 1. The *Master* is Christ, who is the absolute Owner and Proprietor of all persons and things, and in a special manner of his church; into his hands all things are delivered. 2. The *servants* are Christians, his own servants, so they are called; born in his house, bought with his money, devoted to his praise, and employed in his work.

We have three things, in general, in this parable.

I. The trust committed to these servants; Their master *delivered to them his goods*: having appointed them to work (for Christ keeps no servants to be idle), he left them something to work upon. Now observe here,

(1) On what occasion this trust was committed to these servants; The master was *travelling into a far*

country. This is explained, Eph. iv. 8. *When he ascended on high, he gave gifts unto men*.

(2) In what proportion this trust was committed. He gave to some more, to others less; to one *five* talents, to another *two*, to another *one*; to everyone according to his several ability. When Divine Providence has made a difference in men's ability, as to mind, body, estate, relation, and interest, divine grace dispenses spiritual gifts accordingly, but still the ability itself is from him.

II. The different management and improvement of this trust, which we have an account of, *vv.* 16–18.

1. Two of the servants did well.

(1) They were diligent and faithful; *They went, and traded*; they put the money they were entrusted with, to the use for which it was intended—laid it out in goods, and made returns of it; as soon as ever their master was gone, they immediately applied themselves to their business. Those that have so much work to do, as every Christian has, need to set about it quickly, and lose no time.

(2) They were successful; they doubled their stock, and in a little time made *cent. per cent.* of it: he that had *five talents*, soon made them *other five*.

Observe, The returns were in proportion to the receivings. From those to whom he has given but two talents, he expects only the improvement of two, which may encourage those who are placed in a lower and narrower sphere of usefulness; if they lay out themselves to do good according to the best of their capacity and opportunity, they shall be accepted, though they do not so much good as others.

2. The third did ill (*v.* 18); *He that had received one talent, went, and hid his lord's money*. The unfaithful servant was he that had but *one* talent: doubtless there are many that have five talents, and bury them all; great abilities, great advantages, and yet do no good with them.

He hid his *lord's* money; had it been his *own*, he might have done as he pleased; but, whatever abilities and advantages we have, they are not our *own*, we are but stewards of them, and must give account to our Lord, whose goods they are. It was an aggravation of his slothfulness, that his fellow-servants were busy and successful in trading, and their zeal should have provoked his. Are others active, and shall we be idle?

III. The account of this improvement, *v.* 19. 1. The account is deferred; it is not *till after a long time* that they are reckoned with; not that the master neglects his affairs, or that God is *slack concerning his promise* (2 Pet. iii. 9); no, he is *ready to judge* (1 Pet. iv. 5); but every thing must be done in its time and order. 2. Yet the day of account comes at last; *The lord of those servants reckoneth with them*. Now here is,

(1) The good account of the faithful servants; and here observe,

[1] The servants *giving up the account* (*vv.* 20, 22); "*Lord, thou deliveredst to me five talents*, and to me *two*; behold, *I have gained five talents*, and I *two* talents *more*."

First, Christ's faithful servants acknowledge with thankfulness his vouchsafements to them; *Lord, thou deliveredst to me* such and such things.

Secondly, They produce, as an evidence of their faithfulness, what they have gained. Note, God's good stewards have something to show for their diligence; *Show me thy faith by thy works.*

[2] The master's acceptance and approbation of their account, *vv.* 21, 23.

First, He commended them; *Well done, good and faithful servant.*

Secondly, He rewards them. The faithful servants of Christ shall not be put off with bare commendation; no, all their work and labour of love shall be rewarded.

Now this reward is here expressed two ways.

1. In one expression agreeable to the parable; *Thou hast been faithful over a few things, I will make thee ruler over many things.* It is usual in the courts of princes, and families of great men, to advance those to higher offices, that have been faithful in lower.

2. In another expression, which slips out of the parable into the thing signified by it; *Enter thou into the joy of thy Lord.*

(2) The bad account of the slothful servant. Observe,

[1] His apology for himself, *vv.* 24, 25. Though he had received but *one* talent, for that one he is called to account. The smallness of our receiving will not excuse us from a reckoning. None shall be called to an account for more than they have received; but for what we have, we must all account. His excuse bespeaks,

1. The sentiments of an enemy; *I knew thee, that thou art a hard man.* This was like that wicked saying of the house of Israel, *The way of the Lord is not equal,* Ezek. xviii. 25. Thus his *defence* is his *offence. The foolishness of man perverteth his way,* and then, as if that would mend the matter, *his heart fretteth against the Lord.*

2. The spirit of a slave; *I was afraid.* This ill affection toward God arose from his false notions of him; and nothing is more unworthy of God, nor more hinders our duty to him, than slavish fear.

[2] His Lord's answer to this apology.

First, His conviction, *vv.* 26, 27. Two things he is convicted of.

1. Slothfulness; *Thou wicked and slothful servant.* Those that are idle in the affairs of their souls, are not only idle, but something worse, 1 Tim. v. 13. When men sleep, the enemy sows tares.

2. Self-contradiction (*vv.* 26, 27); *Thou knewest that I reap where I sowed not: thou oughtest therefore to have put my money to the exchangers.* Note, The hard thoughts which sinners have of God, though false and unjust, will be so far from justifying their wickedness and slothfulness, that they will rather aggravate and add to their guilt.

Secondly, His condemnation. The slothful servant is sentenced,

1. To be deprived of his talent (*vv.* 28, 29); *Take therefore the talent from him.* The talents were first disposed of by the Master, as an absolute Owner, but this was now disposed of by him as a Judge; he takes it from the unfaithful

servant, to punish him, and gives it
to him that was eminently faithful,
to reward him. And the meaning of
this part of the parable we have in
the reason of the sentence (*v.* 29),
To every one that hath shall be given.
This may be applied, (1) To the
blessings of this life—worldly
wealth and possessions. These we
are entrusted with, to be used for
the glory of God, and the good of
those about us. Now *he that hath*
these things, and useth them for
these ends, he *shall have abundance*; perhaps abundance of the
things themselves, at least, abundance of comfort in them, and of
better things; but *from him that
hath not*, that is, that hath these
things as if he had them not, had
not power to eat of them, or to do
good with them. (2) We may apply
it to the means of grace. They who
are diligent in improving the
opportunities they have, God will
enlarge them, will *set before them
an open door* (Rev. iii. 8); but they
who know not the day of their
visitation, shall have the things that
belong to their peace hid from their
eyes.

2. He is sentenced to be *cast into
outer darkness*, v. 30. Here,

(1) His character is that of an
unprofitable servant.

(2) His doom is, to be *cast into
outer darkness*. Here, as in what
was said to the faithful servants,
our Saviour slides insensibly out of
the parable into the thing intended
by it, and it serves as a key to the
whole; for, *outer darkness, where
there is weeping and gnashing of
teeth*, is, in Christ's discourses, the
common periphrasis of the miseries
of the damned in hell. This will be

the portion of the slothful servant.

SHEEP AND GOATS
(*vv.* 31–46)

We have here a description of the
process of the last judgment in the
great day. There are some passages
in it that are parabolical; as the
separating between the sheep and
the goats, and the dialogues between the judge and the persons
judged: but there is no thread of
similitude carried through the
discourse, and therefore it is rather
to be called a draught or delineation
of the final judgment, than a
parable; it is, as it were, the
explanation of the former parables.
And here we have,

I. The placing of the judge upon
the judgment-seat (*v.* 31); *When the
Son of man shall come*.

II. The appearing of all the
children of men before him (*v.* 32);
*Before him shall be gathered all
nations*.

III. The distinction that will then
be made between the precious and
the vile; *He shall separate them one
from another*, as the tares and wheat
are separated at the harvest, the
good fish and the bad at the shore,
the corn and chaff in the floor.
This separation will be so exact,
that the most inconsiderable saints
shall not be lost in the crowd of
sinners, nor the most plausible
sinner hid in the crowd of saints
(Ps. i. 5), but every one shall go to
his own place. This is compared to
a shepherd's dividing between the
sheep and the goats; it is taken from
Ezek. xxxiv. 17, *Behold, I judge
between cattle and cattle*.

IV. The process of the judgment
concerning each of these.

1. Concerning the godly, on the right hand. Their cause must be first despatched, that they may be assessors with Christ in the judgment of the wicked, whose misery will be aggravated by their seeing Abraham, and Isaac, and Jacob, admitted into the kingdom of heaven, Luke xiii. 28. Observe here,

(1) The *glory* conferred upon them; the sentence by which they shall be not only acquitted, but preferred and rewarded (*v.* 34).

(2) The ground of this (*vv.* 35, 36), *For I was an hungered, and ye gave me meat*. We cannot hence infer that any good works of ours merit the happiness of heaven, by any intrinsic worth or excellency in them: our goodness extends not unto God; but it is plain that Jesus Christ will judge the world by the same rule by which he governs it, and therefore will reward those that have been obedient to that law; and mention will be made of their obedience, not as their title, but as their evidence of an interest in Christ, and his purchase.

Now the good works here mentioned are such as we commonly call works of charity to the poor: not but that many will be found on the right hand who never were in a capacity to feed the hungry, or clothe the naked, but were themselves fed and clothed by the charity of others; but one instance of sincere obedience is put for all the rest, and it teaches us this in general, that faith working by love is all in all in Christianity; *Show me thy faith by thy works*: and nothing will abound to a good account hereafter, but the fruits of righteousness in a good conversation

now. Works of charity and beneficence, according as our ability is, are necessary to salvation; and there will be more stress laid upon them in the judgment of the great day, than is commonly imagined; these must be the proofs of our love, and of our professed subjection to the gospel of Christ, 2 Cor. ix. 13. But they that show no mercy, shall have judgment without mercy.

Now this reason is modestly excepted against by the righteous, but is explained by the Judge himself.

1. It is questioned by the righteous, *vv.* 37–39. Not as if they were loth to inherit the kingdom, or were ashamed of their good deeds, or had not the testimony of their own consciences concerning them: but, (1) The expressions are parabolical, designed to introduce and impress these great truths, that Christ has a mighty regard to works of charity, and is especially pleased with kindnesses done to his people for his sake. Or, (2) They bespeak the humble admiration which glorified saints will be filled with, to find such poor and worthless services, as theirs are, so highly celebrated, and richly rewarded: *Lord, when saw we thee an hungered, and fed thee?* Note, Gracious souls are apt to think meanly of their own good deeds; especially as unworthy to be compared with the glory that shall be revealed.

2. It is explained by the Judge himself (*v.* 40); *Inasmuch as ye have done it to these my brethren*, to the least, to one of the least of them, *ye have done it unto me*. The good works of the saints, when they are produced in the great day, (1) Shall

all be remembered; and not the least, not one of the least, overlooked, no not a cup of cold water. (2) They shall be interpreted most to their advantage, and the best construction that can be put upon them. As Christ makes the best of their infirmities, so he makes the most of their services.

2. Here is the process concerning the wicked, those on the left hand. And in that we have,

(1) The sentence passed upon them, *v.* 41. It was a disgrace to be set on the left hand; but that is not the worst of it, he shall say to them, *Depart from me, ye cursed.*

(2) The reason of this sentence assigned.

Now, [1] All that is charged upon them, on which the sentence is grounded, is, omission; as, before, the servant was condemned, not for wasting his talent, but for burying it; so here, he doth not say, "I was hungry and thirsty, for you took my meat and drink from me; I was a stranger, for you banished me; naked, for you stripped me; in prison, for you laid me there": but, "When I was in these distresses, you were so selfish, so taken up with your own ease and pleasure, made so much of your labour, and were so loth to part with your money, that you did not *minister* as you might have done to my relief and succour. You were like those epicures that were at ease in Zion, and were not *grieved for the affliction of Joseph*," Amos vi. 4–6. Note, Omissions are the ruin of thousands.

[2] It is the omission of works of charity to the poor. They are not sentenced for omitting their sacrifices and burnt-offerings (they abounded in these, Ps. l. 8), but for omitting the weightier matters of the law, *judgment, mercy, and faith.*

Lastly, Here is the execution of both these sentences, *v.* 46. Execution is the life of the law, and Christ will take care that that be done according to the sentence.

1. *The wicked shall go away into everlasting punishment.* Sentence will then be executed speedily, and no reprieve granted, nor any time allowed to move in arrest of judgment. The execution of the wicked is first mentioned; for first the tares are gathered and burned.

2. *The righteous shall go away into life eternal*; that is, they shall *inherit the kingdom*, v. 34. Note, (1) Heaven is life, it is all happiness. The life of the soul results from its union with God by the mediation of Jesus Christ, as that of the body from its union with the soul by the animal spirits. The heavenly life consists in the vision and fruition of God, in a perfect conformity to him, and an immediate uninterrupted communion with him. (2) It is *eternal* life. There is no death to put a period to the life itself, nor old age to put a period to the comfort of it, or any sorrow to embitter it. Thus life and death, good and evil, the blessing and the curse, are set before us, that we may choose our way; and so shall our end be.

CHAPTER TWENTY-SIX

THE PLOT OF THE PRIESTS
(*vv.* 1–5)

Here is, 1. The notice Christ gave his disciples of the near approach of his sufferings, *vv.* 1, 2. While his enemies were preparing trouble for him, he was preparing himself and his followers for it. He had often told them of his sufferings at a distance, now he speaks of them as at the door; *after two days*.

2. The plot of the chief priests, and scribes, and elders of the people, against the life of our Lord Jesus, *vv.* 3–5. Many consultations had been held against the life of Christ; but this plot was laid deeper than any yet, for the grandees were all engaged in it. The chief priests, who presided in ecclesiastical affairs; the elders, who were judges in civil matters, and the scribes, who, as doctors of the law, were directors to both—these composed the sanhedrim, or great council that governed the nation, and these were confederate against Christ.

CHRIST ANOINTED
(*vv.* 6–13)

In this passage of story, we have,

I. The singular kindness of a good woman to our Lord Jesus in anointing his head, *vv.* 6, 7. The woman that did this, is supposed to have been Mary, the sister of Martha and Lazarus. And Dr. Lightfoot thinks it was the same that was called *Mary Magdalene*. She had a *box of ointment very precious*, which she *poured upon the head* of Christ as he sat at meat. This, among us, would be a strange sort of compliment. But it was then accounted the highest piece of respect; for the smell was very grateful, and the ointment itself refreshing to the head. David had his *head anointed*, Ps. xxiii. 5;

Luke vii. 46. Now this may be looked upon,

1. As an act of faith in our Lord Jesus, the Christ, the Messiah, the anointed. To signify that she believed in him as God's anointed, whom he had set king, she anointed him, and made him her king.

2. As an act of love and respect to him. Some think that this was she who *loved much* at first, and *washed Christ's feet with her tears* (Luke vii. 38, 47); and that she had not left her first love, but was now as affectionate in the devotions of a grown Christian as she was in those of a young beginner.

II. The offence which the disciples took at this. They *had indignation* (*vv.* 8, 9), were vexed to see this ointment thus spent, which they thought might have been better bestowed.

1. See how they expressed their offence at it. They said, *To what purpose is this waste?*

2. See how they excused their offence at it, and what pretence they made for it; *This ointment might have been sold for much, and given to the poor*. Note, It is no new thing for bad affections to shelter themselves under specious covers; for people to shift off works of piety under colour of works of charity.

III. The reproof Christ gave to his disciples for the offence at this good woman (*vv.* 10, 11); *Why trouble ye the woman?* He here took part with a good, honest, zealous, well-meaning woman, against all his disciples, though they seemed to have so much reason on their side; so heartily does he espouse the cause of the *offended little ones*, ch. xviii. 10.

Observe his reason; *You have the poor always with you.* Note,

1. There are some opportunities of doing and getting good which are constant, and which we must give constant attendance to the improvement of.

2. There are other opportunities of doing and getting good, which come but seldom, which are short and uncertain, and require more peculiar diligence in the improvement of them, and which ought to be preferred before the other; "*Me ye have not always*, therefore use me while ye have me."

IV. Christ's approbation and commendation of the kindness of this good woman. He calls it a *good work* (*v.* 10), and says more in praise of it than could have been imagined; particularly,

1. That the meaning of it was mystical (*v.* 12); *She did it for my burial.* (1) Some think that she *intended* it so, and that the woman better understood Christ's frequent predictions of his death and sufferings than the apostles did; for which they were recompensed with the honour of being the first witnesses of his resurrection. (2) However, Christ interpreted it so; and he is always willing to make the best, to make the most of his people's well-meant words and actions. This was as it were the embalming of his body; because the doing of that after his death would be prevented by his resurrection, it was therefore done before; for it was fit that it should be done some time, to show that he was still the Messiah, even when he seemed to be triumphed over by death.

2. That the memorial of it

should be honourable (*v.* 13); *This shall be told for a memorial.* This act of faith and love was so remarkable, that the preachers of Christ crucified, and the inspired writers of the history of his passion, could not choose but take notice of this passage, proclaim the notice of it, and perpetuate the memorial of it.

THE TREACHERY OF JUDAS
(*vv.* 14–16)

Immediately after an instance of the greatest kindness done to Christ, follows an instance of the greatest unkindness; such mixture is there of good and bad among the followers of Christ; he hath some faithful friends, and some false and feigned ones. What could be more base than this agreement which Judas here made with the chief priests, to betray Christ to them?

I. The traitor was Judas Iscariot; he is said to be *one of the twelve*, as an aggravation of his villainy.

II. Here is the proffer which he made to the chief priests; he *went to them, and said, What will ye give me?* *v.* 15. They did not send for him, nor make the proposal to him; they could not have thought that one of Christ's own disciples should be false to him.

III. Here is the bargain which the chief priests made with him; *they covenanted with him for thirty pieces of silver.* It should seem, Judas referred himself to them, and was willing to take what they were willing to give; he catches at the first offer, lest the next should be worse.

IV. Here is the industry of Judas, in pursuance of his bargain (*v.* 16); *he sought opportunity to betray him,* his head was still working to find out how he might do it effectually.

THE PASSOVER (*vv.* 17–25)

We have here an account of Christ's keeping the passover. Being made under the law, he submitted to all the ordinances of it, and to this among the rest; it was kept in remembrance of Israel's deliverance out of Egypt, the birth-day of that people; it was a tradition of the Jews, that in the days of the Messiah they should be redeemed on the very day of their coming out of Egypt; and it was exactly fulfilled, for Christ died the day after the passover, in which day they began their march.

I. The time when Christ ate the passover, was the usual time appointed by God, and observed by the Jews (*v.* 17); *the first day of the feast of unleavened bread*, which that year happened on the fifth day of the week, which is our Thursday.

II. The place where, was particularly appointed by himself to the disciples, upon their enquiry (*v.* 17): they asked, *Where wilt thou that we prepare the passover?*

1. They took it for granted that their Master would eat the passover, though he was at this time persecuted by the chief priests, and his life sought; they knew that he would not be put by his duty, either by frightenings without or fears within. Those do not follow Christ's example who make it an excuse for their not attending on the Lord's supper, our gospel passover, that they have many troubles and many enemies, are full of care and fear; for, if so, they have the more need of that ordinance, to help to silence

their fears, and comfort them under their troubles, to help them in forgiving their enemies, and casting all their cares on God.

2. They knew very well that there must be preparation made for it, and that it was their business, as his servants, to make preparation; *Where wilt thou that we prepare?*

3. They knew that he had no house of his own wherein to eat the passover; in this, as in other things, *for our sakes he became poor*. Among all Zion's palaces there was none for Zion's King; but his kingdom was not of this world. See John i. 11.

4. They would not pitch upon a place without direction from him, and from him they had direction; he sent them to *such a man* (*v.* 18), who probably was a friend and follower of his, and to his house he invited himself and his disciples.

III. The preparation was made by the disciples (*v.* 19); *They did as Jesus had appointed*. Note, Those who would have Christ's presence with them in the gospel passover, must strictly observe his instructions, and do as he directs.

IV. They ate the passover according to the law (*v.* 20). By the law, they were to *take a lamb for a household* (Exod. xii. 3, 4), which were to be not less than ten, nor more than twenty; Christ's disciples were his household. Note, They whom God has charged with families, must have their houses with them in serving the Lord.

V. We have here Christ's discourse with his disciples at the passover-supper. The usual subject of discourse at that ordinance, was the deliverance of Israel out of

Egypt (Exod. xii. 26, 27); but the great Passover is now ready to be offered, and the discourse of that swallows up all talk of the other, Jer. xvi. 14, 15. Here is,

1. The general notice Christ gives his disciples of the treachery that should be among them (*v.* 21); *One of you shall betray me.*

2. The disciples' feelings on this occasion, *v.* 22. How did they take it?

(1) *They were exceeding sorrowful.* [1] It troubled them much to hear that their Master should be betrayed. [2] It troubled them more to hear that one of them should do it. [3] It troubled them most of all, that they were left at uncertainty which of them it was, and each of them was afraid for himself, lest, as Hazael speaks (2 Kings viii. 13), he was the *dog* that should *do this great thing*.

(2) *They began every one of them to say, Lord, is it I?*

3. Further information given them concerning this matter (*vv.* 23, 24), where Christ tells them, (1) That the traitor was a familiar friend; *He that dippeth his hand with me in the dish,* that is, One of you that are now with me at the table. He mentions this, to make the treachery appear the more exceeding sinful.

4. The conviction of Judas, *v.* 25. (1) He asked, *Is it I?* to avoid coming under the suspicion of guilt by his silence. He knew very well that it was he, and yet wished to appear a stranger to such a plot. (2) Christ soon answered this question; *Thou hast said,* that is, It is as thou hast said. This is not spoken out so plainly as Nathan's, *Thou*

art the man; but it was enough to convict him, and, if his heart had not been wretchedly hardened, to have broken the neck of his plot, when he saw it discovered to his Master, and discovered by him.

THE LORD'S SUPPER
(*vv.* 26–30)

We have here the institution of the great gospel ordinance of the Lord's supper, which was received of the Lord. Observe,

I. The time when it was instituted —*as they were eating.* At the latter end of the passover-supper, before the table was drawn, because, as a feast upon a sacrifice, it was to come in the room of that ordinance. Christ is to us the Passover-sacrifice by which atonement is made (1 Cor. v. 7); *Christ our Passover is sacrificed for us.* This ordinance is to us the passover-supper, by which application is made, and commemoration celebrated, of a much greater deliverance than that of Israel out of Egypt. All the legal sacrifices of propitiation being summed up in the death of Christ, and so abolished, all the legal feasts of rejoicing were summed up in this sacrament, and so abolished.

II. The institution itself. A sacrament must be instituted; it is no part of moral worship, nor is it dictated by natural light, but has both its being and significancy from the institution, from a divine institution; it is his prerogative who established the covenant, to appoint the seals of it. In which,

1. The body of Christ is signified and represented by bread; he had said formerly (John vi. 35), *I am the bread of life,* upon which metaphor

this sacrament is built; as the life of the body is supported by bread, which is therefore put for all bodily nourishment (*ch.* iv. 4; vi. 11), so the life of the soul is supported and maintained by Christ's mediation.

(1) *He took bread, the loaf*; some loaf that lay ready at hand, fit for the purpose; it was, probably, unleavened bread; but, that circumstance not being taken notice of, we are not to bind ourselves to that, as some of the Greek churches do. His taking the bread was a solemn action, and was, probably, done in such a manner as to be observed by them that sat with him, that they might expect something more than ordinary to be done with it.

(2) *He blessed it*; set it apart for this use by prayer and thanksgiving. We do not find any set form of words used by him upon this occasion; but what he said, no doubt, was accommodated to the business in hand, that new testament which by this ordinance was to be sealed and ratified.

(3) *He brake it*; which denotes, [1] The breaking of Christ's body for us, that it might be fitted for our use; *He was bruised for our iniquities*, as *bread-corn is bruised* (Isa. xxviii. 28). [2] The breaking of Christ's body to us, as the father of the family breaks the bread to the children.

(4) *He gave it to his disciples*, as the Master of the family, and the Master of this feast; it is not said, He gave it *to the apostles*, though they were so, and had been often called so before this, but *to the disciples*, because all the disciples of Christ have a right to this ordinance; and those shall have the

benefit of it who are his disciples indeed; yet he gave it to them as he did the multiplied loaves, by them to be handed to all his other followers.

(5) *He said, Take, eat; this is my body, v.* 26. He here tells them,

[1] What they should do with it; "*Take, eat*; accept of Christ as he is offered to you, receive the atonement, approve of it, consent to it, come up to the terms on which the benefit of it is proposed to you; submit to his grace and to his government." Believing on Christ is expressed by *receiving him* (John i. 12), and *feeding upon him*, John vi. 57, 58. Meat looked upon, or the dish ever so well garnished, will not nourish us; it must be fed upon: so must the doctrine of Christ.

[2] What they should have with it; *This is my body*, not *this bread*, but *this eating and drinking*. Believing carries all the efficacy of Christ's death to our souls. *This is my body*, spiritually and sacramentally; this signifies and represents my body. He employs sacramental language, like that, Exod. xii. 11.

2. The blood of Christ is signified and represented by the wine; to make it a complete feast, here is not only bread to strengthen, but wine to *make glad the heart* (*vv.* 27, 28).

This cup he gave to the disciples,

(1) With a command; *Drink ye all of it.* Thus he welcomes his guests to his table, obliges them all to drink of his cup. Why should he so expressly command them all to drink, and to see that none let it pass them, and press that more expressly in this than in the other part of the ordinance? Surely it was

because he foresaw how in after-ages this ordinance would be dismembered by the prohibition of the cup to the laity.

(2) With an explication; *For this is my blood of the New Testament.* Therefore drink it with appetite, delight, because it is so rich a cordial. Hitherto the blood of Christ had been represented by the blood of beasts, real blood: but, after it was actually shed, it was represented by the blood of grapes, metaphorical blood; so wine is called in an Old-Testament prophecy of Christ, Gen. xlix. 10, 11.

Now observe what Christ saith of his blood represented in the sacrament.

[1] *It is my blood of the New Testament.* The Old Testament was confirmed by the *blood of bulls and goats* (Heb. ix. 19, 20; Exod. xxiv. 8); but the New Testament with the blood of Christ, which is here distinguished from that; *It is my blood of the New Testament.* The covenant God is pleased to make with us, and all the benefits and privileges of it, are owing to the merits of Christ's death.

[2] *It is shed*; it was not shed till next day, but it was now upon the point of being shed, it is as good as done.

[3] *It is shed for many.* Christ came to confirm *a covenant with many* (Dan. ix. 27), and the intent of his death agreed.

[4] *It is shed for the remission of sins*, that is, to purchase remission of sins for us. The redemption which we have through his blood, is *the remission of sins*, Eph. i. 7. The new covenant which is procured and ratified by the blood of Christ,

is a charter of pardon, an act of indemnity, in order to a reconciliation between God and man; for sin was the only thing that made the quarrel, and *without shedding of blood is no remission*, Heb. ix. 22. The pardon of sin is that great blessing which is, in the Lord's supper, conferred upon all true believers; it is the foundation of all other blessings, and the spring of everlasting comfort, *ch.* ix. 2, 3.

He takes leave of such communion; *I will not drink henceforth of this fruit of the vine*, that is, now that I am no more in the world (John xvii. 11); I have had enough of it, and am glad to think of leaving it, glad to think that this is the last meal.

Secondly, He assures them of a happy meeting again at last. It is a long, but not an everlasting, farewell; *until that day when I drink it new with you.*

Lastly, Here is the close of the solemnity with a hymn (*v.* 30); *They sang a hymn* or psalm; whether the psalms which the Jews usually sang at the close of the passover-supper, which they called *the great hallel*, that is, Ps. cxiii. and the five that follow it, or whether some new hymn more closely adapted to the occasion, is uncertain; I rather think the former; had it been new, John would not have omitted to record it.

BEFORE THE COCK CROW
(*vv.* 31–35)

We have here Christ's discourse with his disciples upon the way, as they were going to the mount of Olives. Observe,

I. A prediction of the trial which

both he and his disciples were now to go through. He here foretells,

1. A dismal scattering storm just arising, *v.* 31.

(1) That they should *all be offended because of Christ that very night*; that is, they would all be so frightened with the sufferings, that they would not have the courage to cleave to him in them, but would all basely desert him. [1] There are some temptations and offences, the effects of which are general and universal among Christ's disciples; *All you shall be offended.* [2] We have need to prepare for sudden trials, which may come to extremity in a very little time. [3] The cross of Christ is the great stumbling-block to many that pass for his disciples; both the cross he bore for us (1 Cor. i. 23), and that which we are called out to bear for him, *ch.* xvi. 24.

(2) That herein the scripture would be fulfilled; *I will smite the Shepherd.* It is quoted from Zech. xiii. 7.

2. He gives them the prospect of a comfortable gathering together again after this storm (*v.* 32); "*After I am risen again, I will go before you.* Though you will forsake me, I will not forsake you; though you fall, I will take care you shall not fall finally: we shall have a meeting again in Galilee, *I will go before you*, as the shepherd before the sheep."

II. The presumption of Peter, that he should keep his integrity, whatever happened (*v.* 33); *Though all men be offended, yet will I never be offended.* Peter had a great stock of confidence, and was upon all occasions forward to speak, especially to speak for himself;

sometimes it did him a kindness, but at other times it betrayed him, as it did here.

III. The particular warning Christ gave Peter of what he would do, *v.* 34. He imagined that in the hour of temptation he should come off better than any of them, and Christ tells him that he should come off worse. The warning is introduced with a solemn asseveration; "*Verily, I say unto thee*; take my word for it, who know thee better than thou knowest thyself."

GETHSEMANE (*vv.* 36–46)

Hitherto, we have seen the preparatives for Christ's sufferings; now, we enter upon the bloody scene. In these verses we have the story of his agony in the garden. This was the beginning of sorrows to our Lord Jesus. Observe,

I. The place where he underwent this mighty agony; it was *in a place called Gethsemane.* The name signifies, *torculus olei—an olive-mill*, a press for olives, like a wine-press, where they *trod the olives*, Mic. vi. 15. And this was the proper place for such a thing, at the foot of the mount of Olives. There our Lord Jesus began his passion; there it pleased the Lord to bruise him, and crush him, that fresh oil might flow to all believers from him, that we might partake of the root and fatness of that *good Olive.* There he trod the wine-press of his Father's wrath, and trod it alone.

II. The company he had with him, when he was in this agony.

1. He took all the twelve disciples with him to the garden, except Judas, who was at this time otherwise employed.

2. He took only Peter, and James, and John, with him into that corner of the garden where he suffered his agony. He left the rest at some distance, perhaps at the garden door, with this charge, *Sit ye here, while I go and pray yonder*.

III. The agony itself that he was in; *He began to be sorrowful and very heavy*. It is called an agony (Luke xxii. 44), a conflict. It was not any bodily pain or torment that he was in, nothing occurred to hurt him; but, whatever it was, it was from within; he troubled himself, John xi. 33.

But what was the cause of this? What was it that put him into this agony? Certainly, it was nothing of despair or distrust of his Father, much less any conflict or struggle with him. As the Father loved him because he laid down his life for the sheep, so he was entirely subject to his Father's will in it. But,

1. He engaged in an encounter with the powers of darkness; so he intimates (Luke xxii. 53); *This is your hour, and the power of darkness:* and he spoke of it just before (John xiv. 30, 31).

2. He was now *bearing the iniquities* which the Father laid upon him, and, by his sorrow and amazement, he accommodated himself to his undertaking. The sufferings he was entering upon were for our sins; they were all made to meet upon him, and he knew it.

3. He had a full and clear prospect of all the sufferings that were before him. He foresaw the treachery of Judas, the unkindness of Peter, the malice of the Jews, and their base ingratitude. He knew that he should now in a few hours be scourged, spit upon, crowned with thorns, nailed to the cross; death in its most dreadful appearances, death in pomp, attended with all its terrors, looked him in the face; and this made him sorrowful, especially because it was the wages of our sin, which he had undertaken to satisfy for.

IV. His complaint of this agony. Finding himself under the arrests of his passion, he goes to his disciples (*v.* 38), and,

1. He acquaints them with his condition; *My soul is exceedingly sorrowful, even unto death*. It gives some little ease to a troubled spirit, to have a friend ready to unbosom itself to, and give vent to its sorrows.

2. He bespeaks their company and attendance; *Tarry ye here, and watch with me*.

V. What passed between him and his Father when he was in this agony; *Being in an agony, he prayed*. Prayer is never out of season, but it is especially seasonable in an agony.

The prayer itself; where in we may observe three things,

(1) The title he gives to God; *O my Father*. Thick as the cloud was, he could see God as a Father through it.

(2) The favour he begs; *If it be possible, let this cup pass from me*. He calls his sufferings a *cup*; not a river, not a sea, but a cup, which we shall soon see the bottom of. When we are under troubles, we should make the best, the least, of them, and not aggravate them. His sufferings might be called a *cup*, because allotted him, as at feasts a

cup was set to every mess. He begs that this cup might *pass from him*, that is, that he might avoid the sufferings now at hand; or, at least, that they might be shortened. This intimates no more than that he was really and truly Man, and as a Man he could not but be averse to pain and suffering. This is the first and simple act of man's will—to start back from that which is sensibly grievous to us, and to desire the prevention and removal of it. The law of self-preservation is impressed upon the innocent nature of man, and rules there till over-ruled by some other law; therefore Christ admitted and expressed a reluctance to suffer, to show that he was *taken from among men* (Heb. v. 1), was touched with *the feeling of our infirmities* (Heb. iv. 15), and *tempted as we are; yet without sin.*

(3) His entire submission to, and acquiescence in, the will of God; *Nevertheless, not as I will, but as thou wilt.* Not that the human will of Christ was adverse or averse to the divine will; it was only, in its first act, diverse from it; to which, in the second act of the will, which compares and chooses, he freely submits himself. Note, In conformity to this example of Christ, we must drink of the bitter cup which God puts into our hands, be it ever so bitter; though nature struggle, grace must submit. We then are disposed as Christ was, when our wills are in every thing melted into the will of God, though ever so displeasing to flesh and blood; *The will of the Lord be done*, Acts xxi. 14.

4. The repetition of the prayer; *He went away again the second time, and prayed* (v. 42), and again the third time (v. 44), and all to the same purport; only, as it is related here, he did not, in the second and third prayer, expressly ask that the cup might pass from him, as he had done in the first.

He prayed, saying, Thy will be done. Note, Prayer is the offering up, not only of our desires, but of our resignations, to God.

But what answer had he to this prayer? Certainly it was not made in vain; he that heard him *always*, did not deny him *now*. It is true, the cup did not pass from him, for he withdrew that petition, and did not insist upon it (if he had, for aught I know, the cup had passed away); but he had an answer to his prayer; for, (1) *He was strengthened with strength in his soul*, in the day when he cried (Ps. cxxxviii. 3); and that was a real answer, Luke xxii. 43. (2) He was delivered from that which he feared, which was, lest by impatience and distrust he should offend his Father, and so disable himself to go on with his undertaking, Heb. v. 7. In answer to his prayer, God provided that he should not fail or be discouraged.

VI. What passed between him and his three disciples at this time; and here we may observe,

1. The fault they were guilty of; that when he was in his agony, sorrowful and heavy, sweating and wrestling and praying, they were so little concerned, that they could not keep awake; he comes, and *finds them asleep*, v. 40.

2. Christ's favour to them, notwithstanding. Persons in sorrow are too apt to be cross and peevish with those about them, and to lay it

grievously to heart, if they but seem to neglect them; but Christ in his agony is as meek as ever, and carries it as patiently toward his followers as toward his Father, and is not apt to take things ill.

When Christ's disciples put this slight upon him, he gave them a gentle reproof, for as many as he loves he rebukes; he directed it to Peter, who used to *speak* for them; let him now *hear* for them. The reproof was very melting; *What! could ye not watch with me one hour?* He speaks as one amazed to see them so stupid; every word, when closely considered, shows the aggravated nature of the case. How small a thing it was that he expected from them—only to *watch with him.* If he had bid them do some great thing, had bid them be in an agony with him, or die with him, they thought they could have done it; and yet they could not do it, when he only desired them to *watch with him,* 2 Kings v. 13. How short a time it was that he expected it—but *one hour;* they were not set upon the guard whole nights, as the prophet was (Isa. xxi. 8), only *one hour.* Sometimes he *continued all night in prayer to God,* but did not then expect that his disciples should watch with him; only now, when he had but one hour to spend in prayer.

He gave them good counsel; *Watch and pray, that ye enter not into temptation,* v. 41. Note, When we find ourselves entering into temptation, we have need to watch and pray.

(4) He kindly excused for them; *The spirit indeed is willing, but the flesh is weak.* We do not read of one word they had to say for themselves (the sense of their own weakness stopped their mouth); but then he had a tender word to say on their behalf, for it is his office to be an Advocate; in this he sets us an example of that love *which covers a multitude of sins.* He considered their frame, and did not chide them, for he remembered that they were but flesh; *and the flesh is weak though the spirit be willing,* Ps. lxxviii. 38, 39.

(5) Though they continued dull and sleepy, he did not any further rebuke them for it; for, though we daily offend, yet he will not always chide.

THE ARREST (*vv.* 47–56)

We are here told how the blessed Jesus was seized, and taken into custody; this followed immediately upon his agony, *while he yet spake.*

Now concerning the apprehension of the Lord Jesus, observe,

I. Who the persons were, that were employed in it. 1. Here was *Judas, one of the twelve,* at the head of this infamous guard: *he was guide to them that took Jesus* (Acts i. 16); without his help they could not have found him in this retirement. The rest were the servants and officers of the High Priest, and they were Jews; they that were at variance with each other, agreed against Christ, and Roman guards.

II. How they were armed for this enterprise.

1. What weapons they were armed with; They came *with swords and staves.* The Roman soldiers, no doubt, had swords; the servants of the priests, those of

them that had not swords, brought staves or clubs.

2. What warrant they were armed with; *They came from the chief priests, and elders of the people*; this armed multitude was sent by them upon this errand. It was a sign that he was supported by a divine power, for by all earthly powers he was not only deserted, but opposed; Pilate upbraided him with it; *Thine own nation and the chief priests delivered thee to me,* John xviii. 35.

III. The manner how it was done, and what passed at that time.

1. How Judas betrayed him; he did his business effectually, and his resolution in this wickedness may shame us who fail in that which is good.

2. How the officers and soldiers secured him; *Then came they, and laid hands on Jesus, and took him*; they made him their prisoner. *How were they not afraid to stretch forth their hands against the Lord's Anointed?* They could not have taken him, if he had not surrendered himself, and been *delivered by the determinate counsel and foreknowledge of God,* Acts ii. 23.

Our Lord Jesus was made a prisoner, because he would in all things be treated as a malefactor, punished for our crime, and as a surety under arrest for our debt. The yoke of our transgressions was bound by the Father's hand upon the neck of the Lord Jesus, Lam. i. 14.

3. How Peter fought for Christ, and was checked for his pains. It is here only said to be *one of them that were with Jesus in the garden*; but John xviii. 10, we are told that

it was Peter who signalized himself upon this occasion. Observe,

(1) Peter's rashness (*v.* 51); He *drew his sword*. They had but two swords among them all (Luke xxii. 38), and one of them, it seems, fell to Peter's share; and now he thought it was time to draw it, and he laid about him as if he would have done some great matter; but all the execution he did was the cutting off an ear from a servant of the High Priest; designing, it is likely, to cleave him down the head, because he saw him more forward than the rest in laying hands on Christ, he missed his blow.

(2) The rebuke which our Lord Jesus gave him (*v.* 52); *Put up again thy sword into its place.* As Christ forbade his disciples the sword of justice (*ch.* xx. 25, 26), so here the sword of war. Christ bade Peter put up his sword, and never bade him draw it again; yet that which Peter is here blamed for is his doing it unseasonably; the hour was come for Christ to suffer and die, he knew Peter knew it, the *sword of the Lord was drawn against him* (Zech. xiii. 7), and for Peter to draw his sword for him, was like, *Master, spare thyself*.

Three reasons Christ gives to Peter for this rebuke:

[1] His drawing the sword would be dangerous to himself and to his fellow-disciples; *They that take the sword, shall perish with the sword*; they that use violence, fall by violence; and men hasten and increase their own troubles by blustering bloody methods of self-defence.

[2] It was needless for him to draw his sword in defence of his Master, who, if he pleased, could

summon into his service all the hosts of heaven (*v.* 53); "*Thinkest thou that I cannot now pray to my Father, and he shall send* from heaven effectual succours? Peter, if I would put by these sufferings, I could easily do it without thy hand or thy sword."

[3] It was the wrong time; *For how then shall the scriptures be fulfilled, that thus it must be? v.* 54. It was written, that Christ should be *led as a lamb to the slaughter*, Isa. liii. 7. Should he summon the angels to his assistance, he would not be led to the slaughter at all; should he permit his disciples to fight, he would not be led as a lamb quietly and without resistance; therefore he and his disciples must yield to the accomplishment of the predictions.

4. We are next told how Christ argued the case with them that came to take him (*v.* 55); though he did not resist them, yet he did reason with them. *Are ye come out*, (1) With rage and enmity, *as against a thief*, as if I were an enemy to the public safety, and deservedly suffered this? (2) With all this power and force, as against the worst of thieves, that dare the law, bid defiance to public justice, and add rebellion to their sin?

He further expostulates with them, by reminding them how he had behaved himself hitherto toward them, and they toward him. [1] Of his public appearance; *I sat daily with you in the temple teaching*. And, [2] Of their public connivance; *Ye laid no hold on me*. How comes then this change? They were very unreasonable, in treating him as they did.

But all this was done (so it follows, *v.* 56) *that the scriptures of the prophets might be fulfilled*. Note, The scriptures are in the fulfilling every day; and all those scriptures which speak of the Messiah, had their full accomplishment in our Lord Jesus.

5. How he was, in the midst of this distress, shamefully deserted by his disciples; *They all forsook him, and fled, v.* 56.

THE TRIAL (*vv.* 57–68)

We have here the arraignment of our Lord Jesus in the ecclesiastical court, before the great sanhedrim. Observe,

I. The sitting of the court; the scribes and the elders were assembled, though it was in the dead time of the night, when other people were fast asleep in their beds; yet, to gratify their malice against Christ, they denied themselves that natural rest, and sat up all night, to be ready to fall upon the prey which Judas and his men, they hoped, would *seize*.

II. The setting of the prisoner to the bar; they that had *laid hold on Jesus, led him away*, hurried him, no doubt, with violence, led him as a trophy of their victory, led him as a victim to the altar; he was brought into Jerusalem through that which was called the *sheep-gate*, for that was the way into town from the mount of Olives; and it was so called because the sheep appointed for sacrifice were brought that way to the temple; very fitly therefore is Christ led that way, who is the Lamb of God, that takes away the sin of the world. Christ was led first to the High Priest, for by the law all sacrifices were to be first *presented to the priest, and delivered into his hand,* Lev. xvii. 5.

III. The cowardice and faint-heartedness of Peter (*v.* 58); *But Peter followed afar off.* This comes in here, with an eye to the following story of his denying him. He forsook him as the rest did, when he was seized, and what is here said of his following him is easily reconcilable with his forsaking him; such following was no better than forsaking him.

IV. The trial of our Lord Jesus in this court.

1. They examined witnesses against him, though they were resolved, right or wrong, to condemn him; yet, to put the better colour upon it, they would produce evidence against him. The crimes properly cognizable in their court, were, false doctrine and blasphemy; these they endeavoured to prove upon him. And observe here,

(1) Their search for proof; *They sought false witness against him;* they had seized him, bound him, abused him, and after all have to seek for something to lay to his charge, and can show no cause for his commitment. They tried if any of them could allege seemingly from their own knowledge any thing against him; and suggested one calumny and then another, which, if true, might touch his life.

(2) Their success in this search; in several attempts they were baffled, but at last they met with *two* witnesses, who, it seems, agreed in their evidence, and therefore were hearkened to, in hopes that now the point was gained. The words they swore against him,

were, that he should say, *I am able to destroy the temple of God, and to build it in three days, v.* 61. Now by this they designed to accuse him, [1] As an enemy to the temple, and one that sought for the destruction of it, which they could not bear to hear of; for they valued themselves by *the temple of the Lord* (Jer. vii. 4), and, when they abandoned other idols, made a perfect idol of that. Stephen was accused for *speaking against this holy place,* Acts vi. 13, 14. [2] As one that dealt in witchcraft, or some such unlawful arts, by the help of which he could rear such a building in three days: they had often suggested that he was in league with Beelzebub. Now, as to this, *First,* The words were misrecited; he said, *Destroy ye this temple* (John ii. 19), plainly intimating that he spoke of a temple which his enemies would seek to destroy; they come, and swear that he said, *I am able to destroy* this temple, as if the design against it were his. He said, *In three days I will raise it up— I will raise it to life.* They come, and swear that he said, *I am able to build it;* which is properly used of a house temple. *Secondly,* The words were misunderstood; *he spoke of the temple of his body* (John ii. 21), and perhaps when he said, *this temple,* pointed to, or laid his hane upon, his own body; but they sword that he said the *temple of God,* meaning this holy place.

(3) Christ's silence under all these accusations, to the amazement of the court, *v.* 62. The High Priest, the judge of the court, arose in some heat, and said, "*Answerest thou nothing?*" But Jesus held his peace (*v.* 63), not as one sullen, or

as one self-condemned, or as one astonished and in confusion; not because he lacked something to say, or knew not how to say it, but that the scripture might be fulfilled (Isa. liii. 7); *As the sheep is dumb before the shearer*, and before the butcher, *so he opened not his mouth*.

2. They examined our Lord Jesus himself upon an oath like that *ex officio*; and, since they could not accuse him, they will try, contrary to the law of equity, to make him accuse himself.

(1) Here is the interrogatory put to him by the High Priest.

Observe, [1] The question itself; *Whether thou be the Christ, the Son of God?* That is, Whether thou pretend to be so? For they will by no means admit it into consideration, whether he be really so or no.

[2] The solemnity of the proposal of it; *I adjure thee by the living God, that thou tell us.* If he should refuse to answer when he was thus adjured, they would charge him with contempt of the blessed name of God.

(2) Christ's answer to this interrogatory (*v.* 64), in which,

[1] He owns himself to be *the Christ the Son of God. Thou hast said*; that is, "It is as thou hast said"; for in St. Mark it is, *I am.* Hitherto, he seldom professed himself expressly to be the Christ, the Son of God; the tenor of his doctrine bespoke it, and his miracles proved it: but now he would not omit to make a confession of it, *First*, Because that would have looked like a disowning of that truth which he came into the world to bear witness to. *Secondly*, It would have looked like declining

his sufferings, when he knew the acknowledgment of this would give his enemies all the advantage they desired against him.

[2] He refers himself, for the proof of this, to his second coming, and indeed to his whole estate of exaltation. It is probable that they looked upon him with a scornful disdainful smile, when he said, *I am*"; "A likely fellow," thought they, "to be the Messiah, who is expected to come in so much pomp and power"; and to that this *nevertheless* refers. "Though now you see me in this low and abject state, and think it a ridiculous thing for me to call myself the Messiah, *nevertheless* the day is coming when I shall appear otherwise." *Hereafter ye shall see the Son of man sitting on the right hand of power, to judge the world.*

V. His conviction upon this trial; *The High Priest rent his clothes*, according to the custom of the Jews, when they heard or saw any thing done or said, which they looked upon to be a reproach to God; as Isa. xxxvi. 22; xxxvii. 1; Acts xiv. 14. Caiaphas would be thought extremely tender of the glory of God (*Come, see his zeal for the Lord of hosts*); but, while he pretended an abhorrence of blasphemy, he was himself the greatest blasphemer; he now forgot the law which forbade the High Priest in any case to rend his clothes, unless we will suppose this an excepted case.

Observe, 1. The crime he was found guilty of; *blasphemy. He hath spoken blasphemy*; that is, he hath spoken reproachfully of the living God; that is the notion we have of blasphemy; because we by sin had reproached the Lord, therefore Christ, when *he was made Sin for us*, was condemned as a blasphemer for the truth he told them.

2. The evidence upon which they found him guilty; *Ye have heard the blasphemy*; why should we trouble ourselves to examine *witnesses* any further? He owned the fact, that he did profess himself the *Son of God*; and then they made blasphemy of it, and convicted him upon his confession.

VI. His sentence passed, upon this conviction, *v.* 66.

Here is, 1. Caiaphas's appeal to the bench; *What think ye?*

2. Their concurrence with him; they said, *He is guilty of death*; perhaps they did not all concur: it is certain that Joseph of Arimathea, if he was present, dissented (Luke xxiii. 51); so did Nicodemus, and, it is likely, others with them; however, the majority carried it that way.

VII. The abuses and indignities done to him after sentence passed (*vv.* 67, 68); *Then*, when he was found guilty, they *spat in his face*. Because they had not power to put him to death, and could not be sure that they should prevail with the governor to be their executioner, they would do him all the mischief they could, now that they had him in their hands.

PETER'S DENIAL (*vv.* 69–75)

We have here the story of Peter's denying his Master, and it comes in as a part of Christ's sufferings. Our Lord Jesus was now in the High Priest's hall, not to be tried, but baited rather; and then it would have been some comfort to him to see his friends near him. But we do not find any friend he had about the court, save Peter only, and it would have been better if he had been at a distance. Observe how he fell, and how he got up again by repentance.

I. His sin, which is here impartially related, to the honour of the penmen of scripture, who dealt faithfully. Observe,

1. The immediate occasion of Peter's sin. He sat without in the palace, among the servants of the High Priest. Note, Bad company is to many an occasion of sin.

2. The temptation to it. He was challenged as a retainer to Jesus of Galilee. First one maid, and then another, and then the rest of the servants, charged it upon him; *Thou also wert with Jesus of Galilee, v.* 69. And again, *This fellow was with Jesus of Nazareth, v.* 71. And again (*v.* 73), *Thou also art one of them, for thy speech betrayeth thee* to be a Galilean; whose dialect and pronunciation differed from that of the other Jews.

3. The sin itself. When he was charged as one of Christ's disciples, he denied it, was ashamed and afraid to own himself so, and would have all about him to believe that he had no knowledge of him, nor any kindness or concern for him.

This is written for warning to us, that we sin not after the similitude of Peter's transgression; that we never, either directly or indirectly, deny the Lord that bought us, by rejecting his offers, resisting his Spirit, dissembling our knowledge of him, and being ashamed of him and his words, or afraid of suffering for him and with his suffering people.

4. The aggravations of this sin, which it may be of use to take notice of, that we may observe the like transgressions in our own sins. Consider, (1) Who he was: an apostle, one of the first three, that had been upon all occasions the most forward to speak to the honour of Christ. The greater profession we make of religion, the greater is our sin if in any thing we walk unworthily. (2) What fair warning his Master had given him of his danger; if he had regarded this as he ought to have done, he would not have run himself into the temptation. (3) How solemnly he had promised to adhere to Christ in this night of trial; he had said again and again, "*I will never deny thee*; no, I will die with thee first"; yet he broke these bonds in sunder, and his word was yea and nay. (4) How soon he fell into this sin after the Lord's supper. There to receive such an inestimable pledge of redeeming love, and yet the same night, before morning, to disown his Redeemer, was indeed *turning aside quickly*. (5) How weak comparatively the temptation was; it was not the judge, nor any of the officers of the court, that charged him with being a disciple of Jesus, but a silly maid or two, that probably designed him no hurt, nor would have done him any if he had owned it. (6) How often he repeated it; even after the cock had crowed once he continued in the temptation, and a second and third time relapsed into the sin. Is this Peter? *How art thou fallen!*

II. Peter's repentance for this sin, *v.* 75. The former is written for our admonition, that we may not sin; but, if at any time we be overtaken, this is written for our imitation, that we may make haste to repent. Now observe,

1. What it was, that brought Peter to repentance.

(1) *The cock crew* (*v.* 74); a common contingency; but, Christ having mentioned the crowing of *the cock* in the warning he gave him, that made it a means of bringing him to himself.

(2) *He remembered the words of the Lord*; this was it that brought him to himself, and melted him into tears of godly sorrow; a sense of his ingratitude to Christ, and the slight regard he had had to the gracious warning Christ had given him. Note, A serious reflection upon the words of the Lord Jesus will be a powerful inducement to repentance, and will help to break the heart for sin.

2. How his repentance was expressed; *He went out, and wept bitterly*.

(1) His sorrow was secret; he went out, out of the High Priest's hall, vexed at himself that ever he came into it, now that he found what a snare he was in, and got out of it as fast as he could.

(2) His sorrow was serious; *He wept bitterly*. Sorrow for sin must not be slight, but great and deep, like that for an only son. Those that have sinned sweetly, must weep bitterly; for, sooner or later, sin will be bitterness. Those that have truly sorrowed for sin, will sorrow upon every remembrance of it; yet not so as to hinder, but rather to

increase, their joy in God and in his mercy and grace.

CHAPTER TWENTY-SEVEN
THE DEATH OF JUDAS
(*vv.* 1–10)

We left Christ in the hands of the chief priests and elders, condemned to die, but they could only show their teeth; about two years before this the Romans had taken from the Jews the power of capital punishment; they could put no man to death, and therefore early in the morning another council is held, to consider what is to be done. And here we are told what was done in that morning-council, after they had been for two or three hours consulting with their pillows.

I. Christ is delivered up to Pilate, that he might execute the sentence they had passed upon him.

II. The money which they had paid to Judas for betraying Christ, is by him delivered back to them, and Judas, in despair, hangs himself. The chief priests and elders supported themselves with *this*, in prosecuting Christ, that his own disciple betrayed him to them; but now, in the midst of the prosecution, that string failed them, and even *he* is made to them a *witness* of Christ's innocency and a monument of God's justice; which served, 1, For glory to Christ in the midst of his sufferings, and a specimen of his victory over Satan who had entered into Judas. 2. For warning to his persecutors, and to leave them the more inexcusable. If their heart had not been fully set in them to do this evil, what Judas said and

did, one would think, should have stopped the prosecution.

See here how Judas *repented*: not like Peter, who repented, believed, and was pardoned: no, he repented, despaired, and was ruined.

AT THE BAR OF PILATE
(*vv.* 11–25)

We have here an account of what passed in Pilate's judgment-hall, when the blessed Jesus was brought thither early in the morning. Though it was no court-day, Pilate immediately took his case before him. We have here,

I. The trial Christ had before Pilate.

1. His arraignment; *Jesus stood before the governor*, as the prisoner before the judge.

2. His indictment; *Art thou the king of the Jews?* It was plain that he was not so *de facto—actually*; "But dost thou lay any claim to the government, or pretend a right to rule the Jews?"

3. His plea; *Jesus said unto him*, "*Thou sayest.* It is as thou sayest, though not as thou meanest; I am a king, but not such a king as thou dost suspect me to be." Thus before Pilate he witnessed a good confession, and was not ashamed to own himself a king, though it looked ridiculous, nor afraid, though at this time it was dangerous.

4. The evidence (*v.* 12); He was *accused of the chief priests*. Pilate found *no fault in him*; whatever was said, nothing was proved, and therefore what was wanting in matter they made up in noise and violence, and followed him with repeated accusations, the same as they had given in before; but by

the repetition they thought to force a belief from the governor.

5. The prisoner's silence as to the prosecutors' accusations; *He answered nothing*, (1) Because there was no occasion; nothing was alleged but what carried its own confutation along with it. (2) He was now taken up with the great concern that lay between him and his Father, to whom he was offering up himself a Sacrifice, to answer the demands of his justice, which he was so intent upon, that he minded not what they said against him. (3) His hour was come, and he submitted to his Father's will; *Not as I will, but as thou wilt*. He knew what his Father's will was, and therefore silently *committed himself to him that judgeth righteously*.

Now, [1] Pilate pressed him to make some reply (*v.* 13); *Hearest thou not how many things they witness against thee?* What these things were, may be gathered from Luke xxiii. 3, 5, and John xix. 7. Pilate, having no malice at all against him, was desirous he should clear himself, urges him to it, and believes he could do it. We have,

II. The outrage and violence of the people, in pressing the governor to crucify Christ. The chief priests had a great interest in the people, they called them *Rabbi, Rabbi*, made idols of them, and oracles of all they said; and they made use of this to incense them against him, and by the power of the mob gained the point which they could not otherwise carry. Now here are two instances of their outrage.

1. Their preferring Barabbas before him, and choosing to have him released rather than Jesus.

The proposal was made by Pilate the governor (*v.* 17); *Whom will ye that I release unto you?* It is probable that the judge had the nomination of two, one of which the people were to *choose*. Pilate proposed to them to have Jesus *released*; he was convinced of his innocency, and that the prosecution was malicious; yet had not the courage to acquit him, as he ought to have done, by his own power, but would have him released by the people's election, and so he hoped to satisfy both his own *conscience*, and the *people* too; whereas, finding no fault in him, he ought not to have *put him upon the country*, or brought him *into peril of his life*.

While Pilate was thus labouring the matter, he was confirmed in his unwillingness to condemn Jesus, by a message sent him from his wife (*v.* 19), by way of caution; *Have thou nothing to do with that just man* (together with the reason), *for I have suffered many things this day in a dream because of him*. Probably, this message was delivered to Pilate publicly, in the hearing of all that were present, for it was intended to be a warning not to him only, but to the prosecutors. Observe,

[1] The special providence of God, in sending this dream to Pilate's wife; it is not likely that she had heard any thing, before, concerning Christ, at least not so as to occasion her dreaming of him, but it was immediately from God: perhaps she was one of the *devout and honourable women*, and had some sense of religion; yet God revealed himself by dreams to some

that had not, as to Nebuchadnez-
zar.

[2] The tenderness and care of
Pilate's wife, in sending this
caution, thereupon, to her husband;
*Have nothing to do with that just
man.*

(5) The chief priests and the
elders were busy, all this while, to
influence the people in favour of
Barabbas, *v.* 20. They *persuaded the
multitude*, both by themselves and
their emissaries, whom they sent
abroad among them, *thdt they
should ask Barabbas, and destroy
Jesus*; suggesting that this Jesus was
a deceiver, in league with Satan, an
enemy to their church and temple;
that, if he were let alone, the
Romans would come, and take
away their place and nation; that
Barabbas, though a bad man, yet,
having not the interest that Jesus
had, could not do so much mischief. Thus they managed the mob,
who otherwise were well affected to
Jesus, and, if they had not been so
much at the beck of their priests,
would never have done such a
preposterous thing as to prefer
Barabbas before Jesus.

(6) Being thus over-ruled by the
priests, at length they made their
choice, *v.* 21. *Whether of the twain*
(saith Pilate) *will ye that I release
unto you?* He hoped that he had
gained his point, to have Jesus
released. But, to his great surprise,
they said *Barabbas*; as if his *crimes*
were *less*, and therefore he less
deserved to die; or as if his *merits*
were *greater*, and therefore he
better *deserved to live*. This was it
that Peter charged so home upon
them (Acts iii. 14); *Ye desired a
murderer to be granted to you*; yet

multitudes who choose the world,
rather than God, for their ruler and
portion, thus *choose their own
delusions*.

2. Their pressing earnestly to
have Jesus crucified, *vv.* 22, 23.
Pilate, being amazed at their
choice of Barabbas, was willing to
hope that it was rather from a
fondness for him than from an
enmity to Jesus; and therefore he
puts it to them, "*What shall I do
then with Jesus?* Shall I release him
likewise, for the greater honour of
your feast, or will you leave it to
me? No, *they all said, Let him be
crucified*. That death they desired he
might die, because it was looked
upon as the most scandalous and
ignominious; and they hoped thereby to make his followers ashamed
to own him, and their relation to
him.

Now, as to this demand, we are
further told,

(1) How Pilate objected against
it; *Why, what evil hath he done?* A
proper question to ask before we
censure any in common discourse,
much more for a judge to ask before
he pass a sentence of death.

(2) How they *insisted* upon it;
*They cried out the more, Let him be
crucified*. They do not go about to
show any evil he had done, but,
right or wrong, he must be *crucified*.
Quitting all pretensions to the proof
of the premises, they resolve to hold
the conclusion, and what was
wanting in evidence to make up in
clamour; this unjust judge was
wearied by importunity into an
unjust sentence, as he in the parable
into a just one (Luke xviii. 4, 5),
and the cause carried purely by
noise.

III. Here is the *devolving* of the *guilt* of Christ's blood upon the *people* and *priests*.

1. Pilate endeavours to transfer it from himself, *v.* 24.

(1) He sees it *to no purpose to contend*. What he said, [1] Would do no good; *he could prevail nothing*; he could not convince them what an unjust unreasonable thing it was for him to condemn a man whom he believed innocent, and whom they could not prove guilty. See how strong the stream of lust and rage sometimes is; neither authority nor reason will prevail to give check to it. Nay, [2] It was more likely to *do hurt*; he saw that rather a *tumult was made*.

(2) This puts him into a *great strait*, betwixt the peace of his own mind, and the peace of the city; he is loth to condemn an innocent man, and yet loth to *disoblige* the people, and raise a devil that would not be soon laid. Had he steadily and resolutely adhered to the sacred laws of justice, as a judge ought to do, he had not been in any perplexity; the matter was plain and past dispute, that a man in whom was found *no fault*, ought not to be crucified, upon any pretence whatsoever, nor must an unjust thing be done, to gratify any man or company of men in the world.

(3) Pilate thinks to trim the matter, and to pacify both the people and his own conscience too, by *doing it*, and yet *disowning* it, *acting* the thing, and yet *acquitting* himself from it at the same time.

Now Pilate endeavours to clear himself from the guilt,

[1] By a *sign*; He *took water, and washed his hands before the multitude*; not as if he thought thereby to cleanse himself from any guilt contracted before God, but to acquit himself before the people, from so much as contracting any guilt in this matter; as if he had said, "If it be done, bear witness that it is none of my doing."

[2] By a *saying*; in which, *First*, He *clears* himself; *I am innocent of the blood of this just person*. What nonsense was this, to condemn him, and yet protest that he was innocent of his blood!

2. The priests and people *consented* to take the guilt *upon themselves*; they all said, "*His blood be on us, and on our children*." What a desperate word was this, and how little did they think what was the direful import of it, or to what an abyss of misery it would bring them and theirs! Christ had lately told them, that upon them would come *all the righteous blood shed upon the earth*, from that of the righteous Abel; but as if that were too little, they here imprecate upon themselves the guilt of that blood which was more precious than all the rest, and the guilt of which would lie heavier.

THE SCOURGING (*vv.* 26–32)

Here is,

I. The sentence passed, and the warrant signed for his execution; and this *immediately*, the same hour.

Jesus was *scourged*; this was an ignominious cruel punishment, especially as it was inflicted by the Romans, who were not under the moderation of the Jewish law, which forbade scourgings, above forty stripes; this punishment was most unreasonably inflicted on one that was sentenced to die: the *rods* were not to introduce the axes, but to supersede them.

3. He was then *delivered to be crucified*; though his chastisement was in order to our peace, yet there is no peace made but by the *blood of his cross* (Col. i. 20); therefore the scourging is not enough, he must be *crucified*; a kind of death used only among the Romans; the manner of it is such, that it seems to be the result of wit and cruelty in combination, each putting forth itself to the utmost, to make death in the highest degree terrible and miserable.

II. The barbarous treatment which the soldiers gave him, while things were getting ready for his execution. When he was condemned, he ought to have had some time allowed him to prepare for death. There was a law made by the Roman senate, in Tiberius's time, perhaps upon complaint of this and the like precipitation, that the execution of criminals should be deferred at least *ten days* after sentence. *Sueton in Tiber. cap.* 25. But there were scarcely allowed so many minutes to our Lord Jesus; nor had he any breathing-time during those minutes; it was a *crisis*, and there were no *lucid intervals* allowed him; *deep called unto deep*, and the storm continued without any intermission.

When he was *delivered* to be *crucified*, that was enough; they that *kill the body*, yield that there is no more that they *can do*, but Christ's enemies will *do more*, and, if it be possible, wrap up a thousand deaths in one. Though Pilate pronounced him innocent, yet his soldiers, his guards, set themselves to abuse him, being swayed more by the fury of the people *against him*, than by their master's testimony *for him*; the Jewish *rabble* infected the Roman soldiery, or perhaps it was not so much in spite to him, as to make *sport* for themselves, that they thus abused him. They understood that he *pretended to a crown; to taunt* him with that gave them some diversion, and an opportunity to make themselves and one another merry.

III. The conveying of him to the place of execution. After they had mocked and abused him, as long as they thought fit, they then *took the robe off from him*; to signify their divesting him of all the kingly authority they had invested him with, by putting it on him; and they put his own raiment on him, because that was to fall to the soldiers' share, that were employed in the execution. They took off the robe, but no mention is made of their taking off the *crown of thorns*, whence it is commonly supposed (though there is no certainty of it) that he was crucified with that on his head; for as he is a Priest upon his throne, so he was a King upon his cross. Christ was led to be crucified in *his own raiment*, because he himself was to *bear our sins in his own body upon the tree*. And here,

1. They *led him away* to be *crucified*; he was led *as a lamb to the slaughter*, as a sacrifice to the altar. We may well imagine how they hurried him on, and dragged him along, with all the speed

possible, lest anything should intervene to prevent the glutting of their cruel rage with his precious blood. It is probable that they now loaded him with taunts and reproaches, and treated him as the off-scouring of all things. They led him away *out of the city*; for Christ, that he might sanctify the people with his own blood, *suffered without the gate* (Heb. xiii. 12), as if he that was the glory of them that *waited for redemption* in Jerusalem was not worthy to live among them. To this he himself had an eye, when in the parable he speaks of his being *cast out of the vineyard*, ch. xxi. 39.

2. They compelled Simon of Cyrene *to bear his cross*, v. 32. It seems, at first he *carried the cross* himself, as Isaac carried the wood for the burnt-offering, which was to burn him. And this was intended, as other things, both for pain and shame to him. But after a while they *took the cross* off from him, either, (1) In compassion to him, because they saw it was too great a load for him. We can hardly think that they had any consideration of that, yet it teaches us that God *considers the frame* of his people, and will not *suffer them to be tempted above what they are able*; he gives them some breathing-time, but they must expect that the cross will return, and the lucid intervals only give them space to prepare for the next fit. But, (2) Perhaps it was because he could not, with the cross on his back, go forward so fast as they would have him. Or, (3) They were afraid, lest he should faint away under the load of his cross, and die, and so prevent what their malice further intended to do against him:

thus even the *tender mercies of the wicked* (which seem to be so) *are* really *cruel*. Taking the cross off from him, they *compelled* one Simon of Cyrene to bear it, pressing him to the service by the authority of the governor or the priests. It was a reproach, and none would do it but by compulsion. Some think that this Simon was a disciple of Christ, at least a well-wisher to him, and that they knew it, and therefore put this upon him. Note, All that will approve themselves disciples indeed, must follow Christ, *bearing his cross* (*ch.* xvi. 24), *bearing his reproach*, Heb. xiii. 13. We must know the *fellowship of his sufferings for us*, and patiently submit to all the sufferings for him we are called out to; for those only shall *reign with him*, that *suffer with him*; shall sit with him in his kingdom, that drink of *his cup*, and are baptized with *his baptism*.

THE CRUCIFIXION
(vv. 33–49)

We have here the crucifixion of our Lord Jesus.

I. The place where our Lord Jesus was put to death.

1. They came to a place called *Golgotha*, near adjoining to Jerusalem, probably the common place of execution.

2. There they *crucified* him (*v.* 35), nailed his hands and feet to the cross, and then reared it up, and him hanging on it; for so the manner of the Romans was to crucify. Let our hearts be touched with the feeling of that exquisite pain which our blessed Saviour now endured, and let us look upon him who was thus pierced, and mourn. Was ever

sorrow like unto his sorrow? And when we behold what manner of death he died, let us in that behold with *what manner of love* he *loved us.*

II. The barbarous and abusive treatment they gave him, in which their wit and malice vied which should excel. As if death, so great a death, were not bad enough, they contrived to add to the bitterness and terror of it.

1. By the drink they provided for him before he was nailed to the cross, *v.* 34. It was usual to have a cup of spiced wine for those to drink of, that were to be put to death, according to Solomon's direction (Prov. xxxi. 6, 7), *Give strong drink to him that is ready to perish*; but with that cup which Christ was to drink of, they mingled *vinegar and gall*, to make it sour and bitter. This signified, (1) The *sin of man*, which is a *root of bitterness, bearing gall and wormwood*, Deut. xxix. 18. (2) It signified the *wrath of God*, that cup which his Father *put into his hand*, a bitter cup indeed, like the *bitter water which caused the curse*, Numb. v. 18. This drink they offered him, as was literally foretold, Ps. lxix. 21. And, [1] He *tasted thereof*, and so had the *worst* of it, took the bitter taste into his mouth; he let no bitter cup go by him untasted, when he was making atonement for all our sinful tasting of forbidden fruit; now he was *tasting* death in its full bitterness. [2] He *would not drink it*, because he would not have the *best of it*; would have nothing like an opiate to lessen his sense of pain, for he would die so as to *feel himself die*, because he had so much

work to *do*, as our High Priest, in his suffering work.

2. By the dividing of his garments, *v.* 35. When they nailed him to the cross, they *stripped* him of his garments, at least his *upper garments*; for by sin we were made naked, to our shame, and thus he purchased for us white raiment to cover us. If we be at any time stripped of our comforts for Christ, let us bear it patiently; he was stripped for us. The clothes of those that are executed are the executioner's fee: four soldiers were employed in crucifying Christ, and they must each of them have a share: his upper garment, if it were divided, would be of no use to any of them, and therefore they agreed to *cast lots* for it.

They now *sat down, and watched him*, *v.* 36. The chief priests were careful, no doubt, in setting this guard, lest the people, whom they still stood in awe of, should rise, and rescue him. But Providence so ordered it, that those who were appointed to *watch* him, thereby became unexceptionable witnesses for him; having the opportunity to see and hear that which extorted from them that noble confession (*v.* 54), *Truly this was the Son of God.*

3. By the *title* set up over his head, *v.* 37. It was usual for the vindicating of public justice, and putting the greater shame upon malefactors that were executed, not only by a crier to proclaim before them, but by a writing also over their heads to notify what was the crime for which they suffered; so they set up over Christ's head his accusation written, to give public

notice of the charge against him; *This is Jesus the King of the Jews*. This they designed for his reproach, but God so overruled it, that even his accusation redounded to his honour. Pilate, instead of accusing Christ as a Criminal, proclaimed him a *King*, and that *three times*, in three inscriptions. Thus God makes men to serve *his* purposes, quite beyond *their own*.

4. By his companions with him in suffering, *v*. 38. There were *two thieves crucified with him* at the same time, in the same place, under the same guard; two highway-men, or robbers upon the road, as the word properly signifies. It is probable that this was appointed to be *execution-day*; and therefore they hurried the prosecution of Christ in the morning, that they might have him ready to be executed with the other criminals.

5. By the blasphemies and revilings with which they loaded him when he was hanging upon the cross; though we read not that they cast any reflections on the thieves that were crucified with him.

The taunts and jeers they uttered are here recorded.

First, They upbraided him with his *destroying of the temple*. "*Thou that destroyest the temple*, that vast and strong fabric, try thy strength now in plucking up that *cross*, and drawing those *nails*, and so *save thyself*; if thou hast the power thou hast boasted of, this is a proper time to exert it, and give proof of it; for it is supposed that every man will do his utmost to *save himself*."

Secondly, They upbraided him with his saying that he was *the Son*

of God*; If thou be so, say they, come down from the cross*. Now they take the devil's words out of his mouth, with which he tempted him in the wilderness (*ch*. iv. 3, 6), and renew the same assault; *If thou be the Son of God*. They think that now, or never, he must prove himself to be the *Son of God*; forgetting that he had proved it by the miracles he wrought, particularly his raising of the dead; and unwilling to wait for the complete proof of it by his own resurrection, to which he had so often referred himself and them; which, if they had observed it, would have anticipated the offence of the cross. This comes of judging things by the present aspect of them, without a due remembrance of what is *past*, and a patient expectation of *what may further be produced*.

(2) The *chief priests and scribes*, the church rulers, and the *elders*, the state rulers, they mocked him, *v*. 41. They did not think it enough to invite the rabble to do it, but gave Christ the dishonour, and themselves the diversion, of reproaching him in their own proper persons. They should have been in the temple at their devotion, for it was the first day of the feast of unleavened bread, when there was to be a *holy convocation* (Lev. xxiii. 7); but they were here at the place of execution, spitting their venom at the Lord Jesus. How much below the grandeur and gravity of their character was this!

Two things the priests and elders upbraided him with.

[1] That he could not *save himself*, *v*. 42. He had been before abused in his prophetical and

kingly office, and now in his priestly office as a Saviour. *First,* They take it for granted that he *could not* save himself, and therefore had not the power he pretended to, when really he *would not* save himself, because he would die to *save us.* They should have argued, "He *saved others,* therefore he *could* save himself, and if he do not, it is for some good reason." But, *Secondly,* They would insinuate, that, because he did not now save himself, therefore all his pretence to save others was but sham and delusion, and was never really done; though the truth of his miracles was demonstrated beyond contradiction. *Thirdly,* They upbraid him with being *the King of Israel.* They dreamed of the external pomp and power of the Messiah, and therefore thought *the cross* altogether disagreeable to the King of Israel, and inconsistent with that character. Many people would like the *King of Israel* well enough, if he would but *come down from the cross,* if they could have his kingdom without the tribulation through which they must *enter into* it. But the matter is settled; if no cross, then no Christ, no crown. Those that would reign with him, must be willing to suffer with him, for Christ and his cross are *nailed together* in this world. *Fourthly,* They challenged him to *come down from the cross.* And what had become of us then, and the work of our redemption and salvation? If he had been provoked by these scoffs to *come down from the cross,* and so to have left his undertaking *unfinished,* we had been for ever *undone.* But his unchangeable love and resolution set him above, and

fortified him against, this temptation, so that he did not *fail,* nor was *discouraged. Fifthly,* They promised that, if he would *come down from the cross, they would believe him.* Let him give them that proof of his being the Messiah, and they will own him to be so.

[2] That God, *his Father,* would *not save him* (v. 43); *He trusted in God,* that is, he pretended to do so; for he said, *I am the Son of God.* Those who call God *Father,* and themselves *his children,* thereby profess to put a confidence in him, Ps. ix. 10. Now they suggest, that he did but deceive himself and others, when he made himself so much the *darling of heaven;* for, if he had been the Son of God (as *Job's* friends argued concerning him), he would not have been *abandoned to* all this misery, much less *abandoned in* it.

(3) To complete the reproach, the *thieves also that were crucified with him* were not only not reviled as he was, as if they had been saints compared with him, but, though fellow-sufferers with him, joined in with his prosecutors, and *cast the same in his teeth;* that is, one of them did, who said, *If thou be the Christ, save thyself and us,* Luke xxiii. 39.

Well, thus our Lord Jesus having undertaken to satisfy the justice of God for the wrong done him in his honour by sin, he did it by suffering *in his honour;* not only by divesting himself of that which was due to him as the Son of God, but by submitting to the utmost indignity that could be done to the worst of men; because he was made sin for us, he was thus made a curse for us, to make reproach easy to us, if at any time we suffer it, and have all manner of evil said against us falsely, for righteousness' sake.

III. We have here the frowns of heaven, which our Lord Jesus was under, in the midst of all these injuries and indignities from men. Concerning which, observe,

1. How this was signified—by an extraordinary and miraculous eclipse of the sun, which continued for *three hours*, *v.* 45. There was darkness *over all the earth*; so most interpreters understand it, though our translation confines it to *that land*. An extraordinary light gave intelligence of the birth of Christ (*ch.* ii. 2), and therefore it was proper that an extraordinary darkness should notify his death, for he is the *Light of the world*. Never were there three such hours since the day that God created man upon the earth, never such a dark and awful scene; the *crisis* of that great affair of man's redemption and salvation.

2. How he complained of it (*v.* 46); *About the ninth hour*, when it began to clear up, after a long and silent conflict. *Jesus cried, Eli, Eli, lama sabachthani?* The words are related in the Syriac tongue, in which they were spoken, because worthy of double remark, and for the sake of the perverse construction which his enemies put upon them, in putting *Elias* for *Eli*. Now observe here,

(1) Whence he borrowed this complaint—from Ps. xxii. 1. It is not probable (as some have thought) that he repeated the whole psalm; yet hereby he intimated that the whole was to be applied to him, and that David, in spirit, there

spoke of his humiliation and exaltation.

(2) How he uttered it—*with a loud voice*; which bespeaks the extremity of his pain and anguish, the strength of nature remaining in him, and the great earnestness of his spirit in this expostulation. Now the scripture was fulfilled (Joel iii. 15, 16); *The sun and the moon shall be darkened. The Lord shall also roar out of Zion, and utter his voice from Jerusalem.* David often speaks of his *crying aloud* in prayer, Ps. lv. 17.

(3) What the complaint was— *My God, My God, why hast thou forsaken me?*

Note, [1] That our Lord Jesus was, in his sufferings, for a time, *forsaken by his Father*. So he saith himself, who we are sure was under no mistake concerning his own case. Not that the union between the divine and human nature was in the least weakened or shocked; no, he was *now by the eternal Spirit offering himself*: nor as if there were any abatement of his Father's love to him, or his to his Father; we are sure that there was upon his mind no horror of God, or despair of his favour, nor any thing of the torments of hell; but his Father forsook him; that is, *First*, He delivered him up into the hands of his enemies, and did not appear to deliver him out of their hands. He let loose the powers of darkness against him, and suffered them to do their worst. *Secondly*, He withdrew from him the present comfortable sense of his complacency in him. When *his soul* was first *troubled*, he had a *voice from heaven* to comfort him (John xii.

27, 28); when he was in his agony in the garden, there appeared an angel from heaven strengthening him; but now he had neither the one nor the other. God hid his face from him, and for awhile withdrew his rod and staff in the darksome valley. *Thirdly*, He let out upon his soul an afflicting sense of his wrath against man for sin. Christ was made *Sin* for us, a *Curse* for us; and therefore, though God loved him as a Son, he frowned upon him as a Surety.

[2] That Christ's being *forsaken* of his Father was the most grievous of his sufferings, and that which he complained most of.

[3] That our Lord Jesus, even when he was thus forsaken of his Father, kept hold of him as his God, notwithstanding; *My God, my God*; though forsaking me, yet *mine*. Christ was God's *servant* in carrying on the work of redemption, to him he was to make satisfaction, and by him to be carried through and crowned, and upon that account he calls him *his God*; for he was now *doing his will*. See Isa. xlix. 5–9.

(4) See how his enemies impiously bantered and ridiculed this complaint (*v.* 47); *They said, This man calleth for Elias.* Some think that this was the ignorant mistake of the Roman soldiers, who had heard talk of Elias, and of the Jews' expectation of the coming of Elias, but knew not the signification of *Eli, Eli*, and so made this blundering comment upon these words of Christ, perhaps not hearing the latter part of what he said, for the noise of the people. But others think that it was the wilful mistake

of some of the Jews, who knew very well what he said, but were disposed to abuse him, and make themselves and their companions merry, and to misrepresent him as one who, being forsaken of God, was driven to trust in creatures; perhaps hinting also, that he who had pretended to be himself the Messiah, would now be glad to be beholden to Elias, who was expected to be only the harbinger and forerunner of the Messiah.

IV. The cold comfort which his enemies ministered to him in this agony, which was like all the rest.

1. Some *gave him vinegar to drink* (*v.* 48); instead of some cordial-water to revive and refresh him under this heavy burden, they tantalized him with that which did not only add to the reproach they were loading him with, but did too sensibly represent that cup of trembling which his Father had *put into his hand*.

2. Others, with the same purpose of disturbing and abusing him, refer him to Elias (*v.* 49); "*Let be, let us see whether Elias will come to save him.*"

THE DEATH OF CHRIST
(*vv.* 50–56)

We have here, at length, an account of the death of Christ, and several remarkable passages that attended it.

I. The *manner* how he breathed his last (*v.* 50); between the third and the sixth hour, that is, between nine and twelve o'clock, as we reckon, he was nailed to the cross, and soon after the ninth hour, that is, between three and four o'clock in the afternoon, he *died*. That was the time of the offering of the evening sacrifice, and the time when the paschal lamb was killed; and Christ our Passover was sacrificed for us and offered himself in the evening of the world a sacrifice to God of a sweet-smelling savour.

Two things are here noted concerning the manner of Christ's dying.

1. That he *cried with a loud voice*, as before, *v.* 46. Now,

(1) This was a sign, that, after all his pains and fatigues, his life was *whole* in him, and nature *strong*.

(2) It was significant. This *loud voice* shows that he attacked our spiritual enemies with an undaunted courage, and such a bravery of resolution as bespeaks him hearty in the cause and daring in the encounter. Christ's loud cry was like a trumpet blown over the sacrifices.

2. That then he *yielded up the ghost*. This is the usual periphrasis of dying; to show that the Son of God upon the cross did truly and properly die by the violence of the pain he was put to. His *soul* was separated from his *body*, and so his body was left really and truly dead. He had undertaken to make his soul an *offering for sin*; and he did it, when he *yielded up the ghost*, and voluntarily resigned it.

II. The miracles that attended his death.

1. *Behold, the veil of the temple was rent in twain*. Just as our Lord Jesus expired, at the time of the offering of the evening-sacrifice, and upon a solemn day, when the priests were officiating in the temple, and might themselves be eye-witnesses of it, *the veil of the temple was rent* by an invisible power; that veil which parted between the *holy place* and the *most holy*.

(1) It was in correspondence with the temple of Christ's body, which was now in the dissolving. This was the true temple, in which dwelt *the fulness of the Godhead*; when Christ *cried with a loud voice, and gave up the ghost*, and so dissolved that temple, the literal temple did, as it were, echo to that cry, and answer the stroke, by *rending its veil*.

(2) It signified the revealing and unfolding of the mysteries of the Old Testament. The veil of the temple was for concealment, as was that on the face of Moses, therefore it was called the *veil of the covering*. But now, at the death of Christ, all was laid open, the mysteries were unveiled, so that now he that runs may read the meaning of them. Now we see that the mercy-seat signified *Christ* the great *Propitiation*; the pot of *manna* signified Christ the Bread of life. Thus *we all with open face behold, as in a glass* (which helps the sight, as the veil hindered it), *the glory of the Lord. Our eyes see the salvation*.

(3) It signified the uniting of Jew and Gentile, by the removing of the partition wall between them, which was the ceremonial law, by which the Jews were distinguished from all other people (as a *garden enclosed*), were brought near to God, while others were made to *keep their distance*.

(4) It signified the consecrating and laying open of *a new and living way* to God. The veil kept people off from drawing near to the most holy place, where the *Shechinah*

was. But the rending of it signified that Christ by his death opened a way to God, [1] *For himself.* Though he did not personally ascend into the holy place not made with hands till above forty days after, yet he immediately acquired a right to enter, and had a virtual admission. [2] *For us in him*: so the apostle applies it, Heb. x. 19, 20. We have *boldness to enter into the holiest, by that new and living way which he has consecrated for us through the veil.* We have free access through Christ to the throne of grace, or mercy-seat, now, and to the throne of glory hereafter, Heb. iv. 16; vi. 20.

2. The *earth did quake;* not only mount Calvary, where Christ was crucified, but the *whole land*, and the adjacent countries.

3. The *rocks rent*; the hardest and firmest part of the earth was made to feel this mighty shock.

4. The *graves were opened.* This matter is not related so fully as our curiosity would wish; for the scripture was not intended to gratify that; it should seem, the same earthquake that rent the rocks, *opened the graves*, and many bodies of *saints which slept, arose.* Death to the saints is but the *sleep* of the body, and the *grave* the bed it *sleeps in*; they awoke by the power of the Lord Jesus, and (*v.* 53) came *out of the graves after his resurrection, and went into Jerusalem, the holy city, and appeared unto many.*

III. The conviction of his enemies that were employed in the execution (*v.* 54), which some make no less than another miracle, all things considered. Observe,

1. The persons convinced; *the centurion, and they that were with him watching Jesus*; a captain and his company, that were set on the guard on this occasion. (1) They were *soldiers*, whose profession is commonly hardening, and whose breasts are commonly not so susceptible as some others of the impressions either of fear or pity. But there is no spirit too big, too bold, for the power of Christ to break and humble. (2) They were *Romans, Gentiles*, who knew not the scriptures which were now fulfilled; yet they only were convinced.

2. The means of their conviction; they perceived *the earthquake*, which frightened them, and saw the other *things that were done*. These were designed to assert the honour of Christ in his sufferings, and had their end on these soldiers, whatever they had on others.

3. The expressions of this conviction, in two things.

(1) The *terror* that was *struck* upon them; they *feared greatly*; feared lest they should have been buried in the darkness, or swallowed up in the earthquake.

(2) The *testimony* that was *extorted* from them; they said, *Truly this was the Son of God*; a noble confession; Peter was blessed for it, *ch.* xvi. 16, 17. The best of his disciples could not have said more at any time, and at this time they had not faith and courage enough to say thus much.

IV. The attendance of his friends, that were witnesses of his death, *vv.* 55, 56. Observe,

1. Who they were; *many women who followed him from Galilee*. Not his apostles (only elsewhere we

find John by the cross, John xix. 26), their hearts failed them, they durst not appear, for fear of coming under the same condemnation. But here were a company of women, some would have called them *silly* women, that *boldly* stuck to Christ, when the rest of his disciples had basely deserted him.

2. What they did; they were *beholding afar off*.

(1) They stood *afar off*. Whether their own fear or their enemies' fury kept them at a distance, is not certain; however, it was an aggravation of the sufferings of Christ, that his *lovers and friends stood aloof from his sore*, Ps. xxxviii. 11; Job xix. 13.

(2) They were there *beholding*, in which they showed a concern and kindness for Christ; when they were debarred from doing any other office of love to him, they looked a look of love toward him.

THE BURIAL (vv. 57–66)

We have here an account of Christ's *burial*, and the manner and circumstances of it, concerning which observe, 1. The *kindness* and *good will* of his friends that *laid him in the grave*. 2. The *malice* and *ill will* of his enemies that were very solicitous to keep him there.

I. His friends gave him a *decent burial*. Observe,

1. In general, that Jesus Christ was *buried*; when his precious soul was gone to paradise, his blessed body was deposited in the chambers of the grave, that he might answer the type of Jonas, and fulfil the prophecy of Isaias; he *made his grave with the wicked*. Thus in all things he must be made *like unto his brethren*, sin only excepted, and, like us, unto dust *he must return*. He was buried, to make his death the more certain, and his resurrection the more illustrious. Pilate would not deliver his body to be buried, till he was well assured that he was really dead; while the witnesses lay *unburied*, there were some hopes concerning them, Rev. xi. 8. But Christ, the great Witness, is as one *free among the dead*, *like the slain that lie in the grave*. He was *buried*, that he might take off the terror of the grave, and make it easy to us, might warm and perfume that cold noisome bed for us, and that we might be *buried with him*.

2. The particular circumstances of his burial here related.

(1) The time *when* he was buried; *when the evening was come*; the same evening that he died, before sun-set, as is usual in burying malefactors. It was not deferred till the next day, because it was *the sabbath*; for burying the dead is not proper work either for a day of rest or for a day of rejoicing, as the sabbath is.

(2) The person that took care of the funeral was Joseph of Arimathea. The apostles had all fled, and none of them appeared to show this respect to their Master, which the disciples of John *showed* to him after he was beheaded, who *took up his body, and buried it*, ch. xiv. 12. The women that followed him durst not move in it; then did God stir up this good man to do it; for what work God has to do, he will find out instruments to do it.

(3) The grant of the dead body procured from Pilate, *v.* 58. Joseph *went to* Pilate, the proper person to

be applied to on this occasion, who had the disposal of the body. In Joseph's petition, and Pilate's ready grant of it, *honour* was done to Christ, and a testimony borne to his *integrity*.

(4) The dressing of the body in its grave-clothes (*v.* 59); though he was an honourable counsellor, yet he himself *took the body*, as it should seem, into his own arms, from the infamous and accursed tree (Acts xiii. 29); for where there is true love to Christ, no service will be thought too mean to stoop to for him. Having taken it, he wrapped it in a *clean linen cloth*; for burying in linen was then the common usage, which Joseph complied with.

(5) The depositing of it in the sepulchre, *v.* 60. Here there was nothing of that pomp and solemnity with which the grandees of the world are *brought to the grave, and laid in the tomb*, Job xxi. 32. A private funeral did best befit him whose kingdom came not with observation.

[1] He was laid in a *borrowed* tomb, in Joseph's burying place; as he had not a house of his own, wherein to *lay his head* while he lived, so he had not a grave of his own, wherein to *lay his body* when he was dead, which was an instance of his poverty.

[2] He was laid in a *new tomb*, which Joseph, it is likely, designed *for himself*; it would, however, be *never the worse* for *his* lying in it, who was to rise so quickly, but a *great deal the better* for *his* lying in it, who has altered the property of the grave, and made it *anew* indeed, by turning it into a *bed of rest*, nay into a *bed of spices*, for all the saints.

[3] In a tomb that was *hewn out of a rock*; the ground about Jerusalem was generally rocky. Providence ordered it that Christ's sepulchre should be in a solid entire rock, that no room might be left to suspect his disciples had access to it by some underground passage, or broke through the back wall of it, to steal the body; for there was no access to it but by the door, which was watched.

[4] A *great stone was rolled to the door of his sepulchre*; this also was according to the custom of the Jews in burying their dead, as appears by the description of the grave of Lazarus (John xi. 38), signifying that those who are dead, are *separated* and *cut off from all the living*; if the grave were his prison, now was the prison-door locked and bolted.

(6) The company that attended the funeral; and that was very *small* and *mean—Mary Magdalene, and the other Mary, v.* 56. These, as they had attended him *to the cross*, so they followed him to *the grave*; as if they composed themselves to sorrow, they *sat over against the sepulchre*, not so much to fill their eyes with the sight of what was done, as to empty them in rivers of tears.

II. His enemies did what they could to prevent his resurrection; what they did herein was *the next day that followed the day of the preparation, v.* 62. On that day, the *chief priests and Pharisees*, when they should have been at their devotions, asking pardon for the sins of the week past, were dealing with Pilate about securing the sepulchre, and so *adding rebellion to their sin*. They that had so often quarrelled with Christ for works of the greatest mercy on that day, were themselves busied in a work of the greatest malice. Observe here,

(1) Their address to *Pilate*; they were vexed that the body was given to one that would bury it decently; but, since it must be so, they desire a guard may be set on the sepulchre.

[1] Their petition sets forth, that *that deceiver* (so they call him who is truth itself) *had said, After three days I will rise again*. He had said so, and his disciples *remembered* those very words for the confirmation of their faith, but his persecutors remember them for the provocation of their rage and malice.

[2] It further sets forth their jealousy; *lest his disciples come by night, and steal him away, and say, He is risen*.

First, That which *really* they were afraid of, was, his *resurrection*; that which is most Christ's honour and his people's joy, is most the terror of his enemies.

Secondly, That which they took on them to be afraid of, was, lest *his disciples should come by night, and steal him away*, which was a very improbable thing; for, 1. They had not the courage to own him while he lived, when they might have done him and themselves real service; and it was not likely that his death should put courage into such cowards. 2. What could they promise themselves by stealing away his body, and making people believe he was risen; when, if he should not rise, and so prove himself a deceiver, his disciples, who had left all for him in this world, in

dependence upon a recompence in the other world, would of all others suffer most by the imposture, and would have had reason to throw the first stone at his name?

[3] In consideration hereof, they humbly move to have a guard set upon the sepulchre till the third day; *Command that the sepulchre be made sure*.

(2) Pilate's answer to this address (v. 65); *Ye have a watch, make it sure, as sure as you can*. He was ready to gratify Christ's friends, in allowing them the body, and his enemies, in setting a guard upon it, being desirous to please all sides, while perhaps he laughed in his sleeve at both for making such ado, *pro* and *con*, about the dead body of a man, looking upon the hopes of one side and the fears of the other to be alike ridiculous.

(3) The wonderful care they took, hereupon, to secure the sepulchre (v. 66); *They sealed the stone*. But not trusting too much to that, withal they *set a watch*, to keep *his disciples* from coming to *steal him away*, and, if possible, to hinder *him* from coming out of the grave. To guard the sepulchre against the poor weak disciples, was folly, because *needless*; but to think to guard it against the power of God was folly, because *fruitless* and to no purpose; and yet they thought they had *dealt wisely*.

CHAPTER TWENTY-EIGHT
THE RESURRECTION
(vv. 1–10)

For the proof of Christ's resurrection, we have here the testimony of *the angel*, and of *Christ* himself, concerning his resurrection. Now we may think that it would have been better, if the matter had been so ordered, that a competent number of witnesses should have been present, and have seen the stone rolled away by the angel, and the dead body reviving, as people saw Lazarus come out of the grave, and then the matter had been past dispute; but let us not prescribe to Infinite Wisdom, which ordered that the witnesses of his resurrection should see him *risen*, but not see him *rise*. Christ gave such proofs of his resurrection as were *corroborated* by the scriptures, and by the *word* which he had *spoken* (Luke xxiv. 6, 7–44; Mark xvi. 7); for here we must *walk by faith*, not *by sight*. We have here,

I. The *coming* of the *good women* to the *sepulchre*.

Observe, 1. *When* they came; *in the end of the sabbath, as it began to dawn toward the first day of the week, v.* 1. This fixes the time of Christ's resurrection.

(1) He arose the *third day* after his death; that was the time which he had often pre-fixed, and he kept within it. He was buried in the evening of the sixth day of the week, and arose in the morning of the first day of the following week, so that he lay in the grave about thirty-six or thirty-eight hours. He lay so long, to show that he was really and truly dead; and no longer, that he might not *see corruption*. He arose the third day, to answer the type of the prophet Jonas (*ch.* xii. 40), and to accomplish that prediction (Hos. vi. 2), *The third day he will raise us up, and we shall live in his sight.*

(2) He arose *after the Jewish sabbath*, and it was the passover-sabbath; all that day he lay in the grave, to signify the abolishing of the Jewish feasts and the other parts of the ceremonial law, and that his people must be dead to such observances, and take no more notice of them than he did when he *lay in the grave*. Christ on *the sixth day finished* his work; he said, *It is finished*; on the seventh day he rested, and then on the first day of the next week did as it were begin a new world, and enter upon new work.

(3) He arose upon the *first day of the week*; on the first day of the first week God *commanded the light to shine out of darkness*; on this day therefore did he who was to be the Light of the world, shine out of the darkness of the grave; and the seventh-day sabbath being buried with Christ, it arose again in the first-day sabbath, called the *Lord's day* (Rev. i. 10), and no other day of the week is from henceforward mentioned in all the New Testament than this, and this often, as the day which Christians religiously observed in solemn assemblies, to the honour of Christ, John xx. 19, 26; Acts xx. 7; 1 Cor. xvi. 2.

(4) He arose *as it began to dawn* toward that day; as soon as it could be said that the *third day* was come, the time prefixed for his resurrection, he *arose*; after his withdrawings from his people, he returns with all convenient *speed*, and *cuts the work* as *short in righteousness* as may be.

2. Who they were, that came to the sepulchre; *Mary Magdalene and the other Mary*, the same that

attended the funeral, and *sat over against the sepulchre*, as before they *sat over against the cross*; still they studied to express their love to Christ; still they were enquiring after him. Then shall we *know*, if we thus *follow on to know*. No mention is made of the Virgin Mary being with them; it is probable that the *beloved disciple*, who had taken her to his own home, hindered her from *going to the grave to weep there*.

3. What they *came to do*: the other evangelists say that they came to anoint the body; Matthew saith that they came to *see the sepulchre*, whether it was as they left it; hearing perhaps, but not being sure, that the chief priests had set a guard upon it. They went, to show their good-will in another visit to the dear remains of their beloved Master, and perhaps not without some thoughts of his resurrection, for they could not have quite forgotten all he had said of it.

II. The appearance of an angel of the Lord to them, *vv.* 2–4. We have here an account of the manner of the resurrection of Christ, as far as it was fit that we should know.

1. There was a *great earthquake*. When he died, the earth that *received him*, shook for fear; now that he arose, the earth that *resigned him*, leaped for joy in his exaltation.

2. The *angel of the Lord descended from heaven*. The angels frequently attended our Lord Jesus, at his birth, in his temptation, in his agony; but upon the cross we find no angel attending him: when his Father *forsook him*, the angels withdrew from him; but now that

he is resuming the glory he had before the foundation of the world, now, behold, the *angels of God worship him*.

3. He came, and rolled back the stone from the door, and sat upon it. Our Lord Jesus could have *rolled back the stone* himself by his own power, but he chose to have it done by an angel, to signify that having undertaken to make satisfaction for our sin, imputed to him, and being under arrest pursuant to that imputation, he did not *break prison*, but had a fair and *legal discharge*, obtained from heaven; he did not break prison, but an officer was sent on purpose to *roll away the stone*, and so to open the prison door, which would never have been done, if he had not made a *full satisfaction*.

4. That his *countenance was like lightning, and his raiment white as snow, v.* 3. This was a visible representation, by that which we call *splendid* and *illustrious*, of the *glories* of the invisible world, which know no *difference of colours*. When Christ died, the court of heaven *went into deep mourning*, signified by the *darkening of the sun*; but when he arose, they again put on the *garments of praise*.

5. That *for fear of him the keepers did shake, and became as dead men, v.* 4. They were posted here, to *keep a dead man in his grave*—as easy a piece of service surely as was ever assigned them, and yet it proves too hard for them. They were told that they must expect to be assaulted by a company of feeble faint-hearted disciples, who for fear of them would soon *shake* and become as *dead men*, but are amazed when they find themselves attacked by a

mighty angel, whom they dare not look in the face.

III. The message which this angel delivered to the women, *vv.* 5–7.

1. He *encourages them against their fears*, *v.* 5. "*Fear not ye.* Let not the news I have to tell you, be any surprise to you, for you were told before that your Master would rise; let it be no terror to you, for his resurrection will be your consolation; fear not any hurt, that I will do you, nor any evil tidings I have to tell you. *Fear not ye, for I know that ye seek Jesus.* I know you are friends to the cause. I do not come to frighten you, but to encourage you."

2. He *assures them of the resurrection of Christ*; and there was enough in that to silence their fears (*v.* 6); He *is not here, for he is risen*.

Two things the angel refers these women to, for the confirmation of their faith, touching Christ's resurrection.

[1] To his *word* now *fulfilled*, which they might *remember; He is risen, as he said*. This he vouches as the proper object of faith; "He said that he *would rise*, and you know that he is the *Truth* itself, and therefore have reason to expect that he *should rise*; why should you be backward to *believe* that which he told you would be?"

[2] To his *grave* now *empty*, which they might *look into*; "*Come, see the place where the Lord lay.* Compare what you have *heard*, with what you *see*, and, putting both together, you will *believe*."

3. He *directs them* to go *carry the tidings* of it to his disciples (*v.* 7); Go *quickly, and tell his disciples*. It is probable that they were for

entertaining themselves with the sight of the sepulchre and discourse with the angels. It was good to be here, but they have other work appointed them; *this is a day of good tidings*, and though they have the *first taste* of it, yet they must not have the *monopoly* of it, must not hold their peace, any more than those lepers, 2 Kings vii. 9. They must go *tell the disciples*.

They were directed to appoint the disciples to *meet him in Galilee*. There were other appearances of Christ to them before that in *Galilee*, which were sudden and surprising; but he would have one to be solemn and public, and gave them notice of it before.

Lastly, The angel solemnly affirms upon his word the truth of what he had related to them; "*Lo, I have told you*, you may be assured of it, and depend upon it; *I* have told you, who dare not tell a lie. *The word spoken by angels was steadfast*, Heb. ii. 2.

IV. The women's *departure* from the *sepulchre*, to bring notice to the disciples, *v.* 8. And observe,

1. What frame and temper of spirit they were in; They *departed with fear and great joy*; a strange mixture, fear and joy at the same time, in the same soul. To hear that Christ was risen, was matter of joy; but to be led into his grave, and to see an angel, and talk with him about it, could not but cause fear. It was good news, but they were *afraid* that it was too *good* to be true. But observe, it is said of their *joy*, It was *great* joy; it is not said so of their fear.

2. What haste they made; *They did run*.

3. What errand they went upon; They ran, to *bring his disciples word*.

V. Christ's appearing to the women, to confirm the testimony of the angel, *vv*. 9, 10. These zealous good women not only heard the first tidings of him, but had the first sight of him, after his resurrection.

Here is, 1. Christ's surprising appearance to the women; *As they went to tell his disciples, behold, Jesus met them*.

2. The salutation wherewith he accosted them; *All hail*. We use the old *English form of salutation*, wishing *all health* to those we meet; for so *All hail* signifies, and is expressive of the Greek form of salutation here used, answering to that of the Hebrew, *Peace be unto you*.

3. The affectionate respect they paid him; *They came, and held him by the feet, and worshipped him*.

4. The encouraging words Christ said to them, *v*. 10. Now observe here,

(1) How he rebukes their fear; *Be not afraid*. They must not fear being imposed upon by these repeated notices of his resurrection, nor fear any hurt from the appearance of one from the dead; for the news, though strange, was both *true* and *good*.

(2) How he repeats their message; "*Go, tell my brethren*, that they must prepare for a journey into Galilee, and there *they shall see me*."

A DECEPTION (*vv*. 11–15)

For the further proof of the resurrection of Christ, we have here the confession of the adversaries that were upon the guard; and there are two things which strengthen this testimony—that they were *eye-witnesses*, and did themselves see the glory of the resurrection, which none else did—and that they were *enemies*, set there to oppose and obstruct his resurrection.

The sham was *ridiculous*, and carried along with it its own confutation. If *they slept*, how could they know any thing of the matter, or say who came? If *any one* of them was awake to *observe it*, no doubt, he would awake them all to *oppose it*; for that was the only thing they had in charge. It was altogether improbable that a company of poor, weak, cowardly, dispirited men should expose themselves for so inconsiderable an achievement as the rescue of the dead body. Why were not the houses where they lodged diligently searched, and other means used to discover the dead body; but this was so thin a lie as one might easily see through. But had it been ever so plausible, (2) It was a wicked thing for these priests and elders to hire those soldiers to tell a deliberate lie (if it had been in a matter of ever so small importance), against their consciences. Those know not what they do, who draw others to commit one wilful sin; for that may debauch conscience, and be an inlet to many. But, (3) Considering this as intended to overthrow the great doctrine of Christ's resurrection, this was a sin against the last remedy, and was, in effect, a blasphemy *against the Holy Ghost*, imputing *that* to the roguery of the disciples, which was done by *the power of the Holy Ghost*.

But lest the soldiers should object the penalty they incurred by the Roman law for *sleeping upon the guard*, which was very severe (Acts xii. 19), they promised to interpose with the governor; "*We will persuade him, and secure you.*"

Well, thus was the plot laid; now what success had it?

[1] Those that were *willing to deceive*, took the money, and did as they were taught.

The great argument to prove Christ to be the Son of God, is, his resurrection, and none could have more convincing proofs of the truth of that than these soldiers had; they saw the angel descend from heaven, saw the stone rolled away, saw the body of Christ come out of the grave, unless the consternation they felt hindered them; and yet they were so far from being convinced by it themselves, that they were hired to belie him, and to hinder others from believing in him.

[2] Those that were willing to be deceived, not only credited, but propagated, the story; This *saying is commonly reported among the Jews until this day*. The sham took well enough, and answered the end.

THE GREAT COMMISSION
(*vv.* 16–20)

This evangelist passes over several other appearances of Christ, recorded by Luke and John, and hastens to this, which was of all other the most solemn, as being promised and appointed again and again before his death, and after his resurrection. Observe,

I. How the disciples attended his appearance, according to the appointment (*v.* 16); *They went into Galilee*, a long journey to go for one sight of Christ, but it was worth while. They had seen him several times at Jerusalem, and yet they went into Galilee, to see him there.

II. How they were affected with the appearance of Christ to them, *v.* 17. Now was the time that he was *seen of above five hundred brethren at once*, 1 Cor. xv. 6. We are told,

1. That they *worshipped him*; many of them did so, nay, it should seem, they all did that, they gave divine honour to him, which was signified by some outward expressions of adoration. Note, All that see the Lord Jesus with an eye of faith are obliged to *worship him*.

2. But *some doubted*, some of those that were then present. These doubts were afterward removed, and their faith grew up to a full assurance, and it tended much to the honour of Christ, that the disciples *doubted* before they *believed*; so that they cannot be said to be credulous, and willing to be imposed upon; for they first *questioned*, and *proved all things*, and then *held fast* that which was *true*, and which they found to be so.

III. What Jesus Christ said to them (*vv.* 18–20); *Jesus came, and spoke unto them.* Christ now delivered to his apostles the great charter of his kingdom in the world, was sending them out as his ambassadors, and here gives them their credentials.

In opening this great charter, we may observe two things.

1. The commission which our Lord Jesus received himself from the Father. Being about to *authorize* his apostles, if any ask by what

authority he doeth it, and who gave him that authority, here he tells us, *All power is given unto me in heaven and in earth*; a very great word, and which none but he could say. Hereby he asserts his universal dominion as Mediator, which is the great foundation of the Christian religion. He has *all power*. Observe, (1) *Whence* he hath this power. He did not assume it, or usurp it, but it was *given* him, he was legally entitled to it, and invested in it, by a grant from him who is the Fountain of all being, and consequently of all power. God *set him King* (Ps. ii. 6), inaugurated and enthroned him, Luke i. 32. (2) *Where* he has this power; in *heaven and earth*, comprehending the universe. Christ is the sole universal Monarch, he is *Lord of all*, Acts x. 36.

2. The commission he gives to those whom he sent forth; *Go ye therefore*. This commission is given, (1) To the *apostles* primarily, the chief ministers of state in Christ's kingdom, the architects that laid the foundation of the church. Now those that had followed Christ in the regeneration, were *set on thrones* (Luke xxii. 30); *Go ye*. It is not only a word of command, like that, *Son, go work*, but a word of encouragement, *Go*, and *fear not, have I not sent you?* (2) It is given to their successors, the ministers of the gospel, whose business it is to transmit the gospel from age to age, to the end of the world in time, as it was theirs to transmit it from nation to nation, to the end of the world in place, and no less necessary. The Old-Testament promise of a gospel ministry is made to a succession (Isa. lix.

21); and this must be so understood, otherwise how could Christ be with them always to the *consummation of the world*? Christ, at his ascension, gave not only apostles and prophets, but *pastors and teachers*, Eph. iv. 11. Now observe,

[1] How far his commission is extended; to *all nations*. Go, and disciple *all nations*. Not that they must go all together into every place, but by consent disperse themselves in such manner as might best *diffuse* the light of the gospel. Now this plainly signifies it to be the will of Christ, *First*, That the covenant of peculiarity, made with the Jews, should now be cancelled and disannulled. *Secondly*, That salvation by Christ should be offered to all, and none excluded that did not by their unbelief and impenitence exclude themselves.

[2] What is the principal intention of this commission; to *disciple* all nations. "*Admit them disciples*; do your utmost to make the nations Christian nations"; not, "Go to the nations, and denounce the judgments of God against them, as Jonah against Nineveh, and as the other Old-Testament prophets" (though they had reason enough to expect it for their wickedness), "but go, and *disciple them*."

[3] Their instructions for executing this commission.

First, They must *admit disciples* by the *sacred rite of baptism*; "Go into all nations, preach the gospel to them, work miracles among them, and persuade them to come in themselves, and bring their children with them, into the church of Christ, and then admit them and

273

theirs into the church, by washing them with water."

Secondly, This baptism must be administered *in the name of the Father, and of the Son, and of the Holy Ghost*. That is, 1. *By authority from heaven*, and not *of man*; for his ministers act by authority from the three persons in the Godhead, who all concur, as to our *creation*, so to our *redemption*; they have their commission under the great seal of heaven, which puts an honour upon the ordinance, though to a carnal eye, like him that instituted it, it has *no form or comeliness*. 2. *Calling upon the name* of the Father, Son, and Holy Ghost. Every thing is sanctified by prayer, and particularly the waters of baptism. But, 3. It is *into the name* of *Father, Son, and Holy Ghost*; this was intended as the *summary* of the first principles of the Christian religion, and of the new covenant, and according to it the ancient creeds were drawn up. By our being baptized, we solemnly profess, (1) Our *assent* to the scripture-revelation concerning *God, the Father, Son, and Holy Ghost*. (2) Our *consent* to a covenant-relation to God, *the Father, Son, and Holy Ghost*. Baptism is a *sacrament*, that is, it is *an oath*. It is an oath of *abjuration*, by which we renounce the world and the flesh, as rivals with God for the throne in our hearts; and an oath of *allegiance*, by which we resign and give up *ourselves* to God, to be *his*, our own selves, our whole selves, *body, soul, and spirit*, to be governed by his will, and made happy in his favour.

Thirdly, Those that are thus baptized, and enrolled among the disciples of Christ, must be taught (v. 20); *Teaching them to observe all things, whatsoever I have commanded you*. This denotes two things.

(1) The duty of *disciples*, of all *baptized Christians*; they must observe all things whatsoever Christ has commanded, and, in order to that, must submit to the teaching of those whom he sends.

(2) The duty of the apostles of Christ, and his ministers; and that is, to *teach* the commands of Christ, to expound them to his disciples, to press upon them the necessity of obedience, and to assist them in applying the general commands of Christ to particular cases.

3. Here is the assurance he gives them of his spiritual presence with them in the execution of this commission; *And lo, I am with you always, even unto the end of the world*. Observe,

The favour promised them; *I am with you*. Not, *I will be* with you, but *I am*.

They shall have his *constant* presence; *always, all days*, every day. There is no day, no hour of the day, in which our Lord Jesus is not present with his churches and with his ministers; if there were, that day, that hour, they were undone. Since his resurrection he had appeared to them *now and then*, once a week it may be, and scarcely that. But he assures them that they shall have his spiritual presence continued to them without intermission.

Two solemn farewells we find our Lord Jesus giving to his church, and his parting word at both of them is very encouraging; one was here, when he closed up his personal converse with them, and then his parting word was, "*Lo, I am with you always*; I leave you, and yet still I am with you"; the other was, when he closed up the canon of the scripture by the pen of his beloved disciple, and then his parting word was, "*Surely, I come quickly*. I leave you for awhile, but I will be with you again shortly," Rev. xxii. 20. By this it appears that he did not part in anger, but in love, and that it is his will we should keep up both our communion with him and our expectation of him.

ST. MARK

CHAPTER ONE
JOHN THE BAPTIST
(*vv.* 1–8)

We may observe here,

I. What the New Testament is—the *divine* testament, to which we *adhere* above all that is *human*; the new testament, which we *advance* above that which was old. It is *the gospel of Jesus Christ the Son of God*, v. 1. 1. It is *gospel*; it is God's word, and is *faithful* and *true*; see Rev. xix. 9; xxi. 5; xxii. 6. It is a *good word*, and well *worthy of all acceptation*; it brings us glad tidings. 2. It is the *gospel of Jesus Christ*, the *anointed Saviour*, the Messiah promised and expected.

II. What the *reference* of the New Testament is to the Old, and its *coherence* with it. The gospel of Jesus Christ *begins*, and so we shall find it *goes on*, just *as it is written in the prophets* (v. 2); for it *saith no other things than those which the prophets and Moses said should come* (Acts xxvi. 22).

Quotations are here borrowed from two prophecies—that of Isaiah, which was the *longest*, and that of Malachi, which was the *latest* (and there were above three hundred years between them), both of whom spoke to the same purport concerning *the beginning of the gospel of Jesus Christ*, in the ministry of John.

1. Malachi, in whom we had the Old-Testament *farewell*, spoken very plainly (*ch.* iii. 1) concerning John Baptist, who was to give the New Testament *welcome. Behold, I send my messenger before thy face*, v. 2. Christ himself had taken notice of this, and applied it to John (Matt. xi. 10), who was God's *messenger*, sent to *prepare Christ's way*.

2. Isaiah, the most evangelical of all the prophets, *begins* the evangelical part of his prophecy with this, which points to the *beginning of the gospel of Christ* (Isa. xl. 3); *The voice of him that crieth in the wilderness*, v. 3. Matthew had taken notice of this, and applied it to John, *ch.* iii. 3.

III. What the *beginning of the New Testament* was. The gospel began in John Baptist; for *the law and the prophets were, until John*, the only divine revelation, but then the *kingdom of God began to be preached*, Luke xvi. 16. Peter begins *from the baptism of John*, Acts i. 22. The gospel did not begin *so soon* as the *birth* of Christ, for he took time to *increase in wisdom and stature*, not so late as his entering upon his public ministry, but half a year before, when John began to preach the same doctrine that Christ afterward preached. His baptism was the dawning of the *gospel day*.

In the success of John's preaching, and the disciples he admitted by baptism, there was the *beginning of a gospel church.* He baptized *in the wilderness,* and declined going into the cities; but *there went out unto him all the land of Judea, and they of Jerusalem,* inhabitants both of city and country, families of them, and *were all baptized of him.* They entered themselves his disciples, and bound themselves to his discipline; in token of which, they *confessed their sins;* he admitted them his disciples, in token of which, he *baptized* them. Many of these afterward became followers of Christ, and preachers of his gospel, and this grain of mustard-seed became a *tree.*

BAPTISM OF JESUS
(vv. 9–13)

We have here a brief account of Christ's baptism and temptation, which were largely related Matt. iii. and iv.

CHRIST IN GALILEE
(vv. 14–22)

Here is, I. A general account of Christ's preaching in Galilee. John gives an account of his preaching in Judea, before this (*ch.* ii. and iii.), which the other evangelists had omitted, who chiefly relate what occurred in Galilee, because that was the least known at Jerusalem. Observe,

1. When Jesus began to preach in Galilee; *After that John was put in prison.* When he had *finished* his testimony, then Jesus *began* his.

2. What he preached; *The gospel of the kingdom of God.* Christ came to set up the kingdom of God among men, that they might be brought into *subjection to it,* and might obtain *salvation in it;* and he set it up by the preaching of his gospel, and a power going along with it.

Observe, (1) The great *truths* Christ preached; *The time is fulfilled, and the kingdom of God is at hand.* This refers to the Old Testament, in which the kingdom of the Messiah was promised, and the time fixed for the introducing of it. They were not so well versed in those prophecies, nor did they so well observe the signs of the times, as to understand it themselves, and therefore Christ gives them notice of it.

(2) The great *duties* inferred from thence. Christ tells them, in the prospect of that kingdom approaching, they must *repent, and believe the gospel.* They had broken the *moral law,* and could not be saved by a *covenant of innocency,* for both Jew and Gentile are concluded *under guilt.* They must therefore take the benefit of a *covenant of grace,* must submit to a *remedial law,* and this is it —*repentance towards God, and faith towards our Lord Jesus Christ.*

II. Christ appearing as a teacher, here is next his *calling of disciples,* vv. 16–20. Observe, 1. Christ will have followers. 2. The instruments Christ chose to employ in setting up his kingdom, were the *weak* and *foolish things of the world;* not called from the great sanhedrim, or the schools of the rabbin, but picked up from among the tarpaulins *by the sea-side, that the excellency of the power* might appear to be wholly *of God,* and not at all *of them.* 3. Though Christ needs not the help of man, yet he is pleased to make use of it in setting up his kingdom, that he might deal with us not in a formidable but in a familiar way, and that in his kingdom the *nobles and governors may be of ourselves*, Jer. xxx. 21. 4. Christ puts honour upon those who, though mean in the world, are *diligent in their business*, and *loving to one another*; so those were, whom Christ called. 5. The business of ministers is to *fish for souls*, and *win them to Christ*. 6. Those whom Christ calls, must *leave all*, to follow him; and by his grace he inclines them to do so. *Not that we must needs go out of the world* immediately, but we must sit loose to the world, and forsake every thing that is inconsistent with our duty to Christ, and that cannot be kept without prejudice to our souls.

III. Here is a particular account of his preaching in Capernaum, one of the *cities* of Galilee. Observe, 1. When Christ *came into Capernaum*, he *straightway* applied himself to his work there, and took the *first* opportunity of preaching the gospel. Those will think themselves concerned not to *lose time*, who consider what a deal of work they have to do, and what a little time to do it in. 2. Christ religiously observed the sabbath day, though not by tying himself up to the tradition of the elders, in all the niceties of the *sabbath-rest*, yet (which was far better) by applying himself to, and abounding in, the *sabbath-work*, in order to which the sabbath-rest was instituted. 3. Sabbaths are to be sanctified in *religious assemblies*, if we have opportunity; it is a *holy day*, and must be honoured with a *holy convocation*; this was the *good old way*, Acts xiii. 27; xv. 21. 4. In *religious assemblies* on sabbath-days, the gospel is to be preached, and those to be *taught*, who are willing to learn the *truth as it is in Jesus*. 5. Christ was a non-such preacher; he did not preach *as the scribes*, who expounded the law of Moses by rote, as a school-boy says his lessons, but were neither *acquainted* with it (Paul himself, when a Pharisee, was ignorant of the law), nor *affected* with it; it came not *from the heart*, and therefore came not *with authority*. But Christ taught *as one that had authority*, as one that knew the mind of God, and was commissioned to declare it. 6. There is much in the doctrine of Christ, that is *astonishing*; the more we hear it, the more cause we shall see to *admire it*.

A SABBATH HEALING
(*vv.* 23–28)

As soon as Christ began to preach, he began to work miracles for the confirmation of his doctrine; and they were such as intimated the design and tendency of his doctrine, which were to conquer Satan, and cure sick souls.

In these verses, we have,

I. Christ's *casting the devil* out of a man that was possessed, in the synagogue at Capernaum. Now here we have,

1. The rage which the unclean spirit expressed at Christ; *He cried out*, as one in an agony, at the presence of Christ, and afraid of being dislodged; thus the *devils believe and tremble*, have a horror

of Christ, but no hope in him, nor reverence for him.

2. The victory which Jesus Christ obtained over the unclean spirit; *for this purpose was the Son of God manifested, that he might destroy the works of the devil,* and so he makes it to appear; nor will he be turned back from prosecuting this war, either by his flatteries or by his menaces. It is in vain for Satan to beg and pray, *Let us alone*; his power must be broken, and the poor man must be relieved; and therefore, (1) Jesus *commands.* As he taught, so he healed, *with authority.* Jesus *rebuked him*; he chid him and threatened him, imposed silence upon him; *Hold thy peace; be muzzled.* (2) The unclean spirit *yields,* for there is no remedy (*v.* 26); He *tore him,* put him into a *strong convulsion*; that one could have thought he had been pulled in pieces; when he would not *touch* Christ, in fury at him he grievously disturbed this poor creature.

II. The impression which this miracle made upon the minds of the people, *vv.* 27, 28.

1. It astonished them that saw it; *They were all amazed.* It was evident, beyond contradiction, that the man was possessed—witness the tearing of him, and the *loud voice* with which the *spirit cried*; it was evident that he was *forced out* by the authority of Christ; this was surprising to them, and put them upon considering with themselves, and enquiring of one another, "*What is this new doctrine?*"

2. It raised his reputation among all that heard it; *Immediately his fame spread abroad into the whole*

adjacent region of Galilee, which was a third part of the land of Canaan.

HEALING AND PRAYING
(*vv.* 29–45)

In these verses, we have,

I. A particular account of one miracle that Christ wrought, in the cure of Peter's wife's mother, who was ill of a fever. This passage we had before, in Matthew.

II. A general account of many cures he wrought—diseases healed, devils expelled. It was on the *evening of the sabbath,* when the *sun did set,* or *was set*; perhaps many scrupled bringing their sick to him, till the sabbath was over, but their weakness therein was no prejudice to them in applying to Christ. Though he proved it *lawful to heal on the sabbath days,* yet, if any stumbled at it, they were welcome at another time.

III. His *retirement* to his *private devotion* (*v.* 35); *He prayed,* prayed alone; to set us an example of secret prayer. Though as God he was *prayed to,* as man he *prayed.* Though he was glorifying God, and doing good, in his public work, yet he found time to be alone with his Father; and thus *it became him to fulfil all righteousness.*

IV. His *return* to his *public* work. The disciples thought they were *up early,* but found their Master was up *before them,* and they enquired which way he went, *followed him* to his *solitary place,* and there *found him* at prayer, *vv.* 36, 37. They told him that he was much wanted, that there were a great many patients waiting for him; *All men seek for thee.* "No," saith Christ, "Capernaum must not have the monopoly of the Messiah's preaching and miracles. *Let us go into the next towns*, the *villages* that lie about here, *that I may preach there also*, and work miracles there, *for therefore came I forth*, not to be constantly resident in one place, but to *go about doing good*."

We also have here the story of Christ's *cleansing* a *leper*, which we had before, Matt. viii. 2–4.

CHAPTER TWO

A PARALYTIC HEALED
(vv. 1–12)

Christ, having been for some time preaching about in the country, here returns to Capernaum, his headquarters, and makes his appearance there, in hopes that by this time the talk and crowd would be somewhat abated. Now observe,

I. The great resort there was to him. *There was no room to receive them*, they were so numerous, *no not so much as about the door*. A blessed sight, to see people thus flying like a cloud to Christ's house, though it was but a poor one, and *as the doves to their windows!*

II. The good entertainment Christ gave them, the best his house would afford, and better than any other could; he *preached the word unto them, v*. 2. Many of them perhaps came only for cures, and many perhaps only for curiosity, to get a sight of him; but when he had them together he *preached to them*.

III. The presenting of a poor cripple to him, to be helped by him. The patient was one *sick of the palsy*, it should seem not as that,

Matt. viii. 6, *grievously tormented*, but perfectly disabled, so that he was *borne of four*, was carried upon *a bed*, as if he had been upon *a bier*, by four persons. These kind relations or neighbours thought, if they could but carry this poor man once to Christ, they should not need to carry him any more; and therefore made hard shift to get him to him; and when they could not otherwise get to him, they *uncovered the roof where he was, v*. 4. This bespoke both their *faith* and their *fervency* in this address to Christ. Hereby it appeared that they were in earnest, and would not go away, nor *let Christ go without a blessing*. Gen. xxxii. 26.

IV. The kind word Christ said to this poor patient; *He saw their faith*; perhaps not so much his, for his disability hindered him from the exercise of faith, but *theirs* that brought him. In curing the centurion's servant, Christ took notice of it as an instance of *his faith*, that he did not bring him to Christ, but believed he could cure him at a distance; here he commended *their faith*, because they did bring their friend through so much difficulty. Note, True faith and strong faith may work variously, conquering sometimes the objections of reason, sometimes those of sense; but, however manifested, it shall be accepted and approved by Jesus Christ. Christ said, *Son, thy sins be forgiven thee*. Note, 1. Sin is the procuring cause of all our pains and sicknesses. The word of Christ was to take his thoughts off from the disease, which was the effect, and to lead them to the sin, the cause, that he might be more concerned about that, to get that pardoned. 2. God doth *then* graciously take away the sting and malignity of sickness, when he forgives sin. Pardon of sin strikes at the root of all diseases, and either cures them, or alters their property.

V. The cavil of the scribes at that which Christ said, and a demonstration of the unreasonableness of their cavil. They were expositors of the law, and their doctrine was *true* —that it is blasphemy for any creature to undertake the pardon of sin, and that it is God's prerogative, Isa. xliii. 25. But, as is usual with such teachers, their application was *false*, and was the effect of their ignorance and enmity to Christ. It is *true, None can forgive sins but God only*; but it is false that therefore Christ cannot, who had abundantly proved himself to have a divine power. But Christ *perceived in his spirit that they so reasoned within themselves*; this proves him to be God, and therefore confirmed what was to be proved, that he had authority to *forgive sins*; for he *searched* the heart, and knew *what was in man*, Rev. ii. 23. Now he proves his power to *forgive sin*, by demonstrating his power to cure the *man sick of the palsy*, *vv*. 9–11. He would not have pretended to do *the one*, if he could not have done *the other; that ye may know that the Son of man*, the Messiah, *has power on earth to forgive sin*, that I have that power, *Thou that art* sick of the palsy, *arise, take up thy bed*. Now, 1. This was a *suitable* argument in itself. He could not have cured the disease, which was the effect, if he could not have taken away the sin,

which was the cause. 2. It was suited to them. These carnal scribes would be more affected with such a suitable effect of a pardon as the cure of the disease, and be sooner convinced by it, than by any other more spiritual consequences; therefore it was proper enough to appeal, whether it is easier to say, *Thy sins are forgiven thee*, or to say, *Arise, and walk?* The removing of the punishment as such, was the remitting of the sin; he that could go so far in the cure, no doubt could perfect it. See Isa. xxxiii. 24.

VI. The cure of the sick man, and the impression it made upon the people, *v*. 12. *They were all amazed*, as well they might, and *glorified God*, as indeed they ought; saying, *"We never saw it on this fashion;"* never were such wonders as these done before in our time."

FOLLOW ME (*vv*. 13–17)

Here is,

I. Christ preaching by the *sea-side* (*v*. 13), whither he went *for room*, because he found, upon second trial, no house or street large enough to contain his auditory; but upon the strand there might come as many as would.

II. His calling Levi; the same with Matthew, who had a place in the custom-house at Capernaum, from which he was denominated a *publican*; his place fixed him by the waterside, and thither Christ went to meet with him, and to give him an effectual call. This Levi is here said to be *the son of Alpheus* or *Cleophas*, husband to that Mary who was sister or near kinswoman to the virgin Mary, and if so, he was own brother to James the less, and Jude, and Simon the Canaanite, so that there were four brothers of them apostles. It is probable that Matthew was but a loose extravagant young man, or else, being a Jew, he would never have been a publican. However, Christ called him to *follow him*. Paul, though a Pharisee, had been one of the chief of sinners, and yet was called to be an apostle. With God, through Christ, there is mercy to pardon the greatest sins, and grace to sanctify the greatest sinners.

III. His familiar converse with *publicans and sinners, v.* 15. We are here told, 1. That Christ *sat at meat in Levi's house*, who invited *him and his disciples* to the farewell-feast he made to his friends, when he left all to attend on Christ: such a feast he made, as Elisha did (1 Kings xix. 21), to show, not only with what cheerfulness in himself, but with what thankfulness to God, he quitted all, in compliance with Christ's call. Fitly did he make the *day of his espousals* to Christ a festival day. 2. That *many publicans and sinners* sat with Christ in Levi's house (for *there were many* belonging to that custom-house); and *they followed him*. They followed Levi; so some understand it, supposing that, like Zaccheus, he was *chief among the publicans*, and was *rich*; and for that reason, the inferior sort of them attended him for what they could get. I rather take it, that they *followed Jesus* because of the report they had heard of him. The publicans are here and elsewhere ranked with *sinners*, the worst of *sinners*. (1) Because commonly they *were* such; so general were the corruptions in the execution of that office.

(2) Because the Jews had a particular antipathy to them and their office, as an affront to the liberty of their nation and a badge of their slavery.

IV. The *offence* which the scribes and Pharisees took at this, *v.* 16. They would not come to hear him preach, which they might have been convinced and edified by; but they would come themselves to *see him* sit with publicans and sinners, which they would be provoked by.

V. Christ's justification of himself in it, *v.* 17. He stood to what he did, and would not withdraw, though the Pharisees were offended, as Peter afterwards did, Gal. ii. 12. They thought Christ's character should separate him from them; "No," saith Christ, "my commission directs me to them; *I came not to call the righteous, but sinners to repentance.*"

THE DISCIPLES JUSTIFIED
(*vv.* 18–28)

Christ had been put to *justify* himself in conversing with *publicans and sinners:* here he is put to justify his disciples; and in what they do according to his will he will justify them, and bear them out.

I. He justifies them in their *not fasting*, which was turned to their reproach by the Pharisees.

Two things Christ pleads in excuse of his disciples *not fasting*.

1. That these were *easy days* with them, and fasting was not so *seasonable* now as it would be hereafter, *vv.* 19, 20.

2. That these were *early days* with them, and they were not so able for the severe exercises of

religion as hereafter they would be. The Pharisees had long accustomed themselves to such austerities; and John Baptist himself came neither eating nor drinking. His disciples from the first inured themselves to hardships, and thus found it easier to bear strict and frequent fasting, but it was not so with Christ's disciples; their Master came *eating and drinking*, and had not bred them up to the difficult services of religion as yet, for it was all in good time. To put them upon such frequent fasting at first, would be a discouragement to them, and perhaps drive them off from following Christ; it would be of as ill consequence as *putting new wine into old casks*, or sewing *new cloth* to that which is worn thin and threadbare, *vv.* 21, 22.

II. He justifies them in *plucking the ears of corn on the sabbath day*, which, I will warrant you, a disciple of the Pharisees would not dare to have done; for it was contrary to an express tradition of their elders.

Observe, 1. What a poor breakfast Christ's disciples had on a sabbath-day morning, when they were going to church (*v.* 23); they *plucked the ears of corn*, and that was the best they had. The Jews made it a piece of religion, to eat dainty food on sabbath days, but the disciples were content with any thing.

2. How even this was *grudged them* by the Pharisees, upon supposition that it was not lawful to *pluck the ears of corn* on the sabbath day, that that was as much a servile work as *reaping* (*v.* 24): *Why do they on the sabbath day that which is not lawful?*

3. How Christ defended them in what they did.

(1) By example. They had a good precedent for it in David's eating the *show-bread*, when he was hungry, and there was no other bread to be had (*vv.* 25, 26).

(2) By argument. To reconcile them to the disciples' *plucking the ears of corn*, let them consider,

[1] Whom the sabbath was *made for* (*v.* 27); *it was made for man, and not man for the sabbath*. This we had not in Matthew. The sabbath is a sacred and divine institution; but we must receive and embrace it as a privilege and a benefit, not as a task and a drudgery.

[2] Whom the sabbath was *made by* (*v.* 28); "*The Son of man is Lord also of the sabbath*; and therefore he will not see the kind intentions of the institution of it frustrated by your impositions." Note, The sabbath days are *days of the Son of man*; he is the Lord of the day, and to his honour it must be observed.

CHAPTER THREE

MORE MIRACLES (*vv.* 1–12)

Here, as before, we have our Lord Jesus busy at work *in the synagogue* first, and then by *the sea side*. Now here we have some account of what he did.

I. When he *entered again into the synagogue*, he improved the opportunity he had there, of doing good, and having, no doubt, preached a sermon there, he wrought a miracle for the confirmation of it, or at least for the confirmation of this truth—that *it is lawful to do good on the sabbath day*. We had the narrative, Matt. xii. 9.

1. The patient's case was piteous; he had a *withered hand*, by which he was disabled to work for his living; and those that are so, are the most proper objects of charity; let those be helped that cannot help themselves.

2. The spectators were very unkind, both to the patient and to the Physician; instead of interceding for a poor neighbour, they did what they could to hinder his cure: for they intimated that if Christ cured him now on the sabbath day, they would accuse him as a *Sabbath breaker*.

3. Christ dealt very fairly with the spectators, and dealt with them *first*, if possible to *prevent* the offence.

(1) He laboured to convince their judgment. He bade the man *stand forth* (*v.* 3), that by the sight of him they might be moved with compassion toward him, and might not, for shame, account his cure a crime. And then he appeals to their own consciences; though the thing *speaks itself*, yet *he* is pleased to speak it; "*Is it lawful to do good on the sabbath days*, as I design to do, *or to do evil*, as you design to do? Whether is better, to *save life* or to *kill?*"

(2) When they rebelled against the light, he *lamented their stubbornness* (*v.* 5); *He looked round about on them with anger, being grieved for the hardness of their hearts.*

4. Christ dealt very kindly with the patient; he bade him *stretch forth his hand*, and it was immediately *restored*.

5. The enemies of Christ dealt very barbarously with him. Such a work of *mercy* should have en-

gaged their love *to him*, and such a work of *wonder* their faith *in him*. But, instead of that, the Pharisees, who pretended to be oracles in the church, and the Herodians, who pretended to be the supporters of the state, though of opposite interests one to another, *took counsel together against him, how they might destroy him.*

II. When he withdrew *to the sea*, he did good there. While his enemies sought to *destroy him*, he quitted the place; to teach us in troublous times to shift for our own safety; but see here,

1. How he was followed into his retirement. When some had such an enmity to him, that they drove him out of their country, others had such a value for him, that they followed him wherever he went; and the enmity of their leaders to Christ did not cool their respect to him.

2. What abundance of good he did in his retirement. He did not withdraw to be idle, nor did he send back those who rudely crowded after him when he withdrew, but took it kindly, and gave them what they came for; for he never said to any that sought him diligently, *Seek ye me in vain*. (1) Diseases were effectually cured; He *healed many*; divers sorts of patients, ill of divers sorts of diseases; though numerous, though various, he *healed them*. (2) *Devils* were effectually *conquered*; those whom unclean spirits had got possession of, *when they saw him*, trembled at his presence, and they also *fell down before him*, not to supplicate his favour, but to deprecate his wrath, and by their

own terrors were compelled to own that *he was the Son of God*, v. 11. (3) Christ sought not applause to himself in doing those great things, for *he strictly charged* those for whom he did them, *that they should not make him known* (v. 12).

THE TWELVE CALLED
(vv. 13–21)

In these verses, we have,

I. The choice Christ made of the *twelve apostles* to be his constant followers and attendants, and to be sent abroad as there was occasion, to preach the gospel. Observe,

1. The introduction to this *call* or *promotion* of disciples; He *goes up into a mountain*, and his errand thither was *to pray*. Ministers must be set apart with solemn prayer for the pouring out of the Spirit upon them; though Christ had authority to confer the gifts of the Holy Ghost, yet, to set us an example, he prayed for them.

2. The rule he went by in his choice, and that was his own good pleasure; *He called unto him whom he would*. Christ calls *whom he will*; for he is a free agent, and his grace is his own.

3. The efficacy of the call; He *called them* to separate themselves from the crowd, and stand by him, and they *came unto him*.

4. The end and intention of this call; He *ordained them* (probably by the imposition of hands, which was a ceremony used among the Jews), *that they should be with him* constantly, to be witnesses of *his doctrine, manner of life, and patience*, that they might *fully know it*, and be able to give an account of it; and especially that they might attest the

truth of his miracles; they must be *with him*, to receive instructions *from him*, that they might be qualified to give instructions *to others*.

5. The power he gave them to work miracles; and hereby he put a very great honour upon them, beyond that of the great men of the earth. He ordained them to *heal sicknesses and to cast out devils*. This showed that the power which Christ had to work these miracles was an *original* power; that he had it not *as a Servant*, but *as a Son in his own house*, in that he could confer it upon others, and invest them with it.

6. Their number and names; *He ordained twelve*, according to the number of the twelve tribes of Israel. They are here named not just in the same order as they were in Matthew, nor by couples, as they were there; but as there, so here, Peter is put first and Judas last.

7. Their retirement with their Master, and close adherence to him; *The y went into a house*.

II. The continual crowds that attended Christ's movements (v. 20); The *multitude cometh together again*, unsent for, and unseasonably pressing upon him, some with one errand and some with another; so that he and his disciples could not get time *so much as to eat bread*, much less for a set and full meal. Yet he did not shut his doors against the petitioners, but bade them welcome, and gave to each of them *an answer of peace*.

III. The care of his relations concerning him (v. 21); *When his friends* in Capernaum heard how he was followed, and what pains he took, they *went out, to lay hold on him*, and fetch him home, for they said, *He is beside himself.* 1. Some understand it of an absurd preposterous care, which had more in it of reproach to him than of respect; and so we must take it as we read it, *He is beside himself*; either they suspected it themselves, or it was suggested to them, and they gave credit to the suggestion, that he was *gone distracted*, and therefore his friends ought to bind him, and put him in a dark room, to bring him to his right mind again. 2. Others understand it of a *well-meaning* care; and then they read "*He fainteth*, he has no time to *eat bread*, and therefore his strength will fail him; he will be stifled with the crowd of people, and will have his spirits quite exhausted with constant speaking, and the virtue that *goes out of him* in his miracles; and therefore let us use a friendly violence with him, and get him a little *breathing-time*." In his preaching-work, as well as his suffering-work, he was attacked with, *Master, spare thyself.* Note, They who go on with vigour and zeal in the work of God, must expect to meet with hindrances, both from the groundless disaffection of their enemies, and the mistaken affections of their friends, and they have need to stand upon their guard against both.

BLASPHEMY AGAINST THE HOLY SPIRIT (*vv.* 22–29)

I.˙Here is, The impudent impious brand which the scribes fastened upon Christ's casting out devils, they they might evade and invalidate the conviction of it, and have a poor excuse for not yielding to it.

These *scribes came down from Jerusalem*, *v.* 22. They could not deny but that he cast out devils, which plainly bespoke him sent of God; but they insinuated that *he had Beelzebub* on his side, was in league with him, and by *the prince of the devils cast out devils.* There is a trick in the case; Satan is not *cast out*, he only *goes out* by consent. There was nothing in the manner of Christ's *casting out devils*, that gave any cause to suspect this; he did it *as one having authority*; but so they will have it, who resolve not to believe him.

II. The rational answer which Christ gave to this objection, demonstrating the absurdity of it.

1. Satan is so *subtle*, that he will never voluntarily quit his possession; *If Satan cast out Satan, his kingdom is divided against itself*, and it *cannot stand, vv.* 23–26.

2. Christ is so *wise*, that, being engaged in war with him, he will attack his forces wherever he meets them, whether in the bodies or souls of people, *v.* 27. It is plain, Christ's design is to *enter into the strong man's house*, to take possession of the interest he has in the world, and to *spoil his goods*, and convert them to his own service; and therefore it is natural to suppose that he will thus *bind the strong man*, will forbid him to *speak* when he would, and to *stay* where he would, and thus show that he has gained a victory over him.

III. The awful warning Christ gave them to take heed how they spoke such dangerous words as these; however they might make light of them, as only conjectures, and the language of *free-thinking*, if they persisted in it, it would be of fatal consequence to them; it would be found a sin against the last remedy, and consequently *unpardonable*; for what could be imagined possible to bring *them* to repentance for their sin in blaspheming Christ, who would set aside such a *strong* conviction with such a *weak* evasion?

A FAMILY MISUNDERSTANDING
(vv. 31–35)

Here is, 1. The *disrespect* which Christ's *kindred, according to the flesh*, showed to him, when he was preaching (and they knew very well that he was then in his element); they not only *stood without*, having no desire to come in, and hear him, but they sent in a message to *call him out to them* (vv. 31, 32), as if he must leave his work, to hearken to their *impertinences*.

2. The *respect* which Christ showed to his spiritual kindred upon this occasion. Now, as at other times, he put a *comparative neglect* upon his mother, which seemed purposely designed to obviate and prevent the extravagant respect which men in aftertimes would be apt to pay her. *Our* respect ought to be guided and governed by Christ's; now the virgin Mary, or Christ's mother, is not here regarded as superior to ordinary believers, on whom Christ here puts a *superlative* honour. He looked upon those that *sat about* him, and pronounced those of them that not only heard, but did, the will of God, to be to him as *his brother, and sister, and mother*; as much esteemed, loved,

and cared for, as his nearest relations, *vv.* 33–35. This is a good reason why we should *honour those that fear the Lord*, and choose them for our people; why we should be not hearers of the word only, but doers of the work, that we may share with the saints in this honour.

CHAPTER FOUR

THE SOWER (vv. 1–20)

I. The *way of teaching* that Christ used with the *multitude* (v. 2); He *taught them many things*, but it was *by parables* or similitudes, which would *tempt them to hear*.

II. The way of *expounding* that he used with his *disciples; When he was alone* by himself, not only the *twelve*, but others that were *about him with the twelve*, took the opportunity to *ask him* the meaning of the parables, *v.* 10. And he told them what a distinguishing favour it was to them, that they were made acquainted with the *mystery of the kingdom of God, v.* 11. *The secret of the Lord was with them.*

In particular, we have here,

1. The parable of the sower, as we had it, Matt. xiii. 3, &c.

2. The exposition of it to the disciples. Here is a question Christ put to them before he expounded it, which we had not in Matthew (*v.* 13); *"Know ye not this parable? Know ye not the meaning of it? How then will ye know all parables?"* (1) "If ye know not this, which is so plain, how will ye understand other parables, which will be more dark and obscure?" (2) "If ye know not this, which is intended for your direction in hearing the word, that ye may profit by it; how

shall ye profit by what ye are further to hear? This parable is to teach you to be attentive to the word, and affected with it, that you may *understand* it. If ye receive not this, ye will not know how to use the key by which ye must be let into all the rest."

PARABLES OF THE KINGDOM
(*vv.* 21–34)

The lessons which our Saviour designs to teach us here by parables and figurative expressions are these:—

I. That those who *are good* ought to consider the obligations they are under to *do good*; that is, as in the parable before, to *bring forth fruit*. Those who are lighted as candles, should set themselves *on a candlestick*; that is, should improve all opportunities of doing good, as those that were made for the glory of God, and the service of the communities they are members of; we are not born for ourselves.

II. *If any man have ears to hear, let him hear, v.* 23. Let him give the gospel of Christ a fair hearing; but that is not enough, it is added (*v.* 24), *Take heed what ye hear*, and give a due regard to that which ye do hear; *Consider what ye* hear, so Dr. Hammond reads it. Note, What we hear, doth us no good, unless we consider it. To enforce this caution, consider,

1. As we deal with God, God will deal with us, so Dr. Hammond explains these words, "*With what measure ye mete, it shall be measured to you*. If ye be faithful servants to him, he will be a faithful Master to

you: *with the upright he will show himself upright*."

2. As we improve the talents we are entrusted with, we shall increase them; if we make use of the knowledge we have, for the glory of God and the benefit of others, it shall sensibly grow, as stock in trade doth by being turned; *Unto you that hear, shall more be given; to you that have, it shall be given, v.* 25. If the disciples *deliver* that to the church, which they have *received of the Lord*, they shall be *led* more into the *secret of the Lord*. Gifts and graces multiply by being exercised; and God has promised to bless the *hand of the diligent*.

3. If we do not *use*, we *lose*, what we have; *From him that hath not*, that doeth no good with what he hath, and so hath it in vain, is as if he had it not, *shall be taken even that which he hath*.

III. The good seed of the gospel sown in the world, and sown in the heart, doth by degrees produce wonderful effects, but without noise (*vv.* 26, &c.); *So is the kingdom of God*; so is the gospel, when it is sown, and received, as seed in good ground.

1. It will *come up*; though it seem lost and buried under the clods, it will find or make its way through them.

2. The husbandman cannot describe how it comes up; it is one of the mysteries of nature; It *springs and grows up, he knows not how, v.* 27.

3. The husbandman, when he hath sown the seed, doth nothing toward the springing of it up; *He sleeps, and rises, night and day;*

goes to sleep *at night*, gets up *in the morning*, and perhaps never so much as thinks of the corn he hath sown, or ever looks upon it, but follows his pleasures or other business, and yet *the earth brings forth fruit of itself*, according to the ordinary course of nature, and by the concurring power of the God of nature. Thus the *word of grace*, when it is received in faith, is in the heart a *work of grace*, and the preachers contribute nothing to it. The Spirit of God is carrying it on when *they sleep*, and can do no business (Job xxxiii. 15, 16), or when they rise to go about other business.

4. It grows gradually; *first the blade, then the ear, after that the full corn in the ear*, v. 28. When it is sprung up, it will go forward; nature will have its course, and so will grace.

5. It comes to perfection at last (v. 29); *When the fruit is brought forth*, that is, when it is *ripe*, and ready to be *delivered* into the owner's hand; then he *puts in the sickle*.

IV. The work of grace is small in its beginnings, but comes to be great and considerable at last (vv. 30–32); "*Whereunto shall I liken the kingdom of God*, as now to be set up by the Messiah? How shall I make you to understand the designed method of it?" Christ speaks as one considering and consulting with himself, how to illustrate it with an apt similitude; *With what comparison shall we compare it?* Shall we fetch it from the motions of the sun, or the revolutions of the moon? No, the comparison is borrowed from this earth, it is *like a grain of mustard-seed*; he had compared it before to *seed sown*, here to *that seed*, intending thereby to show,

1. That the beginnings of the *gospel kingdom* would be very small, like that which is *one of the least of all seeds*.

2. That the perfection of it will be very great; *When it grows up, it becomes greater than all herbs*. The gospel kingdom in the world, shall increase and spread to the remotest nations of the earth, and shall continue to the latest ages of time.

After the parables thus specified the historian concludes with this general account of Christ's preaching—that *with many such parables he spoke the word unto them* (v. 33); probably designing to refer us to the larger account of the parables of this kind, which we had before, Matt. xiii.

THE STORM STILLED
(vv. 35–41)

This miracle which Christ wrought for the relief of his disciples, in stilling the storm, we had before (Matt. viii. 23, &c.); but it is here more fully related.

CHAPTER FIVE
LEGION EXPELLED
(vv. 1–20)

We have here an instance of Christ's dispossessing the strong man armed, and disposing of him as he pleased, to make it appear that he was *stronger than he*.

In Matthew, they were said to be *two* possessed with devils; here it is said to be a *man* possessed with an unclean spirit. If there were *two*, there was one, and Mark doth not say that there was *but one*; so that this difference cannot give us any just offence; it is probable that one of them was much more remarkable than the other, and said what was said. Now observe here,

I. The miserable condition that this poor creature was in; he was under the power of an *unclean spirit*, the devil got possession of him, and the effect of it was not, as in many, a silent melancholy, but a raging frenzy; he was raving mad; his condition seems to have been worse than any of the possessed, that were Christ's patients.

1. He had *his dwelling among the tombs*, among the graves of dead people. Their tombs were out of the cities, in *desolate places* (Job iii. 4); which gave the devil great advantage: for *woe to him that is alone*.

2 He was very strong and ungovernable; *No man could bind him*, as it is requisite both for their own good, and for the safety of others, that those who are distracted should be. Not only cords would not hold him, but *chains* and *fetters of iron* would not, *vv.* 3, 4.

3. He was a terror and torment to himself and to all about him, *v.* 5. The devil is a *cruel* master to those that are *led captive* by him, a perfect tyrant; this wretched creature was *night and day in the mountains and in the tombs, crying, and cutting himself with stones*.

II. His application to Christ (*v.* 6); *When he saw Jesus afar off*, coming ashore, he *ran and wor-*

shipped him. He usually *ran upon* others with *rage*, but he *ran to* Christ with *reverence*. That was done by an invisible hand of Christ, which could not be done with chains and fetters; his fury was all on a sudden curbed.

III. The word of command Christ gave to the unclean spirit, to quit his possession (*v.* 8); *Come out of him, thou unclean spirit*. He made the man desirous to be relieved, when he enabled him to *run, and worship him*, and then put forth his power for his relief.

IV. The dread which the devil had of Christ. The *man ran*, and *worshipped Christ*; but it was the devil in the man, that *cried with a loud voice* (making use of the poor man's tongue), *What have I to do with thee? v.* 7.

V. The account Christ took from this unclean spirit of his name. This we had not in Matthew. Christ asked him, *What is thy name?* Not but that Christ could call all the *fallen* stars, as well as the *morning* stars, by their names; but he demands this, that the standers by might be affected with the vast numbers and power of those malignant infernal spirits, as they had reason to be, when the answer was, *My name is Legion, for we are many*; a *legion* of soldiers among the Romans consisted, some say, of six thousand men, others of twelve thousand and five hundred; but the number of a legion with them, like that of a regiment with us, was not always the same.

VI. The request of this legion, that Christ would suffer them to go into a herd of swine that was *feeding nigh unto the mountains* (v. 11), those mountains which the demoniacs haunted, *v.* 5. Their request was, 1. That he *would not send them away out of the country* (v. 10). 2. That he would suffer them to *enter into the swine*, by destroying which they hoped to do more mischief to the souls of all the people in the country, than they could by entering into the body of any particular person, which therefore they did not ask leave to do, for they knew Christ would not grant it.

VII. The permission Christ gave them to enter into the swine, and the immediate destruction of the swine thereby; *He gave them leave* (v. 13), he did not forbid or restrain them, he let them do as they had a mind. The consequence of the devils entering into the swine, was, that they all *ran mad* presently, and ran headlong into the adjoining sea, where they were all drowned, to the number of *two thousand*. The man they possessed did only *cut himself*, for God had said, *He is in your hands, only save his life.* But thereby it appeared, that, if he had not been so restrained, the poor man would have *drowned himself.*

VIII. The report of all this dispersed through the country immediately. They that *fed the swine*, hastened to the owners, to give an account of their charge, *v.* 14. This drew the people together, to see what was done.

IX. An account of the conduct of the poor man after his deliverance. 1. He *desired that he might go along with Christ* (v. 18),

perhaps for fear lest the evil spirit should again seize him; or, rather, that he might receive instruction from him, being unwilling to stay among those heathenish people that desired him to depart. 2. Christ *would not suffer him* to go with him, lest it should savour of ostentation, and to let him know that he could both protect and instruct him at a distance. And besides, he had other work for him to do; he must go home to his friends, and tell them what *great things the Lord had done for him*, the Lord Jesus had done; that Christ might be honoured; and his neighbours and friends might be edified, and invited to believe in Christ.

TWO MIRACLES (vv. 21–43)

The Gadarenes having desired Christ to leave their country, he did not stay to trouble them long, but presently went by water, as he came, back *to the other side* (v. 21), and there *much people gathered to him*. Now among the many that applied themselves to him,

I. Here is one, that comes *openly to beg* a cure for a sick child; and it is no less a person than one of the *rulers of the synagogue*, one that presided in the synagogue-worship or, as some think, one of the judges of the consistory court, which was in every city, consisting of *twenty-three*. He was not named in Matthew, he is here, *Jairus*, or *Jair*, Judg. x. 3. The case is this, He has a *little daughter*, about twelve years old, the darling of the family, and she *lies a dying*; but he believes that if Christ will but come, and *lay his hands upon her*, she will return even from the gates of the grave. He said, at first, when he came, *She lies a dying* (so Mark); but afterward, upon fresh information sent him, he saith, *She is even now dead* (so Matthew); but he still prosecutes his suit; see Luke viii. 42–49. Christ readily agreed, and went with him, *v.* 24.

II. Here is another, that comes *clandestinely* to *steal* a cure (if I may so say) for herself; and she got the relief she came for. This cure was wrought by *the way*, as he was going to raise the ruler's daughter, and was followed by a crowd. See how Christ improved his time, and lost none of the precious moments of it. Many of his discourses, and some of his miracles, are dated *by the way-side*; we should be doing good, not only when we *sit in the house*, but when we *walk by the way*, Deut. vi. 7. We dealt with these two miracles at Matt. ix. 18–26.

THE GIRL RAISED

Diseases and deaths came into the world by the sin and disobedience of the first Adam; but by the grace of the second Adam both are conquered. Christ, having healed an incurable disease, here goes on to triumph over death, as in the beginning of the chapter he had triumphed over an outrageous devil.

I. The melancholy news is brought to Jairus, that his *daughter is dead*, and therefore, if Christ be as other physicians, he comes too late. While there is life, there is hope, and room for the use of means; but when life is gone, it is past recall; *Why troublest thou the Master any further? v.* 35. Ordinarily, the proper thought in this case, is, "The matter is determined, the will of God is done, and I submit, I acquiesce; *The Lord gave, and the Lord hath taken away. While the child was alive, I fasted and wept; for I said, Who can tell but God will yet be gracious to me*, and *the child shall live?* But *now that it is dead, wherefore should I weep? I shall go to it, but it shall not return to me.*" With such words we should *quiet ourselves* at such a time, that our souls may be *as a child that is weaned from his mother*: but here the case was extraordinary; the death of the child doth not, as usually, put an end to the narrative.

II. Christ encourageth the afflicted father yet to hope that his application to Christ on the behalf of his child should not be in vain. Christ had staid to work a cure by the way, but he shall be no sufferer by that, nor loser by the gain of others; *Be not afraid, only believe.* We may suppose Jairus at a pause, whether he should ask Christ to go on or no; but have we not as much occasion for the grace of God, and his consolations, and consequently of the prayers of our ministers and Christian friends, when death is in the house, as when sickness is? Christ therefore soon determines this matter; "*Be not afraid* that my coming will be to no purpose, only believe that I will make it turn to a good account." Note, 1. We must not despair concerning our relations that are dead, nor *sorrow* for them *as those that have no hope.* See what is said to Rachel, who refused to be comforted concerning her children, upon the presumption that they *were not; Refrain thy voice from weeping, and thine eyes from tears; for there is hope in thine end, that thy children shall come again*, Jer. xxxi. 16, 17. Therefore fear not, faint not. 2. Faith is the only remedy against disquieting grief and fear at such a time: let that silence them, *Only believe.* Keep up a confidence in Christ, and a dependence upon him, and he will do what is for the best. Believe the resurrection, and then be not afraid.

III. He went with a select company to the house where the dead child was and raised her.

All who saw them, and heard of them, admired the miracles, and him that wrought them; *They were astonished with a great astonishment.* They could not but acknowledge that there was something extraordinary and very great, and yet they knew not what to make of it, or to infer from it. Their wonder should have worked forward to a lively faith, but it rested in a *stupor* or *astonishment.*

Christ endeavoured to conceal it; *He charged them straitly, that no man should know it.* It was sufficiently known to a competent number, but he would not have it as yet *proclaimed* any further; because his own resurrection was to be the great instance of his power over death, and therefore the divulging of other instances must be reserved till that great proof was given: let one part of the evidence be kept private, till the other part, on which the main stress lies, be made ready.

CHAPTER SIX

CHRIST IN NAZARETH
(vv 1–6)

Here, I. Christ makes a visit to *his own country*, the place not of his birth, but of his education; that was *Nazareth*; where his relations were. He had been in danger of his life among them (Luke iv. 29), and yet he came among them again; so strangely doth he wait to be gracious, and seek the salvation of his enemies.

II. There he *preached* in their *synagogue*, on the *sabbath day*, v. 2. It seems, there was not such flocking to him there as in other places, so that he had no opportunity of preaching till they came together on the sabbath day; and then he expounded a portion of scripture with great clearness.

III. They could not but own that which was very honourable concerning him. 1. That he spoke with great *wisdom*, and that this wisdom was *given to him*, for they knew he had no learned education. 2. That he did *mighty works*, did them with his own hands, for the confirming of the doctrine he taught. They acknowledged the two great proofs of the divine original of his gospel—the *divine wisdom* that appeared in the contrivance of it, and the *divine power* that was exerted for the ratifying and recommending of it; and yet, though they could not deny the premises, they would not admit the conclusion.

IV. They studied to disparage him, and to raise prejudices in the minds of people against him, notwithstanding. All this *wisdom,* and all these *mighty works*, shall be of no account, because he had a home-education, had never travelled, nor been at any university, or bred up at the feet of any of their doctors (*v.* 3); *Is not this the Carpenter?* In Matthew, they upbraid him with being the carpenter's son, his supposed father Joseph being of that trade. But, it seems, they could say further, *Is not this the Carpenter?* our Lord Jesus, it is probable, employing himself in that business with his father, before he entered upon his public ministry, at least, sometimes in journey-work. 1. He would thus *humble himself*, and make himself of no reputation, as one that had taken upon him the form of a servant, and came to minister. Thus low did our Redeemer stoop, when he came to redeem us out of our low estate. 2. He would thus teach us to *abhor idleness*, and to find *ourselves something to do* in this world; and rather to take up with mean and laborious employments, and such as no more is to be got by than a bare livelihood, than indulge ourselves in sloth. 3. He would thus put an honour upon despised mechanics, and encourage those who eat the labour of their hands, though great men look upon them with contempt.

Another thing they upbraided him with, was, the meanness of his relations; "*He is the son of Mary*; his *brethren* and *sisters* are here *with us*; we know his family and kindred"; and therefore, though they were *astonished* at his doctrine (*v.* 2), yet they were *offended* at his person (*v.* 3), were prejudiced against him, and looked upon him with contempt; and for that reason would not receive his doctrine, though ever so well recommended. May we think that if they had not known his pedigree, but he had dropped among them from the clouds, without father, without mother, and without descent, they would have entertained him with any more respect? Truly, no; for in Judea, where this was not known, that was made an objection against him (John ix. 29); *As for this fellow, we know not from whence he is.* Obstinate unbelief will never want excuses.

V. Let us see how Christ bore this contempt.

1. He partly *excused it*, as a common thing, and what might be expected, though not reasonably or justly (*v.* 4); *A prophet is not despised anywhere but in his own country.*

2. He did *some good* among them, notwithstanding the slights they put upon him, for he is kind even to the evil and unthankful; *He laid his hands upon a few sick folks, and healed them.*

3. Yet he *could there do* no such mighty works, at least not so many, as in other places, because of the unbelief that prevailed among the people, by reason of the prejudices which their leaders instilled into them against Christ, *v.* 5. It is a strange expression, as if unbelief tied the hands of omnipotence itself; he *would have done* as many miracles there as he had done elsewhere, but he could not, because people would not make application to him, nor sue for his favours; he could have

wrought them, but they forfeited the honour of having them wrought for them.

4. He *marvelled because of their unbelief, v.* 6. We never find Christ wondering but at the *faith* of the Gentiles that were strangers, as the *centurion* (Matt. viii. 10), and the woman of Samaria, and at the unbelief of Jews that were his own countrymen.

5. He *went round about the villages, teaching.* If we cannot do good where we would, we must do it where we can, and be glad if we may have any opportunity, though but in the villages, of serving Christ and souls.

MIRACLES—AND HEROD'S REACTION (*vv.* 7–29)

Here is the commission given to the twelve apostles, to preach and work miracles; it is the same which we had more largely, Matt. x.

Here is also the opinion of Herod concerning him. He heard of *his name* and fame, of what he said and what he did; and he said, "It is certainly John Baptist, *v.* 14. As sure as we are here, *It is John, whom I beheaded, v.* 16. He is *risen from the dead*; and though while he was with us *he did no miracle,* yet, having removed for awhile to another world, he is come again with greater power, and *now mighty works do show forth themselves in him.*"

Note, 1. Where there is an *idle faith,* there is commonly a *working fancy.* The people said, It is a prophet risen from the dead; Herod said, It is *John Baptist risen from the dead.*

2. They who fight against the cause of God, will find themselves baffled, even when they think themselves conquerors; they cannot gain their point, for the word of the Lord endures for ever.

3. A guilty conscience needs no accuser or tormentor but itself. Herod charges himself with the murder of John, which perhaps no one else dare charge him with; *I beheaded him*; and the terror of it made him imagine that Christ was John risen.

4. There may be the terrors of strong conviction, where there is not the truth of a saving conversion.

Here is also a narrative of Herod's putting John Baptist to death, which is brought in upon this occasion, as it was in Matthew.

FEEDING FIVE THOUSAND (*vv.* 30–44)

In these verses, we have,

I. The return to Christ of the apostles whom he had sent forth (*v.* 7), to preach, and work miracles. They had dispersed themselves into several quarters of the country for some time, but when they had made good their several appointments, by consent they *gathered themselves together,* to compare notes, and came to Jesus, the centre of their unity, to give him an account of what they had done pursuant to their commission: they *told him all things,* both *what they had done, and what they had taught.*

II. The tender care Christ took for their repose, after the fatigue they had (*v.* 31); *He said unto them,* perceiving them to be almost spent, and out of breath,

Come ye yourselves apart into a desert place, and rest awhile. It should seem that John's disciples came to Christ with the mournful tidings of their master's death, much about the same time that his own disciples came to him with the report of their negotiation. Note, Christ takes cognizance of the *frights* of some, and the *toils* of others, of his disciples, and provides suitable relief for both, rest for those that are tired, and refuge for those that are terrified.

III. The diligence of the people to follow him. It was rude to do so, when he and his disciples were desirous, for such good reason, to *retire*; and yet they are not blamed for it, nor bid to go back, but bid welcome.

IV. The entertainment Christ gave them (v. 34); *When he saw much people*, instead of being moved with displeasure, because they disturbed him when he desired to be private, as many a man, many a good man, would have been, he was *moved with compassion toward them*, and looked upon them with concern, because *they* were *as sheep having no shepherd*, they seemed to be well-inclined, and manageable as sheep, and willing to be taught, but they had *no shepherd*, none to lead and guide them in the right way, none to feed them with good doctrine: and therefore, in compassion to them, he not only *healed their sick*, as it is in Matthew, but he *taught them many things*, and we may be sure that they were all true and good, and fit for them to learn.

V. The provision he made for them all; all his hearers he generously made his guests, and treated them at a *splendid* entertainment: so it might truly be called, because a *miraculous* one.

1. The disciples moved that they should be *sent home*.

2. Christ ordered that they should all be fed (v. 37); *Give ye them to eat.*

3. The disciples objected against it as impracticable; *Shall we go, and buy two hundred penny-worth of bread, and give them to eat?*

4. Christ effected it, to universal satisfaction. They had brought with them *five loaves*, for the victualling of their ship, and *two fishes* perhaps they caught as they came along; and that is the bill of fare. This was but a little for Christ and his disciples, and yet this they must give away. We often find Christ entertained at other people's tables, dining with one friend, and supping with another: but here we have him supping a great many at his own charge, which shows that, when others *ministered to him of their substance*, it was not because he could not supply himself otherwise (if he was *hungry*, he needed not *tell them*); but it was a piece of humiliation, that he was pleased to submit to, nor was it agreeable to the intention of miracles, that he should work them for himself. Observe,

A blessing was craved upon the meat; *He looked up to heaven, and blessed.* And by virtue of this blessing the bread strangely multiplied, and so did the fishes, for they did *all eat, and were filled*, though they were to the number of *five thousand*, vv. 42, 44. This miracle was significant, and shows that Christ came into the world, to be the great feeder as well as the great healer; not only to restore, but to preserve and nourish, spiritual life; and in him there is enough for all that come to him, enough to fill the soul, to fill the treasures; none are sent empty away from Christ, but those that come to him full of themselves.

WALKING ON THE WATER
(*vv.* 45–56)

This passage of story we had Matt. xiv. 22, &c., only what was there related concerning Peter, is omitted here.

The disciples were more surprised and astonished at this miracle than did become them, and there was that at the bottom of their astonishment, which was really culpable; *They were sore amazed in themselves*, were in a perfect ecstasy; as if it were a new and unaccountable thing, as if Christ had never done the like before, and they had no reason to expect he should do it now; they ought to admire the power of Christ, and to be confirmed hereby in their belief of his being the Son of God: but why all this confusion about it? It was because they *considered not the miracle of the loaves*; had they given that its due weight, they would not have been so much surprised at this; for his multiplying the bread was as great an instance of his power as his walking on the water. They were strangely stupid and unthinking, and their heart was hardened, or else they would not have thought it a thing incredible

that Christ should command a calm. It is for want of a right understanding of Christ's former works, that we are transported at the thought of his present works, as if there never were the like before.

CHAPTER SEVEN
TRADITIONS OF MEN
(*vv.* 1–23)

One great design of Christ's coming, was, to set aside the ceremonial law which God made, and to put an end to it; to make way for which he begins with the ceremonial law which men had made, and added to the law of God's making, and discharges his disciples from the obligation of that; which here he doth fully, upon occasion of the offence which the Pharisees took at them for the violation of it. These Pharisees and scribes with whom he had this argument, are said to *come from Jerusalem* down to Galilee—fourscore or a hundred miles, to pick quarrels with our Saviour there, where they supposed him to have the greatest interest and reputation. Had they come so far as to be taught by him, their zeal had been commendable; but to come so far to oppose him, and to check the progress of his gospel, was great wickedness. It should seem that the scribes and Pharisees at Jerusalem pretended not only to a pre-eminence above, but to an authority over, the country clergy, and therefore kept up their visitations and sent inquisitors among them, as they did to John when he appeared, John i. 19.

Now in this passage we may observe,

I. What the tradition of the elders was: by it all were enjoined to *wash their hands* before meat; a cleanly custom, and no harm in it; and yet as such to be over-nice in it discovers too great a care about the body, which is *of the earth*; but they placed religion in it, and would not leave it indifferent, as it was in its own nature; people were at their liberty to do it or not to do it; but they interposed their authority, and commanded all to do it upon pain of excommunication; this they kept up as a *tradition of the elders*.

II. What the practice of Christ's disciples was; they knew what the law was, and the common usage; but they understood themselves so well that they would not be bound up by it: they ate bread with *defiled*, that is, with *unwashen*, *hands*, *v*. 2.

III. The offence which the Pharisees took at this; They *found fault* (*v*. 2). They do not ask, Why do not thy disciples *do as we do?* (Though that was what they meant, coveting to make themselves the standard.) But, Why do not they *walk according to the tradition of the elders?* *v*. 5. To which it was easy to answer, that, by receiving the doctrine of Christ, they had *more understanding than all their teachers*, yea *more than the ancients*, Ps. cxix. 99, 100.

IV. Christ's vindication of them; in which,

1. He argues with the Pharisees concerning the authority by which this ceremony was imposed.

(1) He reproves them for their hypocrisy in pretending to honour God, when really they had no such design in their religious observances (*vv*. 6, 7).

(2) He reproves them for placing religion in the inventions and injunctions of their elders and rulers; They *taught for doctrines the traditions of men*.

(3) He reproves them for *laying aside the commandment of God*, and overlooking that, not urging that in their preaching, and in their discipline conniving at the violation of that, as if that were no longer of force, *v*. 8.

This he gives them a particular instance of, and a flagrant one— God commanded children to *honour their parents*, not only by the law of Moses, but, antecedent to that, by the law of nature; and whoso *revileth*, or *speaketh evil of*, father or mother, *let him die the death*, *v*. 10. But if a man will but conform himself in all points to the tradition of the elders, they will find him out an expedient by which he may be discharged from this obligation, *v*. 11. If his parents be in want, and he has wherewithal to help them, but has no mind to do it, let him swear by the *Corban*, that is, by the *gold of the temple*, and the *gift upon the altar*, that his parents shall not be profited by him, that he will not relieve them; and, if they ask any thing of him, let him tell them this, and it is enough; as if by the obligation of this wicked vow he had discharged himself from the obligation of God's holy law. He concludes, *And many such like things do ye*. Where will men stop, when once they have made the word of God give way to their tradition?

2. He instructs the people concerning the principles upon which this ceremony was grounded.

Now that which he goes about to set them right in, is, what the pollution is, which we are in danger of being damaged by, *v.* 15. (1) Not by the *meat we eat*, though it be eaten with unwashen hands; that is but from without, and goes through a man. But, (2) It is by the breaking out of the corruption that is in our hearts; the mind and conscience are defiled, guilt is contracted, and we become odious in the sight of God by that which *comes out* of us; our wicked thoughts and affections, words and actions, these defile us, and these only. Our care must therefore be, to *wash our heart from wickedness*.

3. He gives his disciples, in private, an explication of the instructions he gave the people. They *asked* him, when they had him by himself, *concerning the parable* (*v.* 17); for to them, it seems, it was a parable. Now, in answer to their enquiry, (1) He reproves their dullness; "*Are ye so without understanding also?* Are ye dull *also*, as dull as the people that *cannot* understand, as dull as the Pharisees that *will not*? Are ye *so* dull?" He doth not expect they should understand every thing; "But are ye so weak as not to understand *this*?" (2) He explains this truth to them, that they might *perceive* it, and then they would *believe* it, for it carried its own evidence along with it. If we understand the spiritual nature of God and of his law, and what it is that is offensive to him, and disfits us for communion with him, we shall soon perceive, [1]

That that which we eat and drink cannot defile us, so as to call for any religious washing. But, [2] It is that which *comes out from* the heart, the corrupt heart, that defiles us. As by the ceremonial law, whatsoever (almost) comes out of a man, defiles him (Lev. xv. 2; Deut. xxiii. 13), so what comes out from the *mind* of a man is that which defiles him before God, and calls for a religious washing (*v.* 21); *From within, out of the heart of men*, which they boast of the *goodness* of, and think is the best part of them, thence that which defiles proceeds, thence comes all the mischief.

A GREEK WOMAN
(*vv.* 24–30)

Observe, 1. The application made to Christ by a poor woman in distress and trouble. She was a Gentile, a Greek, *a stranger to the commonwealth of Israel, an alien to the covenant of promise*; she was by extraction a Syrophenician, and not in any degree proselyted to the Jewish religion; she had a *daughter*, a *young* daughter, that was possessed *with the devil*. Her address was, (1) Very humble, pressing, and importunate; *She heard of him, and came, and fell at his feet.* (2) It was very particular; she tells him what she wanted.

2. The discouragement he gave to this address (*v.* 27); He said unto her, "*Let the children first be filled*; let the Jews have all the miracles wrought for them, that they have occasion for, who are in a particular manner God's chosen people; and let not that which was intended for them, be thrown to those who are

not of God's family, and who have not that knowledge of him, and interest in him, which they have, and who are as *dogs in comparison of them*, vile and profane, and who are as *dogs to them*, snarling at them, spiteful toward them, and ready to worry them."

3. The turn she gave to this word of Christ, which made against her, and her improvement of it, to make for her, *v.* 28. She said, "*Yes, Lord, I own it is true that the children's bread* ought not to be cast to the dogs; but they were never denied the *crumbs* of that bread, nay it belongs to them, and they are allowed a place *under the table*, that they may be ready to receive them. I ask not for a *loaf*, no, nor for a *morsel*, only for a *crumb*; do not refuse me that."

4. The grant Christ thereupon made of her request. Is she thus humble, thus earnest? For *this saying, Go thy way*, thou shalt have what thou camest for, *the devil is gone out of thy daughter, v.* 29. This encourages us to *pray* and not to *faint*, to continue instant in prayer, not doubting but to prevail at last; the vision at the end shall *speak, and not lie*.

BE OPENED! (*vv.* 31–37)

Now here we have the story of a cure that Christ wrought, which is not recorded by any other of the evangelists; it is of one that was *deaf* and *dumb*.

I. His case was sad, *v.* 32. There were those that brought to him one that was *deaf*; some think, born deaf, and then he must be dumb of course; others think that by some distemper or disaster he was be-

come deaf, or, at least, thick of hearing; and he had an *impediment in his speech*. He was μογιλάλος some think that he was quite dumb; others, that he could not speak but with great difficulty to himself, and so as scarcely to be understood by those that heard him. He was *tongue-tied*, so that he was perfectly unfit for conversation, and deprived both of the pleasure and of the profit of it; he had not the satisfaction either of hearing other people talk, or of telling his own mind. Let us take occasion from hence to give thanks to God for preserving to us the sense of hearing, especially that we may be capable of hearing the word of God; and the faculty of speech, especially that we may be capable of speaking God's praises; and let us look with compassion upon those that are deaf or dumb, and treat them with great tenderness. They that brought this poor man to Christ, besought him that he would *put his hand upon him*, as the prophets did upon those whom they *blessed* in the name of the Lord. It is not said, They besought him to *cure him*, but to *put his hand upon him*, to take cognizance of his case, and put forth his power to do to him as he pleased.

II. His cure was solemn, and some of the circumstances of it were singular.

1. Christ *took him aside from the multitude, v.* 33. Ordinarily, he wrought his miracles publicly before all the people, to show that they would bear the strictest scrutiny and inspection; but this he did privately, to show that he did not seek his own glory, and to

teach us to avoid every thing that savours of ostentation. Let us learn of Christ to be humble, and to do good where no eye sees, but his that is *all eye*.

2. He used more significant actions, in the doing of this cure, than usual. (1) He *put his fingers into his ears*, as if he would *syringe* them, and fetch out that which stopped them up. (2) He spit upon his own finger, and then *touched his tongue*, as if he would moisten his mouth, and so loosen that with which his tongue was tied; these were no causes that could in the least contribute to his cure, but only signs of the exerting of that power which Christ had in himself to cure him, for the encouraging of his faith, and theirs that brought him. The application was all from himself, it was his own *fingers* that he put into his ears, and his own *spittle* that he put upon his tongue; for he alone heals.

3. He *looked up to heaven*, to give his Father the praise of what he did; for he sought his praise, and did his will, and, as Mediator, acted in dependence on him, and with an eye to him. Thus he signified that it was by a divine power, a power he had as the Lord from heaven, and brought with him thence, that he did this; for the *hearing ear* and the *seeing eye* the Lord has made, and can remake even *both of them*. He also hereby directed his patient who could *see*, though he could not *hear*, to look up to heaven for relief. Moses with his stammering tongue is directed to look that way (Exod. iv. 11); *Who hath made man's mouth? Or who maketh the dumb or deaf, or the*

seeing or the blind? Have not I the Lord?

4. He sighed; not as if he found any difficulty in working this miracle, or obtaining power to do it from his Father; but thus he expressed his pity for the miseries of human life, and his sympathy with the afflicted in their afflictions, as one that was himself *touched with the feeling of their infirmities*.

5. He said, *Ephphatha*; that is, *Be opened*. This was nothing that looked like *spell* or *charm*, such as they used, who had *familiar spirits*, who *peeped and muttered*, Isa. viii. 19. Christ speaks as one having authority, and power went along with the word. *Be opened*, served both parts of the cure; "Let the *ears* be *opened*, let the *lips* be *opened*, let him hear and speak freely, and let the restraint be taken off"; and the effect was answerable (*v.* 35); *Straightway his ears were opened, and the string of his tongue was loosed*, and all was well: and happy he who, as soon as he had his hearing and speech, had the blessed Jesus so near him, to converse with.

Now this cure was, (1) A proof of Christ's being the Messiah; for it was foretold that by his power the *ears of the deaf should be unstopped*, and the *tongue of the dumb* should be made to *sing*, Isa. xxxv. 5, 6. (2) It was a specimen of the operations of his gospel upon the minds of men. The great command of the gospel, and grace of Christ to poor sinners, is *Ephphatha—Be opened*. Grotius applies it thus, that the internal impediments of the mind are removed by the Spirit of Christ, as those bodily impediments were by the word of his power. He *opens the heart*, as he did Lydia's, and thereby opens the ear to receive the word of God, and opens the mouth in prayer and praises.

6. He ordered it to be kept very private, but it was made very public. (1) It was his humility, that he *charged them they should tell no man*, *v.* 36. Most men will proclaim their own goodness, or, at least, desire that others should proclaim it; but Christ, though he was himself in no danger of being puffed up with it, knowing that we are, would thus set us an example of self-denial, as in other things, so especially in praise and applause. We should take pleasure in doing good, but not in its being known. (2) It was their zeal, that, though he charged them to say nothing of it, yet they published it, before Christ would have had it published. But they meant honestly, and therefore it is to be reckoned rather an act of indiscretion than an act of disobedience, *v.* 36. But they that told it, and they that heard it, were *beyond measure astonished*; they were exceedingly affected with it, and this was said by every body, it was the common verdict, *He hath done all things well* (*v.* 37); whereas there were those that hated and persecuted him as an *evil-doer*, they are ready to witness for him, not only that he has done no evil, but that he has done a great deal of good, and has done it well, modestly and humbly, and very devoutly, and all gratis, *without money and without price*, which added much to the lustre of his good works. He *maketh both the deaf to hear, and the dumb to speak*; and that is *well*, it is well for them,

it is well for their relations, to whom they had been a burden; and therefore *they* are inexcusable who speak ill of him.

CHAPTER EIGHT

THE LEAVEN OF THE PHARISEES (*vv.* 1–21)

We had the story of a miracle very like this (*vv.* 1–9) before, in this gospel (*ch.* vi. 35), and of this same miracle (Matt. xv. 32), and here is little or no addition or alteration as to the circumstances.

Still Christ is upon motion; now he visits the parts of Dalmanutha, that no corner of the land of Israel might say that they had not had his presence with them. He came thither *by ship* (*v.* 10); but, meeting with occasions of dispute there, and not with opportunities of doing good, he *entered into the ship again* (*v.* 13), and came back. In these verses, we are told,

I. How he refused to gratify the Pharisees, who challenged him to give them a *sign from heaven*.

1. They demanded of him a *sign from heaven*, as if the signs he gave them on earth, which were more familiar to them, and were more capable of being examined and enquired into, were not sufficient. There was a sign *from heaven* at his baptism, in the descent of the dove, and the voice (Matt. iii. 16, 17); it was public enough; and if they had attended John's baptism as they ought to have done, they might themselves have seen it. Afterward, when he was nailed to the cross, they prescribed a new sign; *Let him come down from the cross, and we will believe him*; thus obstinate infidelity will still have something

to say, though ever so unreasonable. They demanded this sign, *tempting him*; not in hopes that he would give it them, that they might be satisfied, but in hopes that he would not, that they might imagine themselves to have a pretence for their infidelity.

2. He denied them their demand; He *sighed deeply in his spirit, v.* 12. He *groaned* (so some), being grieved for the *hardness of their hearts*, and the little influence that his preaching and miracles had had upon them. (1) He expostulates with them upon this demand; "*Why doth this generation seek after a sign*; this generation, that is so unworthy to have the gospel brought to it, and to have any sign accompanying it; *this generation*, that so greedily swallows the traditions of the elders, without the confirmation of any sign at all?" (2) He refuses to answer their demand; *Verily, I say unto you, there shall no sign*, no such sign, *be given to this generation*. He denied them, and then *left them*, as men not fit to be talked with; if they will not be convinced, they shall not; leave them to their strong delusions.

II. How he warned his disciples against the leaven of the Pharisees and of Herod. Observe here,

1. What the caution was (*v.* 15); "*Take heed, beware*, lest ye partake of the *leaven of the Pharisees*, lest ye embrace the tradition of the elders, which they are so wedded to, lest ye be proud, and hypocritical, and ceremonious, like them."

2. How they misunderstood this caution. It seems, at their putting to sea this time, they had *forgotten to take bread*, and *had not in their ship*

more than one loaf, v. 14. When therefore Christ bid them *beware of the leaven of the Pharisees*, they understood it as an intimation to them, not to apply themselves to any of the Pharisees for relief, when they came to the other side, for they had lately been offended at them for eating with *unwashen hands*.

3. The reproof Christ gave them for their uneasiness in this matter, as it argued a disbelief of his power to supply them, notwithstanding the abundant experience they had had of it. The reproof is given with some warmth, for he knew their hearts, and knew they needed to be thus soundly chidden; "*Perceive ye not yet, neither understand*, that which you have had so many demonstrations of? *Have ye your hearts yet hardened*, so as that nothing will make any impression upon them, or bring them to compliance with your Master's designs? *Do ye not remember* that which was done but the other day, *when I broke the five loaves among the five thousand*, and soon after, the *seven loaves among the four thousand?* Do ye not remember *how many baskets full ye took up* of the fragments?" Yes, they did remember, and could tell that they took up *twelve* baskets full one time, and *seven* another; "Why then," saith he, "*how is it that ye do not understand?* As if he that multiplied *five* loaves, and *seven*, could not multiply one."

A TWO-STAGE HEALING
(*vv.* 22–26)

This cure is related only by this evangelist, and there is something singular in the circumstances.

I. Here is a *blind man* brought to Christ by his friends, with a desire that he would *touch him*, v. 22. Here appears the faith of those that brought him—they doubted not but that one touch of Christ's hand would recover him his sight; but the man himself showed not that earnestness for, or expectation of, a cure that other blind men did.

II. Here is Christ *leading* this blind man, v. 23. He did not bid his friends lead him, but (which bespeaks his wonderful condescension) he himself *took him by the hand, and led him*. Never had poor blind man such a Leader. He led him *out of the town*. Had he herein only designed privacy, he might have led him into a house, into an inner chamber, and have cured him there; but he intended hereby to upbraid Bethsaida with the *mighty works* that had *in vain* been done *in her* (Matt. xi. 21), and was telling her, in effect, she was unworthy to have any more done within her walls. Perhaps Christ took the blind man *out of the town*, that he might have a larger prospect in the *open fields*, to try his sight with, than he could have in the *close streets*.

III. Here is the cure of the blind man, by that blessed Oculist, who came into the world to *preach the recovering of sight to the blind* (Luke iv. 18), and to give what he *preached*. In this cure we may observe, 1. That Christ used a *sign*; he *spat on his eyes* (spat *into* them, so some), and *put his hand upon him*. He could have cured him, as he did others, with a word speaking, but thus he was pleased to assist his faith which was very weak, and to help him against his *unbelief*.

2. That the cure was wrought *gradually*, which was not usual in Christ's miracles. He *asked him if he saw aught*, v. 23. And he *looked up*; so far he *recovered his sight*, that he could open his eyes, and he said, *I see men as trees walking*; he could not distinguish men from trees, otherwise than that he could discern them to move. But, 3. It was soon completed; Christ never doeth *his work* by the halves, nor leaves it till he can say, *It is finished*. He *put his hands again upon his eyes*, to disperse the remaining darkness, and then bade him look up again, and he *saw every man clearly*, v. 25. Now Christ took this way, (1) Because he would not *tie himself to a method*, but would show with what liberty he acted in all he did. He did not cure by *rote*, as I may say, and in a *road*, but *varied* as he thought fit. (2) Because it should be to the patient *according to his faith*; and perhaps this man's faith was at first very weak, but afterward gathered strength, and accordingly his cure was. (3) Thus Christ would show how, and in what method, those are healed by his grace, who by nature are *spiritually blind*; at first, their knowledge is confused, they see *men as trees walking*; but, like the light of the morning, it *shines more and more to the perfect day*, and then they *see all things clearly*, Prov. iv. 18.

IV. The directions Christ gave the man he had cured, not to *tell it to any in the town of Bethsaida*, nor so much as to *go into the town*, where probably there were some expecting him to come back, who had seen Christ lead him out of the town, but, having been eye-witnesses of so many miracles, had not so much as the curiosity to follow him: let not these be gratified with the sight of him when he was cured, who would not show so much respect to Christ as to go a step out of the town, to see this cure wrought. Bethsaida, in the day of her visitation, would not know the things that belonged to her peace, and now they are *hid from her eyes*. They will not see, and therefore shall not see.

THE MEANING OF THE MIRACLES
(*vv.* 27–38)

We have read a great deal of the doctrine Christ preached, and the miracles he wrought, which were many, and strange, and well-attested, of various kinds, and wrought in several places, to the astonishment of the multitudes that were eye-witnesses of them. It is now time for us to pause a little, and to consider what these things mean; the wondrous works which Christ then forbade the publishing of, being recorded in these sacred writings, are thereby published to all the world, to us, to all ages; now what shall we think of them? Is the record of those things designed only for an amusement, or to furnish us with matter for discourse? No, certainly *these things are written, that we may believe that Jesus is the Christ the Son of God* (John xx. 31); and this discourse which Christ had with his disciples, will assist us in making the necessary reflections upon the miracles of Christ, and a right use of them. Three things we are here taught to infer from the miracles Christ wrought.

I. They *prove* that he is *the true Messiah*, the Son of God, and Saviour of the world: this the works he did witnessed concerning him; and this his disciples, who were the eye-witnesses of those works, here profess their belief of; which cannot but be a satisfaction to us in making the same inference from them.

1. Christ enquired of them what the sentiments of the people were concerning him; *Who do men say that I am? v.* 27. Note, Though it is a small thing for us to be judged of men, yet it may sometimes do us good to know what people say of us, not that we may seek our own glory, but that we may hear of our faults. Christ asked them, not that he might be informed, but that they might observe it themselves, and inform one another.

2. The account they gave him, was such as plainly intimated the *high opinion* the people had of him. Though they came short of the truth, yet they were convinced by his miracles that he was an extraordinary person, sent from the invisible world with a divine commission. It is probable that they would have acknowledged him to be the Messiah, if they had not been possessed by their teachers with a notion that the Messiah must be a temporal Prince, appearing in external pomp and power, which the figure Christ made, would not comport with; yet (whatever the Pharisees said, whose copyhold was touched by the strictness and spirituality of his doctrine) none of the people said that he was a Deceiver, but some said that *he was John Baptist*, others *Elias*, others

one of the prophets, v. 28. All agreed that he was one *risen from the dead*.

3. The account they gave him of their own sentiments concerning him, intimated their abundant satisfaction in him, and in their having left all to follow him, which now, after some time of trial, they see no reason to repent; *But whom say ye that I am?* To this they have an answer ready, *Thou art the Christ*, the Messiah often promised, and long expected, v. 29. To be a Christian indeed, is, sincerely to believe that Jesus is the Christ, and to act accordingly; and that he is so, plainly appears by his wondrous works. This they knew, and must shortly publish and maintain; but for the present they must keep it secret (v. 30), till the proof of it was completed, and they were completely qualified to maintain it, by the pouring out of the Holy Ghost; and then *let all the house of Israel know assuredly that God has made this same Jesus, whom ye crucified, both Lord and Christ*, Acts ii. 36.

II. These miracles of Christ *take off the offence of the cross*, and assure us that Christ was, in it, not conquered, but a Conqueror. Now that the disciples are convinced that Jesus is the Christ, they may bear to hear of his sufferings, which Christ now *begins* to give them notice of, v. 31.

1. Christ *taught* his disciples that he must *suffer many things*, Though they had got over the vulgar error of the Messiah's being a temporal Prince, so far as to believe their Master to be the Messiah, notwithstanding his present meanness, yet still they retained it, so far as to

expect that he would *shortly* appear in outward pomp and grandeur, and *restore the kingdom to Israel*; and therefore, to rectify that mistake, Christ here gives them a prospect of the contrary, that he must be *rejected of the elders, and the chief priests*, and *the scribes*, who, they expected, should be brought to own and prefer him; that, instead of being crowned, *he must be killed*, he must be crucified, and *after three days he must rise again* to a heavenly life, and to be *no more in this world*. This he spoke *openly* (v. 32).

2. Peter opposed it; *He took him, and began to rebuke him*. Here Peter showed more love than discretion, a zeal for Christ and his safety, but not according to knowledge. Our Lord Jesus allowed his disciples to be free with him, but Peter here took too great a liberty.

3. Christ checked him for his opposition (v. 33); He *turned about*, as one offended, and *looked on his disciples*, to see if the rest of them were of the same mind, and concurred with Peter in this, that, if they did, they might take the reproof to themselves, which he was now about to give to Peter; and he said, *Get thee behind me, Satan*. Peter little thought to have had such a sharp rebuke for such a kind dissuasive, but perhaps expected as much commendation now for his love as he had lately had for his faith. Note, Christ sees that amiss in what we say and do, which we ourselves are not aware of, and knows what manner of spirit we are of, when we ourselves do not.

III. Here is that which all are concerned to know, and consider, if they expect Christ should heal *their souls.*

1. They must not be *indulgent* of the *ease of the body*; for (*v.* 34), "*Whosoever will come after me* for spiritual cures, as these people do for bodily cures, *let him deny himself*, and live a life of self-denial, mortification, and contempt of the world; let him not pretend to be his own physician, but renounce all confidence in himself and his own righteousness and strength, and let him *take up his cross*, conforming himself to the pattern of a crucified Jesus, and accommodating himself to the will of God in all the afflictions he lies under; and thus let him continue to *follow me*"; as many of those did, whom Christ healed. Those that will be Christ's patients must attend on him, converse with him, receive instruction and reproof from him, as those did that *followed* him, and must resolve they will never forsake him.

2. They must not be *solicitous*, no, not for *the life of the body*, when they cannot keep it without quitting Christ, *v.* 35. Are we invited by the words and works of Christ to follow him? Let us sit down, and count the cost, whether we can prefer our advantages by Christ before life itself, whether we can bear to think of losing our life *for Christ's sake and the gospel's*.

(1) We must *not dread the loss of our lives*, provided it be *in the cause of Christ* (*v.* 35); *Whosoever will save his life*, by declining Christ, and refusing to come to him, or by disowning and denying him after he has in profession come to Christ,

he shall *lose it*, shall lose the comfort of his natural life, the root and fountain of his spiritual life, and all his hopes of eternal life; such a bad bargain will he make for himself. But whosoever *shall lose his life*, shall be truly willing to lose it, shall venture it, shall lay it down when he cannot keep it without denying Christ, he shall *save it*, he shall be an unspeakable gainer; for the loss of his life shall be made up to him in a better life.

(2) We must *dread the loss of our souls*, yea, though we should *gain the whole world* by it (*vv.* 36, 37); *For what shall it profit a man, if he should gain the whole world*, and all the wealth, honour, and pleasure, in it, by denying Christ, and *lose his own soul?* "True it is," said Bishop Hooper, the night before he suffered martyrdom, "that *life is sweet*, and *death is bitter*, but *eternal death is more bitter*, and *eternal life is more sweet*." As the happiness of heaven with Christ, is enough to countervail the loss of life itself for Christ, so the gain of all the world *in sin*, is not sufficient to countervail the ruin of the soul *by sin.*

What that is that men do, to *save their lives*, and *gain the world*, he tells us (*v.* 38), and of what fatal consequence it will be to them; *Whosoever therefore shall be ashamed of me, and of my words, in this adulterous and sinful generation, of him shall the Son of man be ashamed.* Something like this we had, Matt. x. 33. But it is here expressed more fully. Those that are ashamed of Christ in this world where he is despised, he will be ashamed of in that world where he is eternally adored. *They* shall not share with him in his glory then, that were not willing to share with him in his disgrace now.

CHAPTER NINE

THE TRANSFIGURATION
(*vv.* 1–29)

Here is, I. A prediction of Christ's kingdom now near approaching, *v.* 1. That which is foretold, is, 1. That the *kingdom of God* would *come*, and would come so as to be *seen*: the kingdom of the Messiah shall be set up in the world by the utter destruction of the Jewish polity, which stood in the way of it; this was the restoring of the kingdom of God among men, which had been in a manner lost by the woeful degeneracy both of Jews and Gentiles. 2. That it would come *with power*, so as to make its own way, and bear down the opposition that was given to it. It came *with power*, when vengeance was taken on the Jews for crucifying Christ, and when it conquered the idolatry of the Gentile world. 3. That it would come while some now *present were alive*; There are some *standing here, that shall not taste of death*, till they *see* it; this speaks the same with Matt. xxiv. 34, This *generation shall not pass, till all these things be fulfilled.* Those that were standing here with Christ, should see it, when the others could not discern it to be the kingdom of God, for it came not with observation.

II. A specimen of that kingdom in the transfiguration of Christ, *six days* after Christ spoke that prediction. He had begun to give notice to his disciples of his death and sufferings; and, to prevent their offence at that, he gives them this glimpse of his glory, to show that his sufferings were voluntary, and what a virtue the dignity and glory of his person would put into them, and to prevent the *offence of the cross.*

We have had this, and the following miracle—the demon expelled from a boy—in Matt. xvii. 1–21.

THE APOSTLES REPROVED
(*vv.* 30–40)

Here, I. Christ foretells his own approaching sufferings. He *passed through Galilee* with more expedition than usual, and *would not that any man should know it* (*v.* 30); because he had done many mighty and good works among them in vain, they shall not be invited to see them and have the benefit of them, as they had been. The time of his sufferings drew nigh, and therefore he was willing to be private awhile, and to converse only with his disciples, to prepare them for the approaching trial, *v.* 31. He said to them, *The Son of man is delivered* by the determinate counsel and foreknowledge of God *into the hands of men* (*v.* 31), and *they shall kill him.* But still it is observable that when Christ spoke of his death, he always spoke of his resurrection, which took away the reproach of it from himself, and should have taken away the grief of it from his disciples. But they *understood not that saying, v.* 32. The words were plain enough, but they could not be reconciled to the thing, and therefore would suppose them to have

308

some mystical meaning which they did not understand, and they were *afraid to ask him*; not because he was difficult of access, or stern to those who consulted him, but either because they were loth to know the truth, or because they expected to be chided for their backwardness to receive it. Many remain ignorant because they are ashamed to enquire.

II. He rebukes his disciples for magnifying themselves. When he came to Capernaum, he privately asked his disciples what it was that they *disputed among themselves by the way*, v. 33. He knew very well what the dispute was, but he would know it *from them*, and would have them to confess their fault and folly in it.

Now, (1) They were willing to *cover this fault* (*v.* 34); they *held their peace*. As they would not *ask* (*v.* 32), because they were ashamed to own their ignorance, so here they would not *answer* because they were ashamed to own their pride. (2) He was willing to *amend this fault* in them, and to bring them to a better temper; and therefore *sat down*, that he might have a solemn and full discourse with them about this matter; he *called the twelve to him*, and told them, [1] That ambition and affectation of dignity and dominion, instead of gaining them preferment in his kingdom, would but postpone their preferment; *If any man desire* and aim *to be first*, he *shall be last*; he that exalteth himself, shall be abased, and men's *pride* shall *bring them low*. [2] That there is no preferment to be had under him, but an opportunity for, and an obligation to, so

much the more labour and condescension; *If any man desire to be first*, when he is so, he must be much the more busy and serviceable to every body. [3] That those who are most humble and self-denying, do most resemble Christ, and shall be most tenderly owned by him. This he taught them by a sign; *He took a child in his arms*, that had nothing of pride and ambition in it. "Look you," saith he; "*whosoever shall receive* one like this child, *receives me*."

III. He rebukes them for *villifying all but themselves*; while they are striving which of them should be greatest, they will not allow those who are not in communion with them to be any thing. Observe,

1. The account which John gave him, of the restraint they had laid upon one from making use of the name of Christ, because he was not of their society.

2. The rebuke he gave to them for this (*v.* 39); *Jesus said, "Forbid him not*, nor any other that does likewise." Two reasons Christ gives why such should not be forbidden. (1) Because we cannot suppose that any man who makes use of Christ's name in working miracles, should blaspheme his name, as the scribes and Pharisees did. There were those indeed that did *in Christ's name cast out devils*, and yet in other respects were *workers of iniquity*; but they did not *speak evil of Christ*. (2) Because those that differed in communion, while they agreed to fight against Satan under the banner of Christ, ought to look upon one another as on the same side, notwithstanding that difference. *He that is not against us is on our part.*

As to the great controversy between Christ and Beelzebub, he had said, *He that is not with me is against me*, Matt. xii. 30. He that will not own Christ, owns Satan. But as to those that own Christ, though not in the same circumstances, that follow him, though *not with us*, we must reckon that though these differ from us, they are not against us, and therefore are *on our part*, and we must not be any hindrance to their usefulness.

OFFENCES (*vv.* 41–50)

Here, I. Christ promiseth a reward to all those that are any way kind to his disciples (*v.* 41); "*Whosoever shall give you a cup of water*, when you need it, and it will be a refreshment to you, *because ye belong to Christ*, and are of his family, *he shall not lose his reward*."

II. He threatens those that *offend* his *little ones*, that wilfully are the occasion of sin or trouble to them, *v.* 42. Whosoever shall grieve any true Christians, though they be of the weakest, shall oppose their *entrance* into the ways of God, or discourage and obstruct their *progress* in those ways, shall either restrain them from doing good, or draw them in to commit sin, it were *better for him that a millstone were hanged about his neck, and he were cast into the sea*: his punishment will be very great, and the death and ruin of his soul more terrible than such a death and ruin of his body would be. See Matt. xviii. 6.

III. He warns all his followers to take heed of ruining their own souls. This charity must begin at home; if we must take heed of doing any thing to hinder others

from good, and to occasion their sin, much more careful must we be to avoid every thing that will take us off from our duty, or lead us to sin; and that which doth so we must part with, though it be ever so dear to us. This we had twice in Matthew, *ch.* v. 29, 30, and *ch.* xviii. 8, 9. It is here urged somewhat more largely and pressingly; certainly this requires our serious regard, which is so much insisted upon.

CHAPTER TEN

DIVORCE LAWS (*vv.* 1–12)

Here we have our Lord Jesus in the *coasts* of Judea, by the further side of Jordan eastward, as we found him, not long since, in the utmost borders westward, near Tyre and Sidon. Thus was his circuit like that of the sun, from whose light and heat nothing is hid. Now here we have him,

I. *Resorted to* by the *people, v.* 1. Wherever he was, they flocked after him in crowds; they came to him *again*, as they had done when he had formerly been in these parts, and, *as he was wont, he taught them again*. Note, Preaching was Christ's constant practice; it was what he was used to; and, wherever he came, he did *as he was wont*. In Matthew it is said, *He healed them*; here it is said, *He taught them*: his cures were to confirm his doctrine, and to recommend it, and his doctrine was to explain his cures, and illustrate them. His *teaching* was *healing* to poor souls.

II. We have him *disputed with* by the Pharisees, who envied the progress of his spiritual arms, and did all they could to obstruct and oppose it; to divert him, to perplex him, and to prejudice the people against him.

Here is, 1. A question they started concerning divorce (*v.* 2); *Is it lawful for a man to put away his wife?*

2. Christ's reply to them with a question (*v.* 3); *What did Moses command you?* This he asked them, to testify his respect to the law of Moses, and to show that he came not to destroy it; and to engage them to a universal impartial respect for Moses's writings and to compare one part of them with another.

3. The fair account they gave of what they found in the law of Moses, expressly concerning divorce, *v.* 4. They own that Moses only *suffered*, or *permitted*, a man to write his wife a *bill of divorce*, and to put *her away*, Deut. xxiv. 1.

4. The answer that Christ gave to their question, in which he abides by the doctrine he had formerly laid down in this case (Matt. v. 32), *That whosoever puts away his wife, except for fornication, causeth her to commit adultery.* And to clear this he here shows,

(1) That the reason why Moses, in his *law*, permitted divorce, was such, as that they ought not to make use of that permission; for it was only *for the hardness of their hearts* (*v.* 5), lest, if they were not permitted to divorce their wives, they should murder them; so that none must put away their wives but such as are willing to own that their hearts were so hard as to need this permission.

(2) That the account which Moses, in this *history*, *gives* of the institution of marriage, affords

such a reason against divorce, as amounts to a prohibition of it. So that if the question be, *What did Moses command?* (*v.* 3), it must be answered, "Though by a temporary proviso he allowed divorce to the Jews, yet by an eternal reason he forbade it to all the children of Adam and Eve, and that is it which we must abide by."

Now from all this he infers, that men ought not to *put* their wives *asunder* from them, whom God has put so near to them. The bond which God himself has tied, is not to be lightly untied.

5. Christ's discourse with his disciples, in private, about this matter, *vv.* 10–12. No more is here related of this private conference, than the law Christ laid down in this case—That it is adultery for a man to put away his wife, and marry another; it is adultery *against the wife* he puts away, it is a wrong to her, and a breach of his contract with her, *v.* 11. He adds, *If a woman shall put away her husband*, that is, elope from him, leave him by consent, and *be married to another*, she *commits adultery* (*v.* 12), and it will be no excuse at all for her to say that it was with the consent of her husband. Wisdom and grace, holiness and love, reigning in the heart, will make those commands easy which to the carnal mind may be as a heavy yoke.

CHILDREN BROUGHT TO CHRIST (*vv.* 13–16)

Here we have,

I. Little children brought to Christ, *v.* 13. Their parents, or whoever they were that had the nursing of them, brought them to him, that he should *touch them*, in token of his commanding and conferring a blessing on them. It doth not appear that they needed any bodily *cure*, nor were they capable of being *taught*: but it seems, 1. They that had the care of them were mostly concerned *about their souls*, their better part, which ought to be the principal care of all parents for their children; for that is the principal part, and it is well with them, if it be well with their souls. 2. They believed that Christ's blessing would do their souls good; and therefore to him they brought them, that he might *touch* them, knowing that he could reach their hearts, when nothing their parents could say to them, or do for them, would reach them.

II. The *dis*couragement which the disciples gave to the bringing of children to Christ; *They rebuked them that brought them*; as if they had been sure that they knew their Master's mind in this matter, whereas he had lately cautioned them not to *despise the little ones*.

III. The *en*couragement Christ gave to it. 1. He took it very ill that his disciples should keep them off; *When he saw it, he was much displeased, v.* 14. 2. He ordered that they should be *brought to him*, and nothing said or done to hinder them; *suffer little children*, as soon as they are capable, to *come to me*, to offer up their supplications to me, and to receive instructions from me. Little children are welcome betimes to the throne of grace with their Hosannas. 3. He owned them as members of his church, as they had been of the

Jewish church. He came to set up the *kingdom of God* among men, and took this occasion to declare that that kingdom admitted *little children* to be the subjects of it, and gave them a title to the privileges of subjects. 4. That there must be something of the temper and disposition of little children found in all that Christ will own and bless. We must *receive the kingdom of God as little children* (*v.* 15); that is, we must stand affected to Christ and his grace as little children do to their parents, nurses, and teachers. 5. He received the children, and gave them what was desired (*v.* 16); *He took them up in his arms*, in token of his affectionate concern for them; *put his hands upon them*, as was desired, and *blessed them*. See how he outdid the desires of these parents; they begged he would touch them, but he did more. He *blessed* them with the spiritual blessings he came to give. Our children are happy, if they have but the *Mediator's blessing* for their portion. It is true, we do not read that he baptized these children, baptism was not fully settled as the door of admission into the church till after Christ's resurrection; but he asserted their visible church-membership, and by another sign bestowed those blessings upon them, which are now appointed to be conveyed and conferred by baptism, the seal of the promise, which is *to us* and *to our children*.

A HOPEFUL YOUTH
(*vv.* 17–31)

Here is a *hopeful meeting* between Christ and a *young man*; such he is said to be (Matt. xix. 20, 22), and a *ruler* (Luke xviii. 18), a person of quality. Some circumstances here are, which we had not in Matthew, which makes his address to Christ very promising.

1. He came *running* to Christ, which was an indication of his humility; he laid aside the gravity and grandeur of a ruler, when he came to Christ: thus too he manifested his earnestness and importunity; he *ran* as one *in haste*, and longing to be in conversation with Christ.

2. He came to him when he was *in the way*, in the midst of company: he did not insist upon a private conference with him by night, as Nicodemus did, though like him he was a ruler.

3. He *kneeled to him*, in token of the great value and veneration he had for him, as a teacher come from God, and his earnest desire to be taught by him.

4. His address to him was serious and weighty; *Good Master, what shall I do, that I may inherit eternal life?* Most men enquire for good to be *had* in this world (Ps. iv. 6), *any good*; he asks for *good to be done* in this world, in order to the enjoyment of the greatest good in the other world; not, Who will make us to *see good*? But, "Who will make us to *do good*?"

The rest of the account is as in Matt. xix.

THE CUP OF SUFFERING
(*vv.* 32–45)

Here is, I. Christ's prediction of his own sufferings; this string he harped much upon, though in the ears of his disciples it sounded very harsh and unpleasing.

1. See here how bold he was; when they were going up to Jerusalem, *Jesus went before them*, as the *captain of our salvation*, that was now to be *made perfect through sufferings*, v. 32. Thus he showed himself forward to go on with his undertaking, even when he came to the hardest part of it.

2. See here how timorous and faint-hearted his disciples were; *As they followed, they were afraid*, afraid for themselves, as being apprehensive of their own danger; and justly might they be *ashamed* of their being thus *afraid*. Their Master's courage should have put spirit into them.

3. See here what method he took to silence their fears. He did not go about to make the matter better than it was, nor to feed them with hopes that he might escape the storm, but told them *again* what he had often told them before, the *things that should happen to him*. He knew the worst of it, and therefore went on thus boldly, and he will let them know the worst of it. Come, *be not afraid*; for, (1) There is no remedy, the matter is determined, and cannot be avoided. (2) It is only the *Son of man* that shall suffer; their time of suffering was not at hand, he will now provide for their security. (3) He *shall rise again*; the issue of his sufferings will be glorious to himself, and advantageous to all that are his, *vv.* 33, 34.

II. The check he gave to two of his disciples for their ambitious request. This story is much the same here as we had in Matt. xx. 20.

313

Only there they are said to have made their request by their mother, here they are said to make it themselves; she introduced them, and presented their petition, and then they seconded it, and assented to it.

III. The check he gave to the rest of the disciples, for their uneasiness at it. *They began to be much displeased*, to have *indignation about James and John, v.* 41. They were angry at them for affecting precedency, not because it did so ill become the disciples of Christ, but because each of them hoped to have it himself. He shows them,

1. That dominion was generally *abused in the world* (*v.* 42); *They that seem to rule over the* Gentiles, that have the name and title of rulers, *they exercise lordship over them*, that is all they study and aim at, not so much to protect them and provide for their welfare, as to *exercise authority upon them*.

2. That therefore it ought not to be *admitted into the church*; "*It shall not be so among you*; those that shall be put under your charge, must be as sheep under the charge of the *shepherd*, who is to tend them and feed them, and be a servant to them, not as horses under the command of the driver, that works them and beats them, and gets his pennyworths out of them. He that affects to be great and chief, that thrusts himself into a secular dignity and dominion, *he shall be servant of all*, he shall be mean and contemptible in the eyes of all that are wise and good; *he that exalteth himself shall be abased*." Or rather, "He that would be *truly* great and

chief, he must lay out himself to do good to all, must stoop to the meanest services, and labour in the hardest services. Those not only shall be most *honoured* hereafter, but are most *honourable* now, who are most useful." To convince them of this, he sets before them his own example (*v.* 45): "The *Son of man* submits first to the greatest hardships and hazards, and then enters into his glory, and can you expect to come to it any other way; or to have more ease and honour than he has?" (1) He takes upon him *the form of a servant*, comes not to be *ministered to*, and waited upon, but *to minister*, and wait to be gracious. (2) He becomes *obedient to death*, and to its dominion, for he *gives his life a ransom for many*; did he die for the benefit of good people, and shall not we study to live for their benefit?

BLIND BARTIMEUS
(*vv.* 46–52)

This passage of story agrees with that, Matt. xx. 29, &c. Only that there we were told of *two* blind men; here, and Luke xviii. 35, only of *one*: but if there were *two*, there was *one*. This one is named here, being a *blind beggar that* was much talked of; he was called *Bartimeus*, that is, the *son of Timeus*; which, some think, signifies *the son of a blind man*; he was the blind son of a blind father, which made the case the worse, and the cure the more wonderful, and the more proper to typify the spiritual cures wrought by the grace of Christ, on those that not only are born blind, but are born of those that are blind.

CHAPTER ELEVEN

CHRIST ENTERS JERUSALEM
(*vv.* 1–11)

We have here the story of the public entry Christ made into Jerusalem, four or five days before his death. And he came into town thus remarkably, 1. To show that he was not afraid of the power and malice of his enemies in Jerusalem. He did not steal into the city *incognito*, as one that durst not show his face; no, they needed not send spies to search for him, he comes in with observation. This would be an encouragement to his disciples that were timorous, and cowed at the thought of their enemies' power and rage; let them see how bravely their Master sets them all at defiance. 2. To show that he was not cast down or disquieted at the thoughts of his approaching sufferings. He came, not only publicly, but cheerfully, and with acclamations of joy. Though he was now but taking the field, and *girding on the harness*, yet, being fully assured of a complete victory, he thus triumphs as though he had put it off.

The account is as in Matt. xxi. 1–11.

THE FIG-TREE (*vv.* 12–26)

Here is, I. Christ's cursing the fruitless fig-tree. He had a convenient resting-place at Bethany, and therefore thither he went at resting-time; but his work lay at Jerusalem, and thither therefore he returned in the morning, at working-time; and so intent was he upon his work, that he went out from Bethany without breakfast, which,

before he was gone far, he found the want of, and *was hungry* (*v.* 12), for he was subject to all the sinless infirmities of our nature. Finding himself in want of food, he went to a *fig-tree*, which he saw at some distance, and which being well *adorned* with green leaves he hoped to find *enriched* with some sort of fruit. But he *found nothing but leaves*; he hoped to find some fruit, *for* though *the time of* gathering in *figs* was near, it *was not yet*; so that it could not be pretended that it had had fruit, but that it was gathered and gone; for the season had not yet arrived. Or, He found none, for indeed *it was not a season of figs*, it was no good fig-year. But this was worse than any other fig-tree, for there was not so much as one fig to be found upon it, though it was so full of leaves. However, Christ was willing to make an example of it, not to the *trees*, but to the *men*, of that generation, and therefore cursed it with that curse which is the reverse of the first blessing, *Be fruitful*; he said unto it, *Never let any man eat fruit of thee hereafter for ever*, *v.* 14. This was intended to be a type and figure of the doom passed upon the Jewish church, to which he came, *seeking fruit, but found none* (Luke xiii. 6, 7); and though it was not, according to the doom in the parable, immediately cut down, yet, according to this in the history, *blindness* and *hardness* befell them (Rom. xi. 8, 25), so that they were from henceforth *good for nothing*. The *disciples heard* what sentence Christ passed on this tree, and took notice of it.

II. His clearing the temple of the

Christ Enters Jerusalem

market-people that frequented it, and of those that made it a thoroughfare. We do not find that Christ met with food elsewhere, when he missed of it on the fig-tree; but the zeal of God's house so ate him up, and made him forget himself, that he came, hungry as he was, to Jerusalem, and went straight to the temple, and began to reform those abuses which the day before he had marked out; to show that when the Redeemer came to Zion, his errand was, to *turn away ungodliness from Jacob* (Rom. xi. 26), and that he came not, as he was falsely accused, to *destroy* the temple, but to purify and refine it, and reduce his church to its primitive rectitude.

We have had the account in Matt. xxi. 12–17.

III. His discourse with his disciples, upon occasion of the fig-tree's withering away which he had cursed. At *even*, as usual, he *went out of the city* (v. 19), to Bethany; but it is probable that it was in the dark, so that they could not see the fig-tree; but the next morning, as they *passed by*, they observed the *fig-tree dried up from the roots, v.* 20. More is *included* many times in Christ's curses than is *expressed*, as appears by the effects of them. The curse was no more than that it should never bear fruit again, but the effect goes further, *it is dried up from the roots*. If it bear no fruit, it shall bear no leaves to cheat people. Now observe,

1. How the disciples were affected with it. Peter remembered Christ's words, and said, with surprise, *Master, behold, the fig-tree which thou cursedst is withered away, v.* 21. And this seemed very strange to the disciples, and scarcely credible, that the Jews, who had been so long God's own, his only professing people in the world, should be thus abandoned; they could not imagine how that *fig-tree* should *so soon wither away*: but this comes of rejecting Christ, and being rejected by him.

2. The good instructions Christ gave them from it; for of *those* even this *withered* tree was *fruitful*.

(1) Christ teacheth them from hence to *pray in faith* (v. 22); *Have faith in God*. They admired the power of Christ's word of command; "Why," saith Christ, "a lively active faith would put as great a power into your prayers, *vv.* 23, 24. *Whosoever shall say to this mountain*, this mount of Olives, *Be removed, and be cast into the sea*; if he has but any word of God, general or particular, to build his faith upon, and if he *shall not doubt in his heart, but shall believe that those things which he saith*, according to the warrant he has from what God hath said, *shall come to pass, he shall have whatsoever he saith*." Through the strength and power of God in Christ, the greatest difficulty shall be got over, and the thing shall be effected.

(2) To this is added here that necessary qualification of the prevailing prayer, that we freely forgive those who have been any way injurious to us, and be in charity with all men (*vv.* 25, 26); *When ye stand praying*, forgive. This ought to be remembered in prayer, because one great errand we have to the throne of grace, is, to pray for the pardon of our sins: and care

316

about it ought to be our daily care, because prayer is a part of our daily work. Our Saviour often insists on this, for it was his great design to engage his disciples to love one another.

A QUESTION OF AUTHORITY
(vv. 27–33)

We have here Christ examined by the great Sanhedrim concerning his authority; for they claimed a power to call prophets to an account concerning their mission. The great men were vexed to see him followed and heard with attention, and therefore *came to him* with some solemnity, and did as it were arraign him at the bar with this question, *By what authority doest thou these things? v.* 28. Now observe,

I. How they designed hereby to run him aground, and embarrass him. If they could make it out before the people, that he had not a *legal mission*, that he was not duly *ordained*, though he was ever so well qualified, and preached ever so profitably and well, they would tell the people that they *ought not to hear him*.

II. How he effectually ran them aground, and embarrassed them, with this question, "What are your thoughts concerning *the baptism of John? Was it from heaven, or of men?* By what authority did John preach, and baptize, and gather disciples? *Answer me, v.* 30.

1. If they own the baptism of John to be *from heaven*, as really it was, they *shame themselves*; for Christ will presently turn it upon them, *Why did ye not then believe him*, and receive his baptism?

2. If they say, "*It is of men*, he was not sent of God, but his doctrine and baptism were inventions of his own," they *expose themselves*, the people will be ready to do them a mischief, or at least clamour upon them; for *all men counted John that he was a prophet indeed*, and therefore they could not bear that he should be reflected on. Now by this dilemma to which Christ brought them, (1) They were confounded and baffled, and forced to make a dishonourable retreat; to pretend ignorance—*We cannot tell* (and that was mortification enough to those proud men), but really to discover the greatest malice and wilfulness. What Christ did by his wisdom, we must labour to do by our well doing—*put to silence the ignorance of foolish men*, 1 Pet. ii. 15. (2) Christ came off with honour, and justified himself in refusing to give them an answer to their imperious demand; *Neither tell I you by what authority I do these things*. They did not deserve to be told; for it was plain that they contended not for truth, but victory; nor did *he* need to *tell them*, for the works which he did, told them plainly that he had authority from God to do what he did; since no man could do those miracles which he did unless God were with him.

CHAPTER TWELVE
THE HUSBANDMEN
(vv. 1–12)

Christ had formerly in parables showed how he designed to set up the gospel church; now he begins in parables to show how he would lay aside the Jewish church, which it might have been grafted into the *stock of*, but was built upon the *ruins of*. This parable we had just as we have it here, Matt. xxi. 33.

GOD AND CÆSAR
(*vv.* 13-17)

When the enemies of Christ, who thirsted for his blood, could not find occasion against him from what he said against them, they tried to ensnare him by putting questions to him. Here we have him tempted, or *att*empted rather, with a question about the lawfulness of paying tribute to Cæsar. We had this narrative, Matt. xxii. 15.

I. The persons they employed were the *Pharisees* and the *Herodians*, men that in this matter were contrary to one another, and yet concurred against Christ, *v.* 13. The Pharisees were great sticklers for the liberty of the Jews, and, if he should say, It is lawful to give tribute to Cæsar, they would incense the common people against him, and the Herodians would, underhand, assist them in it. The Herodians were great sticklers for the Roman power, and, if he should discountenance the paying of tribute to Cæsar, they would incense the governor against him, yea, and the Pharisees, against their own principles, would join with them in it. It is no new thing for those that are at variance in other things, to join in a confederacy against Christ.

II. The pretence they made was, that they desired him to resolve them a case of conscience, which was of great importance in the present juncture; and they take on them to have a high opinion of his ability to resolve it, *v.* 14.

III. The question they put was, *Is it lawful to give tribute to Cæsar, or not?* They would be thought desirous to know their duty. *As a nation that did righteousness, they ask of God the ordinances of justice*, when really they desired nothing but to know what he would say, in hopes that, which side soever he took of the question, they might take occasion from it to accuse him.

IV. Christ determined the question, and evaded the snare, by referring them to their national concessions already made, by which they were precluded from disputing this matter, *vv.* 15-17. He knew they intended to ensnare him, and therefore contrived the matter so as to ensnare them, and to oblige them by their own words to do what they were unwilling to do, which was, to pay their taxes honestly and quietly, and yet at the same time to screen himself against their exceptions. He made them acknowledge that the current money of their nation was Roman money, had the emperor's image on one side, and his *superscription* on the reverse; and if so, 1. *Cæsar* might command their money for the public benefit, because he has the custody and conduct of the state, wherein he ought to have his charges borne; *Render to Cæsar the things that are Cæsar's.* 2. Cæsar might not command their consciences, nor did he pretend to it; he offered not to make any alteration in their religion. "Pay your tribute, therefore, without murmuring or disputing, but be sure to *render to God the things that are*

God's." Perhaps he referred to the parable he had just now put forth, in which he had condemned them for not *rendering* the fruits to the Lord of the vineyard, *v.* 2. All that heard Christ, *marvelled* at the discretion of his answer, and how ingeniously he avoided the snare; but I doubt none were brought by it, as they ought to be, to render to God themselves and their devotions.

GOD OF THE LIVING
(*vv.* 18–27)

The Sadducees, who were the deists of that age, here attack our Lord Jesus, it should seem, not as the scribes, and Pharisees, and chief-priests, with any malicious design upon his person; they were not bigots and persecutors, but sceptics and infidels, and their design was upon his doctrine, to hinder the spreading of that: they denied that there was any resurrection, any world of spirits, any state of rewards and punishments on the other side of death: now those great and fundamental truths which they denied, Christ had made it his business to establish and prove, and had carried the notion of them much further than ever it was before carried; and therefore they set themselves to perplex his doctrine. The incident we have had at Matt. xxii. 22–33.

THE HOPEFUL SCRIBE
(*vv.* 28–34)

The scribes and Pharisees were (however bad otherwise) enemies to the Sadducees; now one would have expected that, when they heard Christ argue so well against the Sadducees, they would have countenanced him, as they did Paul when he appeared against the Sadducees (Acts xxiii. 9); but it had not that effect: because he did not fall in with them in the ceremonials of religion, his agreeing with them in the essentials, gained him no manner of respect with them. Only we have here an account of *one* of them, a scribe, who had so much civility in him as to take notice of Christ's answer to the Sadducees, and to own that he had *answered well*, and much to the purpose (*v.* 28); and we have reason to hope that he did not join with the other scribes in persecuting Christ; for here we have his application to Christ for instruction, and it was such as became him; not tempting Christ, but desiring to improve his acquaintance with him.

I. He enquired, *Which is the first commandment of all?* *v.* 28. He doth not mean the first in *order*, but the first in *weight* and *dignity*.

II. Christ gave him a direct answer to this enquiry, *vv.* 29–31. Those that sincerely desire to be instructed concerning their duty, Christ will *guide in judgment*, and *teach his way*. He tells him,

1. That the great commandment of all, which is indeed inclusive of all, is, that of *loving God with all our hearts*. Now here in, Mark, our Saviour prefixes to this command the great doctrinal truth upon which it is built (*v.* 29); *Hear, O Israel, The Lord our God is one Lord*; if we firmly believe this, it will follow, that we shall love him *with all our heart*. He is Jehovah, who has all amiable perfections in himself; he is *our God*, to whom we

stand related and obliged; and therefore we ought to *love him*, to set our affections on him, let out our desire toward him, and take a delight in him; and he is *one Lord*, therefore he must be loved with our *whole heart*; he has the sole *right to us*, and therefore ought to have the sole *possession of us*. If he be one, our hearts must be one with him, and since there is no God besides, no rival must be admitted with him upon the throne.

2. That the second great commandment is, to *love our neighbour as ourselves* (v. 31), as truly and sincerely as we love ourselves, and in the same instances, and we must show it by *doing as we would be done by*. As we must therefore love God better than ourselves, because he is Jehovah, a being infinitely better than we are, and must love him with *all our heart*, because he is *one Lord*, and there is no other like him; so we must *love our neighbour as ourselves*, because he is of the same nature with ourselves; our hearts are fashioned alike, and my neighbour and myself are of one body, of one society, that of the world of mankind; and if a fellow-Christian, and of the same sacred society, the obligation is the stronger.

III. The scribe consented to what Christ said, and descanted upon it, *vv.* 32, 33. 1. He commends Christ's decision of this question; *Well, Master, thou hast said the truth*. Christ's assertions needed not the scribe's attestations; but this scribe, being a man in authority, thought it would put some reputation upon what Christ said, to have it commended by him; and it shall be brought in evidence against those who persecuted Christ, as a deceiver, that one of themselves, even a scribe of their own, confessed that he *said the truth*, and said it *well*. And thus must we subscribe to Christ's sayings, must set to our seal that they are true. 2. He comments upon it. Christ had quoted that great doctrine, that *the Lord our God is one Lord*; and this he not only assented to, but added, "*There is none other but he*; and therefore we must have no other God besides." This excludes all rivals with him, and secures the throne in the heart entire for him. Christ had laid down that great law, of loving God *with all our heart*; and this also he explains— that it is loving him *with the understanding*, as those that know what abundant reason we have to love him. Christ had said, "To love God and our neighbour is the greatest commandment of all"; "Yea," saith the scribe, "it is better, it is *more than all whole-burnt-offerings and sacrifices*, more acceptable to God, and will turn to a better account to ourselves." There were those who held, that the law of *sacrifices* was the *greatest commandment* of all; but this scribe readily agreed with our Saviour in this—that the law of love to God and our neighbour is greater than that of *sacrifice*, even than that of *whole-burnt-offerings*, which were intended purely for the honour of God.

IV. Christ approved of what he said, and encouraged him to proceed in his enquiries of him, *v.* 34. 1. He owned that he understood well, as far as he went; so far, so good. 2. He owned that he stood fair for a further advance; "*Thou art not far from the kingdom of God*, the kingdom of grace and glory, thou art in a likely way to be a Christian, a disciple of Christ. For the doctrine of Christ insists most upon these things, and is designed, and has a tendency direct, to bring thee to this." Note, There is hope of those who make a good use of the light they have, and go as far as that will carry them, that by the grace of God they will be led further, by the clearer discoveries God has to make to them.

LORD OF DAVID (vv. 35–40)

Here Christ shows the people how weak and defective the scribes were in their preaching, and how unable to solve the difficulties that occurred in the scriptures of the Old Testament, which they undertook to expound. Of this he gives an instance, which is not so fully related here as it was in Matthew.

THE POOR WIDOW (vv. 41–44)

This passage of story was not in Matthew, but is here and in Luke; it is Christ's commendation of the poor widow, that cast *two mites* into the treasury, which our Saviour busy as he was in preaching, found leisure to take notice of. Observe,

I. There was a *public fund* for charity, into which contributions were brought, and out of which distributions were made; a poor-box, and this in *the temple*; for works of charity and works of piety very fitly go together; where God is honoured by our worship, it is proper he should be honoured by the relief of his poor; and we

often find *prayers* and *alms* in conjunction, as Acts x. 2, 4.

II. Jesus Christ had *an eye* upon it; *He sat over against the treasury, and beheld how the people cast money into it*; not grudging either that he had none to cast in, or had not the disposal of that which was cast in, but observing what was cast in. Note, Our Lord Jesus takes notice of what we contribute to pious and charitable uses; whether we give liberally or sparingly; whether cheerfully or with reluctance and ill-will: nay, he looks at the heart; he observes what principles we act upon, and what our views are, in giving alms; and whether we do it as unto the Lord, or only to be seen of men.

III. He saw *many that were rich cast in much*: and it was a good sight to see rich people charitable, to see *many* rich people so, and to see them not only cast in, but cast in *much*.

IV. There was a *poor widow that cast in two mites, which make a farthing* (v. 42); and our Lord Jesus highly commended her; *called his disciples* to him, and bid them take notice of it (v. 43); told them that she could very ill spare that which she gave, she had scarcely enough for herself, it was *all her living*, all she had to live upon for that day, and perhaps a great part of what she had earned by her labour the day before; and that forasmuch as he knew she did it from a truly charitable disposition, he reckoned it more than all that put together, which the rich people threw in; for they did *cast in of their abundance, but she of her want*, v. 44. Now many would have been ready to censure this *poor widow*, and to think she did ill; why should she give to others, when she had little enough for herself? Charity begins at home; or, if she would give it, why did she not bestow it upon some poor body that she knew? And yet our Saviour commends her, and therefore we are sure that she did very well and wisely. If Christ saith, *Well-done*, no matter who saith otherwise; and we must hence learn, 1. That *giving alms*, is an excellent good thing, and highly pleasing to the Lord Jesus; and if we be humble and sincere in it, he will graciously accept of it, though in some circumstances there may not be all the discretion in the world. 2. Those that have but a *little*, ought to give alms out of *their little*. Those that live by their labour, from hand to mouth, must *give to those that need*, Eph. iv. 28. When we can cheerfully provide for others, out of our own necessary provision, as the widow of Sarepta for Elijah, and Christ for his five thousand guests, and trust God to provide for us some other way, *this is thank-worthy*.

CHAPTER THIRTEEN

GREAT BUILDINGS
(*vv.* 1–4)

We may here see,

I. How apt many of Christ's own disciples are to idolize things that look *great*, and have been long looked upon as *sacred*. They had heard Christ complain of those who had made the temple a *den of thieves*; and yet, when he quitted it, for the wickedness that remained in it, they court him to be as much in love as they were with the stately structure and adorning of it. One of them said to him, "Look, Master, *what manner of stones, and what buildings are here*," v. 1.

II. How little Christ values external pomp, where there is not real purity; "*Seest thou these great buildings*" (saith Christ), "and admirest thou them? I tell thee, the time is at hand when *there shall not be left one stone upon another, that shall not be thrown down*," v. 2. And the sumptuousness of the fabric shall be no security to it, no nor move any compassion in the Lord Jesus towards it.

III. As he was returning to Bethany, he *sat upon the mount of Olives*, *over against the temple*, where he had a full view of it; and there four of the disciples agreed to *ask him privately*, what he meant by the destroying of the temple, which they understood no more than they did the predictions of his own death, so inconsistent was it with their scheme. Probably, though these four proposed the question, yet Christ's discourse, in answer to it, was in the hearing of the rest of the disciples, yet *privately*, that is, apart from the multitude. Their enquiry is, "*When shall these things be?* What presages shall there be of them, and how may we prognosticate their approach?"

THE FUTURE (*vv.* 5–13)

Our Lord Jesus, in reply to their question, sets himself, not so much to satisfy their curiosity as to direct their consciences; leaves them still in the dark concerning the *times* and *seasons*, which the father has *kept in his own power*, and which *it was not for them to know*; but gives them the cautions which were needful, with reference to the events that should now shortly come to pass.

I. They must take heed that they be not *deceived* by the *seducers* and *impostors* that should now shortly arise (*vv.* 5, 6). After the Jews had rejected the true Christ, they were imposed upon, and so *exposed* by many false Christs, but never before; those false Christs *deceived many*; Therefore *take heed lest they deceive you.*

II. They must take heed that they be not *disturbed* at the noise of wars, which they should be alarmed with, *vv.* 7, 8. Sin introduced *wars*, and they come *from men's lusts.* But at some times the nations are more distracted and wasted with wars than at other times; so it shall be now; Christ was born into the world when there was a general peace, but soon after he went out of the world there were general wars; *Nation shall rise against nation, and kingdom against kingdom.* 1. "Let it be no *surprise* to you; you are bid to expect it, and *such things must needs be.*" 2. "Let it be no *terror* to you, as if your interest were in danger of being overthrown, or your work obstructed by these wars; you have no concern in them, and therefore need not be apprehensive of any damage by them." 3. "Let it not be looked upon as an omen of the approaching period of the world, for the *end is not yet*", *v.* 7. 4. "Let it not be looked upon as if in them God had done his worst; be not troubled at the wars you shall hear

of, for they are but *the beginnings of sorrows*, and therefore, instead of being disturbed at *them*, you ought to *prepare for worse*; for there shall also be *earthquakes in divers places*, which shall bury multitudes in the ruins of their own houses, and there *shall be famines*, by which many of the poor shall perish for want of bread, and *troubles* and commotions; so that there shall be no peace to him that *goes out* or *comes in.* The world shall be full of *troubles*, but *not be ye troubled*; without are *fightings*, within are *fears*, but *fear not ye their fear.*"

III. They must take heed that they be not *drawn away* from Christ, and from their duty to him, by the sufferings they should meet with for Christ's sake. Observe,

1. What the trouble is which they must expect.

(1) They shall be *hated of all men*; trouble enough! The world hated them because he loved them.

(2) Their own *relations* shall *betray them*, those to whom they were most nearly allied, and on whom therefore they depended for protection; "They *shall betray you*, shall inform against you, and be your prosecutors."

(3) Their *church-rulers* shall inflict *their censures* upon them; "You shall be *delivered up* to the great Sanhedrim at Jerusalem, and to the inferior courts and consistories in other cities, and shall be *beaten in the synagogues* with forty stripes at a time, as offenders against the law which was read in the synagogue."

(4) *Governors* and *kings* shall use their power against them. They

must resist unto blood, and still resist.

2. What they shall have to comfort themselves with, in the midst of these great and sore troubles.

(1) That the work they were called to should be carried on and prosper, notwithstanding all this opposition which they should meet with in it (*v.* 10).

(2) That their sufferings, instead of obstructing their work, should forward it; "Your being *brought before governors and kings* shall be for a *testimony of them* (so some read it, *v.* 9); it shall give you an opportunity of preaching the gospel to those before whom you are brought as criminals, to whom otherwise you could not have access." Or, as we read it, It shall be for a testimony *against them*, against both the judges and the prosecutors, who pursue those with the utmost rage that appear, upon examination, to be not only innocent but excellent persons.

(3) That, when they were brought before kings and governors for Christ's sake, they should have special assistance from heaven, to plead Christ's cause and their own (*v.* 11); "*Take no thought beforehand what ye shall speak*, but *whatsoever shall be given you in that hour*, whatsoever shall be suggested to you, and put into your minds, and into your mouths that *speak ye*, and fear not the success of it, because it is *off-hand*, for *it is not ye that speak*, purely by the strength of your own wisdom, consideration, and resolution, but it is *the Holy Ghost*."

(4) That heaven at last would *make amends for all*. Perseverance

gains the crown. The salvation here promised is more than a deliverance from evil, it is an everlasting blessedness, which shall be an abundant recompence for all their services and sufferings. All this we have, Matt. x. 17, &c.

THE ABOMINATION
(*vv.* 14–23)

Here we have a prediction of that ruin which came upon them within less than forty years after this: we had it before, Matt. xxiv. 15, &c.

THE SECOND COMING
(*vv.* 24–27)

These verses seem to point at Christ's second coming, to judge the world; the disciples, in their question, had confounded the *destruction* of Jerusalem and the *end of the world* (Matt. xxiv. 3), which was built upon a mistake, as if the temple must needs stand as long as the world stands; this mistake Christ rectifies, and shows that the *end of the world in those days*, those other days you enquire about, the day of Christ's coming, and the day of judgment, shall be *after that tribulation*, and not coincident with it. Let those who live to see the Jewish nation destroyed, take heed of thinking that, because the Son of man doth not visibly come in the clouds *then*, he will never *so* come; no, he will come *after that*. And here he foretells,

1. The final dissolution of the present frame and fabric of the world; even of that part of it which seems least liable to change, the upper part, the purer and more refined part; *The sun shall be dark-*

ened, and the *moon* shall no more *give her light*; for they shall be quite outshone by the glory of the Son of man, Isa. xxiv. 23. The *stars of heaven*, that from the beginning had kept their place and regular motion, shall fall as leaves in autumn; and the *powers that are in heaven*, the heavenly bodies, the fixed stars, *shall be shaken*.

2. The visible appearance of the Lord Jesus, to whom the judgment of that day shall be committed (*v.* 26); *Then shall they see the Son of man coming in the clouds.* Probably he will come over that very place where he sat when he said this; for the clouds are in the lower region of the air. He shall come with *great power and glory*, such as will be suited to the errand on which he comes. *Every eye shall then see him.*

3. The gathering together of all the elect to him (*v.* 27); He shall *send his angels*, and *gather together his elect* to him, to *meet him in the air*, 1 Thess. iv. 17.

THE FIG TREE (*vv.* 28–37)

We have here the application of this prophetical sermon; *now learn* to look forward in a right manner.

I. "As to the *destruction* of Jerusalem, *expect* it to come very *shortly*; as when the *branch of the fig-tree becomes soft*, and the *leaves sprout forth*, ye expect that summer will come shortly," *v.* 28. "*This generation* that is now rising up, shall not all be worn off before *all these things* come to pass, which I have told you of, relating to Jerusalem, and they shall begin to take effect now shortly.

II. "As to the *end of the world*,

do not enquire when it will come, for it is not a question fit to be asked, for of *that day*, and *that hour, knoweth no man*; it is a thing at a great distance; the exact time is fixed in the counsel of God, but is not revealed by any word of God, either to *men* on earth, or to *angels in heaven*." But it follows, *neither the Son*; but is there any thing which the Son is ignorant of? There were those in the primitive times, who taught from this text, that there were some things that Christ, as man, was *ignorant* of; and from thence were called *Agnoetæ*; they said, "It was no more absurd to say so, than to say that his human soul suffered grief and fear"; and many of the orthodox fathers approved of this. "It is certain (says Archbishop Tillotson) that Christ, as God, could not be ignorant of any thing; but the divine wisdom which dwelt in our Saviour, did communicate itself to his human soul, according to the divine pleasure, so that his human nature might sometimes not know some things; therefore Christ is said to grow in wisdom (Luke ii. 52), which he could not be said to do, if the human nature of Christ did necessarily know all things by virtue of its union with the divinity." Dr. Lightfoot explains it thus; Christ calls himself the Son, as Messiah. Now the Messiah, as such, was the Father's servant (Isa. xlii. 1), sent and deputed by him, and as such a one he refers himself often to his Father's will and command, and owns he *did nothing of himself* (John v. 19); in like manner he might be said to *know nothing of himself*. The revelation of Jesus Christ was what *God gave unto him*, Rev. i. 1. He thinks, therefore, that we are to distinguish between those excellencies and perfections of his, which resulted from the personal union between the divine and human nature, and those which flowed from the anointing of the Spirit; from the former flowed the infinite dignity of his person, and his perfect freedom from all sin; but from the latter flowed his power of working miracles, and his foreknowledge of things to come. What therefore (saith he) was to be revealed by him to his church, he was pleased to take, not from the union of the human nature with the divine, but from the revelation of the Spirit, by which he yet knew not this, but *the Father* only knows it; that is, God only, the Deity; for (as Archbishop Tillotson explains it) it is not used here *personally*, in distinction from the Son and the Holy Ghost, but as the Father is, *The Fountain of Deity*.

III. "As to both, your duty is to *watch and pray*. Therefore the time is kept a secret, that you may be engaged to stand always upon your guard (*v.* 33)." This he illustrates, in the close, by a parable.

1. Our Master is gone away, and left us something in trust, in charge, which we must give account of, *v.* 34. He is *as a man taking a far journey*; for he is gone to be away a great while, he has *left his house* on earth, and left his servant, in their offices, given *authority* to some, who are to be overseers, and *work* to others, who are to be labourers. They that have *authority* given them, in that had *work* assigned

them, for those that have the greatest *power* have the most *business*; and to them to whom he gave *work*, he gave some sort of *authority*, to do that work. And when he took his last leave, he *appointed the porter to watch*, to be sure to be ready to open to him at his return; and in the mean time to take care to whom he opened his gates, not to thieves and robbers, but only to his Master's friends and servants. Thus our Lord Jesus, when he *ascended on high*, left something for all his servants to do, expecting they should all do him service in his absence, and be ready to receive him at his return. *All* are appointed to work, and some authorized to rule.

2. We ought to be always upon our watch, in expectation of his return, *v.* 35–37. (1) Our Lord *will come*, and will come as the *Master of the house*, to take account of his servants, of their work, and of the improvement they have made. (2) We know not *when he will come*; and he has very wisely kept us at uncertainty, that we might be always ready. We know not *when he will come*, just at what precise time; the *Master of the house* perhaps will come *at even*, at nine at night; or it may be *at midnight*, or at *cock-crowing*, at three in the morning, or perhaps not till six. This is applicable to his coming to us in particular, at our death, as well as to the general judgment. (3) Our great care must be, that, whenever our Lord comes, he do not *find us sleeping*, secure in ourselves, off our guard, indulging ourselves in ease and sloth, mindless of our work and duty, and

thoughtless of our Lord's coming; *ready* to say, He will not come, and *unready* to meet him. (4) His coming will indeed be *coming suddenly*; it will be a great *surprise* and *terror* to those that are careless, and asleep, it will come upon them as a thief in the night. (5) It is therefore the indispensable duty of all Christ's disciples, to *watch*, to be awake, and keep awake; "*What I say unto you* four (v. 37), I *say unto all* the twelve, or rather to *you* twelve, I say unto all my disciples and followers; what I say to you of this generation, I say to all that shall believe in me, through your word, in every age, *Watch*, *watch*, expect my second coming, prepare for it, that you may be found in peace, without spot, and blameless."

CHAPTER FOURTEEN

CHRIST ANOINTED
(*vv.* 1–11)

We have here instances,

I. Of the *kindness of Christ's friends*, and the provision made of respect and honour for him.

1. Here was *one friend*, that was so kind as to *invite him to sup with him*; and he was so kind as to accept the invitation, *v.* 3.

2. Here was *another friend*, that was so kind as to *anoint his head* with very precious ointment as he *sat at meat*. This was an extraordinary piece of respect paid him by a good woman that thought nothing too good to bestow upon Christ, and to do him honour. It is observable that she took care to pour it all out upon Christ's head. Christ must be honoured with *all*

we have, and we must not think to keep back any part of the price. Do we give him the *precious ointment* of our best affections? Let him have them *all*; love him *with all the heart*.

Now, (1) There were those who put a *worse construction* upon this than it *deserved*. They called it a *waste of the ointment*, v. 4. Because they could not have found in their hearts to put themselves to such an expense for the honouring of Christ, they thought that she was *prodigal*, who did.

(2) Our Lord Jesus put a *better construction* upon it than, for aught that appears, was *designed*. Probably, she intended no more, than to show the great honour she had for him, before all the company, and to complete his entertainment. But Christ makes it to be an act of *great faith*, as well as *great love* (v. 8); "*She is come aforehand*, *to anoint my body to the burying*, as if she foresaw that my resurrection would prevent her doing it afterward." This funeral rite was a kind of presage of, or prelude to, his death approaching. See how Christ's heart was filled with the thoughts of his death, how every thing was construed with a reference to that, and how familiarly he spoke of it upon all occasions.

(3) He recommended this piece of heroic piety to the applause of the church in all ages; *Wherever this gospel shall be preached, it shall be spoken of, for a memorial of her*, v. 9.

II. Of the *malice of Christ's enemies*, and the preparation made by them to do him mischief.

1. The chief priests, his *open*

enemies, consulted how they might *put him to death*, *vv*. 1, 2. The feast of the *passover* was now at hand, and at *that* feast he must be crucified.

2. Judas, his *disguised enemy*, contracted with them for the betraying of him, *vv*. 10, 11. He is said to be *one of the twelve* that were Christ's family, intimate with him, trained up for the service of his kingdom; and he *went to the chief priests*, to tender his service in this affair.

(1) That which he proposed to them, was, to *betray Christ* to them, and to give them notice when and where they might find him, and seize him, without making an *uproar among the people*, which they were afraid of, if they should seize him when he appeared *in public*, in the midst of his admirers.

(2) That which he proposed to himself, was, to *get money* by the bargain; he had what he aimed at, when *they promised- to give him money*. Covetousness was Judas's master-lust, *his own iniquity*, and that betrayed him to the sin of betraying his Master; the devil suited his temptation to *that*, and so conquered him.

(3) Having secured the money, he set himself to make good his bargain; he sought *how he might conveniently betray him*.

THE UPPER ROOM
(*vv.* 12–31)

In these verses we have,

I. Christ's eating the passover with his disciples, the night before he died, with the joys and comforts of which ordinance he prepared himself for his approaching sor-

rows, the full prospect of which did not indispose him for that solemnity.

1. Christ ate the passover at the *usual time* when the other Jews did, as Dr. Whitby has fully made out, and not, as Dr. Hammond would have it, the night before.

2. He directed his disciples how to find the place where he intended to eat the passover; and hereby gave such another proof of his infallible knowledge of things distant and future (which to us seem altogether *contingent*), as he had given when he sent them for the ass on which he rode in triumph (*ch*. xi. 6).

3. He ate the passover in an *upper room furnished, laid with carpets* (so Dr. Hammond); it would seem to have been a very handsome *dining-room*. Christ was far from affecting any thing that looked stately in eating his common meals; on the contrary, he chose that which was homely, sat down on the grass: but, when he was to keep a sacred feast, in honour of that he would be at the expense of as good a room as he could get. God looks not at *outward pomp*, but he looks at the tokens and expressions of *inward reverence* for a divine institution, which, it is to be feared, those lack, who, to save charges, deny themselves decencies in the worship of God.

4. He ate it *with the twelve*, who were his family, to teach those who have the charge of families, not only families of *children*, but families of *servants*, or families of *scholars*, or *pupils*, to keep up religion among them, and worship God with them.

II. Christ's discourse with his disciples, as they were *eating* the passover.

1. They were *pleasing* themselves with the society of *their Master*; but he tells them that they must now presently lose him; *The Son of man is betrayed*; and they knew, for he had often told them, what followed—If he be *betrayed*, the next news you will hear of him, is, that he is *crucified* and *slain*; God hath determined it concerning him, and he agrees to it; *The Son of man goes, as it is written of him. v.* 21.

2. They were *pleasing* themselves with the society *one of another*, but Christ casts a damp upon the joy of that, by telling them, *One of you that eateth with me shall betray me, v.* 18. Christ said this, if it might be, to startle the conscience of Judas, and to awaken him to repent of his wickedness, and to draw back (for it was not too late) from the brink of the pit. But for aught that appears, he who was *most concerned in* the warning, was *least concerned at* it. All the rest were affected with it.

III. The institution of the Lord's supper.

1. It was instituted in the close of a *supper*, when they were sufficiently fed with the *paschal lamb*, to show that in the Lord's supper there is no *bodily repast* intended; to preface it with such a thing, is to revive Moses again. But it is food for *the soul* only, and therefore a very little of that which is for the body, as much as will serve for a *sign*, is enough. It was at the close of the *passover-supper*, which by this was evangelized, and then

superseded and set aside. Much of the doctrine and duty of the eucharist is illustrated to us by the law of the passover (Exod. xii.); for the Old-Testament institutions, though they do not *bind us*, yet *instruct* us, by the help of a gospel-key to them. And these two ordinances lying here so near together, it may be good to compare them, and observe how much shorter and plainer the institution of the Lord's supper is, than that of the passover was.

2. It was instituted by the *example* of Christ himself; not with the ceremony and solemnity of a law, as the ordinance of baptism was, after Christ's resurrection (Matt. xxviii. 19), but by the practice of our Master himself, because intended for those who are already his disciples, and taken into covenant with him: but it has the obligation of a law, and was intended to remain in full force, power, and virtue, till his second coming.

3. It was instituted with *blessing* and *giving of thanks*; the gifts of common providence are to be so received (1 Tim. iv. 4, 5), much more the gifts of special grace. He *blessed* (*v.* 22), and *gave thanks*, *v.* 23. At his other meals, he was wont to *bless*, and *give thanks* (*ch.* vi. 41; viii. 7) so remarkably, that he was known by it, Luke xxiv. 30, 31. And he did the same at this meal.

4. It was instituted to be a *memorial* of his *death*; and therefore he *broke* the bread, to show how it pleased the Lord to *bruise him*; and he called the *wine*, which is the blood of the grape, the *blood*

of the New Testament. The death Christ died was a *bloody death*, and frequent mention is made of the *blood*, the *precious* blood, as the price of our redemption; for the blood is *the life*, and made *atonement for the soul*, Lev. xvii. 11–14. The pouring out of the blood was the most sensible indication of the *pouring out of his soul*, Isa. liii. 12. It is called the *blood of the New Testament*; for the covenant of grace became a *testament*, and of force by the death of Christ, the testator, Heb. ix. 16. It is said to be *shed for many*, to justify *many* (Isa. liii. 11), to bring *many* sons to glory, Heb. ii. 10. It was sufficient for *many*, being of infinite value; it has been of use to *many*; we read of a great multitude which no man could number, that had all *washed their robes, and made them white in the blood of the Lamb* (Rev. vii. 9–14); and still it is a *fountain opened*. How comfortable is this to poor repenting sinners, that the blood of Christ is *shed for many*! And if for *many*, why not for *me*? If for sinners, sinners of the Gentiles, the chief of sinners, then *why not for me*?

5. It was instituted to be a *ratification* of the covenant made with us in him, and a sign of the conveyance of those benefits to us, which were purchased for us by his death; and therefore he broke the bread *to them* (*v.* 22), and said, *Take*, *eat* of it: he gave the cup *to them*, and ordered them to *drink of it*, *v.* 23. Apply the doctrine of Christ crucified to yourselves, and let it be *meat* and *drink* to your souls, strengthening, nourishing, and refreshing, to you, and the

support and comfort of your spiritual life.

6. It was instituted with an eye to the happiness of heaven, and to be an earnest and fore-taste of that, and thereby to put our mouths out of taste for all the pleasures and delights of sense (*v.* 25); *I will drink no more of the fruit of the vine*, as it is a bodily refreshment. I have done with it.

7. It was closed with a *hymn*, *v.* 26. Though Christ was in the midst of his enemies, yet he did not, for fear of them, omit this sweet duty of singing psalms.

IV. Christ's discourse with his disciples, as they were returning to Bethany by moonlight.

1. Christ here foretells that in his sufferings he should be *deserted* by all his disciples; "*You will all be offended because of me, this night.* I know you will (*v.* 27), and what I tell you now, is no other than what the scripture has told you before; *I will smite the shepherd*, and then *the sheep will be scattered.*"

But Christ encourages them with a promise that they shall rally again, shall return both to their duty and to their comfort (*v.* 28); "*After I am risen*, I will *gather you in* from all the places *whither you are scattered*, Ezek. xxxiv. 12. I will *go before you into Galilee*, will see our friends, and enjoy one another there."

2. He foretells that he should be *denied* particularly by Peter.

(1) Peter is confident that he should not *do so ill* as the rest of the disciples (*v.* 29); *Though all should be offended*, all his brethren here present, *yet will not I*. He supposes himself not only stronger

than others, but so much stronger, as to be able to receive the shock of a temptation, and bear up against it, *all alone*; to *stand*, though nobody stood *by him*. It is bred in the bone with us, to *think well* of ourselves, and *trust to our own hearts*.

(2) Christ tells him that he will *do worse* than any of them. They will all *desert* him, but he will *deny* him; not once, but *thrice*; and that presently; *"This day, even this night before the cock crow twice, thou wilt deny* that ever thou hadst any knowledge of me, or acquaintance with me, as one ashamed and afraid to own me."

(3) He stands to his promise; *"If I should die with thee, I will not deny thee*; I will adhere to thee, though it cost me my life:" and, no doubt, he thought as he said. But he that thinks he stands, must learn to take heed lest he fall; and he that *girdeth on the harness*, not boast *as though he had put it off*.

WATCH AND PRAY (*vv.* 32–42)

Christ is here entering upon his sufferings, and begins with those which were the sorest of all his sufferings, those in his *soul*. Here we have him in his *agony*; this melancholy story we had in Matthew *ch. xxvi*; this *agony* in soul was the *wormwood and the gall* in the *affliction and misery*; and thereby it appeared that no sorrow was *forced upon him*, but that it was what he *freely* admitted.

THE BETRAYAL (*vv.* 43–52)

We have here the *seizing* of our Lord Jesus by the officers of the chief priests. This was what his enemies had long aimed at, they had often sent to *take him*; but he had escaped out of their hands, because *his hour was not come*, nor could they now have taken him, had he not freely surrendered himself. He began first to suffer *in his soul*, but afterward suffered in his body, that he might satisfy for sin, which begins in the heart, but afterward makes the members of the body *instruments of unrighteousness*.

I. Here is a band of rude miscreants employed to *take* our Lord Jesus and make him a prisoner; *a great multitude with swords and staves*.

II. Men of no less figure than the *chief priests, and the scribes*, and *the elders*, sent them, and set them on work, who pretended to expect the Messiah, and to be ready to welcome him; and yet, when he *is come*, and has given undeniable proofs that it is he that *should come*, because he doth not make court to them, nor countenance and support their pomp and grandeur, because he appears not as a temporal prince, but sets up a spiritual kingdom, and preaches repentance, reformation, and a holy life, and directs men's thoughts, and affections, and aims, to another world, they set themselves against him, and, without giving the credentials he produces an impartial examination, resolve to run him down.

III. Judas betrayed him *with a kiss*; abusing the freedom Christ used to allow his disciples of kissing his cheek at their return when they had been any time absent. He called him, *Master, Master, and*

kissed him; he said, *Rabbi, Rabbi,*
as if he had been now more respectful to him than ever.

IV. They arrested him, and made
him their prisoner (*v.* 46).

V. Peter laid about him in
defence of his Master, and wounded
one of the assailants, being for the
present mindful of his promise, to
venture his life with his Master.
He was *one of them that stood by*, of
them that *were with him* (so the
word signifies), of *those three*
disciples that were *with him* in the
garden; he *drew a sword*, and aimed,
it is likely, to cut off the head, but
missed his blow, and only *cut off
the ear*, of a servant of the high
priest, *v.* 47.

VI. Christ argues with them that
had seized him, and shows them
the absurdity of their proceedings
against him. 1. That they came out
against him, as against a *thief*,
whereas he was *innocent* of any
crime; he *taught daily in the
temple*, and if he had any wicked
design, there it would some time or
other have been discovered. 2.
That they came to take him thus
privately, whereas he was neither
ashamed nor *afraid* to appear
publicly in the temple. But this was
not all. 3. They came *with swords
and staves*, as if he had been in
arms against the government, and
must have the *posse comitatus*
raised to reduce him.

VII. He reconciled himself to all
this injurious, ignominious treatment, by referring himself to the
Old-Testament predictions of the
Messiah. I am hardly used, *but* I
submit, for *the scriptures must be
fulfilled, v.* 49.

VIII. All Christ's disciples, here-

upon, deserted him (*v.* 50); *They
all forsook him, and fled*. They were
very confident that they should
adhere to him; but even good men
know not what they will do, till
they are tried.

IX. The noise disturbed the
neighbourhood, and some of the
neighbours were brought into
danger by the riot, *vv.* 51, 52. This
passage of story we have not in any
other of the evangelists. Here is an
account of a *certain young man*,
who, as it should seem, was no
disciple of Christ, nor, as some
have imagined, a servant of the
house wherein Christ had eaten the
passover, who *followed him* to see
what would become of him, but
some young man that lived near
the garden, perhaps in the house
to which the garden belonged. Now
observe concerning him.

1. How he was *frightened out of
his bed*, to be a *spectator* of Christ's
sufferings.

2. See how he was *frightened
into his bed* again, when he was in
danger of being made a *sharer* in
Christ's sufferings. His own disciples had run away from him; but
this young man, having no concern
for him, thought he might securely
attend him, especially being so far
from being armed, that he was not
so much as clothed; but *the young
men*, the Roman soldiers, who were
called to assist, *laid hold of him*,
for all was fish that came to their
net. Perhaps they were now vexed
at themselves, that they had
suffered the disciples to *run away*,
and they being got out of their
reach they resolved to seize the
first they could *lay their hands on*.
Finding himself in danger, he *left*

the linen cloth by which they had caught hold of him, and fled away naked.

CHRIST BEFORE CAIAPHAS
(vv. 53–65)

We have here Christ's arraignment, trial, conviction, and condemnation, in the *ecclesiastical* court, before the great sanhedrim, of which the *high priest* was president, or judge of the court; the same Caiaphas that had lately adjudged it expedient he should be put to death, guilty or not guilty (John xi. 50), and who therefore might justly be excepted against as partial.

I. Christ is hurried away to his *house*, his *palace* it is called, such state did he live in. And there, though in the dead of the night, *all the chief priests, and elders, and scribes*, that were in the secret, were *assembled*, ready to receive the prey; so sure were they of it.

II. *Peter followed* at a distance, such a degree of cowardice was his late courage dwindled into, *v.* 54. But when he came to the high priest's palace, he *sneakingly* went, and *sat with the servants*, that he might not be suspected to belong to Christ. The high priest's fire side was no proper place, nor his servants proper company, for Peter, but it was his *entrance into a temptation*.

III. Great diligence was used to procure, for love or money, false witnesses against Christ.

IV. He was at length charged with words spoken some years ago, which, as they were represented, seemed to threaten *the temple*, which they had made no better than an idol of (*vv.* 57, 58); but the witnesses to this matter did not agree (*v.* 59).

V. He was urged to be his own accuser (*v.* 60); The *high priest stood up* in a heat, and said, *Answerest thou nothing?* This he said under pretence of justice and fair dealing, but really with a design to ensnare him, that they might *accuse him*, Luke xi. 53, 54; xx. 20. Still Christ *answered nothing*. But,

VI. When he was asked *whether he was the Christ*, he confessed, and denied not, that *he was*, *vv.* 61, 62. He asked, *Art thou the Son of the Blessed?* that is, the Son of *God*? for, as Dr. Hammond observes, the Jews, when they named *God*, generally added, *blessed for ever*; and thence *the Blessed* is the title of *God*, a peculiar title, and applied to Christ, Rom. ix. 5. And for the proof of his being the *Son of God*, he binds them over to his second coming; "*Ye shall see the Son of man sitting on the right hand of power*; that *Son of man* that now appears so mean and despicable, whom you *see* and trample upon (Isa. liii. 2, 3), you shall shortly see and *tremble before*."

VII. The high priest, upon this confession of his, convicted him as *a blasphemer* (*v.* 63); He *rent his clothes*.

VIII. They agreed that he was a blasphemer, and, as such, was guilty of a capital crime, *v.* 64. The question *seemed* to be put fairly, *What think ye?* But it was really *prejudged*, for the high priest had said, *Ye have heard the blasphemy*; he gave judgment first, who, as president of the court, ought to have voted last. So they *all condemned him* to be *guilty of death*; what friends he had in the great sanhedrim, did not appear, it is probable that they had not notice.

IX. They set themselves to abuse him, and, as the Philistines with Samson, to make sport with him, *v.* 65. If they did not think it below them to abuse Christ, shall we think any thing below us, by which we may do him honour?

PETER'S DENIAL (*vv.* 66–72)

We have here the story of Peter's denying Christ.

1. It began in *keeping at a distance* from him. Peter had followed *afar off* (*v.* 54), and now was *beneath in the palace*, at the lower end of the hall. Those that are *shy* of Christ, are in a fair way to *deny* him, that are shy of attending on holy ordinances, shy of the communion of the faithful, and loth to be seen on the side of despised godliness.

2. It was occasioned by his associating with the high priest's servants, and sitting among them.

3. The temptation was, his being charged as a disciple of Christ; *Thou also wert with Jesus of Nazareth*, *v.* 67. *This is one of them* (*v.* 69), *for thou art a Galilean*, one may know that by thy speaking broad, *v.* 70. Yet, all things considered, the temptation could not be called *formidable*; it was only a *maid* that casually cast her eye upon him, and, for aught that appears, without design of giving him any trouble, said, *Thou art one of them*, to which he needed not to have made any reply, or might have said, "And if I be, I hope that is no treason."

4. The sin was very great; he

denied Christ before men, at a time when he ought to have confessed and owned him, and to have appeared in court a witness for him.

5. His repentance was very speedy. He repeated his denial thrice, and the third was worst of all, for then he *cursed* and *swore*, to confirm his denial; and that third blow, which, one would think, should have *stunned him*, and knocked him down, *startled him*, and roused him up. Then the *cock crew* the second time, which put him in mind of his Master's words, the warning he had given him, with that particular circumstance of the *cock crowing twice*; by recollecting that, he was made sensible of his sin and the aggravations of it; and when he thought thereon, he wept. Some observe that this evangelist, who wrote, as some have thought, by St. Peter's direction, speaks as fully of Peter's sin as any of them, but more briefly of his *sorrow*, which Peter, in modesty, would not have to be magnified, and because he thought he could never sorrow enough for so great a sin.

CHAPTER FIFTEEN

BEFORE PILATE (*vv.* 1–13)

Here we have, I. A *consultation* held by the great Sanhedrim for the effectual prosecution of our Lord Jesus.

II. The delivering of him up a prisoner to Pilate; they *bound him*. He was to be the great sacrifice, and sacrifices must be bound with cords, Ps. cxviii. 27.

III. The examining of him by

Pilate upon interrogatories (*v.* 2); "*Art thou the king of the Jews?* Dost thou pretend to be so, to be that Messiah whom the Jews expect as a temporal prince?"— "Yea," saith Christ, "it is as *thou sayest*, I am that Messiah, but not such a one as they expect."

IV. The articles of impeachment exhibited against him, and his silence under the charge and accusation. The chief priests forgot the dignity of their place, when they turned informers, and did in person *accuse Christ of many things* (*v.* 3), and witness against him, *v.* 4. These priests were very eager and noisy in their accusation; but Christ *answered nothing*, *v.* 3. When Pilate urged him to clear himself, and was desirous he should (*v.* 4), yet still he stood mute (*v.* 5), he *answered nothing*, which Pilate thought very strange. He gave Pilate a direct answer (*v.* 2), but would not answer the prosecutors and witnesses, because the things they alleged, were notoriously false, and he knew Pilate himself was convinced they were so.

V. The proposal Pilate made to the people, to have Jesus released to them, since it was the custom of the feast to grace the solemnity with the release of one prisoner. There was indeed another prisoner, *one Barabbas*, that had an interest, and would have some votes; but he questioned not but Jesus would out-poll him.

VI. The unanimous outrageous clamours of the people to have *Christ put to death*, and particularly to have him *crucified*. It was a great surprise to Pilate, when he found the people so much under the influence of the priests, that they all agreed to desire that Barabbas might be *released*, *v.* 11. Pilate opposed it all he could; "*What will ye that I shall do to him whom ye call the King of the Jews?* Would not ye then have him released too?" *v.* 12. No, say they, *Crucify him*. The priests having put that in their mouths, they insist upon it; when Pilate objected, *Why, what evil has he done?* (a very material question in such a case), they did not pretend to answer it, but *cried out the more exceedingly*, as they were more and more instigated and irritated by the priests, *Crucify him, crucify him*.

THE SCOURGING (*vv.* 15–21)

Here, I. Pilate, to gratify the Jews' malice, delivers Christ to be *crucified*, *v.* 15. *Willing to content the people*, to *do enough* for them (so the word is), and make them easy, that he might keep them quiet, he *released Barabbas unto them*, who was the scandal and plague of their nation, and *delivered Jesus* to be *crucified*, who was the glory and blessing of their nation.

Christ was *crucified*, for that was, 1. A *bloody* death, and *without blood no remission*, Heb. ix. 22. Christ was to lay down *his life* for us, and therefore shed *his blood*. Blood *made atonement for the soul* (Lev. xvii. 11), and therefore in every sacrifice of propitiation special order was given for the *pouring out* of the blood, and the *sprinkling* of that before the Lord. Now, that Christ might answer all these types, he *shed his blood*. 2. It was a *painful* death; the pains were exquisite and acute, for death made its assaults upon the vitals by the exterior parts, which are *quickest of sense*. Christ died, so as that he might feel *himself die*, because he was to be both the priest and the sacrifice; so that he might be *active* in dying, because he was to *make his soul an offering* for sin. 3. It was a *shameful* death, the death of slaves, and the vilest malefactors; so it was accounted among the Romans. The *cross* and the *shame* are put together. God having been injured in his honour by the sin of man, it is *in his honour* that Christ makes him *satisfaction*, not only by denying himself in, and divesting himself of, the honours due to his divine nature, for a time, but by submitting to the greatest reproach and ignominy the human nature was capable of being loaded with. Yet this was not the worst. 4. It was a *cursed* death; thus it was branded by the Jewish law (Deut. xxi. 23); *He that is hanged, is accursed of God*, is under a particular mark of God's displeasure.

II. Pilate, to gratify the gay humour of the Roman soldiers, delivered him to them, to be abused and spitefully treated, while they were preparing for the execution.

III. The soldiers, at the hour appointed, led him away from Pilate's judgment-hall to the place of execution (*v.* 20), as a sheep to the slaughter; he was *led forth with the workers of iniquity*, though he did no sin. But lest his death, under the load of his cross, which he was to carry, should prevent the further cruelties they intended, they compelled one Simon of

Cyrene to carry his cross for him. He *passed by, coming out of the country* or out of the *fields*, not thinking of any such matter.

THE CRUCIFIXION
(*vv.* 22–32)

We have here the *crucifixion* of our Lord Jesus.

I. The *place where* he was crucified; it was called *Golgotha—the place of a skull*: some think, because of the heads of malefactors that were there cut off: it was the common place of execution, as Tyburn, for he was in all respects numbered with the transgressors.

II. The *time when* he was crucified; it was the *third hour, v.* 25. He was brought before Pilate about the sixth hour (John xix. 14), according to the Roman way of reckoning, which John uses, with which ours at this day agrees, that is at six o'clock in the morning; and then, at the *third hour*, according to the Jews' way of reckoning, that is, about nine of the clock in the morning, or soon after, they nailed him to the cross.

III. The indignities that were done him, when he was nailed to the cross; as if that had not been ignominious enough, they added several things to the ignominy of it.

1. It being the custom to give *wine* to persons that were to be *put to death*, they *mingled* his with *myrrh*, which was *bitter*, and made it *nauseous*; he *tasted* it, but would not drink it; was willing to admit the bitterness of it, but not the benefit of it.

2. The garments of those that were crucified, being, as with us, the executioners' fee, the soldiers

cast lots upon his garments (*v.* 24), threw dice for them: so making themselves merry with his misery, and sitting at their sport while he was hanging in pain.

3. They set a superscription over his head, by which they intended to reproach him, but really did him both justice and honour, *The king of the Jews, v.* 26. Here was no crime alleged, but his sovereignty owned.

4. They crucified *two thieves* with him, *one on his right hand, the other on his left,* and him in the midst as the worst of the three (*v.* 27); so great a degree of dishonour did they hereby intend him. In that famous prediction of Christ's sufferings (Isa. liii. 12), it was foretold that he should be numbered with the *transgressors,* because he was made *sin for us.*

5. The spectators, that is, the generality of them, instead of condoling with him in his misery, added to it by insulting over him. Surely never was such an instance of barbarous inhumanity toward the vilest malefactor: but thus the devil showed the utmost rage against him, and thus he submitted to the greatest dishonours that could be done him.

CHRIST'S DYING (*vv.* 33–41)

Here we have an account of Christ's dying, how his enemies abused him, and God honoured him at his death.

I. There was a thick *darkness* over *the whole land* (some think over the whole earth), for three hours, from noon till three of the clock.

II. Toward the close of this darkness, our Lord Jesus, in the agony of his soul, cried out, *My God, my God, why hast thou forsaken me? v.* 34. The darkness signified the present cloud which the human soul of Christ was under, when he was making it an *offering for sin.*

III. Christ's prayer was bantered by them that stood by (*vv.* 35, 36); because he cried, *Eli, Eli,* or (as Mark has it, according to the Syriac dialect) *Eloi, Eloi,* they said, *He calls for Elias,* though they knew very well what he said, and what it signified, *My God, My God.* Thus did they represent him as *praying to saints,* either because he had abandoned God, or God had abandoned him; and hereby they would make him more and more odious to the people. One of them *filled a sponge with vinegar,* and reached it up to him upon a reed; "Let him cool his mouth, with that it is drink good enough for him," *v.* 36. This was intended for a further affront and abuse to him; and whoever it was that checked him who did it, did but add to the reproach; "*Let him alone*; he has called for Elias: *let us see whether Elias will come to take him down*; and if not, we may conclude that he also hath abandoned him."

IV. Christ did again *cry with a loud voice,* and so *gave up the ghost, v.* 37. He was now commending his soul into his Father's hand; and though God is not moved with any *bodily exercise,* yet this loud voice signified the great strength and ardency of affection wherewith he did it.

V. Just at that instant that Christ, died upon *mount Calvary,* the veil of the *temple* was *rent in twain from the top to the bottom*, v. 38. This bespoke a great deal, 1. Of terror to the unbelieving Jews; for it was a presage of the utter destruction of their church and nation, which followed not long after. 2. It bespeaks a great deal of comfort to all believing Christians, for it signifies the consecrating and laying open to us of a *new and living way into the holiest* by the *blood of Jesus*.

VI. The centurion who commanded the detachment which had the oversight of the execution was convinced, and confessed that this Jesus was the *Son of God, v.* 39. But what reason had he to say so? I answer, 1. He had reason to say that he suffered *unjustly*, and had a great deal of wrong done him. 2. He had reason to say that he was a *favourite of heaven*, and one for whom the almighty power was particularly engaged, seeing how Heaven did him honour at his death, and frowned upon his persecutors. This he expresses by such words as denote his eternal generation as God, and his special designation to the office of Mediator, though he meant not so. Our Lord Jesus, even in the depth of his sufferings and humiliation, was the Son of God, and was declared to be so *with power*.

VII. There were some of his friends, the good women especially, that attended him (*v.* 40, 41). These women had followed Christ *from Galilee*, though they were not required to attend the feast, as the males were; but it is probable that they came, in expectation that his temporal kingdom would now shortly be set up, and big with

hopes of preferment for themselves, and their relations under him. It is plain that the mother of Zebedee's children was so (Matt. xx. 21); and now to see *him* upon a cross, whom they thought to have seen upon a throne, could not but be a great disappointment to them. Note, Those that follow Christ, in expectation of great things in this world by him, and by the profession of his religion, may probably live to see themselves sadly disappointed.

THE FUNERAL (*vv.* 42–47)

We are here attending the funeral of our Lord Jesus, a solemn, mournful funeral. O that we may by grace be planted in the likeness of it! Observe,

I. How the body of Christ was *begged*. It was, as the dead bodies of malefactors are, at the disposal of the government. Those that hurried him to the cross, designed that he should make *his grave with the wicked*; but God designed he should make it *with the rich* (Isa. liii. 9), and so he did.

II. How the body of Christ was *buried*. Pilate gave Joseph leave to take down the body, and do what he pleased with it. It was a wonder the chief priests were not too quick for him, and had not first begged the body of Pilate, to expose it and drag it about the streets, but that remainder of their wrath did God restrain, and gave that invaluable prize to Joseph, who knew how to value it; and the hearts of the priests were so influenced, that they did not oppose it.

1. Joseph bought *fine linen* to wrap the body in, though in such a

case old linen that had been worn might have been thought sufficient.

2. He *took down* the body, mangled and macerated as it was, and *wrapt it in the linen* as a treasure of great worth.

3. He *laid it in a sepulchre* of his own, in a private place. This sepulchre was *hewn out of a rock*, for Christ died to make the grave a *refuge* and shelter to the saints, and being hewn out of a rock, it is a *strong* refuge. *O that thou wouldest hide me in the grave!* Christ himself is a *hiding place* to his people, that is, *as the shadow of a great rock*.

4. He *rolled a stone to the door of the sepulchre*, for so the manner of the Jews was to bury.

5. Some of the good women attended the funeral, and *beheld where he was laid*, that they might come after the sabbath to anoint the dead body, because they had not time to do it now.

CHAPTER SIXTEEN
EASTER MORNING
(*vv.* 1–8)

Never was there such a *sabbath* since the sabbath was first instituted as this was, which the first words of this chapter tell us was *now past*; during all this sabbath our Lord Jesus lay in the grave. It was *to him* a sabbath of *rest*, but a *silent* sabbath; it was to his disciples a melancholy sabbath, spent in tears and fears. Never were the sabbath services in the temple such an *abomination to God*, though they had been often so, as they were now, when the chief priests, who presided in them, had their hands full of blood, the blood of Christ.

Well, this sabbath is over, and the first day of the week is the first day of a new world. We have here,

I. The affectionate visit which the good women that had attended Christ, now made to his sepulchre —not a *superstitious* one, but a *pious* one. They had *bought sweet spices* too, and came not only to *bedew* the dead body with their tears (for nothing could more renew their grief than this), but to *perfume* it with their *spices*, *v.* 1. Nicodemus had bought a very large quantity of *dry spices*, *myrrh* and *aloes*, which served to dry the wounds, and dry up the blood, John xix. 39. But these good women did not think that enough; they bought spices, perhaps of another kind, some perfumed oils, to *anoint him*.

II. The care they were in about the rolling away of the stone, and the superseding of that care (*vv.* 3, 4); *They said among themselves*, as they were coming along, and now drew near the sepulchre, *Who shall roll us away the stone from the door of the sepulchre? For it was very great*, more than they with their united strength could move. And there was another difficulty much greater than this, to be got over, which they knew nothing of, to wit, a guard of soldiers set to *keep* the sepulchre. But their gracious love to Christ carried them to the sepulchre; and see how by the time they came thither, both these difficulties were removed, both the *stone* which they *knew of*, and the *guard* which they *knew not of*. They *saw that the stone was rolled away*, which was the first thing that amazed them.

III. The assurance that was given them by an angel, that the Lord Jesus was risen from the dead, and had taken leave of his sepulchre, and had left him there to tell those so who came thither to enquire after him.

1. They *entered into the sepulchre*, at least, a little way in, and saw that the body of Jesus was not there where they had left it the other night.

2. They saw a *young man sitting on the right side* of the sepulchre. This angel was *sitting* on *the right hand* as they went into the sepulchre, *clothed with a long white garment*, a garment down to the feet, such as great men were arrayed with. The sight of him might justly have encouraged them, but they were *affrighted*.

3. He silences their fears by assuring them that here was cause enough for triumph, but none for trembling (*v.* 6); *He saith to them, Be not affrighted*. "We cannot as yet show you *him*, but hereafter you will see him, and you may here see *the place where they laid him*. You see he is gone hence, not stolen either by his enemies or by his friends, but *risen*."

4. He orders them to give speedy notice of this to his disciples.

(1) They must tell the *disciples*, that *he is risen*. "O, go quickly to them," saith the angel, "tell them that *their Master is risen*; this will put some life and spirit into them, and keep them from sinking into despair."

(2) They must be sure to tell Peter. This is particularly taken notice of by this evangelist, who is supposed to have written by Peter's direction. If it were told the disciples, it would be told Peter, for, as a token of his repentance for disowning his Master, he still associated with his disciples; yet it is particularly named: *Tell Peter*, for, [1] It will be good news to him, more welcome to him than to any of them; for he is in sorrow for sin, and no tidings can be more welcome to true penitents than to hear of the resurrection of Christ, because he rose again for *their justification*. [2] He will be afraid, lest the joy of this good news do not belong to him. To obviate that, "Go to Peter by name, and tell him, he shall be as welcome as any of the rest to *see* him in Galilee." Note, A sight of Christ will be very welcome to a true penitent, and a true penitent shall be very welcome to a sight of Christ, for there is joy in heaven concerning him.

(3) They must appoint them all, and Peter by name, to give him the meeting in Galilee, as *he said unto you*, Matt. xxvi. 32. Note, [1] All the meetings between Christ and his disciples are of his own appointing. [2] Christ never forgets his appointment, but will be sure to meet his people with the promised blessing in every place where he records his name. [3] In all meetings between Christ and his disciples, he is the most forward. *He goes before you*.

TWO APPEARANCES
(*vv.* 9–13)

We have here a very short account of two of Christ's appearances, and the little credit which the report of them gained with the disciples.

I. He appeared to Mary Magdalene, to her first in the garden, which we have a particular narrative of, John xx. 14.

2. They could not give credit to the report she brought them. They heard that *he was alive*, and had been seen of her. The story was plausible enough, and yet *they believed not*. They would not say that she made the story herself, or designed to deceive them; but they fear that she is *imposed upon*, and that it was but a fancy that she *saw him*. Had they believed the *frequent* predictions of it from his own mouth, they would not have been now so incredulous of the report of it.

II. He appeared to two of the disciples, *as they went into the country*, *v.* 12. This refers, no doubt, to that which is largely related (Luke xxiv. 13, &c.), of what passed between Christ and the two disciples *going to Emmaus*. He is here said to have appeared to them in *another form*, in another dress than what he usually wore, in the form of a *traveller*, as, in the garden, in such a dress, that Mary Magdalene took him for the gardener; but that he had really his own countenance, appears by this, that *their eyes were holden, that they should not know him*; and when that restraint on *their* eyes was taken off, immediately they *knew him*, Luke xxiv. 16–31. Now,

1. These *two* witnesses gave in their *testimony* to this proof of Christ's resurrection; *They went and told it to the residue*, *v.* 13. Being *satisfied* themselves, they were desirous to give their brethren the *satisfaction* they had, that they might be comforted as they were.

2. This did not gain credit with

all; *Neither believed they them.* They suspected that their eyes also deceived them.

CONVICTION AND COMMISSION (*vv.* 14–18)

Here is, I. The *conviction* which Christ gave his apostles of the truth of his resurrection (*v.* 14); He *appeared to them* himself, when they were all together, *as they sat at meat*, which gave him an opportunity to *eat and drink with them*, for their full satisfaction; see Acts x. 41. And still, when he appeared to them, he *upbraided them with their unbelief and hardness of heart*, for even at the general meeting in *Galilee, some doubted*, as we find Matt. xxviii. 17.

II. The *commission* which he gave them to set up his kingdom among men by the preaching of his *gospel*, the glad tidings of reconciliation to God through a Mediator. Now observe,

1. *To whom* they were to preach *the gospel*. Hitherto they had been sent only to *the lost sheep of the house of Israel*, and were forbidden to go into the *way of the Gentiles*, or into any city of the Samaritans; but now their commission is enlarged, and they are authorized to *go into all the world*, into all parts of the world, the habitable world, and to *preach the gospel* of Christ to *every creature*, to the Gentiles as well as to the Jews; to every human creature that is capable of receiving it.

2. What is the *summary of the gospel* they are to preach (*v.* 16). "Now go and tell them," (1) "That if they *believe the gospel*, and give up themselves to be Christ's

disciples; if they *renounce* the devil, the world, and the flesh, and be *devoted* to Christ as their prophet, priest, and king, and to God in Christ as their God in covenant, and evidence by their constant adherence to this covenant their sincerity herein, they *shall be saved* from the guilt and power of sin, it shall not *rule* them, it shall not *ruin* them. He that is a true Christian, shall be saved through Christ." *Baptism* was appointed to be the *inaugurating* rite, by which those that embraced Christ owned him; but it is here put rather for the *thing signified* than for the sign, for Simon Magus *believed* and was *baptized*, yet was not *saved*, Acts viii. 13. *Believing with the heart, and confessing with the mouth the Lord Jesus* (Rom. x. 9), seem to be much the same with this here. Or thus, We must *a*ssent to gospel-truths, and *con*sent to gospel-terms. (2) "*If they believe not*, if they receive not the record God gives concerning his Son, they cannot expect any other way of salvation, but must inevitably perish; *they shall be damned*, by the sentence of a *despised* gospel, added to that of a broken law."

3. What power they should be endowed with, for the confirmation of the doctrine they were to preach (*v*. 17); *These signs shall follow them that believe*. It added much to the glory and evidence of the gospel, that the preachers not only wrought miracles themselves, but conferred upon others a power to work miracles, which power *followed* some of them that believed, wherever they went to preach. They shall do wonders *in Christ's name*, the

same name into which they were baptized, in the virtue of power derived from him, and fetched in by prayer.

EPILOGUE (*vv.* 19, 20)

Here is, 1. Christ *welcomed* into the *upper world* (*v*. 19): *After the Lord had spoken* what he had to say to his disciples, he *went up into heaven*, in a cloud. Whatever God does concerning us, gives to us, or accepts from us, it is *by his Son*. Now he is glorified with the glory he had before the world.

2. Christ *welcomed* in this *lower world*; his being *believed on in the world*, and *received up into glory*, are put together, 1. Tim. iii. 16. (1) We have here the apostles working diligently for him; they *went forth, and preached every where* far and near. (2) We have here God *working* effectually *with them*, to make their labours successful, by *confirming the word with signs following*, partly by the miracles that were wrought upon the *bodies* of people, which were divine seals to the Christian doctrine, and partly by the influence it had upon the *minds* of people, through the operation of the Spirit of God, see Heb. ii. 4. These were properly *signs following* the word—the reformation of the world, the destruction of idolatry, the conversion of sinners, the comfort of saints; and these signs still follow it, and that they may do so more and more, for the honour of Christ and the good of mankind, the evangelist prays, and teaches us to say *Amen*. Father in heaven, thus let thy name be hallowed, and let thy kingdom come.

THE GOSPEL ACCORDING TO

ST. LUKE

CHAPTER ONE

PREFACE (vv. 1–4)

Complimentary prefaces and dedications, the language of flattery and the food and fuel of pride, are justly condemned by the wise and good; but it doth not therefore follow, that such as are useful and instructive are to be run down; such is this, in which St. Luke dedicates his gospel to his friend Theophilus, not as to his *patron*, though he was a man of honour, to protect it, but as to his *pupil*, to learn it, and hold it fast. It is not certain who this Theophilus was; the name signifies a *friend of God*; some think that it does not mean any particular person, but every one that is a *lover of God*.

Now observe here, I. Why St. Luke wrote this gospel. It is certain that he was moved by the Holy Spirit, not only *to* the writing, but *in* the writing of it; but in both he was moved as a reasonable creature, and not as a mere machine; and he was made to consider,

1. That the things he wrote of were things that were *most surely believed among all Christians*, and therefore things which they ought to be instructed in, that they may know what they believe, and things which ought to be transmitted to posterity (who are as much concerned in them as we are); and,

in order to that, to be committed to writing, which is the surest way of conveyance to the ages to come.

2. That it was requisite there should be a *declaration made in order* of those things; that the history of the life of Christ should be *methodized*, and committed to writing, for the greater certainty of the conveyance. When things are put in order, we know the better where to *find them* for *our own* use, and how to *keep* them for the benefit of *others*.

3. That there were *many who had undertaken* to *publish* narratives of the *life of Christ*, many well-meaning people, who *designed* well, and *did* well, and what they published had *done good*, though not done by divine inspiration, nor so well done as might be, nor intended for perpetuity.

4. That the truth of the things he had to write was *confirmed* by the *concurring testimony* of those who were competent and unexceptionable witnesses of them; what had been published in writing already, and what he was now about to publish, agreed with that which had been delivered by word of mouth, over and over, by those who from the beginning were *eye-witnesses and ministers of the word, v. 2.*

II. Observe why he sent it to *Theophilus*: "I wrote unto thee these things *in order*, not that thou mayest

343

give reputation to the work, but that thou mayest be edified by it (*v.* 4); *that thou mightest know the certainty of those things wherein thou hast been instructed.*" 1. It is implied, that he had been *instructed* in these things either before his baptism, or since, or both, according to the rule, Matt. xxviii. 19, 20. 2. It was intended that he should *know the certainty of those things,* should understand them more clearly and believe them more firmly. There is a *certainty* in the gospel of Christ, there is that therein which we may build upon; and those who have been well instructed in the things of God when they were young should afterwards give diligence to *know the certainty* of those things, to know not only what we believe, but why we believe it, that we may be able to give a *reason of the hope that is in us.*

ZACHARIAS AND THE ANGEL (*vv.* 5–25)

The two preceding evangelists had agreed to begin the gospel with the baptism of John and his ministry, which commenced about six months before our Saviour's public ministry, and therefore this evangelist, designing to give a more particular account than had been given of our Saviour's conception and birth, determines to do so of John Baptist, who in both was his harbinger and forerunner, the morning-star to the Sun of righteousness. Now observe here,

I. The account given of *his parents* (*v.* 5): They lived *in the days of Herod the king,* who was a foreigner, and a deputy for the Romans, who had lately made Judea a province of the empire.

Now the father of John Baptist was a priest, a son of Aaron; his name *Zacharias.*

Now that which is observed concerning Zacharias and Elisabeth is,

1. That they were a very religious couple (*v.* 6): *They were both righteous before God*; they were so in his sight whose judgment, we are sure, is *according to truth*; they were sincerely and really so.

2. That they had been long *childless, v.* 7. Elisabeth was *barren,* and they began to despair of ever having children, for they were both now *well stricken in years,* when the women that have been most fruitful *leave off bearing.* Many eminent persons were born of mothers that had been long childless, as Isaac, Jacob, Joseph, Samson, Samuel, and so here John Baptist, to make their birth the more remarkable and the blessing of it the more valuable to their parents, and to show that when God keeps his people long waiting for mercy he sometimes is pleased to recompense them for their patience by *doubling* the worth of it when it comes.

II. The appearing of an angel to his father Zacharias, as he was ministering in the temple, *vv.* 8–11. Zechariah the prophet was the last of the Old Testament that was conversant with angels, and Zacharias the priest the first in the New Testament. Observe,

1. How Zacharias was employed in the service of God (*v.* 8): He *executed the priest's office, before God, in the order of his course*; it

was his *week of waiting*, and he was *upon duty*.

While Zacharias was burning incense in the temple, *the whole multitude of the people were praying without*, v. 10. Now observe here, (1) That the true Israel of God always were a *praying* people; and prayer is the great and principal piece of service by which we give honour to God, fetch in favours from him, and keep up our communion with him. (2) That *then*, when ritual and ceremonial appointments were in full force, as this of *burning incense*, yet moral and spiritual duties were required to go along with them, and were principally looked at. (3) That it is not enough for us to be where God is worshipped, if our hearts do not join in the worship, and go along with the minister, in all the parts of it. (4) All the prayers we offer up to God here in his courts are acceptable and successful only in virtue of the incense of Christ's intercession in the temple of God above.

2. How, when he was thus employed, he was *honoured* with a messenger, a special messenger sent from heaven to him (v. 11): *There appeared unto him an angel of the Lord.*

3. What impression this made upon Zacharias (v. 12): *When Zacharias saw him*, it was a surprise upon him, even to a degree of terror, for he was *troubled*, and *fear fell upon him*, v. 12.

III. The message which the angel had to deliver to him, v. 13. He began his message, as angels generally did, with, *Fear not.* "*Fear not*, but compose thyself, that thou

mayest with a sedate and even spirit receive the message I have to deliver to thee." Let us see what that is.

1. The *prayers* he has often made shall now receive an *answer of peace: Fear not, Zacharias, for thy prayer is heard.* (1) If he means his particular prayer *for a son* to build up his family, it must be the prayers he had formerly made for that mercy, when he was likely to have children; but we may suppose, now that he and his wife were both *well stricken in years*, as they had done expecting it, so they had done praying for it: like Moses, it *sufficeth them*, and they *speak no more to God of that matter*, Deut. iii. 26. But, (2) If he means the prayers he was *now making*, and offering up with his incense, we may suppose that those were according to the duty of his place, for the Israel of God and their welfare, and the performance of the promises made to them concerning the Messiah and the coming of his kingdom: "This prayer of thine is now *heard*; for thy wife shall shortly conceive him that is to be the Messiah's forerunner." Or, (3) In general, "The prayers thou *now* makest, and all thy prayers, are accepted of God, and *come up for a memorial* before him" (as the angel said to Cornelius, when he visited him at prayer, Acts x. 30, 31); "and this shall be the sign that thou art accepted of God, Elisabeth shall *bear thee a son.*"

2. He shall have a son in his old age, by Elisabeth his wife, who had been long barren, that by his birth, which was *next* to miraculous, people might be prepared to receive

and believe a virgin's bringing forth of a son, which was *perfectly* miraculous. He is directed what name to give his son: *Call him John*, in Hebrew *Johanan*, a name we often meet with in the Old Testament: it signifies *gracious*.

3. This son shall be the joy of his family and of all his relations, *v.* 14. He shall be another Isaac, thy laughter; and some think that is partly intended in his name, *John*. He shall be a *welcome child*.

4. This son shall be a distinguished *favourite of Heaven*, and a distinguished *blessing to the earth*. The honour of having *a son* is nothing to the honour of having *such a son*.

(1) He shall be *great in the sight of the Lord*; those are great indeed that are so in God's sight, not those that are so in the eye of a vain and carnal world.

(2) He shall be a Nazarite, set apart to God from every thing that is *polluting*; in token of this, according to the law of Nazariteship, he *shall drink neither wine nor strong drink*,—or, rather, neither *old* wine nor *new*; for most think that the word here translated *strong drink* signifies some sort of wine, perhaps those that we call *made wines*, or any thing that is *intoxicating*. Those that would be *eminent* servants of God, and employed in *eminent* services, must learn to live a life of self-denial and mortification, must be dead to the pleasures of sense, and keep their minds from every thing that is darkening and disturbing to them.

(3) He shall be abundantly fitted and qualified for those great and eminent services to which in due time he shall be called: *He shall be filled with the Holy Ghost, even from his mother's womb*, and as soon as it is possible he shall appear to have been so.

(4) He shall be instrumental for the conversion of many souls to God, and the preparing of them to receive and entertain the gospel of Christ, *vv.* 16, 17.

He shall go *in the spirit and power of Elias*. That is, *First*, He shall be such a man as Elias was, and do such works as Elias did,—shall, like him, wear a hairy garment and a leathern girdle, and live retired from the world,—shall, like him, preach the necessity of repentance and reformation to a very corrupt and degenerate age,—shall, like him, be bold and zealous in reproving sin and witnessing against it even in the greatest, and be hated and persecuted for it by a Herod and his Herodias, as Elijah was by an Ahab and his Jezebel. He shall be carried on in his work, as Elijah was, by a divine *spirit* and *power*, which shall crown his ministry with wonderful success. As Elias went *before* the *writing* prophets of the Old Testament, and did as it were *usher* in that *signal* period of the Old-Testament dispensation by a little *writing* of his own (2 Chron. xxi. 12), so John Baptist went before Christ and his apostles, and introduced the gospel dispensation by preaching the substance of the gospel doctrine and duty, *Repent, with an eye to the kingdom of heaven*. *Secondly*, He shall be that very person who was prophesied of by Malachi under the name of Elijah (Mal. iv. 5), who should be sent *before the coming of the day of* the Lord. Behold, I *send you a prophet, even Elias*, not Elias the Tishbite (as the LXX. have corruptly read it, to favour the Jews' traditions), but a prophet *in the spirit and power of Elias*, as the angel here expounds it.

He shall *turn many of the children of Israel to the Lord their God*, shall incline their hearts to receive the Messiah, and bid him welcome, by awakening them to a sense of sin and a desire of righteousness.

Hereby he shall *turn the hearts of the fathers to the children*, that is, of the Jews to the Gentiles; shall help to conquer the rooted prejudices which the Jews have against the Gentiles, which was done by the gospel, as far as it prevailed, and was begun to be done by John Baptist, who came *for a witness, that all through him might believe*, who baptized and taught Roman soldiers as well as Jewish Pharisees, and who cured the pride and confidence of those Jews who gloried in their having Abraham to their father, and told them that God would *out of stones raise up children unto Abraham* (Matt. iii. 9), which would tend to *cure* their enmity to the Gentiles. He shall *turn the hearts of the fathers with the children*, that is, the hearts of old and young, shall be instrumental to bring some of every age to be *religious*, to work a great reformation in the Jewish nation, to bring them *of from* a ritual traditional religion which they had rested in, and to bring them up to *substantial serious* godliness: and the effect of this will be, that enmities will be slain and discord made to cease; and they that are at variance, being united in his baptism, will be better reconciled one to another.

Hereby he shall *make ready a people prepared for the Lord*, shall dispose the minds of people to receive the doctrine of Christ, that thereby they may be *prepared* for the comforts of his coming.

IV. Zacharias's unbelief of the angel's prediction, and the rebuke he was laid under for that unbelief. He heard all that the angel had to say, and should have bowed his head, and worshipped the Lord, saying, *Be it unto thy servant according to the word* which thou hast spoken; but it was not so. We are here told,

1. What his unbelief spoke, *v.* 18. He said to the angel, *Whereby shall I know this?* This was not a humble petition for the confirming of his faith, but a peevish objection against what was said to him as altogether incredible; as if he should say, "I can never be made to believe this."

2. How his unbelief was *silenced*, and he *silenced* for it.

(1) The angel *stops his mouth*, by *asserting* his authority. Doth he ask, *Whereby shall I know this?* Let him know it by this, *I am Gabriel, v.* 19. He puts his name to his prophecy, doth as it were sign it with his own hand. He is Gabriel, who *stands in the presence of God*, an immediate attendant upon the throne of God. "Though I am now talking with thee here, yet *I stand in the presence of God*. I know his eye is upon me, and I dare not say any more than I have warrant to say."

(2) The angel *stops his mouth* indeed, by *exerting his power*: "That thou mayest object no more,

behold thou shall be dumb," v. 20.
Thou shalt be both *dumb* and *deaf*;
the same word signifies both, and it
is plain that he lost his hearing as
well as his speech, for his friends
made signs to him (v. 62), as well
as he to them, v. 22.

V. The return of Zacharias to the
people, and at length to his family,
and the conception of this child of
promise, the son of his old age.

1. The people stayed, expecting
Zacharias to come out of the
temple, because he was to pronounce the blessing upon them in
the name of the Lord.

2. When he came out, he was
speechless, v. 22. He was now to
have dismissed the congregation
with a blessing, but was dumb and
not able to do it.

3. He made a shift to give them
to understand that he had *seen a
vision*, by some awful signs he
made, for he *beckoned to them*, and
remained speechless, v. 22.

4. He stayed out the *days of his
ministration*; for, his lot being to
burn incense, he could do that,
though he was *dumb* and *deaf*.
When we cannot perform the
service of God so well as we would,
yet, if we perform it as well as we
can, God will accept of us in it.

5. He then returned to his family,
and his *wife conceived*, vv. 23, 24.
She conceived by virtue of the
promise, and, being aware of it,
she hid herself five months. Now
Elisabeth triumphs, that not only
this reproach is taken away, but
great glory is put upon her instead
of it: *Thus hath the Lord dealt with
me*, beyond any thought or expectation of mine, *in the days wherein
he looked on me*. Note, In God's

gracious dealings with us we ought
to observe his gracious regards to
us. He has *looked on us* with compassion and favour, and therefore
has thus *dealt with us*.

THE ANNUNCIATION
(vv. 26–37)

We have here notice given us of all
that it was fit we should know concerning the incarnation and conception of our blessed Saviour, six
months after the conception of
John. The same angel, Gabriel, that
was employed in making known to
Zacharias God's purpose concerning *his son*, is employed in this also;
for in this, the same glorious work
of redemption, which was *begun* in
that, is *carried on*.

I. We have here an account given
of the mother of our Lord, of
whom he was to be born, whom,
though we are not to pray to, yet
we ought to praise God for.

1. Her name was *Mary*, the same
name with *Miriam*, the sister of
Moses and Aaron; the name signifies *exalted*, and a great elevation
it was to her indeed to be thus
favoured above all the daughters of
the house of David.

2. She was a daughter of the
royal family, lineally descended
from David, and she herself and all
her friends knew it, for she went
under the title and character of the
house of David, though she was
poor and low in the world.

3. She was *a virgin*, a pure unspotted one, but *espoused* to one of
the same royal stock, like her,
however, of low estate; so that
upon both accounts there was (as
it was fit there should be) an
equality between them; his name

was Joseph; he also was *of the house of David*, Matt. i. 20. Christ's mother was a *virgin*, because he was not to be born by ordinary generation, but miraculously; it was necessary that he should be so, that, though he must partake of the nature of man, yet not of the corruption of that nature: but he was born of a *virgin espoused*, made up to be married, and contracted, to put honour upon the married state, that that might not be brought into contempt (which was an ordinance in innocency) by the Redeemer's being born of a virgin.

4. She lived in Nazareth, a *city of Galilee*, a remote corner of the country, and in no reputation for religion or learning, but which bordered upon the heathen, and therefore was called *Galilee of the Gentiles*.

II. The *address* of the angel to her, *v.* 28. We are not told what she was doing, or how employed, when the angel came *unto her*; but he surprised her with this salutation, *Hail, thou that art highly favoured.* This was intended to raise in her, 1. A value for *herself*; and, though it is very rare that any need to have any sparks struck into their breast with such design, yet in some, who like Mary pore only on their *low estate*, there is occasion for it. 2. An expectation of great news, not from abroad, but from above. Heaven designs, no doubt, uncommon favours for one whom an angel makes court to with such respect.

(1) She is dignified: "Thou art *highly favoured*. God, in his choice of thee to be the mother of the Messiah, has put an honour upon thee peculiar to thyself, above that of Eve, who was the mother of *all living*."

(2) She has the presence of God with her: "*The Lord is with thee*, though poor and mean, and perhaps now forecasting how to get a livelihood and maintain a family in the married state."

(3) She has the blessing of God upon her: "*Blessed art thou among women.*" She explains this herself (*v.* 48), *All generations shall call me blessed.*

III. The consternation she was in, upon this address (*v.* 29). *When she saw him*, and the glories with which he was surrounded, she was *troubled* at the sight of him, and much more *at his saying*. She *cast in her mind what manner of salutation this should be*. Was it from heaven or of men? Was it to amuse her? was it to ensnare her? was it to banter her? or was there something substantial and weighty in it?

IV. The message itself which the angel had to deliver to her. Some time the angel gives her to *pause*; but, observing that this did but increase her perplexity, he went on with his errand, *v.* 30. To what he had said she made no reply; he therefore confirms it: "*Fear not, Mary*, I have no other design than to assure thee that *thou hast found favour with God*." Note, Those that have *found favour with God* should not give way to disquieting distrustful fears.

1. Though she is a *virgin*, she shall have the honour of being a *mother*: "*Thou shalt conceive in thy womb, and bring forth a son*, and thou shalt have the naming of him; thou shalt *call his name Jesus*," *v.* 31.

2. Though she lives in *poverty* and *obscurity*, yet she shall have the honour to be the mother of the Messiah; her son shall be named *Jesus—a Saviour*, such a one as the world *needs*, rather than such a one as the Jews *expect*.

(1) He will be very *nearly allied* to the *upper world*. He *shall be great*, truly great, incontestably great; for he shall be called *the Son of the Highest*, the Son of God who is *the Highest*; of the same nature, as the son is of the same nature with the father; and very dear to him, as the son is to the father.

(2) He will be very *highly preferred* in the *lower world*; for, though born under the most disadvantageous circumstances possible, and appearing in the form of a servant, yet *the Lord God shall give unto him the throne of his father David*, v. 32. He assures her, [1] That his kingdom shall be *spiritual*: he shall *reign over the house of Jacob*, not *Israel according to the flesh*, for they neither came into his interests nor did they continue long a people; it must therefore be a *spiritual* kingdom, the house of Israel *according to promise*, that he must *rule over*. [2] That it shall be eternal: he shall reign *for ever*, and *of his kingdom there shall be no end*.

V. The further information given her, upon her enquiry concerning the birth of this prince.

1. It is a just enquiry which she makes: "*How shall this be?*" v. 34. "How can I now presently conceive a child" (for so the angel meant) "when I *know not a man*; must it therefore be otherwise than by ordinary generation? If so, let me know *how*?"

2. It is a satisfactory answer that is given to it, v. 35. (1) She shall conceive by *the power of the Holy Ghost*, whose proper work and office it is to *sanctify*, and therefore to sanctify the virgin for this purpose.

(2) She must *ask no questions* concerning the way and manner how it shall be wrought; for the Holy Ghost, as the *power of the Highest*, shall *overshadow* her, as the *cloud* covered the tabernacle when the glory of God took possession of it, to conceal it from those that would too curiously observe the motions of it, and pry into the mystery of it. The formation of every babe in the womb, and the entrance of the spirit of life into it, is a mystery in nature; none knows *the way of the spirit, nor how the bones are formed in the womb of her that is with child*, Eccl. xi. 5. We were *made in secret*, Ps. cxxxix. 15, 16. Much more was the formation of the child Jesus a *mystery*; without controversy, *great was the mystery of godliness, God manifest in the flesh*, 1 Tim. iii. 16. It is a *new thing created in the earth* (Jer. xxxi. 22), concerning which we must not covet to be *wise above what is written*.

(3) The child she shall conceive is a *holy thing*, and therefore must not be conceived by *ordinary generation*, because he must not share in the common corruption and pollution of the human nature.

3. It was a further encouragement to her faith to be told that *her cousin Elisabeth*, though stricken in years, was *with child*, v. 36. Here is an age of wonders beginning, and therefore be not surprised.

VI. Her acquiescence in the will of God concerning her, *v. 38*. She owns herself, 1. A believing subject to the divine authority: "*Behold, the handmaid of the Lord. Lord, I am at thy service, at thy disposal, to do what thou commandest me.*" She objects not the danger of spoiling her marriage, and blemishing her reputation, but leaves the issue with God, and submits entirely to his will. 2. A believing expectant of the divine favour. She is not only content that it should be so, but humbly desires that it may be so: *Be it unto me according to thy word.*

Hereupon, *the angel departed from her*; having completed the errand he was sent upon, he returned, to give account of it, and receive new instructions.

MARY'S SONG (*vv. 39–56*)

We have here an interview between the two happy mothers, Elisabeth and Mary. Here is,

I. The visit which Mary made to Elisabeth. Mary was the *younger*, and younger with child; and therefore, if they must come together, it was fittest that Mary should take the journey, not insisting on the preference which the greater dignity of her conception gave her, *v. 39*.

II. The meeting between Mary and Elisabeth. Mary entered into the house of Zacharias; but he, being *dumb* and *deaf*, kept his chamber, it is probable, and saw no company; and therefore she *saluted Elisabeth* (*v. 40*), told her that she was come to make her a visit, to know her state, and *rejoice with her* in her joy.

Now, at their first coming together, for the confirmation of the faith of both of them, there was something very extraordinary. Mary knew that Elisabeth was with child, but it does not appear that Elisabeth had been told any thing of her cousin Mary's being designed for the mother of the Messiah; and therefore what knowledge she appears to have had of it must have come by a *revelation*, which would be a great encouragement to Mary.

1. The babe *leaped in her womb*, *v. 41*. It is very probable that she had been several weeks *quick* (for she was six months gone), and that she had often felt the child stir; but this was a more than ordinary motion of the child, which alarmed her to expect something very extraordinary.

2. Elisabeth was herself *filled with the Holy Ghost*, or a Spirit of prophecy, by which, as well as by the particular suggestions of the Holy Ghost she was filled with, she was given to understand that the Messiah was at hand, in whom prophecy should revive, and by whom the Holy Ghost should be more plentifully poured out than ever, according to the expectations of those who *waited for the consolation of Israel*. The uncommon motion of the babe in her womb was a token of the extraordinary emotion of her spirit under a divine impulse.

III. The welcome which Elisabeth, by the Spirit of prophecy, gave to Mary, the mother of our Lord; not as to a common friend making a common visit, but as to one of whom the Messiah was to be born.

1. She congratulates her on her

honour, and, though perhaps she knew not of it till *just now*, she acknowledges it with the greatest assurance and satisfaction. She said, *Blessed art thou among women*, the same word that the angel had said (*v* 28); for thus this will of God, concerning honouring the Son, should be done *on earth* as it is *done in heaven*. But Elisabeth adds a reason, *Therefore blessed art thou* because *blessed is the fruit of thy womb*; thence it was that she derived this excelling dignity.

2. She acknowledges her condescension, in making her this visit (*v.* 43): *Whence is this to me, that the mother of my Lord should come to me?* Observe, (1) She calls the virgin Mary the *mother of her Lord* (as David, in spirit, called the Messiah Lord, *his Lord*), for she knew he was to be *Lord of all*. (2) She not only bids her welcome to her house, though perhaps she came but in mean circumstances, but reckons this visit a great favour, which she thought herself unworthy of.

3. She acquaints her with the concurrence of the babe in her womb, in this welcome to her (*v.* 44). He *leaped* as it were *for joy* that the Messiah, whose harbinger he was to be, would himself come so soon after him.

4. She commends her faith, and encourages it (*v.* 45): *Blessed is she that believed.* They are *blessed* who *believe* the word of God, for that word will not fail them; *there shall*, without doubt, *be a performance of those things which are told her from the Lord*.

IV. Mary's song of praise, upon this occasion.

1. Here are the expressions of joy and praise, and God alone the object of the praise and centre of the joy. Some compare this song with that which her name-sake Miriam, the sister of Moses, sung, upon the triumphant departure of Israel out of Egypt, and their triumphant passage through the Red Sea; others think it better compared with the song of Hannah, upon the birth of Samuel, which, like this, passes from a family mercy to a public and general one. *This* begins, like *that*, *My heart rejoiceth in the Lord*, 1 Sam. ii. 1. Observe how Mary here speaks of God.

(1) With great reverence of him, as *the Lord*: "*My soul doth magnify the Lord*; I never saw him so *great* as now I find him so *good*."

(2) With great complacency in him as *her Saviour: My spirit rejoiceth in God my Saviour*. This seems to have reference to the Messiah, whom she was to be the mother of. She calls him *God her Saviour*; for the angel had told her that he should be the *Son of the Highest*, and that his name should be *Jesus, a Saviour*; this she fastened upon, with application to herself: *He is God my Saviour*.

2. Here are just causes assigned for this joy and praise.

(1) Upon *her own* account, *vv.* 48, 49. [1] Her *spirit rejoiced in the Lord*, because of the *kind* things he had done for her: his *condescension* and *compassion* to her. *He has regarded the low estate of his handmaiden*; that is, he has *looked* upon her *with pity*, for so the word is commonly used. [2] Her *soul magnifies* the Lord, because of the

wonderful things he has done for her (*v.* 49): *He that is mighty has done to me great things.* A great thing indeed, that a *virgin* should *conceive.* A *great* thing indeed, that Messiah, who had been so long ago promised to the church, and so long expected by the church, should now at length be born. He that is *mighty*, even he *whose name is holy*, has *done to me great things.* Glorious things may be expected from him that is both *mighty* and *holy*; who *can do every thing*, and *will* do every thing *well* and *for the best.*

(2) Upon the account of *others.* The virgin Mary, as the mother of the Messiah, is become a kind of public person, wears a public character, and is therefore immediately endued with another spirit, a more public spirit than before she had, and therefore *looks abroad*, looks *about her*, looks *before her*, and takes notice of God's various dealings with the children of men (*vv.* 50, &c.), as Hannah (1 Sam. ii. 3, etc.). In this she has especially an eye to the coming of the Redeemer and God's manifesting himself therein.

[1] It is a certain truth that *God has mercy in store*, mercy in reserve, *for all that have a reverence for his majesty*, and a due regard to his sovereignty and authority. But never did this appear so as in sending his Son into the world to save us (*v.* 50): *His mercy is on them that fear him*; it has always been so; he has ever looked upon *them* with an eye of *peculiar favour* who have looked up to him with an eye of *filial fear.*

[2] It has been a common obser-vation that God in his providence puts *contempt* upon the *haughty* and *honour* upon the *humble*; and this he has done remarkably in the whole economy of the work of man's redemption. This doth especially appear in the methods of gospel grace.

(1.) In the *spiritual honours* it dispenses. When the proud Pharisees were rejected, and Publicans and sinners went *into the kingdom of heaven* before them,—when the Jews, who *followed after the law of righteousness*, did not attain it, and the Gentiles, who never thought of it, attained to righteousness (Rom. ix. 30, 31),—when God chose not the *wise men after the flesh*, not the *mighty*, or the *noble*, to preach the gospel, and plant Christianity in the world, but the *foolish* and *weak* things of the world, and things that were despised (1 Cor. i. 26, 27)—then he *scattered the proud*, and *put down the mighty*, but *exalted them of low degree.*

(2.) In the *spiritual riches* it dispenses, *v.* 53. (1) Those who see their need of Christ, and are importunately desirous of righteousness and life in him, he *fills* with *good things*, with the *best things.* (2) Those who are rich, who are not *hungry*, who, like Laodicea, think they have *need of nothing*, are full of themselves and their own righteousness, and think they have a sufficiency in themselves, those he *sends away* from his door, they are not welcome to him, he sends them *empty* away, they come *full of self*, and are sent away *empty of Christ.*

[3] It was always expected that the Messiah should be, in a special

manner, the strength and glory of his people Israel, and so he is in a peculiar manner (v. 54): *He hath helped his servant Israel*. The sending of the Messiah, on whom *help* was *laid* for poor sinners, was the greatest kindness that could be done, the greatest help that could be provided for his people Israel, and that which magnifies it is,

First, That it is *in remembrance of his mercy*, the mercifulness of his nature, the mercy he has in store for *his servant Israel*.

Secondly, That it is *in performance of his promise*. It is a mercy not only designed, but declared (v. 55); it was *what he spoke to our fathers*.

Lastly, Mary's return to Nazareth (v. 56), after she had continued with Elisabeth about *three months*, so long as to be fully satisfied concerning herself that she was *with child*, and to be confirmed therein by her cousin Elisabeth.

THE BIRTH OF JOHN
(vv. 57–66)

In these verses, we have,

I. The birth of John Baptist, v. 57. Though he was conceived in the womb by miracle, he continued in the womb according to the ordinary course of nature (so did our Saviour).

II. The great joy that was among all the relations of the family, upon this extraordinary occasion (v. 58): *Her neighbours and her cousins heard of it*; for it would be in every body's mouth, as next to miraculous.

III. The dispute that was among them concerning the naming him (v. 59): *On the eighth day*, as God

had appointed, they *came together*, to *circumcise the child*.

Now it was the custom, when they circumcised their children, to *name them*, because, when *Abram* was circumcised God gave him a new name, and called him *Abraham*; and it is not unfit that they should be left *nameless* till they are by name *given up to God*. Now,

1. *Some* proposed that he should be called by his father's name, *Zacharias*.

2. The *mother* opposed it, and would have him called *John*; having learned, either by inspiration of the Holy Ghost (as is most probable), or by information in writing from her husband, that God appointed this to be his name (v. 60).

3. The *relations* objected to that (v. 61).

4. They appealed to the *father*, and would try if they could possibly get to know his mind; for it was his office to *name the child*, v. 62. They *made signs* to him, by which it appears that he was *deaf* as well as *dumb*; nay, it should seem, *mindless* of any thing, else one would think they should at first have desired him to write down his child's name, if he had ever yet communicated any thing by writing since he was *struck*. Whereupon he made signs to them to give him a *table-book*, such as they then used, and with the pencil he wrote these words, *His name is John*, v. 63. Not, "It shall be so," or, "I would have it so," but, "It is so." The matter is determined already; the *angel* had given him that name.

5. He thereupon recovered the use of his speech (v. 64): *His mouth*

was opened immediately. The time prefixed for his being silenced was *till the day that these things shall be fulfilled* (v. 20); not *all the things* going before concerning John's ministry, but those which relate to his birth and name (v. 13). That time was now expired, whereupon the restraint was taken off, and God gave him the *opening of the mouth again*, as he did to Ezekiel, ch. iii. 27.

6. These things were told all the country over, to the great amazement of all that heard them, vv. 65, 66. They said *within* themselves, and said *among* themselves, "*What manner of child shall this be?* What will be the fruit when these are the buds, or rather when the *root* is out of such a *dry ground?*"

Lastly, It is said, *The hand of the Lord was with him*; that is, he was taken under the special protection of the Almighty, from his birth, as one designed for something great and considerable, and there were many instances of it.

THE SONG OF ZACHARIAS
(vv. 67–80)

We have here the song wherewith Zacharias *praised* God when his *mouth* was *opened*; in it he is said to *prophesy* (v. 67), and so he did in the strictest sense of *prophesying*; for he foretold things to come concerning the kingdom of the Messiah, to which all the prophets bear witness. Observe,

I. How he was qualified for this: *He was filled with the Holy Ghost*, was endued with more than ordinary measures and degrees of it, for this purpose; he was divinely inspired.

II. What the matter of his song

was. He is wholly taken up with the kingdom of the Messiah, and the public blessings to be introduced by it. The Old-Testament prophecies are often expressed in *praises* and *new songs*, so is this beginning of New-Testament prophecy: *Blessed be the Lord God of Israel*. The *God of the whole earth shall he be called*; yet Zacharias, speaking of the work of redemption, called him the *Lord God of Israel*, because to Israel the prophecies, promises, and types, of the redemption had hitherto been given, and to them the first proffers and proposals of it were now to be made.

Now Zacharias here blesses God,

1. For the work of *salvation* that was to be wrought out by the Messiah himself, vv. 68–75. This it is that *fills him*, when he is *filled with the Holy Ghost*, and it is that which all who have the *Spirit of Christ* are *full of*.

(1) In sending the Messiah, God has *made a gracious visit* to his people, whom for many ages he had seemed to neglect, and to be estranged from; he hath *visited them* as a friend, to take cognizance of their case.

(2) He has *wrought out redemption* for them: *He has redeemed his people*. This was the errand on which Christ *came into the world*, to redeem those that were sold *for* sin, and sold *under* sin; even God's own people, his Israel, his son, his *firstborn*, his *free-born*, need to be *redeemed*, and are undone if they be not. Christ redeems them by *price* out of the hands of God's justice, and redeems them by *power* out of the hands of Satan's tyranny, as Israel out of Egypt.

(3) He has fulfilled the *covenant of royalty* made with the most famous *Old-Testament prince*, that is, David. Glorious things had been said of his family, that on him, as a *mighty one, help* should be *laid*, that *his horn should be exalted*, and his *seed* perpetuated, Ps. lxxxix. 19, 20, 24, 29. But that family had been long in a manner *cast off* and *abhorred*, Ps. lxxxix. 38. Now here it is gloried in, that, according to the promise, the *horn* of David should again be *made to bud*; for, Ps. cxxxii. 17, he *hath raised up a horn of salvation for us in the house of his servant David* (*v.* 69), there, where it was promised and expected to arise.

He has fulfilled all the precious promises made to the church by the most famous *Old-Testament prophets* (*v.* 70). *As he spoke by the mouth of his holy prophets.* His doctrine of salvation by the Messiah is confirmed by an appeal to the prophets, and the greatness and importance of that salvation thereby evidenced and magnified; it is the same that they spoke of, which therefore ought to be expected and welcomed; it is what they *enquired and searched diligently after* (1 Pet. i. 10, 11), which therefore ought not to be slighted or thought meanly of.

Now what is this *salvation* which was prophesied of?

First, It is a *rescue* from the malice of *our enemies*; it is *a salvation out of our enemies*, from among them, and *out of the power of them that hate us* (*v.* 71). He shall *save his people from their sins*, that they may not have dominion over them, Matt. i. 21.

Secondly, It is a *restoration* to the favour of God; it is to *perform the mercy promised to our forefathers*, *v.* 72. Observe, 1. That which was promised to the fathers, and is performed to us, is *mercy*, pure mercy; nothing in it is owing to our *merit* (we deserve wrath and the curse), but all to the *mercy* of God, which *designed* us grace and life. 2. God herein had an eye to *his covenant*, his *holy* covenant, that covenant with Abraham: I *will be a God to thee and thy seed*.

Thirdly, It is a qualification for, and an encouragement to, the service of God. Thus was *the oath he sware to our Father Abraham*, That he would *give us* power and grace to *serve him*, in an acceptable manner to him and a comfortable manner to ourselves, *vv.* 74, 75. We are hereby enabled, 1. To serve God *without fear*. We are *therefore* put into a state of *holy safety* that we might serve God with a *holy security* and *serenity of mind*, as those that are *quiet from the fears of evil*. 2. To serve him in *holiness and righteousness*, which includes the whole duty of man towards God and our neighbour. It is both the intention and the direct tendency of the gospel to renew upon us that image of God in which man was at first made, which consisted *in righteousness and true holiness*, Eph. iv. 24. 3. To serve him, *before him*, in the duties of his *immediate* worship, wherein we present ourselves *before the Lord*, to serve him as those that have an eye always upon him, and see his eye always upon us, upon our inward man, that is serving him *before him*. 4. To serve him *all the days of our life*. The design of the gospel is to engage us to constancy and perseverance in the service of God, by showing us how much depends upon our not drawing back, and by showing us how Christ *loved us to the end*, and thereby engaged us to *love him to the end*.

2. He *blessed God* for the work of *preparation* for this salvation, which was to be done by John Baptist (*v.* 76): *Thou child*, though now but a child of eight days old, shalt be called *the prophet of the Highest*. John's business was,

(1) To prepare people for the salvation, by preaching repentance and reformation as great gospel duties: *Thou shalt go before the face of the Lord,* and but a little before him, to *prepare his ways,* to call people to make room for him, and get ready for his entertainment.

(2) To give people a general idea of the salvation, that they might know, not only what to do, but what to expect; for the doctrine he preached was that the *kingdom of heaven* is at hand.

In the last verse, we have a short account of the younger years of John Baptist. Though he was the son of a priest, he did not, like Samuel, go up, when he was a child, to minister before the Lord; for he was to prepare the way for a better priesthood. But we are here told,

[1.] Of his *eminence* as to the *inward man*: The *child grew* in the capacities of his mind, much more than other children; so that he *waxed strong in spirit*, had a strong judgment and strong resolution.

[2.] Of his *obscurity* as to the *outward man*: *He was in the deserts*; not that he lived a hermit, cut off

from the society of men. No, we have reason to think that he went up to Jerusalem at the *feasts*, and frequented the synagogues on the sabbath day, but his constant residence was in some of those scattered houses that were in the wilderness of Zuph or Maon, which we read of in the story of David.

CHAPTER TWO

THE BIRTH OF JESUS
(*vv.* 1–7)

The *fulness of time* was now come, when God would send forth his Son, *made of a woman*, and *made under the law*; and it was foretold that he should be born at Bethlehem. Now here we have an account of the time, place, and manner of it.

I. The time when our Lord Jesus was born. Several things may be gathered out of these verses which intimate to us that it was the *proper time*.

1. He was born at the time when the *fourth monarchy* was in its height, just when it was become, more than any of the three before it, a *universal monarchy*. Now this was the time when the Messiah was to be born, according to Daniel's prophecy (Dan. ii. 44): *In the days of these kings*, the kings of the fourth monarchy, *shall the God of heaven set up a kingdom which shall never be destroyed*.

2. He was born when Judea was become a province of the empire, and tributary to it; as appears evidently by this, that when all the Roman empire was taxed, the Jews were taxed among the rest. Now just at this juncture, the

357

The Birth of Jesus

Messiah was to be born, for so was dying Jacob's prophecy, that Shiloh should come when the *sceptre was departed from Judah*, and the *lawgiver from between his feet*, Gen. xlix. 10. This was the *first taxing* that was made in Judea, the first badge of their servitude; therefore now Shiloh must come, to set up his kingdom.

3. There is another circumstance, as to the time, implied in this general enrolment of all the subjects of the empire, which is, that there was now universal peace in the empire. The temple of Janus was now shut, which it never used to be if any wars were on foot; and now it was fit for the Prince of peace to be born, in whose days *swords should be beaten into plough-shares*.

II. The place where our Lord Jesus was born is very observable. He was born at *Bethlehem*; so it was foretold (Mic. v. 2), the scribes so understood it (Matt. ii. 5, 6), so did the common people, John vii. 42.

That which Augustus designed was either to gratify his *pride* in knowing the numbers of his people, and proclaiming it to the world, or he did it in *policy*, to strengthen his interest, and make his government appear the more formidable; but Providence had another reach in it. All the world shall be at the trouble of being *enrolled*, only that Joseph and Mary may. This brought them up from Nazareth in Galilee to Bethlehem in Judea, because they were *of the stock and lineage of David* (vv. 4, 5). Divers ends of Providence were served by this.

1. Hereby the virgin Mary was brought, *great with child*, to Bethlehem, to be *delivered* there,

according to the prediction; whereas she had designed to lie in at Nazareth. See how *man purposes and God disposes*; and how Providence orders all things for the fulfilling of the scripture, and makes use of the projects men have for serving their own purposes, quite beyond their intention, to serve his.

2. Hereby it appeared that Jesus Christ was of the *seed* of David; for what brings his mother to Bethlehem now, but because she *was of the stock and lineage of David?*

3. Hereby it appeared that he was *made under the law*; for he became a subject of the Roman empire as soon as he was born, a *servant of rulers*, Isa. xlix. 7.

III. The circumstances of his birth, which were very mean, and under all possible marks of contempt.

1. He was under some abasements in common with other children; he was *wrapped in swaddling clothes*, as other children are when they are new-born, as if he could be bound, or needed to be kept straight. The Ancient of days became an infant of a span long.

2. He was under some abasements peculiar to himself.

(1) He was born *at an inn*. That son of David that was the glory of his father's house had no inheritance that he could command, no not in the city of David, no nor a friend that would accommodate his mother in distress with lodgings to be brought to bed in. Christ was born *in an inn*, to intimate that he came into the world but to sojourn here for awhile, as in an inn, and to teach us to do likewise.

(2) He was born *in a stable*; so some think the word signifies which we translate *a manger*, a place for cattle to stand to be fed in. His being born in a stable and laid in a manger was an instance, [1] Of the poverty of his parents. Had they been rich, room would have been made for them; but, being poor, they must *shift* as they *could*. [2] Of the corruption and degeneracy of manners in that age; that a woman in reputation for virtue and honour should be used so barbarously. If there had been any common humanity among them, they would not have turned a woman in travail into a stable. [3] It was an instance of the humiliation of our Lord Jesus. We were become by sin like an out-cast infant, helpless and forlorn; and such a one Christ was.

THE SHEPHERDS (*vv*. 8–20)

We had in Matthew an account of the notice given of the arrival of this ambassador, this prince from heaven, to the wise men, who were Gentiles, by a star; here we are told of the notice given of it to the shepherds, who were Jews, by an angel; to each God chose to speak in the language they were most conversant with.

I. See here how the shepherds were employed; they were *abiding in the fields* adjoining to Bethlehem, and *keeping watch over their flocks by night*, *v*. 8. Observe, 1. They were not *sleeping* in their beds, when this news was brought them (though many had very acceptable intelligence from heaven in *slumbering upon the bed*), but *abiding in the fields*, and *watching*. Those that

would hear from God must *stir up themselves*. They were broad awake, and therefore could not be deceived in what they saw and heard, so as those may be who are half asleep. 2. They were employed now, not in acts of devotion, but in the business of their calling; they were *keeping watch over their flock*, to secure them from thieves and beasts of prey, it being probably in the summer time, when they kept their cattle out all night, as we do now, and did not house them. Note, We are not out of the way of divine visits when we are sensibly employed in an honest calling, and abide with God in it.

II. How they were surprised with the appearance of an angel (*v*. 9). This made them *sore afraid*, put them into a great consternation, as fearing some evil tidings.

III. What the message was which the angel had to deliver to the shepherds, *vv*. 10–12. 1. "*Fear not*, for we have nothing to say to you that needs be a terror to you; you *need not* fear your enemies, and *should not* fear your friends." 2. He furnishes them with abundant matter for joy: "Behold, I *evangelize to you great joy*; I solemnly declare it, and you have reason to bid it welcome, for it shall bring *joy to all people*, and not to the people of the Jews only; that *unto you is born this day*, at this time, *a Saviour*, the Saviour that has been so long expected, *which is Christ the Lord, in the city of David*," *v*. 11. Jesus is the Christ, the Messiah, the Anointed; he is *the Lord*, Lord of all; he is a sovereign prince; nay, he is God, for *the Lord*, in the Old Testament, answers to *Jehovah*. He is a Saviour, and he will be a Saviour to those only that accept of him for their Lord. "The Saviour *is born*, he is born *this day*; and, since it is matter of *great joy to all people*, it is not to be kept secret, you may proclaim it, may tell it to whom you please. He is born in the place where it was foretold he should be born, in the *city of David*; and he is born *to you*; to you Jews he is sent in the first place, to *bless you*, to you *shepherds*, though poor and mean in the world." This refers to Isa. ix. 6, *Unto us a child is born, unto us a son is given.* To *you* men, not to *us* angels; he took not on him the nature of angels. This is matter of *joy* indeed to all people, great joy. Long-looked for is come at last. Let heaven and earth rejoice before this Lord, *for he cometh*. 3. He gives them a sign for the confirming of their faith in this matter. "How shall we find out this child in Bethlehem, which is now full of the descendants from David?" "You will find him by this token: he is lying in a *manger*, where surely never any new-born infant was laid before." They expected to be told, "You shall find him, though a babe, dressed up in robes, and lying in the best house in the town, lying in state, with a numerous train of attendants in rich liveries." "No, you will find him wrapped in *swaddling clothes*, and *laid in a manger*. When Christ was here upon earth, he *distinguished* himself, and made himself remarkable, by nothing so much as the instances of his *humiliation*."

IV. The angels' *doxology* to God, and *congratulations* of men, upon this solemn occasion, *vv.* 13, 14.

The message was no sooner delivered by one angel (that was sufficient to go express) than suddenly there was with that angel *a multitude of the heavenly hosts*; sufficient, we may be sure, to make a *chorus*, that were heard by the shepherds, *praising God*; and certainly their song was not like that (Rev. xiv. 3) which *no man could learn*, for it was designed that we should all learn it. 1. Let God have the honour of this work: *Glory to God in the highest.* God's goodwill to men, manifested in sending the Messiah, redounds very much to his praise; and angels in the highest heavens, though not immediately interested in it themselves, will celebrate it to his honour, Rev. v. 11, 12. *Glory to God*, whose kindness and love designed this favour, and whose wisdom contrived it in such a way as that one divine attribute should not be glorified at the expense of another, but the honour of all effectually secured and advanced. Other works of God are for his glory, but the redemption of the world is for his *glory in the highest.* 2. Let men have the joy of it: *On earth peace, good-will toward men.* God's *good-will* in sending the Messiah introduced peace in this lower world, slew the enmity that sin had raised between God and man, and resettled a peaceable correspondence. If God be at peace with us, all peace results from it: peace of conscience, peace with angels, peace between Jew and Gentile. Peace is here put for *all good*, all that good which flows to us from the incarnation of Christ. All the *good* we have, or hope, is owing to God's *good-will*; and, if we have the comfort of it, he must have the glory of it. Nor must any *peace*, any *good*, be expected in a way inconsistent with the glory of God; therefore not in any way of sin, nor in any way but by *a Mediator*. Here was the *peace proclaimed* with great solemnity; whoever will, let them come and take the benefit of it. It is on earth peace, to *men of good-will* (so some copies read it), ἐν ἀνθρώποις εὐδοκίας; to men who have a *good-will to God*, and are willing to be reconciled; or to men whom God has a *good-will to*, though vessels of his mercy. See how well affected the angels are to man, and to his welfare and happiness; how well pleased they were in the incarnation of the Son of God, though he passed by their nature; and ought not we much more to be affected with it? This is a *faithful saying*, attested by an innumerable company of angels, and well *worthy of all acceptation, That the good-will of God toward men is glory to God in the highest, and peace on the earth*.

V. The visit which the shepherds made to the new-born Saviour. 1. They consulted about it, *v*. 15. While the angels were singing their hymn, they could attend to that only; but, *when they were gone away from them into heaven* (for angels, when they appeared, never made any long stay, but returned as soon as they had despatched their business), *the shepherds said one to another, Let us go to Bethlehem*. Note, When extraordinary messages from the upper world are no more to be expected, we must set ourselves to improve the advantages we have for the confirming of our faith, and the keeping up of our communion with God in this lower world. And it is no reflection upon the testimony of angels, no nor upon a divine testimony itself, to get it corroborated by observation and experience. But observe, These shepherds do not speak doubtfully, "Let us go see whether it be so or no"; but with assurance, *Let us go see this thing which is come to pass*; for what room was left to doubt of it, when *the Lord had* thus *made it known to them?* The *word spoken by angels was steadfast* and unquestionably true. 2. They immediately made the visit, *v*. 16. They lost no time, but *came with haste* to the place, which, probably, the angel directed them to more particularly than is recorded ("Go to the stable of such an inn"); and there *they found Mary and Joseph*, and *the babe lying in the manger*. The poverty and meanness in which they found *Christ the Lord* were no shock to their faith, who themselves knew what it was to live a life of comfortable communion with God in very poor and mean circumstances. We have reason to think that the shepherds told Joseph and Mary of the vision of the angels they had seen, and the song of the angels they had heard, which was a great encouragement to them, more than if a visit had been made them by the best ladies in the town. And it is probable that Joseph and Mary told the shepherds what visions they had had concerning the child; and so, by communicating their experiences to each other, they greatly strengthened one another's faith.

VI. The care which the shepherds took to spread the report of this (*v.* 17): *When they had seen it*, though they saw nothing in the child that should induce them to believe that he was *Christ the Lord*, yet the circumstances, how mean soever they were, agreeing with the sign that the angel had given them, they were abundantly satisfied. They made *known abroad* the whole story of what was *told them*, both by the *angels*, and by Joseph and Mary, *concerning this child*, that he was the Saviour, even *Christ the Lord*, that in him there is *peace on earth*, and that he was *conceived by the power of the Holy Ghost*, and *born of a virgin*. This they told every body, and agreed in their testimony concerning it. And now if, when he *is in the world*, the world knows him not, it is *their own fault*, for they have sufficient notice given them.

VII. The use which those made of these things, who did believe them, and receive the impression of them. 1. The virgin Mary made them the matter of her *private meditation*. She said little, but *kept all these things*, and *pondered them in her heart*, *v.* 19. 2. The shepherds made them the matter of their more *public praises*. If others were not affected with those things, yet they themselves were (*v.* 20): They *returned, glorifying and praising God*, in concurrence with the holy angels.

THE PRESENTATION
(*vv.* 21–24)

Our Lord Jesus, being *made of a woman*, was *made under the law*, Gal. iv. 4.

Now here we have two instances of his being *made under* that *law*, and submitting to it.

I. He was *circumcised* on the very day that the law appointed (*v.* 21): *When eight days were accomplished*, that day seven-night that he was born, they *circumcised* him. Christ was circumcised, (1) That he might own himself of the seed of Abraham, and of that nation *of whom, as concerning the flesh, Christ came*, and who was to *take on him the seed of Abraham*, Heb. ii. 16. (2) That he might own himself a surety for our sins, and an undertaker for our safety. Circumcision (saith Dr. Goodwin) was our *bond*, whereby we acknowledged ourselves *debtors to the law*; and Christ, by being circumcised, did as it were set his hand to it, being *made sin for us*. The ceremonial law consisted much in sacrifices; Christ hereby obliged himself to offer, not the blood of bulls or goats, but his own blood, which none that ever were circumcised before could oblige themselves to. (3) That he might justify, and put an honour upon, the dedication of the infant seed of the church to God, by that ordinance which is the instituted seal of the covenant, and of the righteousness which is by faith, as circumcision was (Rom. iv. 11), and baptism is. And certainly his being circumcised at eight days old doth make much more for the dedicating of the seed of the faithful by baptism in their infancy than his being baptized at thirty years old doth for the deferring of it till they are grown up. The change of the ceremony alters not the substance. At his circumcision, according to the custom, he had his name given him; he was called *Jesus* or *Joshua*, for he was *so named of the angel* to his mother Mary *before he was conceived in the womb* (Luke i. 31), and to his supposed father Joseph after, Matt. i. 21.

II. He was *presented* in the temple. This was done with an eye to the law, and at the time appointed by the law, when he was forty days old, *when the days of her purification were accomplished*, *v.* 22. Now, according to the law,

1. The child Jesus, being a first-born son, was *presented to the Lord*, in one of the courts of the temple. The law is here recited (*v.* 23): *Every male that opens the womb shall be called holy to the Lord*, because by a special writ of protection the first-born of Israel were preserved, when the first-born of the Egyptians were slain by the destroying angel; so that Christ, as first-born, was a priest by a title surer than that of Aaron's house.

2. The mother brought her offering, *v.* 24. When she had presented that son of hers unto the Lord who was to be the great sacrifice, she might have been excused from offering any other; but so *it is said in the law of the Lord*, that law which was yet in force, and therefore so it must be done, she must offer *a pair of turtle-doves, or two young pigeons*; had she been of ability, she must have brought a *lamb for a burnt-offering*, and a *dove for a sin-offering*; but, being poor, and not able to reach the price of a lamb, she brings *two doves*, one for a *burnt-offering and the other for a sin-offering* (see Lev. xii. 6, 8), to teach us in every address to God, and

particularly in those upon special occasions, both to give thanks to God for his mercies to us and to acknowledge with sorrow and shame our sins against him; in both we must give glory to him, nor do we ever want matter for both. Christ was not *conceived* and *born* in sin, as others are, so that there was not that occasion in his case which there is in others; yet, because he was made under the law, he complied with it. *Thus it became him to fulfil all righteousness.* Much more doth it become the best of men to join in confessions of sin; for *who can say, I have made my heart clean?*

SIMEON AND ANNA
(*vv.* 25–40)

Even when he humbles himself, still Christ has honour done him to balance the offence of it. Simeon and Anna now do him honour, by the inspiration of the Holy Ghost.

I. A very honourable testimony is borne to him by Simeon. Now observe here,

1. The account that is given us concerning this Simeon, or Simon.

(1) That he was *just* and *devout*, *just* towards men and *devout* towards God; these two must always go together, and each will befriend the other, but neither will atone for the defect of the other. (2) That he *waited for the consolation of Israel*, that is, for the coming of the Messiah, in whom alone the nation of Israel, that was now miserably harassed and oppressed, would find *consolation*. He was long a coming, and they who believed he would come continued *waiting*, *desiring* his coming, and *hoping* for it with

patience; I had almost said, with some degree of *impatience* waiting till it came. (3) The *Holy Ghost* was upon him, not only as a Spirit of holiness, but as a Spirit of prophecy; he was *filled with the Holy Ghost*, and enabled to speak things above himself. (4) He had a gracious promise made him, that before he died he should have a sight of the Messiah, *v.* 26.

2. The seasonable coming of Simeon into the temple, at the time when Christ was presented there, *v.* 27. Just then, when Joseph and Mary brought in the child, to be registered as it were in the church-book, among the first-born, Simeon came, by direction of *the Spirit*, into the temple.

3. The abundant satisfaction wherewith he welcomed this sight: *He took him up in his arms* (*v.* 28), he *embraced* him with the greatest affection imaginable, laid him in his bosom, as near his heart as he could, which was as full of joy as it could hold.

4. The solemn declaration he made hereupon: *He blessed God*, and said, *Lord, now let thou thy servant depart in peace*, *vv.* 29–32.

(1) He has a pleasant prospect *concerning himself*, and (which is a great attainment) is got quite above the love of life and fear of death; nay, he is arrived at a holy contempt of life, and desire of death: "*Lord, now let thou thy servant depart*, for mine eyes have seen the salvation I was promised a sight of before I died." Here is, [1] An acknowledgment that God had been *as good as his word*; there has not failed one tittle of his good promises, as Solomon owns,

1 Kings viii. 56. Note, Never any that hoped in God's word were made ashamed of their hope. [2] A thanksgiving for it. He *blessed God* that he saw that salvation in his arms which many prophets and kings desired to see, and might not. [3] A confession of his faith, that this child in his arms was the *Saviour*, the *Salvation* itself; *thy salvation*, the salvation of thine appointing, the salvation *which thou hast prepared* with a great deal of contrivance. And, while it has been thus long *in the coming*, it hath still been *in the preparing*. [4] It is a farewell to this world: "*Now let thy servant depart*; now mine eyes have been blessed with this sight, let them be closed, and see no more in this world." The eye is not satisfied with seeing (Eccl. i. 8), till it hath *seen Christ*, and then it is.

(2) He has a pleasant prospect concerning the world, and concerning the church. This salvation shall be,

[1] A blessing to the world. It is *prepared before the face of all people*, not to be hid in a corner, but to be made known; to be a *light to lighten the Gentiles* that now sit in darkness: they shall have the knowledge of him, and of God, and another world through him. This has reference to Isa. xlix. 6, *I will give thee for a light to the Gentiles*; for Christ came to be the light of the world, not a candle in the Jewish candlestick, but the *Sun of righteousness*.

[2] A blessing to the church: *the glory of thy people Israel*. It was an honour to the Jewish nation that the Messiah sprang out of one of

their tribes, and was born, and lived, and died, among them. And of those who were Israelites indeed, of the spiritual Israel, he was indeed *the glory*, and will be so to eternity, Isa. lx. 19.

5. The prediction concerning this child, which he delivered, with his blessing, to Joseph and Mary. They *marvelled at those things* which were still more and more fully and plainly spoken concerning this child, *v.* 33. And because they were affected with, and had their faith strengthened by, that which was said to them, here is more said to them.

(1) Simeon shows them what reason they had to *rejoice*; for he *blessed them* (*v.* 34), he pronounced them blessed who had the honour to be related to this child, and were entrusted with the bringing him up. He *prayed* for them, that God would *bless* them, and would have others do so too.

(2) He shows them likewise what reason they had to *rejoice with trembling*, according to the advice given of old, with reference to the Messiah's kingdom, Ps. ii. 11. Lest Joseph, and Mary especially, should be *lifted up* with the abundance of the revelations, here is a *thorn in the flesh* for them, an allay to their joy; and it is what we sometimes need.

[1] It is true, Christ shall be a blessing to Israel; but there are those in Israel whom he is *set for the fall off*, whose corruptions will be provoked, who will be prejudiced and enraged against him, and offended, and whose sin and ruin will be aggravated by the revelation of Jesus Christ. Men will be judged of by the thoughts of

their hearts, their thoughts concerning Christ; are they for *him*, or are they for his *adversaries*? The *word of God* is a discerner of the *thoughts* and *intents of the heart*, and by it we are discovered to ourselves, and shall be judged hereafter.

[2] It is true, Christ shall be a comfort to his mother; but be not thou too proud of it, for *a sword shall pass through thine own soul also*. He shall be a suffering Jesus; and, *First*, "Thou *shalt suffer with him*, by sympathy, more than any other of his friends, because of the nearness of thy relation, and strength of affection, to him." When he was abused, it was *a sword in her bones*. When she stood by his cross, and saw him dying, we may well think her inward grief was such that it might truly be said, *A sword pierced through her soul*, it cut her to the heart. *Secondly*, Thou shalt *suffer for him*. Many understand it as a prediction of her martyrdom; and some of the ancients say that it had its accomplishment in that.

II. He is taken notice of by one *Anna*, or *Ann*, a *prophetess*, that one of each sex might bear witness to him in whom both *men* and *women* are invited to believe, that they may be saved. Observe,

1. The account here given of this Anna, who she was. She was, (1) *A prophetess*; the Spirit of prophecy now began to revive, which had ceased in Israel above three hundred years. (2) She was *the daughter of Phanuel*; her father's name (says Grotius) is mentioned, to put us in mind of Jacob's *Phanuel*, or *Penuel* (Gen. xxxii 30), that now the mystery of

that should be unfolded, when in Christ we should as it were see God face to face, and our lives be preserved; and her name signifies *gracious*. (3) She was of *the tribe of Asher*, which was in Galilee; this, some think, is taken notice of to refute those who said, *Out of Galilee ariseth no prophet*, when no sooner did prophecy revive but it appeared from Galilee. (4) She was of *a great age*, a widow of about eighty-four years. (5) She was a constant resident *in* or at least attendant *on* the temple. Some think she had lodgings in the courts of the temple, either in an alms-house, being maintained by the temple charities; or, as a prophetess, she lodged there, as in a proper place to be consulted and advised with by those that desired to know the mind of God; others think her not *departing from the temple* means no more, than that she was constantly there at the time of divine service: when any good work was to be done, she was ready to join in it.

2. The testimony she bore to our Lord Jesus (*v*. 38): *She came in at that instant* when the child was presented, and Simeon discoursed concerning him; she, who was so *constant* to the temple, could not miss the opportunity.

Now, (1) She *gave thanks likewise to the Lord*, just as Simeon, perhaps like him, wishing now to depart in peace.

(2) She, as a prophetess, instructed others concerning him: She *spoke of him to all them* that believed the Messiah would come, and with him *looked for redemption in Jerusalem*. Redemption was the

thing wanted, waited for, and wished for; redemption *in Jerusalem*, for thence the *word of the Lord was to go forth*, Isa. ii. 3.

Lastly, Here is a short account of the infancy and childhood of our Lord Jesus.

1. *Where* he spent it, *v*. 39. When the ceremony of presenting the child, and purifying the mother, was all over, they *returned into Galilee*.

2. *How* he spent it, *v*. 40. In all things *it behoved him to be made like unto his brethren*, and therefore he passed through infancy and childhood as other children did, yet without sin; nay, with manifest indications of a divine nature in him. As other children, he *grew* in stature of body, and the improvement of understanding in his human soul, that his *natural* body might be a figure of his *mystical* body, which, though animated by a perfect spirit, yet *maketh increase of itself* till it comes to the *perfect man*, Eph. iv. 13, 16. But, (1) Whereas other children are weak in understanding and resolution, he was *strong in spirit*. By the Spirit of God his human soul was endued with extraordinary vigour, and all his faculties performed their offices in an extraordinary manner. He reasoned strongly, and his judgment was penetrating. (2) Whereas other children have *foolishness bound in their hearts*, which appears in what they say or do, he was *filled with wisdom*, not by any advantages of instruction and education, but by the operation of the Holy Ghost; every thing he said and did was wisely said, and wisely done, above his years. (3) Whereas other

children show that the corruption of nature is in them, and *the tares of sin* grow up with the *wheat of reason*, he made it appear that nothing but *the grace of God was upon him* (the wheat sprang up without tares), and that, whereas other children are by nature children of wrath, he was *greatly beloved*, and high in the favour of God; and God loved him, and cherished him, and took a particular care of him.

THE BOY CHRIST
(vv. 41–52)

We have here the only passage of story recorded concerning our blessed Saviour, from his infancy to the day of his showing to Israel at twenty-nine years old, and therefore we are concerned to make much of this, for it is in vain to wish we had more. Here is,

I. Christ's *going up with his parents* to Jerusalem, at the feast of the passover, *vv.* 41, 42. 1. It was their constant practice to attend there, according to the law, though it was a long journey, and they were poor, and perhaps not well able, without straitening themselves, to bear the expenses of it. 2. The child Jesus, at *twelve years old*, went up with them. The Jewish doctors say that at twelve years old children must begin to fast from time to time, that they may learn to fast on the day of atonement; and that at thirteen years old a child begins to be *a son of the commandment*, that is, obliged to the duties of adult church-membership, having been from his infancy, by virtue of his circumcision, *a son of the covenant*.

II. Christ's *tarrying behind his parents at Jerusalem*, unknown to them, in which he designed to give an early specimen of what he was reserved for.

1. His parents did not return till they had *fulfilled the days*; they had stayed there all the seven days at the feast, though it was not absolutely necessary that they should stay longer than the two first days, after which many went home.

2. The child *tarried behind in Jerusalem*, not because he was loth to go home, or shy of his parents' company, but because he had business to do there, and would let his parents know that he had a *Father in heaven*, whom he was to be *observant* of more than of *them*; and respect to *him* must not be construed disrespect *to them*.

3. His parents went the *first day's journey* without any suspicion that he was left behind, for they *supposed him to have been in the company*, *v.* 44. On these occasions, the crowd was very great, especially the first day's journey, and the roads full of people; and they concluded that he came along with some of their neighbours, and they *sought him among their kindred and acquaintance*, that were upon the road, going down.

4. When they found him not at their quarters at night, they *turned back again*, next morning, *to Jerusalem, seeking him*.

5. The *third day* they found him *in the temple*, in some of the apartments belonging to the temple, where the doctors of the law kept, not their courts, but their conferences rather, or their schools for

disputation; and there they found him *sitting in the midst of them* (v. 46), not standing as a *catechumen* to be examined or instructed by them, for he had discovered such measures of knowledge and wisdom that they admitted him to sit among them as a fellow or member of their society. This is an instance, not only that he was *filled with wisdom* (v. 40), but that he had both a desire to increase it and a readiness to communicate it; and herein he is an example to children and young people, who should learn of Christ to delight in the company of those they may get good by, and choose to *sit in the midst of* the doctors rather than in the midst of the players. Let them begin at *twelve years old*, and sooner, to enquire after knowledge, and to associate with those that are able to instruct them; it is a hopeful and promising presage in youth to be desirous of instruction. Many a youth at Christ's age now would have been playing with the *children in the temple*, but he was sitting with the *doctors in the temple*. (1) He *heard* them. Those that would *learn* must be *swift to hear*. (2) He *asked them questions*; whether, as a teacher (he had authority so to ask) or as a learner (he had humility so to ask) I know not, or whether as an associate, or joint-searcher after truth, which must be found out by mutual amicable disquisitions. (3) He returned *answers* to them, which were very surprising and satisfactory, v. 47. And his wisdom and *understanding* appeared as much in the questions he asked as in the answers he gave, so that all who heard him *were astonished*:

they never heard one so young, nor indeed any of their greatest doctors, talk sense at the rate that he did; like David, he had *more understanding than all his teachers*, yea, *than the ancients*, Ps. cxix. 99, 100.

6. His mother talked with him privately about it. When the company broke up, she took him aside, and examined him about it with a deal of tenderness and affection, v. 48. Joseph and Mary were both *amazed* to find him there, and to find that he had so much respect showed him as to be admitted to *sit among the doctors*, and to be taken notice of. His father knew he had only the name of a father, and therefore said nothing. But, (1) His mother told him how ill they took it: "*Son, why hast thou thus dealt with us?* Why didst thou put us into such a fright?" They were ready to say, as Jacob of Joseph, "*A wild beast has devoured him*; or, He is fallen into the hands of some more cruel enemy, who has at length found out that he was the young child whose life Herod had sought some years ago." A thousand imaginations, we may suppose, they had concerning him, each more frightful than another. "Now, why hast thou given us occasion for these fears? *Thy father and I have sought thee, sorrowing*; not only troubled that we lost thee, but vexed at ourselves that we did not take more care of thee, to bring thee along with us." (2) He gently reproved their inordinate solicitude about him (v. 49): "*How is it that you sought me?* You might have depended upon it, I would have followed you home when I had

done the business I had to do here. I could not be lost in Jerusalem. Wist ye not that I *ought to be in my Father's house*?" so some read it; "where else should the Son be, who *abideth in the house for ever*? I ought to be," [1] "*Under my Father's care* and protection; and therefore you should have cast the care of me upon him, and not have burdened yourselves with it." Christ is a shaft hid in his Father's quiver, Isa. xlix. 2. He takes care of his church likewise, and therefore let us never despair of its safety. [2] "*At my Father's work*" (so we take it): "I must be *about my Father's business*, and therefore could not go home as soon as you might. *Wist ye not?* Have you not already perceived that concerning me, that I have devoted myself to the service of religion, and therefore must employ myself in the affairs of it?"

Lastly, Here is their return to Nazareth. This glimpse of his glory was to be short. It was now over, and he did not urge his parents either to come and settle at Jerusalem or to settle him there (though that was the place of improvement and preferment, and where he might have the best opportunities of showing his wisdom), but very willingly retired into his obscurity at Nazareth, where for many years he was, as it were, buried alive. Doubtless, he came up to Jerusalem, to worship at the feasts, three times a year, but whether he ever went again into the temple, to dispute with the doctors there, we are not told; it is not improbable but he might. But here we are told,

1. That he was *subject to his parents*. Though once, to show that he was *more than a man*, he withdrew himself from his parents, to attend his heavenly Father's business, yet he did not, as yet, make that his constant practice, nor for many years after, but was *subject to them*, observed their orders, and went and came as they directed, and, as it should seem, worked with his father at the trade of a carpenter.

2. That his mother, though she did not perfectly understand her son's sayings, yet *kept them in her heart*, expecting that hereafter they would be explained to her, and she should fully understand them, and know how to make use of them.

3. That he improved, and came on, to admiration (*v.* 52): *He increased in wisdom and stature*. In the perfections of his divine nature there could be no increase; but this is meant of his human nature, his body increased in *stature* and bulk, he grew in the growing age; and his soul increased *in wisdom*, and in all the endowments of a human soul. And he increased in *favour with God and man*, that is, in all those graces that rendered him acceptable to God and man.

CHAPTER THREE

JOHN'S MINISTRY (*vv.* 1–14)

John's baptism introducing a new dispensation, it was requisite that we should have a particular account of it. Glorious things were said of John, what a distinguished favourite of Heaven he should be, and what a great blessing to this earth (*ch.* i. 15, 17); but we lost him in

369

the deserts, and there he remains until *the day of his showing unto Israel*, ch. i. 80. And now at last that day dawns, and a welcome day it was to them that waited for it more than they that waited for the morning. Observe here,

I. The date of the beginning of John's baptism, when it was that he appeared; this is here taken notice of, which was not by the other evangelists, that the truth of the thing might be confirmed by the exact fixing of the time. And it is dated,

1. By the government of the heathen, which the Jews were under, to show that they were a conquered people, and therefore it was time for the Messiah to come to set up a spiritual kingdom, and an eternal one, upon the ruins of all the temporal dignity and dominion of David and Judah.

(1) It is dated by the reign of the Roman emperor; it was in the fifteenth year of Tiberius Cæsar, the third of the twelve Cæsars, a very bad man, given to covetousness, drunkenness, and cruelty.

(2) It is dated by the governments of the viceroys that ruled in the several parts of the Holy Land under the Roman emperor, which was another badge of their servitude, for they were all foreigners.

2. By the government of the Jews among themselves, to show that they were a corrupt people, and that therefore it was time that the Messiah should come, to reform them, *v.* 2. Annas and Caiaphas were the high priests. God had appointed that there should be but one high priest at a time, but here were two, to serve some ill turn or

other: one served one year and the other the other year; so some.

II. The origin and tendency of John's baptism.

1. The origin of it was *from heaven*: *The word of God came unto John*, *v.* 2. He received full commission and full instructions from God to do what he did.

2. The scope and design of it were to bring all the people of his country off from their sins and home to their God, *v.* 3. *He came* out of the wilderness *into all the country*, with some marks of distinction, *preaching* a new *baptism*; not a sect, or party, but a *profession*, or distinguishing badge. The sign, or ceremony, was such as was ordinarily used among the Jews, *washing with water*, by which proselytes were sometimes admitted, or disciples to some great master; but the meaning of it was, *repentance for the remission of sins*: that is, all that submitted to his baptism,

(1) Were thereby obliged to *repent of their sins*, to be *sorry* for what they had done amiss, and to *do so no more*.

(2) They were thereby assured of the pardon of their sins, upon their repentance.

III. The fulfilling of the scriptures in the ministry of John. The other evangelists had referred us to the same text that is here referred to, that of Esaias, *ch.* xl. 3.

IV. The general warnings and exhortations which he gave to those who submitted to his baptism, *vv.* 7–9. In Matthew he is said to have preached these same things to *many of the Pharisees and Sadducees*, that *came to his baptism*

(Matt. iii. 7–10); but here he is said to have spoken them *to the multitude, that came forth to be baptized of him, v.* 7. This was the purport of his preaching to all that came to him, and he did not alter it in compliment to the Pharisees and Sadducees, when they came, but dealt as plainly with them as with any other of his hearers. And as he did not flatter the *great,* so neither did he compliment the *many,* or make his court to them, but gave the same reproofs of sin and warnings of wrath to the *multitude* that he did to the Sadducees and Pharisees; for, if they had not the same faults, they had others as bad.

V. The particular instructions he gave to several sorts of persons, that enquired of him concerning their duty: the *people,* the *publicans,* and the *soldiers.* Some of the Pharisees and Sadducees came to his baptism; but we do not find them asking, *What shall we do?* They thought they knew what they had to do as well as he could tell them, or were determined to do what they pleased, whatever he told them. But the *people,* the *publicans,* and the *soldiers,* who knew that they had done amiss, and that they ought to do better, and were conscious to themselves of great ignorance and unacquaintedness with the divine law, were particularly inquisitive: *What shall we do?* Now John gives answer to each, according to their place and station.

(1) He tells the *people* their duty, and that is to be charitable (*v.* 11): *He that has two coats,* and, consequently, one to spare, let him *give,* or *lend* at least, *to him that has none,* to keep him warm. Perhaps

he saw among his hearers some that were overloaded with clothes, while others were ready to perish in rags, and he puts those who had superfluities upon contributing to the relief of those that had not necessaries. The gospel requires *mercy,* and not sacrifice; and the design of it is to engage us to do all the good we can. *Food and raiment* are the two supports of life; he that hath *meat* to spare, let him give to him that is destitute of *daily food,* as well as he that hath clothes to spare: what we have we are but stewards of, and must use it, accordingly, as our Master directs.

(2) He tells the *publicans* their duty, the collectors of the emperor's revenue (*v.* 13): *Exact no more than that which is appointed you.* They must do justice between the government and the merchant, and not oppress the people in levying the taxes, nor any way make them heavier or more burdensome than the law had made them. They must not think that because it was their office to take care that the people did not defraud the prince they might therefore, by the power they had, bear hard upon the people; as those that have ever so little a branch of power are apt to abuse it: "No, keep to your *book of rates,* and reckon it enough that you collect for Cæsar the things that are Cæsar's, and do not enrich yourselves by taking more." The public revenues must be applied to the public service, and not to gratify the avarice of private persons. Observe, He does not direct the publicans to quit their places, and to go no more to the receipt of custom; the employment

is in itself lawful and necessary, but let them be just and honest in it.

(3) He tells the *soldiers* their duty, *v.* 14. Some think that these soldiers were of the Jewish nation and religion: others think that they were Romans; for it was not likely either that the Jews would serve the Romans or that the Romans would trust the Jews in their garrisons in their own nation; and then it is an early instance of Gentiles embracing the gospel and submitting to it. Military men seldom seem inclined to religion; yet these submitted even to the Baptist's strict profession, and desired to receive the *word of command* from him: *What must we do?* Those who more than other men have their lives in their hands, and are in deaths often, are concerned to enquire what they shall do that they may be *found in peace*. In answer to this enquiry, John does not bid them lay down their arms, and desert the service, but cautions them against the sins that soldiers were commonly guilty of; for this is fruit meet for repentance, to *keep ourselves from our iniquity*. [1] They must not be injurious to *the people* among whom they were quartered, and over whom indeed they were set: "*Do violence to no man*. Your business is to keep the peace, and prevent men's doing violence to one another; but do not you *do violence* to any. *Shake no man*" (so the word signifies); "do not put people into fear; for the sword of war, as well as that of justice, is to be a terror only to evil doers, but a protection to those that do well. Be not rude in your quarters; force not money from

people by frightening them. Shed not the blood of war in peace; offer no incivility either to man or woman, nor have any hand in the barbarous devastations that armies sometimes make." Nor must they *accuse any falsely* to the government, thereby to make themselves formidable, and get bribes. [2] They must not be injurious to their *fellow-soldiers*; for some think that caution, not to *accuse falsely*, has special reference to them: "Be not forward to complain one of another to your superior officers, that you may be revenged on those whom you have a pique against, or undermine those above you, and get into their places." *Do not oppress any*; so some think the word here signifies, as used by the LXX. in several passages of the Old Testament. [3] They must not be given to mutiny, or contend with their generals about their pay: "*Be content with your wages*. While you have what you agreed for, do not murmur that it is not more." It is discontent with what they have that makes men oppressive and injurious; they that never think they have enough themselves will not scruple at any the most irregular practices to make it more, by defrauding others.

JOHN'S BAPTISM (*vv.* 15–20)

We are now drawing near to the appearance of our Lord Jesus publicly; the Sun will not be long after the morning-star. We are here told,

I. How the people took occasion, from the ministry and baptism of John, to think of the Messiah, and to think of him as at the door, as now come. Thus the way of the Lord was *prepared*, and people were prepared to bid Christ welcome. Now when they observed what an excellent doctrine John Baptist preached, what a divine power went along with it, and what a tendency it had to reform the world, 1. They began presently to consider that now was the time for the Messiah to appear. 2. Their next thought was, "Is not this he that should come?" *All* thinking men *mused*, or reasoned, *in their hearts*, concerning John, *whether he were the Christ or not*.

II. How John disowned all pretensions to the honour of being himself the Messiah, but confirmed them in their expectations of him that really was the Messiah, *vv.* 16, 17. John's office, as a crier or herald, was to give notice that the *kingdom of God* and the King of that kingdom were *at hand*; and therefore, when he had told all manner of people severally what they must do ("You must do this, and you must do that"), he tells them one thing more which they must all do: they must expect the Messiah now shortly to appear. And this serves as an *answer* to their *musings* and debates concerning himself. Though he knew not their thoughts, yet, in declaring this, he *answered* them.

1. He declares that the utmost he could do was to *baptize* them *with water*. He had no access to *the Spirit*, nor could command *that* or work upon *that*; he could only exhort them to *repent*, and assure them of forgiveness, upon repentance; he could not work repent-

ance in them, nor confer remission on them.

2. He consigns them, and turns them over, as it were, to Jesus Christ, for whom he was sent to *prepare the way*, and to whom he was ready to transfer all the interest he had in the affections of the people, and would have them no longer to *debate* whether John was the Messiah or no, but to look for him that was really so.

(1) John owns the Messiah to have a greater *excellency* than he had, and that he was in all things preferable to him; he is one the *latchet of whose shoe* he does not think himself *worthy to loose*; he does not think himself worthy to be the meanest of his servants, to help him on and off with his shoes.

(2) He owns him to have a greater *energy* than he had: "He is *mightier than I*, and does that which I cannot do, both for the comfort of the faithful and for the terror of hypocrites and dissemblers."

The evangelist concludes his account of John's preaching with an *et cætera* (*v.* 18): *Many other things in his exhortation preached he unto the people*, which are not recorded.

III. How full a stop was put to John's preaching. When he was in the midst of his usefulness, going on thus successfully, he was imprisoned by the malice of Herod (*vv.* 19, 20): *Herod the tetrarch being reproved by him*, not only for living in incest with his brother Philip's wife, but for the many other *evils which Herod had done* (for those that are wicked in one instance are commonly so in many others), he could not *bear it*, but contracted an antipathy to him for his plain dealing, and *added* this wickedness to all the rest, which was indeed *above all*, that he *shut up John in prison*, put that burning and shining light under a bushel.

CHRIST'S PEDIGREE

The evangelist mentioned John's imprisonment before Christ's being baptized, though it was nearly a year after it, because he would finish the story of John's ministry, and then introduce that of Christ. Now here we have,

I. A short account of Christ's baptism, which had been more fully related by St. Matthew. Jesus came, to be baptized of John, and he was so, *vv.* 21, 22.

II. A long account of Christ's pedigree, which had been more briefly related by St. Matthew. Here is,

1. His age: *He now began to be about thirty years of age.* So old Joseph was when he stood before Pharaoh (Gen. xli. 46), David when he began to reign (2 Sam. v. 4), and at this age the priests were to enter upon the full execution of their office, Num. iv. 3.

2. His pedigree, *vv.* 23, &c. Matthew had given us somewhat of this. He goes no higher than Abraham, but Luke brings it as high as Adam. Matthew designed to show that Christ was the son of Abraham, in whom *all the families of the earth are blessed*, and that he was heir to the throne of David; and therefore he begins with Abraham, and brings the genealogy down to Jacob, who was the father of Joseph, an heir-male of the house of David: but Luke, de-

signing to show that Christ was the *seed of the woman*, that should break the serpent's head, traces his pedigree upward as high as Adam, and begins it with Eli, or Heli, who was the father, not of Joseph, but of the virgin Mary.

CHAPTER FOUR

THE TEMPTATION
(*vv.* 1–13)

We have already had this report in full in Matthew.

Christ gave the devil opportunity to say and do all he could against him; he let him try all his force, and yet defeated him.

He then quitted the field: He *departed from him.* He saw it was to no purpose to attack him; he had *nothing in him* for his fiery darts to fasten upon; he had no blind side, no weak or unguarded part in his wall, and therefore Satan gave up the cause. Note, If we resist the devil, he will flee from us.

Yet he continued his malice against him, and departed with a resolution to attack him again; he departed but *for a season*, or till the season when he was again to be let loose upon him, not as a *tempter*, to draw him to *sin*, and so to strike at *his head*, which was what he now aimed at and was wholly defeated in; but as a *persecutor*, to bring him to *suffer* by Judas and the other wicked instruments whom he employed, and so to *bruise his heel*, which it was told him (Gen. iii. 15) he should have to do, and would do, though it would be the breaking of his *own head*. He *departed now* till that season came which Christ calls the *power of darkness* (*ch.* xxii. 53), and when the prince of this world would again *come*, John xiv. 30.

CHRIST IN THE SYNAGOGUE
(*vv.* 14–30)

Observe,

I. What is here said in general of his preaching, and the entertainment it met with *in Galilee*, a remote part of the country, distant from Jerusalem; it was a part of Christ's humiliation that he began his ministry there.

But, 1. Thither he came *in the power of the Spirit*. The same Spirit that qualified him for the exercise of his prophetical office strongly inclined him to it. He was not to wait for a call from men, for he had light and life in himself. 2. There he *taught in their synagogues*, their places of public worship, where they met, not, as in the temple, for ceremonial services, but for the moral acts of devotion, to read, expound, and apply, the word, to pray and praise, and for church-discipline; these came to be more frequent since the captivity, when the ceremonial worship was near expiring. 3. This he did so as that he gained a great reputation. *A fame of him went through all that region* (*v.* 14), and it was a good fame; for (*v.* 15) he *was glorified of all*.

II. Of his preaching at Nazareth, the city where he was brought up; and the entertainment it met with there. And here we are told how he *preached* there, and how he was *persecuted*.

How he preached there. In that observe,

(1) The opportunity he had for it: *He came to Nazareth* when he had gained a reputation in other places, in hopes that thereby something at least of the contempt and prejudice with which his countrymen would look upon him might be worn off.

(2) The call he had to it. [1] He *stood up to read*. [2] The *book of the prophet Esaias* was *delivered to him*, either by the ruler of the synagogue or by the minister mentioned (*v.* 20), so that he was no intruder, but duly authorized *on this occasion*. The second lesson for *that* day being in the prophecy of Esaias, they gave him that volume to read in.

(3) The text he preached upon. Now the book being *delivered to him*, [1] He *opened* it. The books of the Old Testament were in a manner *shut up* till Christ opened them, Isa. xxix. 11. [2] Now his text was taken out of Isa. lxi. 1, 2, which is here quoted at large, *vv.* 18, 19. There was a providence in it that that portion of scripture should be read that day, which speaks so very plainly of the Messiah, that they might be left inexcusable who *knew him not*, though they heard *the voices of the prophets* read *every sabbath day*, which bore witness of him, Acts xiii. 27. This text gives a full account of Christ's undertaking, and the work he came into the world to do.

He was qualified and commissioned,

1. To be a great *prophet*. He was *anointed to preach*; that is three times mentioned here, for that was the work he was now entering upon. Observe, (1) To *whom* he was to preach: to the *poor*; to those that were *poor in the world*. (2) *What* he

375

was to *preach*. In general, he must preach *the gospel*. Not only to preach to them, but to make that preaching effectual; to bring it, not only to their ears, but to their hearts, and deliver them into the mould of it. Three things he is to preach: —

[1] *Deliverance to the captives.* The gospel is a proclamation of liberty, like that to Israel in Egypt and in Babylon.

[2] *Recovering of sight to the blind.* He came not only by the word of his gospel to bring *light* to them that sat *in the dark*, but by the power of his grace to give sight to them that were *blind*.

[3] *The acceptable year of the Lord*, v. 19. He came to let the world know that the God whom they had offended was willing to be reconciled to them, and to *accept* of them upon new terms; that there was yet a way of making their services acceptable to him; that there is now a time of *good will toward men*.

2. Christ came to be a great *Physician*; for he was sent to *heal the broken-hearted*, to comfort and cure afflicted consciences, to give peace to those that were troubled and humbled for sins, and under a dread of God's wrath against them for them, and to bring them to rest who were weary and heavy-laden, under the burden of guilt and corruption.

3. To be a great *Redeemer*. He not only proclaims liberty to the captives. He came in God's name to discharge poor sinners that were debtors and prisoners to divine justice.

(4) Here is Christ's *application* of

this text to himself (v. 21): "*This day is this scripture fulfilled in your ears.* This, which Isaiah wrote by way of prophecy, I have now read to you by way of history." It now began to be fulfilled in Christ's entrance upon his public ministry; *now*, in the report they heard of his preaching and miracles in other places; *now*, in his preaching to them in their own synagogue. It is most probable that Christ went on, and showed particularly how this scripture was fulfilled in the doctrine he preached concerning *the kingdom of heaven at hand*; that that was preaching liberty, and sight, and healing, and all the blessings of *the acceptable year of the Lord*. Many other gracious words proceeded out of his mouth, which these were but the *beginning* of: for Christ often preached long sermons, which we have but a short account of. This was enough to introduce a great deal: *This day is this scripture fulfilled.*

(5) Here is the *attention* and *admiration* of the auditors.

[1] Their *attention* (v. 20): *The eyes of all them that were in the synagogue* (and, probably, there were a great many) *were fastened on him.*

[2] Their *admiration* (v. 22): *They all bore him witness* that he spoke admirably well, and to the purpose. They all commended him, and *wondered at the gracious words that proceeded out of his mouth*; and yet, as appears by what follows, they did not *believe in him*.

(6) Christ's anticipating an objection which he knew to be in the minds of many of his hearers. Observe,

[1] What the objection was (*v.* 23): "*You will surely say to me, Physician, heal thyself.*"

[2] How he answers this objection against the course he took.

First, By a plain and positive reason why he would not make Nazareth his headquarters (*v.* 24), because it generally holds true *that no prophet is accepted in his own country*, at least not so well, nor with such probability of doing good, as in some other country; experience seals this. For this reason, Christ declined working miracles, or doing any thing extraordinary, at Nazareth, because of the rooted prejudices they had against him there.

Secondly, By pertinent examples of two of the most famous prophets of the Old Testament, who chose to dispense their favours among foreigners rather than among their own countrymen, and that, no doubt, by divine direction.

How he was *persecuted* at Nazareth.

(1) That which provoked them was his taking notice of the favour which God by Elijah and Elisha showed to the Gentiles: *When they heard these things, they were filled with wrath* (*v.* 28), they were *all so*; a great change since *v.* 22, when they *wondered at the gracious words that proceeded out of his mouth*; thus uncertain are the opinions and affections of the multitude, and so very fickle.

(2) They were provoked to that degree that they made an attempt upon his life. This was a severe trial, now at his setting out, but a specimen of the usage he met with

when he *came to his own*, and they *received him not*.

(3) Yet he escaped, because his hour was not yet come: He *passed through the midst of them*, unhurt. Either he blinded their eyes, as God did those of the Sodomites and Syrians, or he bound their hands, or filled them with confusion, so that they could not do what they designed; for his work was not done, it was but just begun; his hour was not yet come, when it was come, he freely surrendered himself.

A DEMON EXPELLED
(*vv.* 31–44)

When Christ was expelled Nazareth, he came to Capernaum, another city of Galilee. The account we have in these verses of his preaching and miracles there we had before, Mark i. 21, &c.

CHAPTER FIVE
THE DRAUGHT OF FISHES
(*vv.* 1–11)

This passage of story fell, in order of time, before the two miracles we had in the close of the foregoing chapter, and is the same with that which was more briefly related by Matthew and Mark, of Christ's calling Peter and Andrew to be *fishers of men*, Matt. iv. 18, and Mark i. 16. They had not related this miraculous draught of fishes at that time, having only in view the calling of his disciples; but Luke gives us that story as one of the many signs which Jesus did in the presence of his disciples, which *had not been written* in the foregoing books, John xx. 30, 31. Observe here,

I. What vast *crowds* attended Christ's preaching: *The people pressed upon him to hear the word of God* (v. 1), insomuch that no house would contain them, but he was forced to draw them out to the *strand*. Christ was a popular preacher; and though he was able, at *twelve*, to *dispute* with the *doctors*, yet he chose, at *thirty*, to preach to the capacity of the *vulgar*. See how the people relished *good preaching*, though under all external disadvantages: they pressed to *hear the word of God*; they could perceive it to be the *word of God*, by the divine power and evidence that went along with it, and therefore they coveted to hear it.

II. What poor *conveniences* Christ had for preaching: *He stood by the lake of Gennessareth* (v. 1), upon a level with the crowd, so that they could neither see him nor hear him. So Christ *entered* into that *ship* that belonged to Simon, and begged of him that he would lend it him for a pulpit. There he *sat down*, and *taught the people* the good knowledge of the Lord.

III. What a particular acquaintance Christ, hereupon, fell into with these fishermen. They had had some conversation with him before, which began at John's baptism (John i. 40, 41); they were with him at *Cana of Galilee* (John ii. 2), and in Judea (John iv. 3); but as yet they were not called to attend him constantly, and therefore here we have them at their calling, and now it was that they were called into a more intimate fellowship with Christ.

1. When Christ had done preaching, he ordered Peter to apply himself to the business of his calling again: *Launch out into the deep, and let down your nets*, v. 4.

2. Peter having *attended* upon Christ in his *preaching*, Christ will *accompany* him in his *fishing*.

3. Christ ordered Peter and his ship's crew to *cast their nets into the sea*, which they did, in obedience to him, though they had been hard at it all night, and had *caught nothing*, vv. 4, 5. We may observe here

(1) How melancholy their business had now been: "*Master, we have toiled all the night*, when we should have been asleep in our beds, *and have taken nothing*, but have had our labour for our pains."

(2) How ready their obedience was to the command of Christ: *Nevertheless, at thy word, I will let down the net*. [1] Though **they** had *toiled all night*, yet, if Christ bid them, they will renew their toil, for they know that they who *wait on him shall renew their strength*, as work is renewed upon their hands; for every fresh service they shall have a fresh supply of *grace sufficient*. [2] Though they have *taken nothing*, yet, if Christ bid them *let down for a draught*, they will hope to take *something*. Note, We must not abruptly quit the callings wherein we are called because we have not the success in them we promised ourselves.

4. The draught of fish they caught was so much beyond what was ever known that it amounted to a miracle (v. 6): They *enclosed a great multitude of fishes*, so that *their net broke*, and yet, which is strange, they did not lose their draught.

378

Now by this vast draught of fishes, (1) Christ intended to show his *dominion* in the *seas* as well as on the *dry land*, over its *wealth* as over its *waves*. (2) He intended hereby to confirm the doctrine he had just now preached out of Peter's ship. (3) He intended hereby to repay Peter for the loan of his boat; for Christ's gospel will be sure to make amends, rich amends, for its kind entertainment. (4) He intended hereby to give a specimen, to those who were to be his ambassadors to the world, of the success of their embassy, that though they might for a time, and in one particular place, *toil* and *catch nothing*, yet they should be instrumental to bring in many to Christ, and enclose many in the gospel net.

5. The impression which this miraculous draught of fishes made upon Peter was very remarkable.

(1) All *concerned* were *astonished*, and the more *astonished* for their being *concerned*. All the boat's crew were *astonished at the draught of fishes which they had taken* (v. 9); *and so were also James and John, who were partners with Simon* (v. 10), and who, for aught that appears, were not so well acquainted with Christ, before this, as Peter and Andrew were. Now they were the more *affected* with it, [1] Because they *understood* it better than others did. [2] Because they were most *interested* in it, and *benefited* by it. Peter and his part-owners were gainers by this great draught of fishes; it was a rich booty for them and therefore it transported them, and their *joy* was a *helper* to their *faith*.

(2) Peter, above all the rest, was astonished to such a degree that he *fell down at Jesus's knees*, as he sat in the stern of his boat, and said, as one in an ecstasy or transport, that knew not where he was or what he said, *Depart from me, for I am a sinful man, O Lord*, v. 8. Not that he feared the weight of the fish would sink him because he was a sinful man, but that he thought himself unworthy of the favour of Christ's presence in his boat, and worthy that it should be to him a matter rather of terror than of comfort. [1] His acknowledgment was very just, and what it becomes us all to make: *I am a sinful man, O Lord*. [2] His inference from it was what *might have been* just, though really it was not so. If I be a *sinful man*, as indeed I am, I ought to say, "*Come to me, O Lord*, or let me come to thee, or I am undone, *for ever undone*." But, considering what reason *sinful men* have to tremble before the holy Lord God and to dread his wrath, Peter may well be excused, if, in a sense of his own sinfulness and vileness, he cried out on a sudden, *Depart from me*.

6. The occasion which Christ took from this to intimate to Peter (v. 10), and soon after to James and John (Matt. iv. 21), his purpose to make them his apostles, and instruments of planting his religion in the world. When by Peter's preaching *three thousand souls* were, *in one day*, added to the church, then the type of this great draught of fishes was abundantly answered.

Lastly, The fishermen's farewell to their calling, in order to their constant attendance on Christ (*v.* 11): *When they had brought their ships to land*, instead of going to seek for a market for their fish, that they might make the best hand they could of this miracle, they *forsook all and followed him*, being more solicitous to serve the interests of Christ than to advance any secular interests of their own. It is observable that they *left all to follow Christ*, when their calling prospered in their hands more than ever it had done and they had had uncommon success in it. When *riches increase*, and we are therefore most in temptation to *set our hearts* upon them, then to quit them for the service of Christ, this is *thank-worthy*.

TWO HEALED (*vv.* 12–26)

Here is the cleansing of a leper, *vv.* 12–14. This narrative we had both in Matthew and Mark. It is here said to have been *in a certain city* (*v.* 12); it was in Capernaum, but the evangelist would not name it, perhaps because it was a reflection upon the government of the city that a leper was suffered to be *in it*.

Here is also, I. A general account of Christ's preaching and miracles, *v.* 17. 1. He was *teaching on a certain day*, not in the *synagogue*, but in a *private house*. 2. There he *taught*, he *healed* (as before, *v.* 15): *And the power of the Lord was to heal them.* It was *mighty* to heal them; it was *exerted* and *put forth* to heal them, to heal those whom he *taught* (we may understand it so), to heal their souls, to cure them of their spiritual diseases, and to give them a new life, a new nature.

II. A particular account of the cure of the man *sick of the palsy*, which was related much as it is here by both the foregoing evangelists.

NEW WINE, OLD BOTTLES
(*vv.* 27–39)

All this, except the last verse, we had before in Matthew and Mark; it is not the story of any *miracle in nature* wrought by our Lord Jesus, but it is an account of some of the *wonders of his grace*, which, to those who understand things aright, are no less cogent proofs of Christ's being sent of God than the other.

Christ would train up his followers gradually to the discipline of his family; for no man, having *drank old wine*, will *of a sudden*, straightway, *desire new*, or relish it, but will say, *The old is better*, because he has been *used to it*, *v.* 39. The disciples will be tempted to think their old way of living better, till they are by degrees trained up to this way whereunto they are called. Or, turn it the other way: "Let them be *accustomed* awhile to religious exercises, and then they will *abound* in them as much as you do: but we must not be too hasty with them."

CHAPTER SIX
SABBATH HEALING (*vv.* 1–11)

These two passages of story we had both in Matthew and Mark, and they were there laid together (Matt. xii. 1; Mark ii. 23; iii. 1), because, though happening at some distance of time from each other, both were

380

designed to rectify the mistakes of the scribes and Pharisees concerning the sabbath day, on the *bodily rest* of which they laid greater stress and required greater strictness than the Law-giver intended.

APOSTLES CHOSEN (*vv.* 12–19)

In these verses, we have our Lord Jesus in *secret*, in *his family*, and in *public*; and in all three acting like himself.

I. In *secret* we have him *praying to God*, *v.* 12. This evangelist takes frequent notice of Christ's retirements, to give us an example of secret prayer, by which we must keep up our communion with God daily, and without which it is impossible that the soul should prosper.

II. In his *family* we have him nominating his immediate attendants, that should be the constant auditors of his doctrine and eye-witnesses of his miracles, that hereafter they might be sent forth as *apostles*, his *messengers* to the world, to preach his gospel to it, and plant his church in it, *v.* 13. The number of the apostles was *twelve*. Their names are here recorded; it is the *third time* that we have met with them, and in each of the *three* places the *order* of them differs, to teach both ministers and Christians not to be nice in precedency. He that in Mark was called *Thaddeus*, in Matthew *Lebbeus*, whose surname was *Thaddeus*, is here called *Judas the brother of James*, the same that wrote the epistle of Jude. Simon, who in Matthew and Mark was called the *Canaanite*, is here called *Simon*

Zelotes, perhaps for his great zeal in religion.

III. In *public* we have him *preaching* and *healing*, the two great works between which he divided his time, *v.* 17. He came down with the twelve from the mountain, and *stood in the plain*, ready to receive those that resorted to him; and there were presently gathered about him, not only the *company of his disciples*, who used to attend him, but also a great *multitude of people*, a mixed multitude *out of all Judea and Jerusalem*. 1. They *came to hear him*, and he *preached* to them. Those that have not good preaching near them had better travel far for it than be without it. 2. They came to be *cured* by him, and he *healed* them. Some were troubled *in body*, and some *in mind*; some had *diseases*, some had *devils*; but both the one and the other, upon their application to Christ, were *healed*, for he has power over *diseases* and *devils* (*vv.* 17, 18), over the effects and over the causes.

BLESSINGS AND WOES (*vv.* 20–26)

Here begins a practical discourse of Christ, which is continued to the end of the chapter, most of which is found in the *sermon upon the mount*, Matt. v. and vii. Some think that this was preached at some other time and place, and there are other instances of Christ's preaching the same things, or to the same purport, at different times; but it is probable that this is only the evangelist's abridgment of that sermon, and perhaps that in

Matthew too is but an abridgment; the beginning and the conclusion are much the same; and the story of the cure of the centurion's servant follows presently upon it, both there and here, but it is not material. In these verses, we have,

I. Blessings pronounced upon *suffering saints*, as *happy* people, though the world *pities them* (v. 20).

II. *Woes* denounced against *prospering sinners as miserable people*, though the world *envies them*. These we had not in Matthew. It should seem, the best exposition of *these woes*, compared with the foregoing *blessings*, is the parable of the *rich man* and Lazarus. Lazarus had the blessedness of those that are *poor*, and *hunger*, and *weep*, now, for in Abraham's bosom all the promises made to them who did so were *made good* to him; but the rich man had the *woes* that follow here, as he had the character of those on whom these woes are entailed.

1. Here is a *woe* to them that are *rich*, that is, that *trust in riches*, that have abundance of this world's wealth, and, instead of serving God with it, serve their lusts with it; woe to them, for *they have received their consolation*, that which they placed their happiness in, and were willing to take up with for a portion, v. 24. (1) It is the *folly* of carnal worldlings that they make the things of this world *their consolation*, which were intended only for their *convenience*. (2) It is their misery that they are *put off* with them as *their consolation*. Let them know it, to their terror, when they are parted from these things, there is an end of all their comfort,

a final end of it, and nothing remains to them but everlasting misery and torment.

2. Here is a *woe* to them that are *full* (v. 25), that are *fed to the full*, and have *more than heart could wish* (Ps. lxxiii. 7). They are *full of themselves*, without God and Christ. Woe to such, for *they shall hunger*, they shall shortly be *stripped* and *emptied* of all the things they are so proud of; and, when they shall have *left behind them* in the world all those things which are their fulness, they shall *carry away with them* such appetites and desires as the world they remove to will afford them no gratifications of; for all the delights of sense, which they are now so full of, will in hell be *denied*, and in heaven *superseded*.

3. Here is a *woe* to them that *laugh now*, that have always a *disposition to be merry*, and always something to *make merry with*. *Woe unto such*, for it is but *now*, for a little time, that they *laugh*; they shall *mourn and weep* shortly, shall *mourn and weep* eternally, in a world where there is nothing but *weeping and wailing*, endless, easeless, and remediless sorrow.

4. Here is a *woe* to them *whom all men speak well of*, that is, who make it their great and only care to gain the praise and applause of men, who value themselves upon that more than upon the favour of God and his acceptance (v. 26): "The false prophets indeed, that flattered your fathers in their wicked ways, that *prophesied smooth things* to them, were caressed and spoken well of; and, if you be in like manner cried up,

you will be justly suspected to deal deceitfully as they did."

MORE PRECEPTS (*vv.* 27–49)

Verses 27–36 agree with Matt. v. 38, to the end of that chapter: *I say unto you that hear* (*v.* 27), to all you that hear, and not to disciples only, for these are lessons of universal concern. *He that has an ear, let him hear*. Those that diligently hearken to Christ shall find he has something to say to them well worth their hearing.

The sayings of Christ in *vv.* 37–49 we had before in Matthew; some of them in *ch.* vii., others in other places. They were sayings that Christ often used; they needed only to be mentioned, it was easy to apply them. Grotius thinks that we need not be critical here in seeking for the coherence: they are golden sentences, like Solomon's proverbs or parables.

CHAPTER SEVEN

THE CENTURION'S SERVANT
(vv. 1–10)

Some difference there is between this story of the cure of the centurion's servant as it is related here and as we had it in Matt. viii. 5, &c. There it was said that the centurion came to Christ; here it is said that he sent to him first some of the *elders of the Jews* (*v.* 3), and afterwards some other *friends*, *v.* 6.

This miracle is here said to have been wrought by our Lord Jesus *when he had ended all his sayings in the audience of the people*, *v.* 1. What Christ said he said *publicly*; whoever would might come and hear him: *In secret have I said*

nothing, John xviii. 20. Now, to give an undeniable proof of the *authority* of his *preaching word*, he here gives an incontestable proof of the *power* and *efficacy* of his *healing word*.

THE WIDOW'S SON (*vv.* 11–18)

We have here the story of Christ's raising to life a widow's son at Nain, that was dead and in the carrying out to be buried, which Matthew and Mark had made no mention of; only, in the general, Matthew had recorded it, in Christ's answer to the disciples of John, that *the dead were raised* up, Matt. xi. 5. Observe,

I. Where, and when, this miracle was wrought. It was the *next day after* he had cured the centurion's servant, *v.* 11. Christ was doing good *every day*, and never had cause to complain that he had *lost a day*. It was done at the gate of a small city, or town, called *Nain*, not far from Capernaum, probably the same with a city called *Nais*, which Jerome speaks of.

II. Who were the witnesses of it. It is as well attested as can be, for it was done in the sight of two crowds that met in or near the gate of the city.

III. How it was wrought by our Lord Jesus.

1. The person raised to life was a *young man*, cut off by death in the beginning of his days. That he was really dead was universally agreed. There could be no collusion in the case; for Christ was *entering into the town*, and had not seen him till now that he met him upon the bier. He was *carried out* of the city; for the Jews' burying-places were without their cities, and at some

distance from them. This young man was the *only son of his mother*, and *she a widow*. She depended upon him to be the staff of her old age, but he proves a broken reed; every man at his best estate is so. *Much people of the city was with her*, *condoling* with her loss, to *comfort* her.

2. Christ showed both his *pity* and his *power* in raising him to life, that he might give a specimen of both, which shine so brightly in man's redemption.

(1) See how *tender* his *compassions* are towards the afflicted (*v.* 13): *When the Lord saw* the poor widow following her son to the grave, *he had compassion on her*. Christ said, *Weep not*; and he could give her a reason for it which no one else could: "Weep not for a *dead son*, for he shall presently become a *living one*." This was a reason peculiar to her case; yet there is a reason common to all that sleep in Jesus, which is of equal force against inordinate and excessive grief for their death— that they shall rise again, shall rise in glory; and therefore we must *not sorrow as those that have no hope*, 1 Thess. iv. 13.

(2) See how *triumphant* his *commands* are over even death itself (*v.* 14): *He came, and touched the bier*, or coffin, in or upon which the dead body lay; for to him it would be no pollution. Hereby he intimated to the bearers that they should not proceed; he had something to say to the dead young man. Hereupon *they that bore him stood still*, and probably let down the bier from their shoulders to the ground, and opened the coffin, if it

was closed up; and then with solemnity, as one that had authority, and to whom belonged the issues from death, he said, *Young man, I say unto thee, Arise*. The young man was *dead*, and could not arise by any power of his own (no more can those that are spiritually dead in trespasses and sins); yet it was no absurdity at all for Christ to bid him *arise*, when a power went along with that word to *put life* into him. Christ's dominion over death was evidenced by the immediate effect of his word (*v.* 15): *He that was dead sat up*, without any help. Another evidence of life was that he *began to speak*; for whenever Christ gives us spiritual life he *opens the lips* in prayer and praise. And, *lastly*, he would not oblige this young man, to whom he had given a new life, to go along with him as his disciple, to minister to him (though he owned him even his own self), much less as a trophy or show to get honour by him, but *delivered him to his mother*, to attend her as became a dutiful son; for Christ's miracles were miracles of mercy, and a great act of mercy this was to this widow.

IV. What influence it had upon the people (*v.* 16): *There came a fear on all*; it frightened them all, to see a dead man start up alive out of his coffin in the open street, at the command of a man; they were all struck with wonder at this miracle, and *glorified God*. The Lord and his goodness, as well as the Lord and his greatness, are to be feared. The inference they drew from it was, "*A great prophet is risen up among us*, the great prophet that we have been long looking for; doubtless, he is one divinely inspired who can thus breathe life into the dead, and in him *God hath visited his people*, to redeem them, as was expected," Luke i. 68. This would be *life from the dead* indeed to all them that waited for the consolation of Israel.

TRIBUTE TO JOHN (*vv.* 19–35)

All this discourse concerning John Baptist, occasioned by his sending to ask whether he was the Messiah or no, we had, much as it is here related, Matt. xi. 2–19.

AT SIMON'S HOUSE (*vv.* 36–50)

When and where this passage of story happened does not appear; this evangelist does not observe order of time in his narrative so much as the other evangelists do. Who this woman was that here testified so great an affection to Christ does not appear; it is commonly said to be Mary Magdalene, but I find no ground in scripture for it: she is described (*ch.* viii. 2 and Mark xvi. 9) to be one *out of whom Christ had cast seven devils*; but that is not mentioned here, and therefore it is probable that it was not she. Now observe here,

I. The civil entertainment which a Pharisee gave to Christ, and his gracious acceptance of that entertainment (*v.* 36): *One of the Pharisees desired him that he would eat with him*. It appears that this Pharisee did not believe in Christ, for he will not own him to be a *prophet* (*v.* 39), and yet our Lord Jesus accepted his invitation, *went into his house, and sat down to meat*, that they might see he took the same liberty with Pharisees that he

did with publicans, in hopes of *doing them good*.

II. The great respect which a poor penitent sinner showed him, when he was at meat in the Pharisee's house. It was a woman in the city *that was a sinner*, a Gentile a *harlot*, I doubt, known to be so, and infamous. She *knew that Jesus sat at meat in the Pharisee's house*, and, having been converted from her wicked course of life by his preaching, she came to acknowledge her obligations to him, having no opportunity of doing it in any other way than by *washing* his feet, and anointing them with some sweet ointment that she brought with her for that purpose. The way of sitting at table then was such that their feet were partly *behind them*. Now this woman did not look Christ in the face, but came *behind him*, and did that part of a *maid-servant*, whose office it was to *wash the feet* of the guests (1 Sam. xxv. 41) and to prepare the ointments.

Now in what this good woman did, we may observe,

1. Her *deep humiliation* for sin. She stood behind him *weeping*; her eyes had been the inlets and outlets of sin, and now she makes them fountains of tears.

2. Her *strong affection* for the Lord Jesus. This was what our Lord Jesus took special notice of, that she *loved much*, *vv.* 42, 47. She *washed his feet*, in token of her ready submission to the meanest office in which she might *do him honour*. Nay, she washed them with *her tears*, tears of joy; she was in a transport, to find herself so near her Saviour, whom her soul loved.

She *kissed his feet*. It was a kiss of adoration as well as affection. *She wiped them with her hair*, as one entirely devoted to his honour. She anointed his feet in token of her consent to God's design in anointing his head with the *oil of gladness*. Note, All true penitents have a dear love to the Lord Jesus.

III. The offence which the Pharisee took at Christ, for admitting the respect which this poor penitent paid him (*v.* 39): *He said within himself* (little thinking that Christ knew what he thought), *This man, if he were a prophet*, would then have so much *knowledge* as to perceive that *this woman is a sinner*, is a Gentile, is a woman of ill fame, and so much *sanctity* as *therefore* not to suffer her to come so near him; for can one of such a character approach a prophet, and his heart not rise at it?

IV. Christ's justification of the woman in what she did to him, and of himself in admitting it. Christ knew what the Pharisee spoke *within himself*, and made answer to it: *Simon, I have something to say unto thee*, *v.* 40. Though he was kindly entertained at his table, yet even there he reproved him for what he saw amiss in him, and would not *suffer sin upon him*. Now Christ, in his answer to the Pharisee, reasons thus:—It is true this woman has been a sinner: he knows it; but she is a *pardoned* sinner, which supposes her to be a *penitent* sinner. What she did to him was an expression of her *great love* to her Saviour, by whom her sins were forgiven. If she was pardoned, who had been *so great a sinner*, it might reasonably be expected that she

should love her Saviour more than others, and should give greater proofs of it than others; and if this was the fruit of her love, and flowing from a sense of the pardon of her sins, it became him to accept of it, and it ill became the Pharisee to be offended at it. Now Christ has a further intention in this. The Pharisee doubted whether he was a *prophet* or no, nay, he did in effect deny it; but Christ shows that he was more than a prophet, for he is one that has *power on earth to forgive sins*, and to whom are due the affections and thankful acknowledgments of penitent pardoned sinners. Now, in his answer,

1. He by a parable forces Simon to acknowledge that the greater sinner this woman had been the greater love she ought to show to Jesus Christ when her *sins* were *pardoned*, *vv.* 41–43. A man had *two debtors* that were both insolvent, but one of them owed him *ten times* more than the other. He very freely *forgave them both*, and did not take the advantage of the law against them, did not order them and their children to be sold, or *deliver them to the tormentors*. Now they were both sensible of the great kindness they had received; but *which of them, will love him most*? Certainly, saith the Pharisee, he to *whom he forgave most*; and herein he rightly judged. Now we, being obliged to *forgive*, as we are and hope to be *forgiven*, may hence learn the duty between debtor and creditor.

(1) The *debtor*, if he have *any thing to pay*, ought to make satisfaction to his *creditor*. No man can reckon any thing *his own*, or

have any comfortable enjoyment of it, but that which is so when *all his debts are paid*.

(2) If God in his providence have disabled the debtor to pay his debt, the creditor ought not to be severe with him, nor to go to the utmost rigour of the law with him, but *freely to forgive him. Summum jus est summa injuria—The law stretched into rigour becomes unjust.* Let the unmerciful creditor read that parable, Matt. xviii. 23, &c., and tremble; for *they* shall have judgment without mercy that show no mercy.

(3) The debtor that has found his creditors merciful ought to be very grateful to them; and, if he cannot otherwise recompense them, ought to love them. We may learn here, [1] That *sin is a debt*, and *sinners are debtors* to God Almighty. [2] That some are deeper in debt to God, by reason of sin, than others are: *One owed five hundred pence and the other fifty.* The Pharisee was the less debtor, yet he a debtor too, which was more than he thought himself, but rather that God was his debtor, Luke xviii. 10, 11. [3] That, whether our debt be more or less, it is *more* than we are able to pay: *They had nothing to pay*, nothing at all to make a composition with; for the debt is great, and we have nothing at all to pay it with. [4] That the God of heaven is *ready* to forgive, *frankly* to *forgive*, poor sinners, upon gospel terms, though their debt be ever so great. [5] That those who have their sins *pardoned* are obliged to *love him* that pardoned them; and the more is forgiven them, the more they should love him.

2. He applies this parable to the different temper and conduct of the Pharisee and the sinner towards Christ. Though the Pharisee would not allow Christ to be a prophet, Christ seems ready to allow him to be in a justified state, and that he was one *forgiven*, though to him *less was forgiven*. He did indeed show some love to Christ, in inviting him to his house, but nothing to what this poor woman showed. "Observe," saith Christ to him, "she is one that has much forgiven her, and therefore, according to thine own judgment, it might be expected that she should love much more than thou dost, and so it appears. *Seest thou this woman? v.* 44. (1) "Thou didst not so much as order a basin of water to be brought, to wash my feet in, when I came in, wearied and dirtied with my walk, which would have been some refreshment to me; but she has done much more: *she has washed my feet with tears*, tears of affection to me, tears of affliction for sin, and has *wiped them with the hairs of her head*, in token of her great love to me." (2) "Thou didst not so much as kiss my cheek" (which was a usual expression of a hearty and affectionate welcome to a friend); "but *this woman has not ceased to kiss my feet* (*v.* 45), thereby expressing both a humble and an affectionate love." (3) "Thou didst not provide me a little common oil, as usual, to anoint my head with; but she has bestowed a box of precious *ointment* upon *my feet* (*v.* 46), so far has she outdone thee."

3. He silenced the Pharisee's cavil: *I say unto thee*, Simon, *her*

sins, which are many, are forgiven,
v. 47. He owns that she had been
guilty of *many sins*: "But they are
forgiven her, and therefore it is no
way unbecoming in me to accept her
kindness. They *are forgiven, for she
loved much.*" It should be rendered,
therefore she loved much; for it is
plain, by the tenour of Christ's
discourse, that her loving much was
not the *cause*, but the *effect*, of her
pardon, and of her comfortable
sense of it; for *we love God* because
he first loved us; he did not forgive
us because we first loved him. "But
to whom little is forgiven, as is
to thee, *the same loveth little,* as
thou dost." Hereby he intimates to
the Pharisee that his love to Christ
was so little that he had reason to
question whether he loved him at
all in sincerity; and, consequently,
whether indeed his sins, though
comparatively *little*, were forgiven
him.

4. He silenced her fears, who
probably was discouraged by the
Pharisee's conduct, and yet would
not so far yield to the discouragement as to fly off. (1) Christ said
unto her, *Thy sins are forgiven, v.* 48.
(2) Though there were those present who quarrelled with Christ, in
their own minds, for presuming to
forgive sin, and to pronounce
sinners absolved (*v.* 49), as those
had done (Matt. ix. 3), yet he *stood
to what he had said*; for as he had
there proved that he had *power to
forgive sin,* by curing the man sick
of the palsy, and therefore would
not here take notice of the cavil, so
he would now show that he had
pleasure in forgiving sin, and it was
his delight; he loves to speak
pardon and peace to penitents: *He*

*said to the woman, Thy faith hath
saved thee, v.* 50.

CHAPTER EIGHT
WOMEN DISCIPLES (*vv.* 1–3)

We are here told,

I. *What* Christ *made* the *constant
business* of his *life*—it was *preaching*; in that work he was indefatigable, and went about doing
good (*v.* 1).

II. *Whence* he *had* the *necessary
supports* of life: He lived upon the
kindness of his friends. There were
certain women, who frequently
attended his ministry, that *ministered to him of their substance, vv.*
2, 3.

1. They were such, for the most
part, as had been *Christ's patients,*
and were the monuments of his
power and mercy; they had been
*healed by him of evil spirits and
infirmities.* He is the physician both
of body and soul, and those who
have been *healed by him* ought to
study what they shall *render to him.*

2. One of them was Mary
Magdalene, out of whom had been
cast seven devils; a certain number
for an uncertain. Some think that
she was one that had been *very
wicked,* and then we may suppose
her to be the woman that *was a
sinner* mentioned just before, ch.
vii. 37.

3. Another of them was *Joanna
the wife of Chuza, Herod's steward.*
She had been his wife (so some),
but was now a widow, and left in
good circumstances. If she was now
his wife, we have reason to think
that her *husband,* though preferred
in Herod's court, had received the
gospel, and was very willing that

his wife should be both a hearer of Christ and a contributor to him.

4. There were many of them that *ministered to Christ of their substance*. It was an instance of the meanness of that condition to which our Saviour humbled himself that he needed it, and of his great humility and condescension that he accepted it. Though he was rich, yet for our sakes *he became poor*, and lived upon alms.

THE SOWER (*vv.* 4–21)

The former paragraph began with an account of Christ's industry in *preaching* (*v.* 1); this begins with an account of the people's industry in hearing, *v.* 4.

Now in these verses we have,

I. Necessary and excellent rules and cautions for hearing the word, in the parable of *the sower* and the explanation and application of it, all which we had twice before more largely.

II. Needful instructions given to those that are appointed to preach the word, and to those also that have heard it. 1. Those that have *received the gift* must *minister the same*; for a *candle* must not be *covered with a vessel* nor *put under a bed*, *v.* 16. Ministers and Christians are to be lights in the world, *holding forth the word of life*. Their light must shine before men; they must not only *be good*, but *do good*. 2. We must expect that what is now done *in secret*, and from unseen springs, will shortly be *manifested* and *made known*, *v.* 17. What is committed to you *in secret* should be made manifest *by you*; for your Master did not give you talents to be buried, but to be traded with.

Let that which is now hid be *made known*; for, if it be not manifested *by you*, it will be manifested *against you*, will be produced in evidence of your treachery. 3. The gifts we have will either be continued to us, or taken from us, according as we do, or do not, make use of them for the glory of God and the edification of our brethren: *Whosoever hath, to him shall be given, v.* 18.

III. Great encouragement given to those that prove themselves faithful *hearers of the word*, by being *doers of the work*, in a particular instance of Christ's respect to his disciples, in preferring them even before his nearest relations (*vv.* 19–21), which passage of story we had twice before.

FOUR MIRACLES (*vv.* 22–56)

We have here two illustrious proofs of the power of our Lord Jesus which we had before—his power over the *winds*, and his power over the *devils*. See Mark iv. v.

We also have here two miracles interwoven, as they were in Matthew and Mark—the raising of Jairus's daughter to life, and the cure of the woman that had an issue of blood, as he was going in a crowd to Jairus's house.

CHAPTER NINE

THE DISCIPLES SENT OUT
(*vv.* 1–9)

We have here, I. The method Christ took to spread his gospel, to diffuse and enforce the light of it. He had *himself* travelled about, preaching and healing; but he could be only in one place at a time, and therefore now he *sent* his twelve disciples abroad, who by this time were pretty well instructed in the nature of the present dispensation, and able to instruct others and *deliver to them* what they had *received from the Lord*. For the confirming of their doctrine, because it was new and surprising, and very different from what they had been taught by the scribes and Pharisees, and because so much depended upon men's receiving, or not receiving it, he empowered them to work miracles (*vv.* 1, 2): He *gave them authority over all devils*, to dispossess them, and cast them out, though ever so numerous, so subtle, so fierce, so obstinate. He authorized and appointed them likewise to *cure diseases*, and to *heal the sick*, which would make them welcome wherever they came, and not only convince people's judgments, but gain their affections. This was their commission. Now observe,

1. What Christ directed them to do, in prosecution of this commission at this time, when they were not to *go far* or be *out long*. (1) They must not be solicitous to recommend themselves to people's esteem by their outward appearance. (2) They must depend upon Providence, and the kindness of their friends, to furnish them with what was convenient for them. (3) They must not change their lodgings, as suspecting that those who entertained them were *weary* of them; they have no reason to be so, for the ark is a guest that always pays well for its entertainment: "*Whatsoever house ye enter into there abide* (*v.* 4)."

(4) They must put on authority, and speak *warning* to those who *refused* them as well as comfort to those that *received* them, *v.* 5.

2. What they did, in prosecution of this commission (*v.* 6): *They departed* from their Master's presence; yet, having still his spiritual presence with them, his *eye* and his *arm* going along with them, and, thus borne up in their work, they *went through the towns*, some or other of them, all the towns within the circuit appointed them, *preaching the gospel, and healing every where*. Their work was the same with their Master's, doing good both to souls and bodies.

II. We have here Herod's perplexity and vexation at this. When the country sees such as these *healing the sick* in the name of Jesus it gives it an alarm. Now observe,

1. The *various speculations* it *raised* among the *people*, who, though they thought not *rightly*, yet could not but think *honourably*, of our Lord Jesus, and that he was an extraordinary person, one come from the other world; that either John Baptist, who was lately persecuted and slain for the cause of God, or *one of the old prophets*, that had been persecuted and slain long since in that cause, was *risen again*, to be recompensed for his sufferings by this honour put upon him; or that Elias, who was taken alive to heaven in a fiery chariot, *had appeared* as an express from heaven, *vv.* 7, 8.

2. The *great perplexity* it *created* in the mind of Herod: *When he had heard of all that was done* by

Christ, his guilty conscience flew in his face, and he was ready to conclude with them that *John was risen from the dead.* He *desired to see him*; and why did he not go and see him? Probably, because he thought it *below him* either to go to him or to send for him; he had enough of John Baptist, and cared not for having to do with any more such reprovers of sin. He desired to see him, but we do not find that ever he did, till he saw him at his bar, and then *he and his men of war set him at nought*, Luke xxiii. 11.

REFRESHMENT (*vv.* 10–17)

We have here, I. The account which the twelve gave their Master of the success of their ministry. They were not long out; but, *when they returned, they told him all that they had done*, as became servants who were sent on an errand. They told him *what they had done*, that, if they had done anything amiss, they might mend it next time.

II. Their *retirement*, for a little *breathing*: He *took them, and went aside privately into a desert place*, that they might have some relaxation from business and not be always upon the stretch.

III. The *resort* of the people to him, and the kind *reception* he gave them. They *followed* him, though it was into a *desert place*; for that is no desert where Christ is. 1. He *spoke unto them of the kingdom of God*, the laws of that kingdom with which they must be bound, and the privileges of that kingdom with which they might

be blessed. 2. He *healed them that had need of healing*, and, in a sense of their need, made their application to him.

IV. The plentiful provision Christ made for the multitude that attended him. With *five loaves* of bread, and *two fishes*, he fed *five thousand men.* This narrative we had twice before, and shall meet with it again; it is the only miracle of our Saviour's that is recorded by all the four evangelists.

PETER'S CONFESSION
(*vv.* 18–27)

In these verses, we have Christ discoursing with his disciples about the great things that *pertained to the kingdom of God*; and one circumstance of this discourse is taken notice of here which we had not in the other evangelists — that Christ was *alone praying*, and his *disciples with him*, when he entered into this discourse, *v.* 18. Observe, 1. Though Christ had much public work to do, yet he found some time to be *alone* in private, for converse with himself, with his Father, and with his disciples. 2. When Christ was alone he was *praying*. It is good for us to improve our solitude for devotion, that, *when we are alone*, we may *not be alone*, but may have *the Father with us.* 3. When Christ was alone, praying, his *disciples were with him*, to join with him in his prayer; so that this was a family-prayer.

He discourses with them,

I. Concerning himself; and enquires,

1. What *the people* said of him:

Who say the people that I am?
Christ knew better than they did,
but would have his disciples
made sensible, by the mistakes of
others concerning him, how happy
they were that were led into the
knowledge of him and of the truth
concerning him. Some said that
he was John Baptist, who was
beheaded but the other day;
others Elias, or *one of the old
prophets*; any thing but what he
was.

2. What *they* said of him. "Now
see what an advantage you have
by your discipleship; you know
better." "So we do," saith Peter,
"thanks be to our Master for it;
we know that thou art *the Christ
of God*, the *Anointed* of God, the
Messiah promised." Now one
would have expected that Christ
should have charged his disciples
who were so fully apprized and
assured of this truth, to publish it
to every one they met with; but
no, he *strictly charged them to
tell no man that thing* as yet,
because there is a time for all
things. After his resurrection, which
completed the proof of it, Peter
made the temple ring of it, that
*God had made this same Jesus
both Lord and Christ* (Acts ii. 36);
but as yet the evidence was not
ready to be summed up, and
therefore it must be concealed;
while it was so, we may conclude
that the belief of it was not necessary to salvation.

II. Concerning his own *sufferings* and *death*, of which he had
yet said little. Now that his
disciples were well established in
the belief of his being the Christ,
and able to bear it, he speaks of

them expressly, and with great
assurance, *v.* 22.

III. Concerning their sufferings
for him. So far must they be from
thinking how to *prevent* his sufferings that they must rather
prepare for their own.

1. We must *accustom* ourselves
to all instances of *self-denial* and
patience, v. 23.

2. We must *prefer the salvation
and happiness of our souls* before
any *secular concern* whatsoever.
Observe, In Matthew and Mark
the dreadful issue is a man's
losing his own soul, here it is
losing himself, which plainly intimates that *our souls* are *ourselves*.

3. We must therefore *never be
ashamed* of Christ and his gospel,
nor of any disgrace or reproach
that we may undergo for our
faithful adherence to him and it,
v. 26. *For whosoever shall be
ashamed of me and of my words,
of him shall the Son of man be
ashamed*, and justly. Observe here,
How Christ, to support himself
and his followers under present
disgraces, speaks *magnificently* of
the lustre of his second coming, in
prospect of which he *endured the
cross, despising the shame*. (1) He
shall come *in his own glory*. This
was not mentioned in Matthew
and Mark. He shall come in the
glory of the Mediator, *all that
glory* which the Father *restored to
him*, which he had with God
before the worlds were. (2) He
shall come *in his Father's glory*.
The Father will judge the world
by him, having committed all
judgment to him; and therefore
will publicly own him in the
judgment as the *brightness of his*

glory and the *express image* of his person. (3) He shall come in *the glory of the holy angels*. They shall all *attend* him, and *minister* to him, and add every thing they can to the lustre of his appearance. What a figure will the blessed Jesus make in that day! Did we believe it, we should never be ashamed of him or his words now.

Lastly, To encourage them in suffering for him, he assures them that *the kingdom of God* would now *shortly be set up*, notwithstanding the great opposition that was made to it, *v*. 27. "Though the second coming of the Son of man is at a great distance, the kingdom of God shall come in its power in the present age, while some here present are alive." They *saw the kingdom of God* when the Spirit was poured out, when the gospel was preached to all the world and nations were brought to Christ by it; they saw the kingdom of God triumph over the Gentile nations in their *conversion*, and over the Jewish nation in its *destruction*.

THE TRANSFIGURATION
(*vv*. 28–36)

We have here the narrative of Christ's transfiguration, which was designed for a specimen of that glory of his in which he will come to judge the world, of which he had lately been speaking, and, consequently, an encouragement to his disciples to suffer for him, and never to be ashamed of him. We had this account before in Matthew and Mark.

Here are divers circumstances added and explained, which are very material.

1. We are *here* told that Christ had this honour put upon him when he was *praying*: He *went up into a mountain to pray*, as he frequently did (*v*. 28), and *as he prayed* he was *transfigured*. When Christ *humbled* himself to pray, he was thus *exalted*.

2. Luke does not use the word *transfigured* (which Matthew and Mark used), perhaps because it had been used so much in the Pagan theology, but makes use of a phrase equivalent, *the fashion of his countenance was another thing from what it had been*: his face shone far beyond what Moses's did when he came down from the mount; and *his raiment* was *white and glistering*: it was—*bright like lightning* (a word used only here), so that he seemed to be arrayed all with light, to *cover himself with light as with a garment*.

3. It was said in Matthew and Mark that Moses and Elias *appeared to them*; here it is said that they *appeared in glory*, to teach us that saints departed are *in glory*, are in a *glorious* state; they shine in glory.

4. We are here told what was the subject of the discourse between Christ and the two great prophets of the Old Testament: *They spoke of his decease, which he should accomplish at Jerusalem*—his *exodus*, his *departure*; that is, his *death*.

5. We are here told, which we were not before, that the disciples were *heavy with sleep*, *v*. 32. These three were now asleep, when Christ was in *his glory*, as after-

wards they were, when he was in *his agony*; see the *weakness* and *frailty* of human nature, even in the best, and what need they have of the grace of God.

Lastly, The apostles are here said to have kept this vision private. They *told no man in those days*, reserving the discovery of it for another opportunity, when the evidences of Christ's being the Son of God were completed in the pouring out of the Spirit, and that doctrine was to be published to all the world. As there is a time *to speak*, so there is a time to *keep silence*. Every thing is beautiful and useful in its season.

THE LUNATIC BOY
(vv. 37–50)

This passage of story in Matthew and Mark follows immediately upon that of Christ's transfiguration, and his discourse with his disciples after it; but here it is said to be *on the next day, as they were coming down from the hill*, which confirms the conjecture that Christ was transfigured *in the night*, and, it should seem, though they did not *make tabernacles* as Peter proposed, yet they found some shelter to repose themselves in all night, for it was not till next day that they *came down from the hill*, and then he found things in some disorder among his disciples, though not so bad as Moses did when he came down from the mount. When wise and good men are in their beloved retirements, they would do well to consider whether they are not wanted in their *public stations*.

FIRE FROM HEAVEN
(vv. 51–56)

This passage of story we have not in any other of the evangelists, and it seems to come in here for the sake of its affinity with that next before, for in this also Christ rebuked his disciples, because they envied for his sake. There, under colour of zeal for Christ, they were for silencing and restraining separatists; here, under the same colour, they were for putting infidels to death; and, as for *that*, so for *this* also, Christ reprimanded them, for a spirit of bigotry and persecution is directly contrary to the spirit of Christ and Christianity. Observe here,

I. The *readiness* and *resolution* of our Lord Jesus, in prosecuting his great undertaking for our redemption and salvation. Of this we have an instance, *v.* 51: *When the time was come that he should be received up, he stedfastly set his face to go to Jerusalem.* Observe 1. There was a time fixed for the sufferings and death of our Lord Jesus, and he knew well enough when it was, and had a clear and certain foresight of it, and yet was so far from keeping out of the way that then he appeared most publicly of all, and was most busy, knowing that his time was short. 2. When he saw his death and sufferings approaching, he looked through them and beyond them, to the glory that should follow; he looked upon it as the time when he should be *received up into glory* (1 Tim. iii. 16), received up into the highest heavens, to be enthroned there. 3. On this prospect of the joy set before him, he *stedfastly set his face to go to Jerusalem*, the place where he was to suffer and die. He *did not fail nor was discouraged*, but *set his face as a flint, knowing* that he should be not only *justified*, but glorified (Isa. 1. 7), not only not *run down*, but *received up*. How should this shame us *for*, and shame *us out of*, our backwardness to do and suffer for Christ!

II. The *rudeness* of the Samaritans in a *certain village* (not named, nor deserving to be so) who would not *receive him*, nor suffer him to stay in their town, though his way lay through it. Observe here, 1. How *civil* he was to them: *He sent messengers before his face.* 2. How *uncivil* they were to him, *v.* 53. They did not *receive him*, would not suffer him to come into their village, but ordered their watch to keep him out.

III. The *resentment* which James and John expressed of this affront, *v.* 54. When these two heard this message brought, they were all in a flame presently, and nothing will serve them but Sodom's doom upon this village: "Lord," say they, "give us leave to command fire to come down from heaven, not to *frighten* them only, but to *consume* them."

IV. The *reproof* he gave to James and John for their fiery, furious zeal (*v.* 55): He *turned* with a just displeasure, and *rebuked them*.

1. He shows them in particular their mistake: *Ye know not what manner of spirit ye are of*; that is,

(1) "You *are not aware* what an *evil spirit* and disposition you are of; how much there is of pride, and passion, and personal revenge, covered under this pretence of zeal for your Master." Note, There may be much corruption lurking, nay, and stirring too, in the hearts of good people, and they themselves not be sensible of it. (2) "You *do not consider* what a *good spirit*, directly contrary to this, you *should be of*. Surely you have yet to learn, though you have been so long learning, what the spirit of Christ and Christianity is. Have you not been taught to *love your enemies*, and to *bless them that curse you*, and to call for grace from heaven, not fire from heaven, upon them?"

2. He shows them the general design and tendency of his religion (*v.* 56): *The Son of man* is not himself come, and therefore does not send you abroad *to destroy men's lives, but to save them.*

V. His *retreat* from this village. Christ would not only not punish them for their rudeness, but would not insist upon his right of travelling the road (which was as free to him as to his neighbours), would not attempt to force his way, but quietly and peaceably *went to another village*, where they were not so stingy and bigoted, and there refreshed himself, and went on his way.

THE COST OF FOLLOWING
(*vv.* 57–62)

We have here an account of three different persons who offered themselves to follow Christ, and the answers that Christ gave to each of them. The two former we had an account of in Matt. viii. 19–22.

Here is another that is willing to follow Christ, but he must have a *little time* to *talk with his friends* about it.

Observe, 1. His request for a dispensation, *v.* 61. He said, "*Lord, I will follow thee*; I design no other, I am determined to do it; but *let me first go bid them farewell that are at home*." This seemed reasonable. But that which was amiss in this is, (1) That he looked upon his following Christ as a melancholy, troublesome, dangerous thing; it was to him as if he were *going to die*, and therefore he must take *leave* of all his friends, never to *see them again*, or never *with any comfort*; whereas, in following Christ, he might be more a comfort and blessing to them than if he had continued with them. (2) That he seemed to have his worldly concerns more upon his heart than he ought to have, and than would consist with a close attendance to his duty as a follower of Christ. He seemed to hanker after his relations and family concerns, and he could not part easily and suitably from them, but they stuck to him. (3) That he was willing to enter into a temptation from his purpose of following Christ. To go and bid them *farewell* that were *at home at his house* would be to expose himself to the strongest solicitations imaginable to alter his resolution; for they would all be against it, and would *beg* and *pray* that he would not *leave them*. Now it was presumption in him to thrust himself into such a

temptation. Those that resolve to walk with their Maker, and follow their Redeemer, must resolve that they will not so much as parley with their tempter.

2. The rebuke which Christ gave him for this request (*v.* 62): "*No man, having put his hand to the plough*, and designing to make good work of his ploughing, will *look back*, or look behind him, for then he makes balks with his plough, and the ground he ploughs is *not fit* to be sown; so thou, if thou hast a design to follow me and to reap the advantages of those that do so, yet if thou *lookest back* to a worldly life again and hankerest after that, if thou *lookest back* as Lot's wife did to Sodom which seems to be alluded to here, *thou art not fit for the kingdom of God*." Note, Those who begin with the work of God must resolve to *go on* with it, or they will make nothing of it. Looking back inclines to *drawing back*, and *drawing back* is to *perdition*. Those are not fit for heaven who, having set their faces heavenward, face about. But he, and he only, that *endures to the end, shall be saved*.

CHAPTER TEN

THE SEVENTY SENT OUT
(*vv.* 1–16)

We have here the sending forth of seventy disciples, two and two, into divers parts of the country, to preach the gospel, and to work miracles in those places which Christ himself designed to visit, to make way for his entertainment. This is not taken notice of by the other evangelists: but the instructions here given them are much the same with those given to the twelve. Observe,

I. Their number: they were seventy. As in the choice of twelve apostles Christ had an eye to the twelve patriarchs, the twelve tribes, and the twelve princes of those tribes, so here he seems to have an eye to the *seventy* elders of Israel. Now,

1. We are glad to find that Christ had so many followers fit to be sent forth; his labour was not altogether in vain, though he met with much opposition. Many of those that were the companions of the apostles, whom we read of in the Acts and the Epistles, we may suppose, were of these seventy disciples.

2. We are glad to find there was work for so many ministers, hearers for so many preachers: thus the grain of mustard-seed began to *grow*, and the savour of the leaven to diffuse itself in the meal, in order to the leavening of the whole.

II. Their work and business: He sent them *two and two*, that they might strengthen and encourage one another. *If one fall, the other will help to raise him up*. He sent them, not to all the cities of Israel, as he did the *twelve*, but only *to every city and place whither he himself would come* (v. 1), as his harbingers; and we must suppose, though it is not recorded, that Christ soon after went to all those places whither he now sent them, though he could stay but a little while in a place. Two things they were ordered to do, the same that

Christ did wherever he came:— 1. They must *heal the sick* (v. 9), heal them *in the name of Jesus*, which would make people long to see this Jesus, and ready to entertain him whose name was so powerful. 2. They must publish the approach of the kingdom of God, its approach *to them*: "Tell them this, *The kingdom of God is come nigh to you*, and you now stand fair for an admission into it, if you will but look about you. Now is the *day of your visitation*, know and understand it." It is good to be made sensible of our advantages and opportunities, that we may lay hold of them. When the *kingdom of God comes nigh us*, it concerns us to go forth to meet it.

THE SUCCESS OF THE SEVENTY (vv. 17–24)

Now here we are told,

1. What account they gave him of the success of their expedition: *They returned again with joy* (v. 17); not complaining of the fatigue of their journeys, nor of the opposition and discouragement they met with, but rejoicing in their success, especially in casting out unclean spirits: *Lord, even the devils are subject unto us through thy name*.

II. What acceptance they found with him, and how he received this account.

1. He confirmed what they said, as agreeing with his own observation (v. 18): "My heart and eye went along with you; I took notice of the success you had, and I *saw Satan fall as lightning from*

heaven." Note, Satan and his kingdom fell before the preaching of the gospel. "I see how it is," saith Christ, "as you get ground the devil loseth ground." He falls *as lightning falls from heaven*, so suddenly, so irrecoverably, so visibly, that all may perceive it, and say, "See how Satan's kingdom totters, see how it tumbles." They triumphed in casting devils out of the bodies of people; but Christ sees and rejoices in the fall of the devil from the interest he has in the souls of men, which is called his power *in high places*, Eph. vi. 12.

2. He repeated, ratified, and enlarged their commission: *Behold I give you power to tread on serpents*, v. 19. Note, To him that hath, and useth well what he hath, more shall be given. They had employed their power vigorously against Satan, and now Christ entrusts them with greater power.

3. He directed them to turn their joy into the right channel (v. 20): "*Notwithstanding in this rejoice not, that the spirits are subject unto you*, that they have been so, and shall be still so, but *rather rejoice because your names are written in heaven*, because you are chosen of God to eternal life, and are the children of God through faith." Christ, who knew the counsels of God, could tell them that their *names were written in heaven*, for it is the *Lamb's book of life* that they are written in. Note, Power to become the children of God is to be valued more than a power to work miracles; for we read of those who did *in Christ's name cast out devils*, as Judas did, and yet will be

disowned by Christ in the great day.

4. He offered up a solemn thanksgiving to his Father, for employing such mean people as his disciples were in such high and honourable services, vv. 21, 22. This we had before (Matt. xi. 25–27), only here it is prefixed that *in that hour Jesus rejoiced*. It was fit that particular notice should be taken of *that* hour, because there were so few such, for he was a *man of sorrows*. In *that hour* in which he saw Satan fall, and heard of the good success of his ministers, *in that hour he rejoiced*.

THE GOOD SAMARITAN
(vv. 25–37)

We have here Christ's discourse with a lawyer about some points of conscience, which we are all concerned to be rightly informed in, and are so here, from Christ, though the questions were proposed with no good intention.

I. We are concerned to know what that good is which we should do in *this* life, in order to attain *eternal life*. A question to this purport was proposed to our Saviour by a *certain lawyer*, or *scribe*, only with a design to *try* him, not with a desire to be instructed by him, v. 25. The lawyer *stood up*, and *asked him, Master, what shall I do to inherit eternal life?* Now this question being started, observe,

1. How Christ turned him over to the divine law, and bade him follow the direction of that. Though he knew the thoughts and intents of his heart, he did not

answer him according to the folly of that, but according to the wisdom and goodness of the question he asked. He answered him with a question: *What is written in the law? How readest thou? v.* 26.

2. What a good account he gave of the law, of the principal commandments of the law, to the observance of which we must bind ourselves if we would inherit eternal life. He did not, like a Pharisee, refer himself to the tradition of the elders, but, like a good textuary, fastened upon the two first and great commandments of the law, as those which he thought must be most strictly observed in order to the obtaining of *eternal life*, and which included all the rest, *v.* 27. (1) We must *love God with all our hearts*, must look upon him as the best of beings, in himself most amiable, and infinitely perfect and excellent; as one whom we lie under the greatest obligations to, both in gratitude and interest. We must prize him, and value ourselves by our relation to him; must please ourselves in him, and devote ourselves entirely to him. Our love to him must be sincere, hearty, and fervent; it must be a superlative love, a love that is as strong as death, but an intelligent love, and such as we can give a good account of the grounds and reasons of. It must be an *entire* love; he must have our *whole* souls, and must be served with *all that is within us.* We must love nothing *besides him*, but what we love *for him* and in subordination to him. (2) We must love our neighbours as *ourselves*, which we

shall easily do, if we, as we ought to do, love God *better than ourselves*. We must wish well to all and ill to none; must do all the good we can in the world and no hurt, and must fix it as a rule to ourselves to do to others as we would they should do to us; and this is to love our neighbour *as ourselves*.

3. Christ's approbation of what he said, *v.* 28. Though he came to tempt him, yet what he said that was good Christ commended: *Thou hast answered right.* So far is right; but the hardest part of this work yet remains: *"This do, and thou shalt live*; thou shalt *inherit eternal life.*

4. His care to avoid the conviction which was now ready to fasten upon him. He was *willing to justify himself*, and therefore cared not for carrying on that discourse, but saith, in effect, as another did (Matt. xix. 20), *All these things have I kept from my youth up.*

II. We are concerned to know who is our neighbour, whom by the second great commandment we are obliged to love. This is another of this lawyer's queries, which he started only that he might *drop* the former, lest Christ should have forced him, in the prosecution of it, to *condemn himself*, when he was resolved to *justify* himself. Now observe,

1. What was the corrupt notion of the Jewish teachers in this matter. Dr. Lightfoot quotes their own words to this purport: "Where he saith, *Thou shalt love thy neighbour*, he excepts all Gentiles, for they are not *our neighbours*,

but those only that are of our own nation and religion."

2. How Christ corrected this inhuman notion, and showed, by a parable, that whomsoever we *have need* to receive kindness *from*, and *find ready* to show us the kindness *we need*, we cannot but look upon as *our neighbour*; and therefore ought to look upon all those as such who need our kindness, and to show them kindness accordingly, though they be not of our own nation and religion. Now observe,

(1) The parable itself, which represents to us a poor Jew in distressed circumstances, succoured and relieved by a good Samaritan. Let us see here,

[1] How he was *abused* by his *enemies*. The honest man was travelling peaceably upon his lawful business in the road, and it was a great road that led from Jerusalem to Jericho, *v*. 30. This poor man *fell among thieves*. They not only took his money, but stripped him of his clothes, and, that he might not be able to pursue them, or only to gratify a cruel disposition (for otherwise *what profit was there in his blood?*) they *wounded him*, and left him *half dead*, ready to die of his wounds.

[2] How he was *slighted* by those who should have been his friends, who were not only men of his own nation and religion, but one a priest and the other a Levite, men of a public character and station; nay, they were men of professed sanctity, whose offices obliged them to tenderness and compassion (Heb. v. 2), who ought to have taught others their duty in

such a case as this, which was to *deliver them that were drawn unto death*; yet they would not themselves do it. It is sad when those who should be examples of charity are prodigies of cruelty, and when those who should, by displaying the mercies of God, open the bowels of compassion in others, shut up their own.

[3] How he was *succoured* and *relieved* by a *stranger*, a *certain Samaritan*, of that nation which of all others the Jews most despised and detested and would have no dealings with. This man had some humanity in him, *v*. 33. The priest had his heart hardened against one of *his own people*, but the Samaritan had his opened towards one of *another* people. *When he saw him he had compassion on him*, and never took into consideration what country he was of. See how friendly this good Samaritan was. *First*, He *went to* the poor man, whom the priest and Levite kept at a distance from; he enquired, no doubt, how he came into this deplorable condition, and condoled with him. *Secondly*, He did the surgeon's part, for want of a better. He *bound up his wounds*, making use of his own linen, it is likely, for that purpose; and poured *in oil and wine*, which perhaps he had with him; wine to wash the wound, and oil to mollify it, and close it up. He did all he could to ease the pain, and prevent the peril, of his wounds, as one whose heart bled with them. *Thirdly*, He *set him on his own beast*, and went on foot himself, and *brought him to an inn*. *Fourthly*, He *took care of him* in the inn,

got him to bed, had food for him that was proper, and due attendance, and, it may be, prayed with him. Nay, *Fifthly*, As if he had been his own child, or one he was obliged to look after, when he left him next morning, he left money with the landlord, to be laid out for his use, and passed his word for what he should spend more.

Now this parable is applicable to another purpose than that for which it was intended; and does excellently set forth the kindness and love of God our Saviour towards sinful miserable man. We were like this poor distressed traveller. Satan, our enemy, had *robbed* us, *stripped* us, *wounded* us; such is the mischief that sin hath done us. We were by nature more than *half dead*, twice dead, in trespasses and sins; utterly unable to help ourselves, for we were without strength. The law of Moses, like the priest and Levite, the ministers of the law, *looks upon us*, but has no compassion on us, gives us no relief, *passes by on the other side*, as having neither pity nor power to help us; but then comes the blessed Jesus, that good Samaritan (and they said of him, by way of reproach, *he is a Samaritan*), he has compassion on us, he binds up our bleeding wounds (Ps. cxlvii. 3; Isa. lxi. 1), pours in, not *oil and wine*, but that which is infinitely more precious, *his own blood*. He takes care of us, and bids us put all the expenses of our cure upon his account; and all this though he was none of us, till he was pleased by his voluntary condescension to make himself so, but infinitely

above us. This magnifies the riches of his love, and obliges us all to say, "How much are we indebted, and what shall we render?"

(2) The application of the parable. [1] The truth contained in it is extorted from the lawyer's own mouth. "Now tell me," saith Christ, *"which of these three was neighbour to him that fell among thieves* (v. 36), the priest, the Levite, or the Samaritan? Which of these did the neighbour's part?" To this the lawyer would not answer, as he ought to have done, "Doubtless, the Samaritan was"; but, *"He that showed mercy on him*; doubtless, he was a good neighbour to him, and very neighbourly, and I cannot but say that it was a good work thus to save an honest Jew from perishing." [2] The duty inferred from it is pressed home upon the lawyer's own conscience: *Go, and do thou likewise.*

MARTHA AND MARY
(vv. 38-42)

We may observe in this story,

I. The entertainment which Martha gave to Christ and his disciples at her house, *v.* 38. Observe,

1. Christ's coming to the village where Martha lived: *As they went* (Christ and his disciples together), he and they with him *entered into a certain village*. This village was *Bethany*, nigh to Jerusalem, whither Christ was now going up, and he took this in his way.

2. His reception at Martha's house: *A certain woman, named Martha, received him into her*

house, and made him welcome, for she was the housekeeper.

II. The attendance which Mary, the sister of Martha, gave upon the word of Christ, *v.* 20. She *heard his word*. It seems, our Lord Jesus, as soon as he came into Martha's house, even before entertainment was made for him, addressed himself to his great work of preaching the gospel. He presently took the chair with solemnity; for Mary sat to hear him, which intimates that it was a continued discourse.

III. The care of Martha about her domestic affairs: But Martha *was cumbered about much serving* (*v.* 40), and that was the reason why she was not where Mary was— sitting at Christ's feet, to hear his word. She was providing for the entertainment of Christ and those that came with him. Observe here,

1. Something *commendable*, which must not be overlooked. (1) Here was a commendable *respect to our Lord Jesus*; for we have reason to think it was not for ostentation, but purely to testify her good-will to him, that she made this entertainment. (2) Here was a commendable *care of her household affairs*.

2. Here was something *culpable*, which we must take notice of too. (1) She was for *much serving*. Her heart was upon it, to have a very sumptuous and splendid enter-tainment; great plenty, great variety, and great exactness, ac-cording to the fashion of the place. (2) She was *cumbered* about it; she was just *distracted* with it. Note, Whatever cares the providence of God casts upon us we must not be

cumbered with them, nor be disquieted and perplexed by them. *Care* is good and duty; but *cumber* is sin and folly. (2) She was *then cumbered about much serving* when she should have been with her sister, sitting at Christ's feet to hear his word.

IV. The *complaint* which Martha made to Christ against her sister Mary, for not *assisting* her, upon this occasion, in the *business of the house* (*v.* 40): "*Lord, dost thou not care that my sister*, who is con-cerned as well as I in having things done well, *has left me to serve alone*? Therefore dismiss her from attending thee, and bid her come and help me." Now,

1. This complaint of Martha's may be considered as a *discovery* of her *worldliness*: it was the language of her inordinate care and cumber.

2. It may be considered as a discouragement of Mary's piety and devotion. Her sister should have *commended* her for it, should have told her that she was in the right; but, instead of this, she *condemns* her as wanting in her duty.

V. The reproof which Christ gave to Martha for her inordinate care, *v.* 41. She appealed to him, and he gives judgment against her: *Martha, Martha, thou art careful and troubled about many things*, whereas but *one thing is needful*.

1. He reproved her, though he was at this time her guest. Her fault was her over-solicitude to entertain him, and she expected he should justify her in it, yet he publicly checked her for it.

2. When he reproved her, he

called her by her name, *Martha*;
for reproofs are *then* most likely
to do good when they are *particular*, applied to particular persons and cases, as Nathan's to
David, *Thou art the man.*

3. Christ reproves her, both for
the *intenseness* of her care ("Thou
art *careful and troubled, divided
and disturbed* by thy care"), and
for the *extensiveness of it*, "about
many things; thou dost *grasp* at
many *enjoyments*, and so art
troubled at many *disappointments*.
Poor Martha, thou hast many
things to fret at, and this puts thee
out of humour, whereas less ado
would serve."

4. That which aggravated the
sin and folly of her care was that
but one thing is needful. There is
need of *one heart* to attend upon
the word, not divided and hurried
to and fro, as Martha's was at
this time. *The one thing needful* is
certainly meant of that which
Mary made her choice—*sitting at*
Christ's feet, to hear his word.

VI. Christ's approbation and
commendation of Mary for her
serious piety: *Mary hath chosen
the good part.* Mary said nothing
in her own defence; but, since
Martha has appealed to the
Master, to him she is willing to
refer it, and will abide by his
award; and here we have it.

1. She had justly given the
preference to that which best
deserved it; for *one thing is needful*,
this one thing that she has done, to
give up herself to the guidance of
Christ, and *receive the law* from
his mouth.

2. She had herein wisely done
well for herself. Christ *justified*

Mary against her sister's clamours.
But this was not all; he *applauded*
her for her wisdom: *She hath
chosen the good part*; for she
chose to be with Christ, to take
her part with him; she chose the
better business, and the better
happiness, and took a better way
of *honouring* Christ and of *pleasing*
him, by receiving his word into her
heart, than Martha did by providing for his entertainment in her
house.

CHAPTER ELEVEN

PRAYER (*vv.* 1–13)

Prayer is one of the great laws of
natural religion. That man is a
brute, is a monster, that never
prays, that never gives glory to his
Maker, nor feels his favour, nor
owns his dependence upon him.
One great design therefore of
Christianity is to *assist us in
prayer*, to enforce the duty upon
us, to instruct us in it, and encourage us to expect advantage by
it. Now here,

I. We find Christ himself *praying
in a certain place*, probably where
he used to pray, *v.* 1. As God, he
was *prayed to*; as man, he *prayed*;
and, though he was a Son, yet
learned he this obedience. This
evangelist has taken particular
notice of Christ's *praying often*,
more than any other of the evangelists: when he was baptized
(*ch.* iii. 21), he was *praying*; he
*withdrew into the wilderness, and
prayed* (*ch.* v. 16); he *went out into
a mountain to pray, and continued
all night in prayer* (*ch.* vi. 12); he
was *alone praying* (*ch.* ix. 18);
soon after, he *went up into a*

mountain to pray, and *as he prayed he was transfigured* (*ch.* ix. 28, 29); and here he was *praying in a certain place*. Thus, like a genuine son of David, he *gave himself unto prayer*, Ps. cix. 4.

II. His disciples applied themselves to him for direction in prayer.

Now, 1. Their request is, "*Lord, teach us to pray*; give us a rule or model by which to go in praying, and put words into our mouths."

2. Their plea is, "*As John also taught his disciples.* He took care to instruct his disciples in this necessary duty, and we would be taught as they were, for we have a better Master than they had."

III. Christ gave them direction, much the same as he had given them before in his sermon upon the mount, Matt. vi. 9, &c. In Mathew he had directed them to pray *after this manner*; here, *When ye pray, say*; which intimates that the Lord's prayer was intended to be used both as a form of prayer and a directory.

There are some differences between the Lord's prayer in Matthew and in Luke, by which it appears that it was not the design of Christ that we should be *tied up* to these very words, for then there would have been no variation.

POWER OVER SATAN
(*vv.* 14–26)

The substance of these verses we had in Matt. xii. 22, &c. Christ is here giving a general proof of his divine mission, by a particular proof of his power over Satan, his conquest of whom was an indication of his great design in coming

into the world, which was, to *destroy the works of the devil*. Here too he gives an earnest of the success of that undertaking. He is here casting out *a devil* that made the poor possessed man *dumb*: in Matthew we are told that he was *blind* and *dumb*. When the devil was forced out by the word of Christ, the *dumb* spoke immediately, echoed to Christ's word, and the lips were opened to show forth his praise.

TRUE BLESSING
(*vv.* 27, 28)

We had not this passage in the other evangelists, nor can we tack it, as Dr. Hammond does, to that of Christ's mother and brethren desiring to speak with him (for this evangelist also has related that in *ch.* viii. 19), but it contains an interruption much like that, and, like that, occasion is taken from it for instruction.

1. The applause which an affectionate, honest, well-meaning woman gave to our Lord Jesus, upon hearing his excellent discourses. While the scribes and Pharisees despised and blasphemed them, this good woman (and probably she was a person of some quality) admired them, and the wisdom and power with which he spoke: *As he spoke these things* (*v.* 27), with a convincing force and evidence, a *certain woman of the company* was so pleased to hear how he had confounded the Pharisees, and conquered them, and put them to shame, and cleared himself from their vile insinuations, that she

could not forbear crying out, "*Blessed is the womb that bore thee*. What an admirable, what an excellent man is this! Surely never was there a greater or better born of a woman: happy the woman that has him for her son. I should have thought myself very happy to have been the mother of one that *speaks as never man spoke*, that has so much of the grace of heaven in him, and is so great a blessing to this earth." This was *well said*, as it expressed her high esteem of Christ, and that for the sake of his doctrine; and it was not amiss that it reflected honour upon the virgin Mary his mother, for it agreed with what she herself had said (*ch.* i. 48), *All generations shall call me blessed*; some even of this generation, bad as it was. Note, To all that believe the word of Christ the person of Christ is precious, and he is *an honour*, 1 Pet. ii. 7. Yet we must be careful, lest, as this good woman, we too much magnify the honour of his natural kindred, and so *know him after the flesh*, whereas we must now henceforth *know him so no more*.

2. The occasion which Christ took from this to pronounce *them* more happy who are his faithful and obedient followers than she was who bore and nursed him. He does not deny what this woman said, nor refuse her respect to him and his mother; but leads her from this to that which was of higher consideration, and which more concerned her: *Yea, rather, blessed are they that hear the word of God, and keep it*, v. 28. He thinks them so; and his saying

that they are so makes him so, and should make us of his mind. This is intended partly as a *check* to her, for doting so much upon his bodily presence and his human nature, partly as an *encouragement* to her to hope that she might be as happy as his own mother, whose happiness she was ready to envy, if she would *hear the word of God and keep it*. Note, Though it is a great privilege to hear the word of God, yet those only are truly blessed, that is, blessed of the Lord, that hear it and *keep* it, that keep it in memory, and keep to it as their way and rule.

SIGN OF JONAH
(*vv.* 29–36)

Christ's discourse in these verses shows two things:—

I. What is the *sign* we may *expect* from God for the *confirmation* of our *faith*. The great and most convincing proof of Christ's being sent of God, and which they were yet to wait for, after the many signs that had been given them, was the resurrection of Christ from the dead. Here is,

1. A reproof to the people for demanding other signs than what had already been given them in great plenty. They came *seeking a sign*, they came to gaze, to have something to talk of when they went home; and it is an *evil generation* which nothing will awaken and convince, no, not the most sensible demonstrations of divine power and goodness.

2. A promise that yet there should be *one sign* more given

them, different from any that had yet been given them, even the *sign of Jonas the prophet*, which in Matthew is explained as meaning the *resurrection of Christ*. As Jonas being cast into the sea, and lying there three days, and then coming up alive and preaching repentance to the Ninevites, was a sign to them, upon which they turned from their evil way, so shall the death and resurrection of Christ, and the preaching of his gospel immediately after to the Gentile world, be the last warning to the Jewish nation.

3. A warning to them to improve this sign; for it was at their peril if they did not. (1) The *queen of Sheba* would *rise up in judgment against them*, and condemn *their unbelief*, v. 31. She was a stranger to the commonwealth of Israel, and yet so readily gave credit to the report she heard of the glories of a king of Israel, that, notwithstanding the prejudices we are apt to conceive against foreigners, she came from the uttermost parts of the earth to *hear his wisdom*, not only to satisfy her curiosity, but to inform her mind, especially in the knowledge of the true God and his worship, which is upon record, to her honour; and, behold, a *greater than Solomon is here*, *more than a Solomon is here*; that is, says Dr. Hammond, more of wisdom and more heavenly divine doctrine than ever was in all Solomon's words or writings; and yet these wretched Jews will give no manner of regard to what Christ says to them, though he be in the midst of them. (2) The Ninevites would

rise up in judgment against them, and condemn their impenitency (*v.* 32): They *repented at the preaching of Jonas*; but here is preaching which far exceeds that of Jonas, is more powerful and awakening, and threatens a much sorer ruin than that of Nineveh, and yet none are startled by it, to turn *from their evil way*, as the Ninevites did.

II. What is the *sign* that God *expects* from us for the *evidencing* of our faith, and that is the serious practice of that religion which we profess to believe, and a readiness to entertain all divine truths, when brought to us in their proper evidence. Now observe,

1. They had *the light* with all the advantage they could desire.

2. Having the *light*, their concern was to have the *sight*, or else to what purpose had they the light? Be the *object* ever so *clear*, if the *organ* be not *right*, we are never the better: *The light of the body is the eye* (*v.* 34), which receives the light of the candle when it is brought into the room. So the light of the soul is the understanding and judgment, and its power of discerning between good and evil, truth and falsehood. If the *eye of the* soul be evil,—if the judgment be *bribed* and *biassed* by the corrupt and vicious dispositions of the mind, by pride and envy, by the love of the world and sensual pleasures,—if the understanding be *prejudiced* against divine truths, and resolved not to admit them, though brought with ever so convincing an evidence,—it is no wonder that the *whole body*, the whole soul, should be *full of*

darkness, v. 34. How can they have instruction, information, direction, or comfort, from the gospel, that wilfully shut their eyes against it? and what hope is there of such? what remedy for them? The inference hence therefore is, *Take heed that the light which is in thee be not darkness*, v. 35. Take heed that the eye of the mind be not blinded by partiality, and prejudice, and sinful aims. Be sincere in your enquiries after truth, and ready to receive it in the light, and love, and power of it; and not as the men of *this generation* to whom Christ preached, who never sincerely *desired* to know God's will, nor *designed* to do it, and therefore no wonder that they *walked on in darkness*, wandered *endlessly*, and perished *eternally*.

PHARISEES REPROVED
(vv. 37–54)

Christ here says many of those things to a Pharisee and his guests, in a *private* conversation at table, which he afterwards said in a *public* discourse in the temple (Matt. 23); for what he said in public and private was *of a piece*. Here is,

I. Christ's going to dine with a Pharisee that very civilly invited him to his house (v. 37): *As he spoke*, even while he was speaking, a *certain Pharisee* interrupted him with a request to him to come and *dine with him*, to come *forthwith*, for it was dinner-time. Note, Christ's disciples must learn of him to be *conversable*, and not *morose*. Though we have need to

be *cautious* what company we keep, yet we need not be *rigid*, nor must we therefore *go out of the world*.

II. The offence which the Pharisee took at Christ, as those of that sort had sometimes done at the disciples of Christ, for not *washing before dinner*, v. 38. Was it not strictly commanded by the canons of their church? It was so, and *therefore* Christ would not do it, because he would witness against their assuming a power to impose that as a matter of religion which *God commanded them not*.

III. The sharp reproof which Christ, upon this occasion, gave to the Pharisees, without begging pardon even of the Pharisee whose guest he now was; for we must not flatter our best friends in any evil thing.

1. He reproves them for placing religion so much in those instances of it which are only external, and fall under the eye of man, while those were not only *postponed*, but quite *expunged*, which respect the soul, and fall under the eye of God, vv. 39, 40.

2. He reproves them for laying stress upon trifles, and neglecting the weighty matters of the law, v. 42.

3. He reproves them for their pride and vanity, and affectations of precedency and praise of men (v. 43).

4. He reproves them for their hypocrisy, and their colouring over the wickedness of their hearts and lives with specious pretences (v. 44).

IV. The testimony which he bore also against the lawyers or

scribes, who made it their business to *expound* the law according to the tradition of the elders, as the Pharisees did to *observe* the law according to that tradition.

1. There was one of that profession who resented what he said against the Pharisees (*v.* 45): "*Master, thus saying thou reproachest us also,* for we are scribes; and are we therefore hypocrites?"

2. Our Lord Jesus thereupon took them to task (*v.* 46): *Woe unto you also, ye lawyers*; and again (*v.* 52): *Woe unto you, lawyers.*

(1) The lawyers are reproved for making the services of religion more *burdensome* to others, but more *easy* for themselves, than God had made them (*v.* 46).

(2) They are reproved for pretending a veneration for the memory of the prophets whom their fathers killed, when yet they hated and persecuted those in their own day who were sent to them on the same errand, to call them to repentance, and direct them to Christ, *vv.* 47–49.

(3) They are reproved for opposing the gospel of Christ, and doing all they could to obstruct the progress and success of it, *v.* 52.

Lastly, In the close of the chapter we are told how spitefully and maliciously the scribes and *Pharisees* contrived to draw him into a snare, *vv.* 53, 54. Note, Faithful reprovers of sin must expect to have many enemies, and have need to set a watch before the door of their lips, because of *their observers* that watch for their slips.

CHAPTER TWELVE

CHRIST'S PREACHING
(*vv.* 1–12)

We find here, I. A vast auditory that was got together to hear Christ preach. Though in the morning sermon, when they were *gathered thickly together* (*ch.* xi. 29), he had severely reproved them, as an *evil generation that seek a sign,* yet they renewed their attendance on him; so much better could the people bear *their* reproofs than the Pharisees *theirs.*

II. The instructions which he gave his followers, in the hearing of this auditory.

1. He began with a caution against *hypocrisy.*

(1) The description of that sin which he warns them against: *It is the leaven of the Pharisees.* [1] It is *leaven*; it is *spreading* as leaven, *insinuates* itself into the whole man, and all that he does; it is *swelling* and *souring* as leaven, for it puffs men up with pride, embitters them with malice, and makes their service unacceptable to God. [2] It is the leaven of the Pharisees: "It is the sin they are most of them found in. Make not *your* religion a *cloak of maliciousness,* as they do theirs."

(2) A good reason against it: "*For there is nothing covered that shall not be revealed, vv.* 2, 3. It is to no purpose to dissemble, for, sooner or later, truth will come out; and a *lying tongue is but for a moment.*"

2. To this he added a charge to them to be faithful to the trust reposed in them, and not to betray it, through cowardice or base fear.

(1) "The power of your enemies is a limited power (*v.* 4): *I say unto you, my friends*" (Christ's disciples are his friends, he calls them *friends*, and gives them this *friendly* advice), "*be not afraid*; do not disquiet yourselves with tormenting fears of the power and rage of men." Note, Those whom Christ owns for *his friends* need not be afraid of any enemies.

· (2) God is to be feared more than the most powerful men: "*I will forewarn you whom you shall fear* (*v.* 5): that you may fear man less, fear God more."

(3) The lives of good Christians and good ministers are the particular care of divine Providence, *vv.* 6, 7. To encourage us in times of difficulty and danger, we must have recourse to our first principles, and build upon them. Now a firm belief of the doctrine of God's universal providence, and the extent of it, will be satisfying to us when at any time we are in peril, and will encourage us to trust God in the way of duty.

(4) "You will be owned or disowned by Christ, in the great day, according as you now own or disown him," *vv.* 8, 9. [1] To engage us to *confess Christ before men*, whatever we may lose or suffer for our constancy to him, and how dear soever it may cost us, we are assured that they who *confess Christ* now shall be owned by him in the great day *before the angels of God*, to their everlasting comfort and honour. [2] To deter us from *denying* Christ, and a cowardly *deserting* of his truths and ways, we are here assured that those who *deny Christ*, and

treacherously depart from him, whatever they may save by it, though it were life itself, and whatever they may *gain* by it, though it were a kingdom, will be vast losers at last, for they shall be *denied before the angels of God*.

(5) The errand they were shortly to be sent out upon was of the highest and last importance to the children of men, to whom they were sent, *v.* 10. Let them be bold in preaching the gospel, for a sorer and heavier doom would attend those that rejected them than those that now rejected Christ himself, and opposed him.

(6) Whatever trials they should be called out to, they should be sufficiently furnished for them, and honourably brought through them, *vv.* 11, 12.

THE RICH MAN
(*vv.* 13–21)

We have in these verses,

I. The application that was made to Christ, very unseasonably, by one of his hearers, desiring him to interpose *between him and his brother* in a matter that concerned the estate of the family (*v.* 13): "*Master, speak to my brother*; speak as a prophet, speak as a king, speak with authority; he is one that will have regard to what thou sayest; speak to him, *that he divide the inheritance with me*."

II. Christ's refusal to interpose in this matter (*v.* 14): *Man, who made me a judge or divider over you?* In matters of this nature, Christ will not assume either a *legislative* power to alter the settled rule of inheritances, or a *judicial* power to determine controversies concerning them. Now this shows us what is the nature and constitution of Christ's kingdom. It is a spiritual kingdom, and not of this world. 1. It does not interfere with civil powers, nor take the authority of princes out of their hands. Christianity leaves the matter as it found it, as to civil power. 2. It does not intermeddle with civil rights; it obliges all to do justly, according to the settled rules of equity, but dominion is not founded in grace. 3. It does not *encourage* our *expectations* of worldly advantages by our religion. If this man will be a disciple of Christ, and expects that in consideration of this Christ should give him his brother's estate, he is mistaken; the rewards of Christ's disciples are of another nature. 4. It does not *encourage* our *contests* with our brethren, and our being rigorous and high in our demands, but rather, for peace' sake, to recede from our right.

III. The necessary caution which Christ took occasion from this to give to his hearers. Though he came not to be a *divider* of men's estates, he came to be a director of their consciences about them, and would have all take heed of harbouring that corrupt principle which they saw to be in others the *root* of *so much evil*. Here is,

1. The caution itself (*v.* 15): *Take heed and beware of covetousness.*

2. The reason of it, or an argument to enforce this caution: *For a man's life consisteth not in the abundance of the things which he possesseth*; that is, "our happiness

and comfort do not depend upon our having a great deal of the wealth of this world."

3. The illustration of this by a parable which gives us the life and death of a *rich man*, and leaves us to judge whether he was a *happy* man.

(1) Here is an account of his worldly wealth and abundance (*v.* 16): *The ground of a certain rich man brought forth plentifully.*

(2) Here are the workings of his heart, in the midst of this abundance.

[1] What his *cares* and *concerns* were. When he saw an extraordinary crop upon his ground, instead of *thanking God* for it, or rejoicing in the opportunity it would give him of doing the more good, he afflicts himself with this thought, *What shall I do, because I have no room to bestow my fruits?*

[2] What his *projects* and *purposes* were, which were the result of his cares, and were indeed absurd and foolish like them (*v.* 18): "*This will I do*, and it is the wisest course I can take, *I will pull down my barns*, for they are too little, and I will *build greater, and there will I bestow all my fruits and my goods*, and then I shall be at ease." Now here, *First*, It was folly for him to call the fruits of the ground *his* fruits and *his* goods. It is *my corn* (saith God) and *my wine*, Hos. ii. 8, 9. *Secondly*, It was folly for him to *hoard up* what he had, and then to think it *well bestowed*. There will I bestow it *all*; as if none must be bestowed upon the poor, none upon his family, none upon the Levite and *the stranger*, the

fatherless and the widow, but all in the great barn. *Thirdly*, It was folly for him to let his *mind* rise with his *condition*; when his ground brought forth more plentifully than usual, then to talk of bigger barns, as if the next year must needs be as fruitful as this, and much more abundant, whereas the barn might be as much too big the next year as it was too little this. *Fourthly*, It was folly for him to contrive and resolve all this *absolutely* and *without reserve*. This *I will* do: *I will* pull down my barns and *I will* build greater, yea, that *I will*; without so much as that necessary proviso, *If the Lord will, I shall live*, Jam. iv. 13–15.

[3] What his *pleasing hopes* and *expectations* were, when he should have made good these projects. "Then *I will say to my soul, thou hast much goods laid up for many years* in these barns; now *take thine ease*, enjoy thyself, *eat, drink, and be merry*," v. 19.

(3) Here is God's sentence upon all this; and we are sure that his judgment is according to truth. God said he did ill for himself: *Thou fool, this night thy soul shall be required of thee*, v. 20. Now observe what God said,

[1] The character he gave him: *Thou fool*.

[2] The sentence he passed upon him, a sentence of death: *This night thy soul shall be required of thee; they shall require thy soul* (so the words are), and then *whose shall those things be which thou hast provided?* He thought he had goods that should be his for many years, but he must part from them *this night*; he thought he should

enjoy them himself, but he must leave them to he knows not who.

First, It is a *force*, an *arrest*; it is the *requiring of the soul*, that soul that thou art making such a fool of. God shall require it; he shall require an account of it. "Man, woman, what hast thou done with they soul. Give an account of that stewardship."

Secondly, It is a *surprise*, an *unexpected* force. It is *this night*, this *present* night, without delay; there is no giving bail, or begging a day. This *pleasant* night, when thou art promising thyself many years to come, now thou must die, and go to judgment.

Thirdly, It is the leaving of all *those things* behind *which they have provided*, which they have laboured for, and prepared for hereafter, with abundance of toil and care. All that which they have placed their happiness in, and built their hope upon, and raised their expectations from, they must leave behind.

Fourthly, It is leaving them to they *know not who*: "Then *whose shall those things be*? Not *thine* to be sure, and thou knowest not what *they* will prove for whom thou didst design them."

Fifthly, It is a demonstration of his folly. Then it will appear that he took pains to lay up treasure in a world he was hastening from, but took no care to lay it up in the world he was hastening to.

Lastly, Here is the application of this parable (*v.* 21): *So is he*, such a fool, a fool in God's judgment, a fool upon record, that *layeth up treasure for himself, and is not rich towards God*. This is the way and this is the end of such a man.

MORE PRECEPTS (*vv.* 22–40)

Our Lord Jesus is here inculcating some needful useful lessons upon his disciples, which he had before taught them, Matt. vi. 25, &c.; and the arguments here used are much the same, designed for our encouragement to cast all our care upon God, which is the *right way* to *ease* ourselves of it.

He also charges them to get ready, and to keep in a readiness for Christ's coming, when all those who have laid up their treasure in heaven shall enter upon the enjoyment of it, *vv.* 35, &c.

1. Christ is our *Master*, and we are his *servants*, not only *working* servants, but *waiting* servants, servants that are to do him honour, in *waiting* on him, and attending his motions: *If any man serve me, let him follow me. Follow the Lamb whithersoever he goes.* But that is not all: they must do him honour in *waiting for him*, and expecting his return. We must be as men that *wait for their Lord*, that sit up late while he stays out late, to be ready to receive him.

2. Christ our Master, though now *gone from us*, will *return again*. He *will come* to take cognizance of his servants, and, that being a *critical day*, they shall either stay with him or be turned out of doors, according as they are found in that day.

3. The time of our Master's return is uncertain; it will be *in the night*, it will be *far* in the night, when he has long *deferred* his coming, and when many have done

looking for him; in the *second watch*, just before midnight, or in the *third watch*, next after midnight, *v.* 38. His coming to us, at our death, is uncertain, and to many it will be a great surprise; for *the Son of man cometh at an hour that ye think not* (*v.* 40), without giving notice beforehand.

4. That which he expects and requires from his servants is that they be *ready to open to him immediately*, whenever he comes (*v.* 36), that is, that they be in a frame fit to receive him, or rather to be received by him; that they be found *as* his servants, in the posture that becomes them.

5. Those servants will be happy who shall be found ready, and in a good frame, when their Lord shall come (*v.* 37): *Blessed are those servants.*

6. We are *therefore* kept at uncertainty concerning the precise time of his coming that we may be always ready; for it is no thanks to a man to be ready for an attack, if he know beforehand just the time when it will be made: *The good man of the house, if he had known what hour the thief would have come,* though he were ever so careless a man, *would yet have watched,* and have frightened away the thieves, *v.* 39. But we do not know at what hour the alarm will be given us, and therefore are concerned to watch at all times, and never to be off our guard.

THE DISCIPLES' RESPONSIBILITY (*vv.* 41–53)

Here is, I. Peter's question, which he put to Christ upon occasion of the foregoing parable (*v.* 41). Peter desires Christ to explain himself, and to direct the arrow of the foregoing parable to the mark he intended. Lord, said Peter, was it intended for *us*, or for *all*? To this Christ gives a direct answer (Mark xiii. 37): *What I say unto you, I say unto all*. Yet here he seems to show that the apostles were primarily concerned in it.

II. Christ's reply to this question, directed to Peter and the rest of the disciples. Now our Lord Jesus here tells them,

1. What was their *duty* as *stewards*, and what the *trust* committed to them. (1) They are made *rulers of God's household*, under Christ, whose own the house is. (2) Their business is to give God's children and servants *their portion of meat*, that which is proper for them and allotted to them. (3) To give it to them *in due season*, at that time and in that way which are most suitable to the temper and condition of those that are to be fed. (4) Herein they must approve themselves *faithful* and *wise*.

2. What would be their happiness if they approved themselves faithful and wise (*v.* 43): *Blessed is that servant*, (1) That is *doing*, and is not idle, nor indulgent of his ease; even the rulers of the household must be *doing*, and make themselves *servants of all*. (2) That is *so* doing, doing as he should be, giving them their *portion of meat*, by public preaching and personal application. (3) That is *found* so doing when his Lord comes; that perseveres to the end, notwithstanding the difficulties he may meet with in the way.

3. What a dreadful reckoning there would be if they were treacherous and unfaithful, *vv.* 45, 46. If that servant begin to be quarrelsome and profane, he shall be called to an account, and severely punished. We had all this before in Matthew.

III. A further discourse concerning his own sufferings, which he expected, and concerning the sufferings of his followers, which he would have them also to live in expectation of. In general (*v.* 49): *I am come to send fire on the earth*. By this some understand the preaching of the gospel, and the pouring out of the Spirit, holy fire. But, by what follows, it seems rather to be understood of the fire of *persecution*. Christ is not the Author of it, as it is the sin of the incendiaries, the *persecutors*; but he *permits* it, nay, he *commissions* it, as a *refining* fire for the *trial* of the *persecuted*.

1. He must himself suffer many things; he must pass through this fire that was already kindled (*v.* 50): *I have a baptism to be baptized with*. Afflictions are compared both to *fire* and *water*, Ps. lxvi. 12; lxix. 1, 2. Christ's sufferings were both. He calls them a *baptism* (Matt. xx. 22); for he was watered or sprinkled with them. He must be sprinkled with his own blood, and with the blood of his enemies, Isa. lxiii. 3. Christ in his sufferings *devoted* himself to his Father's honour, and *consecrated* himself a priest for evermore, Heb. vii. 27, 28. He longed for the time when he should suffer and die, having an eye to the glorious issue of his sufferings.

2. He tells those about him that they also must bear with hardships and difficulties (*v.* 51): "*Suppose ye that I came to give peace on earth*, to give you a peaceable possession of the earth, and outward prosperity on the earth?" You will find,

(1) "That the effect of the preaching of the gospel will be *division*." Not but that the design of the gospel and its proper tendency are to unite the children of men to one another, to knit them together in holy love, and, if all would receive it, this would be the effect of it; but there being multitudes that not only will not receive it, but oppose it, and have their corruptions exasperated by it, and are enraged at those that do receive it, it proves, though not the *cause*, yet the *occasion* of *division*.

(2) "That this *division* will reach into private families, and the preaching of the gospel will give occasion for discord among the nearest relations" (*v.* 53). Therefore let not the disciples of Christ promise themselves *peace` upon earth*, for they are sent forth *as sheep in the midst of wolves*.

SEEING THE SIGN (*vv.* 54–59)

Having given his disciples *their* lesson in the foregoing verses, here Christ turns to *the people*, and gives them *theirs*, *v.* 54. Two things he specifies:—

I. Let them learn to *discern the way of God towards them*, that they may *prepare* accordingly. The prognostications here referred to had their origin in repeated observations upon the chain of

causes; from what *has been* we conjecture what *will be*. See the benefit of experience; by *taking notice* we may come to *give notice*.

II. Let them hasten to *make their peace with God* in time, before it be too late, *vv.* 58, 59. This we had upon another occasion, Matt. v. 25, 26.

CHAPTER THIRTEEN

REPENT—OR PERISH
(*vv.* 1–5)

We have here, I. Tidings brought to Christ of the death of some Galileans lately, whose blood *Pilate had mingled with their sacrifices*, *v.* 1. Let us consider,

1. What this tragical story was. It is briefly related here, and is not met with in any of the historians of those times. Josephus indeed mentions Pilate's killing some Samaritans, who, under the conduct of a factious leader, were going in a tumultuous manner to mount Gerizim, where the Samaritans' temple was; but we can by no means allow that story to be the same with this. The Galileans being Herod's subjects, it is probable that this outrage committed upon them by Pilate occasioned the quarrel that was between Herod and Pilate, which we read of in *ch.* xxiii. 12.

2. Why it was related *at this season* to our Lord Jesus. (1) Perhaps merely as a matter of news, which they supposed he had not heard before, and as a thing which they lamented, and believed he would do so too; for the Galileans were their countrymen. (2) Perhaps it was intended as a

confirmation of what Christ had said in the close of the foregoing chapter, concerning the necessity of making our peace with God in time, before we be *delivered to the officer*, that is, to *death*, and so *cast into prison*, and then it will be too late to make agreements. (3) Perhaps they would stir him up, being himself of Galilee, and a prophet, and one that had a great interest in that country, to find out a way to revenge the death of these Galileans upon Herod. (4) Perhaps this was told Christ to *deter* him from going up to Jerusalem, to worship (*v.* 22), lest Pilate should serve him as he had served those Galileans. (5) Christ's answer intimates that they told him this with a spiteful *innuendo*, that, though Pilate was unjust in killing them, yet without doubt they were secretly bad men, else God would not have permitted Pilate thus barbarously to cut them off.

II. Christ's reply to this report, in which,

1. He seconded it with another story, which, like it, gave an instance of people's being taken away by sudden death. It is not long since *the tower of Siloam fell*, and there were eighteen persons killed and buried in the ruins of it.

2. He cautioned his hearers not to make an ill use of these and similar events, nor take occasion thence to censure *great sufferers*, as if they were *therefore* to be accounted *great sinners*: *Suppose ye that these Galileans*, who were slain as they were sacrificing, *were sinners above all the Galileans, because they suffered such things?*

I tell you nay, vv. 2, 3. We cannot judge of men's *sins* by their *sufferings* in this world; for many are thrown into the furnace as gold to be purified, not as dross and chaff to be consumed.

3. On these stories he founded a call to repentance, adding to each of them this awakening word, *Except ye repent, ye shall all likewise perish, vv.* 3–5. (1) This intimates that we all deserve to *perish* as much as *they did*, and had we been dealt with according to our sins, according to the *iniquity of our holy things*, our blood had been long ere this mingled with our sacrifices by the justice of God. (2) That therefore we are all concerned to *repent*, to be sorry for what we have done amiss, and to do so no more. The judgments of God upon others are loud calls to us to *repent*. (3) That repentance is the way to escape perishing, and it is a sure way: *so iniquity shall not be your ruin*, but upon no other terms. (4) That, if we repent not, we shall certainly perish, as others have done before us.

THE FIG TREE (*vv.* 6–9)

This parable is intended to enforce that word of warning immediately going before, "*Except ye repent, ye shall all likewise perish*; except you be reformed, you will be ruined, as the barren tree, except it bring forth fruit, will be cut down."

I. This parable primarily refers to the nation and people of the Jews. God chose them for his own, made them a people near to him, gave them advantages for knowing and serving him above any other people, and expected answerable returns of duty and obedience from them, which, turning to his praise and honour, he would have accounted *fruit*; but they disappointed his expectations: they did not do their duty; they were a reproach instead of being a credit to their profession. Upon this, he justly determined to abandon them, and cut them off, to deprive them of their privileges, to unchurch and unpeople them; but, upon Christ's intercession, as of old upon that of Moses, he graciously gave them further time and further mercy; tried them, as it were, another year, by sending his apostles among them, to call them to repentance, and in Christ's name to offer them pardon, upon repentance. Some of them were wrought upon to *repent*, and bring forth fruit, and with them all was well; but the body of the nation continued impenitent and unfruitful, and ruin without remedy came upon them; about forty years after they were cut down, and cast into the fire, as John Baptist had told them (Matt. iii. 10), which saying of his this parable enlarges upon.

II. Yet it has, without doubt, a further reference, and is designed for the awakening of all that enjoy the means of grace, and the privileges of the visible church, to see to it that the temper of their minds and the tenour of their lives be answerable to their professions and opportunities, for that is the *fruit* required. Now observe here,

1. The advantages which this fig-tree had. It was *planted in a vineyard*, in better soil, and where it had more care taken of it and more pains taken with it, than other fig-trees had, that commonly grew, not in *vineyards* (those are for vines), but by the *way-side*, Matt. xxi. 19.

2. The owner's expectation from it: *He came, and sought fruit thereon*, and he had reason to expect it. Note, The God of heaven requires and expects *fruit* from those that have a place in his vineyard.

3. The disappointment of his expectation: *He found none*, none at all, not one fig. Note, It is sad to think how many enjoy the privileges of the gospel, and yet do nothing at all to the honour of God, nor to answer the end of his entrusting them with those privileges; and it is a disappointment to him and a grief to the Spirit of his grace.

4. The doom passed upon it: *Cut it down*. He saith this to the *dresser of the vineyard*, to Christ, to whom all judgment is committed, to the ministers who are in his name to declare this doom.

5. The dresser's intercession for it. Christ is the great Intercessor; he ever lives, interceding. Now observe,

(1) What it is he prays for, and that is a reprieve: *Lord, let it alone this year also*.

(2) How he promises to improve this reprieve, if it be obtained: *Till I shall dig about it, and dung it*. Unfruitful Christians must be *awakened* by the terrors of the law, which *break up the fallow ground*, and then encouraged by the promises of the gospel, which

are warming and fattening, as manure to the tree. Both methods must be tried; the one prepares for the other, and all little enough.

(3) Upon what foot he leaves the matter: "Let us try it, and try what we can do with it one year more, *and, if it bear fruit, well, v.* 9. It is possible, nay, there is hope, that yet it may be fruitful."

But he adds, *If not, then after that thou shalt cut it down.* Observe here, [1] That, though God bear long, he will not bear always with unfruitful professors. [2] The longer God has *waited*, and the more cost he has been at upon them, the greater will their destruction be. [3] Cutting down, though it is work that shall be done, is work that God does not take pleasure in. [4] Those that now intercede for barren trees, and take pains with them, if they persist in their unfruitfulness will be even content to see them cut down, and will not have one word more to say for them.

INFIRM WOMAN HEALED
(*vv.* 10–17)

Here is, I. The miraculous cure of a woman that had been long under a spirit of infirmity. Our Lord Jesus spent his *sabbaths* in the *synagogues, v.* 10. Now to confirm the doctrine he preached, and recommend it as faithful, and well worthy of all acceptation, he wrought a miracle, a miracle of mercy.

1. The object of charity that presented itself was a woman in the synagogue that had *a spirit of infirmity eighteen years, v.* 11. She had an infirmity, which an evil

spirit, by divine permission, had brought upon her, which was such that she was *bowed together* by strong convulsions, and could *in no wise lift up herself*.

2. The offer of this cure to one that sought it not bespeaks the preventing mercy and grace of Christ: *When Jesus saw her, he called her to him, v.* 12.

3. The cure effectually and immediately wrought bespeaks his almighty power. He *laid his hands on her*, and said, "*Woman, thou art loosed from thine infirmity*; though thou hast been long labouring under it, thou art at length released from it." Let not those despair whose disease is *inveterate*, who have been long in affliction. God can at length relieve them, therefore though he tarry wait for him. Though it was a *spirit of infirmity*, an evil spirit, that she was under the power of, Christ has a power superior to that of Satan, is *stronger than he.* Though *she could in no wise lift up herself*, Christ could lift her up, and enable her to lift up herself.

4. The present effect of this cure upon the *soul* of the patient as well as upon her *body*. She *glorified God*, gave him the praise of her cure to whom all praise is due. When crooked souls are made straight, they will show it by their glorifying God.

II. The offence that was taken at this by the *ruler of the synagogue*, as if our Lord Jesus had committed some heinous crime, in healing this poor woman. He *had indignation* at it, because it was *on the sabbath day, v.* 14.

III. Christ's justification of him-

Infirm Woman Healed

self in what he had done (*v.* 15): *The Lord then answered him*, as he had answered others who in like manner cavilled at him, *Thou hypocrite*. Christ knew that he had a real enmity to him and to his gospel, that he did but cloak this with a pretended zeal for the sabbath day, and that when he bade the people come on the *six days*, and be healed, he really would not have them be healed any day. Christ could have told him this, but he vouchsafes to reason the case with him; and,

1. He *appeals* to the common practice among the Jews, which was never disallowed, that of *watering* their cattle on the sabbath day.

2. He applies this to the present case (*v.* 16): "Must the *ox* and the *ass* have compassion shown them on the sabbath day, and have so much time and pains bestowed upon them *every* sabbath, to be loosed from the stall, led away perhaps a great way to the water, and then back again, and shall not this woman, only with a touch of the hand and a word's speaking, be *loosed* from a much *greater* grievance than that which the cattle undergo when they are kept a day without water?

IV. The different effect that this had upon those that heard him. And now observe,

1. What a confusion this was to the malice of his persecutors: *When he had said these things, all his adversaries were ashamed* (*v.* 17).

2. What a confirmation this was to the faith of his friends: *All the people*, who had a better sense of things, and judged more impartially than their rulers, rejoiced *for all the glorious things that were done by him*. The shame of his foes was the joy of his followers.

SIMILES OF THE KINGDOM
(*vv.* 18–22)

Here is, I. The gospel's progress foretold in two parables, which we had before, Matt. xiii. 31–33. The *kingdom of the Messiah* is the *kingdom of God*, for it advances his glory; this kingdom was yet a mystery, and people were generally in the dark, and under mistakes, about it. Now, when we would describe a thing to those that are strangers to it, we choose to do it by similitudes. So Christ undertakes here to show *what the kingdom of God is like* (*v.* 18).

THE LAST AND THE FIRST
(*vv.* 23–30)

We have here,

1. A question put to our Lord Jesus. The question was, *Are there few that are saved? v.* 23: "*If the saved be few?*"

II. Christ's answer to this question, which directs us what use to make of this truth. Ask not, "How many shall be saved?" But, be they more or fewer, "Shall I be one of them?" Not, "What shall become of such and such, and *what shall this man do?*" But, "What shall I do, and what will become of me?" Now in Christ's answer observe,

1. A quickening exhortation and direction: *Strive to enter in at the strait gate*. This is directed not to him only that asked the question, but to all, to us, it is in the plural number: *Strive ye*.

2. Various awakening considerations, to enforce this exhortation.

(1) Think how many take *some pains* for salvation and yet perish because they do not take *enough*, and you will say that there are *few that will be saved* and that it highly concerns us to *strive*: *Many will seek to enter in, and shall not be able*; they *seek*, but they do not *strive*.

(2) Think of the *distinguishing* day that is coming and the *decisions* of that day, and you will say there are *few that shall be saved* and that we are concerned to strive: The *Master of the house* will *rise up, and shut to the door, v.* 25.

(3) Think how many who were very *confident* that they should be *saved* will be rejected in the day of trial, and their confidences will deceive them, and you will say that there are *few* that *shall be saved* and that we are all concerned to *strive*. Consider,

[1] What an *assurance* they had of *admission*, and how far their hope carried them, even to *heaven's gate*. There they *stand and knock*, knock as if they had authority, knock as those that belong to the house, *saying*, "*Lord, Lord, open to us*, for we think we have a right to enter; take us in among the *saved ones*, for we joined ourselves to them."

[2] What *grounds* they had for this *confidence*. Let us see what their plea is, *v.* 26. *First*, They had been *Christ's guests*, had had an intimate converse with him, and had shared in his favours: *We have eaten and drunk in thy presence*, at thy table. *Secondly*, They had been *Christ's hearers*, had received

instruction from him, and were well acquainted with his doctrine and law.

[3] How their confidence will fail them, and all their pleas be rejected as frivolous. Christ will say to them, *I know you not whence you are, v.* 25. And again (*v.* 27), *I tell you, I know you not, depart from me.* He does not deny that what they pleaded was true; they had *eaten and drunk in his presence*, by the same token that they had no sooner eaten of his bread than they lifted up the heel against him. He had *taught in their streets*, by the same token that they had despised his instruction and would not submit to it. And therefore, *First*, He *disowns* them: "*I know you not*; you do not belong to my family." *Secondly*, He *discards* them: *Depart from me.* It is the hell of hell to depart from Christ, the principal part of the misery of the damned. *Thirdly*, He gives them such a character as is the reason of this doom: *You are workers of iniquity*. This is their ruin, that, under a pretence of piety, they kept up secret haunts of sin, and did the devil's drudgery in Christ's livery.

[4] How terrible their punishment will be (*v.* 28): *There shall be weeping and gnashing of teeth*, the utmost degree of grief and indignation; and that which is the cause of it, and contributes to it, is a sight of the happiness of those that are saved: *You shall see the patriarchs and prophets in the kingdom of God, and yourselves thrust out.*

(4) Think who are they that shall be saved, notwithstanding:

They shall come from the east and the west; and the last shall be first, vv. 29, 30. Those who *sit down in the kingdom of God* are such as had taken pains to get thither, for they came from far — *from the east and from the west, from the north and from the south*; they had passed through different climates, had broken through many difficulties and discouragements. This shows that they who would enter into that kingdom must *strive*. They who *travel* now in the service of God and religion shall shortly *sit down* to rest in the *kingdom of God*.

A MESSAGE TO HEROD
(vv. 31–35)

Here is, I. A suggestion to Christ of his danger from Herod, now that he was in Galilee, within Herod's jurisdiction (*v.* 31).

II. His defiance of Herod's rage and the Pharisees' too; he fears neither the one nor the other: *Go you, and tell that fox* so, *v.* 32. In calling him a *fox*, he gives him his true character; for he was subtle as a fox, noted for his craft, and treachery, and baseness, and preying (as they say of a fox) furthest from his own den. And, though it is a black and ugly character, yet it did not ill become Christ to give it to him, nor was it in him a violation of that law, *Thou shalt not speak evil of the ruler of thy people.* For Christ was a prophet, and prophets always had a liberty of speech in reproving princes and great men.

III. His lamentation for Jerusalem, and his denunciation of wrath against that city, *vv.* 34, 35. This we had Matt. xxiii. 37–39.

CHAPTER FOURTEEN

ANOTHER SABBATH MIRACLE (*vv.* 1–6)

In this passage of story we find,

I. That *the Son of man went into the house of one of the chief Pharisees*, a ruler, it may be, and a magistrate in his country, *to eat bread on the sabbath day*, *v.* 1.

II. That he *went about doing good*. Here was *a certain man before him who had the dropsy, v.* 2. We do not find that he offered himself, or that his friends offered him to be Christ's patient, but Christ *prevented him* with the blessings of his goodness, and *before he called* him. answered. him.

III. That he *endured the contradiction of sinners against himself: They watched him, v.* 1. When Christ asked them *whether* they thought it *lawful to heal on the sabbath day* (and herein he is said to *answer* them, for it was an answer to *their thoughts*, and thoughts are *words* to Jesus Christ), they would say neither *yea* nor *nay*, for their design was to *inform against him*, not to be *informed by him*.

IV. That Christ would not be hindered from *doing good* by the *opposition* and *contradiction* of sinners. He *took him, and healed him, and let him go, v.* 4.

V. That our Lord Jesus *did nothing but what he could justify*, to the conviction and confusion of those that quarrelled with him, *vv.* 5, 6. He still answered their thoughts, and made them *hold their peace* for *shame* who before held their peace for *subtlety*, by an appeal to their own practice, as he had been used to do upon such occasions, that he might show them how in condemning him they condemned themselves.

TABLE TALK (*vv.* 7–14)

Our Lord Jesus here sets us an example of profitable edifying discourse at our tables, when we are in company with our friends.

I. He takes occasion to reprove *the guests* for striving to *sit uppermost*, and thence gives us a lesson of *humility*.

1. He observed how these lawyers and Pharisees affected the *highest seats*, towards the head-end of the table, *v.* 7.

2. He observed how those who were thus aspiring often exposed themselves, and came off *with a slur*; whereas those who were modest, and seated themselves in the lowest seats, often *gained respect* by it.

3. He applied this generally, and would have us all learn not to *mind high things*, but to content ourselves with mean things, as for other reasons, so for this, because pride and ambition are disgraceful before men: for *whosoever exalteth himself shall be abased*; but humility and self-denial are really honourable: *he that humbleth himself shall be exalted, v.* 11. We see in other instances that *a man's pride will bring him low*, but *honour shall uphold the humble in spirit*, and *before honour is humility*.

II. He takes occasion to reprove the master of the feast for inviting so many *rich people*, who had

wherewithal to dine very well at home, when he should rather have *invited the poor*, or, which was all one, have *sent portions to them for whom nothing was prepared*, and who could not afford themselves a good meal's meat. See Neh. viii. 10.

THE GREAT SUPPER
(*vv.* 15–24)

Here is another discourse of our Saviour's.

I. The occasion of the discourse was given by one of the guests, who, when Christ was giving rules about feasting, said to him, *Blessed is he that shall eat bread in the kingdom of God* (*v.* 15), which, some tell us, was a saying commonly used among the rabbin.

1. But with what design does this man bring it in here? (1) Perhaps this man, observing that Christ reproved first the guests and then the master of the house, fearing he should put the company out of humour, started this, to *divert* the discourse to something else. Or, (2) Admiring the good rules of humility and charity which Christ had now given, but despairing to see them lived up to in the present degenerate state of things, he longs for *the kingdom of God*, when these and other good laws shall prevail, and pronounces them *blessed* who shall have a place in that kingdom. Or, (3) Christ having mentioned *the resurrection of the just*, as a recompence for acts of charity to the poor, he here confirms what he said, "Yea, Lord, they that shall be recompensed in the resurrection of the just, shall *eat bread in the kingdom*,

and that is a greater recompence than being reinvited to the table of the greatest man on earth." Or, (4) Observing Christ to be silent, after he had given the foregoing lessons, he was willing to draw him in again to further discourse, so wonderfully well-pleased was he with what he said.

2. Now what this man said was a plain and acknowledged truth. (1) In the kingdom of grace, in the kingdom of the Messiah, which was expected now shortly to be set up. Christ promised his disciples that they should *eat and drink with him in his kingdom*. (2) In the kingdom of glory, at the resurrection. The happiness of heaven is an *everlasting feast*.

II. The parable which our Lord Jesus put forth upon this occasion, *vv*. 16, &c. Now in the parable we may observe,

1. The free grace and mercy of God, shining in the gospel of Christ; it appears,

(1) In the rich provision he has made for poor souls, for their nourishment, refreshment, and entertainment (*v*. 16): *A certain man made a great supper*.

(2) In the gracious invitation given us to come and partake of this provision. Here is, [1] A general invitation given: He *bade many*. Christ invited the whole nation and people of the Jews to partake of the benefits of his gospel. [2] A particular memorandum given, when the supper time was at hand; the servant was sent round to put them in mind of it: *Come, for all things are now ready*. When the Spirit was poured out, and the gospel church planted,

those who before were invited were more closely pressed to come in at once.

2. The cold entertainment which the grace of the gospel meets with. The invited guests declined coming. They did not say flatly and plainly that they *would not come*, but *they all with one consent began to make excuse*, *v*. 18. (1) Here were *two* that were *purchasers*, who were in such haste to go and see their purchases that they could not find time to go to this supper. (2) Here was one that was *newly married*, and could not leave his wife to go out to supper, no, not for once (*v*. 30): *I have married a wife, and therefore*, in short, *I cannot come*. He pretends that he *cannot*, when the truth is he *will not*. Thus many pretend *inability* for the duties of religion when really they have an *aversion* to them.

3. The account which was brought to the master of the feast of the affront put upon him by his friends whom he had invited, who now showed how little they valued him (*v*. 21).

4. The master's just resentment of this affront: *He was angry*, *v*. 21. Note, The ingratitude of those that slight gospel offers, and the contempt they put upon the God of heaven thereby, are a very great provocation to him, and justly so. Abused mercy turns into the greatest wrath.

5. The care that was taken to furnish the table with guests, as well as food. "Go" (saith he to the servants), "*go first into the streets and lanes of the city*, and bring in *hither the poor and the*

maimed, the halt and the blind; pick up the common beggars." They soon gather an abundance of such guests: *Lord, it is done as thou hast commanded.* But *yet there is room* for more guests, and provision enough for them all. "Go, then, *secondly, into the highways and hedges. Compel them to come in*, not by force of arms, but by force of arguments. They will be shy and modest, and will hardly believe that they shall be welcome, and therefore be importunate with them and do not leave them till you have prevailed with them." This refers to the *calling of the Gentiles*, to whom the apostles were to *turn* when the Jews refused the offer, and with them the church was filled. Now observe here, (1) The provision made for precious souls in the gospel of Christ shall appear not to have been made *in vain*; for, if some *reject it*, yet others will thankfully *accept* the offer of it. (2) Those that are very poor and low in the world shall be as welcome to Christ as the rich and great. (3) Many times the gospel has the *greatest success* among those that are *least likely* to have the benefit of it, and whose submission to it was least expected. The publicans and harlots went into the kingdom of God before the scribes and Pharisees; *so the last shall be first, and the first last.* Let us not be *confident* concerning those that are most forward, nor despair of those that are least promising. (4) Christ's ministers must be both very expeditious and very importunate in inviting to the gospel feast: "*Go out quickly* (*v.* 21); lose no

time, because *all things are now ready*. Call to them to come *to-day, while it is called to-day*; and *compel them to come in*, by accosting them kindly, and *drawing them with the cords of a man and the bands of love*."

COUNTING THE COST
(*vv.* 25–35)

See how Christ in his doctrine suited himself to those to whom he spoke, and *gave every one his portion of meat.* To Pharisees he preached humility and charity. He is in these verses directing his discourse to the multitudes that crowded after him, and seemed zealous in following him; and his exhortation to them is to understand the terms of discipleship, before they undertook the profession of it, and to consider what they did. See here.

I. How zealous people were in their attendance on Christ (*v.* 25): *There went great multitudes with him.*

II. How *considerate* he would have them to be in their *zeal*. Those that undertake to follow Christ must count upon the worst, and prepare accordingly.

1. He tells them what the worst is that they must count upon, much the same with what he had gone through *before* them and *for* them.

(1) They must be willing to *quit* that which was *very dear*, and therefore must come to him thoroughly *weaned from* all their creature-comforts, and *dead* to them, so as cheerfully to part with them rather than quit their interest in Christ, *v.* 26. [1] Every good

man loves *his relations*; and yet, if he be a disciple of Christ, he must comparatively *hate them*, must love them *less than Christ*, as Leah is said to be *hated* when Rachel was better loved. Not that their persons must be in any degree hated, but our comfort and satisfaction in them must be lost and swallowed up in our love to Christ. [2] Every man loves *his own life*, no man ever yet *hated it*; and we cannot be Christ's disciples if we do not love him better than our own lives, so as rather to have our lives *embittered* by cruel *bondage*, nay, and *taken away* by cruel *deaths*, than to dishonour Christ, or depart from any of his truths and ways.

(2) That they must be willing to *bear* that which was very *heavy* (v. 27). Though the disciples of Christ are not *all crucified*, yet they all *bear their cross*, as if they counted upon being crucified. They must be content to be put into an ill name, and to be loaded with infamy and disgrace.

2. He bids them count upon it, and then consider of it. It is better never to begin than not to proceed; and therefore before we begin we must consider what it is to proceed. This is to act rationally, and as becomes men, and as we do in other cases. The cause of Christ will bear a scrutiny.

(1) When we take upon us a profession of religion we are like a man that undertakes to *build a tower*, and therefore must consider the *expense of it* (vv. 28–30).

(2) When we undertake to be Christ's disciples we are like a man that *goes to war*, and therefore

must consider the *hazard* of it, and the difficulties that are to be encountered, vv. 31, 32. A king that declares war against a neighbouring prince considers whether he has strength wherewith to make his part good, and, if not, he will lay aside his thoughts of war.

3. He warns them against apostasy and a degeneracy of mind from the truly Christian spirit and temper, for that would make them utterly useless, vv. 34, 35. (1) Good Christians are *the salt of the earth*, and good ministers especially (Matt. v. 13); and this *salt is good* and of great use. (2) Degenerate Christians, who, rather than part with what they have in the world, will throw up their profession, and then of course become carnal, and worldly, and wholly destitute of a Christian spirit, are like *salt that has lost its savour*; it has no manner of virtue or good property in it.

CHAPTER FIFTEEN

THE LOST SHEEP (vv. 1–10)

Here is, I. The diligent attendance of the publicans and sinners upon Christ's ministry. These *drew near*, when perhaps the multitude of the Jews that had followed him had (upon his discourse in the close of the foregoing chapter) *dropped off*; thus afterwards the Gentiles took their turn in hearing the apostles, when the Jews had rejected them.

II. The offence which the *scribes* and *Pharisees* took at this. They *murmured*, and turned it to the reproach of our Lord Jesus: *This man receiveth sinners, and eateth* with them, *v.* 2. They could not, for shame, condemn him for *preaching to them*, though that was the thing they were most enraged at; and therefore they reproached him for *eating with them*, which was more expressly contrary to the tradition of the elders.

III. Christ's justifying himself in it, by showing that the worse these people were, to whom he preached, the more glory would redound to God, and the more joy there would be in heaven, if by his preaching they were brought to repentance. This he here illustrates by two parables, the explication of both of which is the same.

1. The parable of the *lost sheep*. Something like it we had in Matt. xviii. 12. There it was designed to show the care God takes for the preservation of saints, as a reason why we should not offend them; here it is designed to show the pleasure God takes in the conversion of sinners, as a reason why we should rejoice in it.

This is very applicable to the great work of our redemption. Mankind were gone astray, Isa. liii. 6. The value of the whole race to God was not so much as that of one sheep to him that had a hundred; what loss would it have been to God if they had all been left to perish? There is a world of holy angels that are as the ninety-nine sheep, a noble flock; yet God sends his Son to *seek and save that which was lost, ch.* xix. 10. Christ is said to *gather the lambs in his arms*, and carry *them in his bosom*, denoting his pity and tenderness towards poor sinners; here he is

said to bear them *upon his shoulders*, denoting the power wherewith he supports and bears them up; those can never perish whom he carries upon his shoulders.

He *lays it on his shoulders rejoicing* that he has not lost his labour in seeking; and the joy is the greater because he began to be out of hope of finding it; and he *calls his friends and neighbours*, the shepherds that keep their flocks about him, *saying, Rejoice with me.*

2. The parable of the *lost piece of silver.* (1) The *loser* is here supposed to be *a woman*, who will more passionately grieve for her loss, and rejoice in finding what she had lost, than perhaps a man would do, and therefore it the better serves the purpose of the parable. She has *ten pieces of silver*, and out of them loses only one. Let this keep up in us high thoughts of the divine goodness, notwithstanding the sinfulness and misery of the world of mankind, that there are nine to one, nay, in the foregoing parable there are ninety-nine to one, of God's creation, that retain their integrity, in whom God *is* praised, and never *was* dishonoured. O the numberless beings, for aught we know numberless worlds of beings, that never were lost, nor stepped aside from the laws and ends of their creation!

3. The explication of these two parables is to the same purport (*vv.* 7, 10): *There is joy in heaven, joy in the presence of the angels of God, over one sinner that repenteth*, as those publicans and sinners did, some of them at least (and, if but

one of them did repent, Christ would reckon it worth his while), more than *over* a great number of *just persons, who need no repentance*.

Now if there is such *joy in heaven*, for the conversion of sinners, then the Pharisees were very much strangers to a heavenly spirit, who did all they could to hinder it and were grieved at it, and who were exasperated at Christ when he was doing a piece of work that was of all others most grateful to Heaven.

THE PRODIGAL SON
(vv. 11–33)

We have here the parable of the prodigal son, the scope of which is the same with those before, to show how pleasing to God the conversion of sinners is, of great sinners, and how ready he is to receive and entertain such, upon their repentance.

I. The parable represents God as a *common Father* to all mankind, to the whole family of Adam. We are all his *offspring*, have all *one Father*, and *one God created us*, Mal. ii. 10.

II. It represents the children of men as of *different* characters, though all related to God as their common Father. He had *two sons,* one of them a solid grave youth, *reserved* and *austere*, sober himself, but not at all *good-humoured* to those about him; such a one would adhere to his education, and not be easily drawn from it; but the other *volatile* and *mercurial*, and impatient of restraint, roving, and willing to try his fortune, and, if he fall into ill hands, likely to be a

rake, notwithstanding his virtuous education. Now this latter represents the publicans and sinners, whom Christ is endeavouring to bring to repentance, and the Gentiles, to whom the apostles were to be sent forth to *preach repentance*. The former represents the Jews in general, and particularly the Pharisees, whom he was endeavouring to reconcile to that grace of God which was offered to, and bestowed upon, sinners.

The *younger son* is the prodigal, whose character and case are here designed to represent that of a sinner, that of every one of us in our natural state, but especially of some. Now we are to observe concerning him,

1. His *riot* and *ramble* when he was a prodigal, and the extravagances and miseries he fell into. We are told,

(1) What his request to his father was (*v.* 12): *He said to his father*, proudly and pertly enough, *"Father, give me the portion of goods that falleth to me*; not so much as you *think fit* to allot to me, but that which falls to me as *my due."*

(2) How kind his father was to him: *He divided unto them his living*. He computed what he had to dispose of between his sons, and gave the younger son *his share*.

(3) How he managed himself when he had got his portion in his own hands. He set himself to spend it as fast as he could, and, as prodigals generally do, in a little time he made himself a beggar: *not many days after, v.* 13.

Now the condition of the prodigal in this ramble of his

represents to us a *sinful* state, that *miserable* state into which man is *fallen*.

[1] A sinful state is a state of *departure* and *distance* from God. *First*, It is the *sinfulness* of sin that it is an apostasy from God. He *took his journey* from his father's house. Sinners are fled from God. They get as far off him as they can. The world is the *far country* in which they take up their residence, and are as at home; and in the service and enjoyment of it they spend their all. *Secondly*, It is the misery of sinners that they are afar off from God, from him who is the Fountain of all good, and are going further and further from him. What is hell itself, but being *afar off* from God?

[2] A sinful state is a *spending* state: There he *wasted his substance with riotous living* (v. 13), devoured it *with harlots* (v. 30), and in a little time *he had spent all*, v. 14. Wilful sinners *waste* their patrimony; for they misemploy their thoughts and all the powers of their souls, mispend their time and all their opportunities, do not only bury, but embezzle, the talents they are entrusted to trade with for their Master's honour; and the gifts of Providence, which were intended to enable them to serve God and to do good with, are made the food and fuel of their lusts.

[3] A sinful state is a *wanting* state: *When he had spent all* upon his harlots, they left him, to seek such another prey; and *there arose a mighty famine in that land*, every thing was scarce and dear, and he *began to be in want*, v. 14.

Note, Wilful waste brings woeful want. This represents the misery of *sinners*, who have thrown away *their own mercies*, the favour of God, their interest in Christ, the strivings of the Spirit, the admonitions of conscience; these they *gave away* for the pleasure of sense, and the wealth of the world, and then are ready to perish for want of them. Sinners are *wretchedly* and *miserably poor*, and, what aggravates it, they brought themselves into that condition, and keep themselves in it by refusing the supplies offered.

[4] A sinful state is *a vile servile state*. When this young man's riot had brought him to want his want brought him to servitude. *He went, and joined himself to a citizen of that country*, v. 15. The same wicked life that before was represented by *riotous living* is here represented by *servile living*; for sinners are perfect slaves. The devil is the *citizen of that country*; for he is both in city and country. Sinners *join themselves* to him, hire themselves into his service, to do *his work*, to be at *his beck*, and to depend upon him for maintenance and a portion. They that commit sin are the *servants of sin*, John viii. 34.

[5] A sinful state is a state of *perpetual dissatisfaction*. When the prodigal began to be in want, he thought to help himself by *going to service*; and he must be content with the provision which not the house, but the field, afforded; but it is poor provision: *He would fain have filled his belly*, satisfied his hunger, and nourished his body, *with the husks which the*

swine did eat, *v.* 16. A fine pass my young master had brought himself to, to be fellow-commoner with the swine!

[6] A sinful state is a state which *cannot expect relief from any creature*. This prodigal, when he could not earn his bread by *working*, took to *begging*; but *no man gave unto him*, because they knew he had brought all this misery upon himself, and because he was rakish, and provoking to every body; such poor are *least pitied*. This, in the application of the parable, intimates that those who depart from God cannot be helped by any creature.

[7] A sinful state is a *state of death: This my son was dead*, *vv.* 24, 32. A sinner is not only dead in law, as he is under a sentence of death, but dead in state too, dead in trespasses and sins, destitute of spiritual life; no union with Christ, no spiritual senses exercised, no living to God, and therefore *dead*.

[8] A sinful state is a *lost state: This my son was lost*—lost to every thing that was good—lost to all virtue and honour—lost to his father's house; they had no joy of him. Souls that are separated from God are *lost* souls; lost as a *traveller* that is out of his way, and, if infinite mercy prevent not, will soon be lost as a ship that is sunk at sea, lost irrecoverably.

[9] A sinful state is a state of *madness* and *frenzy*. This is intimated in that expression (*v.* 17), *when he came to himself*, which intimates that he had been *beside himself*. Surely he was so when he left his father's house, and much

more so when he joined himself to the citizen of that country.

2. We have here his *return* from this *ramble*, his penitent *return* to his father again. When he was brought to the last extremity, then he bethought himself how much it was his interest to go home. The grace of God can soften the hardest heart, and give a happy turn to the strongest stream of corruption. Now observe here,

(1) What was the *occasion* of his return and repentance. It was his *affliction*; when he was in *want*, then he *came to himself*. Note, Afflictions, when they are sanctified by divine grace, prove happy means of turning sinners from the error of their ways.

(2) What was the *preparative* for it; it was *consideration*. He said within himself, he reasoned with himself, when he recovered his right mind, *How many hired servants of my father's have bread enough!* Note, Consideration is the first step towards conversion.

[1] He considered how bad his condition was: *I perish with hunger*. Not only, "I am *hungry*," but, "*I perish with hunger*, for I see not what way to expect relief."

[2] He considered how much better it might be made if he would but return: *How many hired servants of my father's*, the meanest in his family, the very day-labourers, *have bread enough, and to spare*, such a good house does he keep!

(3) What was the *purpose* of it. Since it is so, that his condition is so bad, and may be bettered by returning to his father, his consideration issues, at length, in this

conclusion: *I will arise, and go to my father*. Note, Good purposes are good things, but still good performances are all in all.

[1] He determined what to do: *I will arise and go to my father*. He will not take any longer time to consider of it, but will *forthwith* arise and go.

[2] He determined what to say. Note, In all our addresses to God, it is good to deliberate with ourselves beforehand what we shall say, that we may *order our cause before him*, and *fill our mouth with arguments*.

First, He would confess his fault and folly: *I have sinned*. The confession of sin is required and insisted upon, as a necessary condition of peace and pardon.

Secondly, He would aggravate it, and would be so far from extenuating the matter that he would *lay a load* upon himself for it: I have sinned *against Heaven*, and *before thee*. Let those that are *undutiful* to their *earthly parents* think of this; they sin *against heaven*, and *before God*. Offences against them are offences against God. Let us all think of this, as that which renders our *sin exceedingly sinful*, and should render us exceedingly sorrowful for it.

Thirdly, He would judge and condemn himself for it, and acknowledge himself to have forfeited all the privileges of the family: *I am no more worthy to be called thy son*, v. 19. Note, It becomes sinners to acknowledge themselves unworthy to receive any favour from God, and to humble and abase themselves before him.

Fourthly, He would nevertheless sue for admission into the family, though it were into the meanest post there: "*Make me as one of thy hired servants*; that is good enough, and too good for me." Note, True penitents have a high value for God's house, and the privileges of it, and will be glad of any place, so they may but be in it, though it be but as *door-keepers*, Ps. lxxxiv. 10.

Fifthly, In all this he would have an eye to his father as a father: "*I will arise, and go to my father, and will say unto him, Father*." Note, Eyeing God as a Father, and our Father, will be of great use in our repentance and return to him. It will make our sorrow for sin genuine, our resolutions against it strong, and encourage us to hope for pardon.

(4) What was the performance of this purpose: *He arose, and came to his father*. His good resolve he put in execution without delay; he struck while the iron was hot, and did not adjourn the thought to some more convenient season.

3. We have here his reception and entertainment with his father: *He came to his father*; but was he welcome? Yes, heartily welcome. Now here observe,

(1) The great love and affection wherewith the father received the son: *When he was yet a great way off his father saw him*, v. 20. He expressed his kindness before the son expressed his repentance; for God precedes us with the blessings of his goodness. Even *before we call he answers*; for he knows what is in our hearts.

(2) The penitent submission which the poor prodigal made to his father (*v.* 21): He *said unto him, Father, I have sinned.* As it commends the good father's kindness that he showed it before the prodigal expressed his repentance, so it commends the prodigal's repentance that he expressed it after his father had shown him so much kindness. When he had received the kiss which sealed his pardon, yet he said, *Father, I have sinned.*

(3) The splendid provision which this kind father made for the returning prodigal. He was going on in his submission, but one word we find in his purpose to say (*v.* 19) which we do not find that he did say (*v.* 21), and that was, *Make me as one of thy hired servants.* We cannot think that he forgot it, much less that he changed his mind, and was now either less desirous to be in the family or less willing to be a hired servant there than when he made that purpose; but his father interrupted him, prevented his saying it: "Hold, son, talk no more of thy unworthiness, thou art heartily welcome, and, though not *worthy to be called a son,* shalt be treated as a *dear son,* as a *pleasant child.*" He who is thus entertained at first needs not ask to be made *as a hired servant.*

But this is not all; here is rich and royal provision made for him, according to his birth and quality, far beyond what he did or could expect. He would have thought it sufficient, and been very thankful, if his father had but taken notice of him, and bid him go to the kitchen, and get his dinner with his servants; but God does for those who return to their duty, and cast themselves upon his mercy, abundantly above what they are able to ask or think. The prodigal came home between hope and fear, fear of being rejected and hope of being received; but his father was not only better to him than his fears, but better to him than his hopes—not only *received* him, but received him with respect.

[1] He came home *in rags*, and his father not only *clothed* him, but *adorned* him.

[2] He came home *hungry*, and his father not only *fed him*, but *feasted him* (*v.* 23). Now he found his own words made good, *In my father's house there is bread enough and to spare.*

(4) The great joy and rejoicing occasioned by his return. The bringing of the fatted calf was designed to be not only a *feast* for him, but a *festival* for the family: "*Let us all eat, and be merry,* for it is a good day; for *this my son was dead,* when he was in his ramble, but his return is as *life from the dead,* he *is alive again*; we thought that he was dead, having heard nothing from him of a long time, but behold *he lives*; he *was lost,* we gave him up for lost, we despaired of hearing of him, but he *is found.*"

4. We have here the *repining and envying of the elder brother,* which is described by way of reproof to the scribes and Pharisees, to show them the folly and wickedness of their discontent at the repentance and conversion of the

publicans and sinners, and the favour Christ showed them. Now concerning the elder brother, observe,

(1) How *foolish* and *fretful* he was upon occasion of his brother's reception, and how he was disgusted at it. It seems he was abroad *in the field*, in the country, when his brother came, and by the time he had returned home the *mirth* was *begun: When he drew nigh to the house he heard music and dancing*, either while the dinner was getting ready, or rather after they had eaten and were full, *v.* 25. He enquired *what these things meant* (*v.* 26), and was informed that his brother was come, and his father had made him a feast for his *welcome home*, and great joy there was because he had received him *safe and sound*, *v.* 27. Now this offended him to the highest degree: *He was angry, and would not go in* (*v.* 28), not only because he was resolved he would not himself join in the mirth, but because he would show his displeasure at it, and would intimate to his father that he should have kept out his younger brother.

Let us observe, 1. He *would not go in*, except his brother were *turned out*; one house shall not hold him and his own brother, no, not his *father's house*. The language of this was that of the Pharisee (Isa. lxv. 5): *Stand by thyself, come not near to me, for I am holier than thou*; and (*ch.* xviii. 11) *I am not as other men are, nor even as this publican.* 2. He would not call him *brother*; but *this thy son*, which sounds arrogantly, and not without reflection upon his father, as if his indulgence had made him a prodigal: "He is *thy son*, thy darling." 3. He *aggravated his brother's faults*, and made the worst of them, endeavouring to incense his father against him: He *is thy son, who hath devoured thy living with harlots.* It is true, he had spent his own portion foolishly enough (whether *upon harlots* or no we are not told before, perhaps that was only the language of the elder brother's jealousy and ill will), but that he had devoured *all his father's living* was false; the father had still a good estate. Now this shows how apt we are, in censuring our brethren, to *make the worst* of every thing, and to set it out in the blackest colours, which is not doing as we would be done by, nor as our heavenly Father does by us, who is not extreme to mark iniquities. 4. He *grudged* him the *kindness* that his father *showed him: Thou hast killed for him the fatted calf*, as if he were such a son as he should be.

(2) Let us now see how *favourable* and *friendly* his father was in *his carriage towards him* when he was thus sour and ill-humoured.

[1] When he would not come in, his *father came out, and entreated him*, accosted him mildly, gave him good words, and desired him to come in. He might justly have said, "If he will not come in, let him stay out, shut the doors against him, and send him to seek a lodging where he can find it. Is not the house my own? and may I not do what I please in it? Is not the fatted calf my own? and may

I not do what I please with it?" No, as he went to meet the younger son, so now he goes to court the elder, did not send a servant out with a kind message to him, but went himself. Now, *First*, This is designed to represent to us the goodness of God; how strangely gentle and winning he has been towards those that were strangely froward and provoking. *Secondly*, It is to teach all superiors to be mild and gentle with their inferiors, even when they are in a fault and passionately justify themselves in it, than which nothing can be more provoking; and yet even in that case let fathers *not provoke their children to more wrath*, and let *masters forebear threatening*, and both show all *meekness*.

[2] His father assured him that the kind entertainment he gave his younger brother was neither any reflection upon him nor should be any prejudice to him (*v.* 31).

[3] His father gave him a good reason for this uncommon joy in the family: *It was meet that we should make merry and be glad*, *v.* 32. He might have insisted upon his own authority: "It was *my will* that the family should make merry and be glad." It is better to give a convincing reason, as the `father does here: *It was meet*, and very becoming, *that we should make merry* for the return of a prodigal son, more than for the perseverance of a dutiful son; for, though the latter is a greater blessing to a family, yet the former is a more emotional pleasure. Any family would be much more transported with joy at the raising of a dead child to life, yea, or

at the recovery of a child from a sickness that was adjudged mortal, than for the continued life and health of many children. We do not find that the elder brother made any reply to what his father said, which intimates that he was entirely satisfied, and acquiesced in his father's will, and was well reconciled to his prodigal brother; and his father put him in mind that he was his brother: *This thy brother*. But as for the scribes and Pharisees, for whose conviction it was primarily intended, for aught that appears they continued the same disaffection to the sinners of the Gentiles, and to the gospel of Christ because it was preached to them.

CHAPTER SIXTEEN
THE UNJUST STEWARD
(*vv.* 1–17)

Let us consider,

I. The parable itself, in which all the children of men are represented as *stewards* of what they have in this world, and we are but stewards. Whatever we have, the property of it is God's; we have only the use of it, and that according to the direction of our great Lord, and for his honour. Now,

1. Here is the *dishonesty* of this steward. He *wasted his lord's goods*, embezzled them, misapplied them, or through carelessness suffered them to be lost and damaged; and for this he was *accused to his lord*, *v.* 1. We are all *liable* to the same charge. We have not made a due improvement of what God has entrusted us with in this

world, but have perverted his purpose; and, that we may not be for this *judged of our Lord*, it concerns us to *judge ourselves*.

2. His *discharge* out of his place. His lord *called for him*, and said, "*How is it that I hear this of thee? I* expected better things from thee." The steward cannot deny it, and therefore there is no remedy, he must make up his accounts, and be gone in a little time, *v.* 2.

3. His *after-wisdom*. Now he began to consider, *What shall I do? v.* 3. He would have done well to have considered this before he had so foolishly thrown himself out of a good place by his unfaithfulness; but it is better to *consider* late than never. He must live; which way shall he have a livelihood? (1) He knows that he has not such a degree of industry in him as to get his living by work: "*I cannot dig*; I cannot earn my bread by my labour." But why can he not dig? It does not appear that he is either old or lame; but the truth is, he is *lazy*. His *cannot* is a *will not*; it is not a natural but a moral disability that he labours under. (2) He knows that he has not such a degree of *humility* as to get his bread by begging: *To beg I am ashamed*. This was the language of his pride, as the former of his slothfulness. (3) He therefore determines to make friends of his lord's debtors, or his tenants that were behind with their rent, and had given notes under their hands for it. Now the way he would take to make them his friends was by striking off a considerable part

of their debt to his lord, and giving it in in his accounts so much less than it was. How hard is it to find one that confidence can be reposed in! *Let God be true, but every man a liar.* Though this steward is turned out for dealing dishonestly, yet still he does so. So rare is it for men to mend of a fault, though they smart for it.

4. The approbation of this: *The lord commended the unjust steward, because he had done wisely, v.* 8. It may be meant of *his lord*, the lord of that servant, who, though he could not but be angry at his knavery, yet was pleased with his ingenuity and policy for himself; but, taking it so, the latter part of the verse must be the words of *our Lord*, and therefore I think the whole is meant of him. Christ did, as it were, say, "Now commend me to such a man as this, that knows how to do well for himself, how to improve a present opportunity, and how to provide for a future necessity." He does not commend him because he had done *falsely* to his master, but because he had done *wisely* for himself. Yet perhaps herein he did well for his master too, and but justly with the tenants. Now this forecast of his, for a comfortable subsistence in this world, shames our improvidence for another world: *The children of this world*, who choose and have their portions in it, *are wiser for their generation*, act more considerately, and better consult their worldly interest and advantage, than the *children of light*, who enjoy the gospel, in *their generation*, that is, in the

concerns of their souls and eternity.

II. The application of this parable, and the inferences drawn from it (*v.* 9): "*I say unto you, you my disciples*" (for to them this parable is directed, *v.* 1), "though you have but little in this world, consider how you may do good with that little." Observe,

1. What it is that our Lord Jesus here exhorts us to; to provide for our comfortable reception to the happiness of another world, by making good use of our possessions and enjoyments in this world: "*Make to yourselves friends of the mammon of unrighteousness*, as the steward with his lord's goods made his lord's tenants his friends." It is the wisdom of the men of this world so to manage their money as that they may have the benefit of it hereafter, and not for the present only; therefore they put it out to interest, buy land with it, put it into this or the other fund. Now we should learn of them to make use of our money so as that we may be the better for it hereafter in another world, as they do in hopes to be the better for it hereafter in this world.

2. With what arguments he presses this exhortation to abound in works of piety and charity.

(1) If we do not make a right use of the *gifts of God's providence*, how can we expect from him those present and future comforts which are the *gifts of his spiritual grace*?

(2) We have no other way to prove ourselves the servants of God than by giving up ourselves so entirely to his service as to make *mammon*, that is, all our

worldly gain, serviceable to us in his service (*v.* 13): *No servant can serve two masters*, whose commands are so inconsistent as those of God and *mammon* are. If a man will *love* the world, and *hold to that*, it cannot be but he will *hate God* and *despise* him. But, on the other hand, if a man will *love God*, and *adhere* to him, he will comparatively *hate* the world (whenever God and the world come into competition) and will *despise* it, and make all his business and success in the world some way or other conducive to his furtherance in the business of religion; and the things of the world shall be made to help him in serving God and working out his salvation.

3. We are here told what entertainment this doctrine of Christ met with among the Pharisees, and what rebuke he gave them.

(1) They wickedly *ridiculed* him, *v.* 14. *The Pharisees, who were covetous, heard all these things*, and could not contradict him, but *they derided him*. Let us consider this, [1] As their *sin*, and the fruit of their *covetousness*, which was their reigning sin, their own iniquity. [2] As *his suffering*. Our Lord Jesus endured not only the *contradiction* of sinners, but their *contempt*; they *had him in derision* all the day.

(2) He justly reproved them; not for *deriding* him (he knew how to *despise the shame*), but for *deceiving* themselves with the shows and colours of piety, when they were strangers to the power of it, *v.* 15. Here is,

[1] Their *specious outside*; nay, it was a *splendid* one. *First*, They

justified themselves before men; they denied whatever ill was laid to their charge, even by Christ himself.

[2] Their *odious inside*, which was under the eye of God: "He *knows your heart*, and it is in his sight an *abomination*; for it is full of all manner of wickedness."

(3) He turned from them to the publicans and sinners, as more likely to be wrought upon by his gospel than those covetous conceited Pharisees (*v.* 16).

(4) Yet still he protests against any design to invalidate the law (*v.* 17): *It is easier for heaven and earth to pass away*, to pass away, though the foundations of the earth and the pillars of heaven are so firmly established, *than for one tittle of the law to fail*. The moral law is confirmed and ratified, and not one tittle of that fails; the duties enjoined by it are duties still; the sins forbidden by it are sins still.

RICH MAN AND LAZARUS
(*vv.* 19–31)

As the parable of the prodigal son set before us the grace of the gospel, which is encouraging to us all, so this sets before us the *wrath to come*, and is designed for our awakening; and very fast asleep those are in sin that will not be awakened by it. In this description (for so I shall choose to call it) we may observe,

I. The different condition of a *wicked rich man*, and a *godly poor man*, in this world. We know that as some of late, so the Jews of old, were ready to make prosperity one of the marks of a true

church, of a good man and a favourite of heaven, so that they could hardly have any favourable thoughts of a *poor man*. This mistake Christ, upon all occasions, set himself to correct, and here very fully, where we have,

1. A wicked man, and one that will be for ever miserable, in the height of prosperity (*v.* 19): *There was a certain rich man.* Now we are told concerning this rich man,

(1) That he was *clothed in purple and fine linen*, and that was his *adorning*. He never appeared abroad but in great magnificence.

(2) He *fared* deliciously and *sumptuously every day*. It is true, eating good meat and wearing good clothes are lawful; but it is as true that they often become the food and fuel of pride and luxury, and so turn into sin to us. The sin of this rich man was not so much his dress or his diet, but his providing only for himself.

2. Here is a godly man, and one that will be for ever happy, in the depth of adversity and distress (*v.* 20): *There was a certain beggar*, named *Lazarus*. Now observe,

[1] His expectations from the rich man's table: *He desired to be fed with the crumbs, v.* 21. He did not look for a feast from off his table, though he ought to have had one, one of the best; but would be thankful for the crumbs from under the table, the broken meat which was the rich man's leavings; nay, the leavings of his dogs. He was *poor*, but he was *poor in spirit*, contentedly poor. This miserable man was a good man, and in favour with God.

[2] The usage he had from the dogs: *The dogs came and licked his sores*. The rich man kept a kennel of hounds, it may be, or other dogs, for his diversion, and to please his fancy, and these were fed to the full, when poor Lazarus could not get enough to keep him alive.

II. Here is the *different condition* of this *godly poor man*, and this *wicked rich man*, *at* and *after death*.

1. They both died (*v.* 22): The *beggar died*; the *rich man also died*. Death is the common lot of rich and poor, godly and ungodly; there they meet together.

2. The beggar *died first*. God often takes godly people out of the world, when he leaves the wicked to flourish still.

3. The rich man *died and was buried*. Nothing is said of the interment of the poor man. They dug a hole any where, and tumbled his body in, without any solemnity. But the rich man had a pompous funeral, lay in state, had a train of mourners to attend him to his grave, and a stately monument set up over it.

4. The beggar died and was *carried by angels into Abraham's bosom*. How much did the honour done to his soul, by this convoy of it to its rest, exceed the honour done to the rich man, by the carrying of his body with so much magnificence to its grave! Observe (1) His soul *existed* in a state of separation from the body. It did not *die*, or *fall asleep*, with the body; his candle was not put out with him; but lived, and acted, and knew what it did, and what

was done to it. (2) His soul *removed* to another world, to the world of spirits; it returned to God who gave it, to its native country; this is implied in its being *carried*. The spirit of a man goes upward. (3) Angels took care of it; it was *carried by angels*. They are ministering spirits to the heirs of salvation, not only while they live, but when they die. (4) It was carried *into Abraham's bosom*. The Jews expressed the happiness of the righteous at death three ways:—they go *to the garden of Eden*; they go *to be under the throne of glory*; and they go *to the bosom of Abraham*, and it is this which our Saviour here makes use of. Abraham was the *father of the faithful*; and whither should the souls of the faithful be gathered but to him, who, as a tender father, lays them *in his bosom*, especially at their first coming, to bid them welcome, and to refresh them when newly come from the sorrows and fatigues of this world?

5. The next news you hear of the *rich man*, after the account of his *death* and *burial*, is, that *in hell he lifted up his eyes, being in torment, v.* 23.

(1) His state is very miserable. *He is in hell*, in *hades*, in the state of separate souls, and there he is in *the utmost misery* and *anguish* possible. This *rich man* had entirely devoted himself to the pleasures of the *world of sense*, was wholly *taken up* with them, and *took up with them* for his portion, and therefore was wholly unfit for the pleasures of the *world of spirits*; to such a carnal mind as

his they would indeed be no pleasure, nor could he have any relish of them, and therefore he is of course excluded from them.

(2) The misery of his state is aggravated by his knowledge of the happiness of Lazarus: He *lifts up his eyes*, and *sees Abraham afar off*, and *Lazarus in his bosom*. It is the soul that is *in torment*, and they are the eyes of the mind that are lifted up.

III. Here is an account of what passed between the rich man and Abraham in the separate state—a state of separation one from another, and of both from this world. Though it is probable that there will not be, nor are, any such dialogues between glorified saints and damned sinners, yet it is very proper to represent what will be the mind and sentiments both of the one and of the other. Now in this discourse we have,

1. The request which the rich man made to Abraham for some mitigation of his present misery, *v.* 24. Observe here,

(1) The title he gives to Abraham: *Father Abraham*. Note, There are many in hell that can call Abraham *father*, that were Abraham's seed after the flesh, nay, and many that were, in name and profession, the children of the covenant made with Abraham.

(2) The representation he makes to him of his present deplorable condition: *I am tormented in this flame*.

(3) His request to Abraham, in consideration of this misery: *Have mercy on me*. Note, The day is coming when those that make light of divine mercy will beg hard

for it. He that had no mercy on Lazarus, yet expects Lazarus should have mercy on him; "for," thinks he, "Lazarus is better natured than ever I was." The particular favour he begs is, *Send Lazarus, that he may dip the tip of his finger in water, and cool my tongue*.

2. The reply which Abraham gave to this request. In general, he did not grant it. He would not allow him one *drop of water*, to *cool* his tongue. See how justly this rich man is paid in his own coin. He that denied a crumb is denied a drop. Now it is said to us, *Ask, and it shall be given you*; but, if we let slip this accepted time, we may ask, and it shall not be given us. But this is not all; had Abraham only said, "You shall have nothing to abate your torment," it had been sad; but he says a great deal which would add to his torment, and make the flame the hotter, for every thing in hell will be tormenting.

(1) He calls him *son*, a kind and civil title, but here it serves only to aggravate the denial of his request, which shut up the bowels of the compassion of a father from him. He had been a son, but a rebellious one, and now an abandoned disinherited one.

(2) He puts him in mind of what had been both his own condition and the condition of Lazarus, in their *life-time*: *Son, remember*; this is a cutting word. The memories of damned souls will be their tormentors, and conscience will then be awakened and stirred up to do its office, which here they would not suffer it to do.

(3) He puts him in mind of

Lazarus's present bliss, and his own misery: *But now* the tables are turned, and so they must abide for ever; *now he is comforted, and thou art tormented.*

(4) He assures him that it was to no purpose to think of having any relief by the ministry of Lazarus; for (*v.* 26), *Besides all this,* worse yet, *between us and you there is a great gulf fixed,* an impassable one, *a great chasm,* that so there can be no communication between glorified saints and damned sinners. In this world, blessed be God, there is no gulf fixed between a state of nature and grace, but we may pass from the one to the other, from sin to God; but if we die in our sins, if we throw ourselves into the pit of destruction, there is no coming out. It is a pit *in which there is no water,* and *out of which there is no redemption.* The decree and counsel of God have fixed this gulf, which all the world cannot unfix.

3. The further request he had to make to his father Abraham, not for himself, his mouth is stopped.

(1) He begs that Lazarus might be *sent to his father's house,* upon an errand thither: *I pray thee therefore, father, v.* 27. "Send him back *to my father's house*; he knows well enough where it is, has been there many a time, having been denied the crumbs that fell from the table. He knows I have *five brethren* there; if he appear to them, they will *know him,* and will regard what he saith, for they knew him to be an honest man. Let him *testify to them*; let him tell them what condition I am in, and that I brought myself to it

by my luxury and sensuality, and my unmercifulness to the poor. Let him warn them not to tread in my steps, nor to go on in the way wherein I led them, and left them, *lest they also come into this place of torment,*" *v.* 28.

(2) Abraham denies him this favour too. There is no request granted in hell. Abraham leaves them to the testimony of Moses and the prophets, the ordinary means of conviction and conversion; they have the written word, which they may read and hear read.

(3) He urges his request yet further (*v.* 30): "*Nay, father Abraham,* give me leave to press this. It is true, they have Moses and the prophets, and, if they would but give a due regard to them, it would be sufficient; but they do not, they will not; yet it may be hoped, *if one went to them from the dead, they would repent,* that would be a more sensible conviction to them."

(4) Abraham insists upon the denial of it, with a conclusive reason (*v.* 31): "*If they hear not Moses and the prophets,* and will not believe the testimony nor take the warning they give, *neither will they be persuaded though one rose from the dead.* If they regard not the public revelation, which is confirmed by miracles, neither would they be wrought upon by a private testimony to themselves." Let us not therefore desire visions and apparitions, nor seek to the dead, but *to the law and to the testimony* (Isa. viii. 19, 20), for that is *the sure word of prophecy,* upon which we may depend,

CHAPTER SEVENTEEN

OFFENCES (*vv.* 1–10)

We are here taught,

I. That the *giving of offences* is a *great sin*, and that which we should every one of us avoid and carefully watch against, *vv.* 1, 2. *It is almost impossible but that offences will come*, and therefore we are concerned to provide accordingly; but *woe to him through whom they come*, his doom will be heavy (*v.* 2), more terrible than that of the worst of the malefactors who are condemned to be thrown into the sea, for they perish under a load of guilt more *ponderous* than that of *millstones*. This includes a woe, 1. To persecutors, who offer any injury to the least of Christ's *little ones*, in word or deed, by which they are discouraged in serving Christ, and doing their duty, or in danger of being driven off from it. 2. To seducers, who corrupt the truths of Christ and his ordinances, and so *trouble the minds of the disciples*; for they are those by whom *offences come*. 3. To those who, under the profession of the Christian name, live scandalously, and thereby weaken the hands and sadden the hearts of God's people.

II. That the *forgiving of offences* is a *great duty*, and that which we should every one of us make conscience of (*v.* 3): *Take heed to yourselves*. This may refer either to what goes before, or to what follows: *Take heed that you offend not one of these little ones*. Ministers must be very careful not to say or do anything that may be a discouragement to weak Chris-

tians; there is need of great caution, and they ought to speak and act very considerately, for fear of this: or, "When *your brother trespasses against you*, does you any injury, puts any slight or affront upon you, if he be accessary to any damage done you in your property or reputation, *take heed to yourselves at such a time*, lest you be put into a passion; lest, when your spirits are provoked, you *speak unadvisedly*, and rashly vow revenge (Prov. xxiv. 29): *I will do so to him as he hath done to me*. Take heed what you say at such a time, lest you say amiss."

1. If you are permitted to *rebuke him*, you are advised to do so. Smother not the resentment, but give it vent.

2. You are commanded, upon his repentance, to forgive him, and to be perfectly reconciled to him: *If he repent, forgive him*; forget the injury, never think of it again, much less upbraid him with it.

3. You are to repeat this every time he repeats his trespass, *v.* 4. If he could be supposed to be either so negligent, or so impudent, as to *trespass against thee seven times in a day*, and as often profess himself sorry for his fault, and promise not again to offend in like manner, continue to *forgive him*.

III. That we have all need to get our *faith* strengthened, because, as that grace grows, all other graces grow. Faith in God's pardoning mercy will enable us to get over the greatest difficulties that lie in the way of our forgiving our brother. Christ assured them of the wonderful efficacy of true faith (*v.* 6): "*If ye had faith as a grain of mustard-seed, so small* as mustard-seed, you might do wonders much beyond what you now do; nothing would be too hard for you, that was fit to be done for the glory of God, and the confirmation of the doctrine you preach, yea, though it were the *transplanting of a tree* from the earth, *to the sea.* See Matt. xvii. 20. As with God *nothing is impossible,* so are all *things possible to him that can believe.*

IV. That, whatever we do in the service of Christ, we must be very humble, and not imagine that we can merit any favour at his hand, or claim it as a debt; even the apostles themselves, who did so much more for Christ than others, must not think that they had thereby made him their debtor. 1. We are all *God's servants* (his *apostles* and *ministers* are in a special manner *so*), and, as servants, are bound to do all we can for his honour. 2. As God's servants, it becomes us to fill up our time with duty, and we have a variety of work appointed us to do; we ought to make the end of one service the beginning of another. 3. Our principal care here must be to do the duty of our relation, and leave it to our Master to give us the comfort of it, when and how he thinks fit. No servant expects that his master should say to him, *Go and sit down to meat*; it is time enough to do that when we have *done our day's work.* Let us be in care to finish our work, and to do that

well, and then the reward will come in due time. 4. It is fit that Christ should be served before us: *Make ready wherewith I may sup, and afterwards thou shalt eat and drink.* Doubting Christians say that they cannot give to Christ the glory of his love as they should, because they have not yet obtained the comfort of it; but this is wrong. First let Christ have the glory of it, let us attend him with our praises, and then we shall *eat and drink* in the comfort of that love, and in this there is a feast. 5. Christ's servants, when they are to wait upon him, must *gird themselves,* must free themselves from every thing that is entangling and encumbering, and fit themselves with a close application of mind to go on, and go through, with their work; they must *gird up the loins of their mind.* 6. Christ's servants do not so much as merit his thanks for any service they do him: "*Does he thank that servant?* Does he reckon himself indebted to him for it? No, by no means." No good works of ours can merit any thing at the hand of God. 7. Whatever we do for Christ, though it should be more perhaps than some others do, yet it is no more than is our duty to do. 8. The best servants of Christ, even when they do the best services, must humbly acknowledge that they are *unprofitable servants*; though they are not those unprofitable servants that bury their talents, and shall be cast into *utter darkness,* yet as to Christ, and any advantage that can accrue to him by their services, they are *unprofitable.* For God is happy

440

without us, but we are undone without him.

TEN LEPERS (*vv.* 11–19)

We have here an account of the cure of ten lepers, which we had not in any other of the evangelists. Observe,

I. The address of these lepers to Christ. They were ten in a company; for, though they were shut out from society with others, yet those that were infected were at liberty to converse with one another. Now observe, 1. They *met* Christ *as he entered into a certain village.* They did not stay till he had refreshed himself for some time after the fatigue of his journey, but met him as he *entered* the town, weary as he was; and yet he did not put them off, nor adjourn their cause. 2. They *stood afar off*, knowing that by the law their disease obliged them to *keep their distance.* A sense of our spiritual leprosy should make us very humble in all our approaches to Christ. 3. Their request was unanimous, and very importunate (*v.* 13): *They lifted up their voices*, being at a distance, and cried, *Jesus, Master, have mercy on us.*

II. Christ sent them to *the priest*, to be *inspected* by him, who was the judge of the leprosy. He did not tell them positively that they should be *cured*, but bade them *go show themselves to the priests*, *v.* 14. This was a trial of their obedience, and it was fit that it should be so tried, as Naaman's in a like case: *Go wash in Jordan.*

III. *As they went, they were cleansed*, and so became fit to be looked upon by the priest, and to have a certificate from him that they were clean. Observe, *Then* we may expect God to meet us with mercy when we are found in the way of duty.

IV. One of them, and but one, *returned, to give thanks, v.* 15. When he *saw that he was healed*, instead of going forward to the priest, to be by him declared clean, and so discharged from his confinement, which was all that the rest aimed at, he *turned back* towards him who was the Author of his cure, whom he wished to have the glory of it, before he received the benefit of it. He appears to have been very hearty and affectionate in his thanksgivings: *With a loud voice he glorified God*, acknowledging it to come originally from *him*. But he also made a particular address of thanks to Christ (*v.* 16): *He fell down at his feet*, put himself into the most humble reverent posture he could, and *gave him thanks.*

V. Christ took notice of this one that had thus distinguished himself; for, it seems, he was a Samaritan, whereas the rest were Jews, *v.* 16. The Samaritans were separatists from the Jewish church, and had not the pure knowledge and worship of God among them that the Jews had, and yet it was one of them that *glorified God*, when the Jews forgot, or, when it was moved to them, *refused*, to do it. Now observe here,

1. The particular notice Christ took of him, of the grateful return he made, and the ingratitude of those that were sharers with him in the mercy—that he who

was a *stranger* to the common-wealth of Israel was the only one that *returned to give glory to God, vv,* 17, 18.

2. The great encouragement Christ gave him, *v.* 19. The rest had their *cure,* and had it not *revoked,* as justly it might have been, for their ingratitude, though they had such a good example of gratitude set before them; but he had his cure confirmed particularly with an encomium: *Thy faith hath made thee whole.* The rest were *made whole* by the power of Christ, in compassion to their distress, and in answer to their prayer; but he was made whole *by his faith,* by which Christ saw him distinguished from the rest. Note, Temporal mercies are *then* doubled and sweetened to us when they are *fetched* in by the prayers of faith, and *returned* by the praises of faith.

THE KINGDOM TO COME
(vv. 20–37)

We have here a discourse of Christ's concerning the *kingdom of God,* that is, the kingdom of the Messiah, which was now shortly to be *set up,* and of which there was great expectation.

I. Here is the demand of the Pharisees concerning it, which occasioned this discourse.

II. Christ's reply to this demand, directed to the Pharisees first, and afterwards to his own disciples, who knew better how to under-stand it (*v.* 22); what he said to both, he saith to us.

1. That the kingdom of the Messiah was to be a *spiritual kingdom,* and not temporal and

external. They asked *when* it would come. "You know not what you ask," saith Christ; "it may come, and you not be aware of it." For it has not an *external show,* as other kingdoms have, the advancements and revolutions of which are taken notice of by the nations of the earth, and fill the newspapers; so they expected this kingdom of God would do. "No," saith Christ, (1) "It will have a silent entrance, without pomp, without noise; it *cometh not with observation.*" (2) "It has a *spiritual* influence: *The kingdom of God is within you.*" It is not of this world, John xviii. 36. Its glory does not strike men's fancies, but affects their spirits, and its power is over their souls and consciences; from them it receives homage, and not from their bodies only. The *kingdom of God* will not change men's outward condition, but their hearts and lives.

2. That the setting up of this kingdom was a work that would meet with a great deal of *opposition* and *interruption, v.* 22. This looks forward to his disciples in after-ages; they must expect much disappointment; the gospel will not be always preached with equal liberty and success. Ministers and churches will sometimes be under *outward restraints.* Teachers will be removed into corners, and solemn assemblies scattered. Then they will wish to see such days of opportunity as they have formerly enjoyed, sabbath days, sacrament days, preaching days, praying days; these are *days of the Son of man,* in which we hear from him, and converse with him. The time

may come when we may in vain
wish for such days. God teaches us
to know the worth of such mercies
by the want of them. It concerns
us, while they are continued, to
improve them, and in the years of
plenty to lay up in store for the
years of famine.

3. That Christ and his kingdom
are not to be looked for in this or
that particular place, but his
appearance will be general in all
places at once (*vv.* 23, 24). The
kingdom of God was not designed
to be the glory of one people
only, but to *give light to the
Gentiles*. The design of the setting
up of Christ's kingdom was not to
make one *nation great*, but to
make *all nations good*—some, at
least, of all nations; and this
point shall be gained, though the
nations rage, and the *kings of the
earth set themselves* with all their
might against it.

4. That the Messiah must *suffer*
before he must *reign* (*v.* 25).
They thought of having the kingdom of the Messiah set up in
external splendour: "No," saith
Christ, "we must go by the cross
to the crown. The *Son of man must
suffer many things*."

5. That the setting up of the
kingdom of the Messiah would
introduce the destruction of the
Jewish nation, whom it would
find in a deep sleep of *security*,
and drowned in *sensuality*, as the
old world was in the days of
Noah, and Sodom in the days of
Lot, *vv.* 26, &c.

6. That it ought to be the care
of his disciples and followers to
distinguish themselves from the
unbelieving Jews in that day, and,

leaving them, their city and
country, to themselves, to flee at
the signal given, according to the
direction that should be given.
This flight of theirs from Jerusalem
must be *expeditious*, and must not
be retarded by any concern about
their worldly affairs (*v.* 31). When
they have made their escape, they
must not think of returning
(*v.* 32): "*Remember Lot's wife*;
and take warning by her not only
to flee from this Sodom (for so
Jerusalem is become, Isa. i. 10),
but to persevere in your flight, and
do not *look back*, as she did; be
not loth to leave a place marked
for destruction, whomsoever or
whatsoever you leave behind you,
that is ever so dear to you."

7. That all good Christians
should certainly escape, but many
of them very *narrowly*, from that
destruction, *vv.* 34–36.

8. That this distinguishing, dividing, discriminating work shall be
done in all places, as far as the
kingdom of God shall extend,
v. 37. *Where, Lord?* They had
enquired concerning the time, and
he would not gratify their curiosity
with any information concerning
that; they therefore tried him with
another question: "*Where, Lord?
Where shall those be safe that are
taken? Where shall those perish
that are left?*" The answer is
proverbial, and may be explained
so as to answer each side of the
question: *Wheresoever the body is,
thither will the eagles be gathered
together.* (1) Wherever the wicked
are, who are marked for perdition,
they shall *be found out* by the
judgments of God; as wherever a
dead carcase is, the birds of prey

will smell it out, and make a prey of it. (2) Wherever the godly are, who are marked for preservation, they *shall be found* happy in the enjoyment of Christ. As the dissolution of the Jewish church shall be extended to all parts, so shall the constitution of the Christian church. Wherever Christ is, believers will flock to him, and meet in him, as eagles about the prey, without being directed or shown the way, by the instinct of the new nature.

CHAPTER EIGHTEEN
THE POOR WIDOW (*vv.* 1–8)

This parable has its key hanging at the door; the drift and design of it are *prefixed*. Christ spoke it with this intent, to teach us that *men ought always to pray and not to faint*, *v.* 1.

I. Christ shows, by a parable, the *power of importunity* among men, who will be swayed by that, when nothing else will influence, to do what is just and right. He gives you an instance of an honest cause that succeeded before an unjust judge, not by the equity or compassionableness of it, but purely by *dint of importunity*. Observe here, 1. The bad character of the judge that was in a certain city. He *neither feared God nor regarded man*; he had no manner of concern either for his conscience or for his reputation; he stood in no awe either of the wrath of God against him or of the censures of men concerning him: or, he took no care to do his duty either to God or man; he was a perfect stranger both to godliness

and honour, and had no notion of either. 2. The distressed case of a poor widow that was necessitated to make her appeal to him, being wronged by some one that thought to bear her down with power and terror. She had manifestly right on her side; but, it should seem, in soliciting to have right done her, she tied not herself to the formalities of the law, but made personal application to the judge from day to day at his own house, still crying, *Avenge me of mine adversary*, that is, *Do me justice against mine adversary*; not that she desired to be revenged on him for any thing he had done against her, but that he might be obliged to restore what effects he had of hers in his hands, and might be disabled any more to oppress her. 3. The difficulty and discouragement she met with in her cause: *He would not for awhile*. According to his usual practice, he frowned upon her, took no notice of her cause, but connived at all the wrong her adversary did her; for she had no bribe to give him, no great man whom he stood in any awe of to speak for her, so that he did not at all incline to redress her grievances; and he himself was conscious of the reason of his dilatoriness, and could not but own within himself that he *neither feared God nor regarded man*. 4. The gaining of her point by continually *dunning* this unjust judge (*v.* 5): "*Because this widow troubleth me*, gives me a continual toil, I will hear her cause, and do her justice; not so much lest by her clamour against me she bring

444

me into an ill name, as lest by her clamour to me she weary me; for she is resolved that she will give me no rest till it is done, and therefore I will do it, to save myself further trouble; as good at first as at last." Thus she got justice done her by continual craving; she begged it at his door, followed him in the streets, solicited him in open court, and still her cry was, *Avenge me of mine adversary*, which he was forced to do, to get rid of her; for his conscience, bad as he was, would not suffer him to send her to prison for an affront upon the court.

II. He applies this for the encouragement of God's praying people to pray with faith and fervency, and to persevere therein.

1. He assures them that God will at length be gracious to them (*v.* 6): *Hear what the unjust judge saith*, how he owns himself quite overcome by a constant importunity, *and shall not God avenge his own elect?* Observe,

(1) What it is that they desire and expect: that God would *avenge his own elect*. God's own elect meet with a great deal of trouble and opposition in this world; there are *many adversaries* that fight against them; Satan is their great adversary. That which is wanted and waited for is God's preserving and protecting them, and the work of his hands in them; his securing the interest of the church in the world and his grace in the heart.

(2) What it is that is required of God's people in order to the obtaining of this: they must *cry day and night to him*; not that he needs their remonstrances, or can be moved by their pleadings, but this he has made their duty, and to this he has promised mercy.

(3) What discouragements they may perhaps meet with in their prayers and expectations. He may *bear long with them*, and may not presently appear for them, in answer to their prayers.

(4) What assurance they have that mercy will come at last, though it be delayed, and how it is supported by what the unjust judge saith: If this widow prevail by being importunate, much more shall God's elect prevail. For, [1] This widow was a *stranger*, nothing related to the judge; but God's praying people are his own elect, whom he knows, and loves, and delights in, and has always concerned himself for. [2] She was but *one*, but the praying people of God are *many*, all of whom come to him on the same errand, and agree to ask what they need, Matt. xviii. 19. [3] She came to a *judge* that bade her *keep her distance*; we come to a *Father* that bids us *come boldly* to him, and teaches us to cry, *Abba, Father*. [4] She came to an *unjust judge*; we come to a *righteous Father* (John xvii. 25), one that regards his own glory and the comforts of his poor creatures, especially those in distress, as *widows* and *fatherless*. [5] She came to this judge purely upon her own account; but God is himself engaged in the cause which we are soliciting; and we can say, *Arise, O Lord, plead thine* own cause; and *what wilt thou do to*

thy great name? [6] She had no friend to speak for her, to add force to her petition, and to use interest for her more than her own; but we have an *Advocate with the Father*, his own Son, who *ever lives to make intercession* for us, and has a powerful prevailing interest in heaven. [7] She had no promise of speeding, no, nor any encouragement given her to ask; but we have the golden sceptre held out to us, are told to ask, with a promise that it shall be given to us. [8] She could have access to the judge only at some certain times; but we may cry to God *day and night*, at all hours, and therefore may the rather hope to prevail by importunity. [9] Her importunity was provoking to the judge, and she might fear lest it should set him more against her; but our importunity is pleasing to God; the prayer of the upright is *his delight*, and therefore, we may hope, shall avail much, if it be an effectual fervent prayer.

2. He intimates to them that, notwithstanding this, they will begin to be weary of waiting for him (*v.* 8): "*Nevertheless*, though such assurances are given that God will avenge his own elect, yet, *when the Son of man cometh, shall he find faith on the earth*?" The question implies a strong negation: No, he will not; he himself foresees it.

TWO KINDS OF PRAYER
(*vv.* 9–14)

The scope of this parable likewise is prefixed to it, and we are told (*v.* 9) who they were whom it was levelled at, and for whom it was calculated. He designed it for the conviction of some who *trusted in themselves that they were righteous, and despised others*. Now Christ by this parable would show such their folly, and that thereby they shut themselves out from acceptance with God.

I. Here are both these addressing themselves to the duty of prayer at the same place and time (*v.* 10): *Two men went up into the temple* (for the temple stood upon a hill) *to pray*.

II. Here is the Pharisee's address to God (for a prayer I cannot call it): He *stood* and *prayed thus with himself* (*vv.* 11, 12); *standing by himself, he prayed thus*, so some read it; he was wholly intent upon himself, had nothing in his eye but *self*, his own praise, and not God's glory. We see,

1. That he *trusted to himself that he was righteous*. A great many good things he said of himself, which we will suppose to be true. Now all this was very well and commendable. Miserable is the condition of those who come short of the righteousness of this Pharisee: yet he was not accepted; and why was he not? (1) His giving God thanks for this, though in itself a good thing, yet seems to be a mere formality. He does not say, *By the grace of God I am what I am*, as Paul did, but turns it off with a slight, *God, I thank thee*, which is intended but for a plausible introduction to a proud vainglorious ostentation of himself. (2) He makes his boast of this, and dwells with delight upon this subject, as if all his

business to the temple was to tell God Almighty how very good he was; and he is ready to say, with those hypocrites that we read of (Isa. lviii. 3), *Wherefore have we fasted, and thou seest not?* (3) He *trusted* to it as a righteousness, and not only mentioned it, but pleaded it, as if hereby he had merited at the hands of God, and made him his debtor. (4) Here is not one word of prayer in all he saith. He went *up to the temple to pray*, but forgot his errand, was so full of himself and his own goodness that he thought he had need of nothing, no, not of the favour and grace of God, which, it would seem he did not think worth asking.

2. That he *despised others*. (1) He thought meanly of all mankind but himself: *I thank thee that I am not as other men are.* He speaks indefinitely, as if he were better than any. We may have reason to thank God that we are not as *some men* are, that are notoriously wicked and vile; but to speak at random thus, as if *we* only were good, and all besides us were reprobates, is to judge by wholesale. (2) He thought meanly in a particular manner of this publican, whom he had left behind, it is probable, in the court of the Gentiles, and whose company he had fallen into as he came to the temple. He knew that he was a publican, and therefore very uncharitably concluded that he was an *extortioner*, *unjust*, and all that is evil. Suppose it had been so, and he had known it, what business had he to take notice of it? There could not be a plainer evidence,

not only of the want of humility and charity, but of reigning pride and malice, than this was.

III. Here is the publican's address to God, which was the reverse of the Pharisee's, as full of *humility* and *humiliation* as his was of *pride* and *ostentation*; as full of *repentance* for sin, and *desire* towards God, as his was of *confidence* in *himself* and his own righteousness and sufficiency.

1. He expressed his repentance and humility in *what he did*; and his gesture, when he addressed himself to his devotions, was *expressive* of great seriousness and humility, and the proper clothing of a broken, penitent, and obedient heart. (1) He *stood afar off*. The Pharisee *stood*, but crowded up as high as he could, to the upper end of the court; the publican *kept at a distance* under a sense of his unworthiness to draw near to God. (2) He *would not lift up so much as his eyes to heaven*, much less his *hands*, as was usual in prayer. The dejection of his looks is an indication of the dejection of his mind at the thought of sin. (3) He *smote upon his breast*, in a holy indignation at himself for sin: "Thus would I smite this wicked heart of mine, the poisoned fountain out of which flow all the streams of sin, if I could come at it."

2. He expressed it *in what he said*. His prayer was *short*. Fear and shame hindered him from saying much; sighs and groans swallowed up his words; but what he said was to the purpose: *God, be merciful to me a sinner.* And blessed be God that we have this

prayer upon record as an answered prayer, and that we are sure that he who prayed it went to his house justified; and so shall we, if we pray it, as he did, through Jesus Christ: "*God, be merciful to me a sinner.*"

IV. Here is the publican's *acceptance with God*. We have seen how differently these two addressed themselves to God; it is now worth while to enquire how they sped. There were those who would cry up the Pharisee, by whom he would go to his house applauded, and who would look with contempt upon this sneaking whining publican. But our Lord Jesus, to whom all hearts are open, all desires known, and from whom no secret is hid, who is perfectly acquainted with all proceedings in the court of heaven, assures us that this poor, penitent, brokenhearted publican *went to his house justified, rather than the other.*

The reason given for this is because God's glory is to *resist the proud, and give grace to the humble.* 1. Proud men, who *exalt themselves*, are *rivals with God*, and therefore *they shall* certainly be *abased*. 2. Humble men, who *abase themselves*, are *subject to God*, and they shall be *exalted*. God has preferment in store for those that will take it as a favour, not for those that demand it as a debt.

ACTIONS AND REACTIONS
(*vv.* 15–34)

This passage we had both in Matthew (xix and xx) and Mark;

it very fitly follows here after the story of the publican, as a confirmation of the truth which was to be illustrated by that parable, that those shall be accepted with God, and honoured, who humble themselves, and for them Christ has *blessings in store*, the choicest and best of blessings.

A BLIND BEGGAR
(*vv.* 35–43)

Christ came not only to bring *light* to a *dark* world, and so to set before us the *objects* we are to have in view, but also to give *sight* to blind *souls*, and by healing the *organ* to enable them to view those objects. As a token of this, he cured many of their bodily blindness; we have now an account of one to whom he *gave sight* near Jericho. Mark gives us an account of one, and names him, whom he cured *as he went out of Jericho*, Mark x. 46. Matthew speaks of two whom he cured *as they departed* from Jericho, Matt. xx. 30. Luke says it was *when he was near* to Jericho, which might be when he was going out of it as well as when he was coming into it.

CHAPTER NINETEEN
ZACCHEUS (*vv.* 1–10)

Many, no doubt, were converted to the faith of Christ of whom no account is kept in the gospels; but the conversion of some, whose case had something in it extraordinary, is recorded, as this of Zaccheus. Observe,

I. Who, and what, this Zaccheus was. His name bespeaks him a

Jew. *Zaccai* was a common name among the Jews; they had a famous rabbi, much about this time, of that name. Observe, 1. His calling, and the post he was in: *He was the chief among the publicans*, receiver-general; other publicans were officers under him; he was, as some think, farmer of the customs. We often read of publicans coming to Christ; but here was one that was *chief* of the publicans, was in authority, that enquired after him. God has his remnant among all sorts. Christ came to save even the *chief of sinners*, and therefore even the *chief of publicans*. 2. His circumstances in the world were very considerable: *He was rich*. The inferior publicans were commonly men of broken fortunes, and low in the world; but he that was *chief of the publicans* had raised a good estate. Christ had lately shown how *hard* it is for *rich people to enter into the kingdom of God*, yet presently produces an instance of one rich man that had been lost, and was found, and that not as the prodigal by being reduced to want.

II. How he came in Christ's way, and what was the occasion of his acquaintance with him. 1. He had a great *curiosity to see Jesus*, what kind of a man he was, having heard great talk of him, *v.* 3. 2. He could not get his curiosity gratified in this matter because he was *little*, and the crowd was *great*. Zaccheus was *low of stature*, and over-topped by all about him, so that he could not get a sight of Jesus. Many that are little of stature have large

souls, and are lively in spirit. 3. Because he would not disappoint his curiosity he *forgot his gravity*, as chief of the publicans, and *ran before*, like a boy, and *climbed up into a sycamore-tree, to see him*.

III. The notice Christ took of him, the call he gave him to a further acquaintance (*v.* 5), and the efficacy of that call, *v.* 6. 1. Christ *invited himself* to Zaccheus's house, not doubting of his hearty welcome there. He bade him *make haste, and come down*. Those that Christ calls must *come down*, must humble themselves, and not think to climb to heaven by any righteousness of their own; and they must *make haste* and come down, for delays are dangerous. Zaccheus must not hesitate, but hasten; he knows it is not a matter that needs consideration whether he should welcome such a guest to his house. He must *come down*, for Christ intends this day to *wait at his house*, and stay an hour or two with him. *Behold, he stands at the door and knocks*. 2. Zaccheus was *overjoyed* to have such an honour put upon his house (*v.* 6): *He made haste, and came down, and received him joyfully*; and his receiving him *into his house* was an indication and token of his receiving him *into his heart*.

IV. The offence which the people took at this *kind greeting* between Christ and Zaccheus. Those narrow-souled censorious Jews *murmured*, saying that he was *gone to be a guest with a man that is a sinner*; and were not they themselves sinful men? Was it not Christ's errand into the world to seek and save *men* that are *sinners*? But Zaccheus they think to be a sinner above all men that dwelt in Jericho, such a sinner as was not fit to be conversed with.

V. The proofs which Zaccheus gave publicly that, though he had been a *sinner*, he was now a *penitent*, and a true *convert*, v. 8. He does not expect to be justified by his works as the Pharisee who boasted of what he had done, but by his *good works* he will, through the grace of God, evidence the *sincerity* of his *faith* and *repentance*; and here he declares what his determination was. He *stood*, which denotes his saying it deliberately and with solemnity, in the nature of a vow to God. He makes it appear that there is a change *in his heart* (and that is repentance), for there is a change in his way.

1. Zaccheus had a good estate, and, whereas he had been in it hitherto laying up treasure for himself, and doing hurt to himself, now he resolves that for the future he will be all towards God, and do good to others with it: *Behold, Lord, the half of my goods I give to the poor*. Not, "I *will* give it by my will when I die," but, "I *do* give it now."

2. Zaccheus was conscious to himself that he had not got all he had honestly and fairly, but some by indirect and unlawful means, and of what he had got by such means he promises to make restitution: "If *I have taken any thing from any man by false accusation*, or if I have wronged any man in the way of my business as a *publican*, exacting more than was appointed, I promise to

restore him *four-fold*." This was the restitution that a thief was to make, Exod. xxii. 1.

VI. Christ's *approbation* and *acceptance* of Zaccheus's conversion, by which also he cleared himself from any imputation in going to be a guest with him, vv. 9, 10.

1. Zaccheus is declared to be now a *happy man*. Now he is turned from sin to God; now he has bidden Christ welcome to his house, and is become an honest, charitable, good man: *This day is salvation come to this house.*

2. What Christ had done to make him, in particular, a happy man, was consonant to the great design and intention of his coming into the world, v. 10. With the same argument he had before justified his conversing with publicans, Matt. ix. 13. He came from heaven to earth (a long journey) to *seek* that which was *lost* (which had *wandered and gone astray*), and to bring it back (Matt. xviii. 11, 12), and to *save* that which was lost, which was perishing, and in a manner destroyed and cut off. Christ undertook the cause when it was given up for *lost*; undertook to bring those to themselves that were *lost* to God and all goodness. He seeks those that were not worth seeking; he seeks those that sought him not, and asked not for him, as Zaccheus here.

TRUE SERVANTS (vv. 11–27)

Our Lord Jesus is now upon his way to Jerusalem, to his last passover, when he was to suffer and die; now here we are told,

I. How the expectations of his friends were *raised* upon this occasion: *They thought that the kingdom of God would immediately appear*, *v.* 11. The Pharisees expected it about this time (*ch.* xvii. 20), and, it seems, so did Christ's own disciples; but they both had a mistaken notion of it.

II. How their expectations were *checked*, and the mistakes *rectified* upon which they were founded; and this he does in three things:—

1. They expected that he should appear in his glory now *presently*, but he tells them that he must not be publicly installed in his kingdom for a great while yet. He is like *a certain nobleman* who *goes into a far country, to receive for himself a kingdom*. Christ must go to heaven, to sit down at the right hand of the Father there, and to receive from him *honour and glory*, before the Spirit was poured out by which his kingdom was to be set up on earth, and before a church was to be set up for him in the Gentile world. He must receive the kingdom, and then *return*.

2. They expected that his apostles and immediate attendants should be advanced to dignity and honour, that they should all be made princes and peers, privy-counsellors and judges, and have all the pomp and preferments of the court and of the town. But Christ here tells them that, instead of this, he designed them to be *men of business*; they must expect no other preferment in this world than that of the trading end of the town; he would set them up with a stock under their hands, that they

might employ it themselves, in serving him and the interest of his kingdom among men.

They have a *great work* to do now. Their Master leaves them, to receive his kingdom, and, at parting, he gives each of them a *pound*. This signifies the same thing with the talents in the parable that is parallel to this (Matt. xxv.), all the gifts with which Christ's apostles were endued, and the advantages and capacities which they had of serving the interests of Christ in the world, and others, both ministers and Christians, like them in a lower degree.

3. Another thing they expected was, that, when the kingdom of God should appear, the body of the Jewish nation would immediately fall in with it, and submit to it, and all their aversions to Christ and his gospel would immediately vanish; but Christ tells them that, after his departure, the generality of them would persist in their obstinacy and rebellion, and it would be their ruin.

PALM SUNDAY (*vv.* 28–48)

We have here the same account of Christ's riding in some sort of triumph (such as it was) into Jerusalem which we had before in Matthew (xxi) and Mark.

But also observe,

I. The *tears he shed* for the *approaching ruin* of the *city* (*v.* 41): *When he was come near, he beheld the city, and wept over it*.

1. What a tender spirit Christ was of; we never read that he

laughed, but we often find him in tears.

2. That Jesus Christ *wept* in the midst of his triumphs, *wept* when all about him were *rejoicing*, to show how little he was elevated with the applause and acclamation of the people.

3. That he *wept over Jerusalem*. Note, There are cities to be wept over, and none to be more lamented than Jerusalem, that had been the holy city, and the joy of the whole earth, if it be degenerated. But why did Christ weep at the sight of Jerusalem?

(1) Jerusalem has not improved the day of her opportunities. He wept, and said, *If thou hadst known, even thou at least in this thy day, the things that belong to thy peace*, the making of thy peace with God, and the securing of thine own spiritual and eternal welfare—but thou *dost not know the day of thy visitation, v.* 44.

(2) Jerusalem cannot escape the day of her desolation. The *things of her peace* are now in a manner hidden from her eyes; they will be shortly. The *peaceful things* are not *hidden from the eyes* of particular persons; but it is too late to think now of the nation of the Jews, *as such*, becoming a Christian nation, by embracing Christ. And therefore they are marked for ruin. And there was scarcely one stone *left upon another*. This was for their crucifying Christ; this was because they *knew not the day of their visitation*. Let other cities and nations take warning.

II. The *zeal he showed* for the *present purification of the temple*. Though it must be destroyed ere

long, it does not therefore follow that no care must be taken of it in the meantime. See Matt. xxi. 12.

TEACHING IN THE TEMPLE
(vv. 1–47)

The whole of this passage we have dealt with already, at Matt. xxi–xxiii. Luke adds no more to this.

THE POOR WIDOW
(vv. 1–4)

This short passage of story we had before in Mark xii.

JUDGMENTS TO COME
(vv. 5–28)

Most of this is common to Matt. (xxiv) and Mark (xiii), so we confine ourselves to what is unique to Luke.

1. "God will stand by you, and own you, and assist you, in your trials; you are his advocates, and you shall be well furnished with instructions, *vv.* 14, 15. *Settle it in your hearts*, impress it upon them, take pains with them to persuade them *not to meditate before what you shall answer*; do not *depend* upon your own wit and ingenuity, your own prudence and policy, and do not *distrust* or *despair* of the immediate and extraordinary aids of the divine grace. I promise you the special assistance of divine grace: *I will give you a mouth and wisdom.*" This proves Christ to be God; for it is God's prerogative to *give wisdom*, and he it is that *made man's mouth*. Note, *First*, A *mouth* and *wisdom* together com-

pletely fit a man both for services and sufferings; *wisdom* to know what to say, and a *mouth* wherewith to say it as it should be said. *Secondly*, Those that plead Christ's cause may depend upon him to give them *a mouth and wisdom*, which way soever they are called to plead it, especially when they are brought before magistrates for his name's sake. It is not said that he will send an angel from heaven to answer for them, though he could do this, but that he will give them a *mouth* and *wisdom* to enable them to answer for themselves, which puts a greater honour upon them, which requires them to use the gifts and graces Christ furnishes them with, and redounds the more to the glory of God, who *stills the enemy and the avenger out of the mouths of babes and sucklings*. *Thirdly*, When Christ gives to his witnesses a *mouth and wisdom*, they are enabled to say that both for him and themselves which *all their adversaries are not able to gainsay or resist*, so that they are silenced, and put to confusion. This was remarkably fulfilled after the pouring out of the Spirit, by whom Christ gave his disciples this *mouth* and *wisdom*, when the apostles were brought before the priests and rulers, and answered them so as to make them ashamed, Acts iv. v. and vi.

(1) "You shall suffer no real damage by all the hardships they shall put upon you (*v.* 18): *There shall not a hair of your head perish*." Shall some of them lose their heads, and yet not lose a hair? It is a proverbial expression, denoting the greatest indemnity and security imaginable; it is frequently used both in the Old Testament and New, in that sense. "Not a hair of your head shall perish but," *First*, "I will take *cognizance* of it." To this end he had said (Matt. x. 30), *The hairs of your head are all numbered*; and an account is kept of them, so that none of them shall perish but he will miss it. *Secondly*, "It shall be upon a *valuable consideration*." We do not reckon that *lost* or *perishing* which is laid out for good purposes, and will turn to a good account. *Thirdly*, "It shall be abundantly recompensed; when you come to balance profit and loss, you will find that nothing has perished, but, on the contrary, that you have great gain in present comforts, especially in the joys of a life eternal;" so that though we may be losers for Christ we shall not, we cannot be losers by him in the end.

(2) "It is therefore your duty and interest, in the midst of your own sufferings and those of the nation, to maintain a holy sincerity and serenity of mind, which will keep you always easy (*v.* 19): *In your patience possess ye your souls*; get and keep possession of your souls." Some read it as a promise, "You *may* or *shall* possess your souls." It comes all to one.

2. Having given them an idea of the times for about thirty-eight years next ensuing, he here comes to show them what all those things would issue in at last, namely, the destruction of Jerusalem, and the utter dispersion of the Jewish nation, which would be a little day of judgment, a type and figure of Christ's second coming, which was not so fully spoken of here as in the

parallel place (Matt. xxiv.), yet glanced at; for the destruction of Jerusalem would be as it were the destruction of the world to those whose hearts were bound up in it.

III. He foretells the terrible havoc that should be made of the Jewish nation (*v.* 22): *Those are the days of vengeance* so often spoken of by the Old-Testament prophets, which would complete the ruin of that provoking people. All their predictions must now be fulfilled, and the blood of all the Old-Testament martyrs must now be required. *All things that are written must be fulfilled* at length.

IV. He describes the issue of the struggles between the Jews and the Romans, and what they will come to at last; in short, 1. Multitudes of them *shall fall by the edge of the sword.* It is computed that in those wars of the Jews there fell by the sword above eleven hundred thousand. And the siege of Jerusalem was, in effect, a military execution. 2. The rest shall be *led away captive*; not into *one* nation, as when they were conquered by the Chaldeans, which gave them an opportunity of keeping together, but *into all nations*, which made it impossible for them to *correspond* with each other, much less to *incorporate*. 3. Jerusalem itself was *trodden down of the Gentiles.* The Romans, when they had made themselves masters of it, laid it quite waste, as a *rebellious and bad city, hurtful to kings and provinces*, and therefore hateful to them.

V. He describes the great frights that people should generally be in. Many frightful *sights* shall be *in the sun, moon and stars*, prodigies in the heavens, and here in this lower world, the *sea and the waves roaring*, with terrible storms and tempests, such as had not been known, and above the ordinary working of natural causes. The effect of this shall be universal confusion and consternation *upon the earth, distress of nations with perplexity, v.* 25. *Men's hearts shall fail them for fear* (*v.* 26), *men being quite* dispirited, *unsouled*, dying away for fear. When *judgment begins at the house of God*, it will not end there; it shall be as if all the world were falling in pieces; and where can any be secure then? The *powers of heaven shall be shaken*, and then the pillars of the earth cannot but tremble. Thus shall the present Jewish policy, religion, laws, and government, be all entirely dissolved by a series of unparalleled calamities, attended with the utmost confusion.

VI. He encourages all the faithful disciples in reference to the terrors of that day (*v.* 28): "*When these things begin to come to pass*, when Jerusalem is besieged, and everything is concurring to the destruction of the Jews, *then* do you look *up*, when others are looking down, look heavenward, in faith, hope, and prayer, and *lift up your heads* with cheerfulness and confidence, *for your redemption draws nigh.*" 1. When Christ came to destroy the Jews, he came to redeem the Christians that were persecuted and oppressed by them; *then had the churches rest.* 2. When he comes to judge the world at the last day, he will *redeem* all that are his, from all their grievances. When they see that day approaching, they can *lift up their heads with joy*, knowing that *their redemption draws nigh*, their removal to their Redeemer.

VII. Here is one word of prediction that looks further than the destruction of the Jewish nation, which is not easily understood; we have it in *v.* 24: *Jerusalem shall be trodden down of the Gentiles, till the times of the Gentiles be fulfilled*. 1. Some understand it of what is past; so Dr. Hammond. The Gentiles, who have conquered Jerusalem, shall keep possession of it, and it shall be purely Gentile, till the times of the Gentiles be fulfilled, till a great part of the Gentile world shall have become Christian, and many of the Jews shall turn Christians, shall join with the Gentile Christians, to set up a church in Jerusalem, which shall flourish there for a long time. 2. Others understand it of what is yet to come; so Dr. Whitby. Jerusalem shall be possessed by the Gentiles, of one sort or other, for the most part, till the time come when the nations that yet remain infidels shall embrace the Christian faith, when the kingdoms of this world shall become Christ's kingdoms, and then all the Jews shall be converted. Jerusalem shall be inhabited by them, and neither they nor their city any longer trodden down by the Gentiles.

BE READY (*vv.* 29–38)

Here, in the close of this discourse,

I. Christ appoints his disciples to observe the signs of the times. This we had at Matt. xxiv. 32 ff.

He also cautions them against security and sensuality, by which they would unfit themselves for the trying times that were coming on, and make them to be a great surprise and terror to them (*vv.* 34, 35): *Take heed to yourselves*. This is the word of command given to all Christ's disciples: "*Take heed to yourselves*, that you be not overpowered by temptations, nor betrayed by your own corruptions." Note, We cannot be *safe* if we be *secure*. It concerns us at *all* times, but especially at *some* times, to be very cautious. See here, 1. What our *danger* is: that *the day* of death and judgment should *come upon us unawares*, when we do not *expect* it, and are not *prepared* for it. 2. What our *duty* is, in consideration of this danger: we must *take heed lest our hearts be overcharged*, lest they be burdened and overloaded, and so unfitted and disabled to do what must be done in preparation for death and judgment. Two things we must watch against, lest our hearts be overcharged with them:— (1) The indulging of the appetites of the body, and allowing of ourselves in the gratifications of sense to an excess: *Take heed lest you be overcharged with surfeiting and drunkenness*. (2) The inordinate pursuit of the good things of this world. The heart is overcharged with the *cares of this life*. The former is the snare of those that are given to their pleasures: this is the snare of the men of business, that *will be rich* We have need to guard on both hands, not only lest at the time when death comes, but lest *at any time* our hearts should be thus overcharged. Our caution against sin, and our care of our own souls, must be *constant*.

II. He counsels them to prepare and get ready for this great day, *v.* 36. Here see. 1. What should be *our aim*: that we may be *accounted worthy to escape all these things*; that, when the judgments of God are abroad, we may be preserved from the malignity of them. Yet we must aim not only to *escape that*, but to *stand before the Son of man*; not only to stand *acquitted* before him as our Judge (Ps. i. 5), to have boldness in the day of Christ (that is supposed in our *escaping* all those things), but to *stand before him*, to attend on him as our Master. 2. What should be our *actings* in these aims: *Watch therefore, and pray always*. Watching and praying must go together, Neh. iv. 9. Those that would escape the wrath to come, and make sure of the joys to come, must *watch* and *pray*, and must do so always, must make it the constant business of their lives.

In the last two verses we have an account how Christ disposed of himself during those three or four days between his riding in triumph into Jerusalem and the night in which he was betrayed. 1. He was *all day teaching in the temple*. Christ preached on week-days as well as sabbath days. He was an indefatigable preacher; he preached in the face of opposition, and in the midst of those that he knew sought occasion against him. 2. At night he went out to lodge at a friend's house, in the mount of Olives, about a mile out of town. 3. Early in the morning he was in the temple again, where he had a morning lecture for those that were willing to attend it; and the people were forward to hear one that they saw forward to preach (*v.* 38).

CHAPTER TWENTY-TWO

THE UPPER ROOM
(*vv.* 1–20)

Most of this narrative is also found in Matt. xxvi. and Mark xiv. Again we note the distinctively Lucan material.

The institution of the Lord's supper, *vv.* 19, 20. The *passer* and the *deliverance* out of Egypt were *typical* and *prophetic signs* of a Christ to come, who should by dying deliver us from sin and death, and the tyranny of Satan. Therefore the Lord's supper is instituted to be a commemorative sign or memorial of a Christ already come, that *has* by dying delivered us; and it is his death that is in a special manner set before us in that ordinance.

1. The *breaking of Christ's body* as a *sacrifice for us* is here commemorated by the *breaking of bread*; and the sacrifices under the law were called the *bread of our God* (Lev. xxi. 6, 8, 17): *This is my body which is given for you*. And there is a feast upon that sacrifice instituted, in which we are to apply it to ourselves, and to take the benefit and comfort of it. This bread that was given for us is given *to us* to be food for our souls, for nothing can be more *nourishing* and *satisfying* to our souls than the doctrine of Christ's making atonement for sin, and the assurance of our interest in that atonement; this bread that was *broken* and *given for us*, to satisfy for the guilt

of our sins, is *broken* and *given to us*, to satisfy the desire of our souls. And this we do in *remembrance* of what he did for us, when he died for us, and for a *memorial* of what we *do*, in making ourselves *partakers of him*, and joining ourselves to him in an everlasting covenant.

2. The *shedding* of *Christ's blood*, by which the atonement was made (for *the blood made atonement for the soul*, Lev. xvii. 11), as represented by the wine in the cup; and that cup of wine is a sign and token of the New Testament, or new covenant, made with us. It *commemorates* the purchase of the covenant by the blood of Christ, and *confirms* the promises of the covenant, which are all *Yea* and *Amen* in him. This will be reviving and refreshing to our souls, as wine that *makes glad the heart*. In all our commemorations of the shedding of Christ's blood, we must have an eye to it as shed for us; we needed it, we take hold of it, we hope to have benefit by it; *who loved me, and gave himself for me*. And in all our regards to the New Testament we must have an eye to the *blood of Christ*, which gave life and being to it, and seals to us all the promises of it. Had it not been for the blood of Christ, we had never had the New Testament; and, had it not been for the New Testament, we had never known the meaning of Christ's blood shed.

DISCOURSE
WITH THE DISCIPLES
(vv. 21–38)

We have here Christ's discourse with his disciples after supper, much of which is new here; and in St. John's gospel we shall find other additions.

I. He discoursed with them concerning him that should betray him, who was now present. 1. He signifies to them that the traitor was now among them, and one of them, *v.* 21. By placing this after the institution of the Lord's supper, though in Matthew and Mark it is placed before it, it seems plain that Judas did receive the Lord's supper, did *eat of that bread* and *drink of that cup*; for, after the solemnity was over, Christ said, *Behold, the hand of him that betrayeth me is with me on the table*. There have been those that have eaten bread with Christ and yet have betrayed him. 2. He foretells that the treason would take effect (*v.* 22): *Truly the Son of man goes as it was determined*, goes to the place where he will be betrayed; for he is delivered up by the counsel and foreknowledge of God, else Judas could not have delivered him up. Christ was not driven to his sufferings, but cheerfully *went to them*. He said, *Lo, I come*. 3. He threatens the traitor: *Woe to that man by whom he is betrayed*. 4. He frightens the rest of the disciples into a suspicion of themselves, by saying that it was one of them, and not naming which (*v.* 23): *They began to enquire among themselves*, to interrogate themselves, to put the question to themselves, *who it was that should do this thing*, that could be so base to so good a Master. The enquiry was not, *Is it you?* or, *Is it such a one?* but, *Is it I?*

II. Concerning the strife that was among them for precedency or supremacy.

1. See what the dispute was: *which of them should be accounted the greatest*. Such and so many contests among the disciples for dignity and dominion, *before* the Spirit was poured upon them, were a sad presage of the like strifes for, and affections of, supremacy in the churches, after the Spirit should be provoked to depart from them.

2. See what Christ said to this dispute.

(1) This was to make themselves like the *kings of the Gentiles*, who affect worldly pomp, and worldly power, *v.* 25.

(2) It was to make themselves unlike the disciples of Christ, and unlike Christ himself: "*You shall not be so*," *vv.* 26, 27. See here, [1] What is the rule Christ gave to his disciples: He that is *greater among you*, that is *senior*, to whom precedency is due upon the account of his age, let him be as the *younger*, both in point of *lowness of place* (let him condescend to sit with the younger, and be free and familiar with them) and in point of *labour* and *work*. [2] What was the example which he himself gave to this rule: *Whether is greater, he that sitteth at meat or he that serveth?* he that attendeth or he that is attended on? Now Christ was among his disciples just like one that waited at table. Shall those take upon them the form of princes who call themselves followers of him that *took upon him the form of a servant?*

(3) They ought not to strive for worldly honour and grandeur, because he had better honours in reserve for them, of another nature,

a *kingdom*, a *feast*, a *throne*, for each of them, wherein they should all share alike and should, have no occasion to strive for precedency, *vv.* 28–30. Where observe,

[1] Christ's commendation of his disciples for their faithfulness to him; and this was honour enough for them, they needed not to strive for any greater.

[2] The recompence he designed them for their fidelity: *I appoint, I bequeath, unto you a kingdom*. Or thus, *I appoint to you, as my Father has appointed a kingdom to me, that you may eat and drink at my table*. Understand it, *First*, Of what should be done for them in this world. God gave his Son a *kingdom among men*, the gospel church, of which he is the living, quickening, ruling, Head. This *kingdom* he *appointed* to his apostles and their successors in the ministry of the gospel. Or, *Secondly*, Of what should be done for them in the other world, which I take to be chiefly meant. Let them go on in their services in this world; their preferments shall be in the other world.

III. Concerning Peter's denying him. And in this part of the discourse we may observe,

1. The general notice Christ gives to Peter of the devil's design upon him and the rest of the apostles (*v.* 31): *The Lord said, Simon, Simon*, observe what I say; *Satan hath desired to have you*, to have you all in his hands, *that he may sift you as wheat*. Peter, who used to be the *mouth* of the rest in speaking to Christ, is here made the *ear* of the rest; and what is designed for warning to them all (*all*

you shall be offended, because of me) is directed to Peter, because he was principally concerned, being in a particular manner struck at by the tempter: *Satan has desired to have you*.

2. The particular encouragement he gave to Peter, in reference to this trial: "*I have prayed for thee*, because, though he desires to have them all, he is permitted to make his strongest onset upon thee only: thou wilt be most violently assaulted, *but I have prayed for thee, that thy faith fail not*, that it may not totally and finally fail." Note, (1) If faith be kept up in an hour of temptation, though we may fall, yet we shall not be utterly cast down. Faith will quench Satan's fiery darts. (2) Though there may be many failings in the faith of true believers, yet there shall not be a total and final failure of their faith. It is their seed, their root, remaining in them. (3) It is owing to the mediation and intercession of Jesus Christ that the faith of his disciples, though sometimes sadly shaken, yet is not sunk.

3. The charge he gives to Peter to help others as he should himself be helped of God: "*When thou art converted, strengthen thy brethren*; when thou art recovered by the grace of God, and brought to repentance, do what thou canst to recover others." Note, (1) Those that have fallen into sin must be *converted from it*; those that have turned aside must *return*; those that have left their first love must do their first works. (2) Those that through grace are converted from sin must do what they can to strengthen their brethren that stand, and to prevent *their*

falling; see Ps. li. 1–13; 1 Tim. i. 13.

4. Peter's declared resolution to cleave to Christ, whatever it cost him (*v.* 33): *Lord, I am ready to go with thee, both into prison and to death*. This was a great word, and yet I believe no more than he meant at this time, and thought he should *make good* too.

5. Christ's express prediction of his denying him thrice (*v.* 34): "*I tell thee, Peter the cock shall not crow this day before thou even deny that thou knowest me*." Note, Christ knows us better than we know ourselves, and knows the evil that is in us, and will be done by us, which we ourselves do not suspect.

IV. Concerning the condition of all the disciples.

1. He appeals to them concerning what had been, *v.* 35, He had owned that they had been faithful servants to him, *v.* 28. Now he expects, at parting, that they should acknowledge that he had been a kind and careful Master to them ever since they left all to follow him: *When I sent you without purse, lacked you any thing?*

2. He gives them notice of a very great change of their circumstances now approaching. For, (1) He that was their Master was now entering upon his sufferings, which he had often foretold (*v.* 37). (2) They must therefore expect troubles, and must not think now to have such an easy and comfortable life as they had had; no, the scene will alter. They must now in some degree suffer *with* their Master; and, when he is gone, they must expect to suffer *like* him. The servant is not better than his Lord.

GETHSEMANE (*vv.* 39–53)

We have here the awful story of Christ's *agony in the garden,* just before he was betrayed, which was largely related by the other evangelists.

There are three things in this passage which we had not in the other evangelists:—

1. That, when Christ was in his agony, *there appeared* to him *an angel from heaven, strengthening him, v.* 43. (1) It was an instance of the deep humiliation of our Lord Jesus that he *needed* the assistance of an angel, and would *admit* it. (2) When he was not delivered from his sufferings, yet he was *strengthened* and supported under them, and that was *equivalent.* (3) The angels ministered to the Lord Jesus in his sufferings. He could have had legions of them to rescue him; nay, this one could have done it, could have chased and conquered the whole band of men that came to take him; but he made use of his ministration only to *strengthen him;* and the very visit which this angel made him now in his grief, when his enemies were awake and his friends asleep, was such a seasonable token of the divine favour as would be a very great strengthening to him. Yet this was not all: he probably *said something* to him to strengthen him; put him in mind that his sufferings were in order to his Father's glory, to his own glory, and to the salvation of those that were given him, represented to him the joy set before him, the seed he should see; with these and the like suggestions he encouraged him to go on cheerfully;

and what is comforting is strengthening.

2. That, *being in an agony, he prayed more earnestly, v.* 44. As his sorrow and trouble grew upon him, he grew more importunate in prayer; not that there was before any coldness or indifferency in his prayers, but there was now a greater vehemency in them, which was expressed in his voice and gesture.

3. That, in this agony, *his sweat was as it were great drops of blood falling down to the ground.* Sweat came in with sin, and was a branch of the curse, Gen. iii. 19. And therefore, when Christ was made sin and a curse for us, he underwent a grievous sweat, that *in the sweat of his face* we might eat bread, and that he might sanctify and sweeten all our trials to us. There is some dispute among the critics whether this *sweat* is only *compared to* drops of *blood,* being much *thicker* than drops of sweat commonly are, the pores of the body being more than ordinarily opened, or whether *real* blood out of the capillary veins mingled with it, so that it was in colour like blood, and might truly be called a *bloody sweat;* the matter is not great. Some reckon this one of the times when Christ shed his blood for us, *for without the shedding of blood there is no remission.* Every pore was as it were a bleeding wound, and his blood stained all his raiment. This showed the *travail of his soul.*

The other evangelists tell us what was the check Christ gave to Peter for striking the servant of the high priest. Luke here tells us, 1. How Christ excused the blow:

Suffer ye thus far, v. 51. Dr. Whitby thinks he said this to his enemies who came to take him, to pacify them, that they might not be provoked by it to fall upon the disciples, whom he had undertaken the preservation of. 2. How he cured the wound, which was more than amends sufficient for the injury: *He touched his ear, and healed him.* Christ hereby gave them a proof, (1) Of his power. He that could *heal* or could *destroy* if he pleased, which should have obliged them in interest to submit to him. (2) Of his mercy and goodness. Christ here gave an illustrious example to his own rule of *doing good to them that hate us,* as afterwards he did of *praying for them that despitefully use us.* Those who render good for evil do as Christ did.

PETER'S DENIAL (*vv.* 54–62)

This is recorded and commented upon at Matt. xxvi. 69 ff.

CHRIST BEFORE THE SANHEDRIM
(*vv.* 63–71)

We are here told, as before in the other gospels,

I. How our Lord Jesus was *abused* by the servants of the high priest.

II. How he was accused and condemned by the great sanhedrim, consisting of the *elders of the people, the chief priests, and the scribes,* who were all up betimes, and got together *as soon as it was day,* about five of the clock in the morning, to prosecute this matter. It is but a short account that we have here of his trial in the ecclesiastical court.

CHAPTER TWENTY-THREE
PILATE AND HEROD
(*vv.* 1–12)

Our Lord Jesus was condemned as a blasphemer in the spiritual court, but it was the most *impotent malice* that could be that this court was actuated by; for, when they had *condemned* him, they knew they could not *put him to death,* and therefore took another course.

I. They accused him before Pilate. The *whole multitude of them arose,* when they saw they could go no further with him in their court, and *led him unto Pilate.*

1. Here is the indictment drawn up against him (*v.* 2), in which they pretended a zeal for Cæsar, only to ingratiate themselves with Pilate, but it was all *malice* against Christ, and nothing else. They misrepresented him, (1) As making the people *rebel against Cæsar.* Christ had particularly taught that they *ought to give tribute to Cæsar,* though he knew there were those that would be offended at him for it; and yet he is here falsely accused as *forbidding to give tribute to Cæsar.* Innocency is no fence against calumny. (2) As making himself a *rival with Cæsar,* though the very reason why they rejected him, and would not own him to be the Messiah, was because he did not appear in worldly pomp and power, and did not set up for a temporal prince.

2. His pleading to the indictment: *Pilate asked him, Art thou the king of the Jews? v.* 3. To which he answered, *Thou sayest it;* that is, "It is as thou sayest," Christ's

kingdom is wholly spiritual, and will not interfere with Cæsar's jurisdiction. Or, "*Thou sayest it*; but canst thou prove it? What evidence hast thou for it?"

3. Pilate's declaration of his innocency (*v.* 4): He *said to the chief priests, and the people* that seemed to join with them in the prosecution, "*I find no fault in this man.*"

4. The continued fury and outrage of the prosecutors, *v.* 5. Instead of being moderated by Pilate's declaration of his innocency, and considering, as they ought to have done, whether they were not bringing the guilt of innocent blood upon themselves, they were the more exasperated, more exceedingly *fierce*.

II. They accused him before Herod. 1. Pilate removed him and his cause to Herod's court. 2. Herod was very willing to have the examining of him (*v.* 8): *When he saw Jesus he was exceedingly glad.* He had *heard many things of him* in Galilee, where his miracles had for a great while been all the talk of the country; and he *longed to see him*, not for any affection he had for him or his doctrine, but purely out of curiosity. 3. His prosecutors appeared against him before Herod, for they were restless in the prosecution: *They stood, and vehemently accused him* (*v.* 10), *impudently* and *boldly*, so the word signifies. They would make Herod believe that he had poisoned Galilee too with his seditious notions. 4. Herod was very *abusive* to him: He, with *his men of war*, his attendants, and officers, and great men, *set him at nought*. They *made nothing* of him;

so the word is. 5. Herod sent him back to Pilate, and it proved an occasion of the making of them friends, they having been for some time before at variance.

SECOND TRIAL BEFORE PILATE (*vv.* 13–25)

We have here the blessed Jesus run down by the mob, and hurried to the cross in the storm of a popular noise and tumult, raised by the malice and artifice of the *chief priests*, as agents for the prince of the power of the air.

I. Pilate solemnly protests that he believes he has done nothing worthy of death or of bonds.

II. He appeals to Herod concerning him (*v.* 15): "*I sent you to him*, who is supposed to have known more of him than I have done, and he has *sent him back*, not convicted of any thing, nor under any mark of his displeasure; in his opinion, his crimes are not capital."

III. He proposes to release him, if they will but consent to it.

IV. The people choose rather to have Barabbas released, a wretched fellow, that had nothing to recommend him to their favour but the daringness of his crimes.

V. When Pilate urged the second time that Christ should be released, they cried out, *Crucify him, crucify him*, *vv.* 20, 21.

VI. When Pilate the third time reasoned with them, to show them the unreasonableness and injustice of it, they were the more peremptory and outrageous (*v.* 22).

VII. Pilate's yielding, at length, to their importunity. The voice of the people and of the *chief priests* prevailed, and were too hard for

Pilate, and overruled him to go contrary to his convictions and inclinations.

THE WAY OF SORROW
(vv. 26–31)

We have here the blessed Jesus, the Lamb of God, led as *a lamb to the slaughter*, to the sacrifice. Now as they led him away to death we find,

I. One that was a *bearer*, that carried his cross, *Simon* by name, *a Cyrenian*.

II. Many that were *mourners*; true mourners, who followed him, *bewailing* and *lamenting* him. He diverts their lamentation into another channel, *v.* 28.

1. He gives them a general direction concerning their lamentations: *Daughters of Jerusalem, weep not for me*, but rather let them *weep for themselves and for their children*, with an eye to the destruction that was coming upon Jerusalem, which some of them might live to see and share in the calamities of, or, at least their children would, for whom they ought to be solicitous.

2. He gives them a particular reason why they should *weep for themselves and for their children*: "*For behold* sad times are coming upon your city; it will be destroyed, and you will be involved in the common destruction."

3. He shows how natural it was for them to infer this desolation from his sufferings. *If they do these things in a green tree, what shall be done in the dry? v.* 31. Christ was a *green tree*, fruitful and flourishing; now, if such things were done to

him, we may thence infer what would have been done to the whole race of mankind if he had not *interposed*, and what shall be done to those that continue dry trees, notwithstanding all that is done to make them fruitful.

THE TWO MALEFACTORS
(vv. 32–43)

In these verses we have,

I. Divers passages which we had before in Matthew and Mark concerning Christ's sufferings.

II. Here are two passages which we had not before, and they are very remarkable ones.

1. Christ's prayer for his enemies (*v.* 34): *Father, forgive them*. Seven remarkable words Christ spoke after he was nailed to the cross, and before he died, and this is the first. Observe,

(1) The petition: *Father, forgive them*. Now he made intercession for transgressors, as was foretold (Isa. liii. 12), and it is to be added to his prayer (John xvii.), to complete the specimen he gave of his intercession within the veil: that for saints, this for sinners. Now the sayings of Christ upon the cross as well as his sufferings had a further intention than they seemed to have. This was a mediatorial word, and explicatory of the intent and meaning of his death: "*Father, forgive them*, not only these, but all that shall repent, and believe the gospel"; and he did not intend that these should be forgiven upon any other terms. "Father, that which I am now suffering and dying for is in order to this, that poor sinners may be pardoned."

(2) The plea: *For they know not what they do*; for, *if they had known*, they would not have crucified him, 1 Cor. ii. 8. There was a veil upon his glory and upon their understandings; and how could they see through two veils? They wished his blood on them and their children: but, had they known what they did, they would have unwished it again.

2. The conversion of the thief upon the cross. Christ was crucified between two thieves, and in them were represented the different effects which the cross of Christ would have upon the children of men, to whom it would be *brought near* in the preaching of the gospel. They are all malefactors, all guilty before God. Now the cross of Christ is to some a *savour of life unto life*, to others of *death unto death*.

(1) Here was one of these malefactors that was *hardened to the last*. Near to the cross of Christ, he *railed on him*, as others did (*v.* 39): he said, *If thou be the Christ*, as they say thou art, *save thyself and us*.

(2) Here was the other of them that was *softened at the last*. This malefactor, when just ready to fall into the hands of Satan, was snatched as a brand out of the burning, and made a monument of divine mercy and grace, and Satan was left to roar as a lion disappointed of his prey. This gives no encouragement to any to put off their repentance to their death-bed, or to hope that then they shall find mercy; for, though it is certain that true repentance is never too late, it is as certain that late repentance is seldom true. He never had any

offer of Christ, nor day of grace, before now: he was designed to be made a singular instance of the power of Christ's grace now at a time when he was *crucified in weakness*. We shall see the case to be extraordinary if we observe,

[1] The extraordinary operations of God's grace upon him, which appeared in what he said. Here were so many evidences given in a short time of a blessed change wrought in him that more could not have been given in so little a compass.

[2] The extraordinary grants of Christ's favour to him: *Jesus said unto him*, in answer to his prayer, "*Verily I say unto thee*, I the *Amen*, the faithful Witness, I say *Amen* to this prayer, put my *fiat* to it: nay, thou shalt have more than thou didst ask, *This day thou shalt be with me in paradise*," *v.* 43.

See here how the happiness of heaven is set forth to us. (1) It is *paradise*, a garden of pleasure, the *paradise of God* (Rev. ii. 7), alluding to the garden of Eden, in which our first parents were placed when they were innocent. (2) It is being *with Christ* there. That is the happiness of heaven, to see Christ, and sit with him, and share in his glory, John xvii. 24. (3) It is immediate upon death: *This day shalt thou be with me*, to-night, before to-morrow. *The souls of the faithful, after they are delivered from the burden of the flesh*, immediately *are in joy and felicity*; the spirits of just men are immediately *made perfect*. Lazarus departs, and is immediately *comforted*; Paul departs, and is immediately with Christ, Phil. i. 23.

CHRIST'S DEATH (*vv.* 44–56)

We have here the dying and burying of the Lord Jesus, as earlier recorded by Matt. xxvii. 45 ff, and Mark.

CHAPTER TWENTY-FOUR

FIRST DAY OF THE WEEK
(*vv.* 1–12)

The manner of the re-uniting of Christ's soul and body in his resurrection is a mystery, one of the *secret things* that *belong not to us*. But that he did indeed rise from the dead, and was thereby proved to be the Son of God, are *things revealed, which belong to us and to our children*. Some of them we have here in these verses, which relate the same story for substance that we had in Matthew and Mark.

I. We have here the affection and respect which the good women that had followed Christ showed to him, after he was dead and buried, *v.* 1. As soon as ever they could, after the sabbath was over, they *came to the sepulchre*, to embalm his body.

II. The surprise they were in, when they found the stone rolled away and the grave empty (*vv.* 2, 3).

III. The plain account which they had of Christ's resurrection from two angels, who appeared to them *in shining garments*, not only white, but bright, and casting a lustre about them. They first saw *one* angel without the sepulchre, who presently *went in*, and sat with another angel in the sepulchre, *one at the head and the other at the feet, where the body of Jesus had lain*; so

the evangelists may be reconciled.

IV. Their satisfaction in this account, *v.* 8. The women seemed to acquiesce; they *remembered his words*, when they were thus put in mind of them, and thence concluded that if he was risen it was no more than they had reason to expect.

V. The report they brought of this to the apostles: *They returned from the sepulchre, and told all these things to the eleven, and to all the rest* of Christ's disciples, *v.* 9. *Their words seemed to them as idle tales, and they believed them not.* One cannot but be amazed at the stupidity of these disciples,—who had themselves so often professed that they believed Christ to be the Son of God and the true Messiah, had been so often told that he must die and rise again, and then enter into his glory, had seen him more than once raise the dead,—that they should be so backward to believe in his raising himself.

VI. The enquiry which Peter made hereupon, *v.* 12. It was Mary Magdalene that brought the report to him, as appears, John xx. 1, 2, where this story of his running to the sepulchre is more particularly related. 1. Peter hastened to the sepulchre upon the report. He now *ran to the sepulchre*, who but the other day *ran from his Master*. 2. He looked into the sepulchre, and took notice how orderly the linen clothes in which Christ was wrapped were taken off, and folded up, and laid by themselves, but the body gone. 3. He went away, as he thought, not much the wiser, *wondering in himself at that which was come to pass*.

THE EMMAUS ROAD
(vv. 13–35)

This appearance of Christ to the *two disciples* going to Emmaus was mentioned, and but just mentioned, before (Mark xvi. 12); here it is largely related. It happened the same day that Christ rose, the first day of the new world that rose with him. One of these two disciples was *Cleopas* or *Alpheus*, said by the ancients to be the brother of Joseph, Christ's supposed father; who the other was is not certain. Now in this passage of story we may observe,

I. The *walk* and *talk* of these two disciples: *They went to a village called Emmaus*, which is reckoned to be about two hours' walk from Jerusalem; it is here said to be about sixty furlongs, seven measured miles, *v.* 13. But as they travelled they *talked together of all those things which had happened*, *v.* 14. They *talked over these things*, reasoning with themselves concerning the probabilities of Christ's resurrection; for, according as these appeared, they would either go forward or return back to Jerusalem.

II. The good company they met with upon the road, when Jesus himself came, and joined himself to them (*v.* 15): *They communed together, and reasoned*, and perhaps were warm at the argument, one hoping that their Master was risen, and would set up his kingdom, the other despairing. *Jesus himself drew near*, as a stranger who, seeing them travel the same way that he *went*, told them that he should be *glad of their company*. But, though they had Christ with them, they were not at first aware of it (*v.* 16): *Their eyes were held, that they should not know him*. It should seem, there were both an alteration of the *object* (for it is said in Mark that now *he appeared in another form*) and a restraint upon the organ (for here it is said that *their eyes were held* by a divine power).

III. The conference that was between Christ and them, when he knew them, and they knew not him. Now Christ and his disciples, as is usual when friends meet incognito, or in a disguise, are here crossing questions.

1. Christ's first question to them is concerning *their* present *sadness*, which plainly appeared in their countenances. Observe,

(1) They were *sad*; it appeared to a stranger that they were so. [1] They had lost their dear Master, and were, in their own apprehensions, quite disappointed in their expectations from him. They had given up the cause, and knew not what course to take to retrieve it. [2] Though he was risen from the dead, yet either they did not know it or did not believe it, and so they were still in sorrow. [3] Being sad, they had *communications one with another* concerning Christ. Joint-mourners should be mutual comforters; comforts sometimes come best from such.

(2) Christ came up to them, and enquired into the matter of their talk, and the cause of their grief: *What manner of communications are these?* Though Christ had now entered into his state of exaltation, yet he continued tender of his disciples, and concerned for their

comfort. He speaks as one troubled to see their melancholy: *Wherefore look ye so sadly to-day?* Gen. xl. 7.

2. In answer to this, they put a question to him concerning *his strangeness. Art thou only a stranger in Jerusalem, and hast not known the things that are come to pass there in these days?* Observe, (1) Cleopas gave him a civil answer. He does not rudely ask him, "As for what we are talking of, what is that to you?" and bid him go about his business. (2) He is full of Christ himself and of his death and sufferings, and wonders that every body else is not so too: "What! art thou such a stranger in Jerusalem as not to know what has been done to our Master there?" (3) He is very willing to inform this stranger concerning Christ, and to draw on further discourse with him upon this subject. (4) It appears, by what Cleopas says, that the death of Christ made a great noise in Jerusalem, so that it could not be imagined that any man should be such a stranger in the city as not to know of it; it was all the talk of the town, and discoursed of in all companies. Thus the matter of fact came to be universally *known*, which, after the pouring out of the Spirit, was to be *explained*.

3. Christ, by way of reply, asked concerning *their knowledge* (*v.* 19): *He said unto them, What things?* thus making himself yet more a stranger.

4. They, hereupon, gave him a particular account concerning Christ, and the present posture of his affairs. Observe the story they tell, *v.* 19, &c.

(1) Here is a summary of Christ's

life and *character*. The *things* they are full of are concerning *Jesus of Nazareth* (so he was commonly called), who *was a prophet*, a teacher come from God. He preached a true and excellent doctrine, which had manifestly its rise from heaven, and its tendency towards heaven. He confirmed it by many glorious miracles, miracles of mercy, so that he was *mighty in deed and word before God and all the people*. He had great acceptance with God, and a great reputation in the country.

(2) Here is a modest narrative of his sufferings and death, *v.* 20. "Though he was so dear both to God and man, yet the *chief priests and our rulers*, in contempt of both, *delivered him* to the Roman power, *to be condemned to death*, and *they have crucified him*."

(3) Here is an intimation of their disappointment in him, as the reason of their sadness: "*We trusted that it had been he who should have redeemed Israel, v.* 21. We are of those who not only looked upon him to be a prophet, like Moses, but, like him, a redeemer too." He was depended upon, and great things expected from him, by them that *looked for redemption*, and in it for the consolation of Israel. Now, if *hope deferred makes the heart sick*, hope disappointed, especially such a hope, kills the heart.

(4) Here is an account of their present amazement with reference to his resurrection.

(5) Our Lord Jesus, though not known by face to them, makes himself known to them by his word. [1] He reproves them for their

incogitancy, and the weakness of their faith in the scriptures of the Old Testament: *O fools, and slow of heart to believe*, v. 25. That which is condemned in them as their *foolishness* is, *First*, Their *slowness to believe*. Believers are branded as fools by atheists, and infidels, and free-thinkers, and their most holy faith is censured as a fond credulity; but Christ tells us that those are *fools* who are *slow of heart to believe*, and are kept from it by prejudices never impartially examined. *Secondly*, Their slowness to believe *the writings of the prophets*. He does not so much blame them for their slowness to believe the testimony of the women and of the angels, but for that which was the cause thereof, their *slowness to believe* the prophets.

[2] He shows them that the sufferings of Christ, which were such a stumbling-block to them, and made them unapt to believe his glory, were really the appointed way to his glory, and he could not go to it any other way (*v.* 26): "*Ought not the Christ* (the Messiah) to *have suffered these things, and to enter into his glory?* Was it not decreed, and was not that decree *declared*, that the promised Messiah must first suffer and then reign, that he must go by his cross to his crown?" Had they never read the fifty-third of Isaiah and the ninth of Daniel, where the prophets speak so very plainly of the *sufferings of Christ* and the *glory that should follow?* 1 Pet. i. 11.

[3] He expounded to them the scriptures of the Old Testament, which spoke of the Messiah, and showed them how they were fulfilled in Jesus of Nazareth, and now can tell them more concerning him than they could before tell him (*v.* 27). You cannot go far in any part of scripture but you meet with something that has reference to Christ, some prophecy, some promise, some prayer, some type or other; for he is the true *treasure hid in the field* of the Old Testament. A golden thread of gospel grace runs through the whole web of the Old Testament.

IV. Here is the discovery which Christ at length made of himself to them. *They drew nigh to the village whither they went* (*v.* 28), where, it should seem, they determined to *take up* for that night. And now,

1. They courted his stay with them: *He made as though he would have gone further*. Christ yielded to their importunity: He *went in, to tarry with them*. Thus ready is Christ to give further instructions and comforts to those who improve what they have received.

2. He manifested himself to them, *vv.* 30, 31. (1) They began to suspect it was he, when, as they *sat down to meat*, he undertook the office of the Master of the feast, which he performed so like himself, and like what he used to do among his disciples, that by it they discerned him: *He took bread, and blessed it*, and *brake, and gave to them*. (2) Presently *their eyes were opened*, and then they saw who it was, and *knew him* well enough. See how Christ by his Spirit and grace makes himself known to the souls of his people. [1] He opens the scriptures to them, for they are they which testify of him to those who

search them, and search for him in them. [2] He meets them at his table, in the ordinance of the Lord's supper, and commonly there makes further discoveries of himself to them, is *known to them in the breaking of bread*. But, [3] The work is completed by the opening of the eyes of their mind, and causing the scales to fall off from them, as from Paul's in his conversion.

3. He immediately disappeared: *He vanished out of their sight*. He *withdrew himself* from them, slipped away of a sudden, and went *out of sight*. Or, he *became not visible by them*, was made inconspicuous by them. Such short and transient views have we of Christ in this world; we see him, but in a little while lose the sight of him again. When we come to heaven the vision of him will have no interruptions.

V. Here is the reflection which these disciples made upon this conference, and the report which they made of it to their brethren at Jerusalem.

1. The reflection they each of them made upon the influence which Christ's discourse had upon them (v. 32): *They said one to another, Did not our hearts burn within us?* They found the preaching powerful, even when they knew not the preacher. See here, (1) What *preaching* is likely to *do good*— such as Christ's was, *plain preaching*, and that which is familiar and level to our capacity—*he talked with us by the way*; and *scriptural* preaching—*he opened to us the scriptures*, the scriptures relating to himself. (2) What *hearing* is likely to *do good*—that which makes the

heart burn; when we are much affected with the things of God, especially with the love of Christ in dying for us, then we may say, "Through grace our hearts are thus inflamed."

2. The report they brought of this to their brethren at Jerusalem (v. 33). Observe, (1) How they found them, just when they came in among them, discoursing on the same subject, and relating another proof of the resurrection of Christ. *The Lord is risen indeed, and hath appeared to Simon, v. 34.* That Peter had a sight of him before the rest of the disciples had appears 1. Cor. xv. 5, where it is said, *He was seen of Cephas, then of the twelve.* (2) How they seconded their evidence with an account of what they had seen (v. 35): *They told what things were done in the way.* The words that were spoken by Christ to them in the way, having a wonderful effect and influence upon them, are here called the *things* that were *done in the way*; for the words that Christ speaks are not an empty sound, but *they are spirit and they are life*, and wondrous things are *done* by them.

THE RISEN CHRIST
(vv. 36–49)

Five times Christ was seen the same day that he rose: by Mary Magdalene alone in the garden (John xx. 14), by the women as they were going to tell the disciples (Matt. xxviii. 9), by Peter alone, by the two disciples going to Emmaus, and now at night by the eleven, of which we have an account in these verses, as also John xx. 19. Observe,

1. The great *surprise* which his

appearing gave them. 2. The *fright* which they put themselves into upon it (*v.* 37): They were *terrified*, supposing that *they had seen a spirit*, because he came in among them without any noise, and was in the midst of them ere they were aware. The word used (Matt. xiv. 26), when they said *It is a spirit*, is a *spectre*, and *apparition*; but the word here used properly signifies *a spirit*; they supposed it to be a spirit not clothed with a real body.

II. The great *satisfaction* which has discourse gave them, wherein we have,

1. The reproof he gave them for their causeless fears: *Why are you troubled, and why do* frightful *thoughts arise in your hearts?* *v.* 38.

2. The proof he gave them of his resurrection. Two proofs he gives them:—

(1) He shows them his body, particularly *his hands and his feet*. They saw that he had the shape, and features, and exact resemblance, of their Master; but is it not his ghost? "No," saith Christ, "*behold my hands and my feet.*" He lays down this principle—that a *spirit has not flesh and bones*. He does not tell us what a *spirit* is (it is time enough to know that when we go to the world of spirits), but what it is not: *It has not flesh and bones.*

(2) He *eats* with them, to show that he had a real and true body, and that he was willing to converse freely and familiarly with his disciples, as one friend with another. Peter lays a great stress upon this (Acts x. 41): We *did eat and drink with him after he rose from the dead.*

3. The *insight* he gave them into

the word of God, which they had *heard* and read, by which faith in the resurrection of Christ is wrought in them, and all the difficulties are cleared. (1) He refers them to the *word* which they had *heard* from him when he was with them, and puts them in mind of that as the angel had done (*v.* 44): *These are the words which I said unto you* in private, many a time, *while I was yet with you.* (2) He refers them to the *word* they had read in the Old Testament, to which the word they had heard from him directed them: *All things must be fulfilled which were written.* (3) By an immediate present work upon their minds, of which they themselves could not but be aware he gave them to apprehend the true intent and meaning of the Old-Testament prophecies of Christ, and to see them all fulfilled in him: *Then opened he their understanding, that they might understand the scriptures, v.* 45.

4. The instructions he gave them as *apostles*, who were to be employed in setting up his kingdom in the world. "You are now to enter upon them; *you are* to be *witnesses of these things* (*v.* 48), to carry the notice of them to all the world; not only to *report* them as matter of news, but to *assert* them as evidence upon the trial of the great cause that has been so long depending between God and Satan, the issue of which must be the casting down and casting out of the *prince of this world.* You are fully assured of these things yourselves, you are eye and ear-witnesses of them; go, and assure the world of them; and the same Spirit that has

enlightened you shall go along with you for the enlightening of others."

Whither must they carry these proposals, and how far does their commission extend? They are here told, [1] That they must preach this *among all nations*. The prophets had preached *repentance* and *remission* to the *Jews*, but the apostles must preach them to *all the world*. [2] That they must *begin at Jerusalem*. There they must preach their first *gospel sermon*; there the *gospel church* must be first formed; there the gospel day must dawn, and thence that light shall go forth which must take hold on the ends of the earth.

It is a vast undertaking that they are here called to, a very large and difficult province, especially considering the opposition this service would meet with, and the sufferings it would be attended with. If therefore they ask, *Who is sufficient for these things?* here is an answer ready: *Behold, I send the promise of my Father upon you*, and *you shall be endued with power from on high*, v. 49. He here assures them that in a little time the Spirit should be poured out upon them in greater measures than ever, and they should thereby be furnished with all those gifts and graces which were necessary to their discharge of this great trust; and therefore they must *tarry at Jerusalem*, and not enter upon it till this be done.

EPILOGUE (vv. 50–53)

How solemnly Christ took leave of his disciples. Probably, it was very early in the morning that he ascended, before people were stirring; for he never showed himself openly to all the people after his resurrection, but only to *chosen witnesses*. The disciples did not see him rise out of the grave, because his resurrection was capable of being proved by their seeing him alive afterwards; but they saw him *ascend* into heaven, because they could not otherwise have an *ocular* demonstration of his ascension. They were *led out* on purpose to see him ascend, had their eye upon him when he ascended, and were not looking another way. He did not go away in displeasure, but in love; he left a blessing behind him; *he lifted up his hands*, as the high priest did when he blessed the people; see Lev. ix. 22. *While he was blessing them, he was parted from them*; not as if he were taken away before he had said all he had to say, but to intimate that his being parted from them did not put an end to his blessing them, for the intercession which he went to heaven to make for all his is a continuation of the blessing.

How cheerfully his disciples continued their attendance on him, and on God through him, even now that he was parted from them. They *returned to Jerusalem with great joy*. There they were ordered to continue till the Spirit should be poured out upon them, and thither they went accordingly, though it was into the mouth of danger. They abounded in acts of devotion while they were in expectation of the promise of the Father, v. 53. (1) They attended the temple-service at the hours of prayer. God had not as yet quite forsaken it, and therefore they did not. (2) Temple-sacrifices, they knew, were superseded by Christ's sacrifice, but the temple-songs they joined in.

The *amen* that concludes seems to be added by the church and every believer to the reading of the gospel, signifying an assent to the truths of the gospel, and a hearty concurrence with all the disciples of Christ in praising and blessing God. *Amen.* Let him be continually praised and blessed.

THE GOSPEL ACCORDING TO

ST. JOHN

CHAPTER ONE
PROLOGUE (*vv.* 1–5)

The evangelist here lays down the great truth he is to prove, that Jesus Christ is God, one with the Father. Observe,

I. Of whom he speaks—*The Word*. This is an idiom peculiar to John's writings. See 1 John i. 1; v. 7; Rev. xix. 13. Yet some think that Christ is meant by *the Word* in Acts xx. 32; Heb. iv. 12; Luke i. 2. Even the Jews were taught that the *Word of God* was the same with God. The evangelist, in the close of his discourse (*v.* 18), plainly tells us why he calls Christ *the Word*— *because he is the only begotten Son, who is in the bosom of the Father, and has declared him. Word* is twofold: *word conceived*; and *word uttered; intelligence* and *utterance*. 1. There is the *word conceived*, that is, *thought*, which is the first and only immediate product and conception of the soul (all the operations of which are performed by *thought*), and it is one with the soul. And thus the second person in the Trinity is fitly called *the Word*; for he is the *first-begotten of the Father*, that eternal essential Wisdom which *the Lord possessed*, as the soul does its thought, *in the beginning of his way*, Prov. viii. 22. There is nothing we are more sure of than *that we think*, yet nothing

we are more in the dark about than *how we think*; who can declare the generation of *thought* in the soul? Surely then the generations and births of the eternal mind may well be allowed to be great mysteries of godliness, the bottom of which we cannot fathom, while yet we adore the depth. 2. There is the *word uttered*, and this is *speech*, the chief and most natural indication of the mind. And thus Christ is *the Word*, for *by him* God has in *these last days spoken to us* (Heb. i. 2), and has directed us to *hear him*, Matt. xvii. 5. He has made known God's mind to us, as a man's word or speech makes known his thoughts, as far as he pleases, and no further. Christ is called that *wonderful speaker* (see notes on Dan. viii. 13), the *speaker of things hidden* and *strange*. He is *the Word* speaking *from* God to us, and *to God* for us. John Baptist was *the voice*, but Christ *the Word*: being *the Word*, he is *the Truth*, the *Amen*, the *faithful Witness* of the mind of God.

II. What he saith of him, enough to prove beyond contradiction that *he is God*. He asserts,

1. His existence in the beginning: *In the beginning was the Word*. This bespeaks his existence, not only before his incarnation, but before all time. The Word had a being before the world had a beginning.

He that *was* in the beginning *never* began, and therefore was *ever*,— *without beginning of time*. So Nonnus.

2. His co-existence with the Father: *The Word was with God, and the Word was God.* Let none say that when we invite them to Christ we would draw them from God, for Christ is *with God* and *is God*; it is repeated in *v.* 2: *the same*, the very same that we believe in and preach, was *in the beginning with God*, that is, he was so from eternity. The Word was with God, (1) In respect of *essence* and *substance*; for *the Word was God*: a distinct person or substance, for he was *with God*; and yet the same in substance, for he *was God*, Heb. i. 3. (2) In respect of *complacency* and *felicity*. There was a glory and happiness which Christ had *with God* before the world was (*ch.* xvii. 5), the Son infinitely happy in the enjoyment of his Father's bosom, and no less the Father's delight, the Son of his love, Prov. viii. 30. (3) In respect of *counsel* and *design*. The mystery of man's redemption by this Word incarnate was *hid in God* before all worlds, Eph. iii. 9.

3. His agency in making the world, *v.* 3. This is here, (1) Expressly asserted: *All things were made by him.* By him, not as a subordinate instrument, but as a co-ordinate agent, God *made the world* (Heb. i. 2), not as the workman cuts by his axe, but as the body sees by the eye. (2) The contrary is denied: *Without him was not any thing made that was made*, from the highest angel to the meanest worm. God the Father did nothing without him in that work.

Now, [1] This proves that *he is God*; for he that *built all things is God*, Heb. iii. 4. [2] This proves the excellency of the Christian religion, that the author and founder of it is the same that was the author and founder of the world. [3] This shows how well qualified he was for the work of our redemption and salvation. Help was laid upon one that was mighty indeed; for it was laid upon him that made all things; and he is appointed the author of our bliss who was the author of our being.

4. The original of life and light that is in him: *In him was life, v,* 4. This further proves that he is God, and every way qualified for his undertaking; for, (1) He has *life in himself*; not only the *true God*, but the *living God*. God is life; he swears by himself when he saith, *As I live.* (2) All living creatures have their life in him; not only all the *matter* of the creation was *made* by him, but all the *life* too that is in the creation is derived from him and supported by him. (3) Reasonable creatures have their *light* from him; that *life* which is *the light of men* comes from him. Life in man is something greater and nobler than it is in other creatures; it is *rational*, and not merely *animal*. When man became a *living soul*, his life was *light*, his capacities such as distinguished him from, and dignified him above, the beasts that perish.

5. The manifestation of him to the children of men. It might be objected, If this eternal Word was all in all thus in the creation of the world, whence is it that he has been so little taken notice of and regarded? To this he answers (*v.* 5),

The light shines, but the darkness comprehends it not. Observe,

The disability of the degenerate world to receive this discovery: *The darkness comprehended it not*; the most of men received the grace of God in these discoveries in vain.[1]

THE WORD REJECTED
(vv. 6–14)

The evangelist designs to bring in John Baptist bearing an honourable testimony to Jesus Christ. Now in these verses, before he does this,

I. He gives us some account of the witness he is about to produce. His name was *John*, which signifies *gracious*; his conversation was austere, but he was not the less *gracious*. Now,

1. We are here told concerning him, in general, that he was a *man sent of God*. God gave him both his mission and his message, both his credentials and his instructions.

2. We are here told what his office and business were (*v.* 7): *The same came for a witness*, an eye-witness, a leading witness. Now observe, (1) The matter of his testimony: *He came to bear witness to the light.* Light is a thing which witnesses for itself, and carries its own evidence along with it; but to those who shut their eyes against the light it is necessary there should be those that bear witness to it. Christ's light needs not man's testimony, but the world's darkness

does. (2) The design of his testimony: *That all men through him might believe*; not in him, but in Christ, whose way he was sent to prepare. He taught men to look through him, and pass through him, to Christ; through the doctrine of repentance for sin to that of faith in Christ.

3. We are here cautioned not to mistake him for the light who only came to bear witness to it (*v.* 8): *He was not that light* that was expected and promised, but only was sent to bear witness of that great and ruling light.

II. Before he goes on with John's testimony, he returns to give us a further account of this Jesus to whom John bore record. Having shown in the beginning of the chapter the glories of his Godhead, he here comes to show the graces of his incarnation, and his favours to man as Mediator.

1. Christ was the *true light* (*v.* 9); not as if John Baptist were a false light, but, in comparison with Christ, he was a very small light. Christ is the great light that deserves to be called so. But how does Christ enlighten every man that comes into the world? (1) By his creating power he enlightens every man with the light of reason; that life which is the light of men is from him; all the discoveries and directions of reason, all the comfort it gives us, and all the beauty it puts upon us, are from Christ. (2) By the publication of his gospel to all nations he does in effect enlighten every man. (3) By the operation of his Spirit and grace he enlightens all those that are enlightened to salvation; and those

[1] Editor's note: The author has, in common with most of his contemporaries, misunderstood the Greek here. See RV, RSV, NEB etc.

that are not enlightened by him perish in darkness.

2. Christ *was in the world*, v. 10. The Son of the Highest was here in this *lower* world; that *light* in this *dark* world; that *holy thing* in this sinful polluted world. He left a world of bliss and glory, and was here in this melancholy miserable world. He undertook to reconcile the world to God, and therefore was *in the world*, to treat about it, and settle that affair; to satisfy God's justice for the world, and discover God's favour to the world. Now observe here, (1) What reason Christ had to expect the most affectionate and respectful welcome possible in this world; for *the world was made by him*. (2) What cold entertainment he met with, notwithstanding: *The world knew him not*. They did not own him, did not bid him welcome, because they did not *know him*; and they did not know him because he did not make himself known in the way that they expected—in external glory and majesty.

3. He *came to his own* (v. 11); not only to the world, which was *his own*, but to the people of Israel, that were peculiarly *his own* above all people; of them he came, among them he lived, and to them he was *first sent*. He was sent to the lost sheep of the house of Israel, for it was he whose own the sheep were. Now observe,

(1) That the generality *rejected* him: *His own received him not*. They had the oracles of God, which told them beforehand *when* and *where* to expect him, and of what tribe and family he should arise. He came among them him-

self, introduced with signs and wonders, and himself the greatest; and therefore it is not said of them, as it was of the world (v. 10), that they *knew him not*; but *his own*, though they could not but know him, yet *received him not*; did not receive his doctrine, did not welcome him as the Messiah, but fortified themselves against him.

(2) That yet there was a remnant who *owned* him, and were faithful to him. Though his own received him not, yet there were those that *received* him (v. 12). Observe here,

[1] The true Christian's *description* and *property*; and that is, that he *receives Christ*, and *believes on his name*; the latter explains the former.

[2] The true Christian's dignity and privilege are twofold:—

First, The *privilege of adoption*, which takes them into the number of God's children: *To them gave he power to become the sons of God*. The Son of God became a Son of man, that the sons and daughters of men might become the sons and daughters of God Almighty.

Secondly, The *privilege of regeneration* (v. 13): *Which were born*. Now here we have an account of the original of this new birth. 1. Negatively. (1) It is not *propagated* by natural generation from our parents. It is *not of blood, nor of the will of the flesh*, nor of *corruptible seed*, 1 Pet. i. 23. Man is called *flesh and blood*, because thence he has his original: but we do not become the children of God as we become the children of our natural parents. (2) It is not *produced* by the natural power of our own will. As it is not of *blood*, nor of *the will of the flesh*, so neither is it of the *will of man*, which labours under a moral impotency of determining itself to that which is good; so that the principles of the divine life are not of our own planting, it is the grace of God that makes us willing to be *his*.

4. The *word was made flesh, v.* 14. This expresses Christ's incarnation more clearly than what went before. By his divine presence he always *was in the world*, and by his prophets he *came to his own*. But now that the fulness of time was come he was sent forth after another manner, *made of a woman* (Gal. iv. 4); God manifested in the flesh, according to the faith and hope of holy Job; *Yet shall I see God in my flesh*, Job xix. 26. Observe here,

(1) The *human nature of Christ* with which he was veiled; and that expressed two ways.

[1] *The word was made flesh.* The voice that ushered in the gospel cried, *All flesh is grass* (Isa. xl. 6), to make the Redeemer's love the more wonderful, who, to *redeem* and *save* us, was made flesh, and withered as grass; but the *Word of the Lord*, who was made flesh, *endures for ever*; when made flesh, he ceased not to be the Word of God.

[2] He *dwelt among us*, here in this lower world. Having taken upon him the nature of man, he put himself into the place and condition of other men. But that the eternal Word was *made flesh*, was clothed with a body as we are, and dwelt in this world as we do, this has put an honour upon them both, and should make us willing to abide in the flesh while God has any work

for us to do; for Christ dwelt in this lower world, bad as it is, till he had finished what he had to do here, *ch.* xvii. 4.

(2) The *beams of his divine glory* that *darted* through this *veil of flesh: We beheld his glory, the glory as of the only begotten of the Father, full of grace and truth.* Observe,

[1] Who were the witnesses of this glory: *we*, his disciples and followers, that conversed most freely and familiarly with him; we among whom he *dwelt*. Other men discover their weaknesses to those that are most familiar with them, but it was not so with Christ; those that were most intimate with him saw most of his glory.

[2] What evidence they had of it: *We saw it.* The word signifies a fixed abiding sight, such as gave them an opportunity of making their observations.

[3] What the glory was: *The glory as of the only begotten of the Father.* The glory of the *Word made flesh* was such a glory as became the only *begotten Son of God*, and could not be the glory of any other. God's goodness is his glory, and he went about doing good; he spoke and acted in every thing as an incarnate Deity.

[4] What advantage those he dwelt among had from this. He dwelt among them, *full of grace and truth.* In the old tabernacle wherein God dwelt was the *law*, in *this* was grace; in that were *types*, in this was *truth*.

GRACE FOR GRACE (*vv.* 15–18)

In these verses,

I. The evangelist begins again to give us John Baptist's testimony concerning Christ, *v.* 15. He had said (*v.* 8) that he *came for a witness*; now here he tells us that he did accordingly *bear witness*. Here, Observe,

1. *How he expressed* his testimony: He *cried*, according to the prediction that he should be *the voice of one crying*. This intimates, (1) That it was an open *public* testimony, proclaimed, that all manner of persons might take notice of it, for all are concerned in it. (2) That he was free and hearty in bearing this testimony.

2. What his *testimony* was.

(1) He had given the preference to this Jesus: *He that comes after me*, in the time of his birth and public appearance, is preferred before me; he that *succeeds* me in preaching and making disciples is a more excellent person, upon all accounts; as the prince or peer that *comes after* is preferred before the harbinger or gentleman-usher that makes way for him.

(2) He here gives a good reason for it: *For he was before me, He was my first*, or *first to me*; he was my first Cause, my original.

II. He presently returns again to speak of Jesus Christ, and cannot go on with John Baptist's testimony till *v.* 19. The 16th verse has a manifest connection with *v.* 14, where the incarnate Word was said to be *full of grace and truth*. Now here he makes this the matter, not only of our adoration, but of our thankfulness, because *from the fulness* of his *we all have received. He received gifts for men* (Ps. lxviii. 18), that he might *give gifts to men*, Eph. iv. 8. He was filled, that he might *fill all in all* (Eph. i. 23),

might *fill our treasures*, Prov. viii. 21. Let us see what it is that we have received.

1. We have received *grace for grace*. Our receivings by Christ are all summed up in this one word, *grace*. It is repeated, *grace for grace*; for to every stone in this building, as well as *to the top-stone*, we must cry, *Grace, grace*.

2. We have received *grace and truth*, *v.* 17. He had said (*v.* 14) that Christ was *full of grace and truth*; now here he says that by him *grace and truth* came to us. From Christ we *receive grace*; this is a string he delights to harp upon, he cannot go off from it. Two things he further observes in this verse concerning this grace:—(1) Its *preference* above the law of Moses. (2) Its *connection* with truth: *grace and truth*. The law was only *made known* by Moses, but the *being* of this grace and truth, as well as the discovery of them, is owing to Jesus Christ; this was *made* by him, as the world at first was; and by him this *grace and truth* do consist.

3. Another thing we receive from Christ is a clear revelation of God to us (*v.* 18): He hath *declared* God to us, whom *no man hath seen at any time*. This was the grace and truth which came by Christ, the knowledge of God and an acquaintance with him. Observe,

(1) The insufficiency of all other discoveries: *No man hath seen God at any time*.

(2) The all-sufficiency of the gospel discovery proved from its author: *The only-begotten Son, who is in the bosom of the Father, he has declared him*.

JOHN'S TESTIMONY (*vv.* 19–28)

We have here the testimony of John, which he delivered to the messengers who were sent from Jerusalem to examine him. Observe here,

I. Who they were that sent to him, and who they were that were sent: *the Jews at Jerusalem*, the great sanhedrim or high-commission court, which sat at Jerusalem, and was the representative of the Jewish church, who took cognizance of all matters relating to religion.

II. On what errand they were sent; it was to enquire concerning John and *his baptism*.

III. What was the answer he gave them, and his account, both concerning himself and concerning his baptism, in both which he witnessed to Christ.

1. Concerning himself, and what he professed himself to be. He answers their interrogatory,

(1) *Negatively*. He was not that great one whom some took him to be. God's faithful witnesses stand more upon their guard *against undue respect* than against *unjust contempt*.

(2) *Affirmatively*. *I am the voice of one crying in the wilderness*. Observe,

[1] He gives his answer in the words of scripture, to show that the scripture was fulfilled in him, and that his office was supported by a divine authority.

[2] He gives in his answer in very humble, modest, self-denying expressions. He chooses to apply that scripture to himself which denotes not his dignity, but his duty and

dependence, which bespeaks him little.

[3] He gives such an account of himself as might be profitable to them, and might excite and awaken them to hearken to him; for he *was the voice* (see Isa. xl. 3), a voice to alarm, an articulate voice to instruct. He came to prepare and dispose people for the reception and entertainment of Christ and his gospel. It is an allusion to the harbingers of a prince or great man, that cry, *Make room*.

2. Here is his testimony concerning *his baptism*.

(1) The enquiry which the committee made about it: *Why baptizest thou, if thou be not the Christ, nor Elias, nor that prophet? v.* 25. [1] They readily apprehended baptism to be fitly and properly used as a sacred rite or ceremony. [2] They expected it would be used in the days of the Messiah, because it was promised that then there should be a *fountain opened* (Zech. xiii. 1), and *clean water sprinkled*, Ezek. xxxvi. 25. It is taken for granted that Christ, and Elias, and *that prophet*, would baptize, when they came to *purify* a *polluted* world. [3] They would therefore know by what authority John baptized. His denying himself to be Elias, or *that prophet*, subjected him to this further question, *Why baptizest thou?*

(2) The account he gave of it, *vv.* 26, 27.

[1] He owned himself to be only the minister of the outward sign: "*I baptize with water*, and that is all; I am no more, and do no more, than what you see; I have no other title than *John the Baptist*; I

cannot confer the spiritual grace signified by it."

[2] He directed them to one who was greater than himself, and would do that for them, if they pleased, which he could not do. *First*, He tells them of Christ's *presence among them* now at this time: *There stands one among you*, at this time, *whom you know not.* Note, 1. Much true worth lies hid in this world; obscurity is often the lot of real excellency. Saints are God's *hidden ones*, therefore *the world knows them not.* 2. God himself is often nearer to us than we are aware of. *The Lord* is *in this place*, and *I knew it not.*

Lastly, Notice is taken of the place where all this was done: *In Bethabara beyond Jordan*, v. 28. It was at a great *distance* from Jerusalem, beyond Jordan; probably because what he did *there* would be least offensive to the government.

THE LAMB OF GOD (*vv.* 29–36)

Now here are *two testimonies* borne by John to Christ, but those two *agree in one.*

I. Here is his testimony to Christ on the first day that he saw him coming from the wilderness; and here four things are witnessed by him concerning Christ, when he had him before his eyes: —

1. That he is *the Lamb of God which taketh away the sin of the world*, v. 29. Let us learn here,

(1) That Jesus Christ is the *Lamb of God*, which bespeaks him the great sacrifice, by which atonement is made for sin, and man reconciled to God. He is the Lamb *of God*; he is appointed by *him*

(Rom. iii. 25), he was devoted to him (*ch.* xvii. 19), and he was accepted with him; in him he was well pleased.

(2) That Jesus Christ, as the *Lamb of God, takes away the sin of the world.* This ground of hope we have—Jesus Christ is *the Lamb of God.* [1] He *takes away sin.* He, being Mediator between God and man, takes away that which is, above any thing, offensive to the *holiness* of God, and destructive to the *happiness* of man. [2] He takes away the *sin of the world*; purchases pardon for all those that repent, and believe the gospel, of what country, nation, or language, soever they be. The legal sacrifices had reference only to the sins of Israel, to make atonement for them; but the Lamb of God was offered to be a propitiation for the *sin of the whole world*; see 1 John ii. 2. This is encouraging to our faith; if Christ takes away the sin of the world, then why not my sin? [3] He does this by *taking it upon himself.* He is the Lamb of God, that *bears the sin of the world*; so the margin reads it. He bore sin *for us*, and so bears it *from us*; he *bore the sin of many*, as the scapegoat had the sins of Israel put upon his head, Lev. xvi. 21. God could have taken away the sin by taking away the sinner, as he took away the sin of the old world; but he has found out a way of abolishing the sin, and yet sparing the sinner, by making his Son *sin for us.*

(3) That it is our duty, with an eye of faith, to *behold* the Lamb of God thus taking away the *sin of the world.*

2. That this was he of whom he

had spoken before (*vv.* 30, 31). Observe, (1) This honour John had above all the prophets, that, whereas they spoke of him as one that should come, he saw him already come. *This is he.* Such a difference there is between present *faith* and future *vision.* (2) John calls Christ *a man*; after me comes a man—a *strong man*: like *the man*, the branch, or the *man of God's right hand.* (3) He refers to what he had himself said of him before: *This is he of whom I said.* (4) He protests against any confederacy or combination with this Jesus: *And I knew him not.* Though there was some relation between them (Elisabeth was cousin to the virgin Mary), yet there was no acquaintance at all between them; John had no personal knowledge of Jesus till he saw him come to his baptism. (5) The great intention of John's ministry and baptism was to introduce Jesus Christ. That he should be *made manifest to Israel, therefore am I come baptizing with water.* Observe, [1] Though John did not know Jesus by face, yet he knew that he should be made manifest. [2] The general assurance John had that Christ *should be made manifest* served to carry him with diligence and resolution through his work, though he was kept in the dark concerning particulars. [3] God reveals himself to his people by degrees. At first, John knew no more concerning Christ but that he should be made manifest; in confidence of that, he came baptizing, and now he is favoured with a sight of him. They who, upon God's word, believe what they do not see, shall shortly see what they now believe. [4] The ministry of the word and sacraments is designed for no other end than to lead people to Christ, and to make him more and more manifest. [5] Baptism with water made way for the manifesting of Christ, as it supposed our corruption and filthiness, and signified our cleansing by him who is the *fountain opened.*

3. That this was he *upon whom the Spirit descended from heaven like a dove.* For the confirming of his testimony concerning Christ, he here vouches the extraordinary appearance at his baptism, in which God himself bore witness to him. This was a considerable proof of Christ's mission.

Observe, [1] The spirit descended *from heaven*, for every good and perfect gift is *from above.* [2] He descended *like a dove*—an emblem of meekness, and mildness, and gentleness, which makes him *fit to teach.* The dove brought the olive-branch of peace, Gen. viii. 11. [3] The Spirit that descended upon Christ *abode upon him*, as was foretold, Isa. xi. 2. The Spirit did not *move him at times*, as Samson (Judg. xiii. 25), but *at all times.*

4. That he is *the Son of God.* This is the conclusion of John's testimony, that in which all the particulars centre: *I saw, and bore record, that this is the Son of God.* (1) The truth asserted is, *that this is the Son of God.* The voice from heaven proclaimed, and John subscribed to it, not only that he should baptize with the Holy Ghost by a divine authority, but that he has a divine nature. (2) John's testimony to it: "*I saw, and bore record.*" Christ's witnesses

were eye-witnesses, and therefore the more to be credited: they did not speak by hear-say and report, 2 Pet. i. 16.

II. Here is John's testimony to Christ, the next day after, *vv.* 35, 36. Where observe, 1. He took every opportunity that offered itself to lead people to Christ. 2. He repeated the same testimony which he had given to Christ the day before, though he could have delivered some other great truth concerning him; but thus he would show that he was uniform and constant in his testimony, and consistent with himself. 3. He intended this especially for his two disciples that stood with him; he was willing to turn them over to Christ, for to this end he bore witness to Christ in their hearing that they might leave all to follow him, even that they might leave *him*.

ANDREW AND SIMON
(*vv.* 37–42)

We have here the turning over of two disciples from John to Jesus, and one of them fetching in a third, and these are the first-fruits of Christ's disciples; see how small the church was in its beginnings, and what the dawning of the day of its great things was.

I. Andrew and another with him were the two that John Baptist had directed to Christ, *v.* 37.

1. Here is their readiness to go over to Christ: They *heard* John *speak* of Christ as the *Lamb of God*, and they *followed Jesus*. The strongest and most prevailing argument with a sensible awakened soul to follow Christ is that

it is he, and he only, that *takes away sin*.

2. The kind notice Christ took of them, *v.* 38. They came behind him; but, though he had his back towards them, he was soon aware of them, and *turned*, and *saw them following*.

3. Their modest enquiry concerning the place of his abode: *Rabbi, where dwellest thou?*

4. The courteous invitation Christ gave them to his lodgings: *He saith unto them, Come and see.* Thus should good desires towards Christ and communion with him be countenanced.

5. Their cheerful and (no doubt) thankful acceptance of his invitation: *They came and saw where he dwelt*, and *abode with him that day*. It had been greater modesty and manners than had done them good if they had refused this offer.

II. Andrew brought his brother Peter to Christ. Observe,

1. The *information* which Andrew gave to Peter, with an intimation to come to Christ.

(1) He *found him: He first finds his own brother Simon*; his finding implies his seeking him. Simon came along with Andrew to attend John's ministry and baptism, and Andrew knew where to look for him.

(2) He told him whom they had found: *We have found the Messias. We have found* that pearl of great price, that true treasure; and, having found it, he proclaims it as those lepers, 2 Kings vii. 9, for he knows that he shall have never the less in Christ for others sharing. He speaks *intelligently: We have found the Messias*, which was more than

had yet been said. John had said, *He is the Lamb of God, and the Son of God*, which Andrew compares with the scriptures of the Old Testament, and, comparing them together, concludes that he is the Messiah promised to the fathers, for it is now that the fulness of time is come.

(3) He *brought him to Jesus*; would not undertake to instruct him himself, but brought him to the fountain-head, persuaded him to come to Christ and introduced him.

2. The *entertainment* which Jesus Christ gave to Peter, who was never the less welcome for his being influenced by his brother to come, *v.* 42. Observe,

(1) Christ called him by his name: *When Jesus beheld him, he said, Thou art Simon, the son of Jona*. It should seem that Peter was utterly a stranger to Christ, and if so, [1] It was a proof of Christ's omniscience that upon the first sight, without any enquiry, he could tell the name both of him and of his father. However, [2] It was an instance of his condescending grace and favour, that he did thus freely and affably call him by his name. Some observe the signification of these names: *Simon—obedient, Jona—a dove*. An obedient dove-like spirit qualifies us to be the disciples of Christ.

(2) He gave him a new name: *Cephas*. [1] His giving him a name intimates *Christ's favour* to him. A new name denotes some great dignity, Rev. ii. 17; Isa. lxii. 2. [2] The name which he gave him bespeaks his *fidelity* to Christ: *Thou shalt be called Cephas* (that is Hebrew for *a stone*), *which is by*

interpretation Peter; so it should be rendered. Peter's natural temper was stiff, and hardy, and resolute, which I take to be the principal reason why Christ called him *Cephas—a stone*. When Christ afterwards prayed for him, that his faith might not fail, that so he might be firm to Christ himself, and at the same time bade him *strengthen his brethren*, and lay out himself for the support of others, then he *made him* what he here called him, *Cephas—a stone*.

PHILIP AND NATHANAEL
(*vv.* 43–51)

We have here the call of Philip and Nathanael.

I. Philip was called immediately by Christ himself, not as Andrew, who was directed to Christ by John, or Peter, who was invited by his brother. God has various methods of bringing his chosen ones home to himself. Philip was brought to be a disciple by the power of Christ going along with that word, *Follow me*. See the nature of true Christianity; it is *following Christ*, devoting ourselves to his *converse* and *conduct*, attending his movements, and treading in his steps. See the efficacy of the grace of Christ making the call of his word to prevail; it is the *rod of his strength*.

II. Nathanael was invited to Christ by Philip, and much is said concerning him. In which we may observe,

1. What passed between Philip and Nathanael. Here is,

(1) The joyful news that Philip brought to Nathanael, *v.* 45. As Andrew before, so Philip here,

having got some knowledge of Christ himself, rests not till he has *made manifest the savour of that knowledge*.

(2) The objection which Nathanael made against this, *Can any good thing come out of Nazareth?* v. 46. Here, [1] His *caution* was commendable, that he did not lightly assent to every thing that was said, but took it into examination; our rule is, *Prove all things*. But, [2] His objection arose from ignorance. If he meant that no good thing could come out of Nazareth it was owing to his ignorance of the divine grace, as if that were less affected to one place than another, or tied itself to men's foolish and ill-natured observations.

(3) The short reply which Philip gave to this objection: *Come and see*. [1] It was his *weakness* that he could not give a satisfactory answer to it; yet it is the common case of young beginners in religion. We may *know* enough to *satisfy* ourselves, and yet not be able to *say* enough to *silence* the cavils of a subtle adversary. [2] It was his *wisdom* and zeal that, when he could not answer the objection himself, he would have him go to one that could: *Come and see*.

2. What passed between Nathanael and our Lord Jesus. He came and *saw*, not in vain.

(1) Our Lord Jesus bore a very honourable testimony to Nathanael's integrity: *Jesus saw him* coming, and met him with favourable encouragement; he said of him to those about him, Nathanael himself being within hearing, *Behold an Israelite indeed*. Observe,

[1] That he *commended* him;

not to flatter him, or puff him up with a good conceit of himself, but perhaps because he knew him to be a *modest* man.

[2] That he commended him for his *integrity*. The whole nation were Israelites in name, but *all are not Israel that are of Israel* (Rom. ix. 6); here, however, was *an Israelite indeed*. 1. A sincere follower of the good example of Israel, whose character it was that he was a *plain man*, in opposition to Esau's character of a *cunning man*. 2. A sincere professor of the faith of Israel; he was true to the religion he professed, and lived up to it: he was really as good as he seemed, and his practice was *of a piece* with his profession.

(2) Nathanael is much surprised at this.

[1] Here is Nathanael's modesty, in that he was soon put out of countenance at the kind notice Christ was pleased to take of him: "*Whence knowest thou me*, me that am unworthy of thy cognizance? *who am I, O Lord God?*" 2 Sam. vii. 18. This was an evidence of his sincerity, that he did not catch at the praise he met with, but declined it.

[2] Here is Christ's further *manifestation* of himself to him: *Before Philip called thee, I saw thee. First*, He gives him to understand that he *knew him*, and so manifests his divinity. *Secondly*, That before Philip called him he saw him under the fig-tree; this manifests a particular kindness for him. 1. His eye was towards him before Philip called him, which was the first time that ever Nathanael was acquainted with Christ. Christ has knowledge

of us before we have any knowledge of him; see Isa. xlv. 4; Gal. iv. 9. 2. His eye was upon him when he was *under the fig-tree*; this was a private token which nobody understood but Nathanael. It is most probable that Nathanael under the fig-tree was employed, as Isaac in the field, in meditation, and prayer, and communion with God. Perhaps then and there it was that he solemnly joined himself to the Lord in an inviolable covenant. Christ saw in secret, and by this public notice of it did in part reward him openly.

(3) Nathanael hereby obtained a full assurance of faith in Jesus Christ, expressed in that noble acknowledgment (*v.* 49): *Rabbi, thou art the Son of God, thou art the king of Israel*; that is, in short, thou art the true Messiah.

(4) Christ hereupon raises the hopes and expectations of Nathanael to something further and greater than all this, *vv.* 50, 51.

He promises him much greater helps for the confirmation and increase of his faith than he had had for the first production of it.

First, In general: "*Thou shalt see greater things than these*, stronger proofs of my being the Messiah"; the miracles of Christ, and his resurrection.

Secondly, In particular: "Not thou only, but you, all you my disciples, whose faith this is intended for the confirmation of, you *shall see heaven opened*." Through Christ we have communion with and benefit by the holy angels, and things in heaven and things on earth are *reconciled* and *gathered together*. Christ is to

us as Jacob's ladder (Gen. xxviii. 12), by whom angels continually ascend and descend for the good of the saints.

CHAPTER TWO

WATER INTO WINE (*vv.* 1–11)

We have here the story of Christ's miraculous conversion of water into wine at a marriage in Cana of Galilee. Now observe,

I. The occasion of this miracle. Observe,

1. The time: the *third day* after he came into Galilee. The evangelist keeps a journal of occurrences, for no day passed without something extraordinary done or said.

2. The place: it was at Cana in Galilee. Christ began to work miracles in an obscure corner of the country, remote from Jerusalem, which was the public scene of action, to show that he *sought not honour from men* (*ch.* v. 41), but would put honour *upon the lowly*.

3. The occasion itself was a *marriage*; probably one or both of the parties were akin to our Lord Jesus. The *mother of Jesus* is said to be *there*, and not to be *called*, as Jesus and his disciples were, which intimates that she was there as one at home. Observe the honour which Christ hereby put upon the ordinance of marriage, that he graced the solemnity of it, not only with his presence, but with his first miracle. Marriages were usually celebrated with festivals (Gen. xxix. 22; Judg. xiv. 10), in token of joy and friendly respect, and for the confirming of love.

4. Christ and his mother and

485

disciples were principal guests at this entertainment.

II. The miracle itself. In which observe,

1. They *wanted wine*, v. 3. (1) There was *want* at a *feast*; though much was provided, yet all was spent.

2. The *mother of Jesus* solicited him to assist her friends in this strait. We are told (*vv.* 3–5) what passed between Christ and his mother upon this occasion.

(1) She acquaints him with the difficulty they were in (*v.* 3): *She saith unto him, They have no wine.*

(2) He gave her a reprimand for it, for he saw more amiss in it than we do, else he had not treated it thus. — Here is,

[1] The rebuke itself: *Woman, what have I to do with thee?* As many as Christ loves, he rebukes and chastens. The question might be read, *What is that to me and thee?* What is it to us if they do want?

[2] The reason of this rebuke: *Mine hour is not yet come.* For every thing Christ did, and that was done to him, he had *his hour*, the *fixed* time and the *fittest* time, which was punctually observed. "Mine hour for *working miracles* is not yet come." Yet afterwards he wrought this, before the hour, because he foresaw it would confirm the faith of his infant disciples (*v.* 11), which was the end of all his miracles: so that this was an earnest of the many miracles he would work when his *hour was come.*

(3) Notwithstanding this, she encouraged herself with expectations that he would help her friends in this strait, for she bade the

servants *observe his orders*, v. 5. She directed the servants to have an eye *to him* immediately, and not to make their applications to her, as it is probable *they had done.* Note, Those that expect Christ's *favours* must with an implicit obedience observe his *orders.* The way of duty is the way to mercy; and Christ's methods must not be objected against.

(4) Christ did at length miraculously supply them; for he is often better than his word, but never worse.

[1] The miracle itself was *turning water into wine*; the substance of water acquiring a new form, and having all the accidents and qualities of wine.

[2] The circumstances of it magnified it and freed it from all suspicion of cheat or collusion; for,

First, It was done in water-pots (*v.* 6): *There were set there six water-pots of stone.*

Secondly, The water-pots were filled *up to the brim* by the servants at Christ's word, v. 7.

Thirdly, The miracle was wrought suddenly, and in such a manner as greatly magnified it.

a. As soon as they had filled the water-pots, presently he said, *Draw out now* (*v.* 8), and it was done, (*a*) Without any ceremony, in the eye of the spectators. (*b*) Without any hesitation or uncertainty in his own breast. As he knew what he *would* do, so he knew what he *could* do, and made no essay in his work; but all was good, very good, even in the beginning.

b. Our Lord Jesus directed the servants, (*a*) To draw it out; not to let it alone in the vessel, to be admired, but to *draw it out*, to be drank. Christ's works are all *for use*; he gives no man a talent to be *buried*, but to be *traded with*. (*b*) To present it to *the governor of the feast*.

Fourthly, The wine which was thus miraculously provided was of the best and richest kind, which was acknowledged by the governor of the feast; and that it was really so, and not his fancy, is certain, because he knew not whence it was, *vv*. 9, 10. This the governor of the feast takes notice of to the bridegroom, with an air of pleasantness, as *uncommon*. (1) The common method was otherwise. Good wine is brought out to the best advantage at the beginning of a feast. (2) This bridegroom obliged his friends with a reserve of the best wine for the grace-cup: *Thou hast kept the good wine until now*; not knowing to whom they were indebted for this good wine, he returns the thanks of the table to the bridegroom.

III. In the conclusion of this story (*v*. 11) we are told, 1. That this was *the beginning of miracles* which Jesus did. 2. That herein he *manifested his glory*; hereby he proved himself to be the Son of God, and his glory to be that of the only-begotten of the Father.

THE TEMPLE CLEANSED
(*vv*. 12–22)

Here we have,

I. The short visit Christ made to Capernaum, *v*. 12. It was a large and populous city, about a day's journey from Cana; it is called *his own city* (Matt. ix. 1), because he made it his headquarters in Galilee, and what little rest he had was there.

II. The passover he kept at Jerusalem; it is the *first* after his baptism, and the evangelist takes notice of all the passovers he kept henceforward, which were four in all, the *fourth* that at which he suffered (three years after this), and half a year was now past since his baptism. Christ kept the passover at Jerusalem yearly, ever since he was twelve years old, in obedience to the law; but now that he has entered upon his public ministry we may expect something more from him than before; and two things we are here told he did there:—

1. He *purged the temple, vv*. 14–17. Observe here,

(1) The first place we find him in at Jerusalem was the *temple*, and, it should seem, he did not make any public appearance till he came thither; for his presence and preaching there were that glory of the latter house which was to *exceed the glory of the former*, Hag. ii. 9. It was foretold (Mal. iii. 1): *I will send my messenger*, John Baptist; he never preached in the temple, but *the Lord, whom ye seek*, he shall *suddenly come to his temple*, suddenly after the appearing of John Baptist; so that this was the time, and the temple the place, when, and where, the Messiah was to be expected.

(2) The first work we find him at in the temple was the *purging* of it; for so it was foretold there (Mal. iii. 2, 3): *He shall sit as a refiner and purify the sons of Levi*. Now was come the *time of reformation*. See here,

[1] What were the corruptions that were to be purged out. He found a market in one of the courts of the temple, that which was called the *court of the Gentiles*, within the *mountain of that house*.

[2] What course our Lord took to purge out those corruptions. He did not complain to the chief priests, for he knew they countenanced those corruptions. But he himself,

First, Drove out the sheep and oxen, and those that *sold them*, out of the temple. He never used *force* to drive any *into* the temple, but only to drive those out that profaned it.

Secondly, He *poured out the changers' money*. In *pouring out* the money, he showed his contempt of it; he threw it to the ground, to the earth as it *was*. In *overthrowing* the tables, he showed his displeasure against those that make religion a matter of worldly gain. Moneychangers in the temple are the scandal of it.

Thirdly, He *said to them that sold doves* (sacrifices for the poor), *Take these things hence*. The doves, though they took up less room, and were a less nuisance than the oxen and sheep, yet must not be allowed there. The sparrows and swallows were welcome, that were left to God's providence (Ps. lxxxiv. 3), but not the doves, that were appropriated to man's profit.

Fourthly, He gave them a good reason for what he did: *Make not my Father's house a house of merchandise*. Reason for conviction should accompany force for correction.

Fifthly, Here is the remark which

his disciples made upon it (*v.* 17): *They remembered that it was written, The zeal of thine house hath eaten me up*. They were somewhat surprised at first to see him to whom they were directed as the *Lamb of God* in such a heat, and him whom they believed to be the *King of Israel* take so little state upon him as to do this himself; but one scripture came to their thoughts, which taught them to reconcile this action both with the meekness of the *Lamb of God* and with the majesty of the *King of Israel*; for David, speaking of the Messiah, takes notice of his *zeal for God's house*, as so great that it even *ate him up*, it made him forget himself, Ps. lxix. 9.

2. Christ, having thus purged the temple, gave a sign to those who demanded it to prove his authority for so doing. Observe here,

(1) Their demand of a sign: *Then answered the Jews*, that is the multitude of the people, with their leaders. Being Jews, they should rather have stood by him, and assisted him to vindicate the honour of their temple; but, instead of this, they objected against it.

(2) Christ's answer to this demand, *v.* 19. He did not immediately work a miracle to convince them, but gave them a sign in something *to come*, the truth of which must appear by the event, according to Deut. xviii. 21, 22.

Now, [1] The sign that he gives them is his own *death* and *resurrection*.

[2] He foretells his death and resurrection, not in plain terms, as he often did to his disciples, but in figurative expressions; as after-

wards, when he gave this for a sign, he called it the *sign of the prophet Jonas*, so here, *Destroy this temple, and in three days I will raise it up.* Thus he spoke in parables to those who were willingly ignorant, that *they might not perceive*, Matt. xiii. 13, 14. Those that will not see shall not see.

[3] He chose to express this by *destroying* and *re-edifying* the temple, *First*, Because he was now to justify himself in purging the temple, which they had profaned. *Secondly*, Because the death of Christ was indeed the destruction of the Jewish temple, the procuring cause of it; and his resurrection was the raising up of another temple, the gospel church, Zech. vi. 12.

(3) Their cavil at this answer: "*Forty and six years was this temple in building, v.* 20. Temple work was always slow work, and canst thou make such quick work of it?"

(4) A vindication of Christ's answer from their cavil. The difficulty is soon solved by explaining the terms: *He spoke of the temple of his body, v.* 21. Some think that when he said, Destroy *this* temple, he pointed to his own body, or laid his hand upon it; however, it is certain that he *spoke of the temple of his body.* Note, The body of Christ is the true temple, of which that at Jerusalem was a type.

(5) A reflection which the disciples made upon this, long after, inserted here, to illustrate the story (*v.* 22): *When he was risen from the dead*, some years after, *his disciples remembered that he had said this.* We found them, *v.* 17, remembering what had been *written before of him*, and here we find them re-membering what they had *heard from him*.

MANY BELIEVED (*vv.* 23–25)

We have here an account of the success, the poor success, of Christ's preaching and miracles at Jerusalem, while he kept the pass-over there.

Yet *Jesus did not commit himself unto them* (*v.* 24): *He did not trust himself with them*. It is the same word that is used for *believing* in him. So that to believe in Christ is to *commit ourselves* to him and to his guidance. Christ did not see cause to repose any confidence in these new converts at Jerusalem, where he had many enemies that sought to destroy him, either, 1. Because they were *false*, at least some of them, and would betray him if they had an opportunity, or were strongly tempted to do so. Or, 2. Because they were *weak*, and I would hope that this was the worst of it; not that they were *treacherous* and designed him a mischief.

The reason he did not *commit himself* to them was because he *knew* them (*v.* 25), knew the wickedness of some and the weakness of others. The evangelist takes this occasion to assert Christ's omniscience.

CHAPTER THREE

CHRIST AND NICODEMUS
(vv. 1–21)

We found, in the close of the foregoing chapter, that few were brought to Christ at Jerusalem; yet here was *one*, a considerable one. It is worth while to go a great way for the salvation though but of *one soul*. Observe,

I. Who this Nicodemus was. Not many mighty and noble are called; yet some are, and here was one. He was a *ruler of the Jews*, a member of the great sanhedrim, a senator, a privy-counsellor, a man of authority in Jerusalem.

II. His solemn address to our Lord Jesus Christ, *v.* 2. See here,

1. When he came: *He came to Jesus by night*, which may be considered, [1] As an act of *prudence* and *discretion*. [2] As an act of *zeal* and *forwardness*. Nicodemus was a man of business, and could not spare time all day to make Christ a visit, and therefore he would rather take time from the diversions of the *evening*, or the rest of the *night*, than not converse with Christ. Or, [3] As an act of *fear* and *cowardice*. He was afraid, or ashamed, to be *seen* with Christ, and therefore came *in the night*.

2. What he said. He tells Christ how far *he had attained*: We *know that thou art a teacher*. Observe, (1) His *assertion* concerning Christ: *Thou art a teacher come from God*. (2) His *assurance* of it: *We know*, not only *I*, but *others*; so he took it for granted, the thing being so plain and self-evident. (3) The ground of this assurance: *No man can do those miracles that thou doest, except God be with him*. Here, [1] We are assured of the truth of Christ's miracles, and that they were not counterfeit. Here was Nicodemus, a judicious, sensible, inquisitive man, one that had all the *reason* and *opportunity* imaginable to examine them, so fully satisfied that they were real miracles that he was wrought upon by them to go contrary to his interest, and to the stream of those of his own rank, who were prejudiced against Christ. [2] We are directed what inference to draw from Christ's miracles: Therefore we are to receive him as a *teacher come from God*.

III. The discourse between Christ and Nicodemus hereupon, or, rather, the sermon Christ preached to him; the contents of it, and that perhaps an abstract of Christ's public preaching; see *vv.* 11, 12. Four things our Saviour here discourses of:

1. Concerning the *necessity and nature of regeneration* or the *new birth*, *vv.* 3–8. Observe,

(1) What it is that is required: to be *born again*; that is, *First*, We must *live a new life*. Birth is the beginning of life; to be *born again* is to begin anew, as those that have hitherto lived either much amiss or to little purpose. We must not think to patch up the old building, but begin from the foundation. *Secondly*, We must have a new *nature*, new principles, new affections, new aims. By our *first birth* we are corrupt, shapen in sin and iniquity; we must therefore undergo a second birth; our souls must be *fashioned* and *enlivened* anew. We must be born *from above*, so the word is used by the evangelist, *ch.* iii. 31; xix. 11; for to be born *from above* supposes being *born again*. But this new birth has its rise *from* heaven (*ch.* i. 13) and its tendency *to* heaven: it is to be born to a *divine* and *heavenly* life, a life of communion with God and the upper world, and, in order to this, it is to

partake of a *divine nature* and bear the *image of the heavenly*.

(2) The indispensable necessity of this: "Except *a man be born again, he cannot see the kingdom of God*, the kingdom of the Messiah begun in *grace* and perfected in *glory*." Except we be *born from above*, we cannot *see* this. That is, *First*, We cannot *understand* the *nature* of it. *Secondly*, We cannot *receive the comfort* of it, cannot expect any benefit by Christ and his gospel, nor have any part or lot in the matter.

This great truth of the necessity of regeneration being thus solemnly laid down,

a. It is objected against by Nicodemus (*v.* 4): *How can a man be born when he is old? Can he enter the second time into his mother's womb, and be born?*

b. It is opened and further explained by our Lord Jesus, *vv.* 5–8. From the objection he takes occasion,

(*a*) To repeat and confirm what he had said (*v.* 5): "*Verily, verily, I say unto thee*, the very same that I said before."

(*b*) To expound and clear what he had said concerning regeneration; for the explanation of which he further shows,

[*a*] The *author* of this blessed change, and who it is that works it. To be born again is to be *born of the Spirit*, *vv.* 5–8. The change is not wrought by any wisdom or power of our own, but by the power and influence of the blessed Spirit of grace.

[*b*] The *nature* of this change, and what that is which is wrought; it is *spirit, v.* 6. Those that are regenera-ted are made *spiritual*, and refined from the dross and dregs of sensuality.

[*c*] The *necessity* of this change. *First*, Christ here shows that it is necessary in the *nature of the thing*, for we are not fit to enter into the kingdom of God till we are born again: *That which is born of the flesh is flesh*, *v.* 6. Here is our malady, with the causes of it, which are such that it is plain there is no remedy but we must be *born again*.

[*d*] This change is illustrated by two comparisons. *First*, The regenerating work of the Spirit is compared to *water, v.* 5. 1. That which is primarily intended here is to show that the Spirit, in sanctifying a soul, (1) *Cleanses* and purifies it as water, takes away its filth, by which it was unfit for the kingdom of God. It is the *washing of regeneration*, Tit. iii. 5. *You are washed*, 1 Cor. vi. 11. See Ezek. xxxvi. 25. (2) Cools and refreshes it, as water does the hunted hart and the weary traveller. The Spirit is compared to *water, ch.* vii. 38, 39; Isa. xliv. 3. 2. It is probable that Christ had an eye to the ordinance of baptism, which John had used and he himself had begun to use, "You must be born again of the Spirit," which regeneration by the Spirit should be signified by washing with water, as the visible sign of that spiritual grace: not that all they, and they only, that are baptized, are saved; but without that new birth which is wrought by the Spirit, and signified by baptism, none shall be looked upon as the *protected privileged* subjects of the *kingdom of heaven*. *Secondly*,

It is compared to *wind*: *The wind bloweth where it listeth, so is every one that is born of the Spirit, v.* 8. The same word signifies both the wind and the Spirit. The Spirit came upon the apostles in a *rushing mighty wind* (Acts ii. 2), his *strong* influences on the hearts of sinners are compared to the *breathing of the wind* (Ezek. xxxvii. 9), and his *sweet* influences on the souls of saints to the north and south wind, Cant. iv. 16. This comparison is here used to show, 1. That the Spirit, in regeneration, works *arbitrarily*, and as a free agent. 2. That he works *powerfully*, and with evident effects: *Thou hearest the sound thereof*; though its causes are hidden, its effects are manifest. 3. That he works *mysteriously*, and in secret hidden ways: *Thou canst not tell whence it comes, nor whither it goes.* How it gathers and how it spends its strength is a riddle to us; so the manner and methods of the Spirit's working are a mystery.

2. Here is a discourse concerning the *certainty and sublimity of gospel truths*, which Christ takes occasion for from the weakness of Nicodemus. Here is,

(1) The objection which Nicodemus still made (*v.* 9): *How can these things be?* Christ's explanation of the doctrine of the necessity of regeneration, it should seem, made it no clearer to him.

(2) The reproof which Christ gave him for his dullness and ignorance: "*Art thou a master in Israel, a teacher*, a tutor, one who sits in Moses's chair, and yet not only unacquainted with the doctrine of regeneration, but incapable of understanding it?"

(3) Christ's discourse, hereupon, of the certainty and sublimity of gospel truths (*vv.* 11–13), to show the folly of those who make strange of these things, and to recommend them to our search. Observe here,

[1] That the truths Christ taught were very *certain* and what we may venture upon (*v.* 11): *We speak that we do know.* Observe, *First*, That the truths of Christ are of undoubted certainty. He spoke not upon hearsay, but upon the clearest evidence, and therefore with the greatest assurance. *Secondly*, That the unbelief of sinners is greatly aggravated by the infallible certainty of the truths of Christ.

[2] The truths Christ taught, though communicated in language and expressions borrowed from common and earthly things, yet in their own nature were most sublime and heavenly. The things of the gospel are *heavenly* things, out of the road of the enquiries of human reason, and much more out of the reach of its discoveries. Earthly things are despised because they are *vulgar*, and heavenly things because they are *abstruse*; and so, whatever method is taken, still some fault or other is found with it (Matt. xi. 17), but Wisdom is, and will be, *justified of her children*, notwithstanding.

[3] Our Lord Jesus, and he alone, was fit to reveal to us a doctrine thus certain, thus sublime: *No man hath ascended up into heaven but he, v.* 13.

First, None but Christ was able to reveal to us the will of God for our salvation.

Secondly, Jesus Christ is able, and fit, and every way qualified, to reveal the will of God to us; for it is *he that came down from heaven* and *is in heaven.*

3. Christ here discourses of the *great design of his own coming into the world, and the happiness of those that believe in him,* vv. 14–18. Here we have the very marrow and quintessence of the whole gospel, that *faithful saying* (1 Tim. i. 15), that Jesus Christ came to seek and to save the children of men from death, and recover them to life.

[1] Jesus Christ came to save us by *healing* us, as the children of Israel that were stung with fiery serpents were cured and *lived* by looking up to the brazen serpent; we have the story of it, Num. xxi. 6–9. It was the *last* miracle that passed through the hand of Moses before his death. Now in this type of Christ we may observe,

First, The *deadly* and *destructive* nature of *sin,* which is implied here. The guilt of sin is like the *pain* of the biting of a fiery serpent; the power of corruption is like the *venom* diffused thereby.

Secondly, The powerful remedy provided against this fatal malady. The case of poor sinners is deplorable; but is it desperate? Thanks be to God, it is not; there is balm in Gilead. The *Son of man is lifted up,* as the *serpent of brass* was by Moses, which cured the stung Israelites. 1. It was a *serpent of brass* that cured them. It was made in the shape of a *fiery serpent,* and yet had no poison, no sting, fitly representing Christ, who was *made sin for us* and yet knew no sin; was *made in the likeness of sinful flesh* and yet not sinful; as harmless as a serpent of brass. The serpent was a

cursed creature; Christ was made a *curse.* That which cured them reminded them of their plague; so in Christ sin is set before us most fiery and formidable. 2. It was lifted up upon a pole, and so *must* the Son of man be lifted up; thus it *behoved him,* Luke xxiv. 26, 46.

Thirdly, The way of *applying* this remedy, and that is by *believing,* which plainly alludes to the Israelites' *looking up* to the brazen serpent, in order to their being healed by it. If any stung Israelite was either so little sensible of his pain and peril, or had so little confidence in the word of Moses as not to look up to the brazen serpent, justly did he die of his wound; but every one that *looked up to it* did well, Num. xxi. 9. If any so far slight either their disease by sin or the method of cure by Christ as not to embrace Christ upon his own terms, their blood is upon their own head. He hath said, *Look, and be saved* (Isa. xlv. 22), look and live.

Fourthly, The great encouragements given us by faith to look up to him. 1. It was for this end that he was *lifted up,* that his followers might be saved; and he will pursue his end. 2. The offer that is made of salvation by him is general, that *whosoever believes* in him, without exception, might have benefit by him. 3. The salvation offered is complete. (1) They *shall not perish,* shall not die of their wounds; though they may be pained and ill frightened, iniquity shall not be their ruin. But that is not all. (2) They shall *have eternal life.* They shall not only not die of their wounds in the wilderness, but they shall reach Canaan (which they were then just ready to enter into); they shall enjoy the promised rest.

[2] Jesus Christ came to save us by *pardoning us*, that we might not die by the sentence of the law, *vv.* 16, 17.

First, Here is God's *love,* in *giving his Son for the world* (*v.* 16), where we have the great *gospel mystery* revealed: *God so loved the world that he gave his only-begotten Son.* The love of God the Father is the original of our regeneration by the Spirit and our reconciliation by the lifting up of the Son. Note, (1) Jesus Christ is the *only-begotten Son of God.* (2) To achieve the redemption and salvation of man, it pleased God to *give his only-begotten Son.* (3) Herein God has commended his *love to the world:* God so *loved the world,* so really, so richly. Now his creatures shall see that he loves them, and wishes them well. He so loved the world of fallen man as he did not love that of fallen angels; see Rom. v. 8; 1 John iv. 10. Behold, and wonder, that the *great God* should love such a *worthless* world!

Secondly, Here is God's design in sending his Son into the world: it was *that the world through him might be saved.* He came into the world with salvation in *his eye,* with salvation *in his hand.* Therefore the aforementioned offer of life and salvation is sincere, and shall be made good to all that by faith accept it (*v.* 17). 1. He did not come to *condemn the world.* We had reason enough to expect that he should, for it is a guilty world; it is *convicted,* and what cause can be shown why judgment should not be given, and execution awarded, according to law? 2. He came *that the world through him might be saved,* that a door of salvation might be opened to the world, and whoever would might enter in by it. God was in Christ *reconciling the world to himself,* and so *saving* it.

[3] From all this is inferred the happiness of true believers: *He that believeth on him is not condemned, v.* 18. Though he has been a sinner, a great sinner, and *stands convicted,* yet, upon his believing, process is stayed, judgment is arrested, and he is *not condemned.*

4. Christ, in the close, discourses concerning the *deplorable condition of those that persist in unbelief and wilful ignorance, vv.* 18–21.

(1) Read here the doom of those that will not *believe in Christ:* they *are condemned already.* The curse has already taken hold of them; the wrath of God now fastens upon them. They are condemned already, for their own hearts condemn them. Unbelief may truly be called *the great damning sin,* because it leaves us under the guilt of all our other sins; it is a sin against the *remedy,* against our *appeal.*

(2) Read also the doom of those that would not so much as *know him, v.* 19. And *this is the condemnation,* the sin that ruined them, *that light is come into the world, and they loved darkness rather.* Now here observe, [1] That the gospel is light, and, when the gospel came, *light came into the world.* Light is *self-evidencing,* so is the gospel; it proves its own divine origin. [2] It is the unspeakable folly of the most of men that they loved darkness rather than light, rather than *this*

light. [3] The true reason why men love darkness rather than light is *because their deeds are evil.* They love darkness because they think it is an excuse for their evil deeds, and they hate the light because it robs them of the good opinion they had of themselves, by showing them their sinfulness and misery. [4] Wilful ignorance is so far from excusing sin that it will be found, at the great day, to aggravate the condemnation. We must account in the judgment, not only for the knowledge we *had*, and *used not*, but for the knowledge we *might have had*, and *would not.*

On the other hand, upright hearts, that approve themselves to God in their integrity, bid this light welcome (*v.* 21): *He that doeth truth cometh to the light.* It seems, then, that though the gospel had many enemies it had some friends. It is a common observation that *truth seeks no corners.* Those who mean and act honestly dread not a scrutiny, but desire it rather. Now this is applicable to the gospel light; as it *convinces* and *terrifies* evil-doers, so it *confirms* and *comforts* those that walk in their integrity.

Thus far we have Christ's discourse with *Nicodemus*; it is probable that much more passed between them, and it had a good effect, for we find (*ch.* xix. 39) that Nicodemus, though he was puzzled at first, yet afterwards became a faithful disciple of Christ.

JOHN'S WITNESS (*vv.* 22–36)

In these verses we have,

I. Christ's removal into the land of Judea (*v.* 22), and there he tarried with his disciples. *After these things*, after he had had this discourse with Nicodemus, he came into the land of Judea; not so much for *greater privacy* (though mean and obscure places best suited the humble Jesus in his humble state) as for *greater usefulness.* He did not retire into the country for his ease and pleasure, but for more free conversation with his disciples and followers.

II. John's continuance in his work, as long as his opportunities lasted, *vv.* 23, 24. Here we are told,

1. That *John was baptizing.* Christ's baptism was, for substance, the same with John's, for John bore witness to Christ, and therefore they did not at all clash or interfere with one another.

2. That he baptized in Enon near Salim, places we find nowhere else mentioned. He chose a place where there was much water, *many waters*, that is, many *streams* of water; so that wherever he met with any that were willing to submit to his baptism water was at hand to baptize them with.

3. That thither people *came to him* and *were baptized.* Though they did not come in such vast crowds as they did when he first appeared, yet now he was not without encouragement, but there were still those that attended and owned him.

4. It is noted (*v.* 24) that *John was not yet cast into prison*, to clear the order of the story, and to show that these passages are to come in before Matt. iv. 12.

III. A contest between *John's disciples and the Jews about purify-*

ing, v. 25. See how the gospel of Christ came not to *send peace upon earth*, but *division*, 1. Who were the disputants: *some of John's disciples, and the Jews* who had not submitted to his baptism of repentance. 2. What was the matter in dispute: *about purifying*, about *religious washing*. Thus objections are made against the gospel from the advancement and improvement of gospel light, as if childhood and manhood were contrary to each other, and the superstructure were against the foundation. There was no reason to object Christ's baptism against John's, for they consisted very well together.

IV. A complaint which John's disciples made to their master concerning Christ and his baptizing, v. 26. If these disciples of John had not undertaken to dispute about *purifying*, before they understood the *doctrine of baptism*, they might have answered the objection without being put into a passion. In their complaint, they speak respectfully to their own master, *Rabbi*; but speak very slightly of our Saviour, though they do not name him. 1. They suggest that Christ's setting up a baptism of his own was a piece of presumption, very unaccountable. 2. They suggest that it was a piece of ingratitude to John. He *to whom thou barest witness* baptizes; as if Jesus owed all his reputation to the honourable character John gave of him, and yet had very unworthily improved it to the prejudice of John. But Christ needed not John's testimony, *ch*. v. 36. 3. They conclude

that it would be a total eclipse to John's baptism: "*All men come to him*; they that used to follow with us now flock after him, it is therefore time for us to look about us." It was not indeed strange that *all men came to him*. As far as Christ is *manifested* he will be *magnified*; but why should John's disciples grieve at this?

V. Here is John's answer to this complaint which his disciples made, *vv*. 27, &c. His disciples expected that he would have resented this matter as they did; but Christ's *manifestation to Israel* was no *surprise* to John, but what he looked for; it was no *disturbance* to him, but what he wished for.

1. John here *abases himself in comparison with Christ, vv*. 27–30.

(1) *John acquiesces* in the divine disposal, and satisfies himself with that (*v*. 27).

(2) John appeals to the testimony he had formerly given concerning Christ (*v*. 28): You can bear me witness that I said, again and again, *I am not the Christ, but I am sent before him*. See how steady and constant John was in his testimony to Christ, and not as a *reed shaken with the wind*; neither the frowns of the chief priests, nor the flatteries of his own disciples, could make him change his note.

(3) John professes the great satisfaction he had in the advancement of Christ and his interest. He was so far from *regretting* it, as his disciples did, that he *rejoiced* in it. This he expresses (*v*. 29) by an elegant similitude.

(4) He owns it highly fit and necessary that the reputation and interest of Christ should be ad-

vanced, and his own diminished (v. 30): *He must increase, but I must decrease.*

2. John Baptist here *advances* Christ, and instructs his disciples concerning him, that, instead of grieving that so many come to him, they might come to him themselves.

(1) He instructs them concerning the *dignity of Christ's person* (v. 31): *He that cometh from above, that cometh from heaven, is above all.*

(2) Concerning the *excellency and certainty of his doctrine.* His disciples were displeased that Christ's preaching was admired, and attended upon, more than his; but he tells them that there was reason enough for it. For,

[1] He, for his part, *spoke of the earth, and so do all those that are of the earth.*

[2] But he that cometh from heaven is not only in his person, but in his doctrine, above all the prophets that ever lived on earth; none teacheth like him.

From the *certainty* of Christ's doctrine, John takes occasion, [1] To lament the infidelity of the most of men: though he testifies what is infallibly true, yet *no man* receiveth his testimony, that is, very few, next to none, none in comparison with those that refuse it. [2] He takes occasion to commend the faith of the chosen remnant (v. 33): *He that hath received his testimony* (and some such there were, though very few) hath *set to his seal that God is true.* God is true, though we do not *set our seal to it*; let God be true, and every man a liar; his

truth needs not our faith to support it, but by faith we do ourselves the honour and justice to subscribe to his truth, and hereby God reckons himself honoured. By believing in Christ we set to our seal, *First,* That God is true to all the promises which he has made *concerning Christ,* that which he spoke by the mouth of *all his holy prophets*; what he *swore to our fathers* is all accomplished, and not one iota or tittle of it fallen to the ground, Luke i. 70, &c. Acts xiii. 32, 33. *Secondly,* That he is true to all the promises he has made *in Christ*; we venture our souls upon God's veracity, being satisfied that he is *true.*

It is recommended to us as a *divine* doctrine; not his own, but *his that sent* him (v. 34): *For he whom God hath sent speaketh the word of God,* which he was sent to speak, and enabled to speak; *for God giveth not the Spirit by measure unto him.* The prophets were as messengers that brought letters from heaven; but Christ came under the character of an *ambassador,* and treats with us as such; for, 1. He spoke the *words of God,* and nothing he said savoured of human infirmity; both substance and language were divine. 2. He spoke as no other prophet did; for *God giveth not the Spirit by measure to him.* None can speak the *words of God* without the *Spirit of God,* 1 Cor. ii. 10, 11. The Old-Testament prophets had the Spirit, and in different degrees, 2 Kings ii. 9, 10. But, whereas God gave them the Spirit by *measure* (1 Cor. xii. 4), he gave him to Christ *without measure*; all fulness dwelt in him, the fulness of the Godhead, an immeasurable fulness.

(3) Concerning *the power and authority he is invested with*, which gives him the pre-eminence above all others, and a more excellent name than they.

[1] He is the *beloved Son of the Father* (*v.* 35): *The Father loveth the Son*. The prophets were faithful as servants, but Christ as a Son.

[2] He is *Lord of all*. The Father, as an evidence of his love for him, *hath given all things into his hand*. Having given *him the Spirit without measure*, he gave him *all things*; for he was hereby qualified to be master and manager of all.

[3] He is the object of that faith which is made the great condition of eternal happiness, and herein he has the pre-eminence above all others: *He that believeth on the Son, hath life*, *v.* 36. Here is,

First, The blessed state of all true Christians: *He that believes on the Son hath everlasting life*. Grace is glory begun.

Secondly, The wretched and miserable condition of unbelievers: *He that believeth not the Son* is undone. The word includes both *incredulity* and *disobedience*. He is not only under the *wrath of God*, which is as surely *the soul's death* as his favour is *its life*, but it *abides upon him*.

CHAPTER FOUR

THE WOMAN AT THE WELL
(*vv.* 1-26)

We have here an account of the good Christ did in Samaria, when he *passed through* that country in his way to Galilee. The Samaritans, both in *blood* and *religion* were *mongrel Jews*. They worshipped the God of Israel only, to whom they erected a temple on mount Gerizim, in competition with that at Jerusalem. There was great enmity between them and the Jews. Now observe,

I. Christ's coming into Samaria. He charged his disciples not to *enter into any city of the Samaritans* (Matt. x. 5), that is, not to preach the gospel, or work miracles; nor did he here preach publicly, or work any miracle, his eye being to *the lost sheep of the house of Israel*. What kindness he here did them was *accidental*; it was only a *crumb* of the children's bread that casually *fell from the master's table*.

1. His *road* from Judea to Galilee lay through the *country* of Samaria (*v.* 4): *He must needs go through Samaria*. There was no other way, unless he would have fetched a compass on the other side *Jordan*, a great way about.

2. His baiting place happened to be at a *city of Samaria*. Now observe,

(1) The place described. It was called *Sychar*; probably the same with *Sichem*, or *Shechem*, a place which we read much of in the Old Testament. [1] Here lay Jacob's ground, the *parcel of ground which Jacob* gave to his son Joseph, whose bones were buried in it, Gen. xlviii. 22; Josh. xxiv. 32. [2] Here was Jacob's well which he digged, or at least used, for himself and his family. We find no mention of this well in the Old Testament; but

the tradition was that it was Jacob's well.

(2) The posture of our Lord Jesus at this place: *Being wearied with his journey, he sat thus on the well*.

II. His discourse with a Samaritan woman, which is here recorded at large, while Christ's dispute with the doctors, and his discourse with Moses and Elias on the mount, are buried in silence. This discourse is reducible to four heads:—

1. They discourse *concerning the water*, vv. 7–15.

(1) Notice is taken of the *circumstances* that gave occasion to this discourse.

[1] There comes a *woman* of Samaria to *draw water*. This intimates her poverty, she had no servant to be a *drawer of water*; and her industry, she would do it herself. The grace of God sometimes brings people unexpectedly under the means of conversion and salvation. He is found of them that sought him not.

[2] His disciples were *gone away into the city to buy meat*. Now this gave Christ an opportunity of discoursing with this woman about spiritual concerns, and he improved it; he often preached to multitudes that crowded after him for instruction, yet here he condescends to teach a single person, a woman, a poor woman, a stranger, a Samaritan, to teach his ministers to do likewise.

(2) Let us observe the *particulars* of this discourse.

[1] Jesus begins with a modest request for a draught of water: *Give me to drink*. He that *for our sakes became poor* here becomes a beggar, that those who are in want, and cannot dig, may not be ashamed to beg.

[2] The woman, though she does not deny his request, yet quarrels with him because he did not carry on the mood of his own nation (*v.* 9): *How is it?* Observe, *First*, What a mortal feud there was between the Jews and the Samaritans: *The Jews have no dealings with the Samaritans*. *Secondly*, How ready the woman was to upbraid Christ with the haughtiness and ill nature of the Jewish nation: *How is it that thou, being a Jew, askest drink of me?* By his dress or dialect, or both, she knew him to be a Jew, and *thinks it strange* that he runs not to the same excess of riot against the Samaritans with other Jews.

[3] Christ takes this occasion to instruct her in divine things: *If thou knewest the gift of God, thou wouldst have asked, v.* 10. Observe,

First, He waives her objection of the feud between the Jews and Samaritans, and takes no notice of it.

Secondly, He fills her with an apprehension that she had now an opportunity (a fairer opportunity than she was aware of) of gaining that which would be of unspeakable advantage to her.

a. He hints to her what she *should know*, but was ignorant of: *If thou knewest the gift of God*, that is, as the next words explain it, *who it is that saith, Give me to drink*. If thou knewest *who I am*. She saw him to be a Jew, a poor weary traveller; but he would have her know something more concerning him than did yet appear.

b. He hopes concerning her, what she would have done if she had known him: *Thou wouldest have asked.* Note, (*a*) Those that would have any benefit by Christ must ask for it, must be earnest in prayer to God for it. (*b*) Those that have a right knowledge of Christ will seek to him, and if we do not seek unto him it is a sign that we do not know him, Ps. ix. 10.

c. He assures her what he would have done for her if she had applied to him: "He *would have given thee* (and not have upbraided thee as thou dost me) *living water.*" By this living water is meant the *Spirit*, who is not like the water in the bottom of the well, for some of which he asked, but like *living* or *running* water, which was much more valuable. Note, (*a*) The Spirit of grace is as *living water*; see *ch.* vii. 38. Under this similitude the blessings of the Messiah had been promised in the Old Testament, Isa. xii. 3; xxxv. 7; xliv. 3; lv. 1; Zech. xiv. 8. The graces of the Spirit, and his comforts, satisfy the thirsting soul, that knows its own nature and necessity. (*b*) Jesus Christ *can* and *will* give the Holy Spirit to them that ask him; for he *received* that he might *give*.

[4] The woman objects against and cavils at the gracious intimation which Christ gave her (*vv.* 11, 12): *Thou hast nothing to draw with*; and besides, *Art thou greater than our father Jacob?* What he spoke figuratively, she took literally; Nicodemus did so too.

First, She does not think him capable of furnishing her with any water, no, not this in the well that is just at hand: *Thou hast nothing to draw with*, and *the well is deep.*

Secondly, She does not think it possible that he should furnish her with any better water than this which she could come at, but he could not: *Art thou greater than our father Jacob, who gave us the well?*

[5] Christ answers this cavil, and makes it out that the *living water* he had to give was far better than that of Jacob's well, *vv.* 13, 14. Though she spoke perversely, Christ did not cast her off, but instructed and encouraged her. He shows her,

First, That the water of Jacob's well yielded but a *transient* satisfaction and supply: "*Whoso drinketh of this water shall thirst again.*"

Secondly, That the living waters he would give should yield a lasting satisfaction and bliss, *v.* 14. Christ's gifts appear most valuable when they come to be compared with the things of this world; for there will appear no comparison between them. Whoever partakes of the Spirit of grace, and the comforts of the everlasting gospel,

a. He shall *never thirst*, he shall never want that which will abundantly satisfy his soul's desires; they are *longing*, but not *languishing*. A *desiring* thirst he has, nothing more *than* God, still more and more *of* God; but not a *despairing* thirst.

b. Therefore he shall never thirst, because this water that Christ gives *shall be in him a well of water*. *He* can never be reduced to extremity that has in himself a *fountain* of supply and satisfaction.

[6] The woman (whether in jest or earnest is hard to say) begs of him to give her some of this water (*v.* 15): *Give me this water, that I thirst not.*

2. The next subject of discourse with this woman is *concerning her husband*, *vv.* 16–18. It was not to let fall the discourse of the water of life that Christ started this, as many who will bring in any *impertinence* in conversation that they may drop a serious subject; but it was with a gracious design that Christ mentioned it. What he had said concerning his grace and eternal life he found had made little impression upon her, because she had not been convinced of sin: therefore, waiving the discourse about the living water, he sets himself to awaken her conscience.

Observe, (1) How discreetly and decently Christ introduces this discourse (*v.* 16): *Go, call thy husband, and come hither.*

(2) How industriously the woman seeks to evade the conviction, and yet insensibly convicts herself, and, ere she is aware, owns her fault; she said, *I have no husband.* Her saying this intimated no more than that she did not care to have her husband spoken of, nor that matter mentioned any more.

(3) How closely our Lord Jesus brings home the conviction to her conscience. It is probable that he said more than is here recorded, for she thought that he told her all that ever she did (*v.* 29), but

that which is here recorded is concerning her husbands. Here is, [1] A *surprising narrative* of her *past* way of life. *Thou hast had five husbands.* Doubtless, it was not her *affliction* (the burying of so many husbands), but her *sin*, that Christ intended to upbraid her with; either she had *eloped* (as the law speaks), had run away from her *husbands*, and married others, or by her undutiful, unclean, disloyal conduct, had provoked them to *divorce her*, or by indirect means had, contrary to law, *divorced them*. [2] A severe reproof of her present state of life: *He whom thou now hast is not thy husband.* Either she was never married to him at all, or he had some other wife, or, which is most probable, her former husband or husbands were living: so that, in short, *she lived in adultery*.

3. The next subject of discourse with this woman is concerning *the place of worship*, *vv.* 19–24. Observe,

(1) A case of conscience proposed to Christ by the woman, concerning the place of worship, *vv.* 19, 20.

[1] The inducement she had to put this case: *Sir, I perceive that thou art a prophet.* She does not deny the truth of what he had charged her with, but by her silence owns the justice of the reproof. But this is not all; she goes further: *First*, She speaks respectfully to him, calls him *Sir.* Thus should we *honour* those that deal faithfully with us. This was the effect of Christ's meekness in reproving her; he gave her no ill language, and then she gave him

none. *Secondly*, She acknowledges him to be a *prophet*, one that had a correspondence with Heaven.

[2] The case itself that she propounded concerning the *place of religious worship in public*. Some think that she started this to shift off further discourse concerning her sin. Controversies in religion often prove great prejudices to serious godliness; but, it should seem, she proposed it with a good design; she knew she must worship God, and desired to do it aright; and therefore, meeting with a prophet, begs his direction. Observe how she states the case: —

First, As for the Samaritans: *Our fathers worshipped in this mountain*, near to this city and this well; there the Samaritan temple was built by Sanballat.

Secondly, As to the Jews: *You say* that *in Jerusalem is the place where men ought to worship*. The Samaritans governed themselves by the five books of Moses, and (some think) received *only them* as canonical. Now, though they found frequent mention there of the place God would choose, yet they did not find it named there; and they saw the temple at Jerusalem stripped of many of its ancient glories, and therefore thought themselves at liberty to set up another place, altar against altar.

(2) Christ's answer to this case of conscience, *vv.* 21, &c. Those that apply themselves to Christ for instruction shall find him *meek*, *to teach the meek his way*. Now here,

[1] He puts *a slight* upon the question, as she had proposed it, concerning the place of worship (*v.* 21). *First*, The object of worship is supposed to continue still the same—*God*, as a Father; under this notion the very heathen worshipped God, the Jews did so, and probably the Samaritans. *Secondly*, But a period shall be put to all scruples and all differences about the place of worship.

[2] He *lays a stress* upon other things, in the matter of religious worship. When he made so light of the place of worship he did not intend to lessen our concern about the thing itself, of which therefore he takes occasion to discourse more fully.

First, As to the present state of the controversy, he *determines* against the Samaritan worship, and in favour of the Jews, *v.* 22. He tells her here, 1. That the Samaritans were certainly *in the wrong*. 2. That the Jews were certainly *in the right*. For, "*We know what we worship*. We go upon sure grounds in our worship, for our people are catechised and trained up in the knowledge of God, as he has revealed himself in the scripture."

Secondly, He describes the evangelical worship which alone God would accept and be well pleased with. Having shown that the place is *indifferent*, he comes to show what is *necessary* and *essential*— that we worship God *in spirit and in truth*, *vv.* 23, 24. The stress is not to be laid upon the *place* where we worship God, but upon the state of *mind* in which we worship him. Observe,

a. The great and glorious revolution which should introduce this change: *The hour cometh, and now is*—the fixed stated time, concerning which it was of old determined when it should come, and how long it should last. The *perfect day is coming*, and now it *dawns*.

b. The blessed change itself. In gospel times the *true worshippers shall worship the Father in spirit and in truth*. As creatures, we worship the Father of *all*: as Christians, we worship *the Father of our Lord Jesus*. Now the change shall be, (*a*) In the *nature* of the worship. Christians shall worship God, not in the ceremonial observances of the Mosaic institution, but in *spiritual* ordinances, consisting less in *bodily exercise*, and animated and invigorated more with divine power and energy. (*b*) In the *temper* and *disposition* of the worshippers; and so the true worshippers are good Christians, distinguished from hypocrites; all *should*, and they will, worship God *in spirit and in truth*. Spirit is sometimes put for the new nature, in opposition to the *flesh*, which is the corrupt nature; and so to worship God *with our spirits* is to worship him *with our graces*, Heb. xii. 28. *In truth*, that is, in *sincerity*. God requires not only the *inward part* in our worship, but *truth in the inward part*, Ps. li. 6. We must mind the power more than the form, must aim at God's glory, and not to be *seen of men*; draw near with a *true heart*, Heb. x. 22.

Thirdly, He intimates the reasons why God must be thus worshipped.

a. Because in gospel times they, and they only, are accounted the

true worshippers. The gospel erects a spiritual way of worship, so that the professors of the gospel are not true in their profession, do not live up to gospel light and laws, if they do not worship God *in spirit and in truth*.

b. Because *the Father seeketh such worshippers of him*. This intimates, (*a*) That such worshippers are very rare, and seldom met with, Jer. xxx. 21. (*b*) That God is greatly well pleased with and graciously accepts such worship and such worshippers.

c. Because *God is a spirit*. Christ came to *declare God* to us (*ch*. i. 18), and this he has declared concerning him. Note, (*a*) *God is a spirit*, for he is an infinite and eternal mind, an intelligent being, incorporeal, immaterial, invisible, and incorruptible. It is easier to say what God is not than what he is; a spirit *has not flesh and bones*, but *who knows the way of a spirit*? If God were not *a spirit*, he could not be *perfect*, nor infinite, nor eternal, nor independent, nor the Father of spirits. (*b*) The spirituality of the divine nature is a very good reason for the spirituality of divine worship. If we do not worship God, who is *a spirit, in the spirit*, we neither *give him the glory due to his name*, and so do not perform the *act* of worship, nor can we hope to obtain his favour and acceptance, and so we miss of the *end* of worship, Matt. xv. 8, 9.

4. The last subject of discourse with this woman is concerning the Messiah, *vv*. 25, 26. Observe here,

(1) The faith of the woman, by

which she expected the Messiah: *I know that Messias cometh—and he will tell us all things*. She had nothing to object against what Christ had said; his discourse was, for aught she knew, what might become the Messiah then expected; but *from him* she would receive it, and in the mean time she thinks it best to suspend her belief.

(2) The favour of our Lord Jesus in making himself known to her: *I that speak to thee am he*, v. 26. Christ did never make himself known so expressly to any as he did here to this poor Samaritan, and to the blind man (*ch.* ix. 37); no, not to John Baptist, when he sent to him (Matt. xi. 4, 5); no, not to the Jews, when they challenged him to tell them whether he was the Christ, *ch.* x. 24.

THE HARVEST (*vv.* 27–42)

We have here the remainder of the story of what happened when Christ was in Samaria, after the long conference he had with the woman.

I. The *interruption given to this discourse* by the disciples' coming. 1. They wondered at Christ's converse with this woman, marvelled that he talked thus earnestly (as perhaps they observed at a distance) with a woman, a strange woman alone, especially with a Samaritan woman. 2. Yet they acquiesced in it; they knew it was for some good reason, and some good end, of which he was not bound to give them an account, and therefore none of them asked,

What seekest thou? or, *Why talkest thou with her?*

II. The notice which the woman gave to her neighbours of the extraordinary person she had happily met with, *vv.* 28, 29. Observe here,

1. How she *forgot her errand to the well*, v. 28. Therefore, because the disciples were come, and broke up the discourse, and perhaps she observed they were not pleased with it, she *went her way*.

2. How she *minded her errand to the town*, for her heart was upon it. She *went into the city*, and said to *the men*, probably the aldermen, the men in authority, whom, it may be, she found met together upon some public business; or to *the men*, that is, to every man she met in the streets; she proclaimed it in the chief places of concourse: *Come, see a man who told me all things that ever I did. Is not this the Christ?* Observe,

(1) How *solicitous* she was to *have her friends and neighbours* acquainted with Christ.

(2) How fair and ingenuous she was in the notice she gave them concerning this stranger she had met with. [1] She *tells them* plainly what induced her to admire him: *He has told me all things that ever I did.* [2] She *invites them* to *come and see* him of whom she had conceived so high an opinion. Not barely, "Come and look upon him" (she does not invite them to him as a *show*), but, "Come and converse with him; come and *hear his wisdom*, as I have done, and you will be of my mind." [3] She

resolves to *appeal to themselves*, and their own sentiments upon the trial? *Is not this the Christ?* She will not impose her faith upon them, but only propose it to them.

(3) What success she had in this invitation: *They went out of the city, and came to him*, v. 30. Though it might seem very improbable that a woman of so *small* a figure, and so *ill* a character, should have the honour of the first discovery of the Messiah among the Samaritans, yet it pleased God to incline their hearts to take notice of her report, and not to slight it as an idle tale.

III. Christ's discourse with his disciples while the woman was absent, *vv.* 31–38. Two things are observable in this discourse:—

1. How Christ *expresses the delight* which he himself had in his work. His work was to *seek and save* that which was lost, to go about doing good. Now with this work we here find him wholly taken up.

2. See here how Christ, having expressed his delight in *his* work, excites his disciples to diligence in *their* work; they were workers *with him*, and therefore should be workers *like him*, and make their work their *meat*, as he did. The work they had to do was to *preach the gospel*, and to set up the kingdom of the Messiah. Now this work he here compares to *harvest work*, the gathering in of the fruits of the earth; and this similitude he prosecutes throughout the discourse, *vv.* 35–38. The disciples were to gather in a harvest of souls for Christ. Now he here

suggests three things to them to quicken them to diligence:—

(1) That it was *necessary work*, and the *occasion* for it very urgent and pressing (*v.* 35): *You say, It is four months to harvest*; but I say, *The fields are already white*.

(2) That it was *profitable* and *advantageous* work, which they themselves would be gainers by (*v.* 36): "*He that reapeth receiveth wages*, and so shall you." Christ has undertaken to pay those well whom he employs in his work. He that reapeth, not only *shall* but *does* receive wages. There is a present reward in the service of Christ, and his work is *its own wages*.

(3) That it was *easy work*, and work that was half done to their hands by those that were gone before them: *One soweth, and another reapeth*, *vv.* 37, 38. This sometimes denotes a grievous judgment upon him that sows, Mic. vi. 15; Deut. xxviii. 30, *Thou shalt sow, and another shall reap*; as Deut. vi. 11, *Houses full of all good things, which thou fillest not*. So here. Moses, and the prophets, and John Baptist, had *paved* the way to the gospel, had sown the good seed which the New-Testament ministers did in effect but gather the fruit of. *I sent you to reap that whereon you bestowed*, in comparison, no *labour*. Isa. xl. 3–5. [1] This intimates *two things* concerning the Old-Testament ministry:—*First*, That it was very much *short* of the New-Testament ministry. Moses and the *prophets* sowed, but they could not be said to *reap*, so little did they see

of the fruit of their labours. *Secondly*, That it was very *serviceable* to the New-Testament ministry, and made way for it. [2] This also intimates *two things* concerning the ministry of the *apostles of Christ*. *First*, That it was a *fruitful* ministry: they were reapers that gathered in a great harvest of souls to Jesus Christ, and did more in seven years towards the setting up of the kingdom of God among men than the prophets of the Old Testament had done in twice so many ages. *Secondly*, That it was much *facilitated*, especially among the Jews, to whom they were first sent, by the writings of the prophets.

IV. The *good effect* which this visit Christ made to the Samaritans had upon them, and the fruit which was now presently gathered among them, *vv*. 39–42. See what impressions were made on them,

1. By the *woman's testimony* concerning *Christ*; though a single testimony, and of one of no good report, and the testimony no more than this, *He told me all that ever I did*, yet it had a good influence upon many. And *two things* they were brought to: —

(1) To *credit* Christ's *word* (*v*. 39): *Many of the Samaritans of that city believed on him for the saying of the woman*.

(2) They were brought to *court his stay* among them (*v*. 40): When they were come to him *they besought him that he would tarry with them*. Now we are told that Christ granted their request.

He *abode there*. Though it was a city of the Samaritans nearly adjoining to their temple, yet,

when he was *invited*, he *tarried* there.

2. We are also told what impressions were made upon them by Christ's own word, and his personal converse with them (*vv*. 41, 42); what he *said* and *did* there is not related, whether he healed their sick or no; but it is intimated, in the effect, that he said and did that which convinced them that he was the Christ; and the labours of a minister are best told by the good fruit of them.

Thus was the seed of the gospel sown in Samaria. What effect there was of this afterwards does not appear, but we find that four or five years after, when Philip preached the gospel in Samaria, he found such blessed remains of this good work now wrought that the *people with one accord gave heed to those things which Philip spoke*, Acts viii. 5, 6, 8. But as some were pliable to good so were others to evil, whom Simon Magus bewitched with his sorceries, *vv*. 9, 10.

THE NOBLEMAN'S SON
(*vv*. 43–54)

In these verses we have,

I. Christ's *coming* into Galilee, *v*. 43. *He went into Galilee*, for there he spent much of his time. Now see here,

1. Whither Christ went; into Gaililee, into the country of Galilee, but not to Nazareth, which was strictly *his own* country. He went among the villages, but declined going to Nazareth, the head city, for a reason here given, which *Jesus himself testified*, who knew the temper of his country-

men, the hearts of all men, and the experiences of all prophets, and it is this, That *a prophet has no honour in his own country*. Men's pride and envy make them scorn to be instructed by those who once were their school-fellows and play-fellows.

2. What entertainment he met with among the Galileans in the country (*v.* 45): They *received him*, bade him welcome, and cheerfully attended on his doctrine.

3. What city he went to. When he would go to a city, he chose to go to Cana of Galilee, *where he had made the water wine* (*v.* 46); thither he went, to see if there were any good fruits of that miracle remaining; and, if there were, to confirm their faith, and water what he had planted.

II. His *curing* the *nobleman's son* that was sick of a fever. This story is not recorded by any other of the evangelists; it comes in Matt. iv. 23.

Observe, 1. Who the *petitioner* was, and who the *patient*: the petitioner was a *nobleman*; the patient was his son: *There was a certain nobleman*. It was fifteen miles from Capernaum where this nobleman lived to Cana, where Christ now was; yet this affliction in his family sent him so far to Christ.

2. How the petitioner made *his application* to the physician. Having heard that *Jesus was come out of* Judea to Galilee, and finding that he did not come towards Capernaum, but turned off towards the other side of the country, he *went to him* himself, and *besought him to come and heal his son*, *v.* 47. See

here, (1) His *tender affection* to his son, that when he was sick he would spare no pains to get help for him. (2) His *great respect* to our Lord Jesus, that he would come himself to wait upon him, when he might have sent a servant. As to the errand he came upon, we may observe a mixture in *his faith*. [1] There was *sincerity* in it; he did believe that Christ could heal his son, though his disease was dangerous. [2] Yet there was *infirmity* in his faith; he believed that Christ could heal his son, but, as it should seem, he thought he could not heal him at a distance, and therefore he besought him that he would *come down* and heal him.

3. The gentle rebuke he met with in this address (*v.* 48): *Jesus said to him*, "I see how it is; *except you see signs and wonders, you will not believe*, as the Samaritans did, though they saw no signs and wonders, and therefore I must work miracles among you." Though he was a *nobleman*, and now in *grief* about his son, and had shown great respect to Christ in coming so far to him, yet Christ gives him a reproof. Men's dignity in the world shall not exempt them from the rebukes of the word or providence.

4. His continued importunity in his address (*v.* 49): *Sir, come down ere my child die. Lord*; so it should be rendered. In this reply of his we have, (1) Something that was commendable: he took the reproof patiently; he spoke to Christ respectfully. (2) Something that was blameworthy, that was his infirmity; for, [1] He seems to take no notice of the reproof

Christ gave him, says nothing to it, by way either of confession or of excuse, for he is so wholly taken up with concern about his child that he can mind nothing else. [2] He still discovered the weakness of his faith in the power of Christ. *First*, He must have Christ to come down, thinking that else he could do the child no kindness. *Secondly*, He believes that Christ could heal a *sick* child, but not that he could raise a *dead* child, and therefore, "O come down, ere my child die," as if then it would be too late.

5. The answer of peace which Christ gave to his request at last (*v*. 50): *Go thy way, thy son liveth*. Observe, His power was exerted by his word. In saying, *Thy son lives*, he showed that he has *life in himself*, and power to *quicken whom he will*.

6. The nobleman's belief of the word of Christ: He *believed*, and *went away*. Though Christ did not gratify him so far as to go down with him, he is satisfied with the method Christ took, and reckons he has gained his point. How quickly, how easily, is that which is lacking in our faith perfected by the word and power of Christ. Now he *sees no sign or wonder*, and yet *believes* the wonder done.

7. The further confirmation of his faith, by comparing notes with his servants at his return. (1) His servants met him with the agreeable news of the child's recovery, *v*. 51. (2) He enquired what hour the child began to recover (*v*. 52); not as if he doubted the influence of Christ's word upon the child's recovery, but he was desirous to

have his faith confirmed. They told him, *Yesterday, at the seventh hour* (at one o'clock in the afternoon, or, as some think this evangelist reckons, at seven o'clock at night) the *fever left him*. So *the father knew that it was at the same hour* when Jesus said to him, *Thy son liveth*.

8. The *happy effect and issue of this*. The bringing of the cure to the family brought salvation to it. (1) The nobleman *himself believed*. (2) His *whole house* believed likewise. [1] Because of the *interest* they all had in the miracle, which preserved the *blossom* and *hopes* of the family; this affected them all, and endeared Christ to them, and recommended him to their best thoughts. [2] Because of the *influence* the master of the family had upon them *all*.

9. Here is the evangelist's remark upon this cure (*v*. 54); *This is the second miracle*, referring to *ch*. ii. 11, where the turning of water into wine is said to be the first; that was soon after his first return out of Judea, this soon after his second.

CHAPTER FIVE

THE POOL OF BETHESDA
(*vv*. 1–16)

This miraculous cure is not recorded by any other of the evangelists, who confine themselves mostly to the miracles wrought in Galilee, but John relates those wrought at Jerusalem. Concerning this observe,

I. *The time when* this cure was wrought: it was at a *feast of the*

Jews, that is, the passover, for that was the most celebrated feast.

II. The *place where* this cure was wrought: at the *pool of Bethesda*, which had a miraculous healing virtue in it, and is here particularly described, *vv.* 2–4.

III. The patient on whom this cure was wrought (*v.* 5): one that *had been infirm thirty-eight years*. 1. His *disease* was *grievous*: He had an *infirmity*, a weakness; he had lost the use of his limbs, at least on one side, as is usual in palsies.

IV. The cure and the circumstances of it briefly related, *vv.* 6–9.

1. *Jesus saw him lie.* Observe, When Christ came up to Jerusalem he visited not the palaces, but the hospitals, which is an instance of his humility, and condescension, and tender compassion, and an *indication* of his great design in coming into the world, which was to seek and save the sick and wounded. There was a great multitude of poor cripples here at Bethesda, but Christ fastened his eye upon this one, and singled him out from the rest, because he was *senior* of the house, and in a more deplorable condition than any of the rest; and Christ delights to help the helpless, and hath mercy *on whom he will have mercy*.

2. He knew and considered *how long he had lain* in this condition. Those that have been long in affliction may comfort themselves with this, that God keeps account *how long*, and knows our frame.

3. He asked him, *Wilt thou be made whole?* A strange question to be asked one that had been so long ill. Christ put it to him,

(1) To *express* his own pity and concern for him. (2) To try him whether he would be beholden for a cure to him against whom the great people were so prejudiced and sought to prejudice others. (3) To teach him to value the mercy, and to excite in him desires after it.

4. The poor impotent man takes this opportunity to renew his complaint, and to set forth the misery of his case, which makes his cure the more illustrious: *Sir, I have no man to put me into the pool*, *v.* 7. (1) He does not think of any other way of being cured than by these waters, and desires no other friendship than to be helped into *them*; therefore, when Christ cured him, his imagination or expectation could not contribute to it, for he thought of no such thing. (2) He complains for want of friends to help him in: "*I have no man*, no friend to do me that kindness." (3) He bewails his infelicity, that very often when *he* was coming *another stepped in before him*. But a step between him and a cure, and yet he continues impotent.

5. Our Lord Jesus hereupon cures him with a word speaking, though he neither asked it nor thought of it. Here is,

(1) The word he said: *Rise, take up thy bed*, *v.* 8. [1] He is bidden to *rise and walk*; a strange command to be given to an *impotent* man, that had been long disabled; but this divine word was to be the vehicle of a divine power; it was a command to the disease to *be gone*, to nature to *be strong*, but it is expressed as a command

to him to *bestir himself*. [2] He is bidden to *take up his bed*. *First*, To make it to appear that it was a *perfect cure*, and purely miraculous. *Secondly*, It was to *proclaim* the cure, and make it public; for, being the sabbath day, whoever carried a burden through the streets made himself very remarkable, and every one would enquire what was the meaning of it; thereby notice of the miracle would spread, to the honour of God. *Thirdly*, Christ would thus witness against the tradition of the elders, which had stretched the law of the sabbath beyond its intention; and would likewise show that he was *Lord of the sabbath*, and had power to make what alterations he pleased about it, and to over-rule the law. *Fourthly*, He would hereby try the faith and obedience of his patient. By carrying his bed publicly, he exposed himself to the censure of the ecclesiastical court, and was liable, at least, to be *scourged in the synagogue*. Now, will he run the hazard of this, in obedience to Christ? Yes, he will. Those that have been *healed by Christ's word* should be *ruled by his word*, whatever it cost them.

(2) The efficacy of this word (*v*. 9): a divine power went along with it, and immediately he was *made whole*, *took up his bed*, *and walked*.

V. What became of the poor man after he was cured. We are here told,

1. What passed between him and the Jews who saw him carry his bed on the sabbath day; for on that day this cure was wrought, and it was the sabbath that fell

within the passover week, and therefore a *high day*, ch. xix. 31. Now here,

(1) The Jews quarrelled with the man for carrying his bed on the sabbath day, telling him that *it was not lawful*, *v*. 10.

(2) The man justified himself in what he did by a warrant that would bear him out, *v*. 11. "I do not do it in contempt of the law and the sabbath, but in obedience to one who, by *making me whole*, has given me an undeniable proof that he is greater than either."

(3) The Jews enquired further who it was that gave him this warrant (*v*. 12): *What man is that?* In their question, observe, [1] They resolve to look upon Christ as a *mere man*: *What man is that?* [2] They resolve to look upon him as a bad *man*, and take it for granted that he who bade this man carry his bed, whatever divine commission he might *produce*, was certainly a delinquent, and as such they resolve to prosecute him.

(4) The poor man was unable to give them any account of him: *He wist not who he was*, *v*. 13.

[1] Christ was *unknown* to him when he healed him. Probably he had heard of the name of Jesus, but had never seen him, and therefore could not tell that this was he.

[2] For the present he *kept himself unknown*; for as soon as he had wrought the cure he *conveyed himself away*, he *made himself unknown* (so some read it), *a multitude being in that place*. Christ left the miracle to commend

itself, and the man on whom it was wrought to justify it.

2. What passed between him and our Lord Jesus at their next interview, *v.* 14. Observe here,

(1) Where Christ found him: *in the temple*, the place of public worship. There Christ found him the same day, as it should seem, that he was healed; thither he straightway went, *First*, Because he had, *by his infirmity*, been so long *detained* thence. *Secondly*, Because he had *by his recovery* a good errand thither; he went up to the temple to return thanks to God for his recovery. *Thirdly*, Because he had, by *carrying his bed*, seemed to put a contempt on the sabbath, he would thus show that he had an honour for it, and made conscience of sabbath-sanctification, in that on which the chief stress of it is laid, which is the *public worship* of God. Works of necessity and mercy are allowed; but when they are over we must *go to the temple*.

(2) What he said to him. When Christ has cured us, he has not done with us; he now applies himself to the healing of his soul, and this *by the word* too. [1] He gives him a *memento* of his cure: *Behold thou art made whole.* [2] He gives him a caution against sin, in consideration hereof, *Being made whole*, *sin no more.* This implies that his disease was the punishment of sin; whether of some remarkably flagrant sin, or only of sin in general, we cannot tell, but we know that sin is the procuring cause of sickness, Ps. cvii. 17, 18. [3] He gives him warning of his danger, in case he should return to

his former sinful course: *Lest a worse thing come to thee.*

VI. Now, after this interview between Christ and his patient, observe in the two following verses, 1. The notice which the poor simple man gave to the Jews concerning Christ, *v.* 15. He told them it was Jesus that had *made him whole.* 2. The rage and enmity of the Jews against him: *Therefore did the* rulers of the Jews *persecute Jesus.* This was the pretended crime, *Because he had done these things on the sabbath day.* Thus hypocrites often cover their real enmity against the *power* of godliness with a pretended zeal for the *form* of it.

FROM DEATH TO LIFE
(*vv.* 17–30)

We have here Christ's discourse upon occasion of his being accused as a sabbath-breaker. Observe,

I. The doctrine laid down, by which he justified what he did on the sabbath day (*v.* 17): *He answered them.* 1. He pleads that he was the *Son of God*, plainly intimated in his calling *God his Father*; and, if so, his holiness was *unquestionable* and his sovereignty *incontestable*; and he might make what alterations he pleased of the divine law. 2. That he was a worker together with God. (1) *My Father worketh hitherto.* The example of God's resting on the seventh day from all his work is, in the fourth commandment, made the ground of our observing it as a *sabbath* or *day of rest*. Now God rested only from such work as he had done the six days before;

otherwise he *worketh hitherto*, he is every day working, sabbath days and week-days; upholding and governing all the creatures, and concurring by his common providence to all the motions and operations of nature, *to his own glory*; therefore, when we are appointed to rest on the sabbath day, yet we are not restrained from doing that which has a direct tendency *to the glory of God*, as the man's carrying his bed had. (2) *I work*; not only therefore I *may* work, *like him*, in doing good on sabbath days as well as other days, but I also *work with him*. As God created all things by Christ, so he supports and governs all by him, Heb. i. 3.

II. The offence that was taken at his doctrine (*v.* 18): *The Jews sought the more to kill him*. They sought to kill him,

1. Because he had broken the sabbath; for, let him say what he would in his own justification, they are resolved, right or wrong, to *find him guilty* of sabbath breaking.

2. Not only so, but he had said also *that God was his Father*. Now they pretend a jealousy for *God's honour*, as before for the sabbath day, and charge Christ with it as a heinous crime that he made himself equal with God; and a heinous crime it had been if he had not really been so.

III. Christ's discourse upon this occasion, which continues without interruption to the end of the chapter.

1. *In general*. He is one with the Father in all he does as Mediator, and there was a perfectly good understanding between them in the whole matter. It is ushered in with a solemn preface (*v.* 19): *Verily, verily, I say unto you*; I the Amen, the Amen, say it. Two things he says in general concerning the Son's oneness with the Father in working:—

[1] That the Son *conforms to the Father* (*v.* 19): *The Son can do nothing of himself but what he sees the Father do*; for *these things does the Son*. The Lord Jesus, as Mediator, is, *First, Obedient to his Father's will*; so entirely obedient that he *can do nothing of himself*, in the same sense as it is said, *God cannot* lie, *cannot deny* himself, which expresses the perfection of his truth, not any imperfection in his strength; so here, Christ was so entirely devoted to his Father's will that it was impossible for him in any thing to act separately. *Secondly*, He is *observant of his Father's counsel*; he can, he will, do nothing *but what he sees the Father do*. No man can *find out the work of God*, but the only-begotten Son, who lay in his bosom, sees what he does, is intimately acquainted with his purposes, and has the plan of them ever before him.

[2] That the Father *communicates* to the Son, *v.* 20. Observe,

First, The inducement to it: *The Father loveth the Son*; he declared, *This is my beloved Son*.

Secondly, The instances of it. He shows it, 1. In what he *does* communicate to him: *He shows him all things that himself doth*. 2. In what he *will* communicate; he will *show him*, that is, will appoint and direct him to do *greater works than these.* (1) Works of greater *power* than the *curing of the impotent man*; for he should raise the dead, and should himself rise from the dead. (2) Works of greater *authority* than warranting the man to *carry his bed on the sabbath day.*

2. *In particular.* He proves his equality with the Father, by specifying some of those works which he does that are the peculiar works of God. This is enlarged upon, *vv.* 21–30. He does, and shall do, that which is the peculiar work of God's almighty power— *raising the dead* and *giving life, vv.* 21, 25, 26, 28. He does, and shall do, that which is the peculiar work of God's sovereign dominion and jurisdiction—*judging* and *executing judgment, vv.* 22–24, 27. These two are interwoven, as being nearly connected; and what is said once is repeated and inculcated; put both together, and they will prove that Christ said not amiss when he made himself *equal with God.*

Now observe here,

a. When this resurrection shall be: *The hour is coming*; it is *fixed* to an hour, so very punctual is this great appointment. The judgment is not adjourned *sine die*—*to some time not yet pitched upon*; no, *he hath appointed a day. The hour is coming.* (*a*) It is *not yet* come, it is not the hour spoken of at *v.* 25, that is coming, and *now is.* Those erred dangerously who said that the *resurrection was past already,* 2 Tim. ii. 18. But, (*b*) It *will certainly* come, it is coming on, nearer every day than other; it is at the door. How

far off it is we know not; but we know that it is infallibly designed and unalterably determined.

b. Who shall be raised: *All that are in the graves,* all that have died from the beginning of time, and all that shall die to the end of time.

c. How they shall be raised. Two things are here told us:— (*a*) The efficient of this resurrection: *They shall hear his voice*; that is, he shall cause them to hear it, as Lazarus was made to hear that word, *Come forth*; a divine power shall go along with the voice, to put life into them, and enable them to obey it. (*b*) The effect of it: *They shall come forth* out of their graves, as prisoners out of their prison-house; they shall *arise out* of the dust, and shake themselves from it; see Isa. lii. 1, 2, 11. But this is not all; they shall *appear* before Christ's tribunal, shall *come forth* as those that are to be tried, *come forth* to the bar, publicly to receive their doom.

d. To what they shall be raised; to a different state of happiness or misery, according to their different character; to a state of retribution, according to what they did in the state of probation.

(*a*) *They that have done good shall come forth to the resurrection of life*; they shall live again, to live for ever.

(*b*) *They that have done evil to the resurrection of damnation*; they shall live again, to be for ever dying.

IV. Observe what is here said concerning the Mediator's *authority to execute judgment, vv.* 22–24, 27. Here is,

[1] Christ's commission or dele-

gation to the office of a judge, which is twice spoken of here (*v.* 22): *He hath committed all judgment to the Son*; and again (*v.* 27): *He hath given him authority.*

First, The *Father judges no man*; not that the Father hath resigned the government, but he is pleased to govern by Jesus Christ; so that man is not under the terror of dealing with God immediately, but has the comfort of access to him by a Mediator.

Secondly, He has committed all judgment to the Son, has constituted him *Lord of all* (Acts x. 36; Rom. xiv. 9). All judgment is committed to our Lord Jesus; for, 1. He is *entrusted* with the administration of the *providential kingdom,* is *head over all things* (Eph. i. 22), head of every man, 1 Cor. xi. 3. All things consist by him, Col. i. 17. 2. He is empowered to make laws immediately to bind conscience. *I say unto you* is now the form in which the statutes of the kingdom of heaven run. *Be it enacted* by the Lord Jesus, and by *his* authority. All the acts now in force are touched with his sceptre. 3. He is authorized to appoint and settle the terms of the new covenant, and to draw up the articles of peace between God and man; it is God in Christ that reconciles the world, and to him he has given power to confer eternal life. The book of life is the Lamb's book; by his award we must stand or fall. 4. He is commissioned to carry on and complete the war with the powers of darkness; to cast out and *give judgment against the prince of this world, ch.* xii. 31. He is commissioned not only to judge, but to *make war,* Rev. xix. 11. All that will fight *for God against Satan* must enlist themselves under *his* banner. 5. He is constituted sole manager of the judgment of the great day.

Thirdly, He has *given him authority to execute judgment also, v.* 27. Observe, 1. What the authority is which our Redeemer is invested with: *An authority to execute judgment*; he has not only a legislative and judicial power, but an *executive* power too. 2. Whence he has that authority: the Father *gave it to him.* Christ's authority as Mediator is delegated and derived; he acts as the Father's Viceregent, as the Lord's Anointed, the Lord's Christ.

[2] Here are the reasons (reasons of state) for which this commission was given him. He has all judgment committed to him for two reasons:—

First, Because he is the *Son of man*; which denotes these three things:—1. His humiliation and gracious condescension. 2. His affinity and alliance to us. The Father has committed the government of the children of men to him, because, being the *Son of man,* he is of the same nature with those whom he is *set over,* and therefore the more unexceptionable, and the more acceptable, as a Judge. 3. His being the Messiah promised. In that famous vision of his kingdom and glory, Dan. vii. 13, 14, he is called the *Son of man*; and Ps. viii. 4–6 Thou hast made the Son of man have *dominion over the works of thy hands.* He is the Messiah, and therefore is invested with all this power.

Secondly, That all men should honour the Son, v. 23. The honouring of Jesus Christ is here spoken of as God's great design (the Son intended to glorify the Father, and therefore the Father intended to glorify the Son, *ch.* xii. 32); and as man's great duty, in compliance with that design. If God will have the Son honoured, it is the duty of all to whom he is made known to honour him.

[3] Here is the rule by which the Son goes in executing this commission, so those words seem to come in (*v.* 24): *He that heareth and believeth* hath *everlasting life.* Here we have the substance of the whole gospel.

First, The *character* of a Christian: *He that heareth my word, and believeth on him that sent me.* To be a Christian indeed is, 1. To *hear the word of Christ.* It is not enough to be within hearing of it, but we must *attend on* it, as scholars on the instructions of their teachers; and *attend to* it, as servants to the commands of their masters; we must hear and obey it, must abide by the gospel of Christ as the fixed rule of our faith and practice. 2. To *believe on him that sent him*; for Christ's design is to *bring us to God*; and, as he is the first original of all grace, so is he the last object of all faith. Christ is our *way*; God is our rest.

Secondly, The *charter* of a Christian, in which all that are Christians indeed are interested. See what we get by Christ. 1. A charter of pardon: *He shall not come into condemnation.* The grace of the gospel is a full discharge

from the curse of the law. 2. A charter of privileges: He is *passed out of death to life*, is invested in a present happiness in spiritual life and entitled to a future happiness in eternal life.

[4] Here is the righteousness of his proceedings pursuant to this commission, *v.* 30. All judgment being committed to him, we cannot but ask *how he manages it.* And here he answers, *My judgment is just.* All Christ's acts of government, both *legislative* and *judicial*, are exactly agreeable to the rules of equity; see Prov. viii. 8. His judgments are certainly just, for they are directed.

First, By the Father's *wisdom*: *I can of my ownself do nothing*, nothing without the Father, but *as I hear I judge*, as he had said before (*v.* 19), The Son *can do nothing but what he sees the Father do*; so here, nothing but what he hears the Father *say*: *As I hear*, 1. From the secret eternal counsels of the Father, *so I judge.* Would we know what we may depend upon in our dealing with God? *Hear the word* of Christ. 2. From the published records of the Old Testament. Christ, in all the execution of his undertaking, had an eye to the scripture, and made it his business to conform to this, and *fulfil* it: *As it was written in the volume of the book.* Thus he taught us to do *nothing of ourselves*, but, *as we hear* from the word of God, *so to judge* of things, and act accordingly.

Secondly, By the Father's *will*: *My judgment is just*, and cannot be otherwise, *because I seek not my own will*, but *his who sent me.*

CHRIST'S MISSION (*vv.* 31–47)

In these verses our Lord Jesus proves and confirms the commission he had produced, and makes it out that he was sent of God to be the Messiah.

I. He *sets aside* his own testimony of himself (*v.* 31). Now, 1. This reflects reproach upon the sons of men, and their veracity and integrity. 2. It reflects honour on the Son of God, and bespeaks his wonderful condescension, that, though he is the *faithful witness*, the truth itself, yet he is pleased to *waive his privilege*, and, for the confirmation of our faith, refers himself to his *vouchers*, that we may have full satisfaction.

II. He produces other witnesses that bear testimony to him that he was sent of God.

1. The Father himself bore testimony to him (*v.* 32): *There is another that beareth witness*.

2. John Baptist witnessed to Christ, *vv.* 33, &c. John came to *bear witness of the light* (ch. i. 7); his business was to prepare his way, and direct people to him: *Behold the Lamb of God*.

Two things are added concerning John's testimony:—

[1] That it was a testimony *more than he needed to vouch* (*v.* 34): *I receive not testimony from man*. Though Christ saw fit to quote John's testimony, it was with a protestation that it shall not be deemed or construed so as to prejudice the prerogative of his self-sufficiency.

[2] That it was a testimony *to the man*, because John Baptist was one whom *they* had a respect for

(*v.* 35): *He was a light* among you. Observe,

First, The character of John Baptist: *He was a burning and a shining light*. It denotes his *activity*, zeal, and fervency, burning in love to God and the souls of men; fire is always working on itself or something else, so is a good minister.

Secondly, The affections of the people to him: *You were willing for a season to rejoice in his light*. 1. It was a *transport* that they were *in*, upon the appearing of John. 2. It was but *transient*, and soon over: "You were fond of him *for an hour*, for *a season*, as little children are fond of a new thing, you were pleased with John awhile, but soon grew weary of him and his ministry, and said that *he had a devil*, and now you have him in prison." Now, (1) Christ mentions their respect to John, to *condemn* them for their present opposition to himself, to whom John bore witness. If they had continued their veneration for John, as they ought to have done, they would have embraced Christ. (2) He mentions the passing away of their respect, to justify God in depriving them, as he had now done, of John's ministry, and putting that light under a bushel.

3. Christ's own works witnessed to him (*v.* 36): *I have a testimony greater than that of John*; for *if we believe the witness of men* sent of God, as John was, the *witness of God* immediately, and not by the ministry of men, *is greater*, 1 John v. 9. Now this greater testimony was that of the *works*

which *his Father had given him to finish*.

4. He produces, more fully than before, his Father's testimony concerning him (*v.* 37): *The Father that sent me hath borne witness of me*. Where God demands belief, he will not fail to give sufficient *evidence*, as he has done concerning Christ. That which was to be witnessed concerning Christ was chiefly this, that the God we had offended was willing to accept of him as a Mediator. Now concerning this he has *himself* given us full satisfaction (and he was fittest to do it), declaring himself well-pleased in him; if we be so, the work is done. Now, it might be suggested, if God himself thus bore witness of Christ, how came it to pass that he was not universally received by the Jewish nation and their rulers? To this Christ here answers that it was not to be thought strange, nor could their infidelity weaken his credibility, for two reasons:—[1] Because they were not acquainted with such extraordinary revelations of God and his will: *You have neither heard his voice at any time, nor seen his shape*, or *appearance*. They showed themselves to be as ignorant of God, though they professed relation to him, as we are of a man we never either saw or heard. [2] Because they were not affected, no, not with the ordinary ways by which God·had revealed himself to them: *You have not his word abiding in you*, *v.* 38. They had the scriptures of the Old Testament; might they not by them be disposed to

receive Christ? Yes, if they had had their due influence upon them. But, *First*, The word of God was not in them; it was *among them*, in their country, in their hands, but not *in them*, in their hearts: not ruling in their souls, but only shining in their eyes and sounding in their ears. What did it avail them that they had the oracles of God *committed* to them (Rom. iii. 2), when they had not these oracles *commanding* in them? If they had, they would readily have embraced Christ. *Secondly*, It did not *abide*. Many have the word of God coming into them, and making some impressions for a while, but it does not *abide* with them; it is not constantly in them, as a man at home, but only now and then, as a *wayfaring man*. If the word *abide in* us, if we converse with it by frequent meditation, consult with it upon every occasion, and conform to it in our conversation, we shall then readily receive the witness of the Father concerning Christ; see *ch.* vii. 17.

5. The last witness he calls is the Old Testament, which witnessed of him, and to it he appeals (*vv.* 39, &c.): *Search the scriptures*.

(1) This may be read, either, [1] "*You search the scriptures*, and you do well to do so." Note, It is possible for men to be very studious in the letter of the scripture, and yet to be strangers to the power and influence of it. Or, [2] As we read it: *Search the scriptures*; and so, *First*, It was spoken to *them* in the nature of an *appeal*: "You profess to receive and believe the scripture; here I

will *join issue* with you, let this be the judge, provided you will not *rest in the letter* but will *search* into it." Note, when appeals are made to the scriptures, they must be searched.

(2) Now there are two things which we are here directed to have in our eye, in our searching the scripture: *heaven* our end, and *Christ* our way. [1] We must search the scriptures for *heaven* as our *great end: For in them you think you have eternal life.* [2] We must *search the scriptures* for *Christ*, as the new and living *way* that leads to this *end.* These are *they*, the great and principal witnesses, *that testify of me.*

(3) To this testimony he annexes a reproof of their infidelity and wickedness in four instances; particularly,

[1] Their *neglect of him* and his doctrine: "*You will not come to me, that you might have life*, v. 40. You search the scriptures, you believe the prophets, who you cannot but see testify of me; and yet you will not *come to me*, to whom they direct you."

[2] Their *lack of the love of God* (v. 42): "*I know you* very well, *that you have not the love of God in you.* Why should I wonder that you do not come to me, when you lack even the first principle of *natural religion*, which is the *love of God?*"

[3] Another crime charged upon them is their readiness to entertain false Christs and false prophets, while they obstinately opposed him who was the true Messias (v. 43).

[4] They are here charged with pride and vain-glory, and unbelief, the effect of them, v. 44. Having sharply reproved their unbelief, like a wise physician, he here searches into the cause, lays the axe to the root. They *therefore* slighted and undervalued Christ because they *admired* and *overvalued* themselves.

6. The last witness here called is Moses, vv. 45, &c. The Jews had a great veneration for Moses, and valued themselves upon their being the *disciples* of Moses, and pretended to adhere to Moses, in their opposition to Christ; but Christ here shows them,

(1) That Moses was a witness against the unbelieving Jews, *and accused them to the Father: There is one that accuses you, even Moses.* This may be understood either, [1] As showing the difference between the law and the gospel. Or, [2] As showing the manifest unreasonableness of their infidelity. "Moses himself says enough to convict you of, and condemn you for, your unbelief."

(2) That Moses was a witness for Christ and to his doctrine (vv. 46, 47): *He wrote of me.* Moses did particularly prophesy of Christ, as the Seed of the woman, the Seed of Abraham, the Shiloh, the great Prophet; the ceremonies of the law of Moses were *figures of him that was to come.* The Jews made Moses the patron of their opposition to Christ; but Christ here shows them their error, that Moses was so far from writing against Christ that he wrote *for him*, and *of him.*

Thus ends Christ's plea for himself, in answer to the charge exhibited against him. What effect it had we know not; it would seem to have had this, their *mouths* were *stopped* for the present, and they could not for shame but drop the prosecution, and yet their *hearts* were *hardened*.

CHAPTER SIX

FEEDING FIVE THOUSAND
(vv. 1–14)

We have here an account of Christ's feeding five thousand men with five loaves and two fishes, which miracle is in *this* respect remarkable, that it is the only passage of the actions of *Christ's life* that is recorded by all the four evangelists. John, who does not usually relate what had been recorded by those who wrote before him, yet relates this, because of the reference the following discourse has to it.

Notice the influence which this miracle had upon the people who tasted of the benefit of it (v. 14): *They said, This is of a truth that prophet*. Note, 1. Even the vulgar Jews with great assurance expected the Messiah to come into the world, and to be a *great prophet*. They speak here with assurance of his coming. The Pharisees despised them as *not knowing the law*; but, it should seem, they knew more of him that is the *end of the law* than the Pharisees did. 2. The miracles which Christ wrought did clearly demonstrate that he was the Messiah promised, a teacher come from God, the great prophet, and could not but convince the amazed spectators that this was he that should come. There were many who were convinced he was that prophet that should come into the world who yet did not cordially receive his doctrine, for they did not continue in it. Such a wretched incoherence and inconsistency there is between the faculties of the corrupt unsanctified soul, that it is possible for men to acknowledge that Christ is that prophet, and yet to turn a deaf ear to him.

WALKING ON THE WATER
(vv. 15–21)

Here is, I. Christ's retirement from the multitude.

1. Observe what induced him to retire; because he perceived that those who acknowledged him to be that prophet that should come into the world would come, and *take him by force, to make him a king*, v. 15. Now here we have an instance,

(1) Of the irregular zeal of some of Christ's followers; nothing would serve but they would make him *a king*. It was intended to carry on a *secular* design; they hoped this might be a fair opportunity of shaking off the Roman yoke, of which they were weary. If they had one to head them who could victual an army cheaper than another could provide for a family, they were sure of the sinews of the war, and could not fail of success, and the recovery of their ancient liberties. Thus is religion often prostituted to a secular interest, and Christ is served only to *serve a turn*, Rom. xvi. 18.

(2) Here is an instance of the humility and self-denial of the

Lord Jesus, that, when they would have made him a king, he *departed*; so far was he from countenancing the design that he effectually quashed it.

2. Observe *whither* he retired: *He departed again into a mountain*, the mountain where he had preached (*v.* 3), whence he came down into the plain, to feed the people, and then returned to it alone, to be private.

II. Here is the disciples' distress at sea.

1. Here is their *going down to the sea* in a ship (*vv.* 16, 17).

2. Here is the *stormy wind* arising and *fulfilling the word of God*. They were Christ's disciples, and were now in the way of their duty, and Christ was now in the mount praying for them; and yet they were in this distress. Let it comfort good people, when they happen to be in storms at sea, that the disciples of Christ were so; and let the promises of a gracious God balance the threats of an angry sea. Though in a storm, and *in the dark*, they are no worse off than Christ's disciples were. Clouds and darkness sometimes surround the children of the light, and of the day.

3. Here is Christ's seasonable approach to them when they were in this peril, *v.* 19. *They had rowed* (being forced by the contrary winds to betake themselves to their oars) *about twenty-five or thirty furlongs*. And, when they were got off a good way at sea, they *see Jesus walking on the sea*. See here, (1) The power Christ has over the laws and customs of nature, to control and dispense

with them at his pleasure. It is natural for heavy bodies to sink in water, but Christ walked *upon* the water as upon dry land, which was more than Moses's dividing the water and walking *through* the water. (2) The concern Christ has for his disciples in distress: *He drew nigh to the ship*; for *therefore* he walked upon the water, as he *rides upon the heavens, for the help of his people*, Deut. xxxiii. 26. (3) The relief Christ gives to his disciples in their fears. They *were afraid*, more afraid of an apparition (for so they supposed him to be) than of the winds and waves. But, when they were in this fright, how affectionately did Christ silence their fears with that compassionate word (*v.* 20), *It is I, be not afraid!* When trouble is nigh Christ is nigh.

4. Here is their speedy arrival at the port they were bound for, *v.* 17. (1) They *welcomed* Christ into the ship; they *willingly received him*. (2) Christ brought them safely to the shore: *Immediately the ship was at the land whither they went*. The disciples had rowed hard, but could not make their point till they had got Christ in the ship, and then the work was *done suddenly*.

CHRIST ADDRESSES THE CROWD (*vv.* 22–27)

In these verses we have,

I. The careful enquiry which the people made after Christ, *vv.* 23, 24.

1. They were *much at a loss* for him. He was gone, and they knew not what was become of him.

2. They were very *industrious in seeking* him. They searched the

places thereabouts, and when *they saw that Jesus was not there, nor his disciples* (neither he nor any one that could give tidings of him), they resolved to search elsewhere.

3. They laid hold of the opportunity that offered itself, and *they also took shipping, and came to Capernaum, seeking for Jesus.*

II. The success of this enquiry: *They found him on the other side of the sea, v.* 25.

III. The question they put to him when they found him: *Rabbi, when camest thou hither?* It should seem by *v.* 59 that they found him *in the synagogue.* Their enquiry refers not only to the *time*, but to the *manner*, of his conveying himself thither; not only *When*, but, "*How*, camest thou hither?" for there was no boat for him to come in. They were curious in asking concerning Christ's motions, but not solicitous to observe their own.

IV. The answer Christ gave them, not direct to their question (what was it to them *when* and *how* he came thither?) but such an answer as their case required.

1. He discovers the *corrupt principle* they acted from in following him (*v.* 26). These followed Christ, (1) Not for his doctrine's sake: *Not because you saw the miracles.* But, (2) It was for their own bellies' sake: *Because you did eat of the loaves, and were filled*; not because he taught them, but because he fed them. Note, Many follow Christ for *loaves*, and not for *love.*

2. He directs them to better principles (*v.* 27): *Labour for that meat which endures to everlasting life.* His design is,

(1) To moderate our worldly pursuits: *Labour not for the meat that perishes.* This does not forbid honest labour for food convenient, 2 Thess. iii. 12. But we must not make the things of this world our chief care and concern. Note, [1] The things of the world are *meat that perishes.* [2] It is therefore folly for us inordinately to labour after them.

(2) To quicken and excite our gracious pursuits: "Bestow your pains to better purpose, and *labour for that meat* which belongs to the soul," of which he shows,

[1] That it is *unspeakably desirable*: It is meat which *endures to everlasting life*; it is a happiness which will last as long as we must, which not only itself endures eternally, but will nourish us up to everlasting life.

[2] It is *undoubtedly attainable.* We are told to *labour for it*, as if it were to be got by our own industry. But, when we have laboured ever so much for it, we have not merited it as our *hire*, but the Son of man *gives it.* And what more free than gift? It is an encouragement that he who has the giving of it is the *Son of man*, for then we may hope the *sons of men* that seek it, and labour for it, shall not fail to have it. *Secondly*, What authority he has to give it; for *him has God the Father sealed, for him the Father has sealed* (proved and evidenced) *to be God*; so some read it; he has declared him to be the Son of God with power. He has *sealed him*, that is, has given him full authority to deal between God and man, as God's *ambassador* to man and

man's *intercessor* with God, and has proved his commission by miracles. Having given him *authority*, he has given us *assurance* of it; having entrusted him with *unlimited powers*, he has satisfied us with *undoubted proofs* of them; so that as he might go on with confidence in his undertaking for us, so may we in our resignations to him.

BREAD OF HEAVEN
(*vv.* 28–59)

I. Christ having told them that *they* must *work for the meat* he spoke of, must *labour* for it, they enquire what work they must do, and he answers them, *vv.* 28, 29. 1. Their *enquiry* was *pertinent* enough (*v.* 28): *What shall we do, that we may work the works of God?* Some understand it as a pert question: "What works of God can we do more and better than those we do in obedience to the law of Moses?" But I rather take it as a humble serious question, showing them to be, at least for the present, in a good mind, and willing to know and do their duty. 2. Christ's answer was plain enough (*v.* 29): *This is the work of God that ye believe.* Note, (1) The work of faith is the work of God. They enquire after the *works* of God (in the plural number), being careful about *many things*; but Christ directs them to one work, which includes all, the one thing needful: that *you believe*, which supersedes all the works of the ceremonial law; the work which is necessary to the acceptance of all the other works, and which produces them, for without faith

you cannot please God. (2) That faith is the work of God which closes with Christ, and relies upon him. It is to *believe on him* as one whom God *hath sent*, as God's commissioner in the great affair of peace between God and man, and as such to *rest* upon him, and *resign ourselves* to him. See *ch.* xiv. 1.

II. Christ having told them that the *Son of man* would *give them this meat*, they enquire concerning him, and he answers their enquiry.

1. Their enquiry is after *a sign* (*v.* 30): *What sign showest thou?* But *herein* they missed it,

(1) That they overlooked the many miracles which they had seen wrought by him, and which amounted to an abundant proof of his divine mission.

(2) That they preferred the miraculous feeding of Israel in the wilderness before all the miracles Christ wrought (*v.* 31): *Our fathers did eat manna in the desert*; and, to strengthen the objection, they quote a scripture for it: *He gave them bread from heaven* (taken from Ps. lxxviii. 24), *he gave them of the corn of heaven.* [1] Christ reproved them for their fondness of the miraculous bread, and bade them not set their hearts upon *meat which perisheth.* [2] Christ had fed five thousand men with five loaves, and had given them that as one sign to prove him *sent of God*; but, under colour of *magnifying* the miracles of Moses, they tacitly *undervalue* this miracle of Christ, and *evade* the evidence of it.

2. Here is Christ's reply to this enquiry, wherein,

(1) He *rectifies* their *mistake* concerning the *typical* manna. It was true that their fathers did *eat manna* in the desert. But, [1] It was not Moses that gave it to them, nor were they obliged to him for it; he was but the instrument, and therefore they must look beyond him to God. [2] It was not given them, as they imagined, *from heaven*, from the highest heavens, but only from *the clouds*, and therefore not so much superior to that which had its rise from the earth as they thought. Because the scripture saith, *He gave them bread from heaven*, it does not follow that it was *heavenly bread*, or was intended to be the nourishment of souls. Misunderstanding scripture language occasions many mistakes in the things of God.

(2) He *informs* them concerning the *true* manna, of which that was a type: *But my Father giveth you the true bread from heaven.* That which is truly and properly the *bread from heaven*, of which the manna was but a shadow and figure, is *now given*, not to *your fathers*, who are dead and gone, but *to you* of this present age, for whom the *better things were reserved*: he is *now giving* you that *bread from heaven*, which is *truly* so called.

III. Christ, having replied to their enquiries, takes further occasion from their objection concerning the *manna* to discourse of *himself* under the similitude of *bread*, and of *believing* under the similitude of *eating and drinking*; to which, together with his putting both together in the *eating* of his *flesh* and *drinking* of his *blood*, and with the remarks made upon it by the hearers, the rest of this conference may be reduced.

1. Christ having spoken of *himself* as the great *gift of God*, and the *true bread* (v. 32), largely *explains* and *confirms* this, that we may rightly know him.

(1) He here shows that he is the *true bread*; this he repeats again and again, vv. 33, 35, 48–51. *First*, He is the *living bread* (so he explains himself, v. 51): *I am the living bread.* Bread is itself a dead thing, and nourishes not but by the help of the faculties of a living body; but Christ is himself *living bread*, and nourishes by his own power. *Secondly, He gives life unto the world* (v. 33), spiritual and eternal life; the life of the soul in union and communion with God here, and in the vision and fruition of him hereafter; a life that includes in it all happiness. The *manna* did only preserve and support life, did not preserve and perpetuate life, much less restore it; but Christ *gives* life to those that were dead in sin.

(2) He here shows what his undertaking was, and what his errand into the world. Laying aside the metaphor, he speaks plainly, and speaks no proverb, giving us an account of his business among men, vv. 38–40.

[1] He assures us, in general, that he came from heaven upon his Father's business (v. 38), not to *do his own will, but the will of him that sent him.* That is, *First*, Christ did not come into the world as a *private* person, that acts for himself only, but under a *public character*, to act for others as an ambassador, or plenipotentiary,

authorized by a public commission; he came into the world as God's great agent and the world's great physician. *Secondly*, Christ, when he was in the world, did not carry on any *private* design, nor had any *separate interest* at all, distinct from theirs for whom he acted. The scope of his whole life was to glorify God and do good to men.

[2] He acquaints us, in particular, with that will of the Father which he came to do; he here *declares the decree*, the instructions he was to pursue.

First, The *private instructions* given to Christ, that he should be sure to save all the chosen remnant; and this is the *covenant of redemption* between the Father and the Son (*v.* 38): *This is the Father's will, who hath sent me*; this is the charge I am entrusted with, that *of all whom he hath given me I should lose none*." Those whom God chose to be the objects of his special love he lodged as a trust in the hands of Christ. Christ's undertaking for those that are given him extends to the resurrection of their bodies. *I will raise it up again at the last day*, which supposes all that goes before, but this is to crown and complete the undertaking.

Secondly, The *public instructions* which were to be given to the children of men, in what way, and upon what terms, they might obtain salvation by Christ; and this is the *covenant of grace* between God and man. "*This is the will*, the revealed will, *of him that sent me*, the method agreed upon, upon which to proceed with the children of men, that

every one, Jew or Gentile, that *sees the Son, and believes on him*, may have *everlasting life*, and *I will raise him up*." This is *gospel* indeed, good news. This everlasting life is sure to all those who believe in Christ, and to them only. He that *sees the Son*, and *believes on him*, shall be saved. Some understand this *seeing* as a *limitation* of this condition of salvation to those only that have the revelation of Christ and his grace made to them. Every one that has the opportunity of being acquainted with Christ, and improves this so well as to *believe* in him, shall have everlasting life, so that none shall be condemned for unbelief (however they may be for other sins) but those who have had the gospel preached to them, who, like these Jews here (*v.* 36), have *seen*, and yet have *not* believed; have known Christ, and yet not trusted in him. But I rather understand *seeing* here to mean the same thing with *believing*. Every one that *sees the Son*, that is, *believes on him*, sees him with an eye of faith, by which we come to be duly acquainted and affected with the doctrine of the gospel concerning him. It is to look upon him, as the stung Israelites upon the brazen serpent. Those who believe in Jesus Christ, shall be raised up by his power at the last day. He had it in charge as his Father's will (*v.* 39), and here he solemnly makes it his own undertaking.

2. Now Christ discoursing thus concerning himself, as the *bread of life* that came down from heaven, let us see what remarks his hearers made upon it.

(1) When they heard of such a thing as the *bread of God*, which *gives life*, they heartily prayed for it (*v.* 34): *Lord, evermore give us this bread.*

(2) But, when they understood that by this *bread of life* Jesus meant *himself*, then they *despised* it. Whether they were the same persons that had prayed for it (*v.* 34), or some others of the company, does not appear; it seems to be some others, for they are called *Jews.* Now it is said (*v.* 41), *They murmured at him.* This comes in immediately after that solemn declaration which Christ had made of God's will and his own undertaking concerning man's salvation (*vv.* 39, 40), which certainly were some of the most weighty and gracious words that ever proceeded out of the mouth of our Lord Jesus, the most faithful, and best worthy of all acceptation. Now, [1] That which offended them was Christ's asserting his origin to be *from heaven*, *vv.* 41, 42. How is it that he saith, *I came down from heaven?* [2] That which they thought justified them herein was that they knew his extraction on earth: *Is not this Jesus the son of Joseph, whose father and mother we know?* They took it amiss that he should say that he came down from heaven, when he was *one of them.*

3. Christ, having spoken of faith as the great *work of God* (*v.* 29), discourses largely concerning this work, instructing and encouraging us in it.

(1) He shows what it is to *believe in Christ.* [1] To believe in Christ is to *come to Christ.* He that *comes to* me is the same with him that *believes in me* (*v.* 35), and again (*v.* 37): *He that comes unto me*; so *vv.* 44, 45. [2] It is to *feed upon Christ* (*v.* 51): *If any man eat of this bread.* The former denotes applying ourselves to Christ; this denotes applying Christ to ourselves, with appetite and delight, that we may receive life, and strength, and comfort from him.

(2) He shows what is to be got by believing in Christ.

[1] They shall never want, *never hunger, never thirst*, *v.* 35. Desires they have, earnest desires, but these so suitably, so seasonably, so abundantly satisfied, that they cannot be called hunger and thirst, which are uneasy and painful.

[2] They shall *never die*, not die eternally; for, *First*, He that believes on Christ *has everlasting life* (*v.* 47); he has the assurance of it, the grant of it, the earnest of it; he has it in the promise and first-fruits. *Secondly*, Whereas they that did *eat manna* died, Christ is such bread as a man may eat of and never die, *vv.* 49, 50. *Not die*, that is, not perish, not come short of the heavenly Canaan, as the Israelites did of the earthly, for want of *faith*, though they had *manna.* This is further explained by that promise in the next words: *If any man eat of this bread, he shall live for ever, v.* 51. This is the meaning of this *never dying*: though he go down *to death*, he shall pass through it to that world where there shall be *no more death.*

(3) He shows what encouragements we have to believe in Christ.

Christ here speaks of some who *had seen him and yet believed not, v.* 36. Two things we are here assured of, to encourage our faith: —

[1] That the Son will bid all those welcome that come to him (*v.* 37): *Him that cometh to me I will in no wise cast out.* There are two negatives: *I will not, no, I will not.*

[2] That the Father will, without fail, bring all those to him in due time that were given him. Though he lose many of his *creatures*, yet none of his *charge*: *All that the Father gives him shall come to him* notwithstanding. The giving of the chosen remnant to Christ is spoken of (*v.* 39) as a thing *done*; he *hath given* them. Here it is spoken of as a thing *in the doing*; he *giveth them*; because, *when the first begotten was brought into the world*, it should seem, there was a renewal of the grant; see Heb. x. 5, &c. God was now about to *give him the heathen for his inheritance* (Ps. ii. 8), to put him in possession of *the desolate heritages* (Isa. xlix. 8), to *divide him a portion with the great*, Isa. liii. 12. And though the Jews, who *saw* him, *believed not* on him, yet these (saith he) shall *come to me*; the other sheep, which are not of this fold, shall be *brought, ch.* x. 15, 16. See Acts xiii. 45–48. *They shall come to me.* This is not in the nature of a *promise*, but a *prediction*, that as many as were in the counsel of God ordained to life shall be brought to life by being brought to Christ. He that *formed the spirit of man within him* by his creating power, and *fashions the*

hearts of men by his providential influence, knows how to new-mould the soul, and to alter its bent and temper, and make it conformable to himself and his own will, without doing any wrong to its natural liberty (*v.* 44). It is such a drawing as works not only a *compliance*, but a cheerful compliance, a complacency: *Draw us, and we will run after thee. No man*, in this weak and helpless state, can come to Christ without it. As we *cannot* do any natural action without the concurrence of *common providence*, so we cannot do any action morally good without the influence of *special grace*, in which the *new man* lives, and moves, and has its being, as much as the *mere man* has in the divine providence. The Father, having sent Christ, would not send him on a fruitless errand. Christ having undertaken to bring souls to glory, God promised him to bring them to him, and so to give him possession of those to whom he had given him a right.

4. Christ, having thus spoken of himself as the *bread of life*, and of faith as *the work of God*, comes more particularly to show *what of himself* is this bread, namely, his flesh, and that to believe is to eat of that, *vv.* 51–58, where he still prosecutes the metaphor of food. Observe, here, the *preparation* of this food: *The bread that I will give is my flesh* (*v.* 51), *the flesh of the Son of man and his blood*, *v.* 53. *His flesh is meat indeed, and his blood is drink indeed*, *v.* 55. Observe, also, the *participation* of this food: We must *eat the flesh of the Son of*

man and drink his blood (v. 53); and again (v. 54), *Whoso eateth my flesh and drinketh my blood*; and the same words (vv. 56, 57), he that *eateth me.* This is certainly a parable or figurative discourse, wherein the actings of the soul upon things spiritual and divine are represented by bodily actions about things sensible, which made the truths of Christ more intelligible to some, and less so to others, Mark iv. 11–12. Now,

(1) Let us see how this discourse of Christ was liable to mistake and misconstruction, that *men might see, and not perceive.* [1] It was misconstrued by the carnal *Jews,* to whom it was first delivered (v. 52). [2] It has been wretchedly misconstrued for the support of the doctrine of transubstantiation. The Lord's supper was not yet instituted, and therefore it could have no reference to that; it is a *spiritual* eating and drinking that is here spoken of, not a *sacramental.* Therefore,

(2) Let us see how this discourse of Christ to be understood.

[1] What is meant by the *flesh and blood of Christ.* It is called (v. 53), *The flesh of the Son of man, and his blood, his* as Messiah and Mediator: the *flesh and blood* which he *assumed* in his incarnation (Heb. ii. 14), and which he *gave up* in his *death* and *suffering*: *my flesh which I will give* to be crucified and slain. It is said to be *given for the life of the world,* that is, *First, Instead* of the *life of the world,* which was *forfeited* by sin, Christ gives his own flesh as a ransom or counter-price. *Secondly, In order to* the *life of the world,* to purchase a *general* offer of eternal life to all the world, and the *special* assurances of it to all believers.

[2] What is meant by *eating this flesh* and *drinking* this *blood,* which is so necessary and beneficial; it is certain that it means neither more nor less than believing in Christ. As we partake of meat and drink by eating and drinking, so we partake of Christ and his benefits by faith.

(3) Having thus explained the general meaning of this part of Christ's discourse, the particulars are reducible to two heads:—

[1] The *necessity* of our *feeding upon Christ* (v. 53): *Except you eat the flesh of the Son of man, and drink his blood, you have no life in you.* That is, *First,* "It is a certain sign that you *have no* spiritual *life* in you if you have no *desire* towards Christ, nor *delight* in him." *Secondly,* "It is certain that you *can have* no spiritual life, unless you derive it from Christ by faith; separated from him you can do nothing."

[2] The *benefit* and *advantage* of it, in two things:—

First, We shall be *one with Christ,* as our bodies are with our food when it is digested (v. 56).

Secondly, We shall *live,* shall live eternally, *by him,* as our bodies live by our food.

a. We shall *live by him* (v. 57): *As the living Father hath sent me, and I live by the Father, so he that eateth me, even he shall live by me.* We have here the series and order of the divine life. (*a*) God is the *living Father,* hath life in and of himself. *I am that I am* is his name for ever. (*b*) Jesus Christ, as Mediator, lives *by the Father*; he has life *in himself* (*ch.* v. 26), but he has it of the Father. (*c*) True believers receive this divine life by virtue of their union with Christ, which is inferred from the union between the Father and the Son, as it is compared to it, *ch.* xvii. 21.

b. We shall live *eternally* by him (*v.* 54): *Whoso eateth my flesh, and drinketh my blood*, as prepared in the gospel to be the food of souls, he *hath eternal life*, he hath it now, as *v.* 40. He has that in him which is eternal life begun; he has the earnest and foretaste of it, and the hope of it; he shall live *for ever, v.* 58. His happiness shall run parallel with the longest line of eternity itself.

Lastly, The historian concludes with an account *where* Christ had this discourse with the Jews (*v.* 59): *In the synagogue as he taught*, implying that he taught them many other things besides these, but this was that in his discourse which was new.

WORDS OF LIFE (*vv.* 60–71)

We have here an account of the effects of Christ's discourse. Some were offended and others edified by it; some driven *from him* and others brought nearer *to him*.

I. To some it was a *savour of death unto death*. Now here we have,

1. Their murmurings at the doctrine they heard (*v.* 60); not a few, but many of them, were offended at it. Of the several sorts of ground that received the seed, only one in four brought

forth fruit. See what they say to it (*v.* 60): *This is a hard saying, who can hear it?*

2. Christ's comments upon their murmurings.

(1) He well enough knew their murmurings, *v.* 61. Their cavils were secret in their own breasts, or whispered among themselves in a corner. But, [1] Christ *knew* them; he saw them, he heard them. [2] He knew it *in himself*, not by any information given him, nor any external indication of the thing, but by his own divine omniscience.

(2) He well enough knew how to answer them: "*Doth this offend you? Is this a stumbling-block to you?*"

[1] He gives them a hint of his ascension into heaven, as that which would give an irresistible evidence of the truth of his doctrine (*v.* 62): *What and if you shall see the Son of man ascend up where he was before?* And what then? Those who stumble at smaller difficulties should consider how they will get over greater. *Secondly*, "When you see the Son of man ascend, this will much more offend you, for then my body will be less capable of being eaten by you in that gross sense wherein you now understand it"; so Dr. Whitby. Let us wait awhile, till the mystery of God shall be finished, and then we shall see that there was no reason to be offended at any of Christ's sayings.

[2] He gives them a general key to this and all such parabolical discourses, teaching them that they are to be understood spiritually, and not after a corporal

and carnal manner: *It is the spirit that quickeneth, the flesh profiteth nothing,* v. 63.

[3] He gives them an intimation of his *knowledge of them,* and that he had expected no better from them, though they called themselves his disciples, *vv.* 64, 65. Now was fulfilled that of the prophet, speaking of Christ and his doctrine (Isa. liii. 1), *Who hath believed our report? and to whom is the arm of the Lord revealed?* Both these Christ here takes notice of.

II. This discourse was to others a *savour of life unto life. Many went back,* but, thanks be to God, all did not; even then the *twelve* stuck to him. Though the *faith of some be overthrown,* yet the *foundation of God stands sure.* Observe here,

1. The affectionate question which Christ put to the twelve (*v.* 67): *Will you also go away?*

2. The believing reply which Peter, in the name of the rest, made to this question, *vv.* 68, 69.

(1) Here is a good resolution to adhere to Christ, and so expressed as to intimate that they would not entertain the least thought of leaving him: "*Lord, to whom shall we go?* It were folly to go from thee, unless we knew where to better ourselves; no, Lord, we like our choice too well to change."

(2) Here is a good reason for this resolution. It was not the inconsiderate resolve of a blind affection, but the result of mature deliberation. The disciples were resolved never to go away from Christ,

[1] Because of the *advantage* they

promised themselves by him: *Thou hast the words of eternal life.*

[2] Because of the assurance they had concerning him (*v.* 69): *We believe, and are sure, that thou art that Christ.* If he be the promised Messiah, he must *bring in an everlasting righteousness* (Dan. ix. 24), and therefore has the *words of eternal life,* for *righteousness reigns to eternal life,* Rom. v. 21.

3. The melancholy remark which our Lord Jesus made upon this reply of Peter's (*vv.* 70, 71): *Have not I chosen you twelve, and one of you is a devil?* And the evangelist tells us whom he meant: *he spoke of Judas Iscariot.* Peter had undertaken for them all that they would be faithful to their Master. Now Christ does not condemn his charity (it is always good to hope the best), but he tacitly corrects his confidence. We must not be too sure concerning any. God knows those that are his; we do not.

CHAPTER SEVEN

CHRIST AND HIS BROTHERS
(*vv.* 1–13)

We have here, I. The reason given why Christ spent more of his time in Galilee than in Judea (*v.* 1): *because the Jews,* the people in Judea and Jerusalem, sought to *kill him,* for curing the impotent man on the sabbath day, *ch.* v. 16.

II. The approach of the *feast of tabernacles* (*v.* 2), one of the three solemnities which called for the personal attendance of all the males at Jerusalem; see the institution of it, Lev. xxiii. 34, &c., and the revival of it after a long disuse, Neh. viii. 14.

III. Christ's discourse with his *brethren*, some of his kindred, whether by his mother or his supposed father is not certain; but they were such as pretended to have an interest in him, and therefore interposed to advise him in his conduct. And observe,

1. Their ambition and vain-glory in urging him to make a more public appearance than he did: "*Depart hence*," said they, "*and go into Judea* (*v.* 3), where thou wilt make a better figure than thou canst here."

2. The prudence and humility of our Lord Jesus, which appeared in his answer to the advice his brethren gave him, *vv.* 6–8. Though there were so many base insinuations in it, he answered them mildly.

(1) He shows the difference between himself and them, in two things:—[1] His *time* was *set*, so was not *theirs*: *My time is not yet come, but your time is always ready*. Understand it of the time of his going up to the feast. It was an indifferent thing to them when they went, for they had nothing of moment to do either where they were, to *detain* them *there*, or where they were going, to *hasten* them *thither*; but every minute of Christ's time was precious, and had its own particular business allotted to it. [2] His *life* was *sought*, so was not *theirs*, *v.* 7. They, in *showing themselves* to the world, did not expose themselves. Christ was not only *slighted*, as inconsiderable in the world (*the world knew him not*), but *hated*, as if he had been hurtful to the world; thus ill was

he requited for his love to the world: reigning sin is a rooted antipathy and enmity to Christ.

(2) He dismisses them, with a design to stay behind for some time in Galilee (*v.* 8): *Go you up to this feast, I go not up yet.* [1] He allows their going to the feast, though they were carnal and hypocritical in it. [2] He denies them his company when they went to the feast, because they were carnal and hypocritical.

3. Christ's continuance in Galilee till his *full time* was come, *v.* 9. He, saying these things to them, *abode still in Galilee*; because of this discourse he continued there.

4. His going up to the feast when his time was come. Observe, (1) *When* he went. *When his brethren were gone up.* He would not go up *with them*, lest they should make a noise and disturbance, under pretence of *showing him to the world*. But he went up *after them*. (2) *How* he went—*as if he were hiding himself: not openly, but as it were in secret*, rather for fear of *giving offence* than of *receiving injury*. He went up to the feast, because it was an opportunity of honouring God and doing good; but he went up as it were in secret, because he would not provoke the government.

5. The great expectation that there was of him among the Jews at Jerusalem, *vv.* 11–14. Having formerly come up to the feasts, and signalized himself by the miracles he wrought, he had made himself the subject of much discourse and observation.

(1) They could not but think of him (*v.* 11): *The Jews sought him*

at the feast, and said, Where is he?

(2) The people differed much in their sentiments concerning him (*v.* 12): *There was much murmuring,* or *muttering* rather, *among the people concerning him.* The enmity of the rulers against Christ, and their enquiries after him, caused him to be so much the more talked of and observed among the people. This ground the gospel of Christ has got by the opposition made to it, that it has been the more enquired into, and, by being *everywhere spoken against,* it has come to be every where *spoken of,* and by this means has been spread the further, and the merits of his cause have been the more *searched into.* This murmuring was not *against* Christ, but *concerning* him.

Now what were the sentiments of the people concerning him? [1] Some said, *He is a good man.* This was a truth, but it was far short of being the *whole truth.* He was not only a *good man,* but more than a man, he was the *Son of God.* [2] Others said, *Nay, but he deceiveth the people;* if this had been true, he had been a very bad man. [3] They were frightened by their superiors from speaking much of him (*v.* 13): *No man spoke openly of him, for fear of the Jews.* Either, *First,* They durst not openly speak *well* of him. While any one was at liberty to censure and reproach him, none durst vindicate him. Or, *Secondly,* They durst not speak *at all* of him openly. Because nothing could justly be said *against* him, they would not suffer any thing to be said *of* him.

AT THE FEAST OF TABERNACLES (*vv.* 14–36)

Here is, I. Christ's public preaching in the temple (*v.* 14): He *went up into the temple, and taught,* according to his custom when he was at Jerusalem.

II. His discourse with the Jews; and the conference is reducible to four heads:

1. Concerning *his doctrine.* See here,

(1) How the Jews *admired* it (*v.* 15): *They marvelled,* saying, *How knoweth this man letters, having never learned?* [1] That Christ *had letters,* though he had never *learned* them; was mighty in the scriptures, though he never had any doctor of the law for his tutor. [2] That Christ's having learning, though he had not been taught it, made him truly great and wonderful; the Jews speak of it here with wonder.

(2) What he *asserted* concerning it; three things:—

[1] That his *doctrine* is *divine* (*v.* 16): *My doctrine is not mine, but his that sent me.* They were offended because he undertook to *teach* though he had never learned, in answer to which he tells them that his doctrine was such as was not to be *learned,* for it was not the product of *human thought* and natural powers enlarged and elevated by reading and conversation, but it was a *divine revelation.*

[2] That the most competent judges of the truth and divine authority of Christ's doctrine are those that with a sincere and upright heart desire and endeavour to do the will of God (*v.* 17): *If*

any man be willing to do the will of God, have his will melted into the *will of God, he shall know of the doctrine whether it be of God or whether I speak of myself*.

2. They discourse concerning the *crime* that was laid to his charge for curing the impotent man, and bidding him carry his bed on the sabbath day, for which they had formerly prosecuted him, and which was still the pretence of their enmity to him.

(1) He argues against them by way of *recrimination*, convicting them of far worse practices, *v*. 19. How could they for shame censure him for a breach of the law of Moses, when they themselves were such notorious breakers of it? *Did not Moses give you the law?*

Here the *people* rudely interrupted him in his discourse, and contradicted what he said (*v*. 20): *Thou hast a devil; who goes about to kill thee?* This intimates, [1] The *good opinion* they had of their rulers, who, they think, would never attempt so atrocious a thing as to kill him; no, such a veneration they had for their elders and chief priests that they would swear for them they would do no harm to an innocent man. [2] The *ill opinion* they had of our Lord Jesus: "*Thou hast a devil*, thou art possessed with a lying spirit, and art a *bad man* for saying so"; so some: or rather, "Thou art melancholy, and art a *weak man*; thou frightenest thyself with causeless fears, as hypochondriacal people are apt to do." Let us not think it strange if the best of men are put under the worst of characters. To this vile

calumny our Saviour returns no direct answer, but seems as if he took no notice of it.

(2) He argues by way of appeal and vindication.

[1] He appeals to *their own sentiments* of this miracle: "*I have done one work, and you all marvel*, *v*. 21. You cannot choose but marvel at it as truly great, and altogether supernatural; you must all own it to be marvellous," Or, "Though I have done but *one work* that you have any colour to find fault with, yet you marvel, you are offended and displeased as if I had been guilty of some heinous or enormous crime."

[2] He appeals to their own practice in other instances: "*I have done one work* on the sabbath, and it was done easily, with a word's speaking, and you all marvel, you make a mighty strange thing of it, that a religious man should dare do such a thing, whereas you yourselves *many a time* do that which is a much more servile work on the sabbath day, in the case of circumcision; if it be lawful for you, nay, and your duty, to circumcise a child on the sabbath day, when it happens to be the eighth day, as no doubt it is, much more was it lawful and good for me to heal a diseased man on that day."

He concludes this argument with that rule (*v*. 24): *Judge not according to the appearance, but judge righteous judgment*. This may be applied, either, *First*, In particular, to this work which they quarrelled with as a violation of the law. Or, *Secondly*, In general, to Christ's person and preaching, which they were offended at and prejudiced against. Those things that are false, and designed to impose upon men, commonly appear best when they are judged of *according to the outward appearance*, they appear most plausible *prima facie — at the first glance*. It was this that gained the Pharisees such an interest and reputation, that they *appeared right* unto men (Matt. xxiii. 27, 28), and men judged of them by that appearance, and so were sadly mistaken in them. "But," saith Christ, "be not too confident that all are real saints who are seeming ones." With reference to himself, his *outward appearance* was far short of his real dignity and excellency, for he took upon him the *form of a servant* (Phil. ii. 7), was in the *likeness of sinful flesh* (Rom. viii. 3), had *no form nor comeliness*, Isa. liii. 2. So that those who undertook to judge whether he was the Son of God or no by his *outward appearance* were not likely to *judge righteous judgment*.

3. Christ's discourses with them here concerning *himself*, whence he came, and whither he was going, *vv*. 25–36.

(1) *Whence he came*, *vv*. 25–31. In the account of this observe,

[1] The objection concerning this stated by some of the inhabitants of Jerusalem, who seem to have been of all others most prejudiced against him, *v*. 25. These people of Jerusalem showed their ill-will to Christ,

First, By their reflecting on the rulers, because they let him alone: *Is not this he whom they seek to kill?*

Secondly, By their exception against his being the Christ, in which appeared more malice than matter, *v*. 27. "If the rulers think him to be the Christ, we neither can nor will believe him to be so, for we have this argument against it, that *we know this man, whence he is; but when Christ comes no man knows whence he is.*"

[2] Christ's answer to this objection, *vv*. 28, 29.

First, He spoke freely and boldly, he *cried in the temple, as he taught*, he spoke this louder than the rest of his discourse, 1. To express his earnestness, being *grieved for the hardness of their hearts*. 2. The priests and those that were prejudiced against him, did not come near enough to hear his preaching, and therefore he must speak louder than ordinary what he will have them to hear.

Secondly, His answer to their cavil is, 1. By way of *concession*, granting that they did or might know his origin as to the flesh: "*You both know me, and you know whence I am*. You know I am of your own nation, and one of yourselves." They knew *whence* he came perhaps, and *where* he had his birth, but he will tell them what they knew not, *from whom* he came. (1) That he did not *come of himself*. (2) That he was sent of his Father; this is twice mentioned: *He hath sent me*. (3) That he was *from his Father — I am from him*; not only sent from him as a servant from his master, but from him by eternal generation, as a son from his father, by essential emanation, as the beams from the sun. (4) *That the Father* _who sent him is true_; he had promised to give the Messiah, and, though the Jews had forfeited the promise, yet he that made the promise is _true_, and has performed it. (5) That these unbelieving Jews did _not know the Father: He that sent me, whom you know not._ There is much ignorance of God even with many that have a _form of knowledge_; and the true reason why people reject Christ is because they do not _know God._ (6) Our Lord Jesus was intimately acquainted with the Father that _sent him: but I know him._ He knew him so well that he was not at all _in doubt_ concerning his mission from him, but perfectly _assured_ of it; nor at all _in the dark_ concerning the work he had to do, but perfectly _apprized_ of it, Matt. xi. 27.

[3] The provocation which this gave to his enemies, who hated him because he _told them the truth_, v. 30. _They sought therefore to take him_, to lay violent hands on him, not only to do him a mischief, but some way or other to be the death of him; but by the restraint of an invisible power it was prevented; nobody touched him, _because his hour was not yet come_; this was not their reason why they did it not, but God's reason why he hindered them from doing it.

[4] The good effect which Christ's discourse had, notwithstanding this, upon some of his hearers (_v._ 31). _Many of the people believed on him._

(2) _Whither he was going_, vv. 32–36. Here observe,

[1] The design of the Pharisees and chief priests against him, _v._ 32.

[2] The discourse of our Lord Jesus hereupon (_vv._ 33, 34): _Yet a little while I am with you, and then I go to him that sent me; you shall seek me, and shall not find me; and where I am, thither you cannot come._ These words, like the pillar of cloud and fire, have a _bright_ side and a _dark_ side.

First, They have a _bright side_ towards our Lord Jesus himself, and speak abundance of comfort to him and all his faithful followers that are exposed to difficulties and dangers for his sake. Three things Christ here comforted himself with:—1. That he had but _a little time_ to continue here in this troublesome world. 2. That when he should quit this troublesome world, he should _go to him that sent him; I go._ Not, "I am driven away by force," but, "I voluntarily _go_; having finished my embassy, I return to him on whose errand I came. When I have done my work with you, then, and not till then, I go to him _that sent me_, and will _receive me_, will prefer me, as ambassadors are preferred when they return." 3. That, though they persecuted him here, wherever he went, yet none of their persecutions could follow him to heaven: _You shall seek me, and shall not find me._

Secondly, These words have a _black and dark side_ towards those wicked Jews that hated and persecuted Christ. They now longed to be rid of him, _Away with him from the earth_; but let them know, 1. That according to their choice so shall their doom be. They were industrious to *drive him* from them, and their sin shall be their punishment; he will not trouble them long, yet a little while and he will *depart* from them. 2. That they would certainly repent their choice when it was too late. (1) They should in vain seek the presence of the Messiah. Those who rejected the true Messiah when he did come were justly abandoned to a miserable and endless expectation of one that should never come. (2) They should in vain expect a place in heaven: *Where I am*, and where all believers shall be with me, *thither ye cannot come*. Not only because they are *excluded* by the just and irreversible sentence of the judge, and the sword of the angel at every gate of the new Jerusalem, to keep *the way of the tree of life* against those who have *no right to enter*, but because they are disabled by their own iniquity and infidelity: *You cannot come*, because you *will not*."

[3] Their descant upon this discourse (*vv.* 35, 36): *They said among themselves, Whither will he go?* See here, *First*, Their wilful ignorance and blindness. *Secondly*, Their daring contempt of Christ's threatenings. *Thirdly*, Their inveterate malice and rage against Christ. All they dreaded in his *departure* was that he would be out of the reach of their power: "*Whither will he go, that we shall not find him?*" *Fourthly*, Their proud disdain of the Gentiles, whom they here call the *dispersed of the Gentiles*; meaning either the Jews that were *scattered* abroad among the Greeks (James i. 1; 1 Pet. i. 1); will he go and make an interest among those silly people? or, the Gentiles *dispersed* over the world, in distinction from the Jews, who were *incorporated* into one church and nation; will he make his court to them? *Fifthly*, Their jealousy of the least intimation of favour to the Gentiles: "Will he go and *teach the Gentiles?*" They now made a *jest* of his going *to teach the Gentiles*; but not long after he did it *in good earnest* by his apostles and ministers, and gathered those *dispersed* people, sorely to the grief of the Jews, Rom. x. 19.

THE LAST DAY OF THE FEAST (*vv.* 37–44)

In these verses we have,

I. Christ's discourse, with the explication of it, *vv.* 37–39. It is probable that these are only short hints of what he enlarged upon, but they have in them the substance of the whole gospel; here is a *gospel invitation* to *come to Christ*, and a *gospel promise* of comfort and happiness in him. Now observe,

1. *When* he gave this invitation: *On the last day* of the feast of tabernacles, *that great day*. The *eighth day*, which concluded that solemnity, was to be a *holy convocation*, Lev. xxiii. 36. Now on this day Christ published this gospel-call, because, (1) Much people were gathered together, and, if the invitation were given to *many*, it might be hoped that *some* would accept of it, Prov. i. 20. (2) The people were now returning to their homes, and he would give

them this to carry away with them as his parting word. Christ made this offer *on the last day of the feast*, [1] To those who had turned a deaf ear to his preaching on the foregoing days of this sacred week; he will try them once more, and, if they will yet hear his voice, they shall live. [2] To those who perhaps might never have such another offer made them.

2. *How* he gave this invitation: *Jesus stood and cried*, which denotes, (1) His great earnestness and importunity. (2) His desire that all might take notice, and take hold of this invitation.

3. The invitation itself is very general: *If any man* thirst, whoever he be, he is invited to Christ be he high or low, rich or poor, young or old, bond or free, Jew or Gentile. It is also very *gracious*: "*If any man thirst, let him come to me and drink*. If any man desires to be truly and eternally happy, let him apply himself to me, and be ruled by me, and I will undertake to make him so."

(1) The persons invited are such as *thirst*, which may be understood, either, [1] Of their need; either as to their *outward* condition (if any man be destitute of the comforts of this life, or fatigued with the crosses of it, let his poverty and afflictions draw him to Christ for that peace which the world can neither give nor take away), or as to their *inward* state: "If any man want spiritual blessings, he may be supplied by me." Or, [2] Of the *inclination* of their souls and their desires towards a spiritual happiness. If any man hunger and thirst after righteousness, that is, truly desire the good will of God towards him, and the good work of God in him.

(2) The invitation itself: *Let him come to me*. Let him not go to the ceremonial law, nor let him go to the heathen philosophy, which does but beguile men, lead them into a wood, and leave them there; but let him *go to Christ*, admit his doctrine, submit to his discipline, believe in him; come to him as the fountain of living waters, the giver of all comfort.

(3) The satisfaction promised: Let him come *and drink*, he shall have what he comes for, and abundantly more, shall have that which will not only *refresh*, but *replenish*, a soul that desires to be happy."

4. A gracious promise annexed to this gracious call (*v.* 38): *He that believeth on me, out of his belly shall flow*—(1) See here what it is to come to Christ: It is *to believe on him, as the scripture hath said*; it is to receive and entertain him as he is offered to us in the gospel. (2) See how thirsty souls, that come to Christ, shall be made *to drink*. Israel, that believed Moses, drank of the *rock that followed them*, the streams followed; but believers drink of a rock *in them, Christ in them*; he is in them a *well of living water, ch.* iv. 14. Provision is made not only for their *present* satisfaction, but for their *continual perpetual* comfort. Here is, [1] *Living water, running* water, which the Hebrew language calls *living*, because still in motion. [2] *Rivers* of living water, denoting both plenty and

536

constancy. [3] These flow out *of his belly*, that is, out of his heart or soul, which is the subject of the Spirit's working and the seat of his government. Believers shall have the comfort, not of a vessel of water fetched from a pool, but of a river flowing from themselves. The joy of the law, and the pouring out of the water, which signified this, are not to be compared with the joy of the gospel in the wells of salvation.

5. Here is the evangelist's exposition of this promise (*v.* 39): *This spoke he of the Spirit*: not of any outward advantages accruing to believers (as perhaps some misunderstood him), but of the gifts, graces, and comforts of the Spirit. See how scripture is the best interpreter of scripture. Observe,

(1) It is promised to *all that believe* on Christ that they shall *receive the Holy Ghost*. Some received his miraculous gifts (Mark xvi. 17, 18); all receive his sanctifying graces.

(2) The Spirit dwelling and working in believers is as a *fountain of living* running *water*, out of which plentiful streams flow, cooling and cleansing as water, mollifying and moistening as water, making them fruitful, and others joyful; see *ch.* iii. 5. When the apostles spoke so *fluently* of the things of God, as the Spirit gave them utterance (Acts ii. 4), and afterwards preached and wrote the gospel of Christ with such a *flood* of divine eloquence, then this was fulfilled, *Out of his belly shall flow rivers*.

(3) This plentiful effusion of the Spirit was yet the matter of a promise; for *the Holy Ghost was not yet given, because Jesus was not yet glorified*. See here, [1] That *Jesus was not yet glorified*. [2] That *the Holy Ghost was not yet given*. The Spirit of God was from eternity, for in the beginning he *moved upon the face of the waters*. He was in the Old-Testament prophets and saints, and Zacharias and Elisabeth were both *filled with the Holy Ghost*. This therefore must be understood of that eminent, plentiful, and general effusion of the Spirit which was promised, Joel ii. 28, and accomplished, Acts ii. 1, &c. *The Holy Ghost was not yet given* in that visible manner that was intended. [3] That the reason why *the Holy Ghost was not given* was because *Jesus was not yet glorified*. *First*, The death of Christ is sometimes called his glorification (*ch.* xiii. 31); for in his cross he conquered and triumphed. Now the gift of the Holy Ghost was purchased by the blood of Christ: this was the *valuable consideration* upon which the *grant* was grounded, and therefore till this *price* was *paid* (though many other gifts were bestowed upon its being *secured* to be paid) the Holy Ghost was not given. *Secondly*, There was not so much need of the Spirit, while Christ himself was here upon earth, as there was when he was gone, to supply the want of him. *Thirdly*, The giving of the Holy Ghost was to be both an *answer* to Christ's *intercession* (*ch.* xiv. 16), and an *act* of his *dominion*; and therefore till he is glorified, and enters upon both these, the Holy Ghost is not given. *Fourthly*, The

conversion of the Gentiles was the glorifying of Jesus.

II. The consequence of this discourse: *There was a division among the people because of him*, v. 43. Observe what the debate was:—

1. Some were *taken with him*, and well affected to him. (1) Some of them said, *Of a truth this is the prophet*, that prophet whom Moses spoke of to the fathers, who should be *like unto him*. (2) Others went further, and said, *This is the Christ* (v. 41), not the *prophet* of the Messiah, but the Messiah himself.

2. Others were *prejudiced against him*. No sooner was this great truth started, that *Jesus is the Christ*, than immediately it was contradicted and argued against: and this one thing, that his rise and origin were (as they took it for granted) out of Galilee, was thought enough to answer all the arguments for his being the Christ. For, *shall Christ come out of Galilee?* Has not *the scripture said that Christ comes of the seed of David?* See here, (1) A laudable knowledge of the scripture. They were so far in the right, that the Messiah was to be a *rod out of the stem of Jesse* (Isa. xi. 1), that out of Bethlehem should *arise the Governor*, Mic. v. 2. (2) A culpable ignorance of our Lord Jesus. They speak of it as certain and past dispute that *Jesus was of Galilee*, whereas by enquiring of himself, or his mother, or his disciples, or by consulting the genealogies of the family of David, or the register at Bethlehem, they might have known that he was the Son of David, and a native of Bethlehem; but *this they willingly are ignorant of*.

3. Others were *enraged against him*, and they *would have taken him*, v. 44. Though what he said was most sweet and gracious, yet they were exasperated against him for it. They *would have taken him*; but no man *laid hands on him*, being restrained by an invisible power, because his hour was not come.

A PROPHET FROM GALILEE?
(vv. 45–53)

The chief priests and Pharisees are here in a close cabal, contriving how to suppress Christ. Now here we are told,

I. What passed between them and their own officers, who returned without him. Observe,

1. The reproof they gave the officers for not executing the warrant they gave them: *Why have you not brought him?*

2. The reason which the officers gave for the non-execution of their warrant: *Never man spoke like this man*, v. 46. Now, (1) This was a very great truth, that *never any man spoke with* that wisdom, and power, and grace, that convincing clearness, and that charming sweetness, wherewith Christ spoke; none of the prophets, no, not Moses himself. (2) The very officers that were sent to take him were taken with him, and acknowledged this. (3) They said this to their lords and masters, who could not endure to hear anything that tended to the honour of Christ and yet could not avoid hearing this.

3. The Pharisees endeavour to secure their officers to their interest, and to beget in them prejudices against Christ, to whom they saw them begin to be well affected. They suggest two things:—

(1) That if they embrace the gospel of Christ they will *deceive themselves* (v. 47): *Are you also deceived?*

(2) That they will *disparage themselves*. Most men, even in their religion, are willing to be governed by the example of those of the *first rank*; these officers therefore, whose preferments, such as they were, gave them a *sense of honour*, are desired to consider,

[1] That, if they become disciples of Christ, they go contrary to those who were persons of quality and reputation.

[2] That they will link themselves with the despicable vulgar sort of people (v. 43): *But this people, who know not the law, are cursed*, meaning especially those that were well-affected to the doctrine of Christ.

II. What passed between them and Nicodemus, a member of their own body, vv. 50, &c. Observe,

1. The just and rational objection which Nicodemus made against their proceedings. Observe,

(1) Who it was that appeared against them; it was Nicodemus, *he that came to Jesus by night*, *being one of them*, v. 50. Observe, concerning him, [1] That, though he had been with Jesus, and taken him for his teacher, yet he retained his place in the council, and his vote among them. Some impute this to his *weakness* and cowardice,

and think it was his fault that he did not quit his place, but Christ had never said to him, *Follow me*, else he would have done as others that left all to follow him; therefore it seems rather to have been his *wisdom* not immediately to throw up his place, because there he might have opportunity of serving Christ and his interest, and stemming the tide of the Jewish rage, which perhaps he did more than we are aware of. [2] That though at first he came to Jesus *by night*, for fear of being known, and still continued in his post; yet, when there was occasion, he boldly appeared in defence of Christ, and opposed the whole council that were set against him.

(2) What he alleged against their proceedings (v. 51). Observe, [1] He prudently argues from the principles of their own law, and an incontestable rule of justice, that no man is to be condemned *unheard*. [2] Whereas they had reproached the people, especially the followers of Christ, as *ignorant of the law*, he here tacitly retorts the charge upon themselves, and shows how ignorant they were of some of the first principles of the law, so unfit were they to give law to others.

Now we may suppose that the motion Nicodemus made in the house upon this was, That Jesus should be desired to come and give them an account of himself and his doctrine, and that they should favour him with an impartial and unprejudiced hearing; but, though none of them could gainsay his maxim, none of them would second his motion.

2. What was said to this objection. Here is no direct reply given to it; but, when they could not resist the force of his argument, they fell foul upon him, and what was to seek in *reason* they made up in railing and reproach. As to what they said to Nicodemus, we may observe,

(1) How *false* the grounds of their argument were, for, [1] They supposed that Christ was of Galilee, and this was false, and if they would have been at the pains of an impartial enquiry they would have found it so. [2] They suppose that because most of his disciples were Galileans they were all such, whereas he had abundance of disciples in Judea. [3] They suppose that out of Galilee no prophet had *risen*, and for this appeal to Nicodemus's search; yet this was false too: Jonah was of Gath-hepher, Nahum an Elkoshite, both of Galilee.

(2) How *absurd* their arguings were upon these grounds, such as were a shame to *rulers* and *Pharisees*. Supposing no prophet had risen out of Galilee, yet it is not impossible that any should arise thence.

3. The hasty adjournment of the court hereupon. They broke up the assembly in confusion, and with precipitation, and *every man went to his own house*.

CHAPTER EIGHT

THE WOMAN TAKEN IN ADULTERY (vv. 1–11)

His dealing with those that brought to him the *woman taken in adultery*, *tempting* him. Observe here,

1. The case proposed to him by the scribes and Pharisees, who herein contrived to pick a quarrel with him, and bring him into a snare, *vv.* 3–6.

(1) They set the prisoner to the bar (*v.* 3): they brought him *a woman taken in adultery*. Those that were *taken in adultery* were by the Jewish law to be put to death, which the Roman powers allowed them the execution of, and therefore she was brought before the ecclesiastical court. The scribes and Pharisees bring her to Christ, and set her in the midst of the assembly, as if they would leave her wholly to the judgment of Christ, he having *sat down*, as a judge upon the bench.

(2) They prefer an indictment against her: *Master, this woman was taken in adultery, v.* 4. Here they call him *Master* whom but the day before they had called a *deceiver*, in hopes with their flatteries to have ensnared him, as those, Luke xx. 20. But, though men may be imposed upon with compliments, he that searches the heart cannot.

[1] The crime for which the prisoner stands indicted is no less than adultery, which even in the patriarchal age, before the law of Moses, was looked upon as *an iniquity to be punished by the judges*, Job xxxi. 9–11; Gen. xxxviii. 24. The Pharisees, by their vigorous prosecution of this offender, seemed to have a great zeal against the sin, when it appeared afterwards that they themselves were not free from it; nay, they were within *full of all uncleanness*, Matt. xxiii. 27, 28.

Note, It is common for those that are indulgent to their own sin to be severe against the sins of others.

[2] The proof of the crime was from the notorious evidence of the fact, an incontestable proof; she was *taken in the act*, so that there was no room left to plead not guilty.

(3) They produce the statute in this case made and provided, and upon which she was indicted, *v.* 5. Moses in the law commanded *that such should be stoned.* Moses commanded that they should be *put to death* (Lev. xx. 10; Deut. xxii. 22), but not that they should be stoned, unless the adulteress was espoused, not married, or was a priest's daughter, Deut. xxii. 21.

(4) They pray his judgment in the case. But *this they said tempting him, that they might have to accuse him, v.* 6. [1] If he should confirm the sentence of the law, and let it take its course, they would censure him as inconsistent with himself (he having received publicans and harlots) and with the character of the Messiah, who should be meek, and have salvation, and proclaim a year of release. But, [2] If he should acquit her, and give his opinion that the sentence should not be executed (as they expected he would), they would represent him, *First,* As an enemy to the law of Moses, and *secondly,* As a friend to sinners, and, consequently, a favourer of sin.

2. The method he took to resolve this case, and so to break this snare.

(1) He seemed to slight it, and turned a deaf ear to it: He *stooped down, and wrote on the ground.* It is impossible to tell, and therefore needless to ask, what he wrote; but this is the only mention made in the gospels of Christ's writing.

(2) When they importunately, or rather impertinently, pressed him for an answer, he turned the conviction of the prisoner upon the prosecutors, *v.* 7.

[1] They *continued asking him,* and his seeming not to take notice of them made them the more vehement.

[2] At last he put them all to shame and silence with one word: *He lifted up himself,* and *said unto them, He that is without sin among you, let him first cast a stone at her.*

First, Here Christ avoided the snare which they had laid for him, and effectually saved his own reputation. He neither reflected upon the law nor excused the prisoner's guilt, nor did he on the other hand encourage the prosecution or countenance their heat.

Secondly, In the net which they spread is their own foot taken. They came with design to accuse him, but they were forced to accuse themselves. Christ owns it was fit the prisoner should be prosecuted, but appeals to their consciences whether they were fit to be the prosecutors.

a. He here refers to that rule which the law of Moses prescribed in the execution of criminals, that the *hand of the witnesses must be first upon them* (Deut. xvii. 7), as in the stoning of Stephen, Acts vii. 58. The scribes and Pharisees were the witnesses against this woman. Now Christ puts it to them whether, according to their own law, they would dare to be the executioners.

b. He builds upon an uncontested maxim in morality, that it is very absurd for men to be zealous in punishing the offences of others, while they are every whit as guilty themselves. "If there be any of you who is *without sin*, without sin of this nature, that has not some time or other been guilty of fornication or adultery, let him cast the first stone at her."

[3] Having given them this startling word, he left them to consider of it, *and again stooped down, and wrote on the ground, v.* 8. As when they made their address he seemed to slight their question, so now that he had given them an answer he slighted their resentment of it, not caring what they said to it; nay, they needed not to make any reply; the matter was lodged in their own breasts, let them make the best of it there.

[4] The scribes and Pharisees were so strangely thunderstruck with the words of Christ that they let fall their persecution of Christ, whom they durst no further tempt, and their prosecution of the woman, whom they durst no longer accuse (*v.* 9): *They went out one by one.*

What he said frightened them by sending them to their own consciences; he had *shown them to themselves*, and they were afraid if they should stay till he lifted up himself again his next word would show them to the world, and shame them before men, and therefore they thought it best to withdraw. The order of their departure is taken notice of,

beginning at the eldest, either because they were most guilty, or first aware of the danger they were in of being put to the blush; and if the eldest quit the field, and retreat ingloriously, no marvel if the younger follow them.

[5] When the *self-conceited* prosecutors quitted the field, and *fled for the same*, the *self-condemned* prisoner stood her ground, with a resolution to abide by the judgment of our Lord Jesus.

[6] Here is the conclusion of the trial, and the issue it was brought to: *Jesus lifted up himself, and he saw none but the woman, vv.* 10, 11. The woman, it is likely, stood trembling at the bar, as one doubtful of the issue. Christ was *without sin*, and might cast the first stone; but though none more severe than he against sin, for he is infinitely just and holy, none more compassionate than he to sinners, for he is infinitely gracious and merciful, and this poor malefactor finds him so, now that she *stands upon her deliverance*.

First, The prosecutors are called: *Where are those thine accusers? Hath no man condemned thee?*

Secondly, They do not appear when the question is asked: *Hath no man condemned thee?* She said, *No man, Lord.* She speaks respectfully to Christ, calls him *Lord*, but is silent concerning her prosecutors, says nothing in answer to that question which concerned them, *Where are those thine accusers?* She does not triumph in their retreat nor insult over them as witnesses against themselves, not against her.

Thirdly, The prisoner is therefore

542

discharged: *Neither do I condemn thee; go, and sin no more.* Consider this,

a. As her discharge from the temporal punishment: "If they do not condemn thee to be *stoned to death*, neither *do I*."

b. As her discharge from the eternal punishment. For Christ to say, *I do not condemn thee* is, in effect, to say, *I do forgive thee*; and the *Son of man had power on earth to forgive sins*, and could upon good grounds give this absolution. Christ will not condemn those who, though they have sinned, will *go and sin no more*, Ps. lxxxv. 8; Isa. lv. 7. He will not take the advantage he has against us for our former rebellions, if we will but lay down our arms and return to our allegiance.

CHRIST'S CONTRADICTORS
(*vv.* 12–20)

The rest of the chapter is taken up with debates between Christ and contradicting sinners, who cavilled at the most gracious words that proceeded out of his mouth. In these verses we have,

I. A great doctrine laid down, with the application of it.

1. The doctrine is, *That Christ is the light of the world* (*v.* 12). God is light, and Christ is *the image of the invisible God*; God of gods, Light of lights. He was expected to be a *light to enlighten the Gentiles* (Luke ii. 32), and so the *light of the world*, and not of the Jewish church only. The visible light of the world is the sun, and Christ is the *Sun of righteousness*.

2. The inference from this doctrine is, *He that followeth me*, as a traveller follows the light in a dark night, *shall not walk in darkness*, but *shall have the light of life*. It is the happiness of those who follow Christ that they *shall not walk in darkness*. They shall not be left destitute of those instructions in the way of truth which are necessary to keep them from destroying error, and those directions in the way of duty which are necessary to keep them from damning sin. They shall have the *light of life*, that knowledge and enjoyment of God which will be to them the light of spiritual life in this world and of everlasting life in the other world, where there will be no death nor darkness.

II. The objection which the Pharisees made against this doctrine, and it was very trifling and frivolous: *Thou bearest record of thyself; thy record is not true*, *v.* 13. In this objection they went upon the suspicion which we commonly have of men's self-commendation, which is concluded to be the native language of self-love, such as we are all ready to condemn in others, but few are willing to own in themselves. But in this case the objection was very unjust, for, 1. They made that his crime, and a diminution to the credibility of his doctrine, which in the case of one who introduced a divine revelation was necessary and unavoidable. 2. They overlooked the testimony of all the other witnesses, which corroborated the testimony he bore of himself.

III. Christ's reply to this objection, *v.* 14. He is the light of the world, and it is the property of light to be self-evidencing. First principles prove themselves. He urges three things to prove that his testimony, though of himself, was true and cogent.

1. That he was conscious to himself of his own authority, and abundantly satisfied in himself concerning it: *I know whence I came, and whither I go*.

2. That they are very incompetent judges of him, and of his doctrine, and not to be regarded. (1) Because they were *ignorant*, willingly and resolvedly *ignorant*: *You cannot tell whence I came, and whither I go*. (2) Because they were *partial* (*v*. 15): *You judge after the flesh*. When fleshly wisdom gives the rule of judgment, and outward appearances only are given in evidence, and the case decided according to them, then men *judge after the flesh*. (3) Because they were *unjust* and *unfair* towards him, intimated in this: "*I judge no man*; I neither make nor meddle with your political affairs, nor does my doctrine or practice at all intrench upon, or interfere with, your civil rights or secular powers." He thus *judged no man*. Now, if he did not *war after the flesh*, it was very unreasonable for them to *judge him after the flesh*.

3. That his testimony of himself was sufficiently supported and corroborated by the testimony of his Father *with him and for him* (*v*. 16): *And yet, if I judge, my judgment is true*. He did in his doctrine judge (*ch*. ix. 39), though not *politically*. Consider him then,

(1) As a judge, and his own judgment was valid. Now that

which makes his judgment un-exceptionable is, [1] His Father's concurrence with him: *I am not alone, but I and the Father*. [2] His Father's commission to him: "It is the Father that *sent me*."

(2) Look upon him as *a witness*, and now he appeared no otherwise (having not as yet taken the throne of judgment), and as such his testimony was true and un-exceptionable; this he shows, *vv*. 17, 18, where,

[1] He quotes a maxim of the Jewish law, *v*. 17. That *the testimony of two men is true*.

[2] He applies this to the case in hand (*v*. 18): *I am one that bear witness of myself, and the Father that sent me bears witness of me*. Behold two witnesses! Though in human courts, where two witnesses are required, the criminal or candidate is not admitted to be a witness for himself; yet in a matter purely divine, which can be proved only by a divine testimony, and God himself must be the witness, if the formality of two or three witnesses be insisted on, there can be no other than the eternal Father, the eternal Son of the Father, and the eternal Spirit. Now this proves not only that the Father and the Son are two distinct persons (for their respective testimonies are here spoken of as the testimonies of two several persons), but that these two are one, not only one in their testimony, but equal in power and glory, and therefore the same in substance.

This was the sum of the first conference between Christ and these carnal Jews, in the conclusion of which we are told how their tongues were let loose, and their hands tied.

MORE CONTRADICTIONS
(vv. 21–30)

Christ here gives fair warning to the careless unbelieving Jews to consider what would be the consequence of their infidelity, that they might prevent it before it was too late; for he spoke words of terror as well as words of grace. Observe here,

I. The wrath threatened (*v.* 21): *Jesus said again unto them* that which might be likely to do them good. Four things are here threatened against the Jews.

1. Christ's departure from them. They said to him, *Depart from us, we desire not the knowledge of thy ways*; and he takes them at their word; but woe to those from whom Christ departs.

2. Their enmity to the true Messiah, and their fruitless and infatuated enquiries after another Messiah when he was gone away, which were both their sin and their punishment.

3. Their final impenitency: *You shall die in your sins*.

4. Their eternal separation from Christ and all happiness in him: *Whither I go you cannot come*. When Christ left the world, he went to a state of perfect happiness; he went to paradise. Thither he took the penitent thief with him, that did not die in his sins; but the impenitent not only *shall not* come to him, but they *cannot*; it is morally impossible, for heaven would not be heaven to those that

die unsanctified and unmeet for it.

II. The jest they made of this threatening. Instead of trembling at this word, they bantered it, and turned it into ridicule (*v.* 22): *Will he kill himself?*

III. The confirmation of what he had said.

1. *You are from beneath, I am from above; you are of this world, I am not of this world*.

2. He had said, *You shall die in your sins*, and here he stands to it: "Therefore I said, You shall die in your sins, because *you are from beneath*"; and he gives this further reason for it, *If you believe not that I am he, you shall die in your sins*, *v.* 24. See here, (1) What we are required to believe: *that I am he—that I am*, which is one of God's names, Exod. iii. 14. (2) How necessary it is that we believe this. If we have not this faith, *we shall die in our sins*; for the matter is so settled that without this faith we cannot be saved from the power of sin while we live, and therefore shall certainly continue in it to the last. Unbelief is the damning sin; it is a sin against the remedy.

IV. Here is a further discourse concerning *himself*, occasioned by his requiring faith in himself as the condition of salvation, *vv.* 25–29. Observe,

1. The question which the Jews put to him (*v.* 25): *Who art thou?*

2. His answer to this question, wherein he directs them three ways for information:—

(1) He refers them to *what he had said* all along: "Do you ask who I am? *Even the same that I said unto you from the beginning*."

(2) He refers them to his Father's

judgment, and the instructions he had from him (*v.* 26). Here,

[1] He suppresses his accusation of them. He had *many things* to charge them with, and many evidences to produce against them; but for the present he had said enough.

[2] He enters his appeal against them to his Father: *He that sent me.* Here two things comfort him:— *First*, That he had been *true to his Father*, and to the trust reposed in him. *Secondly*, That his Father would be *true to him*; true to the promise that he would *make his mouth like a sharp sword*; true to his purpose concerning him, which was a *decree* (Ps. ii. 7); true to the threatenings of his wrath against those that should reject him.

[3] He refers them to *their own convictions* hereafter, *vv.* 28, 29. He finds they will not understand him, and therefore adjourns the trial till further evidence should come in; they that *will not see shall see*, Isa. xxvi. 11. Now observe here,

a. What they should ere long be *convinced*, *of*: "*You shall know that I am he*, that Jesus is the true Messiah." Two things they should be convinced of, in order to this:— *First*, That he did nothing *of himself*, not of himself as man, of himself alone, of himself without the Father, with whom he was *one*. *Secondly*, That as *his Father taught him*, so he *spoke these things*, that he was not *self-taught*, but *taught of God*.

b. When they should be convinced of this: *When you have lifted up the Son of man*, lifted him up upon the cross, as the

brazen serpent upon the pole (*ch.* iii. 14), as the sacrifices under the law (for Christ is the great sacrifice), which, when they were offered, were said to be *elevated*, or *lifted up*. Or the expression denotes that his death was his exaltation.

c. What supported our Lord Jesus in the mean time (*v.* 29): *He that sent me is with me*, in my whole undertaking; *for the Father* (the fountain and first spring of this affair, from whom as its great cause and author it is derived) *hath not left me alone*, to manage it myself, hath not deserted the business nor me in the prosecution of it, for *do I always those things that please him.*

V. Here is the good effect which this discourse of Christ's had upon some of his hearers (*v.* 30): *As he spoke these words many believed on him.* Note, 1. Though multitudes perish in their unbelief, yet there is a remnant according to the election of grace, who *believe to the saving of the soul.* 2. The words of Christ, and particularly his *threatening* words, are made effectual by the grace of God to bring in poor souls to believe in him.

TRUE FREEDOM (*vv.* 31–37)

We have in these verses,

I. A comfortable doctrine laid down concerning the *spiritual liberty* of Christ's disciples, intended for the encouragement of *those* Jews *that believed*. See here,

1. How graciously the Lord Jesus looks to those that *tremble at his word*, and are ready to receive it; he has something to say

to those who have hearing ears, and will not pass by those who set themselves in his way, without speaking to them.

2. How carefully he cherishes the beginnings of grace, and meets those that are coming towards him. In what he said to them, we have two things, which he saith to all that should at any time believe:—

(1) The character of a true disciple of Christ: *If you continue in my word, then are you my disciples indeed.* Those only that *continue in Christ's word* shall be accepted as his *disciples indeed,* that adhere to his word in every instance without partiality, and abide by it to the end without apostasy.

(2) The privilege of a true disciple of Christ. Here are two precious promises made to those who thus approve themselves disciples indeed, *v.* 32.

[1] "*You shall know the truth,* shall know all that truth which it is needful and profitable for you to know, and shall be more confirmed in the belief of it, shall know the certainty of it."

[2] *The truth shall make you free;* that is, *First,* The truth which Christ teaches tends to make men free, Isa. lxi. 1. *Secondly,* The knowing, entertaining, and believing, of this truth does actually *make us free,* free from prejudices, mistakes, and false notions, than which nothing more *enslaves* and *entangles* the soul, free from the dominion of lust and passion; and restores the soul to the government of itself, by reducing it into obedience to its Creator.

II. The offence which the carnal Jews took at this doctrine, and their objection against it. See here,

1. What it was that they were grieved at: it was an *innuendo* in those words, *You shall be made free,* as if the Jewish church and nation were in some sort of bondage, which reflected on the Jews in general, and as if all that did not believe in Christ continued in that bondage, which reflected on the Pharisees in particular.

2. What it was that they alleged against it; whereas Christ intimated that they needed to be made free, they urge, (1) "We are Abraham's seed." Abraham was in covenant with God, and his children by his right, Rom. xi. 28. Now that covenant, no doubt, was a free charter, and invested them with privileges not consistent with a state of slavery, Rom. ix. 4. And therefore they thought they had no occasion with so *great a sum* as they reckoned faith in Christ to be *to obtain this freedom,* when they were thus free-born. (2) *We were never in bondage to any man.* Now observe, [1] How false this allegation was. I wonder how they could have the assurance to say a thing in the face of a congregation which was so notoriously *untrue.* Were not the seed of Abraham in bondage to the Egyptians? Were they not often in bondage to the neighbouring nations in the time of the judges? Were they not seventy years captives in Babylon? Nay, were they not at this time tributaries to the Romans? [2] How foolish the application was. Christ had spoken of a liberty wherewith the *truth* would make them free,

which must be meant of a *spiritual* liberty; and yet they plead against the offer of *spiritual* liberty that they were never in *corporal* bondage, as if, because they were never in bondage to any *man*, they were never in bondage to any *lust*.

III. Our Saviour's vindication of his doctrine from these objections, and the further explication of it, *vv.* 34–37, where he does these four things:—

1. He shows that, notwithstanding their civil liberties and their visible church-membership, yet it was possible that they might be in a state of bondage (*v.* 34): *Whosoever commits sin*, though he be of Abraham's seed, and was never in bondage to any man, is the servant of sin.

2. He shows them that, being in a state of bondage, their having a place in the house of God would not entitle them to the inheritance of sons; for (*v.* 35) *the servant*, though he be in the house for awhile, yet, being but a *servant*, *abideth not in the house for ever*.

3. He shows them the way of deliverance out of this state of bondage into the *glorious liberty of the children of God*, Rom. viii. 21. Note,

(1) Jesus Christ in the gospel offers us *our freedom*; he has authority and power to *make free*. [1] To *discharge prisoners*; this he does *in justification*, by making satisfaction for *our guilt* and for *our debts*, for which we were by the law arrested and in execution. [2] He has a power to rescue *bond-slaves*, and this he does in *sanctification*; by the powerful arguments of his gospel, and the powerful operations of his Spirit, he breaks the power of corruption in the soul, rallies the scattered forces of reason and virtue, and fortifies God's interest against sin and Satan, and so the soul is made free. [3] He has a power to *naturalize strangers and foreigners*, and this he does in *adoption*.

(2) Those whom Christ makes free are *free indeed*. It denotes, [1] The truth and certainty of the promise. The servants of sin promise themselves liberty, and fancy themselves free, when they have broken religion's bands asunder; but they cheat themselves. None are *free indeed* but those whom Christ *makes free*. [2] It denotes the singular excellency of the freedom promised; it is a freedom that deserves the name, in comparison with which all other liberties are no better than slaveries.

4. He applies this to these unbelieving cavilling Jews, in answer to their boasts of relation to Abraham (*v.* 37): "*I know* very well *that you are Abraham's seed, but now you seek to kill me*, and therefore have forfeited the honour of your relation to Abraham, *because my word hath no place in you.*"

Why were they that were Abraham's seed so very inveterate against Abraham's promised seed, in whom they and *all the families of the earth* should be *blessed*? Our Saviour here tells them, It is because *my word hath no place in you*. They *sought to kill him*, and so effectually to *silence him*, not

because he had done them any
harm, but because they could
not bear the convincing, commanding power of his word.

HEARING GOD'S WORDS
(*vv.* 38–47)

Here Christ and the Jews are still
at issue; he sets himself to convince
and convert them, while they still
set themselves to contradict and
oppose him.

I. He here traces the difference
between his sentiments and theirs
to a different rise and origin
(*v.* 38): *I speak that which I have
seen with my Father*, and *you* do
*what you have seen with your
father*. Here are two fathers
spoken of, according to the two
families into which the sons of
men are divided—God and the
devil, and without controversy
these are contrary the one to the
other.

II. He takes off and answers
their vain-glorious boasts of relation to Abraham and to God as
their fathers, and shows the
vanity and falsehood of their
pretensions.

1. They pleaded relation to Abraham, and he replies to this plea.
"Abraham's children will do the
works of Abraham, but you do
not do Abraham's works, therefore
you are not Abraham's children."

[1] Those only are reckoned
the seed of Abraham, to whom
the promise belongs, who *tread in
the steps* of his faith and obedience,
Rom. iv. 12.

[2] The assumption is evident
likewise: *But you do not do* the
works of Abraham, for *you seek
to kill me, a man that has told you*

the truth, which I have heard of
God; this did not Abraham*, v. 40.

[3] The conclusion follows of
course (*v.* 41): "Whatever your
boasts and pretensions be, you
are not Abraham's children, but
father yourselves upon another
family (*v.* 41); there is *a father
whose deeds you do*, whose spirit
you are of, and whom you resemble."

2. So far were they from owning
their unworthiness of relation to
Abraham that they pleaded relation
to God himself as their Father:
"We are *not born of fornication*,
we are not bastards, but legitimate
sons; *we have one Father, even
God*."

Now our Saviour gives a full
answer to this fallacious plea
(*vv.* 42, 43), and proves, by two
arguments, that they had no
right to call God Father.

First, They did not love Christ:
*If God were your Father, you
would love me*. He had disproved
their relation to Abraham by
their going about to kill him
(*v.* 40), but here he disproves their
relation to God by their not loving
and owning him.

Secondly, They did not understand him. It was a sign they did
not belong to God's family that
they did not understand the
language and dialect of the family.
Christ spoke the words of God
(*ch.* iii. 34) in the dialect of the
kingdom of God; and yet they,
who pretended to belong to the
kingdom, understood not the
idioms and properties of it, but
like strangers, and rude ones
too, ridiculed it. And the reason
why they did not understand

Christ's speech made the matter much worse: *Even because you cannot hear my word*, that is, "You cannot persuade yourselves to hear it attentively, impartially, and without prejudice, as it should be heard."

III. Having thus disproved their relation both to Abraham and to God, he comes next to tell them plainly whose children they were: *You are of your father the devil*, v. 44. If they were not God's children, they were the devil's, for God and Satan divide the world of mankind.

This is a high charge, and sounds very harsh and horrid, that any of the children of men, especially the church's children, should be called *children of the devil*, and therefore our Saviour fully proves it,

1. By a general argument: *The lusts of your father you will do*.

2. By two particular instances, wherein they manifestly resembled the devil—*murder* and *lying*. The devil is an enemy to life, because God is the God of life and life is the happiness of man; and an enemy to truth, because God is the God of truth and truth is the bond of human society.

IV. Christ, having thus proved all murderers and all liars to be the devil's children, leaves it to the consciences of his hearers to say, *Thou art the man*. Two things he charges upon them:—

1. That they would not *believe the word of truth* (v. 45). "*If I say the truth, why do you not believe me?* If you cannot convince me of error, you must own that I *say the truth*, and why do you not

then *give me credit*? Why will you not deal witth me upon trust?"

2. Another thing charged upon them is that they would not hear the words of God (v. 47), which further shows how groundless their claim of relation to God was. Here is,

(1) A doctrine laid down: *He that is of God heareth God's words*; that is, [1] He is *willing* and *ready* to hear them, is sincerely desirous to know what the mind of God is, and cheerfully embraces whatever he knows to be so. [2] He *apprehends* and *discerns* them, he so hears them as to perceive the *voice of God* in them, which the natural man does not, 1 Cor. ii. 14.

(2) The application of this doctrine, for the conviction of these unbelieving Jews: *You therefore hear them not*. If the word of the kingdom do not bring forth fruit, the blame is to be laid upon the soil, not upon the seed, as appears by the parable of the sower, Matt. xiii. 3.

CHRIST INSULTED (vv. 48–50)

Here is, I. The malice of hell breaking out in the base language which the unbelieving Jews gave to our Lord Jesus. Hitherto they had cavilled at his doctrine, and had made invidious remarks upon it; but, having shown themselves uneasy when he complained (vv. 43, 47) that they would not hear him, now at length they fall to downright railing, v. 48. See here,

1. What was the blasphemous character commonly given of our Lord Jesus among the wicked Jews, to which they refer. (1) That

he was a Samaritan, that is, that he was an enemy to their church and nation, one that they hated and could not endure. (2) That *he had a devil*. Either, [1] That he was *in league with the devil*. Or rather, [2] That he was possessed with a devil, or a mad man, and that which he said was no more to be believed than the extravagant rambles of a distracted man, or one in a delirium.

2. How they undertook to justify this character, and applied it to the present occasion: *Say we not well that thou art so?* They value themselves on their enmity to Christ, as if they had never spoken *better* than when they spoke the worst they could of Jesus Christ.

II. The meekness and mercifulness of Heaven shining in Christ's reply to this vile calumny, *vv.* 49, 50.

1. He denies their charge against him: *I have not a devil*; as Paul (Acts xxvi. 25), *I am not mad*. The imputation is unjust; "I am neither actuated by a devil, nor in compact with one"; and this he evidenced by what he did against the devil's kingdom.

2. He asserts the sincerity of his own intentions: But *I honour my Father*.

3. He complains of the wrong they did him by their calumnies: *You do dishonour me*. Christ honoured his Father so as never man did, and yet was himself dishonoured so as never man was; for, though God has promised that those who honour him he will honour, he never promised that men should honour them.

4. He clears himself from the imputation of vain glory, in saying this concerning himself, *v.* 50. See here, (1) His *contempt* of worldly honour: *I seek not mine own glory*. (2) His *comfort* under worldly dishonour: *There is one that seeketh and judgeth*. In two things Christ made it appear that he *sought not his own glory*; and here he tells us what satisfied him as to both. [1] He did not *court* men's respect, but was indifferent to it. [2] He did not *revenge* men's affronts, but was unconcerned at them.

BEFORE ABRAHAM
(*vv.* 51–59)

In these verses we have,

I. The doctrine of the immortality of believers laid down, *v.* 51. Here we have, 1. The *character* of a believer: he is one that *keeps the sayings* of the Lord Jesus. 2. The *privilege* of a believer: *He shall by no means see death for ever*; so it is in the original. Though now they cannot avoid seeing death, and tasting it too, yet they shall shortly be there where it will be *seen no more for ever*, Exod. xiv. 13.

II. The Jews cavil at this doctrine. Instead of laying hold of this precious promise of immortality, which the nature of man has an ambition of (who is there that does not love life, and dread the sight of death?) they lay hold of this occasion to reproach him that makes them so kind an offer: *Now we know that thou hast a devil*. Abraham *is dead*. Observe here,

1. Their *railing*: "*Now we know that thou hast a devil*, that thou art a madman; thou ravest, and sayest thou knowest no what." See how these swine trample underfoot the precious pearls of gospel promises.

2. Their *reasoning*, and the colour they had to *run him down* thus. In short, they look upon him as guilty of an insufferable piece of arrogance, in making himself greater than *Abraham and the prophets: Abraham is dead*, and *the prophets*, they are dead too. Now their arguing goes upon two mistakes:—[1] They understood Christ of an immortality in this world, and this was a mistake. In the "sense that Christ spoke, it was not true that *Abraham and the prophets* were *dead*, for God is still the *God of Abraham* and the *God of the holy prophets* (Rev. xxii. 6); now God is not the God of the dead, but of the living; therefore Abraham and the prophets are still alive, and, as Christ meant it, they had not *seen* nor *tasted* death. [2] They thought none could be greater than Abraham and the prophets, whereas they could not but know that the Messiah would be greater than Abraham or any of the prophets; they did virtuously, but he excelled them all; nay, they borrowed their greatness from him.

III. Christ's reply to this cavil; still he vouchsafes to reason with them, that every mouth may be stopped.

1. In his answer he insists not upon his own testimony concerning himself, but waives it as not sufficient nor conclusive (*v.* 54):

If I honour myself, my honour is nothing.

2. He refers himself to *his* Father, God; and to *their* father, Abraham.

(1) To his Father, *God*: *It is my Father that honoureth me*. By this he means, [1] That he *derived* from his Father all the honour he now claimed. [2] That he *depended* upon his Father for all the honour he further *looked for*. He courted not the applauses of the age, but despised them; for his eye and heart were upon the glory which the Father had promised him, and *which he had with the Father before the world was*. "You *say of him that he is your God, yet you have not known him*." Here observe,

a. The profession they made of relation to God.

b. Their ignorance of him, and estrangement from him, notwithstanding this profession: *Yet you have not known him*. (*a*) *You know him not at all*. These Pharisees were so taken up with the study of their traditions concerning things foreign and trifling that they never minded the most needful and useful knowledge. Or, (*b*) *You know him not aright*, but mistake concerning him; and this is as bad as not knowing him at all, or worse. Men may be able to dispute subtly concerning God, and yet may think him such a one as themselves, and *not know him*. You say that he is *yours*, and it is natural to us to desire to know *our own*, yet you *know him not*.

(2) Christ refers them to *their* father, whom they boasted so much of a relation to, and that was

Abraham, and this closes the discourse.

[1] Christ asserts Abraham's prospect of him, and respect to him: *Your father Abraham rejoiced to see my day, and he saw it, and was glad, v.* 56. And by this he proves that he was not at all out of the way when he *made himself greater than Abraham.*

[2] The Jews cavil at this, and reproach him for it (*v.* 57): *Thou art not yet fifty years old, and hast thou seen Abraham?*

[3] Our Saviour gives an effectual answer to this cavil, by a solemn assertion of his own seniority even to Abraham himself (*v.* 58): "*Verily, verily, I say unto you;* I do not only say it in private to my own disciples, who will be sure to say as I say, but *to you* my enemies and persecutors; I say it to your faces, take it how you will: *Before Abraham was, I am.*" *Before Abraham was made or born, I am.* The change of the word is observable, and bespeaks Abraham a creature, and himself the Creator; well therefore might he make himself *greater* than Abraham. *Before Abraham he was, First,* As God. *I am,* is the name of God (Exod. iii. 14); it denotes his self-existence; he does not say, *I was,* but *I am,* for he is the first and the last, immutably the same (Rev. i. 8); thus he was not only before Abraham, but before *all worlds, ch.* i. 1; Prov. viii. 23. *Secondly,* As Mediator. He was the appointed Messiah, long before Abraham; the *Lamb slain from the foundation of the world* (Rev. xiii. 8), the channel of conveyance of light, life, and love from God to

man. This supposes his divine nature, that he is the same in himself from eternity (Heb. xiii. 8), and that he is the same to man ever since the fall. If Christ was before Abraham, his doctrine and religion were no novelty, but were, in the substance of them, prior to Judaism, and ought to take place of it.

[4] This great word ended the dispute *abruptly,* and put a period to it. Observe here,

First, How they were *enraged* at Christ for what he said: *They took up stones to cast at him, v.* 59.

Secondly, How he made his *escape* out of their hands. 1. He *absconded;* Jesus *hid himself.* 2. He *departed,* he *went out of the temple,* going *through the midst of them,* undiscovered, and *so passed by.* As *the kingdom of God comes not,* so it *goes not, with observation.* See Judg. xvi. 20. *Samson wist not that the Lord was departed from him.* Thus it was with these forsaken Jews, God left them, and they never missed him.

CHAPTER NINE

LIGHT SHINES (*vv.* 1–7)

We have here sight given to a poor beggar that had been blind from his birth. Observe,

I. The notice which our Lord Jesus took of the piteous case of this poor blind man (*v.* 1): *As Jesus passed by he saw a man which was blind from his birth.* If the light is sweet, how melancholy must it needs be for a man, all his days, *to eat in darkness!* He that is *blind* has no *enjoyment* of the light, but he that is *born blind* has no *idea* of it.

II. The discourse between Christ and his disciples concerning this man. Observe,

1. The question which the disciples put to their Master upon this blind man's case, *v.* 2. Now this question of theirs was,

(1) *Uncharitably censorious.* They take it for granted that this extraordinary calamity was the punishment of some uncommon wickedness, and that this man was a sinner above all men that dwelt at Jerusalem, Luke xiii. 4.

(2) It was *unnecessarily curious.* Concluding this calamity to be inflicted for some very heinous crime, they ask, *Who were the criminals, this man or his parents?* And what was this to them? Or what good would it do them to know it?

2. Christ's answer to this question. He was always *apt to teach,* and to rectify his disciples' mistakes.

(1) He gives the reason of this poor man's blindness: "*Neither has this man sinned nor his parents,* but he was born blind, and has continued so to this day, that now at last *the works of God should be made manifest in him,*" *v.* 3. Here Christ, who perfectly knew the secret springs of the divine counsels, told them two things concerning such uncommon calamities:—[1] That they are not always inflicted as punishments of sin. [2] That they are sometimes intended purely *for the glory of God,* and the *manifesting of his works.*

(2) He gives the reason of his own forwardness and readiness to help and heal him, *vv.* 4, 5.

[1] It was his Father's will: *I must work the works of him that sent me.*

[2] Now was his opportunity: I must work *while it is day,* while the time lasts which is appointed to work in, and while the light lasts which is given to work by. Christ himself had *his day.*

[3] The period of his opportunity was at hand, and therefore he would be busy: *The night comes when no man can work.*

[4] His business in the world was to enlighten it (*v.* 5): *As long as I am in the world,* and that will not be long, *I am the light of the world.* He had said this before, *ch.* viii. 12. He is the *Sun of righteousness,* that has not only light in his wings for those that can see, but healing in his wings, or beams, for those that are blind and cannot see, therein far exceeding in virtue that great light which rules *by day.* Christ would cure this blind man, the representative of a blind world, because he came to be *the light of the world,* not only to give *light,* but to give *sight.*

III. The manner of the cure of the blind man, *vv.* 6, 7. In the cure observe,

1. The preparation of the eyesalve. Christ *spat on the ground, and made clay of the spittle.* He could have cured him with a word, as he did others, but he chose to do it in this way to show that he is not *tied* to any method.

2. The application of it to the place: *He anointed the eyes of the blind man with the clay.* Now Christ did this, (1) To magnify his power in making a blind man to see by that method which one

would think more likely to make a seeing man blind. Daubing clay on the eyes would *close them* up, but never *open them*. (2) To give an intimation that it was his mighty hand, the very same that at first made man out of *the clay*; for by him God *made the worlds*, both the great world, and man the little world. (3) To represent and typify the healing and opening of the eyes of the mind by the grace of Jesus Christ. The design of the gospel is to *open men's eyes*, Acts, xxvi. 18. Now the eye-salve that does the work is of Christ's preparing; it is made up, not as this, of his spittle, but of his blood, the blood and water that came out of his pierced side; we must come to Christ for *the eye-salve*, Rev. iii. 18. He only is *able*, and he only is *appointed*, to make it up, Luke iv. 18.

3. The directions given to the patient, *v.* 7. His physician said to him, *Go, wash in the pool of Siloam*. Not that this washing was needful to effect the cure; but, (1) Christ would hereby try his obedience, and whether he would with an implicit faith obey the orders of one he was so much a stranger to. (2) He would likewise try how he stood affected to the tradition of the elders, which taught, and perhaps had taught him (for many that are *blind* are very knowing), that it was not lawful to wash the eyes, no not with spittle medicinally, on the sabbath day, much less to go to a pool of water to wash them. (3) He would hereby represent the method of spiritual healing, in which, though the effect is owing purely to his power and grace, there is duty to be done by us.

4. The patient's obedience to these directions: *He went his way therefore*, and *he washed his eyes*; probably the disciples, or some stander by, informed him that he who bade him do it was that Jesus whom he had heard so much of, else he would not have gone, at his bidding, on that which looked so much like a fool's errand; in confidence of Christ's power, as well as in obedience to his command, he went, and washed.

5. The cure effected: *He came seeing*. There is more glory in this concise narrative, *He went* and *washed*, and *came seeing*, than in Cæsar's *Veni, vidi, vici—I came, I saw, I conquered*.

LIGHT REFLECTS (*vv.* 8–12)

Such a wonderful event as the giving of sight to a man born blind could not but be the talk of the town. Two things are debated in this conference about it:—

I. Whether this was the same man that had before been blind, *v.* 8.

1. The neighbours that lived near the place where he was born and bred, and knew that he had been blind, could not but be amazed when they saw that he had his eye-sight, had it on a sudden, and perfectly; and they said, *Is not this he that sat and begged?*

2. In answer to this enquiry, (1) Some said, *This is he*, the very same man; and these are witnesses to the truth of the miracle, for they had long known him stone-blind. (2) Others, who could not

think it possible that a man born blind should thus on a sudden receive his sight, for that reason, and no other, said, *He is not he, but is like him,* and so, by their confession, if it be he, it is a great miracle that is wrought upon him.

3. This controversy was soon decided by the man himself: *He said, I am he,* the very man that so lately sat and begged. Applying it spiritually, it teaches us that those who are savingly enlightened by the grace of God should be ready to own what they were before that blessed change was wrought, 1 Tim. i. 13, 14.

II. How he came to have his eyes opened, *vv.* 10–12. Two things these neighbours enquire after:—

1. The manner of the cure: *How were thine eyes opened?* In answer to this enquiry the poor man gives them a plain and full account of the matter: *A man that is called Jesus made clay,—and I received sight, v.* 11.

2. The author of it (*v.* 12): *Where is he?* In answer to this, he could say nothing: *I know not.* As soon as Christ had sent him to the pool of Siloam, it should seem, he withdrew immediately (as he did, *ch.* v. 13), and did not stay till the man returned, as if he either doubted of the effect or waited for the man's thanks. For the way of the Spirit is like that of the wind, which thou hearest the sound of, but canst not tell *whence it comes* nor *whither it goes.*

LIGHT REJECTED (*vv.* 13–34)

One would have expected that such a miracle as Christ wrought upon the blind man would have settled his reputation, and silenced and shamed all opposition, but it had the contrary effect; instead of being embraced as a prophet for it, he is prosecuted as a criminal.

I. Here is the information that was given in to the Pharisees concerning this matter: *They brought to the Pharisees him that aforetime was blind, v.* 13.

II. The ground which was pretended for this information, and the colour given to it. That which is good was never maligned but under the imputation of something evil. And the crime objected here (*v.* 14) was that *it was the sabbath day when Jesus made the clay, and opened his eyes.*

III. The trial and examination of this matter by the Pharisees, *v.* 15. Let us see how they teased this man.

1. They interrogated him concerning the cure itself.

(1) They doubted whether he had indeed been *born blind,* and demanded proof of that which even the prosecutors had acknowledged (*v.* 18): They *did not believe,* that is, they would not, that he was *born blind.*

[1] The questions that were put to the parents (*v.* 19): They *asked them* in an imperious threatening way, "*Is this your son?* Dare you swear to it? *Do you say he was born blind?* Are you sure of it? Or did he but pretend to be so, to have an excuse for his begging? *How then doth he now see?* That is impossible, and therefore you had better unsay it."

[2] Their answers to these interrogatories, in which,

First, They fully attest that which they could safely say in this matter; *safely*, that is, upon their own knowledge, and *safely*, that is, without running themselves into trouble (*v.* 20): *We know that this is our son*; and we know that he was *born blind*.

Secondly, They cautiously decline giving any evidence concerning his cure; partly because they were not themselves eyewitnesses of it, and could say nothing to it *of their own knowledge*; and partly because they found it was a *tender point*, and would not bear to be meddled with.

a. Observe how warily they express themselves (*v.* 21): "*By what means he now seeth we know not*, or *who has opened his eyes we know not*, otherwise than by *hearsay*; we can give no account either by what means or by whose hand it was done."

b. See the reason why they were so cautious (*vv.* 22, 23): *Because they feared the Jews*. Here is,

(*a*) The *late law* which the sanhedrim had made. It was agreed and enacted by their authority that, if any man within their jurisdiction did *confess* that Jesus *was Christ, he should be put out of the synagogue*.

(*b*) The influence which this law had upon the parents of the blind man. They declined saying any thing of Christ, and shuffled it off to their son, *because they feared the Jews*. Well, the parents have thus disentangled themselves, and are discharged from any further attendance; let us now go on with the examination of the man himself; the doubt of the

Pharisees, whether he was *born blind*, was put out of doubt *by them*; and therefore,

(2) They enquired of *him* concerning the *manner of the cure*, and made their remarks upon it, *vv.* 15, 16.

[1] The same question which his neighbours had put to him *now again the Pharisees asked him, how he had received his sight*.

[2] The same answer, in effect, which he had before given to his neighbours, he here repeats to the Pharisees. In the former account he said, *I washed, and received sight*; but lest they should think it was only a glimpse for the present, which a heated imagination might fancy itself to have, he now says, "*I do see*: it is a complete and lasting cure."

[3] The remarks made upon this story were very different, and occasioned a debate in the court, *v.* 16.

First, Some took this occasion to censure and condemn Christ for what he had done. Some of the Pharisees said, *This man is not of God*, as he pretends, *because he keepeth not the sabbath day*.

Secondly, Others spoke in his favour, and very pertinently urged, *How can a man that is a sinner do such miracles?* It seems that even in this *council of the ungodly* there were some that were capable of a *free thought*, and were witnesses for Christ, even in the midst of his enemies.

2. After their enquiry concerning the cure, we must observe their enquiry concerning the *author* of it. And here observe,

(1) What the man said of him,

in answer to their enquiry. They ask him (*v.* 17), "*What sayest thou of him, seeing that he has opened thine eyes?*" To this question the poor man makes a short, plain, and direct answer: "*He is a prophet*, he is one inspired and sent of God to preach, and work miracles, and deliver to the world a divine message." This poor blind beggar had a clearer judgment of the things pertaining to the kingdom of God, and saw further into the proofs of a divine mission, than the *masters in Israel*, that assumed an authority to judge of prophets.

(2) What they said of him, in reply to the man's testimony. Having in vain attempted to invalidate the evidence of the fact, and finding that indeed a *notable miracle was wrought*, and they *could not deny it*, they renew their attempt to banter it, and run it down, and do all they can to shake the good opinion the man had of him that opened his eyes, and to convince him that Christ was a bad man (*v.* 24): *Give God the praise, we know that this man is a sinner.* Two ways this is understood: [1] By way of *advice*, to take heed of ascribing the praise of his cure to a sinful man, but to give it all to God, to whom it was due. [2] By way of *adjuration*; so some take it. "We know (though thou dost not, who hast but lately come, as it were, into a new world) that this man is *a sinner*, a great impostor, that cheats the country; this we are sure of, therefore *give God praise*" (as Joshua said to Achan) "by making an ingenuous confession of the fraud and collusion which we are confident there is in this matter; in God's name, man, tell the truth."

3. The debate that arose between the Pharisees and this poor man concerning Christ. They say, *He is a sinner*; he says, *He is a prophet.* Now in the parley between the Pharisees and this poor man we may observe three steps:—

(1) He sticks to the certain matter of fact the evidence of which they endeavour to shake. That which is doubtful is best resolved into that which is plain, and therefore, [1] He adheres to that which to himself at least, and to his own satisfaction, was past dispute (*v.* 25): "*If he be a sinner, I know it not*, I see no reason to say so, but the contrary; for this *one thing I know*, and can be more sure of than you can be of that of which you are so confident, *that whereas I was blind, now I see*, and therefore must not only say that he has been a good friend to me, but that he is a *prophet*; I am both able and bound to speak well of him." The poor man does not here give a nice account of the method of the cure, nor pretend to describe it *philosophically*, but in short, *Whereas I was blind, now I see.* Thus in the work of grace in the soul, though we cannot tell when and how, by what instruments and by what steps and advances, the blessed change was wrought, yet we may take the comfort of it if we can say, through grace, "*Whereas I was blind, now I see.* I did live a carnal, worldly, sensual life, but, thanks be to God, it is now

otherwise with me," Eph. v. 8. [2] They endeavour to baffle and stifle the evidence by a needless repetition of their enquiries into it (*v.* 26): *What did he to thee? How opened he thine eyes?* They asked these questions, *First*, Because they wanted something to say, and would rather speak *impertinently* than seem to be silenced or run a-ground. *Secondly*, Because they hoped, by putting the man upon repeating his evidence, to catch him tripping in it, or wavering, and then they would think they had gained a good point.

(2) He upbraids them with their obstinate infidelity and invincible prejudices, and they revile him as a disciple of Jesus, *vv.* 27–29, where the man is more bold with them and they are more sharp upon him than before.

[1] The man boldly upbraids them with their wilful and unreasonable opposition to the evidence of this miracle, *v.* 27.

[2] For this they scorn and revile him, *v.* 28. When they could not resist the wisdom and spirit by which he spoke, they broke out into a passion, and scolded him, began to call names, and give him ill language. See what Christ's faithful witnesses must expect from the adversaries of his truth and cause; let them count upon *all manner of evil* to be said of them, Matt. v. 11. The method commonly taken by unreasonable man is to make out with railing what is wanting in truth and reason.

In this argument of theirs observe, 1. How impertinently they

allege, in defence of their enmity to Christ, that which none of his followers ever denied: *We know that God spoke unto Moses*, and, thanks be to God, we know it too, more plainly to Moses than to any other of the prophets; but what then? God spoke to Moses, and does it therefore follow that Jesus is an impostor? Moses was a prophet, it is true, and might not Jesus be a prophet also? 2. How absurdly they urge their ignorance of Christ as a reason to justify their contempt of him; *As for this fellow*, this sorry fellow, *we know not whence he is*. It was not long ago that the Jews had made the contrary to this an objection against Christ (*ch.* vii. 27): *We know this man whence he is, but when Christ comes no man knows whence he is*. Thus they could with the greatest assurance either affirm or deny the same thing, according as they saw it would serve their turn.

(3) He reasons with them concerning this matter, and they excommunicate him.

[1] The poor man, finding that he had reason on his side, which they could not answer, grows more bold, and, in prosecution of his argument, is very close upon them.

First, He wonders at their obstinate infidelity (*v.* 30). Two things he wonders at:—1. That they should be strangers to a man so *famous*. 2. That they should question the divine mission of one that had undoubtedly wrought a divine miracle. When they said, *We know not whence he is*, they meant, "We know not any proof that his doctrine and ministry are from heaven." "Now this is strange," saith the poor man, "that the miracle wrought upon me has not convinced you, and put the matter out of doubt,— that you, whose education and studies give you advantages above others of discerning the things of God, should thus shut your eyes against the light."

Secondly, He argues strongly against them, *vv.* 31–33. They had determined concerning Jesus that he was not of God (*v.* 16), but was a *sinner* (*v.* 24), in answer to which the man here proves not only that he was *not a sinner* (*v.* 31), but that he was *of God*, *v.* 33.

a. He argues here, (*a*) With great knowledge. Though he could not read a letter of the book, he was well acquainted with the scripture and the things of God. (*b*) With great zeal for the honour of Christ, whom he could not endure to hear run down, and evil spoken of. (*c*) With great boldness, and courage, and undauntedness, not terrified by the proudest of his adversaries.

b. His argument may be reduced into form, somewhat like that of David, Ps. lxvi. 18–20.

(*a*) He lays it down for an undoubted truth that none but good men are the favourites of heaven (*v.* 31).

[*b*] The application of these truths is very pertinent to prove that he, at whose word such a divine power was put forth as cured one born blind, was not a bad man, but, having manifestly such an interest in the holy God

as that he *heard him always* (*ch.* xi. 41, 42), was certainly a holy one.

[2] The Pharisees, finding themselves unable either to answer his reasonings or to bear them, fell foul upon him, and with a great deal of pride and passion broke off the discourse, *v.* 34. Here we are told,

First, What they *said*. Having nothing to reply to his argument, they reflected upon his person: *Thou wast altogether born in sin, and dost thou teach us?* They take that amiss which they had reason to take kindly, and are cut to the heart with rage by that which should have pricked them to the heart with penitence.

Secondly, What they did: They *cast him out*. There was a law made that if any confessed Jesus to be the Christ he should be *cast out of the synagogue*, *v.* 22. But this man had only said of Jesus that he was a prophet, was *of God*: and yet they stretch the law to bring him under the lash of it, as if he had confessed him to be the Christ.

LIGHT ACCEPTED (*vv.* 35–38)

In these verses we may observe,

I. The tender care which our Lord Jesus took of this poor man (*v.* 35). Jesus Christ will graciously find and receive those who for his sake are unjustly rejected and cast out by men. He will be a hiding place to his outcasts, and appear, to the joy of those whom their brethren hated and cast out.

II. The conversation Christ had with him. He had well improved the knowledge he had, and now

Christ gives him further instruction; for he that is faithful in a little shall be entrusted with more, Matt. xiii. 12.

1. Our Lord Jesus examines his faith: "*Dost thou believe on the Son of God?*"

2. The poor man solicitously enquires concerning the Messiah he was to believe in, professing his readiness to embrace him and close with him (*v.* 36): *Who is he, Lord, that I may believe on him?* (1) Some think he did know that Jesus, who cured him, was the Son of God, but did not know which was Jesus, and therefore, supposing this person that talked with him to be a follower of Jesus, desired him to do him the favour to direct him to his master; not that he might satisfy his curiosity with the sight of him, but that he might the more firmly believe in him, and profess his faith, and *know whom he had believed.* See Cant. v. 6, 7; iii. 2, 3. It is Christ only that can direct us to himself. (2) Others think he did know that this person who talked with him was Jesus, the same that cured him, whom he believed a great and good man and a prophet, but did not yet know that he was the Son of God and the true Messiah.

3. Our Lord Jesus graciously reveals himself to him as that Son of God on whom he must believe: *Thou hast both seen him, and it is he that talketh with thee, v.* 37.

4. The poor man readily entertains this surprising revelation, and, in a transport of joy and wonder, he said, *Lord, I believe, and he worshipped him.*

TRUE BLINDNESS (*vv.* 39–41)

Christ, having spoken comfort to the poor man that was persecuted, here speaks conviction to his persecutors, a specimen of the distributions of trouble and rest at the great day, 2 Thess. i. 6, 7. Here is,

I. The account Christ gives of his design in coming into the world (*v.* 39): *For judgment I am* come to order and administer the great affairs of the *kingdom of God among men.*

1. His business into the world was *great*; he came to keep the assizes and general gaol-delivery.

2. This great truth he explains by a metaphor borrowed from the miracle which he had lately wrought. That *those who see not might see, and that those who see might be made blind.* Such a difference of Christ's coming is often spoken of; to some his gospel is a *savour of life unto life,* to others of *death unto death.*

II. The Pharisees cavil at this. They were *with him,* not desirous to learn any good from him, but to form evil against him; and they said, *Are we blind also?*

III. Christ's answer to this cavil, which, if it did not convince them, yet silenced them: *If you were blind you should have no sin; but now you say, We see, therefore your sin remaineth.* They gloried that they were not blind, as the common people, were not so credulous and manageable as they, but would *see with their own eyes,* having abilities, as they thought, sufficient for their own guidance, so that they needed not anybody to lead them. This very thing which they gloried in, Christ here tells them, was their shame and ruin. For,

1. *If you were blind, you would have no sin.* (1) "If you had been really ignorant, your sin had not been so deeply aggravated, nor would you have had so much sin to answer for as now you have."

2. "*But now you say, We see*; now that you have knowledge, and are instructed out of the law, your sin is highly aggravated; and now that you have a conceit of that knowledge, and think you see your way better than any body can show it you, *therefore your sin remains*, your case is desperate, and your disease incurable."

CHAPTER TEN
I AM THE GOOD SHEPHERD (*vv.* 1–18)

The Pharisees supported themselves in their opposition to Christ with this principle, that they were the *pastors of the church*, and that Jesus, having no commission from them, was an intruder and an impostor, and therefore the people were bound in duty to stick to *them*, against *him*. In opposition to this, Christ here describes who were the false shepherds, and who the true, leaving them to infer what they were.

I. Here is the parable or similitude proposed (*vv.* 1–5); it is borrowed from the custom of that country, in the management of their sheep.

1. In the parable we have,

(1) The evidence of a thief and a robber, that comes to do mischief to the flock, and damage to the owner, *v.* 1. *He enters not by the door*, as having no lawful cause of entry, but *climbs up some other way*, at a window, or some breach in the wall. (2) The character that distinguishes the rightful owner, who has a property in the sheep, and a care for them: *He enters in by the door*, as one having authority (*v.* 2), and he comes to do them some good office or other, to *bind up that which is broken*, and *strengthen that which is sick*, Ezek. xxxiv. 16. (3) The ready entrance that the shepherd finds: *To him the porter openeth*, *v.* 3. (4) The care he takes and the provision he makes for his sheep. The *sheep hear his voice*, when he speaks familiarly to them, when they come into the fold, as men now do to their dogs and horses; and, which is more, he *calls his own sheep by name*, so exact is the notice he takes of them, the account he keeps of them; and he leads them out from the fold to the green pastures; and (*vv.* 4, 5) when he *turns them out* to graze he does not drive them, but (such was the custom in those times) he goes before them, to prevent any mischief or danger that might meet them, and they, being used to it, *follow him*, and are safe. (5) The strange attendance of the sheep upon the shepherd: *They know his voice*, so as to discern his mind by it, and to distinguish it from that of a stranger.

2. Let us observe from this parable, (1) That good men are

fitly compared to sheep. Men, as creatures depending on their Creator, are called the *sheep of his pasture*. (2) The church of God in the world is a *sheepfold*, into which the *children of God* that were scattered abroad are *gathered together* (*ch.* xi. 52). (3) This sheepfold lies much exposed to thieves and robbers; crafty seducers that debauch and deceive, and cruel persecutors that destroy and devour; *grievous wolves* (Acts xx. 29). (4) The great Shepherd of the sheep takes wonderful care of the flock and of all that belong to it. God is the great Shepherd, Ps. xxiii. 1; lxxx. 1. He knows those that are his, calls them by name, marks them for himself, leads them out to fat pastures, makes them both feed and rest there, speaks comfortably to them, guards them by his providence, guides them by his Spirit and word, and goes before them, *to set them in the way of his steps*. (5) The undershepherds, who are entrusted to feed the flock of God, ought to be careful and faithful in the discharge of that trust. (6) Those who are truly the sheep of Christ will be very observant of their Shepherd, and very cautious and shy of strangers.

II. The Jews' ignorance of the drift and meaning of this discourse (*v.* 6): *Jesus spoke this parable* to them, *but they understood not what the things were which he spoke unto them*, were not aware whom he meant by the *thieves and robbers* and whom by the *good Shepherd*.

III. Christ's explication of this parable, opening the particulars of it fully. Christ, in the parable, had distinguished the shepherd from the robber by this, that he *enters in by the door*. Now, in the explication of the parable, he makes himself to be both *the door* by which the shepherd enters and the shepherd that enters in by the door. Though it may be a solecism in rhetoric to make the same person to be both the *door* and the *shepherd*, it is no solecism in divinity to make Christ to have his authority from himself, as he has life in himself; and *himself* to *enter by his own blood*, as the door, *into the holy place*.

1. Christ is *the door*.

(1) In general, [1] He is as a *door shut*, to keep out thieves and robbers, and such as are not fit to be admitted. [2] He is as a *door open* for passage and communication. *First*, By Christ, as the door, we have our first admission into the flock of God, *ch.* xiv. 6. *Secondly*, We go in and out in a religious conversation, assisted by him, accepted in him; walking up and down in his name, Zech. x. 12. *Thirdly*, By him God comes to his church, visits it, and communicates himself to it. *Fourthly*, By him, as the door, the sheep are at last admitted into the heavenly kingdom, Matt. xxv. 34.

(2) More particularly,

[1] Christ is the door of *the shepherds*, so that none who come not in by him are to be accounted *pastors*.

[2] Christ is the door of *the sheep* (*v.* 9): *By me if any man enter into the sheepfold*, as one of the flock, he *shall be saved*; shall

not only be safe from thieves and robbers, but he shall be happy, he *shall go in and out*. Here are, *First*, Plain directions how to come into the fold: we must come in *by Jesus Christ* as the door. *Secondly*, Precious promises to those who observe this direction. 1. They *shall be saved hereafter*; this is the privilege of *their home*. 2. In the mean time they shall *go in and out and find pasture*; this is the privilege of *their way*.

2. Christ is the *shepherd*, *vv.* 11, &c. He was prophesied of under the Old Testament as a *shepherd*, Isa. xl. 11; Ezek. xxxiv. 23; xxxvii. 24; Zech xiii. 7. In the New Testament he is spoken of as the *great Shepherd* (Heb. xiii. 20), the *chief Shepherd* (1 v. 4), the *Shepherd and bishop of our souls*, 1 Pet. ii. 25.

(1) Christ is *a shepherd*, and not as the thief, not as those that *came not in by the door*. Observe,

[1] The mischievous design of the thief (*v.* 10): *The thief cometh not* with any good intent, but to *steal, and to kill, and to destroy*.

[2] The gracious design of the shepherd; he is come,

First, To *give life to the sheep*. In opposition to the design of the thief, which is to *kill and destroy* (which was the design of the *scribes* and *Pharisees*) Christ saith, *I am come among men*, 1. That *they might have life*. He came to put life into the flock, the church in general, which had seemed rather like a valley full of dry bones than like a pasture covered over with flocks. 2. That they might have it *more abundantly*. As we read it, it is *comparative*, that they

might have a life *more abundant* than that which was lost and forfeited by sin. But it may be construed without a note of comparison, *that they might have abundance*, or might *have it abundantly*. Life in abundance is *eternal life*, life without death or fear of death, life and *much more*.

Secondly, To *give his life for the sheep*, and this that he might give life *to them* (*v.* 11): *The good shepherd giveth his life for the sheep*. 1. It is the property of every good shepherd to hazard and expose his life for the sheep. 2. It was the prerogative of the great Shepherd to give his life to purchase his flock (Acts xx. 28), to satisfy for their trespass, and to shed his blood to wash and cleanse them.

(2) Christ is *a good shepherd*, and not as a hireling. There were many that were not thieves, aiming to kill and destroy the sheep, but passed for shepherds, yet were very careless in the discharge of their duty, and through their neglect the flock was greatly damaged; *foolish shepherds, idle shepherds*, Zech. xi. 15, 17.

Here are two great instances of the shepherd's goodness.

a. His *acquainting* himself with his flock, with all that belong or in any wise appertain to his flock, which are of two sorts, both known to him:—

(*a*) He is acquainted with all that *are now of his flock* (*vv.* 14, 15), as the good Shepherd (*vv.* 3, 4): *I know my sheep and am known of mine*.

(*b*) He is acquainted with those that are *hereafter to be of this flock* (*v.* 16): *Other sheep I have*, have a right to and an interest in, *which are not of this fold*, of the Jewish church; *them also I must bring*.

The happy effect and consequence of this is in two things:— *First*, "They shall hear my voice. Not only my voice shall be heard *among them* (whereas they have not heard, and therefore could not believe, now the *sound* of the gospel shall *go to the ends of the earth*), but it shall be heard *by them*; I will speak, and give to them to hear." Faith comes by hearing, and our diligent observance of the voice of Christ is both a means and an evidence of our being brought to Christ, and to God by him. *Secondly, There shall be one fold and one shepherd.* As there is one shepherd, so there shall be one fold. Both Jews and Gentiles, upon their turning to the faith of Christ, shall be incorporated in one church, be joint and equal sharers in the privileges of it, without distinction.

b. Christ's *offering up himself for his sheep* is another proof of his being a *good shepherd*, and in this he yet more *commended his love*, *vv.* 15, 17, 18.

(*a*) He declares his purpose of *dying for his flock* (*v.* 15): *I lay down my life for the sheep.*

(*b*) He takes off the offence of the cross, which to many is a stone of stumbling, by four considerations:—

[*a*] That his *laying down his life for the sheep* was the condition, the performance of which entitled him to the honours and powers of his exalted state (*v.* 17).

[*b*] That his laying down his

life was in order to his resuming it: *I lay down my life, that I may receive it again.*

[*c*] That he was perfectly voluntary in his sufferings and death (*v.* 18): "No one doth or can force my life from me against my will, but I freely *lay it down of myself*, I deliver it as my own act and deed, for I *have* (which no man has) *power to lay it down, and to take it again.*"

[*d*] That he did all this by the express order and appointment of his Father, into which he ultimately resolves the whole affair: *This commandment have I received of my Father.*

THE JEWS DIVIDED
(*vv.* 19–21)

We have here an account of the people's different sentiments concerning Christ, on occasion of the foregoing discourse. See what the debate was in particular.

I. Some upon this occasion spoke ill of Christ and of his sayings, either openly in the face of the assembly, for his enemies were very impudent, or privately among themselves.

II. Others stood up in defence of him and his discourse, and, though the stream ran strong, dared to swim against it; and, though perhaps they did not believe on him as the Messiah, they could not bear to hear him thus abused. Two things they plead:—1. The excellency of his doctrine: "*These are not the words of him that hath a devil*; they are not idle words; distracted men are not used to talk at this rate." 2. The power of his miracles: *Can a devil*, that is, a man that has a devil, *open the eyes of the blind*? Neither mad men nor bad men can work miracles. Therefore Jesus *had not a devil*.

BELIEVE MY WORKS
(vv. 22–38)

We have here another encounter between Christ and the Jews in the temple.

I. We have here the time when this conference was: *It was at the feast of dedication, and it was winter*, a feast that was annually observed by consent, in remembrance of the dedication of a new altar and the purging of the temple, by Judas Maccabæus, after the temple had been profaned and the altar defiled.

II. The place where it was (v. 23): *Jesus walked in the temple in Solomon's porch*; so called (Acts iii. 11), not because built by Solomon, but because built in the same place with that which had borne his name in the first temple, and the name was kept up for the greater reputation of it.

III. The conference itself, in which observe,

1. A weighty question put to him by the Jews, v. 24. *How long dost thou make us to doubt? If thou be the Christ tell us.*

2. Christ's answer to this question, in which,

(1) He justifies himself as not at all accessary to their infidelity and scepticism, referring them, [1] To what he had said: *I have told you.* He had told them that he was the Son of God, the Son of man, that he had life in himself, that

he had *authority to execute judgment*, &c. And is not this the Christ then? [2] He refers them to his works, to the example of his life, which was not only perfectly pure, but highly beneficent, and of a piece with his doctrine; and especially to his miracles, which he wrought for the confirmation of his doctrine. It was certain that no man could do those miracles except God were with him, and God would not be with him to attest a forgery.

(2) He condemns them for their obstinate unbelief. But the reason he gives is very surprising: "*You believed not, because you are not of my sheep*: you believe not in me, because you belong not to me." [1] "You are not disposed to be my followers, are not of a tractable teachable temper." [2] "You are not *designed* to be my followers; you are not of those that were given me by my Father, to be brought to grace and glory."

(3) He takes this occasion to describe both the gracious disposition and the happy state of those that are his sheep; for such there are, though *they* are not.

[1] To convince them that they were not his sheep, he tells them what were the characters of his sheep. *First*, They *hear his voice* (v. 27), for they know it to be his (v. 4), and he has undertaken that they shall hear it, v. 16. *Secondly*, They *follow him*; they submit to his guidance by a willing obedience to all his commands, and a cheerful conformity to his spirit and pattern. [2] To convince them that it was their great unhappiness and misery not to be of Christ's sheep, he

here describes the blessed state and case of those that are.

First, Our Lord Jesus *takes cognizance* of his sheep: They *hear my voice*, and *I know them*.

Secondly, He has provided a happiness for them, suited to them: *I give unto them eternal life*, v. 28.

Thirdly, He has undertaken for their security and preservation to this happiness.

a. They shall be *saved from everlasting perdition. They shall by no means perish for ever*; so the words are.

b. They cannot be kept from their *everlasting happiness*; it is in reserve, but he that gives it to them will preserve them to it. Christ had himself experienced the power of his Father *upholding* and *strengthening* him, and therefore puts all his followers into his hand too. He that secured the glory of the Redeemer will secure the glory of the redeemed. Further to corroborate the security, that the sheep of Christ may have strong consolation, he asserts the union of these two undertakers: "*I and my Father are one*, and have jointly and severally undertaken for the protection of the saints and their perfection." This denotes more than the harmony, and consent, and good understanding, that were between the Father and the Son in the work of man's redemption. Every good man is so far one with God as to concur with him; therefore it must be meant of the *oneness of the nature* of Father and Son, that they are the same in substance, and equal in power and glory. He proves

that none could pluck them out *of his hand* because they could not pluck them out *of the Father's hand*, which had not been a conclusive argument if the Son had not had the same almighty power with the Father, and consequently been one with him in essence and operation.

IV. The rage, the outrage, of the Jews against him for this discourse: *The Jews took up stones again*, v. 31.

V. Christ's tender expostulation with them upon occasion of this outrage (v. 32). When he could have answered them with fire from heaven, he mildly replied, *Many good works have I shown you from my Father: for which of those works do you stone me?*

VI. Their vindication of the attempt they made upon Christ, and the cause upon which they grounded their prosecution, v. 33.

1. They would not be thought such enemies to their country as to persecute him for a good work: *For a good work we stone thee not.*

2. They would be thought such friends to God and his glory as to prosecute him for blasphemy: *Because that thou, being a man, makest thyself God.* Here is,

(1) A pretended zeal for the law. They seem mightily concerned for the honour of the divine majesty, and to be seized with a religious horror at that which they imagined to be a reproach to it.

(2) A real enmity to the gospel, on which they could not put a greater affront than by representing Christ as a blasphemer. [1] The crime laid to his charge is *blas-*

phemy, speaking reproachfully and despitefully of God. [2] The proof of the crime: *Thou, being a man, makest thyself God*. Now, *First*, Thus far they were in the right, that what Christ said of himself amounted to this—that he was God, for he had said that he was *one with the Father* and that he would *give eternal life*; and Christ does not deny it, which he would have done if it had been a mistaken inference from his words. But, *Secondly*, They were much mistaken when they looked upon him as a *mere man*, and that the Godhead he claimed was a usurpation, and of his own making.

VII. Christ's reply to their accusation of him (for such their vindication of themselves was), and his making good those claims which they imputed to him as blasphemous (*vv.* 34, &c.), where he proves himself to be no blasphemer, by two arguments:—

1. By an argument taken from *God's word*. He appeals to what was *written in their law*, that is, in the Old Testament; whoever opposes Christ, he is sure to have the scripture *on his side*. It is written (Ps. lxxxii. 6), *I have said, You are gods*. It is an argument *from the less to the greater*. If they were gods, much more am I. Observe,

(1) *From what* he argues—from his works, which he had often vouched as his credentials, and the proofs of his mission. As he proved himself sent of God by the *divinity* of his works, so we must prove ourselves allied to Christ by the *Christianity* of ours.

(2) *For what* he argues—*that*

you may know and believe, may believe it intelligently, and with an entire satisfaction, that *the Father is in me and I in him*; which is the same with what he had said (*v.* 30): *I and my Father are one*. The Father was so in the Son as that in him *dwelt all the fulness of the Godhead*, and it was by a divine power that he wrought his miracles; the Son was so in the Father as that he was perfectly acquainted with the whole of his mind, not by communication, but by consciousness, having lain in his bosom. This we must *know*; not know and *explain* (for we cannot by searching find it out to perfection), but know and *believe* it; acknowledging and adoring the depth, when we cannot find the bottom.

MANY BELIEVE (*vv*. 39–42)

We have here the issue of the conference with the Jews. One would have thought it would have convinced and melted them, but their hearts were hardened. Here we are told,

I. How they attacked him by force. Therefore *they sought again to take him*, *v.* 39. Therefore, 1. Because he had fully answered their charge of blasphemy, and wiped off that imputation, so that they could not for shame go on with their attempts to stone him, therefore they contrived to seize him, and prosecute him as an offender against the state. Or, 2. Because he persevered in the same testimony concerning himself, they persisted in their malice against him.

II. How he avoided them by

flight; not an inglorious retreat, in
which there was any thing of
human infirmity, but a glorious
retirement, in which there was
much of a divine power.

III. How he disposed of himself
in his retirement: He *went away
again beyond Jordan*, v. 40. Now
observe,

1. What *shelter* he found there.
He went into a private part of the
country, and *there he abode*; there
he found some rest and quietness,
when in Jerusalem he could find
none.

2. What *success* he found there.
He did not go thither merely for
his own security, but to do good
there; and he chose to go thither,
where John at first baptized
(*ch.* i. 28), because there could not
but remain some impressions of
John's ministry and baptism thereabouts, which would dispose them
to receive Christ and his doctrine;
for it was not three years since
John was baptizing, and Christ
was himself baptized here at
Bethabara. The event in some
measure answered expectation; for
we are told,

(1) That they flocked after him
(v. 41): *Many resorted to him*.

(2) That they reasoned in his
favour, and sought arguments to
induce them to close with him as
much as those at Jerusalem
sought objections against him.
They said very judiciously, *John
did no miracle, but all things that
John spoke of this man were true*.

(3) That many believed on him
there. Believing that he who wrought
such miracles, and in whom
John's predictions were fulfilled,
was what he declared himself to
be, the Son of God, they gave up
themselves to him as his disciples,
v. 42.

CHAPTER ELEVEN

LAZARUS DIES (*vv.* 1–16)

We have in these verses,

I. A particular account of the
parties principally concerned in
this story, *vv.* 1, 2. 1. They lived at
Bethany, a village not far from
Jerusalem, where Christ usually
lodged when he came up to the
feasts. 2. Here was a brother
named *Lazarus*; his *Hebrew* name
probably was *Eleazar*, which being
contracted, and a Greek termination put to it, is made *Lazarus*.
3. Here were two sisters, *Martha*
and *Mary*, who seem to have
been the housekeepers, and to
have managed the affairs of the
family, while perhaps Lazarus
lived a retired life, and gave
himself to study and contemplation. 4. One of the sisters is
particularly described to be *that
Mary which anointed the Lord with
ointment*, v. 2. I think it refers
to that anointing of Christ which
this evangelist relates (*ch.* xii. 3).
This was she *whose brother Lazarus
was sick*; and the sickness of
those we love is our affliction.

II. The tidings that were sent to
our Lord Jesus of the sickness of
Lazarus, v. 3. *His sisters* knew
where Jesus was, a great way off
beyond Jordan, and they sent a
special messenger to him, to
acquaint him with the affliction
of their family. The message they
sent was very short, not *petitioning*,
much less *prescribing* or *pressing*,
but barely relating the case with

the tender insinuation of a powerful plea, *Lord, behold, he whom thou lovest is sick*. We have great encouragement in our prayers for those who are sick, if we have ground to hope that they are such as Christ loves; and we have reason to love and pray for those whom we have reason to think Christ loves and cares for.

III. An account how Christ entertained the tidings brought him of the illness of his friend.

1. He prognosticated the event and issue of the sickness, and probably sent it as a message to the sisters of Lazarus by the express, to support them while he delayed to come to them. Now one would think it should follow, *When he heard therefore that he was sick* he made all the haste that he could to him; if he loved them, now was a time to show it by hastening to them, for he knew they impatiently expected him. But he took the contrary way to show his love: it is not said, He loved them and *yet* he lingered; but he loved them and *therefore* he lingered; when he heard that his friend was sick, instead of coming post to him, he abode *two days still in the same place where he was*. (1) He *loved them*, that is, had a great opinion of Martha and Mary, of their wisdom and grace, of their faith and patience, above others of his disciples, and therefore he deferred coming to them, that he might try them, that their trial might at last *be found to praise and honour*. (2) He *loved them*, that is, he designed to do something great and extraordinary for them, to work such a miracle for their relief as he had not wrought for any of his friends; and therefore he delayed coming to them, that Lazarus might be *dead* and *buried* before he came. If Christ had come presently, and cured the sickness of Lazarus, he had done no more than he did for *many*; if he had raised him to life when newly dead, no more than he had done for *some*: but, deferring his relief so long, he had an opportunity of doing more for him than for *any*.

IV. The discourse he had with his disciples when he was about to visit his friends at Bethany, *vv.* 7–16. Two things he discourses about—his own *danger* and Lazarus's *death*.

1. His own danger in going into Judea, *vv.* 7–10.

(1) Here is the notice which Christ gave his disciples of his purpose to go into Judea towards Jerusalem.

(2) Their objection against this journey (*v.* 8): *Master, the Jews of late sought to stone thee, and goest thou thither again?* Here, [1] They remind him of the danger he had been in there not long since. [2] They marvel that he will *go thither again*. "Wilt thou favour those with thy presence that have expelled thee out of their coasts?"

(3) Christ's answer to this objection (*vv.* 9, 10): *Are there not twelve hours in the day?* Man's life is a *day*; this day is divided into various ages, states, and opportunities, as into hours shorter or longer, as God has appointed; the consideration of this should make us not only *very busy*, as to the *work* of life, but also *very*

easy as to the perils of life; our day shall be lengthened out till our work be done, and our testimony finished. This Christ applies to his case, and shows why he must go to Judea, because he had a *clear call* to go. For the opening of this, [1] He shows the comfort and satisfaction which a man has in his own mind while he keeps in the way of his duty, as it is in general prescribed by the word of God, and particularly determined by the providence of God: *If any man walk in the day, he stumbles not.* [2] He shows the pain and peril a man is in who walks not according to this rule (*v.* 10): *If a man walk in the night, he stumbles*; that is, If a man walk in the way of his heart, and the sight of his eyes, and according to the course of this world, he falls into temptations and snares, is liable to great uneasiness, and frightful apprehensions.

2. The death of Lazarus is here discoursed of between Christ and his disciples, *vv.* 11–16, where we have,

(1) The notice Christ gave his disciples of the death of Lazarus, and an intimation that his business into Judea was to look after him, *v.* 11. After he had prepared his disciples for this dangerous march into an enemy's country, he then gives them,

[1] Plain intelligence of the death of Lazarus, though he had received no advice of it: *Our friend Lazarus sleepeth.* He calls the death of a believer a *sleep*: *he sleepeth.* It is good to call death by such names and titles as will help to make it more *familiar* and less *formidable*

to us. The death of Lazarus was in a peculiar sense a sleep, as that of Jairus's daughter, because he was to be raised again speedily; and, since we are sure to *rise again at last*, why should that make any great difference?

[2] Particular intimations of his favourable intentions concerning Lazarus: *but I go, that I may awake him out of sleep.* He could have done it, and yet have staid where he was: he that restored at a distance one that was *dying* (*ch.* iv. 50) could have raised at a distance one that was *dead*; but he would put this honour upon the miracle, to work it by the grave side: *I go, to awake him.*

(2) Their mistake of the meaning of this notice, and the blunder they made about it (*vv.* 12, 13): They said, *Lord, if he sleep, he shall do well.* This intimates, [1] *Some concern* they had for their friend Lazarus; they hoped he would recover; *he shall be saved* from dying at this time. [2] A *greater concern* for themselves; for hereby they insinuate that it was now needless for Christ to go to him, and expose himself and them.

(3) This mistake of theirs rectified (*v.* 13): *Jesus spoke of his death.* See here, [1] How dull of understanding Christ's disciples as yet were. [2] How carefully the evangelist corrects this error: *Jesus spoke of his death.* Those that speak in an unknown tongue, or use similitudes, should learn hence to *explain themselves*, and pray that they may interpret, to prevent mistakes.

(4) The plain and express dec-

laration which Jesus made to them of the death of Lazarus, and his resolution to go to Bethany, *vv.* 14, 15. [1] He gives them notice of the death of Lazarus; what he had before said darkly he now says plainly, and without a figure: *Lazarus is dead, v.* 14. [2] He gives them the reason why he had delayed so long to go and see him: *I am glad for your sakes that I was not there.* If he had been there time enough, he would have healed his disease and prevented his death, which would have been much for the comfort of Lazarus's friends; but then his disciples would have seen no further proof of his power than what they had often seen, and, consequently, their faith had received no improvement. [3] He resolves now to go to Bethany, and take his disciples along with him: *Let us go unto him.*

(5) Thomas exciting his fellow-disciples cheerfully to attend their Master's motions (*v.* 16). *Let us also go that we may die with him; with him,* that is,

[1] With Lazarus, who was now dead; so some take it.

[2] "Let us go and die *with our Master,* who is now exposing himself to death by venturing into Judea"; and so I rather think it is meant.

THE RAISING OF LAZARUS
(*vv.* 17–32)

To Bethany Christ came, and observe,

I. What posture he found his friends there in.

1. He found his friend Lazarus *in the grave, v.* 17. When he came near the town, probably by the burying-place belonging to the town, he was told by the neighbours, or some persons whom he met, that Lazarus had been *four days buried.*

2. He found his friends that survived *in grief.* Martha and Mary were almost swallowed up with sorrow for the death of their brother, which is intimated where it is said that *many of the Jews came to Martha and Mary to comfort them.*

II. What passed between him and his surviving friends at this interview.

1. The interview between Christ and Martha.

(1) We are told that she *went and met him, v.* 20. [1] It should seem that Martha was earnestly expecting Christ's arrival, and enquiring for it. [2] Martha, when the good news was brought that Jesus was coming, threw all aside, and *went and met him,* in token of a most affectionate welcome. She waived all ceremony and compliment to the Jews who came to visit her, and hastened to go and meet Jesus. [3] When Martha went to meet Jesus, Mary *sat still in the house.* Some think she did *not* hear the tidings, being in her drawing-room, receiving visits of condolence, while Martha who was busied in the household-affairs had early notice of it. Perhaps Martha would not tell her sister that Christ was coming, being ambitious of the honour of receiving him first. Others think she *did* hear that Christ was come, but was so overwhelmed with sorrow that she did not care to stir,

choosing rather to indulge her sorrow, and to sit poring upon her affliction, and saying, *I do well to* mourn. Comparing this story with that in Luke x. 38, &c., we may observe the different tempers of these two sisters, and the temptations and advantages of each.

(2) Here is fully related the discourse between Christ and Martha.

[1] Martha's address to Christ, *vv.* 21, 22.

First, She complains of Christ's long absence and delay. She said it, not only with grief for the death of her brother, but with some resentment of the seeming unkindness of the Master: *Lord, if thou hadst been here, my brother had not died. If thou hadst been here*; whereas she ought to have known that Christ could cure at a distance, and that his gracious operations were not limited to his bodily presence.

Secondly, Yet she corrects and comforts herself with the thoughts of the prevailing interest Christ had in heaven; at least, she blames herself for blaming her Master, and for suggesting that he comes too late: *for I know that even now*, desperate as the case is, *whatsoever thou wilt ask of God, God will give it to thee.*

[2] The comfortable word which Christ gave to Martha, in answer to her pathetic address (*v.* 23): *Jesus saith unto her, Thy brother shall rise again.*

[3] The faith which Martha mixed with this word, and the unbelief mixed with this faith, *v.* 24.

First, She accounts it a *faithful saying* that *he shall rise again at the last day*. Though the doctrine of the resurrection was to have its full proof from Christ's resurrection, yet, as it was already revealed, she firmly believed it, Acts xxiv. 15. 1. That there shall be a *last day*, with which all the days of time shall be numbered and finished. 2. That there shall be a *general* resurrection at that day, when the earth and sea shall give up their dead. 3. That there shall be a *particular* resurrection of each one: "I know that I shall rise again, and this and the other relation that was dear to me." As bone shall return to his bone in that day, so friend to his friend.

Secondly, Yet she seems to think this saying not so well worthy of all acceptation as really it was: "*I know he shall rise again at the last day*; but what are we the better for that now?" As if the comforts of the resurrection to eternal life were not worth speaking of, or yielded not satisfaction sufficient to balance her affliction.

[4] The further instruction and encouragement which Jesus Christ gave her; for he will not quench the smoking flax nor break the bruised reed. He said to her, *I am the resurrection and the life*, *vv.* 25, 26. Two things Christ possesses her with the belief of, in reference to the present distress; and they are the things which our faith should fasten upon in the like cases.

First, The power of Christ, his sovereign power: *I am the resurrection and the life*, the fountain of life, and the head and author of the resurrection. Martha believed that at his prayer God would give any thing, but he would have her know that by his word he could work any thing. Martha believed a resurrection at the *last day*; Christ tells her that he had that power lodged in his own hand, that the dead were to *hear his voice* (*ch.* v. 25), whence it was easy to infer, He that could raise a world of men that had been dead many ages could doubtless raise one man that had been dead but *four days*.

Secondly, The promises of the new covenant, which give us further ground of hope that *we shall live*. Observe,

a. To whom these promises are made—to those that believe in Jesus Christ, to those that consent to, and confide in, Jesus Christ as the only Mediator of reconciliation and communion between God and man, that receive the record God has given in his word concerning his Son, sincerely comply with it, and answer all the great intentions of it. The condition of the latter promise is thus expressed: *Whosoever liveth and believeth in me*, which may be understood, either, (*a*) Whoever during *life*, while he is here in this state of probation, *believes in me*, shall be happy in me, but after death it will be too late. Or, (*b*) Of *spiritual* life: He that *lives* and *believes* is he that by faith is born again to a heavenly and divine life, to whom *to live is Christ*—that makes Christ the life of his soul.

b. What the promises are (*v.* 25): *Though he die, yet shall he live,*

nay, *he shall never die, v.* 26. Man consists of body and soul, and provision is made for the happiness of both.

(*a*) For the *body*; here is the promise of a *blessed resurrection*. Though the body be dead because of sin (there is no remedy but it will die), yet it *shall live again*.

(*b*) For the *soul*; here is the promise of a *blessed immortality*. He that *liveth and believeth*, who, being united to Christ by faith, lives spiritually by virtue of that union, he shall *never die*. Christ asks her, "*Believest thou this?* Canst thou *assent* to it with application? Canst thou take my word for it?"

[5] Martha's unfeigned assent yielded to what Christ said, *v.* 27. We have here Martha's creed, the good confession she witnessed, the same with that for which Peter was commended (Matt. xvi. 16, 17), and it is the *conclusion of the whole matter*.

First, Here is the *guide of her faith*, and that is the word of Christ; without any alteration, exception, or proviso, she takes it entire as Christ had said it: *Yea Lord*, whereby she subscribes to the truth of all and every part of that which Christ had promised, in his own sense: *Even so*. Faith is an echo to divine revelation, returns the same words, and resolves to abide by them: *Yea, Lord*.

Secondly, The *ground of her faith*, and that is the authority of Christ; she believes *this* because she believes that he who saith it is Christ. She has recourse to the foundation for the support of the superstructure. Observe here, *a*. What she believed and confessed concerning Jesus; three things, all to the same effect:— (*a*) That he was the Christ, or Messiah, promised and expected under this name and notion, the *anointed one*. (*b*) That he was the *Son of God*; so the Messiah was called (Ps. ii. 7), not by office only, but by nature. (*c*) That it was *he who should come* into the world.

b. What she inferred hence, and what she alleged this for. If she admits this, that Jesus is the Christ, there is no difficulty in believing that he is the resurrection and the life.

2. The interview between Christ and Mary the other sister. And here observe,

(1) The notice which Martha gave her of Christ's coming (*v*. 28): *When she had so said*, as one that needed to say no more, *she went her way*, easy in her mind, and *called Mary her sister*.

(2) The haste which Mary made to Christ upon this notice given her (*v*. 29): *As soon as she heard* this good news, that the *Master was come*, she *arose quickly*, and came to him.

(3) We are told (*v*. 30) where she found the Master; he was not yet come into Bethany, but was at the town's end, *in that place where Martha met him*.

(4) The misconstruction which the Jews that were with Mary made of her going away so hastily (*v*. 31): They said, *She goes to the grave, to weep there*. Martha bore up better under this affliction than Mary did, who was a woman of a tender and sorrowful spirit; such was her natural temper. Those that

are so have need to watch against melancholy, and ought to be pitied and helped. These comforters found that their formalities did her no service, but that she hardened herself in sorrow: and therefore concluded when she went out, and turned that way, it was to go *to the grave* and *weep there*.

(5) Mary's address to our Lord Jesus (*v*. 32): She came, attended with her train of comforters, and *fell down at his feet*, as one overwhelmed with a passionate sorrow, and said with many tears (as appears *v*. 33), *Lord, if thou hadst been here, my brother had not died*, as Martha said before, for they had often said it to one another. Mary added no more, as Martha did; but it appears, by what follows, that what she fell short in words she made up in tears; she said less than Martha, but wept more; and tears of devout affection have a voice, a loud prevailing voice, in the ears of Christ; no rhetoric like this.

AT THE TOMB (*vv*. 33–44)

Here we have, I. Christ's tender *sympathy* with his afflicted friends, and the share he took to himself in their sorrows, which appeared three ways:—

1. By the inward groans and troubles of his spirit (*v*. 33): *Jesus saw Mary weeping* for the loss of a loving brother, and the *Jews that came with her weeping* for the loss of a good neighbour and friend; when he saw what a *place of weepers*, a *bochim*, this was, *he groaned in the spirit, and was troubled*.

2. His concern for them appeared by his *kind enquiry* after the poor remains of his deceased friend (*v.* 34): Where *have you laid him?*

3. It appeared by *his tears.* Those about him did not tell him where the body was buried, but desired him to *come and see*, and led him directly to the grave, that his eye might yet more affect his heart with the calamity.

(1) As he was going to the grave, as if he had been following the corpse thither, *Jesus wept, v.* 35. A very short verse, but it affords many useful instructions. [1] That Jesus Christ was really and truly man, and partook with the children, not only of flesh and blood, but of a human soul, susceptible of the impressions of joy, and grief, and other affections. Christ gave this proof of his humanity, in both senses of the word; that, as a man, he could weep, and, as a merciful man, he *would weep*, before he gave this proof of his divinity. [2] That he was *a man of sorrows*, and *acquainted with grief*, as was foretold, Isa. liii. 3. We never read that he laughed, but more than once we have him in tears. [3] Tears of compassion well become Christians, and make them most to resemble Christ.

(2) Different constructions were put upon Christ's weeping. [1] Some made a kind and candid interpretation of it, and what was very natural (*v.* 36): *Then said the Jews, Behold how he loved him!* [2] Others made a peevish unfair reflection upon it, as if these tears bespoke his inability to help his friend (*v.* 37): *Could not this man,*

who opened the eyes of the blind, have prevented the death of Lazarus? Here it is slily insinuated, *First*, That the death of Lazarus being (as it seemed by his tears) a great grief to him, if he could have prevented it he would, and therefore because he *did not* they incline to think that he *could not.* *Secondly*, That therefore it might justly be questioned whether he did indeed *open the eyes of the blind*, that is, whether it was not a sham.

II. Christ's approach to the grave, and the preparation that was made for working this miracle.

1. Christ repeats his groans upon his coming near the grave (*v.* 38): *Again groaning in himself, he comes to the grave*; he groaned, (1) Being displeased at the unbelief of those who spoke doubtingly of his power, and blamed him for not preventing the death of Lazarus; he was *grieved for the hardness of their hearts.* (2) Being affected with the fresh lamentations which, it is likely, the mourning sisters made, when they came near the grave, more passionately and pathetically than before, his tender spirit was sensibly touched with their wailings. (3) Some think that he *groaned in spirit* because, to gratify the desire of his friends, he was to bring Lazarus again into this sinful troublesome world, from that rest into which he was newly entered; it would be a kindness to Martha and Mary, but it would be to him like thrusting one out to a stormy sea again who was newly got into a safe and quiet harbour. (4) Christ groaned as

one that would affect himself with the calamitous state of the human nature, as subject to death, from which he was now about to redeem Lazarus.

2. The grave wherein Lazarus lay is here described: *It was a cave, and a stone lay upon it.*

3. Orders are given to remove the stone (*v.* 39): *Take away the stone.* He would have this stone removed that all the standers-by might see the body lie dead in the sepulchre, and that way might be made for its coming out, and it might appear to be a true body, and not a *ghost* or *spectre.*

4. An objection made by Martha against the opening of the grave: *Lord, by this time he stinketh.* He is *four days old* in the other world; a citizen and inhabitant of the grave of four days' standing. Probably Martha perceived the body to smell, as they were removing the stone, and therefore cried out thus.

5. The gentle reproof Christ gave to Martha for the weakness of her faith (*v.* 40): *Said I not unto thee that if thou wouldest believe thou shouldest see the glory of God?* This word of his to her was not before recorded; it is probable that he said it to her when she had said (*v.* 27), *Lord, I believe*: and it is enough that it is recorded here, where it is repeated.

6. The opening of the grave, in obedience to Christ's order, notwithstanding Martha's objection (*v.* 41): *Then they took away the stone.*

III. The miracle itself wrought. Their expectations being raised, our Lord Jesus addresses himself to his work.

1. He applies himself to his *living Father in heaven,* so he had called him (*ch.* vi. 17), and so eyes him here.

(1) The gesture he used was very significant: *He lifted up his eyes,* an outward expression of the elevation of his mind, and to show those who stood by whence he derived his power.

(2) His address to God was with great assurance, and such a confidence as became him: *Father, I thank thee that thou hast heard me.*

[1] He has here taught us, by his own example, *First,* In prayer to call God Father, and to draw nigh to him as children to a father, with a humble reverence, and yet with a holy boldness. *Secondly,* In our *prayers* to *praise him,* and, when we come to beg for further mercy, thankfully to acknowledge former favours.

[2] But our Saviour's thanksgiving here was intended to express the unshaken assurance he had of the effecting of this miracle, which he had in his own power to do in concurrence with his Father.

First, Christ speaks of this miracle as an answer to prayer, 1. Because he would thus *humble himself*; though he was a Son, yet *learned he this obedience,* to ask and receive. 2. Because he was pleased thus to *honour prayer,* making it the key wherewith even he unlocked the treasures of divine power and grace.

Secondly, Christ, being assured that his prayer was answered, professes,

a. His thankful acceptance of

this answer: *I thank thee that thou hast heard me.*

b. His cheerful assurance of a ready answer at any time (*v.* 42): *And I know that thou hearest me always.* Let none think that this was some uncommon favour granted him now, such as he never had before, nor should ever have again; no, he had the same divine power going along with him in his whole undertaking, and undertook nothing but what he knew to be agreeable to the counsel of God's will.

Thirdly, But why should Christ give this public intimation of his obtaining this miracle by prayer? He adds, It is *because of the people who stand by, that they may believe that thou hast sent me*; for *prayer may preach.*

2. He now applies himself to his *dead friend in the earth.* He *cried with a loud voice, Lazarus come forth.*

(1) He could have raised Lazarus by a silent exertion of his power and will, and the indiscernible operations of the Spirit of life; but he did it by a call, a loud call,

[1] To be significant of the power then put forth for the raising of Lazarus, how he *created this new thing*; he *spoke, and it was done.*

[2] To be typical of other works of wonder, and particularly other resurrections, which the power of Christ was to effect. This loud call was a figure, *First,* Of the gospel call, by which dead souls were to be brought out of the grave of sin, which resurrection Christ had formerly spoken of (*ch.* v. 25), and of his word as

the means of it (*ch.* vi. 63), and now he gives a specimen of it.

(2) This *loud call* was but *short,* yet *mighty through God* to the battering down of the strongholds of the grave.

(3) This miracle was wrought, [1] *Speedily.* Nothing intervenes between the command, *Come forth,* and the effect, *He came forth.* Thus the change in the resurrection will be *in a moment, in the twinkling of an eye,* 1 Cor. xv. 52. [2] *Perfectly.* He was so thoroughly revived that he got up out of his grave as strongly as ever he got up out of his bed, and returned not only to life, but health. He was not raised to serve a present turn, but to live as other men. [3] With this additional miracle, as some reckon it, that he came out of his grave, though he was fettered with his grave-clothes, with which he was *bound hand and foot,* and *his face bound about with a napkin* (for so the manner of the Jews was to bury); and he came forth in the same dress wherein he was buried, that it might appear that it was he himself and not another, and that he was not only alive, but strong, and able to walk, after a sort, even in his grave-clothes. Lazarus being *come forth,* hampered and embarrassed with his grave-clothes, we may well imagine that those about the grave were exceedingly surprised and frightened at it; we should be so if we should see a dead body rise; but Christ, to make the thing familiar, sets them to work: "*Loose him,* slacken his grave-clothes, that they may serve for day-clothes till he comes to his house, and then he will go

himself, so clad, without guide or supporter to his own house."

REACTIONS (*vv.* 45–57)

We have here an account of the consequences of this glorious miracle, which were as usual; to some it was a savour of life unto life, to others of death unto death.

I. Some were invited by it, and induced to believe. Many of the Jews, when they *saw the things that Jesus did, believed on him,* and well they might, for it was an incontestable proof of his divine mission.

II. Others were irritated by it, and hardened in their unbelief.

1. The *informers* were so (*v.* 46): *Some of them,* who were eye-witnesses of the miracle, were so far from being convinced that they *went to the Pharisees,* whom they knew to be his implacable enemies, and *told them what things Jesus had done.*

2. The judges, the leaders, the *blind leaders,* of the people were no less exasperated by the report made to them, and here we are told what they did.

(1) A special council is called and held (*v.* 47).

(2) The case is proposed, and shown to be weighty and of great consequence.

[1] The matter to be debated was what course they should take with this Jesus, to stop the growth of his interest.

[2] That which made this matter weighty was the peril they apprehended their church and nation to be in from the Romans (*v.* 48): "If we do not silence him, and take him off, *all men will believe*

on him"; and, this being the setting up of a new king, the Romans will take umbrage at it, *and will come* with an army, and *take away our place and nation,* and therefore it is no time to trifle."

(3) Caiaphas makes a malicious but mystical speech in the council on this occasion.

[1] The *malice* of it appears evident at first view, *vv.* 49, 50. He, being the high priest, and so president of the council, took upon him to decide the matter before it was debated. Here,

First, The counsellor was Caiaphas, who was *high priest that same year.*

Secondly, The drift of the advice was, in short, this, That some way or other must be found out to put Jesus to death. We have reason to think that they strongly suspected him to be indeed the Messiah; but his doctrine was so contrary to their darling traditions and secular interest, and his design did so thwart their notions of the Messiah's kingdom, that they resolve, be he who he will, he must be put to death.

Thirdly, This is plausibly insinuated, with all the subtlety as well as malice of the old serpent. 1. He suggests his own sagacity, which we must suppose him as high priest to excel in, though the *Urim* and *Thummim* were long since lost. 2. He takes it for granted that the case is plain and past dispute, and that those are very ignorant who do not see it to be so. 3. He insists upon a maxim in politics, That the welfare of communities is to be preferred before that of particular persons.

It is expedient for us as priests, whose all lies at stake, that *one man die for the people*. Thus far it holds true, that it is *expedient*, and more than so, it is truly *honourable*, for a man to hazard his life in the service of his country (Phil. ii. 17; 1 John iii. 16); but to put an innocent man to death under colour of consulting the public safety is the devil's policy.

[2] The *mystery* that was in this counsel of Caiaphas does not appear at first view, but the evangelist leads us into it (*vv.* 51, 52). Here is a precious comment upon a pernicious text; the counsel of cursed Caiaphas so construed as to fall in with the counsels of the blessed God.

(4) The evangelist explains and enlarges upon Caiaphas's words.

[1] He explains what he said, and shows how it not only was, but was intended to be, accommodated to an excellent purpose. He did not *speak it of himself*. As it was an artifice to stir up the council against Christ, he spoke it of himself, or of the devil rather; but as it was an *oracle*, declaring it the purpose and design of God by the death of Christ to save God's spiritual Israel from sin and wrath, he did not speak it of himself, for he knew nothing of the matter, he *meant not so*, *neither did his heart think so*, for nothing was in his heart but to destroy and cut off, Isa. x. 7.

First, He *prophesied*, and those that prophesied did not, in their prophesying, *speak of themselves*.

Secondly, He prophesied, *being high priest that year*; not that his being high priest did at all dispose or qualify him to be a prophet; we cannot suppose the pontifical mitre to have first inspired with prophecy the basest head that ever wore it; but, 1. Being high priest, and therefore of note and eminence in the conclave, God was pleased to put this significant word into his mouth rather than into the mouth of any other, that it might be the more observed or the non-observance of it the more aggravated. 2. Being high priest *that year*, that famous year, in which there was to be such a plentiful effusion of the Spirit, more than had ever been yet, according to the prophecy (Joel ii. 28, 29, compared with Acts ii. 17), some drops of the blessed shower light upon Caiaphas, as the crumbs (says Dr. Lightfoot) of the children's bread, which fall from the table among the dogs. This year was the year of the expiration of the Levitical priesthood; and out of the mouth of him who was that year high priest was extorted an implicit resignation of it to him who should not (as they had done for many ages) offer beasts for that nation, but offer himself, and so make an end of the *sin-offering*. This resignation he made *unwittingly*, as Isaac gave the blessing to Jacob.

Thirdly, The matter of his prophecy was *that Jesus should die for that nation*, the very thing to which all the prophets bore witness, who *testified beforehand the sufferings of Christ* (1 Pet. i. 11), that the death of Christ must be the life and salvation of Israel. He so died for *that nation* as that *the whole nation should not perish*, but that *a remnant should be saved*, Rom. xi. 5.

[2] The evangelist enlarges upon this word of Caiaphas (*v.* 52), *not for that nation only*, how much soever it thought itself the darling of Heaven, but *that also he should gather together in one the children of God that were scattered abroad.*

He died to *gather in* those who wandered, and to *gather together in one* those who were scattered; to invite those to him who were at a distance from him, and to unite those in him who were at a distance from each other.

(5) The result of this debate is a resolve of the council to put Jesus to death (*v.* 53): *From that day they took counsel together, to put him to death.*

(6) Christ hereupon absconded, knowing very well what was the vote of their close cabal, *v.* 54.

[1] He suspended his public appearances: *He walked no more openly among the Jews.*

[2] He withdrew into an obscure part of the country, so obscure that the name of the town he retired to is scarcely met with any where else. It was not because he either feared the power of his enemies or distrusted his own power; he had many ways to save himself, and was neither averse to suffering nor unprepared for it; but he retired, *First*, To put a mark of his displeasure upon Jerusalem and the people of the Jews. *Secondly*, To render the cruelty of his enemies against him the more inexcusable. *Thirdly*, His hour was *not yet come*. *Fourthly*, His retirement, for a while, was to make his return into

Jerusalem, when his hour was come, the more remarkable and illustrious.

(7) The strict enquiry made for him during his recess, *vv.* 55–57.

[1] The occasion of it was the approach of the passover, at which they expected his presence, according to custom (*v.* 55).

[2] The enquiry was very solicitous: *They said, What think you, that he will not come to the feast?* *v.* 56.

First, Some think this was said by those who wished well to him, and expected his coming, that they might hear his doctrine and see his miracles.

Secondly, It should rather seem that they were his enemies who made this enquiry after him, who wished for an opportunity to lay hands on him.

[3] The orders issued out by the government for the apprehending of him were very strict, *v.* 57. Yet such was his interest in the affections of some, and such God's hold of the consciences of others, that he continued undiscovered, for the *Lord hid him.*

CHAPTER TWELVE

RETURN TO BETHANY
(*vv.* 1–11)

In these verses we have,

I. The *kind visit* our Lord Jesus paid to his friends at Bethany, *v.* 1. His coming to Bethany now may be considered,

1. As a preface to the passover he intended to celebrate, to which reference is made in assigning the date of his coming: *Six days before the passover.*

2. As a voluntary exposing of himself to the fury of his enemies; now that his hour was at hand he came within their reach, and freely offered himself to them, though he had shown them how easily he could evade all their snares.

3. An instance of his kindness to his friends at Bethany, whom he loved, and from whom he was shortly to be taken away.

II. The *kind entertainment* which his friends there gave him. Lazarus was *one of those that sat at meat*. It proved the truth of his resurrection, as it did of Christ's, that there were those who did *eat and drink with him*, Acts x. 41.

III. The particular respect which Mary showed him, above the rest, in anointing his feet with sweet ointment, *v*. 3. She had a *pound of ointment of spikenard, very costly*, which probably she had by her for her own use; but the death and resurrection of her brother had quite weaned her from the use of all such things, and with this she *anointed the feet of Jesus*, and, as a further token of her reverence for him and negligence of herself, she *wiped them with her hair*, and this was taken notice of by all that were present, for *the house was filled with the odour of the ointment*. See Prov. xxvii. 16.

IV. Judas's dislike of Mary's compliment, or token of her respect to Christ, *vv*. 4, 5, where observe,

1. The person that carped at it was Judas, *one of his disciples*; not one of their nature, but only one of their number.

2. The pretence with which he covered his dislike (*v*. 5). (1) Here

is a foul iniquity gilded over with a specious and plausible pretence, for Satan transforms himself into an angel of light. (2) Here is worldly wisdom passing a censure upon pious zeal, as guilty of imprudence and mismanagement. (3) Here is charity to the poor made a colour for opposing a piece of piety to Christ, and secretly made a cloak for covetousness.

3. The detection and discovery of Judas's hypocrisy herein, *v*. 6. Here is the evangelist's remark upon it, by the direction of him who *searches the heart: This he said, not that he cared for the poor*, as he pretended, *but because he was a thief, and had the bag*.

V. Christ's justification of what Mary did (*vv*. 7, 8): *Let her alone*. For Mary's justification,

1. Christ puts a favourable construction upon what she did, which those that condemned it were not aware of: *Against the day of my burying she has kept this*. Or, *She has reserved this for the day of my embalming*; so Dr. Hammond.

2. He gives a sufficient answer to Judas's objection, *v*. 8. (1) It is so ordered in the kingdom of Providence that *the poor we have always with us*, some or other that are proper objects of charity (Deut. xv. 11); such there will be as long as there are in this lapsed state of mankind so much folly and so much affliction. (2) It is so ordered in the kingdom of grace that the church should not always have the bodily presence of Jesus Christ: "*Me you have not always*, but only now for a

little time." Note, We need wisdom, when two duties come in competition, to know which to give the preference to, which must be determined by the circumstances.

VI. The public notice which was taken of our Lord Jesus here at this supper in Bethany (*v.* 9). 1. They came to see Jesus, whose name was very much magnified, and made considerable by the late miracle he had wrought in raising Lazarus. 2. They came to see Lazarus and Christ together, which was a very inviting sight.

VII. The indignation of the chief priests at the growing interest of our Lord Jesus, and their plot to crush it (*vv.* 10, 11). Here observe,

1. How vain and unsuccessful their attempts against Christ had hitherto been. They had done all they could to alienate the people from him, and exasperate them against him, and yet many of the Jews, their neighbours, their creatures, their admirers, were so overcome by the convincing evidence of Christ's miracles that they *went away* from the interest and party of the priests, went off from obedience to their tyranny, *and believed on Jesus*; and it was by reason of Lazarus; his resurrection put life into their faith, and convinced them that this Jesus was undoubtedly the Messiah, and had life in himself, and power to give life. This miracle confirmed them in the belief of his other miracles, which they had heard he wrought in Galilee: what was impossible to him that could raise the dead?

2. How absurd and unreasonable

this day's vote was—that Lazarus must be put to death. For, (1) If they had feared God, they would not have done such an act of defiance to him. God will have Lazarus to live by miracle, and they will have him to die by malice. (2) If they had regarded man, they would not have done such an act of injustice to Lazarus, an innocent man, to whose charge they could not pretend to lay any crime.

PALM SUNDAY (*vv.* 12–19)

This story of Christ's riding in triumph to Jerusalem is recorded by all the evangelists, as worthy of special remark. We may observe,

I. The respect that was paid to our Lord Jesus by the common people, *vv.* 12, 13.

II. The posture Christ puts himself into for receiving the respect that was paid him (*v.* 14): *When he had found*, or procured, *a young ass*, he *sat thereon*. It was but a poor sort of figure he made, he alone upon an ass, and a crowd of people about him shouting *Hosanna*.

III. The fulfilling of the scripture in this: *As it is written, Fear not, daughter of Sion*, *v.* 15. This is quoted from Zech. ix. 9. To him bore all the prophets witness, and particularly to this concerning him.

IV. The remark made by the evangelist respecting the disciples (*v.* 16): *They understood not at first* why Christ did this, and how the scripture was fulfilled; but when *Jesus was glorified*, and thereupon the Spirit poured out, then they remembered that *these things were written of him* in the

Old Testament, and that they and others had, in pursuance thereof, *done these things to him*.

V. The reason which induced the people to pay this respect to our Lord Jesus upon his coming into Jerusalem, though the government was so much set against him. It was because of the illustrious miracle he had lately wrought in raising Lazarus.

VI. The indignation of the Pharisees at all this; some of them probably, saw, and they all soon heard of, Christ's public entry. The committee appointed to find out expedients to crush him thought they had gained their point when he had retired unto privacy, and that he would soon be forgotten in Jerusalem, but they now rage and fret when they see they imagined but a *vain thing*.

GREEKS ASK FOR JESUS
(*vv.* 20–26)

Honour is here paid to Christ by certain Greeks that enquired for him with respect.

I. We are told who they were that paid this honour to our Lord Jesus: *Certain Greeks among the people who came to worship at the feast*, *v.* 20. Some think they were *Jews of the dispersion*, some of the twelve tribes that were scattered among the Gentiles, and were called *Greeks*, Hellenist Jews; but others think they were Gentiles, those whom they called *proselytes of the gate*, such as the eunuch and Cornelius.

II. What was the honour they paid him: they desired to be acquainted with him, *v.* 21. Their business is, they would *see Jesus*;

not only see his face, that they might be able to say, when they came home, they had seen one that was so much talked of (it is probable they had seen him when he appeared publicly); but they would have some free conversation with him, and be taught by him, for which it was no easy thing to find him at leisure, his hands were so full of public work.

III. Christ's acceptance of this honour paid him, signified by what he said to the people hereupon, *vv.* 23, &c., where he foretells both the honour which he himself should have in being followed (*vv.* 23, 24) and the honour which those should have that followed him, *vv.* 25, 26. This was intended for the direction and encouragement of these Greeks, and all others that desired acquaintance with him.

1. He foresees that plentiful harvest, in the conversion of the Gentiles, of which this was as it were the first-fruits, *v.* 23. Observe,

(1) The end designed hereby, and that is the glorifying of the Redeemer.

(2) The strange way in which this end was to be attained, and that was by the death of Christ, intimated in that similitude (*v.* 24): "*Verily, verily, I say unto you*, you to whom I have spoken of my death and sufferings, *except a corn of wheat* fall not only *to*, but *into, the ground*, and *die*, and be buried and lost, it *abideth alone*, and you never see any more of it; but *if it die* according to the course of nature (otherwise it would be a miracle) it *bringeth forth much fruit*, God giving to

every seed its own body." Christ is the corn of wheat, the most valuable and useful grain. Now here is,

[1] The necessity of Christ's humiliation intimated. He must *pour out his soul unto death*, else he cannot *divide a portion with the great*, Isa. liii. 12.

[2] The advantage of Christ's humiliation illustrated. He *fell to the ground* in his incarnation, seemed to be buried alive in this earth, so much was his glory veiled; but this was not all: *he died*. The salvation of souls hitherto, and henceforward to the end of time, is all owing to the dying of this *corn of wheat*.

2. He foretells and promises an abundant recompence to those who should cordially embrace him and his gospel and interest, and should make it appear that they do so by their faithfulness in suffering for him or in serving him.

(1) In suffering for him (*v.* 25). This doctrine Christ much insisted on, it being the great design of his religion to wean us from this world, by setting before us another world.

(2) In serving him (*v.* 26). The Greeks desired to see Jesus (*v.* 21), but Christ lets them know that it was not enough to see him, they must *serve him*. He did not come into the world, to be a show for us to gaze at, but a king to be ruled by.

[1] Here is the work which Christ expects from his servants; and it is very easy and reasonable, and such as becomes them.

First, Let them attend their Master's movements: *If any man serve me, let him follow me.*

Secondly, Let them attend their Master's repose: *Where I am, there let my servant be*, to wait upon me. Christ is where his church is, in the assemblies of his saints, where his ordinances are administered; and *there let his servants be*.

[2] Here are the wages which Christ promises to his servants; and they are very rich and noble.

First, They shall be happy with him: *Where I am, there shall also my servant be*. Those that follow him in the way shall be with him in the end.

Secondly, They shall be honoured by his Father. Those that wait on Christ God will put honour upon, such as will be taken notice of another day, though now under a veil.

A VOICE FROM HEAVEN
(*vv.* 27–36)

Honour is here done to Christ by his Father in a voice from heaven, occasioned by the following part of his discourse, and which gave occasion to a further conference with the people. In these verses we have,

I. Christ's address to his Father, upon occasion of the trouble which seized his spirit at this time: *Now is my soul troubled, v.* 27. Observe,

1. Christ's dread of his approaching sufferings: *Now is my soul troubled*. Now the black and dismal scene began, now were the first throes of the travail of his soul, now his agony began, his soul *began to be exceedingly sorrowful*.

2. The strait he seems to be in hereupon, intimated in those words,

And what shall I say? This does not imply his consulting with any other, as if he needed advice, but considering with himself what was fit to be said now.

3. His prayer to God in this strait: *Father, save me from this hour—out of this hour*, praying, not so much that it might not come as that he might be brought through it.

4. His acquiescence in his Father's will, notwithstanding. He presently corrects himself, and, as it were, recalls what he had said: *But for this cause came I to this hour*. Innocent nature got the first word, but divine wisdom and love got the last.

5. His regard to his Father's honour herein. Upon the withdrawing of his former petition, he presents another, which he will abide by: *Father, glorify thy name*, to the same purport with *Father, thy will be done*; for God's will is for his own glory.

II. The Father's answer to this address; for he heard him always, and does still. Observe, 1. How this answer was given. By a voice from heaven. 2. What the answer was. It was an express return to that petition, *Father, glorify thy name: I have glorified it* already, and *I will glorify it yet again*. When we pray as we are taught, *Our Father, hallowed be thy name*, this is a comfort to us, that it is an answered prayer; answered to Christ here, and in him to all true believers.

III. The opinion of the standers-by concerning this voice, *v.* 29. We may hope there were some among them whose minds were so well prepared to receive a divine revelation that they understood what was said and bore record of it. But notice is here taken of the perverse suggestion of the multitude: some of them said that *it thundered*; others, who took notice that there was plainly an articulate intelligible voice, said that certainly *an angel spoke to him*. Now this shows, 1. That it was a real thing, even in the judgment of those that were not at all well affected to him. 2. That they were loth to admit so plain a proof of Christ's divine mission. They would rather say that it was this, or that, or any thing, than that God spoke to him in answer to his prayer.

IV. The account which our Saviour himself gives of this voice.

1. Why it was sent (*v.* 30): "It came *not because of me*, not merely for my encouragement and satisfaction" (then it might have been whispered in his ear privately), "*but for your sakes*". (1) "That all you who heard it may *believe that the Father hath sent me*." (2) "That you my disciples, who are to follow me in sufferings, may therein be comforted with the same comforts that carry me on."

2. What was the meaning of it.

(1) That by the death of Christ Satan should be conquered (*v.* 31): *Now is the judgment*. He speaks with a divine exultation and triumph.

(2) That by the death of Christ souls should be converted, and this would be the casting out of Satan (*v.* 32): *If I be lifted up from the earth, I will draw all men unto me*. Here observe two things:—

[1] The great design of our Lord Jesus, which was to *draw all men to him*, not the Jews only, who had been long in profession a people *near to God*, but the Gentiles also, who had been *afar off*; for he was to be the *desire of all nations* (Hag. ii. 7), and *to him must the gathering of the people be*.

[2] The strange method he took to accomplish his design by *being lifted up from the earth*. What he meant by this, to prevent mistake, we are told (*v.* 33): *This he spoke signifying by what death he should die*, the death of the cross, though they had designed and attempted to stone him to death. He that was crucified was first nailed to the cross, and then lifted up upon it. He was *lifted up as a spectacle to the world*; lifted up between heaven and earth, as unworthy of either; yet the word here used signifies an honourable advancement—*If I be exalted*; he reckoned his sufferings his honour. Now Christ's drawing all men to him followed his being *lifted up from the earth*. *First*, It followed after it in time. The great increase of the church was after the death of Christ. *Secondly*, It followed upon it as a blessed consequence of it. Note, There is a powerful virtue and efficacy in the death of Christ to draw souls to him.

V. The people's exception against what he said, and their cavil at it, *v.* 34. Christ had called himself the *Son of man* (*v.* 23), which they knew to be one of the titles of the Messiah, Dan. vii. 13. He had also said that the *Son of man must be lifted up* which they understood of his dying, and probably he

explained himself. Now against this,

1. They alleged those scriptures of the Old Testament which speak of the perpetuity of the Messiah, that he should be so far from being cut off in the midst of his days that he should be a *priest for ever* (Ps. cx. 4), and a king *for ever* (Ps. lxxxix. 29, &c.), that he should have *length of days for ever and ever*, and *his years as many generations* (Ps. xxi. 4; lxi. 6), from all which they inferred that the Messiah should not die. Their perverseness in opposing this to what Jesus had said will appear if we consider, (1) That, when they vouched the scripture to prove that the Messiah *abideth for ever*, they took no notice of those texts which speak of the Messiah's death and sufferings. (2) That, when they opposed what Christ said concerning the sufferings of the Son of man, they took no notice of what he had said concerning his glory and exaltation.

2. They asked hereupon, *Who is this Son of man?* This they asked, not with a desire to be instructed, but tauntingly and insultingly, as if now they had baffled him, and run him down.

VI. What Christ said to this exception, or rather what he said *upon* it. "*Yet a little while*, and but a little while, *is the light with you*; therefore be wise for yourselves, and *walk while you have the light*."

1. In general, we may observe here, (1) The concern Christ has for the souls of men, and his desire of their welfare.

2. Particularly we have here,

(1) The advantage they enjoyed in having Christ and his gospel among them, with the shortness and uncertainty of their enjoyment of it: *Yet a little while is the light with you.*

(2) The warning given them to make the best of this privilege while they enjoyed it, because of the danger they were in of losing it: *Walk while you have the light.*

(3) The sad condition of those who have sinned away the gospel, and are come to the period of their day of grace. *They walk in darkness,* and know neither *where* they go, nor *whither* they go; neither the way they are walking in, nor the end they are walking towards.

(4) The great duty and interest of every one of us inferred from all this (*v.* 36): *While you have light, believe in the light.* The Jews had now Christ's presence with them, let them improve it; afterwards they had the first offers of the gospel made to them by the apostles wherever they came; now this is an admonition to them not to out-stand their market, but to accept the offer when it was made to them: the same Christ saith to all who enjoy the gospel.

VII. Christ's retiring from them, hereupon: *These things spoke Jesus,* and said no more at this time, but left this to their consideration, *and departed, and did hide himself from them.* He hid himself from their rage and fury, retreating, it is probable, to Bethany, where he lodged. By this it appears that what he said irritated and exasperated them, and they were made worse by that which should have made them better.

HARD HEARTS (*vv.* 37–41)

We have here the honour done to our Lord Jesus by the Old-Testament prophets, who foretold and lamented the infidelity of the many that believed not on him. Two things are here said concerning this untractable people, and both were foretold by the evangelical prophet Isaiah, that they *did not* believe, and that they *could not* believe.

I. They did not believe (*v.* 37): *Though he had done so many miracles before them,* which, one would think, should have convinced them, yet they believed not, but opposed him.

II. They could not believe, and *therefore* they could not *because Esaias said, He hath blinded their eyes.* This is a hard saying, who can explain it? We are sure that God is infinitely just and merciful, and therefore we cannot think there is in any such an impotency to good, resulting from the counsels of God, as lays them under a fatal necessity of being evil. God damns none by mere sovereignty; yet it is said, *They could not believe.*

1. They *could not* believe, that is, they *would not*; they were obstinately resolved in their infidelity; thus Chrysostom and Austin incline to understand it; and the former gives divers instances of scripture of the putting of an impotency to signify the invincible refusal of the will, as Gen. xxxvii. 4, *They could not speak peaceably to him.* And

ch. vii. 7. This is a *moral* impotency, like that of one that is accustomed to do evil, Jer. xiii. 23. But,

2. They could not because Esaias had said, *He hath blinded their eyes*. Here the difficulty increases; it is certain that God is not the author of sin, and yet,

(1) There is a righteous hand of God sometimes to be acknowledged in the blindness and obstinacy of those who persist in impenitency and unbelief, by which they are justly punished for their former resistance of the divine light and rebellion against the divine law.

Observe the method of conversion implied here, and the steps taken in it. [1] Sinners are brought to *see with their eyes*, to discern the reality of divine things and to have some knowledge of them. [2] To *understand with their heart*, to apply these things to themselves; not only to assent and approve, but to consent and accept. [3] To *be converted*, and effectually turned from sin to Christ, from the world and the flesh to God, as their felicity and portion. [4] Then God will *heal* them, will justify and sanctify them; will *pardon* their sins, which are as bleeding wounds, and mortify their corruptions, which are as lurking diseases. Now when God denies his grace nothing of this is done; the alienation of the mind from, and its aversion to, God and the divine life, grow into a rooted and invincible antipathy, and so the case becomes desperate.

(2) Judicial blindness and hardness are in the word of God

threatened against those who wilfully persist in wickedness, and were particularly foretold concerning the Jewish church and nation. Known unto God are all his works, and all ours too. Christ knew before who would betray him, and spoke of it, *ch.* vi. 70. This is a confirmation of the truth of scripture prophecies, and thus even the unbelief of the Jews may help to strengthen our faith. It is also intended for caution to particular persons, to *beware lest that come upon them which was spoken of in the prophets*, Acts xiii. 40.

(3) What God has foretold will certainly come to pass, and so, by a necessary consequence, in order of arguing, it might be said that *therefore* they *could not believe*, because God by the prophets had foretold they would not; for such is the knowledge of God that he cannot be deceived in what he foresees, and such his truth that he cannot deceive in what he foretells, so that the scripture cannot be broken.

Lastly, The evangelist, having quoted the prophecy, shows (*v.* 41) that it was intended to look further than the prophet's own days, and that its principal reference was to the days of the Messiah: *These things said Esaias when he saw his glory, and spoke of him.* 1. We read in the prophecy that this was said to Esaias, Isa. vi. 8, 9. But here we are told that it was said *by him* to the purpose. 2. The vision which the prophet there had of the *glory of God* is here said to be his *seeing the glory* of Jesus Christ: He *saw his glory*. Jesus Christ therefore is equal in power and glory with the Father, and his praises are equally celebrated.

FEAR OF MAN (*vv*. 42, 43)

Some honour was done to Christ by these rulers: for they *believed on him*, were convinced that he was sent of God, and received his doctrine as divine; but they did not do him honour enough, for they had not courage to own their faith in him. Many professed more kindness for Christ than really they had; these had more kindness for him than they were willing to profess. See here what a struggle was in these rulers between their convictions and their corruptions.

A LAST WARNING (*vv*. 44–50)

We have here the honour Christ not assumed, but asserted, to himself, in the account he gave of his mission and his errand into the world. Probably this discourse was not at the same time with that before (for then *he departed, v*. 36), but some time after, when he made another public appearance; and, as this evangelist records it, it was Christ's farewell sermon to the Jews, and his last public discourse; all that follows was private with his disciples. So Christ here takes leave of the temple, with a solemn declaration of three things:—

I. The privileges and dignities of those that believe; this gives great encouragement to us to believe in Christ and to profess that faith. It is a thing of such a nature that we need not be shy either of doing it or of owning it; for,

1. By believing in Christ we are brought into an *honourable acquaintance with God* (*vv*. 44, 45): *He that believes on me*, and so *sees me, believes on him that sent me*, and so *sees him*.

2. We are hereby brought into a comfortable enjoyment of ourselves (*v*. 46): *I am come a light into the world, that whoever believes in me*, Jew or Gentile, *should not abide in darkness*. [1] They do not continue in that dark condition in which they were by nature; they are *light in the Lord*. They were without any true comfort, or joy, or hope, but do not continue in that condition; light is sown for them. [2] Whatever darkness of affliction, disquietment, or fear, they may afterwards be in, provision is made that they may not long abide in it. [3] They are delivered from that darkness which is perpetual, and which *abideth for ever*, that utter darkness where there is not the least gleam of light nor hope of it.

II. The peril and danger of those that believe not, which gives fair warning to take heed of persisting in unbelief (*vv*. 47, 48). Observe,

1. Who they are whose unbelief is here condemned: those who *hear Christ's words* and yet *believe them not*. Those shall not be condemned for their infidelity that never had, nor could have, the gospel; every man shall be judged according to the dispensation of light he was under: *Those that have sinned without law shall be judged without law*. But those

that have heard, or might have heard, and would not, lie open to this doom.

2. What is the constructive malignity of their unbelief: not receiving Christ's word; it is interpreted (*v.* 48) a *rejecting* of Christ.

3. The wonderful patience and forbearance of our Lord Jesus, exercised towards those who slighted him when he was come here upon earth: *I judge him not*, not now. Note, Christ was not quick or hasty to take advantage against those who refused the first offers of his grace, but continued waiting to be gracious.

4. The certain and unavoidable judgment of unbelievers at the great day, the day of the revelation of the righteous judgment of God: unbelief will certainly be a damning sin. (1) There is *one that judgeth them*. Nothing is more dreadful than abused patience, and grace trampled on; though for awhile *mercy rejoiceth against judgment*, yet there will be *judgment without mercy*. (2) Their final judgment is reserved to the *last day*; to that day of judgment Christ here binds over all unbelievers, to answer then for all the contempts they have put upon him. (3) The word of Christ will judge them then: *The words that I have spoken*, how light soever you have made of them, *the same shall judge* the unbeliever *in the last day*.

III. A solemn declaration of the authority Christ had to demand our faith, and require us to receive his doctrine upon pain of damnation, *vv.* 49, 50, where observe,

1. The commission which our Lord Jesus received from the Father to deliver his doctrine to the world (*v.* 49): *I have not spoken of myself*, as a mere man, much less as a common man; *but the Father gave me a commandment what I should say*.

2. The scope, design, and tendency of this commission: *I know that his commandment is life everlasting*, *v.* 50. The commission given to Christ had a reference to the everlasting state of the children of men, and was in order to their everlasting life and happiness in that state: the instructions given to Christ as a prophet were to reveal eternal life (1 John v. 11); the power given to Christ as a king was to give eternal life, *ch.* xvii. 2. Thus the command given him was life everlasting.

3. Christ's exact observance of the commission and instructions given him, and his steady acting in pursuance of them: *Whatsoever I speak*, it is *as the Father said unto me*. In the midst of all the respect paid to him, this is the honour he values himself upon, that what the Father had said to him that he spoke, and in the manner as he was directed so he spoke.

CHAPTER THIRTEEN

WASHING FEET (*vv.* 1–17)

In these verses we have the story of Christ's washing his disciples' feet; it was an action of a singular nature; no miracle, unless we call it a miracle of humility.

I. Christ washed his disciples' feet that he might give a proof of that great love wherewith he loved them; loved them to the end, *vv.* 1, 2.

1. It is here laid down as an undoubted truth that our Lord Jesus, *having loved his own that were in the world, loved them to the end, v.* 1.

(1) This is true of the disciples that were his immediate followers, in particular the twelve.

(2) It is true of all believers, for these twelve patriarchs were the representatives of all the tribes of God's spiritual Israel.

2. Christ manifested his love to them by washing their feet, as that good woman (Luke vii. 38) showed her love to Christ by washing his feet and wiping them. Thus he would show that as his love to them was constant so it was condescending.

3. He chose this time to do it, a little before his last passover, for two reasons:—

(1) Because now *he knew that his hour was come*, which he had long expected, *when he should depart out of this world to the Father*. Observe here, [1] The change that was to pass over our Lord Jesus; he must *depart*. This began at his death, but was completed at his ascension. [2] The time of this change: *His hour was come*. It is sometimes called his enemies' hour (Luke xxii. 53), the hour of their triumph; sometimes his hour, the hour of his triumph, the hour he had had in his eye all along. The time of his sufferings was fixed to an hour, and the continuance of them but for an hour. [3] His foresight of it: He *knew that his hour was come*; he knew from the beginning that it

would come, and when, but now he knew that it *was come*.

(2) Because the *devil had now put it into the heart of Judas to betray him, v.* 2. These words in a parenthesis may be considered, [1] As tracing Judas's treason to its origin; it was a sin of such a nature that it evidently bore the devil's image and superscription. [2] As intimating a reason why Christ now washed his disciples' feet. *First*, Judas being now resolved to betray him, the time of his departure could not be far off; if this matter be determined, it is easy to infer with St. Paul, *I am now ready to be offered*. *Secondly*, Judas being now got into the snare, and the devil aiming at Peter and the rest of them (Luke xxii. 31), Christ would fortify his own against him. *Thirdly*, Judas, who was now plotting to betray him, was *one of the twelve*. Now Christ would hereby show that he did not design to cast them all off for the faults of one.

II. Christ washed his disciples' feet that he might give an instance of his own wonderful humility, and show how lowly and condescending he was, and let all the world know how low he could stoop in love to his own. This is intimated, *vv.* 3–5.

1. Here is the rightful advancement of the Lord Jesus. Glorious things are here said of Christ as Mediator.

(1) *The Father had given all things into his hands*; had given him a propriety in all, and a power over all, as possessor of heaven and earth, in pursuance of

the great designs of his undertaking; see Matt. xi. 27.

(2) He *came from God*. This implies that he was in the beginning with God, and had a being and glory, not only before he was born into this world, but before the world itself was born.

(3) He *went to God*, to be glorified with him with the same glory which he had with God from eternity.

(4) He *knew* all this; was not like a prince in the cradle, that knows nothing of the honour he is born to, or like Moses, who *wist not that his face shone*; no, he had a full view of all the honours of his exalted state, and yet stooped thus low.

2. Here is the voluntary abasement of our Lord Jesus notwithstanding this. Now that which Christ humbled himself to was to *wash his disciples' feet*.

(1) The action itself was mean and servile, and that which servants of the lowest rank were employed

(2) The condescension was so much the greater that he did this for his own disciples, who in themselves were of a low and despicable condition, not curious about their bodies; their feet, it is likely, were seldom washed, and therefore very dirty. In relation to him, they were his scholars, his servants, and such as should have washed his feet, whose dependence was upon him, and their expectations from him.

(3) He *rose from supper* to do it. Though we translate it (*v.* 2) *supper being ended*, it might be better read, *there being a supper*

made, or *he being at supper*, for he sat down again (*v.* 12), and we find him dipping a sop (*v.* 26), so that he did it in the midst of his meal.

(4) He put himself into the garb of a servant, to do it: he *laid aside* his loose and upper *garments*, that he might apply himself to this service the more expeditely.

(5) He did it with all the humble ceremony that could be, went through all the parts of the service distinctly, and passed by none of them; he did it as if he had been used thus to serve; did it himself alone, and had none to minister to him in it. He *girded himself with the towel*, as servants throw a napkin on their arm, or put an apron before them; he *poured water into the basin* out of the water-pots that stood by (*ch.* ii. 6), and then *washed their feet*; and, to complete the service, *wiped them*.

(6) Nothing appears to the contrary but that he washed the feet of Judas among the rest, for he was present, *v.* 26. The blessed Jesus here washed the feet of a sinner, the worst of sinners, the worst to him, who was at this time contriving to betray him.

III. Christ washed his disciples' feet that he might signify to them spiritual washing, and the cleansing of the soul from the pollutions of sin. This is plainly intimated in his discourse with Peter upon it, *vv.* 6–11, in which we may observe,

1. The surprise Peter was in when he saw his Master go about this mean service (*v.* 6). Very willingly would Peter have taken

the basin and towel, and washed his Master's feet, and been proud of the honour, Luke xvii. 7, 8.

2. The immediate satisfaction Christ gave to this question of surprise. This was at least sufficient to silence his objections (v. 7). Here are two reasons why Peter must submit to what Christ was doing:—

(1) Because he was at present in the dark concerning it, and ought not to oppose what he did not understand.

(2) Because there was something considerable in it, of which he should hereafter know the meaning.

3. Peter's peremptory refusal, notwithstanding this, to let Christ wash his feet (v. 8).

4. Christ's insisting upon his offer, and a good reason given to Peter why he should accept it. This may be taken, (1) As a severe caution against disobedience: "*If I wash thee not*, if thou continue refractory, and wilt not comply with thy Master's will in so small a matter, thou shalt not be owned as one of my disciples, but be justly discarded and cashiered for not observing orders." Or, (2) As a declaration of the necessity of spiritual washing; and so I think it is to be understood: "*If I wash not* thy soul from the pollution of sin, *thou hast no part with me*, no interest in me, no communion with me, no benefit by me."

5. Peter's more than submission, his earnest request, to be washed by Christ, v. 9. Observe,

(1) How ready Peter is to recede from what he had said. Now that

the washing of him appeared to be an act of Christ's authority and grace he admits it; but disliked it when it seemed only an act of humiliation.

(2) How importunate he is for the purifying grace of the Lord Jesus, and the universal influence of it, even upon his hands and head.

6. Christ's further explication of this sign, as it represented spiritual washing.

(1) With reference to his disciples that were faithful to him (v. 10): *He that is washed* all over in the bath (as was frequently practised in those countries), when he returns to his house, *needeth not save to wash his feet*, his hands and head having been washed, and he having only dirtied his feet in walking home. Peter had gone from one extreme to the other. At first he would not let Christ wash his feet; and now he overlooks what Christ had done for him in his baptism, and what was signified thereby, and cries out to have his hands and head washed. Now Christ directs him into the meaning; he must have his feet washed, but not his hands and head. [1] See here what is the comfort and privilege of such as are in a justified state; they are washed by Christ, and are *clean every whit*, that is, they are graciously accepted of God, as if they were so; and, though they offend, yet they need not, upon their repentance, be again put into a justified state, for then should they often be baptized. Though we have occasion to repent daily, God's gifts and callings are without

repentance. [2] See what ought to be the daily care of those who through grace are in a justified state, and that is to wash their feet; to cleanse themselves from the guilt they contract daily through infirmity and inadvertence, by the renewed exercise of repentance, with a believing application of the virtue of Christ's blood. The provision made for our cleansing should not make us presumptuous, but the more cautious. *I have washed my feet, how shall I defile them?* From yesterday's pardon, we should fetch an argument against this day's temptation.

(2) With reflection upon Judas: *And you are clean, but not all, vv.* 10, 11.

IV. Christ washed his disciples' feet to set before us an example. This explanation he gave of what he had done, when he had done it, *vv.* 12–17. Observe,

1. With what solemnity he gave an account of the meaning of what he had done (*v.* 12): *After he had washed their feet,* he said, *Know you what I have done?*

2. Upon what he grounds that which he had to say (*v.* 13): "*You call me Master and Lord,* you give me those titles, in speaking of me, in speaking to me, and *you say well,* for *so I am*; you are in the relation of scholars to me, and I do the part of a master to you."

Our calling Christ Master and Lord is an obligation upon us to receive and observe the instructions he gives us.

3. The lesson which he hereby taught: *You also ought to wash one another's feet, v.* 14. Doubtless

it is to be understood figuratively; it is an instructive sign, but not sacramental, as the eucharist. This was a parable to the eye; and three things our Master hereby designed to teach us:— [1] A humble condescension. We must learn of our Master to be *lowly in heart* (Matt. xi. 29), and walk with all lowliness. [2] A condescension to be serviceable. To wash one another's feet is to stoop to the meanest offices of love, for the real good and benefit one of another. [3] A serviceableness to the sanctification one of another: *You ought to wash one another's feet,* from the pollutions of sin. We cannot satisfy for one another's sins, this is peculiar to Christ, but we may help to purify one another from sin.

4. Here is the ratifying and enforcing of this command from the example of what Christ had now done: *If I your Lord and Master have* done it to you, you ought to do it *to one another.* He shows the cogency of this argument in two things:—

(1) I am *your Master,* and you are my disciples, and therefore you ought to *learn of me* (*v.* 15).

(2) I am *your Master,* and you are my disciples, and therefore you cannot think it below you to do that, how mean soever it may seem, which you have seen me do, for (*v.* 16) *the servant is not greater than his Lord, neither he that is sent,* though sent with all the pomp and power of an ambassador, *greater than he that sent him.*

5. Our Saviour closes this part of his discourse with an intimation

of the necessity of their obedience to these instructions: *If you know these things*; or, seeing you know them, *happy are you if you do them.* Most people think, Happy are those that rise and rule. Washing one another's feet will never get estates and preferments; but Christ saith, notwithstanding this, Happy are those that stoop and obey.

JUDAS DEPARTS (*vv.* 18–30)

We have here the discovery of Judas's plot to betray his Master. Now here,

I. Christ gives them a general intimation of it (*v.* 18): *I speak not of you all*, I cannot expect you will all do these things, for *I know whom I have chosen*, and whom I have passed by; but the scripture will be fulfilled (Ps. xli. 9), *He that eateth bread with me hath lifted up his heel against me.*

II. He gives them a reason why he told them beforehand of the treachery of Judas (*v.* 19): "*Now I tell you before it come*, before Judas has begun to put his wicked plot in execution, *that when it is come to pass you may*, instead of stumbling at it, be confirmed in your *belief that I am he*, he that should come."

III. He gives a word of encouragement to his apostles, and all his ministers whom he employs in his service (*v.* 20): *He that receiveth whomsoever I send receiveth me.* The purport of these words is the same with what we have in other scriptures, but it is not easy to make out their coherence here. Christ had told his disciples that they must humble and abase themselves. "Now," saith he, "though there may be those that will despise you for your condescension, yet there will be those that will do you honour, and shall be honoured for so doing."

IV. Christ more particularly notifies to them the plot which one of their number was now hatching against him (*v.* 21). He had often spoken of his own sufferings and death, without any such trouble of spirit as he here manifested when he spoke of the ingratitude and treachery of Judas. This touched him in a tender part.

V. The disciples quickly take the alarm. They knew their Master would neither deceive them nor jest with them; and therefore *looked one upon another*, with a manifest concern, *doubting of whom he spoke.*

VI. The disciples were solicitous to get their Master to explain himself, and to tell them particularly whom he meant; for nothing but this can put them out of their present pain, for each of them thought he had as much reason to suspect himself as any of his brethren; now,

1. Of all the disciples John was most fit to ask, because he was the favourite, and sat next his Master (*v.* 23): *There was leaning on Jesus's bosom one of the disciples whom Jesus loved.* It appears that this was John, by comparing ch. xxi. 20, 24.

2. Of all the disciples Peter was most forward to know, *v.* 24. Peter, sitting at some distance, beckoned to John, by some sign or other, to ask. It were a desirable

thing, we should think, to know who in the church will deceive us; yet let this suffice—Christ knows, though we do not.

3. The question was asked accordingly (*v.* 25): *He then, lying at the breast of Jesus*, and so having the convenience of whispering with him, *saith unto him, Lord, who is it?*

4. Christ gave a speedy answer to this question, but whispered it in John's ear; for it appears (*v.* 29) that the rest were still ignorant of the matter. *He it is to whom I shall give a sop, a morsel, a crust, when I have dipped it* in the sauce. And *when he had dipped the sop*, John strictly observing his motions, *he gave it to Judas*.

VII. Judas himself, instead of being convinced hereby of his wickedness, was the more confirmed in it, and the warning given him was to him a *savour of death unto death*; for it follows,

1. The devil hereupon took possession of him (*v.* 27): *After the sop, Satan entered into him.* But,

(1) Was not Satan in him before? How then is it said that now *Satan entered into him*? Judas was all along a devil (*ch.* vi. 70), a son of perdition, but now Satan gained a more full possession of him, had a *more abundant entrance* into him.

(2) How came Satan to enter into him *after the sop*? Perhaps he was presently aware that it was the discovery of him, and it made him desperate in his resolutions. Many are made worse by the gifts of Christ's bounty, and are confirmed in their impenitency

by that which should have led them to repentance. The *coals of fire heaped upon their heads*, instead of melting them, harden them.

2. Christ hereupon dismissed him, and delivered him up to his own heart's lusts: *Then said Jesus unto him, What thou doest, do quickly.* This is not to be understood as either advising him to his wickedness or warranting him in it; but either, (1) As abandoning him to the conduct and power of Satan. Or, (2) As challenging him to do his worst.

3. Those that were at table understood not what he meant, because they did not hear what he whispered to John (*vv.* 28, 29).

4. Judas hereupon sets himself vigorously to pursue his design against him: He *went away*.

A NEW COMMANDMENT
(*vv.* 31–35)

This and what follows, to the end of *ch.* xiv., was Christ's table-talk with his disciples. Now our Lord Jesus discourses with them (and probably discourses much more largely than is here recorded),

I. Concerning the great mystery of his own death and sufferings, about which they were as yet so much in the dark that they could not persuade themselves to expect the thing itself, much less did they understand the meaning of it; and therefore Christ gives them such instructions concerning it as made the offence of the cross to cease.

1. Here is something which Christ instructs them in, concerning

his sufferings, that was very *comforting*.

(1) That he should himself be glorified in them.

(2) That God the Father should be glorified in them. The sufferings of Christ were, [1] The satisfaction of God's justice, and so God was glorified in them. [2] They were the manifestation of his holiness and mercy.

(3) That he should himself be greatly glorified after them, in consideration of God's being greatly glorified by them, *v.* 32.

2. Here is something that Christ instructs them in, concerning his sufferings, which was *awakening*, for as yet they were slow of heart to understand it (*v.* 33).

(1) That his stay in this world, to be with them here, they would find to be very short. Whether we understand this as referring to his death or his ascension it comes much to one; he had but a little time to spend with them.

(2) That their following him to the other world, to be with him there, they would find to be very difficult. Christ tells them here, [1] That when he was gone they would feel the want of him: *You shall seek me*, that is, "you shall wish you had me again with you." [2] That whither he went they *could not come*, which suggests to them high thoughts of him, who was going to an invisible inaccessible world, to dwell in that *light which none can approach unto*; and also low thoughts of themselves, and serious thoughts of their future state. Christ tells them that they could not follow him (as Joshua told the people

that they could not serve the Lord) only to quicken them to so much the more diligence and care.

II. He discourses with them concerning the great duty of brotherly love (*vv.* 34, 35): *You shall love one another*. Three arguments for mutual love are here urged:—

1. The command of their Master (*v.* 34): *A new commandment I give unto you.* He not only commends it as amiable and pleasant, not only counsels it as excellent and profitable, but commands it, and makes it one of the fundamental laws of his kingdom; it goes abreast with the command of believing in Christ, 1 John iii. 23; 1 Pet. i. 22. It is *a new commandment*; that is, (1) It is a renewed commandment; it was a commandment *from the beginning* (1 John ii. 7), as old as the law of nature, it was the second great commandment of the law of Moses; yet, because it is also one of the great commandments of the New Testament, of Christ the new Lawgiver, it is called a new commandment; it is like an old book in a new edition corrected and enlarged. (2) It is an excellent command, as a *new song* is an excellent song, that has an uncommon gratefulness in it. (3) It is an everlasting command; so strangely new as to be always so; as the *new covenant*, which shall never decay (Heb. viii. 13). (4) As Christ gives it, it is *new*. Before it was, *Thou shalt love thy neighbour*; now it is, You shall love *one another*.

2. The example of their Saviour is another argument for brotherly

love: *As I have loved you.* It is this
that makes it a *new commandment*
—that this rule and reason of
love (*as I have loved you*) is perfectly new, and such as had been
hidden from ages and generations.

3. The reputation of their profession (*v.* 35): *By this shall all
men know that you are my disciples,
if you have love one to another.*
Note, Brotherly love is the badge
of Christ's disciples. By this he
knows them, by this they may
know themselves (1 John iii. 14),
and by this others may know them.

PETER WARNED (*vv.* 36–38)

In these verses we have,

I. Peter's curiosity, and the check
given to that.

1. Peter's question was bold
and blunt (*v.* 36): *Lord, whither
goest thou?* referring to what
Christ had said (*v.* 33), *Whither I
go, you cannot come.*

2. Christ's answer was instructive. Let this suffice, *thou canst
not follow me now, but shalt
follow me hereafter.* (1) We may
understand it of his following
him to the cross. (2) We may
understand it of his following
him to the crown. Christ was now
going to his glory, and Peter was
very desirous to go with him:
"No," saith Christ, "*thou canst
not follow me now*, thou art not yet
ripe for heaven, nor hast thou
finished thy work on earth. The
forerunner must *first enter to
prepare a place* for thee, but
thou shalt follow me afterwards,
after thou hast fought the good
fight, and at the time appointed."

II. Peter's confidence, and the
check given to that.

1. Peter makes a daring protestation of his constancy. See here,
(1) What an affectionate love Peter
had to our Lord Jesus: "*I will
lay down my life for thy sake*, and
I can do no more." I believe
Peter spoke as he thought, and
though he was inconsiderate he
was not insincere, in his resolution.
(2) How ill he took it to have it
questioned, intimated in that expostulation, "*Lord, why cannot I
follow thee now?* Dost thou suspect
my fidelity to thee?"

2. Christ gives him a surprising
prediction of his inconstancy,
v. 38. Jesus Christ knows us better
than we know ourselves, and has
many ways of discovering those
to themselves whom he loves, and
will hide pride from. He plainly
foretells his cowardice in the
critical hour. To stop the mouth
of his boasting, lest Peter should
say it again, Yea Master, that I
will, Christ solemnly asserts it
with, *Verily, verily, I say unto
thee, the cock shall not crow till
thou hast denied me thrice.* Note,
The most secure are commonly
the least safe; and those most
shamefully betray their own weakness that most confidently presume
upon their own strength, 1 Cor. x.
12.

CHAPTER FOURTEEN
MANY MANSIONS (*vv.* 1–3)

In these verses we have,

I. A general caution which Christ
gives to his disciples against
trouble of heart (*v.* 1): *Let not your
heart be troubled.* They now
began to be troubled, were entering
into this temptation.

II. Here is a particular direction

to act in faith upon the promise of eternal life, *vv.* 2, 3. He had directed them to trust to God, and to trust in him; but what must they trust God and Christ for? Trust them for a happiness to come when this body and this world shall be no more, and for a happiness to last as long as the immortal soul and the eternal world shall last. Let us see how this is suggested here.

1. Believe and consider that really there is such a happiness: *In my Father's house there are many mansions; if it were not so, I would have told you, v.* 2.

(1) See under what notion the happiness of heaven is here represented: as *mansions*, many mansions in Christ's Father's house. [1] Heaven is a house, not a tent or tabernacle; it is *a house not made with hands, eternal in the heavens.* [2] It is a Father's house: *my Father's house*; and his Father is our Father, to whom he was now ascending. [3] There are *mansions* there; that is, *First*, Distinct dwellings, an apartment for each. *Secondly*, Durable dwellings. The house itself is lasting; our estate in it is not for a term of years, but a perpetuity. [4] There are *many* mansions, for there are many sons to be brought to glory, and Christ exactly knows their number, nor will be stretched for room by the coming of more company than he expects.

(2) See what assurance we have of the reality of the happiness itself, and the sincerity of the proposal of it to us: "*If it were not so, I would have told you.*" If either there were no such mansions,

or none designed for them, who had left all to follow him, he would have given them timely notice of the mistake, that they might have made an honourable retreat to the world again, and have made the best they could of it.

2. Believe and consider that the design of Christ's going away was to prepare a place in heaven for his disciples. He went to prepare a place for us; that is, (1) To take possession for us, as our advocate or attorney, and so to secure our title as indefeasible. (2) To make provision for us as our friend and father.

3. Believe and consider that *therefore* he would certainly come again in due time, to fetch them to that blessed place which he was now going to possess for himself and prepare for them (*v.* 3). Now these are comfortable words indeed. (1) That Jesus Christ will come again; *I do come*, intimating the certainty of it, that he will come and that he is daily coming. (2) That he will come again to receive all his faithful followers to himself. He sends for them privately at death, and gathers them one by one; but they are to make their public entry in solemn state all together at the last day, and then Christ himself will come to receive them, to conduct them in the abundance of his grace, and to welcome them in the abundance of his love. (3) *That where he is there they shall be also.* This intimates what many other scriptures declare, that the quintessence of heaven's happiness is being with Christ *there*, ch. xvii. 24; Phil. i. 23; 1 Thess. iv. 17.

WAY, TRUTH, LIFE (*vv.* 4–11)

Christ, having set the happiness of heaven before them as the end, here shows them himself as the way to it, and tells them that they were better acquainted both with the end they were to aim at and with the way they were to walk in than they thought they were.

This word of Christ gave occasion to two of his disciples to address themselves to him, and he answers them both.

I. Thomas enquired concerning the way (*v.* 5), without any apology for contradicting his Master.

Thomas here shows more modesty than Peter, who thought he could follow Christ now. Peter was the more solicitous to know *whither Christ went*. Thomas here, though he complains that he did not know this, yet seems more solicitous to know *the way*. Had Thomas understood, as he might have done, that Christ was going to the invisible world, the world of spirits, to which spiritual things only have a reference, he would not have said, *Lord, we do not know the way*.

II. Now to this complaint of their ignorance, which included a desire to be taught, Christ gives a full answer, *vv.* 6, 7. Believe in God as the end, and in me as the way (*v.* 1), and you do all you should do.

(1) He speaks of himself as the way, *v.* 6. Dost thou *not know the way? I am the way*, and I only, for *no man comes to the Father but by me*. Great things Christ here saith of himself, showing us,

[1] The nature of his mediation: He is *the way, the truth, and the life*.

First, Let us consider these first distinctly. 1. Christ is *the way, the highway* spoken of, Isa. xxxv. 8. Christ was his own way, for by *his own blood he entered into the holy place* (Heb. ix. 12), and he is our way, for we enter by him. 2. He is *the truth*. (1) As truth is opposed to figure and shadow. Christ is the substance of all the Old-Testament types, which are therefore said to be *figures of the true*, Heb. ix. 24. Christ is *the true manna* (*ch.* vi. 32), *the true tabernacle*, Heb. viii. 2. (2) As truth is opposed to falsehood and error; the doctrine of Christ is true doctrine. When we enquire for truth, we need learn no more than *the truth as it is in Jesus*. (3) As truth is opposed to fallacy and deceit; he is true to all that trust in him, as true as truth itself, 2 Cor. i. 20. 3. He is *the life*; for we are *alive unto God* only in and *through Jesus Christ*, Rom. vi. 11. Christ formed in us is that to our souls which our souls are to our bodies. Christ is *the resurrection and the life*.

Secondly, Let us consider these jointly, and with reference to each other. Christ is *the way, the truth, and the life*; that is, 1. He is the beginning, the middle, and the end. In him we must set out, go on, and finish. As *the truth*, he is the guide of our way; as *the life*, he is the end of it. 2. He is *the true and living way* (Heb. x. 20); there are *truth and life* in the way, as well as at the end of it. 3. He is *the true way to life*, the only true way; other ways may seem right, but the end of them is *the way of death*.

[2] The necessity of his mediation: *No man cometh to the Father but by me*. Fallen man must come to God as Judge, but cannot come to him as a Father, otherwise than by Christ as Mediator.

(2) He speaks of his Father as the end (*v. 7*). They knew him, and yet did not know him so well as they might and should have known him. They knew him to be the Christ, but did not follow on to know God in him.

II. Philip enquired concerning the Father (*v. 8*), and Christ answered him, *vv. 9–11*, where observe,

1. Philip's request for some extraordinary discovery of the Father.

2. Christ's reply, referring him to the discoveries already made of the Father, *vv. 9–11*.

(1) He refers him to what he had seen, *v. 9*. He upbraids him with his ignorance and inadvertency: "*Have I been so long time with you*, now above three years intimately conversant with you, *and yet hast thou not known me, Philip?* Now, *he that hath seen me hath seen the Father; and how sayest thou then, Show us the Father?* Wilt thou ask for that which thou hast already?" Now here,

[1] He reproves him for two things: *First*, For not improving his acquaintance with Christ, as he might have done, to a clear and distinct knowledge of him.

[2] He instructs him, and gives him a maxim which not only in general magnifies Christ and leads us to the knowledge of God in him, but justifies what Christ had said (*v. 7*): *You know the Father, and have seen him*; and answered what Philip had asked, *Show us the Father*. Why, saith Christ, the difficulty is soon over, for *he that hath seen me hath seen the Father. First*, All that saw *Christ in the flesh* might *have seen the Father* in him, if Satan had not *blinded their minds*, and kept them from a sight of Christ, *as the image of God*, 2 Cor. iv. 4. *Secondly*, All that saw Christ by faith did *see the Father* in him, though they were not suddenly aware that they did so. In the light of Christ's doctrine they saw God as *the Father of lights*; in the miracles they saw God *as the God of power, the finger of God*. The holiness of God shone in the spotless purity of Christ's life, and his grace in all the acts of grace he did.

(2) He refers him to what he had reason to believe (*vv. 10, 11*): "*Believest thou not that I am in the Father, and the Father in me*, and therefore that in *seeing me* thou hast *seen the Father*? Hast thou not believed this? If not, take my word for it, and believe it now."

[1] See here what it is which we are to believe: *That I am in the Father, and the Father in me*; that is, as he had said (*ch. x. 30*), *I and my Father are one*.

[2] See here what inducements we have to believe this; and they are two:—We must believe it, *First*, For his word's sake: *The words that I speak to you, I speak not of myself*. See *ch. vii. 16, My*

doctrine is not mine. Secondly, For his works' sake: *The Father that dwelleth in me, he doeth them*; and therefore *believe me for their sake.* Many works of power, and works of mercy, Christ did, and the Father did them in him; and the work of redemption in general was God's own work.

GREATER WORKS (*vv.* 12–14)

The disciples, as they were full of grief to think of parting with their Master, so they were full of care what would become of themselves when he was gone. Now, to silence these fears, Christ here assures them that they should be clothed with powers sufficient to bear them out. As Christ had *all power*, they, in his name, should have great *power, both in heaven and in earth.*

I. Great power on earth (*v.* 12): *He that believeth on me* (as I know you do), *the works that I do shall he do also.*

1. Two things he assures them of: —

(1) That they should be enabled to do such works as he had done, and that they should have a more ample power for the doing of them than they had had when he first sent them forth, Matt. x. 8.

(2) That they should do *greater works than these.* [1] In the kingdom of nature they should work greater miracles. No miracle is little, but some to our apprehension seem greater than others. Christ had healed with the hem of his garment, but Peter with his shadow (Acts v. 15), Paul by the handkerchief that had touched him, Acts xix. 12. [2] In the kingdom of

grace. They should obtain greater victories by the gospel than had been obtained while Christ was upon earth. I think this refers especially to *the gift of tongues*; this was the immediate effect of the *pouring out of the Spirit*, which was a constant miracle upon the mind, in which words are framed, and which was made to serve so glorious an intention as that of spreading the gospel to all nations *in their own language*. This was a greater *sign to them that believed not* (1 Cor. xiv. 22), and more powerful for their conviction, than any other miracle whatever.

2. The reason Christ gives for this is, *Because I go unto my Father,* (1) "*Because I go,* it will be requisite that you should have such a power, lest the work suffer damage by my absence." (2) "*Because I go to the Father,* I shall be in a capacity to furnish you with such a power, for *I go to the Father, to send the Comforter,* from whom *you shall receive power,*" Acts i. 8.

II. Great *power in heaven*: "*Whatsoever you shall ask, that will I do* (*vv.* 13, 14), as Israel, who was a prince with God. Therefore you shall do such mighty works, because you have such an interest in me, and I in *my Father.*"

ANOTHER COMFORTER
(*vv.* 15–17)

Christ not only proposes such things to them as were the matter of their comfort, but here promises to send the Spirit, whose office it should be to be their Comforter, to *impress* these things upon them.

I. He premises to this a memento of duty (*v.* 15): *If you love me, keep my commandments.*

II. He promises this great and unspeakable blessing to them, *vv.* 16, 17.

1. It is promised that they shall have *another comforter.* Observe here,

(1) The blessing promised: "Paraclete". The word is used only here in these discourses of Christ's, and 1 John ii. 1, where we translate it an *advocate.* [1] You shall have another *advocate.* The office of the Spirit was to be Christ's advocate with them and others, to plead his cause, and take care of his concerns, on earth. [2] You shall have another *master* or *teacher*, another *exhorter.* While they had Christ with them he excited and exhorted them to their duty; but now that he is going he leaves one with them that shall do this as effectually, though silently. [3] Another *comforter.* Christ was expected as the consolation of Israel. One of the names of the Messiah among the Jews was *Menahem—the Comforter.* The Targum calls the days of the Messiah *the years of consolation.* Christ comforted his disciples when he was with them, and now that he was leaving them in their greatest need he promises them *another.*

(2) The giver of this blessing: *The Father* shall give him, *my Father* and *your Father*; it includes both. The same that gave the Son to be our Saviour will give his Spirit to be our comforter, pursuant to the same design. The

Son is said to send the Comforter (*ch.* xv. 26), but the Father is the prime agent.

(3) How this blessing is procured—by the intercession of the Lord Jesus: *I will pray the Father.* He said (*v.* 14) *I will do it*; here he saith, *I will pray for it*, to show not only that he is both God and man, but that he is both king and priest.

(4) The continuance of this blessing: *That he may abide with you for ever.*

2. This comforter is the *Spirit of truth, whom you know*, *vv.* 16, 17.

(1) The comforter promised is *the Spirit*, one who should do his work in a spiritual way and manner, inwardly and invisibly, by working on men's spirits.

(2) "He is the *Spirit of truth.* He will *teach you the truth*, will enlighten your minds with the knowledge of it, will strengthen and confirm your belief of it, and will increase your love to it."

(3) He is one *whom the world cannot receive*; but *you know him. Therefore he abideth with you.* The gift of the Holy Ghost is a peculiar gift, bestowed upon the disciples of Christ in a distinguishing way—them, and not the world; it is to them *hidden manna*, and the *white stone.* No comforts comparable to those which make no show, make no noise. This is the favour God bears to his chosen; it is the *heritage of those that fear his name.*

I WILL COME TO YOU
(*vv.* 18–24)

When friends are parting, it is a common request they make to each other, "Pray let us hear from you as often as you can": this Christ engaged to his disciples, that out of sight they should not be out of mind.

I. He promises that he would continue his care of them (v. 18): "*I will not leave you orphans*, or *fatherless*; for, though I leave you, yet I leave you this comfort, *I will come to you*." "I will be coming daily to you in my Spirit"; in the tokens of his love, and visits of his grace, he is still coming. "I will come certainly at the end of time; surely I will come quickly to introduce you into the joy of your Lord."

II. He promises that they should continue their acquaintance with him and interest in him (vv. 19, 20). The world sees him no more till his second coming; but his disciples have communion with him in his absence.

1. *You see me*, and shall continue to see me, when *the world sees me no more*. They saw him with their bodily eyes after his resurrection, for he showed himself to them *by many infallible proofs*, Acts i. 8. And *then were the disciples glad when they saw the Lord*. They saw him with an eye of faith after his ascension, sitting at God's right hand, as Lord of all; saw that in him which the world saw not.

2. *Because I live, you shall live also*. That which grieved them was, that their Master was dying, and they counted upon nothing else but to die with him. No, saith Christ, (1) *I live*; this the great God glories in, *I live*, saith the Lord, and Christ saith the same. (2) Therefore *you shall live*

also. Note, The life of Christians is bound up in the life of Christ.

3. You shall have the assurance of this (v. 20): *At that day*, when I am glorified, when the Spirit is poured out, *you shall know* more clearly and certainly than you do now that *I am in my Father, and you in me, and I in you*. The knowledge of this union is their unspeakable joy and satisfaction; they were now in Christ, and he in them, but he speaks of it as a further act of grace that they should know it, and have the comfort of it. An interest in Christ and the knowledge of it are sometimes separated.

III. He promises that he would love them, and manifest himself to them, vv. 21–24. Here observe,

1. Who they are whom Christ will look upon, and accept, as lovers of him; those that *have his commandments, and keep them*.

2. What returns he will make to them for their love; rich returns; there is no love lost upon Christ. (1) They shall have the Father's love: *He that loveth me shall be loved of my Father*. (2) They shall have Christ's love: *And I will love him*, as God-man, as Mediator. (3) They shall have the comfort of that love: *I will manifest myself to him*. Some understand it of Christ's showing himself alive to his disciples after his resurrection; but, being promised to all that *love him and keep his commandments*, it must be construed so as to extend to them. There is a spiritual manifestation of Christ and his love made to all believers.

3. What occurred upon Christ's making this promise.

(1) One of the disciples expresses his wonder and surprise at it, *v.* 22. Observe, [1] Who it was that said this—*Judas, not Iscariot.* [2] What he said—*Lord how is it?* which intimates either, *First,* the weakness of his understanding. So some take it. Or, *Secondly,* as expressing the strength of his affections, and the humble and thankful sense he had of Christ's distinguishing favours to them: *Lord, how is it?* He is amazed at the condescensions of divine grace, as David, 2 Sam. vii. 18. What is there in us to deserve so great a favour?

(2) Christ, in answer hereto, explains and confirms what he had said, *vv.* 23, 24. He overlooks what infirmity there was in what Judas spoke, and goes on with his comforts.

[1] He further explains the condition of the promise, which was loving him, and keeping his commandments. And, as to this, he shows what an inseparable connection there is between love and obedience; love is the root, obedience is the fruit.

[2] He further explains the promise (*v.* 23): *If a man thus love me, I will manifest myself to him.* 1. Not only, *I will,* but, *We will, I and the Father,* who, in this, *are one.* See *v.* 9. 2. Not only, "*I will show myself to him* at a distance," but, "*We will come to him,* to be near him, to be with him," such are the powerful influences of divine graces and comforts upon the souls of those that love Christ in sincerity. 3. Not only, "I will give him a transient view of me, or make him a short and running

visit," but, *We will take up our abode with him,* which denotes complacency in him and constancy to him.

[3] He gives a good reason both to bind us to observe the condition and encourage us to depend upon the promise. *The word which you hear is not mine, but his that sent me, v.* 24.

PEACE (*vv.* 25–27)

Two things Christ here comforts his disciples with:—

I. That they should be under the tuition of his Spirit, *vv.* 25, 26.

II. That they should be under the influence of his peace (*v.* 27): *Peace I leave with you.* When Christ was about to leave the world he *made his will.* His soul he committed to his Father; his body he bequeathed to Joseph, to be decently interred; his clothes fell to the soldiers; his mother he left to the care of John: but what should he leave to his poor disciples, that had left all for him? Silver and gold he had none; but he left them that which was infinitely better, *his peace.*

THE PRINCE OF THIS WORLD (*vv.* 28–31)

Christ here gives his disciples another reason why their hearts should not be troubled for his going away; and that is, because his heart was not. He comforted himself,

I. That, though he went away, he should *come again.*

II. That he *went to his Father.* His departure had a bright side as well as a dark side. Therefore he sent this message after his resurrection (*ch.* xx. 17), *I ascend to my Father and your Father*, as most comfortable. 2. The reason of this is, because *the Father is greater than he*, which, if it be a proper proof of that for which it is alleged (as no doubt it is), must be understood thus, that his state with his Father would be much more excellent and glorious than his present state; his returning to his Father (so Dr. Hammond) would be the advancing of him to a much higher condition than that which he was now in. Or thus, His going to the Father himself, and bringing all his followers to him there, was the ultimate end of his undertaking, and therefore greater than the means. 3. The disciples of Christ should show that they love him by their rejoicing in the glories of his exaltation, rather than by lamenting the sorrows of his humiliation.

III. That his going away, compared with the prophecies which went before it, would be a means of confirming the faith of his disciples (*v.* 29): *I have told you before it come to pass* that I must die and rise again, and ascend to the Father, and send the Comforter, *that, when it is come to pass, you might believe.*" See this reason, *ch.* xiii. 19; xvi. 4.

IV. That he was sure of a victory over Satan, with whom he knew he was to have a struggle in his departure (*v.* 30). One reason why he would not talk much with them was because he had now other work to apply himself to: *The prince of this world comes.* He called the devil the *prince of this world*, *ch.* xii. 31. 2. The assurance

he had of good success in the conflict: *He hath nothing in me, He hath nothing at all.* (1) There was no guilt in Christ to give authority to the *prince of this world* in his terrors. (2) There was no corruption in Christ, to give advantage to *the prince of this world* in his temptations.

V. That his departure was in compliance with, and obedience to, his Father. Satan could not force his life from him, and yet he would die: *that the world may know that I love the Father, v.* 31.

CHAPTER FIFTEEN

THE FRUITS OF THE SPIRIT
(*vv.* 1–8)

Here Christ discourses concerning the fruits, *the fruits of the Spirit*, which his disciples were to bring forth, under the similitude of a vine. Observe here,

I. The doctrine of this similitude; what notion we ought to have of it.

1. That Jesus Christ is *the vine, the true vine.* (1) He is *the vine*, planted in the vineyard, and not a spontaneous product; planted in the earth, for he is *the Word made flesh.* The vine has an unsightly unpromising outside; and Christ had *no form nor comeliness*, Isa. liii. 2. The vine is a spreading plant, and Christ will be known as *salvation to the ends of the earth.* The fruit of the vine honours God and cheers man (Judg. ix. 13), so does the fruit of Christ's mediation; it is *better than gold*, Prov. viii. 19. (2) He is *the true vine*, as truth is opposed to pretence and counterfeit; he is really a fruitful plant, a plant of renown.

2. That believers are branches of this vine, which supposes that Christ is the root of the vine. The root is unseen, and our *life is hid with Christ*; the root bears the tree (Rom. xi. 18), diffuses sap to it, and is all in all to its flourishing and fruitfulness; and in Christ are all supports and supplies. Believers, like the branches of the vine, are weak, and insufficient to stand of themselves, but as they are borne up. See Ezek. xv. 2.

3. That *the Father is the husbandman—the land-worker*. Though *the earth is the Lord's*, it yields him no fruit unless he work it. God has not only a propriety in, but a care of, the vine and all the branches. He *hath planted, and watered, and gives the increase*; for *we are God's husbandry*, 1 Cor. iii. 9. See Isa. v. 1, 2; xxvii. 2, 3.

II. The duty taught us by this similitude, which is to *bring forth fruit*, and, in order to do this, to *abide* in Christ.

1. We must be fruitful. From a vine we look for grapes (Isa. v. 2), and from a Christian we look for Christianity; this is the *fruit*, a Christian temper and disposition, a Christian life and conversation, Christian devotions and Christian designs. To persuade them to this, he urges,

(1) The doom of the unfruitful (*v.* 2): They are *taken away*.

(2) The promise made to the fruitful: *He purgeth them, that they may bring forth more fruit*. The purging of fruitful branches, in order to their greater fruitfulness, is the care and work of the great husbandman, for his own glory.

(3) The benefits which believers

have by the doctrine of Christ, the power of which they should labour to exemplify in a fruitful conversation: *Now you are clean, v.* 3. [1] Their society was clean, now that Judas was expelled by that word of Christ. [2] They were each of them clean, that is, sanctified, by the truth of Christ (*ch.* xvii. 17); that faith by which they received the word of Christ *purified their hearts*, Acts xv. 9. The disciples had now been three years under Christ's instruction; and *now you are clean*.

(4) The glory that will redound to God by our fruitfulness, with the comfort and honour that will come to ourselves by it, *v.* 8. And the more fruit we bring forth, the more we abound in that which is good, the more he is glorified.

2. In order to achieve our fruitfulness, we must abide in Christ, must keep up our union with him by faith, and do all we do in religion in the virtue of that union. Here is,

(1) The duty enjoined (*v.* 4): *Abide in me, and I in you.*

(2) The necessity of our abiding in Christ, for our fruitfulness (*vv.* 4, 5). [1] He that is constant in the exercise of faith in Christ and love to him, that lives upon his promises and is led by his Spirit, *bringeth forth much fruit*. [2] It is necessary to our doing any good. It is not only a means of cultivating and increasing what good there is already in us, but it is the root and spring of all good: "*Without me you can do nothing.*"

(3) The fatal consequences of forsaking Christ (*v.* 6): *If any man abide not in me, he is cast forth as a*

branch. This is a description of the fearful state of hypocrites that are *not in Christ*, and of apostates that *abide not in Christ*.

(4) The blessed privilege which those have that *abide in Christ* (*v.* 7): *If my words abide in you, you shall ask what you will* of my Father in my name, *and it shall be done.*

ABIDING IN LOVE (*vv.* 9–17)

Christ, who is love itself, is here discoursing concerning love, a fourfold love.

I. Concerning the Father's love to him; and concerning this he here tells us, 1. That the Father did love him (*v.* 9): *As the Father hath loved me.* 2. That he abode in his Father's love, *v.* 10. He continually loved his Father, and was beloved of him. 3. That therefore he abode in his Father's love because he kept his Father's law: *I have kept my Father's commandments,* as Mediator, and so *abide in his love.*

II. Concerning his own love to his disciples. Though he leaves them, he loves them. And observe here,

1. The pattern of this love: *As the Father has loved me, so have I loved you.* A strange expression of the condescending grace of Christ! As the Father loved him, who was most worthy, he loved them, who were most unworthy.

2. The proofs and products of this love, which are four:—

(1) Christ loves his disciples, for he laid down his life for them (*v.* 13).

(2) Christ loved his disciples, for he took them into a covenant of friendship with himself, *vv.* 14, 15. "If you approve yourselves by your obedience my disciples indeed, *you are my friends,* and shall be treated as friends."

(3) Christ loved his disciples, for he was very free in communicating his mind to them (*v.* 15). The great things relating to man's redemption Christ declared to his disciples, that they might declare them to others; they were the men of his counsel, Matt. xiii. 11.

(4) Christ loved his disciples, for he chose and ordained them to be the prime instruments of his glory and honour in the world (*v.* 16): *I have chosen you, and ordained you.* His love to them appeared,

[1] In their election, their election to their apostleship (*ch.* vi. 70): *I have chosen you twelve.* It did not begin on their side: *You have not chosen me,* but I first *chose you.*

[2] In their ordination: *I have ordained you;* "I have put you into the ministry (1 Tim. i. 12), put you into commission."

[3] His love to them appeared in the interest they had at the throne of grace: *Whatsoever you shall ask of my Father, in my name, he will give it you.* Probably this refers in the first place to the power of working miracles which the apostles were clothed with, which was to be drawn out by prayer.

III. Concerning the disciples' love to Christ, enjoined in consideration of the great love wherewith he had loved them. Three things he exhorts them to:—

1. To continue in his love, *v.* 9. "Continue in your love to me, and in mine to you."

2. To let his joy remain in them, and fill them, v. 11. This he designed in those precepts and promises given them.

3. To evidence their love to him by keeping his commandments. "This will be an evidence of the fidelity and constancy of your love to me, and then you may be sure of the continuance of my love to you."

IV. Concerning the *disciples' love one to another*, enjoined as an evidence of their love to Christ, and a grateful return for his love to them. We must keep his commandments, and this is his commandment, that we *love one another*, v. 12, and again, v. 17. He speaks as if he were about to give them many things in charge, and yet names this only, *that you love one another*; not only because this includes many duties, but because it will have a good influence upon all.

FRUITS OF ENMITY
(vv. 18–25)

Here Christ discourses concerning *hatred*, which is the character and genius of the devil's kingdom, as love is of the kingdom of Christ. Observe here,

I. Who they are in whom this hatred is found—the world, the children of this world, as distinguished from the children of God; those who are in the interests of the god of this world, whose image they bear, and whose power they are subject to.

II. Who they are against whom this hatred is levelled—against the disciples of Christ, against Christ himself, and against the Father.

1. The world hates the disciples of Christ: *The world hateth you* (v. 19); and he speaks of it as that which they must expect and count upon, v. 18, as 1 John iii. 13.

(2) Observe what is here included.

[1] The world's enmity against the followers of Christ: it *hateth them*. Note, Whom Christ blesseth the world curseth.

[2] The fruits of that enmity, two of which we have here, v. 20. *First*, They will persecute you, because they hate you, for hatred is a restless passion. *Secondly*, Another fruit of their enmity is implied, that they would reject their doctrine. When Christ says, *If they have kept my sayings, they will keep yours*, he means, They will keep yours, and regard yours, no more than they have regarded and kept mine.

[3] The causes of that enmity. The world will hate them,

First, Because they do not belong to it (v. 19). They swim against the stream of the world, and are not conformed to it; they witness against it, and are not conformed to it. This would support them under all the calamities which the world's hatred would bring upon them, that they were hated because they were the choice and the chosen ones of the Lord Jesus, and were not of the world.

Secondly, "Another cause of the world's hating you will be because you do belong to Christ (v. 21): *For my name's sake*." Here is the core of the controversy; whatever is pretended, this is the ground of the quarrel, they hate Christ's disciples because they *bear his name*, and *bear up his name* in the world.

Thirdly, After all, it is the world's ignorance that is the true cause of its enmity to the disciples of Christ (*v.* 21): *Because they know not him that sent me.*

2. The world hates Christ himself. And this is spoken of here for two ends:—

(1) To mitigate the trouble of his followers, arising from the world's hatred, and to make it the less strange, and the less grievous (*v.* 18): *You know that it hated me before you.* We read it as signifying priority of time; he began in the bitter cup of suffering, and then left us to pledge him; but it may be read as expressing his superiority over them: "*You know* that it hated me, *your first*, your chief and captain, your leader and commander."

(2) To aggravate the wickedness of this unbelieving world, and to discover its exceeding sinfulness; to hate and persecute the apostles was bad enough, but in them to hate and persecute Christ himself was much worse. The world is generally in an ill name in scripture, and nothing can put it into a worse name than this, that it hated Jesus Christ. There is a world of people that are haters of Christ. Two things he insists upon to aggravate the wickedness of those that hated him:—

[1] That there was the greatest reason imaginable why they should love him; men's good words and good works usually recommend them; now as to Christ,

First, His words were such as merited their love (*v.* 22): "*If I*

had not spoken unto them, to court their love, *they had not had sin*, their opposition had not amounted to a hatred of me, their sin had been comparatively no sin. But now that I have said so much to them to recommend myself to their best affections they have no pretence, no excuse for their sin."

Secondly, His works were such as merited their love, as well as his words (*v.* 24): "*If I had not done among them*, in their country, and before their eyes, such works as *no other man ever did, they had not had sin*; their unbelief and enmity had been excusable, and they might have had some colour to say that my word was not to be credited, if not otherwise confirmed"; but he produced satisfactory proofs of his divine mission, *works which no other man did.*

[2] That there was no reason at all why they should hate him. "*This comes to pass*, this unreasonable hatred of me, and of my disciples for my sake, *that the word might be fulfilled which is written in their law*" (that is, in the Old Testament, which is a law, and was received by them as a law), "*They hated me without a cause*"; this David speaks of himself as a type of Christ, Ps. xxxv. 19; lxix. 4.

3. In Christ the world hates God himself; this is twice said here (*v.* 23): *He that hateth me*, though he thinks his hatred goes no further, yet really he *hates my Father also*. And again, *v.* 24, They have *seen and hated both me and my Father*. God will have all men to honour the Son as

611

they honour the Father, and therefore what entertainment the Son has, that the Father has.

A DOUBLE WITNESS
(vv. 26–27)

I. It is here promised that the blessed Spirit shall maintain the cause of Christ in the world, notwithstanding the opposition it should meet with. We have more in this verse concerning the Holy Ghost than in any one verse besides in the Bible; and, being baptized into his name, we are concerned to acquaint ourselves with him as far as he is revealed.

1. Here is an account of him in his essence, or subsistence rather. He is *the Spirit of truth, who proceedeth from the Father*. Here, (1) He is spoken of as a distinct person; not a quality or property, but a person under the proper name of a *Spirit*, and proper title of the *Spirit of truth*, a title fitly given him where he is brought in testifying. (2) As a divine person, that *proceedeth from the Father*, by out-goings that were of old, *from everlasting*. The *Nicene* Creed says, The Spirit *proceedeth from the Father and the Son*, for he is called the *Spirit of the Son*, Gal. iv. 6. And the Son is here said to *send him*. The Greek church choose rather to say, *from the Father by the Son*.

2. In his mission. (1) He will come in a more plentiful effusion of his gifts, graces, and powers, than had ever yet been. (2) *I will send him to you from the Father*. He had said (*ch.* xiv. 16), *I will pray the Father, and he shall send you the Comforter*, which

bespeaks the Spirit to be the fruit of the intercession Christ makes within the veil: here he says, *I will send him*, which bespeaks him to be the fruit of his dominion within the veil. The Spirit was sent, [1] By Christ as Mediator, now *ascended on high* to *give gifts unto men*, and all power being given to him. [2] From the Father: "Not only from heaven, my Father's house" (the Spirit was given in a *sound from heaven*, Acts ii. 2), "but according to my Father's will and appointment, and with his concurring power and authority." [3] To the apostles to instruct them in their preaching, enable them for working, and carry them through their sufferings. He was given to them and their successors, both in Christianity and in the ministry; to them and their seed, and their seed's seed, according to that promise, Isa. lix. 21.

3. In his office and operations, which are two:—(1) One implied in the title given to him; he is the *Comforter*, or *Advocate*. And advocate for Christ, to maintain his cause against the world's infidelity, a comforter to the saints against the world's hatred. (2) Another expressed: *He shall testify of me*. He is not only an advocate, but a witness for Jesus Christ; he is one of the three that *bear record in heaven*, and the first of the three that *bear witness on earth*, 1 John v. 7, 8.

II. It is here promised that the apostles also, by the Spirit's assistance, should have the honour of being Christ's witnesses (*v.* 27): *And you also shall bear witness* of me, being competent witnesses, for *you have been with* me from the beginning of my ministry. Note. (1) We have great reason to receive the record which the apostles gave of Christ, for they did not speak by hearsay, but what they had the greatest assurance of imaginable, 2 Pet. i. 16; 1 John i. 1, 3. (2) Those are best able to bear witness for Christ that have themselves been with him, by faith, hope, and love, and by living a life of communion with God in him. Ministers must first learn Christ, and then preach him. Those speak best of the things of God that speak experimentally.

CHAPTER SIXTEEN

PERSECUTION FORETOLD
(*vv.* 1–6)

Christ dealt faithfully with his disciples when he sent them forth on his errands, for he told them the worst of it, that they might sit down and count the cost. He had told them in the chapter before to expect the world's hatred; now here in these verses,

I. He gives them a reason why he alarmed them thus with the expectation of trouble: *These things have I spoken unto you, that you should not be offended*, or *scandalized, v.* 1.

II. He foretells particularly what they should suffer (*v.* 2): "Those that have power to do it shall *put you out of their synagogues*; and this is not the worst, *they shall kill you.*"

1. The sword of ecclesiastical censure; this is drawn against

them by the Jews, for they were the only pretenders to church-power. Note, It has often been the lot of Christ's disciples to be unjustly excommunicated. Many a good truth has been branded with an anathema, and many a child of God *delivered to Satan*.

2. The sword of civil power: "The time cometh, *the hour is come*; now things are likely to be worse with you than hitherto they have been; when you are expelled as heretics, they will *kill you, and think they do God service*, and others will think so too." It is common to patronise an enmity to religion with a colour of duty to God, and service to his church. God's people have suffered the greatest hardships from conscientious persecutors.

III. He gives them the true reason of the world's enmity and rage against them (*v.* 3): "*These things will they do unto you*, not because you have done them any harm, but *because they have not known the Father, nor me*. Let this comfort you, that none will be your enemies but the worst of men."

IV. He tells them why he gave them notice of this now, and why not sooner.

1. Why he told them of it now (*v.* 4), not to discourage them, or add to their present sorrow; nor did he tell them of their danger that they might contrive how to avoid it, but that, "when *the time shall come* (and you may be sure it will come), you may *remember that I told you*." Note, When suffering times come it will be of use to us to remember what Christ has told us of sufferings.

2. Why he did not tell them of it sooner: "*I spoke not this to you from the beginning* when you and I came to be first acquainted, because *I was with you*. (1) While he was with them, he bore the shock of the world's malice, and stood in the front of the battle. (2) It seems rather to be meant of the promise of *another comforter*. This he had said little of to them *at the beginning*, because he was himself with them to instruct, guide, and comfort them, and then they needed not the promise of the Spirit's extraordinary presence.

V. He expresses a very affectionate concern for the present sadness of his disciples, upon occasion of what he had said to them (*vv.* 5, 6).

1. He had told them that he was about to leave them: *Now I go my way*. He was not driven away by force, but voluntarily departed; his life was not extorted from him, but deposited by him.

2. He had told them what hard things they must suffer when he was gone, and that they must not expect such an easy quiet life as they had had. Now, if these were the legacies he had to leave to them, who had *left all* for him, they would be tempted to think they had made a sorry bargain of it, and were, for the present, in a consternation about it, in which their Master sympathizes with them, yet blames them, (1) That they were careless of the means of comfort, and did not stir up themselves to seek it: *None of you asks me, Whither goest thou?* Peter had started this question (*ch.* xiii. 36), and Thomas had seconded it (*ch.* xiv. 5), but they

did not pursue it, they did not take the answer; they were in the dark concerning it, and did not enquire further, nor seek for fuller satisfaction; they did not continue seeking, continue knocking.

(2) That they were too intent, and pored too much, upon the occasions of their grief: *Sorrow has filled their hearts*. Christ had said enough to fill them with joy (*ch.* xv. 11); but by looking at that only which made against them, and overlooking that which made for them, they were so full of sorrow that there was no room left for joy.

THE COMFORTER (*vv.* 7–15)

Three things we have here concerning *the Comforter's coming*:—

I. That Christ's departure was absolutely necessary to the Comforter's coming, *v.* 7. Now he here tells them,

1. In general, *It was expedient for them that he should go away*. This was strange doctrine, but if it was true it was comfortable enough, and showed them how absurd their sorrow was. *It is expedient*, not only for me, but *for you* also, *that I go away*; though they do not see it, and are loth to believe it, so it is.

2. *It was therefore expedient* because its object was the sending of the Spirit. Now observe,

(1) That Christ's going was so that the Comforter may come.

[1] This is expressed negatively: *If I go not away, the Comforter will not come*. And why not? *First*, So it was settled in the

divine counsels concerning this affair, and the measure must not be altered; *shall the earth be forsaken for them? Secondly*, It is congruous enough that the ambassador extraordinary should be recalled, before the envoy come, that is constantly to reside. *Thirdly*, The sending of the Spirit was to be the fruit of Christ's purchase, and that purchase was to be made by his death, which was his going away. *Fourthly*, It was to be an answer to his intercession within the veil. See *ch.* xiv. 16.

[2] It is expressed positively: *If I depart I will send him to you.* Though he *departs*, he sends the *Comforter*; nay, he departs on purpose to send him.

(2) That the presence of Christ's Spirit in his church is so much better, and more desirable, than his bodily presence, that it was really expedient for us that he should go away, to send the Comforter.

II. That the coming of *the Spirit* was absolutely necessary to the carrying on of Christ's interests on earth (*v.* 8).

1. See here what the office of the Spirit is, and on what errand he is sent. (1) To *reprove*. The Spirit, by the word and conscience, is a reprover; ministers are reprovers by office, and by them the Spirit reproves. (2) To *convince*. It is a law-term, and speaks the office of the judge in summing up the evidence, and setting a matter that has been long canvassed in a clear and true light.

2. See who they are whom he is to reprove and convince: *The world*, both Jew and Gentile.

3. See what the Spirit shall convince the world of.

(1) *Of sin* (*v.* 9), *because they believe not on me.* [1] The Spirit is sent to convince sinners of sin, not barely to tell them of it. [2] The Spirit, in conviction, fastens especially upon the sin of unbelief, their not believing in Christ, *First*, As the great reigning sin. There was, and is, a world of people, that believe not in Jesus Christ, and they are not sensible that it is their sin. *Secondly*, As the great ruining sin. Every sin is so in its own nature; no sin is so to them that believe in Christ; so that it is unbelief that damns sinners.

(2) *Of righteousness, because I go to my Father, and you see me no more, v.* 10. We may understand this, [1] Of Christ's personal righteousness. He shall convince the world that Jesus of Nazareth was Christ the righteous (1 John ii. 1), as the centurion owned (Luke xxiii. 47), *Certainly this was a righteous man.* [2] Of Christ's righteousness communicated to us for our justification and salvation; that everlasting righteousness which Messiah was to bring in, Dan. ix. 24.

(3) *Of judgment, because the prince of this world is judged, v.* 11. Observe here, [1] The devil, *the prince of this world*, was judged, was discovered to be a great deceiver and destroyer, and as such judgment was entered against him, and execution in part done. He was cast out of the Gentile world when his oracles were silenced and his altars deserted, cast out of the bodies of

many in Christ's name, which miraculous power continued long in the church; he was cast out of the souls of people by the grace of God working with the gospel of Christ; he *fell as lightning from heaven*. [2] This is a good argument wherewith the Spirit convinces the world of judgment, that is, *First*, Of inherent holiness and sanctification, Matt. xii. 18. By *the judgment of the prince of this world*, it appears that Christ is stronger than Satan, and can disarm and dispossess him, and set up his throne upon the ruins of his. *Secondly*, Of a new and better dispensation of things. He shall show that Christ's errand into the world was to set things to right in it, and to introduce times of reformation and regeneration; and he proves it by this, that *the prince of this world*, the great master of misrule, is judged and expelled. *Thirdly*, Of the power and dominion of the Lord Jesus. He shall convince the world that *all judgment is committed to him*, and that he is the *Lord of all*, which is evident by this, that he has judged the prince of this world, has broken *the serpent's head*, *destroyed him that had the power of death*, *and spoiled principalities*. *Fourthly*, Of the final day of judgment: all the obstinate enemies of Christ's gospel and kingdom shall certainly be reckoned with at last, for the devil, their ringleader, is judged.

III. That the coming of the Spirit would be of unspeakable advantage to the disciples themselves.

1. He intimates to them the tender sense he had of their present weakness (*v.* 12).

2. He assures them of sufficient assistances, by the pouring out of the Spirit.

(1) To guide the apostles. He will take care,

[1] That they do not miss their way: *He will guide you*.

[2] That they do not come short of their end: *He will guide them into all truth*. But how into *all truth*? The meaning is,

First, Into the whole truth relating to their embassy.

Secondly, Into nothing but the truth. All that *he shall guide you into* shall be *truth* (1 John ii. 27); *the anointing is truth*. In the following words he proves both these:—1. "The Spirit shall teach nothing but the truth, *for he shall not speak of himself* any doctrine distinct from mine, *but whatsoever he shall hear*, and knows to be the mind of the Father, *that*, and that only, *shall he speak*." This intimates, (1) That the testimony of the Spirit, in the word and by the apostles, is what we may rely upon. (2) That the testimony of the Spirit always concurs with the word of Christ, *for he does not speak of himself*, has no separate interest or intention of his own, but, as in essence so in records, he *is one with the Father and the Son*, 1 John v. 7.

(2) The Spirit undertook to glorify Christ, *vv.* 14, 15. [1] Even the sending of the Spirit was the glorifying of Christ. God the Father glorified him in heaven, and the Spirit glorified him on earth. [2] The Spirit glorified Christ by leading his followers

into *the truth as it is in Jesus*, Eph. iv. 21.

LASTING JOY (*vv.* 16–22)

Our Lord Jesus, for the comfort of his sorrowful disciples, here promises that he would visit them again.

I. Observe the intimation he gave them of the comfort he designed them, *v.* 16. Here he tells them,

1. That they should now shortly lose the sight of him.

2. That yet they should speedily recover the sight of him: *Again a little while, and you shall see me*, and therefore you ought not to *sorrow as those that have no hope*. His farewell was not a final farewell; they should see him again, (1) At his resurrection, soon after his death, when *he showed himself alive*, by many infallible proofs, and this in a very little while, not forty hours. See Hos. vi. 2. (2) By the pouring out of the Spirit, soon after his ascension, which scattered the mists of ignorance and mistake they were almost lost in, and gave them a much clearer insight into the mysteries of Christ's gospel than they had yet had. (3) At his second coming.

3. He assigns the reason: "*Because I go to the Father.*"

It should seem, all this refers rather to his going away at death, and return at his resurrection, than his going away at his ascension, and his return at the end of time; for it was his death that was their grief, not his ascension (Luke xxiv. 52), and between his

death and resurrection it was indeed a *little while*.

II. The perplexity of the disciples upon the intimation given them; they were at a loss what to make of it (*vv,* 17, 18). When they were at a loss about the meaning of Christ's words, they conferred together upon it, and asked help of one another.

III. The further explication of what Christ had said.

1. See here *why* Christ explained it (*v.* 19); because he *knew they were desirous to ask him*, and designed it.

2. See here *how* he explained it; not by a nice and critical descant upon the words, but by bringing the thing more closely to them; he had told them of *not seeing him, and seeing him*, and they did not apprehend his meaning, and therefore he explains it by their sorrowing and rejoicing, because we commonly measure things according as they affect us (*v.* 20): *You shall weep and lament*, for my departure, *but the world shall rejoice* in it; *and you shall be sorrowful*, while I am absent, *but*, upon my return to you, *your sorrow will be turned into joy*. But he says nothing of the *little while*, because he saw that this perplexed them more than any thing; and it is of no consequence to us to know *the times and the seasons*.

(1) What Christ says here, and *vv.* 21, 22, of their sorrow and joy, is primarily to be understood of the present state and circumstances of the disciples.

(2) It is applicable to all the faithful followers of the Lamb, and describes the common case of

Christians. *Gladness is sown for the upright in heart, that sow in tears*, and without doubt *they will shortly reap in joy*. Their sorrow will not only be followed with joy, but turned into it; for the most precious comforts take rise from pious griefs. This he illustrates by a similitude taken from a woman in travail, to whose sorrows he compares those of his disciples, for their encouragement; for it is the will of Christ that his people should be a comforted people.

First, Here is the similitude or parable itself (*v.* 21): *A woman*, we know, *when she is in travail, hath sorrow*, she is in exquisite pain, *because her hour is come*, the hour which nature and providence have fixed, which she has expected, and cannot escape; *but as soon as she is delivered of the child*, then *she remembers no more the anguish.*

Secondly, The application of the similitude (*v.* 22): "*You now have sorrow*, and are likely to have more, *but I will see you again*, and you me, and then all will be well." Men will attempt to take their joy from them; they would if they could; but they shall not prevail. Some understand it of the eternal joy of those that are glorified; those that have *entered into the joy of the Lord shall go no more out.* I rather understand it of the spiritual joys of those that are sanctified, particularly the apostles' joy in their apostleship.

AN ANSWER TO ASKING
(*vv.* 23–27)

An answer to their askings is here promised, for their further comfort. Now there are two ways of asking: asking by way of enquiry, which is the asking of the ignorant; and asking by way of request, which is the asking of the indigent. Christ here speaks of both.

I. By way of enquiry, they should not need to ask (*v.* 23). In the story *of the apostles' Acts* we seldom find them asking questions, as David, *Shall I do this?* Or, *Shall I go thither?* For they were constantly under a divine guidance.

Now for this he gives a reason (*v.* 25), which plainly refers to this promise, that they should not need to ask questions: "*These things have I spoken unto you in proverbs*, in such a way as you have thought not so plain and intelligible as you could have wished, *but the time cometh when I shall show you plainly*, as plainly as you can desire, *of the Father*, so that you shall not need to ask questions."

1. The great thing Christ would lead them into was the knowledge of God: "*I will show you the Father*, and bring you acquainted with him."

2. Of this he had hitherto spoken to them in proverbs, which are wise and instructive sayings, but figurative, and resting in generals.

3. He would speak to them *plainly—with freedom*, of the Father. When the Spirit was poured out, the apostles attained to a much greater knowledge of divine things than they had before, as appears by the utterance the Spirit gave them, Acts ii. 4.

II. He promises that by way of

request they should ask nothing in vain. Now,

1. Here is an express promise of a grant, *v.* 23. For he says, *Whatsoever you shall ask the Father in my name, he will give it to you.* We had it before, *ch.* xiv. 13. What would we more? The promise is as express as we can desire.

2. Here is an invitation for them to petition. It is thought sufficient if great men permit addresses, but Christ calls upon us to petition, *v.* 24.

(1) He looks back upon their practice hitherto: *Hitherto have you asked nothing in my name.*

(2) He looks forward to their practice for the future: *Ask, and you shall receive, that your joy may be full.*

3. Here are the grounds upon which they might hope to speed (*vv.* 26, 27), which are summed up in short by the apostle (1 John ii. 1): "*We have an advocate with the Father.*"

(1) We have an advocate; as to this, Christ saw cause at present not to insist upon it, only to make the following encouragement shine the brighter: "*I say not unto you that I will pray the Father for you.*" He speaks as if they needed not any further favours, when he had prevailed for the gift of the Holy Ghost to *make intercession within them*, as a Spirit of adoption, crying *Abba, Father*; as if they had no further need of him to pray for them now; but we shall find that he does more for us than he says he will. Men's performances often come short of their promises, but Christ's go beyond them.

(2) We have to do with a Father, which is so great an encouragement that it does in a manner supersede the other. Observe what an emphasis is laid upon this. The Father himself, whose favour you have forfeited, and whose wrath you have incurred, and with whom you need an advocate, he himself now loves you. Observe, [1] Why the Father loved the disciples of Christ: *Because you have loved me, and have believed that I came out from God*, that is, because you are my disciples indeed: not as if the love began on their side, but when by his grace he has wrought in us a love to him he is well pleased with the work of his own hands. [2] What encouragement this gave them in prayer. They need not fear speeding when they came to one that loved them, and wished them well.

CHRIST'S MISSION
(*vv.* 28–33)

Two things Christ here comforts his disciples with:—

I. With an assurance that, though he was leaving the world, he was returning to his Father, from whom he came forth, *vv.* 28–32, where we have,

1. A plain declaration of Christ's mission from the Father, and his return to him (*v.* 28): *I came forth from the Father, and am come*, as you see, *into the world. Again, I leave the world*, as you will see shortly, *and go to the Father.*

(1) These two great truths are here, [1] Contracted, and put into a few words. Brief summaries of Christian doctrine are of great use to young beginners. [2] Compared,

and set the one over against the other. There is an admirable harmony in divine truths; they both corroborate and illustrate one another; Christ's coming and his going do so.

(2) If we ask concerning the Redeemer *whence he came*, and *whither he went*, we are told, [1] That he *came from the Father*, who sanctified and sealed him. [2] That, when he had done his work on earth, he left the world, and went back to his Father at his ascension.

2. The disciples' satisfaction in this declaration (*vv.* 29, 30): *Lo, now speakest thou plainly*. It should seem, this one word of Christ did them more good than all the rest, though he had said many things likely enough to fasten upon them. Two things they improved in by this saying:—

(1) In knowledge: *Lo, now speakest thou plainly*.

(2) In faith: *Now are we sure*. Observe,

[1] What was the matter of their faith: *We believe that thou camest forth from God*.

[2] What was the motive of their faith—his omniscience. This proved him a teacher come from God, and more than a prophet, that he knew all things, which they were convinced of by this that he resolved those doubts which were hid in their hearts, and answered the scruples they had not confessed.

3. The gentle rebuke Christ gave the disciples for their confidence that they now understood him, *vv.* 31, 32. Here we have,

(1) A question, designed to put them upon consideration: *Do you now believe?*

(2) A prediction of their fall, that, how confident soever they were now of their own stability, in a little time they would all desert him, which was fulfilled that very night, when, upon his being seized by a party of the guards, *all his disciples forsook him and fled*, Matt. xxvi. 56.

(3) An assurance of his own comfort notwithstanding: *Yet I am not alone*. He would not be thought to complain of their deserting him, as if it were any real damage to him; for in their absence he should be sure of his Father's presence.

II. He comforts them with a promise of peace in him, by virtue of his victory over the world, whatever troubles they might meet with in it (*v.* 33). Observe,

1. The end Christ aimed at in preaching this farewell sermon to his disciples: *That in him they might have peace*.

2. The entertainment they were likely to meet with in the world: "You shall not have outward peace, never expect it."

3. The encouragement Christ gives them with reference hereto: *But be of good cheer*.

4. The ground of that encouragement: *I have overcome the world*. Christ's victory is a Christian's triumph. Never was there such a conqueror of the world as Christ was, and we ought to be encouraged by it, (1) Because Christ has overcome the world before us; so that we may look upon it as a conquered enemy, that has many a time been baffled. Nay, (2) He has conquered it for us, as the captain of our salvation. We are interested in his victory; by his cross the

world is *crucified to us*, which bespeaks it completely conquered and put into our possession; all is yours, even *the world*. Christ having overcome the world, believers have nothing to do but to pursue their victory, and divide the spoil; and this we do by faith, 1 John v. 4. *We are more than conquerors through him that loved us.*

CHAPTER SEVENTEEN

CHRIST'S PRAYER I

(*vv.* 1–5)

Here we have, I. The circumstances of this prayer, *v.* 1. Observe,

1. The time when he prayed this prayer; when he had *spoken these words*, had given the foregoing farewell to his disciples, he prayed this prayer in their hearing; so that, (1) It was a prayer after sermon; when he had spoken from God to them, he turned to speak to God for them. (2) It was a prayer after sacrament; after Christ and his disciples had eaten the passover and the Lord's supper together, and he had given them a suitable exhortation, he closed the solemnity with this prayer, that God would preserve the good impressions of the ordinance upon them. (3) It was a family-prayer. Christ's disciples were his family. (4) It was a parting prayer. When we and our friends are parting, it is good to part with prayer, Acts xx. 36. (5) It was a prayer that was a preface to his sacrifice, which he was now about to offer on earth, specifying the favours and blessings designed to be purchased by the merit of his death for those that were his.

(6) It was a prayer that was a specimen of his intercession, which he ever lives to make for us within the veil.

(2) The outward expression of fervent desire which he used in this prayer: He *lifted up his eyes to heaven*, as before (*ch.* xi. 41). It is significant of the lifting up of the soul to God in prayer, Ps. xxv. 1.

II. The first part of the prayer itself, in which Christ prays for himself. Observe here,

1. He prays to God as a Father: He *lifted up his eyes, and said, Father.* Note, As prayer is to be made to God only, so it is our duty in prayer to eye him as a Father, and to call him *our Father.* All that have the Spirit of adoption are taught to cry *Abba, Father,* Rom. viii. 15; Gal. iv. 6.

2. He prayed for himself first. Though Christ, as God, was prayed to, Christ, as man, prayed; thus *it became him to fulfil all righteousness. Glorify me, that I may glorify thee,* in doing what is agreed upon to be yet done, *vv.* 1–3. And to the performance of his undertaking hitherto: "*Glorify me, for I have glorified thee.* I have done my part, and now, Lord, do thine," *vv.* 4, 5.

(1) Christ here prays to be *glorified*, in order to *glorify God* (*v.* 1): *Glorify thy Son* according to thy promise, *that thy Son may glorify thee* according to his undertaking. Here observe,

[1] What he prays for—that he might be glorified in this world: "*The hour is come* when all the powers of darkness will combine to vilify thy Son; now, Father, glorify him."

[2] What he pleads to enforce this request.

First, He pleads relation: *Glorify thy Son*; thy Son as God, as Mediator. Note, Those that have received the adoption of sons may in faith pray for the inheritance of sons; if sanctified, then glorified: *Father, glorify thy Son*.

Secondly, He pleads the time: *The hour is come*; the season prefixed to an hour. The hour of Christ's passion was determined in the counsel of God. He had often said his hour was not yet come; but now it was come, and he knew it.

Thirdly, He pleads the Father's own interest and concern herein: *That thy Son may also glorify thee*; for he had consecrated his whole undertaking to his Father's honour. He desired to be carried triumphantly through his sufferings to his glory, that he might glorify the Father two ways:—By *the death of the cross*, which he was now to suffer. 2. By the doctrine of the cross, which was now shortly to be published to the world, by which God's kingdom was to be re-established among men.

Fourthly, He pleads his commission (*vv.* 2, 3); he desires to glorify his Father, in conformity to, and in pursuance of, the commission given him. Now see here the power of the Mediator.

a. The origin of his power: *Thou hast given him power*; he has it from God, *to whom all power belongs*.

b. The extent of his power: He has *power over all flesh*, (*a*) Over all mankind. He has power in and over the world of spirits, the powers of the upper and unseen world are subject to him (1 Peter iii. 22); but,

being now mediating between God and man, he here *pleads his power over all flesh*. (*b*) Over mankind considered as corrupt and fallen, for so he is called *flesh*, Gen. vi. 3. If he had not in this sense been flesh, he had not needed a Redeemer.

c. The grand intention and design of this power: *That he should give eternal life to as many as thou hast given him*. Here is the mystery of our salvation laid open.

(*a*) Here is the Father making over the elect to the Redeemer, and giving them to him as his charge and trust; as the crown and recompence of his undertaking.

(*b*) Here is the Son undertaking to secure the happiness of those that were given him, that he would *give eternal life to them*.

(*c*) Here is the subserviency of the Redeemer's universal dominion to this: He has *power over all flesh*, on purpose that he might give eternal life to the select number. Note, Christ's dominion over the children of men is in order to achieve the salvation of the children of God.

d. Here is a further explication of this grand design (*v.* 3).

(*a*) The great end which the Christian religion sets before us, and that is, eternal life, the happiness of an immortal soul in the vision and fruition of an eternal God.

(*b*) The sure way of attaining this blessed end, which is, by the right knowledge of God and Jesus Christ: "*This is life eternal, to know thee*," which may be taken two ways: —[*a*] "*Life eternal* lies in the knowledge of God and Jesus Christ.

[*b*] The knowledge of God and Christ leads to life eternal; this is the way in which Christ gives eternal life, by the knowledge of him that has called us (2 Peter i. 3), and this is the way in which we come to receive it.

(2) Christ here prays to be glorified in consideration of his having glorified the Father hitherto, *vv.* 4, 5. The meaning of the former petition was, Glorify me in this world; the meaning of the latter is, Glorify me in the other world. *I have glorified thee on the earth, and now glorify thou me.*

Thus we must be taught that those, and only those, who glorify God on earth, and persevere in the work God hath given them to do, shall be glorified with the Father, when they must be no more in this world. Not that we can merit that glory, as Christ did, but our glorifying God is required as an evidence of our interest in Christ, through whom eternal life is God's free gift.

CHRIST'S PRAYER II
(*vv.* 6–10)

Christ, having prayed for himself, comes next to pray for those that are his, and he knew them by name, though he did not here name them. Now observe here,

I. Whom he did not pray for (*v.* 9): *I pray not for the world.* Note, There is a world of people that Jesus Christ did not pray for. It is not meant of the world of mankind in general (he prays for that here, *v.* 21, *That the world may believe that thou hast sent me*); nor is it meant of the Gentiles, in distinction from the Jews; but the world is

here opposed to the elect, who are given to Christ out of the world.

II. Whom he did pray for; not for angels, but for the children of men. 1. He prays *for those that were given him*, meaning primarily the disciples that had attended *him in the regeneration*; but it is doubtless to be extended further, to all who come under the same character, who receive and believe the words of Christ, *vv.* 6, 8. 2. He prays *for all that should believe on him* (*v.* 20), and it is not only the petitions that follow, but those also which went before, that must be construed to extend to all believers, in every place and every age; for he has a concern for them all, and calls *things that are not as though they were.*

III. What encouragement he had to pray for them, and what are the general pleas with which he introduces his petitions for them, and recommends them to his Father's favour; they are five:—

1. The charge he had received concerning them: *Thine they were, and thou gavest them me* (*v.* 6), and again (*v.* 9), *Those whom thou hast given me.*

2. The care he had taken of them to teach them (*v.* 6): *I have manifested thy name to them. I have given to them the words which thou gavest to me, v.* 8.

3. The good effect of the care he had taken of them, and the pains he had taken with them (*v.* 6): *They have kept thy word* (*v.* 7), *they have known that all things are of thee* (*v.* 8); *they have received thy words*, and embraced them, have given their assent and consent to them, *and have known surely that I came out*

from thee, and have believed that thou didst send me.

4. He pleads the Father's own interest in them (*v.* 9): *I pray for them, for they are thine*; and this by virtue of a joint and mutual interest, which he and the Father have in what pertained to each: *All mine are thine, and thine are mine.* Between the Father and Son there can be no dispute (as there is among the children of men) about *mine and thine*, for the matter was settled from eternity; *all mine are thine, and thine are mine.*

5. He pleads his own concern in them: *I am glorified in them.* (1) *I have been glorified in them.* What little honour Christ had in this world was among his disciples; he had been glorified by their attendance on him and obedience to him, their preaching and working miracles in his name; and therefore *I pray for them.* (2) "*I am to be glorified in them,* when I am gone to heaven; they are to bear up my name." The apostles preached and wrought miracles *in Christ's name; the Spirit in them glorified Christ* (*ch.* xvi. 14).

CHRIST'S PRAYER III
(*vv.* 11–16)

After the general pleas with which Christ recommended his disciples to his Father's care follow the particular petitions he puts up for them; and, 1. They all relate to spiritual blessings in heavenly things. 2. They are such blessings as were suited to their present state and case, and their various exigencies and occasions. 3. He is large and full in the petitions, orders them before his Father, and *fills his*

mouth with arguments, to teach us fervency and importunity in prayer, to be large in prayer, and dwell upon our errands at the throne of grace, wrestling as Jacob, *I will not let thee go, except thou bless me.*

Now the first thing Christ prays for, for his disciples, is their preservation. He commits them all to his Father's custody. Now observe,

I. The request itself: *Keep them from the world.* There were two ways of their being delivered from the world:—

1. By taking them out of it; and he does not pray that they might be so delivered: *I pray not that thou shouldest take them out of the world.*

2. Another way is by keeping them from the corruption that is in the world; and he prays they may be thus kept, *vv.* 11, 15. Here are three branches of this petition:—

(1) *Holy Father, keep those whom thou hast given me.*

[1] Christ was now leaving them; but let them not think that their defence was departed from them; no, he does here, in their hearing, commit them to the custody of his Father and their Father.

[2] The titles he gives to him he prays to, and them he prays for, enforce the petition. *First,* He speaks to God as a *holy Father.* In committing ourselves and others to the divine care, we may take encouragement, 1. From the attribute of his holiness, for this is engaged for the preservation of his holy ones; he hath *sworn by his holiness,* Ps. lxxxix. 35. 2. From this relation of a Father, wherein he stands to us through Christ. If he be a Father, he will take care of his

own children, will teach them and keep them; who else should? *Secondly*, He speaks of them as those whom the Father had *given him*. What we receive as our Father's gifts, we may comfortably remit to our Father's care.

(2) *Keep* them *through thine own name*: That is, [1] Keep them for thy name's sake; so some. [2] Keep them in thy name; so others; the original is so, "Keep them in the knowledge and fear of thy name; keep them in the profession and service of thy name, whatever it cost them. Keep them in the interest of thy name, and let them ever be faithful to this; keep them in thy truths, in thine ordinances, in the way of thy commandments." [3] Keep them by or through thy name; so others. "Keep them by thine own power, in thine own hand; keep them thyself, undertake for them, let them be thine own immediate care. Keep them by those means of preservation which thou hast thyself appointed, and by which thou hast made thyself known. Keep them by thy word and ordinances; let thy name be their strong tower, thy tabernacle their pavilion."

(3) *Keep them from the evil*, or out of the evil. He had taught them to pray daily, *Deliver us from evil*, and this would encourage them to pray.

II. The reasons with which he enforces these requests for their preservation, which are five:—

1. He pleads that hitherto he had kept them (*v.* 12).

2. He pleads that he was now under a necessity of leaving them, and could no longer watch over them in the way that he had hitherto done (*v.* 11): "Keep them now, that I may not lose the labour I bestowed upon them while I was with them. Keep them, *that they may be one* with us *as we are* with each other." We shall have occasion to speak of this, *v.* 21.

3. He pleads what a satisfaction it would be to them to know themselves safe, and what a satisfaction it would be to him to see them easy: *I speak this, that they may have my joy fulfilled in themselves*, *v.* 13.

4. He pleads the ill usage they were likely to meet with in the world, for his sake (*v.* 14): "*I have given them thy word* to be published to the world, *and they have received it*, have believed it themselves, and accepted the trust of transmitting it to the world; and therefore *the world hath hated them*, as also because they are *not of the world*, any more than I."

5. He pleads their conformity to himself in a holy non-conformity to the world (*v.* 16): "Father, keep them, for they are of my spirit and mind, *they are not of the world, even as I am not of the world*." Those may in faith commit themselves to God's custody, (1) Who are *as Christ was in this world*, and tread in his steps. God will love those that are like Christ. (2) Who do not engage themselves in the world's interest, nor devote themselves to its service.

CHRIST'S PRAYER IV
(*vv.* 17–19)

The next thing he prayed for for them was that they might be sanctified; not only kept from evil, but made good.

I. Here is the petition (*v.* 17): *Sanctify them through thy truth*, through thy word, for *thy word is truth*; it is true—it is truth itself. He desires they may be sanctified,

1. As Christians. Father, make them holy, and this will be their preservation, 1 Thess. v. 23.

2. As ministers. "*Sanctify them*, set them apart for thyself and service; let their call to the apostleship be ratified in heaven." Prophets were said to be sanctified, Jer. i. 5. Priests and Levites were so. *Sanctify them*; that is, (1) "Qualify them for the office, with Christian graces and ministerial gifts, to make them able ministers of the New Testament." (2) "Separate them to the office, Rom. i. 1. I have called them, they have consented; Father, say *Amen* to it." (3) "Own them in the office; let thy hand go along with them; sanctify them by or in thy truth, as truth is opposed to figure and shadow."

II. We have here two pleas or arguments to enforce the petition for the disciples' sanctification:—

1. The mission they had from him (*v.* 18): "*As thou hast sent me into the world*, to be thine ambassador to the children of men, so now that I am recalled *have I sent them into the world*, as my delegates." Now here,

(1) Christ speaks with great assurance of his own mission: *Thou hast sent me into the world.*

(2) He speaks with great satisfaction of the commission he had given his disciples: "*So have I sent them* on the same errand, and to carry on the same design"; to preach the same doctrine that he preached, and to confirm it with the same proofs, with a charge likewise to commit to other faithful men that which was committed to them. He gave them their commission (*ch.* xx. 21) with a reference to his own, and it magnifies their office that it comes from Christ, and that there is some affinity between the commission given to the ministers of reconciliation and that given to the Mediator; he is called an *apostle* (Heb. iii. 1), a *minister* (Rom. xv. 8), a *messenger*, Mal. iii. 1. Only they are sent as servants, he as a Son. Now this comes in here as a reason, [1] Why Christ was concerned so much for them, and laid their case so near his heart; because he had himself put them into a difficult office, which required great abilities for the due discharge of it. [2] Why he committed them to his Father; because he was concerned in their cause, their mission being in prosecution of his, and as it were an assignment out of it.

2. The merit he had for them is another thing here pleaded (*v.* 19): *For their sakes I sanctify myself.* Here is, (1) Christ's designation of himself to the work and office of Mediator: *I sanctified myself.* (2) Christ's design of kindness to his disciples herein; it is *for their sakes*, that *they may be sanctified*, that is, that they may be martyrs; so some. But I rather take it more generally, that they may be saints and ministers, duly qualified and accepted of God. And he that designed the end designed also the means, that they might be sanctified *by the truth*, the truth which Christ came into

the world to bear witness to, and died to confirm.

CHRIST'S PRAYER V
(*vv.* 20–23)

Next to their purity he prays for their unity; for the wisdom from above is *first pure, then peaceable*; and amity is amiable indeed when it is like the ointment on Aaron's holy head, and the dew on Zion's holy hill. Observe,

I. Who are included in this prayer (*v.* 20): "*Not these only*, not these only that are now my disciples" (the eleven, the seventy, with others, men and women that followed him when he was here on earth), "but *for those also who shall believe on me through their word*, either preached by them in their own day or written by them for the generations to come; I pray *for them all*, that they all may be one in their interest in this prayer, and may all receive benefit by it."

II. What is intended in this prayer (*v.* 21): *That they all may be one*. The same was said before (*v.* 11), *that they may be one as we are*, and again, *v.* 22. The heart of Christ was much upon this. It is the prayer of Christ for all that are his, and we may be sure it is an answered prayer—*that they all may be one*, one in us (*v.* 21), one *as we are one* (*v.* 22), made *perfect in one*, *v.* 23. It includes three things:—

1. That they might all be *incorporated in one body*. As Christ died, so he prayed, to *gather them all in one*, ch. xi. 52; Eph. i. 10.

2. That they might all be animated by one Spirit. This is plainly implied in this—*that they may be one in us*. Union with the Father

and Son is obtained and kept up only by the Holy Ghost.

3. That they might all be *knit together* in the bond of love and charity, all of one heart. *That they all may be one*, (1) In judgment and sentiment; not in every little thing—this is neither possible nor needful, but in the great things of God. (2) In disposition and inclination. All that are sanctified have the same divine nature and image; they have all a new heart, and it is *one heart*. (3) They are all one in their designs and aims. Every true Christian, *as far as he is so*, eyes the glory of God as his highest end, and the glory of heaven as his chief good. (4) They are all one in their desires and prayers; though they differ in words and the manner of expressions, yet, having all received the same *spirit of adoption*, and observing the same rule, they pray for the same things in effect. (5) All one in love and affection. Every true Christian has that in him which inclines him to love all true Christians as such. But this prayer of Christ will not have its complete answer till all the saints come to heaven, for then, and not till then, they shall be *perfect in one*, *v.* 23; Eph. iv. 13.

III. What is intimated by way of plea or argument to enforce this petition; three things:—

1. The oneness that is between the Father and the Son, which is mentioned again and again, *vv.* 11, 21–23.

2. The design of Christ in all his communications of light and grace to them (*v.* 22): "*The glory which thou gavest me*, as the trustee or channel of conveyance, *I have*

accordingly *given them*, to this intent, *that they may be one, as we are one*; so that those gifts will be in vain, if they be not one."

3. He pleads the happy influence their oneness would have upon others, and the furtherance it would give to the public good. This is twice urged (*v*. 21): *That the world may believe that thou hast sent me.* And again (*v*. 23): *That the world may know it*, for without knowledge there can be no true faith.

[1] In general, it will recommend Christianity to the world, and to the good opinion of those outside. When Christianity, instead of causing quarrels about itself, makes all other strifes to cease,—when it cools the fiery, smooths the rugged, and disposes men to be kind and loving, courteous and beneficent, to all men, studious to preserve and promote peace in all relations and societies, this will recommend it to all that have any thing either of natural religion or natural affection in them.

[2] In particular, it will beget in men good thoughts, *First*, Of Christ: They will know and believe that *thou hast sent me. Secondly*, Of Christians: They will *know that thou hast loved them as thou hast loved me.*

CHRIST'S PRAYER VI
(*vv*. 24–26)

Here is, I. A petition for the glorifying of all those that were given to Christ (*v*. 24), not only these apostles, but all believers: *Father, I will that they may be with me.* Observe,

1. The connection of this request with those foregoing. He had prayed that God would preserve, sanctify, and unite them; and now he prays that he would crown all his gifts with their glorification.

2. The manner of the request: *Father, I will.* Here, as before, he addresses himself to God as a Father, and therein we must do likewise; but when he says, *I will*, he speaks a language peculiar to himself, and such as does not become ordinary petitioners, but very well became him who paid for what he prayed for.

3. The request itself—that all the elect might come to be with him in heaven at last, to see his glory, and to share in it. Now observe here,

(1) Under what notion we are to hope for heaven? wherein does that happiness consist? three things make heaven:—[1] It is to be where Christ is: *Where I am.* [2] It is to be with him where he is; this is no tautology, but intimates that we shall not only be in the same happy place where Christ is, but that the happiness of the place will consist in his presence; this is *the fulness of its joy*. [3] It is to *behold his glory, which the Father* has given him.

(2) Upon what ground we are to hope for heaven; no other than purely the mediation and intercession of Christ, because he hath said, *Father, I will.*

4. The argument to back this request: *for thou lovedst me before the foundation of the world.* This is a reason, (1) Why he expected this glory himself. Thou wilt *give it to me, for thou lovedst me.* The honour and power given to the Son as Mediator were founded in the Father's love to him (*ch*. v. 20). Or, (2) Why he expected that those

who *were given to him* should be with him to share in his glory: "*Thou lovedst me*, and them in me, and canst deny me nothing I ask for them."

II. The conclusion of the prayer, which is designed to enforce all the petitions for the disciples, especially the last, that they may be glorified. Two things he insists upon, and pleads:—

1. The respect he had to his Father, *v*. 25. Observe,

(1) The title he gives to God: *O righteous Father*. When he prayed that they might be sanctified, he called him *holy Father*; when he prays that they may be glorified, he calls him *righteous Father*; for it is a *crown of righteousness which the righteous Judge shall give*.

(2) The character he gives of the world that lay in wickedness: *The world has not known thee*. Note, Ignorance of God overspreads the world of mankind; this is the darkness they sit in.

(3) The plea he insists upon for himself: *But I have known thee*. Christ knew the Father as no one else ever did. We are unworthy, but he is worthy.

(4) The plea he insists upon for his disciples: *And they have known that thou hast sent me*; and, [1] Hereby they are distinguished from the unbelieving world. [2] Hereby they are interested in the mediation of Christ, and partake of the benefit of his acquaintance with the Father. Knowing Christ as sent of God, they have, in him, known the Father, and are introduced to an acquaintance with him; therefore, "Father, look after them for my sake."

2. The respect he had to his disciples (*v*. 26): "I have led them into the knowledge of thee, and will do it yet more and more; with this great and kind intention, *that the love wherewith thou hast loved me may be in them, and I in them*."

It is *Christ in us* that is *the* only *hope of glory* that will *not make us ashamed*, Col. i. 27. All our communion with God, the reception of his love to us with our return of love to him again, passes through the hands of the Lord Jesus, and the comfort of it is owing purely to him. Christ had said but a little before, *I in them* (*v*. 23), and here it is repeated (though the sense was complete without it), and the prayer closed with it, to show how much the heart of Christ was set upon it; all his petitions centre in this, and with this *the prayers of Jesus, the Son of David, are ended*: "*I in them*; let me have this, and I desire no more." It is the glory of the Redeemer to dwell in the redeemed: it is his *rest for ever*, and he has desired it. Let us therefore make sure our union with Christ, and then take the comfort of his intercession. *This* prayer had an end, but *that* he ever lives to make.

CHAPTER EIGHTEEN

THE ARREST (*vv*. 1–12)

I. Our Lord Jesus, like a bold champion, takes the field first (*vv*. 1, 2). Observe,

1. That our Lord Jesus entered upon his sufferings *when he had spoken these words*, as Matt. xxvi. 1, *When he had finished all these sayings*. Here it is intimated, (1) That our Lord Jesus took his work

before him. The office of the priest was to teach, and pray, and offer sacrifice. Christ, after teaching and praying, applies himself to make atonement. (2) That having by his sermon prepared his disciples for this hour of trial, and by his prayer prepared himself for it, he then courageously went out to meet it.

2. That *he went forth with his disciples*. Judas knew what house he was in in the city, and he could have stayed and met his sufferings there; but, (1) He would do as he was wont to do, and not alter his method, either to meet the cross or to miss it, when his hour was come. (2) He was as unwilling that there should be *an uproar among the people* as his enemies were, for it was not his way *to strive or cry*. (3) He would set us an example in the beginning of his passion, as he did at the end of it, of retirement from the world.

3. That he went *over the brook Cedron*. He must go over this to go to *the mount of Olives*.

4. That he entered into a garden. This circumstance is taken notice of only by this evangelist, that Christ's sufferings began in a garden. In the garden of Eden sin began; there the curse was pronounced, there the Redeemer was promised, and therefore in a garden that promised seed entered the lists with the old serpent. Christ was buried also in a garden.

5. That he had his disciples with him, (1) Because he used to take them with him when he retired for prayer. (2) They must be witnesses of his sufferings, and his patience under them, that they might with the more assurance and affection

preach them to the world (Luke xxiv. 48), and be themselves prepared to suffer. (3) He would take them into the danger to show them their weakness, notwithstanding the promises they had made of fidelity. Christ sometimes brings his people into difficulties, that he may magnify himself in their deliverance.

6. That Judas the traitor *knew the place*, knew it to be the place of his usual retirement, and probably, by some word Christ had dropped, knew that he intended to be there that night, for want of a better closet.

II. *The captain of our salvation* having taken the field, the enemy presently comes upon the spot, and attacks him (*v*. 3). Observe,

1. The persons employed in this action—*a band of men and officers from the chief priests, with Judas*.

2. The preparation they had made for an attack: They came *with lanterns, and torches, and weapons. The weapons of his warfare were spiritual*, and at these *weapons* he had often beaten them, and *put them to silence*, and therefore they have now recourse to other *weapons, swords and staves*.

III. Our Lord Jesus gloriously repulsed the first onset of the enemy, *vv*. 4–6, where observe,

1. How he received them, with all the mildness imaginable towards them, and all the calmness imaginable in himself.

2. See how he terrified them, and obliged them to retire (*v*. 6). Hereby he showed plainly,

(1) What he could have done with them. When he struck them down, he could have struck them

dead; when he spoke them *to the ground*, he could have spoken them to hell, and have sent them, like Korah's company, the next way thither; but he would not do so, [1] Because the hour of his suffering was come, and he would not put it by; he would only show that his life was not forced from him, but *he laid it down of himself*, as he had said. [2] Because he would give an instance of his patience and forbearance with the worst of men, and his compassionate love to his very enemies.

IV. Having given his enemies a repulse, he gives his friends a protection, and that by his word too, *vv.* 7–9, where we may observe,

1. How he continued to expose himself to their rage, *v.* 7. They did not lie long where they fell, but, by divine permission, got up again; it is only in the other world that God's judgments are everlasting.

2. How he contrived to secure his disciples from their rage. He charges them therefore as *one having authority*: "*Let these go their way*; it is at your peril if you meddle with them."

3. Now herein he confirmed the word which he had spoken a little before (*ch.* xvii. 12), *Of those whom thou gavest me, I have lost none.*

V. Having provided for the safety of his disciples, he rebukes the rashness of one of them, and represses the violence of his followers, as he had repulsed the violence of his persecutors, *vv.* 10, 11, where we have,

1. Peter's rashness. He had a sword; and *he smote one of the high priest's servants*, who was probably one of the forwardest, and aiming,

it is likely, to cleave him down the head, missed his blow, and only *cut off his right ear*. *The servant's name*, for the greater certainty of the narrative, is recorded; it *was Malchus*, or *Malluch*, Neh. x. 4.

2. The rebuke his Master gave him (*v.* 11): *Put up thy sword into the sheath*, or scabbard; it is a gentle reproof, because it was his zeal that carried him beyond the bounds of discretion. Christ did not aggravate the matter, only bade him *do so no more*.

3. The reason for this rebuke: *The cup which my Father has given me, shall I not drink it?* Matthew relates another reason which Christ gave for this rebuke, but John preserves this, which he had omitted; in which Christ gives us, (1) A full proof of his own submission to his Father's will. (2) A fair pattern to us of submission to God's will in every thing that concerns us. [1] It is but a *cup*; a small matter comparatively, be it what it will. [2] It is a cup that is given us; sufferings are gifts. [3] It is given us by a Father, who has a Father's authority, and does us no wrong; a Father's affection, and means us no hurt.

VI. Having entirely reconciled himself to the dispensation, he calmly surrendered, and yielded himself a prisoner, not because he could not have made his escape, but because he would not. One would have thought the cure of Malchus's ear should have made them relent, but nothing would win upon them.

PETER'S DENIAL (*vv.* 13–27)

We have here an account of Christ's arraignment before the high priest, and some circumstances that occurred therein which were omitted by the other evangelists; and Peter's denying him, which the other evangelists had given the story of entire by itself, is interwoven with the other passages. The crime laid to his charge having relation to religion, the judges of the spiritual court took it to fall directly under their cognizance. Both Jews and Gentiles seized him, and so both Jews and Gentiles tried and condemned him, for he died for the sins of both. Let us go over the story in order.

I. Having seized him, they *led him away to Annas first*, before they brought him to the court that was sat, expecting him, in the house of Caiaphas, *v.* 13. 1. They *led him away*, led him in triumph, as a trophy of their victory; led him *as a lamb to the slaughter*, and they led him through the sheep-gate spoken of Neh. iii. 1. 2. They led him away to their masters that sent them. 3. They led him to Annas first. Probably his house lay in the way, and was convenient for them to call at to refresh themselves, and, as some think, to be paid for their service. 4. This Annas was father-in-law to Caiaphas the high priest; this kindred by marriage between them comes in as a reason either why Caiaphas ordered that this piece of respect should be done to Annas, to favour him with the first sight of the prisoner, or why Annas was willing to countenance Caiaphas in a matter his heart was so much upon.

II. Annas did not long detain them, being as willing as any of them to have the prosecution pushed on, and therefore sent him bound to Caiaphas. Observe here,

1. The power of Caiaphas intimated (*v.* 13). He was *high priest that same year*. It was the ruin of Caiaphas that he was high priest that year, and so became a ringleader in the putting of Christ to death.

2. The malice of Caiaphas, which is intimated (*v.* 14) by the repeating of what he had said some time before, that, right or wrong, guilty or innocent, *it was expedient that one man should die for the people*, which refers to the story *ch.* xi. 50.

3. The concurrence of Annas in the prosecution of Christ.

III. In the house of Caiaphas, Simon Peter began to deny his Master, *vv.* 15–18.

1. It was with much ado that Peter got into the hall where the court was sitting, an account of which we have *vv.* 15, 16. Here we may observe,

2. Peter, having got in, was immediately assaulted with the temptation, and foiled by it, *v.* 17. Observe here,

(1) How slight the attack was. It was but a silly maid, of so small account that she was set to keep the door, that challenged him, and she only asked him carelessly, *Art not thou one of this man's disciples?* probably suspecting it by his sheepish look, and coming in timorously.

(2) How speedy the surrender was. Without taking time to recollect himself, he suddenly answered, *I am not*.

(3) Yet he goes further into the temptation: *And the servants and*

officers stood there, and Peter with them, v. 18.

Peter was much to be blamed, 1. Because he associated with these wicked men, and kept company with them. 2. Because he desired to be thought *one of them*, that he might not be suspected to be a disciple of Christ.

IV. Peter, Christ's friend, having begun to deny him, the high priest, his enemy, begins to accuse him, or rather urges him to accuse himself, *vv.* 19–21. Observe,

1. The articles or heads upon which Christ was examined (*v.* 19): concerning *his disciples and his doctrine.* Observe,

(1) The irregularity of the process; it was against all law and equity.

(2) The intention. The *high priest then*, because he had resolved that Christ must be sacrificed to their private malice under colour of the public good, examined him upon those interrogatories which would touch his life. He examined him, [1] Concerning his disciples, that he might charge him with sedition, and represent him as dangerous to the Roman government, as well as to the Jewish church. [2] Concerning his doctrine, that they might charge him with heresy, and bring him under the penalty of the law against false prophets, Deut. xiii. 9, 10.

2. The appeal Christ made, in answer to these interrogatories. (1) As to his disciples, he said nothing, because it was an impertinent question; if his doctrine was sound and good, his having disciples to whom to communicate it was no more than what was prac-

tised and allowed by their own doctors. (2) As to his doctrine, he said nothing in particular, but in general referred himself to those that heard him, being not only made manifest to God, but made manifest also in their consciences, *vv.* 20, 21.

[1] He tacitly charges his judges with illegal proceedings. *First, "Why ask you me now* concerning my doctrine, when you have already condemned it?" They had made an order of court for excommunicating all that owned him (*ch.* ix. 22), had issued out a proclamation for apprehending him; and now they come to ask what his doctrine is! Thus was he condemned, as his doctrine and cause commonly are, unheard. *Secondly, "Why ask you me?* Must I accuse myself, when you have no evidence against me?"

[2] He insists upon his fair and open dealing with them in the publication of his doctrine, and justifies himself with this. The crime which the sanhedrim by the law was to enquire after was the clandestine spreading of dangerous doctrines, enticing secretly, Deut. xiii. 6. As to this, therefore, Christ clears himself very fully. *First,* As to the manner of his preaching. He spoke openly. *Secondly,* As to the persons he preached to: *He spoke to the world*, to all that had *ears to hear*, and were willing to hear him, high or low, learned or unlearned, Jew or Gentile, friend or foe, *Thirdly,* As to the places he preached in. When he was in the country, he preached ordinarily in the synagogues—the places of meeting for worship, and on the

sabbath-day—the time of meeting; when he came up to Jerusalem, he preached the same doctrine in the temple at the time of the solemn feasts, when the Jews from all parts assembled there; and though he often preached in private houses, and on mountains, and by the sea-side, to show that his word and worship were not to be confined to temples and synagogues, yet what he preached in private was the very same with what he delivered publicly. *Fourthly*, As to the doctrine itself. He *said nothing in secret* contrary to what he said in public, but only by way of repetition and explanation: *In secret have I said nothing*.

[3] He appeals to those that had heard him, and desires that they might be examined what doctrine he had preached, and whether it had that dangerous tendency that was surmised.

V. While the judges were examining him, the servants that stood by were abusing him, *vv*. 22, 23.

1. It was a base affront which one of the officers gave him; though he spoke with so much calmness and convincing evidence, this insolent fellow *struck him with the palm of his hand*, probably on the side of his head or face, saying, *Answerest thou the high priest so?* as if he had behaved himself rudely to the court.

2. Christ bore this affront with wonderful meekness and patience (*v*. 23). Christ could have answered him with a miracle of wrath, could have struck him dumb or dead, or have withered the hand that was lifted up against him. But this was the day of his patience and suffer-

ing, and he answered him with the *meekness of wisdom*.

VI. While the servants were thus abusing him, Peter was proceeding to deny him, *vv*. 25–27. It is a sad story, and none of the least of Christ's sufferings.

1. He repeated the sin the second time, *v*. 25.

(1) It was his great folly to thrust himself into the temptation, by continuing in the company of those that were unsuitable for him, and that he had nothing to do with.

(2) It was his great unhappiness that he was again assaulted by the temptation; and no other could be expected, for this was a place, this an hour, of temptation.

(3) It was his great weakness, nay, it was his great wickedness, to yield to the temptation, and to say, *I am not one* of his disciples, as one ashamed of that which was his honour, and afraid of suffering for it, which would have been yet more his honour. See how the *fear of man brings a snare*.

2. He repeated the sin the third time, *vv*. 26, 27. Here he was attacked by one of the servants, who was kinsman to Malchus, who, when he heard Peter deny himself to be a disciple of Christ, gave him the lie with great assurance: "*Did not I see thee in the garden with him?* Witness my kinsman's ear." Peter then denied again, as if he knew nothing of Christ, nothing of the garden, nothing of all this matter.

Immediately the cock crew; and this is all that is here said of his repentance, it being recorded by the other evangelists. The crowing of the cock to others was an accidental thing, and had no significancy; but to Peter it was the voice of God, and had a blessed tendency to awaken his conscience, by putting him in mind of the word of Christ.

BEFORE PILATE (*vv.* 28–40)

We have here an account of Christ's arraignment before Pilate, the Roman governor, in the *prætorium* (a Latin word made Greek), the prætor's house, or *hall of judgment*; thither they hurried him, to get him condemned in the Roman court, and executed by the Roman power. Here is,

I. Pilate's conference with the prosecutors. They were called first, and stated what they had to say against the prisoner, as was very fit, *vv.* 29–32.

1. The judge calls for the indictment. Looking upon Pilate as a magistrate, that we may give every one his due, here are three things commendable in him:—(1) His diligent and close application to business. (2) His condescending to the humour of the people, and receding from the honour of his place to gratify their scruples. (3) His adherence to the rule of justice, in demanding the accusation, suspecting the prosecution to be malicious: "*What accusation bring you against this man?*"

2. The prosecutors demand judgment against him upon a general surmise that he was a criminal, not alleging, much less proving, any thing in particular *worthy of death or of bonds* (*v.* 30). Note, It is no new thing for the best of benefactors to be branded and run down as the worst of malefactors.

3. The judge remands him to their own court (*v.* 31): "*Take you him, and judge him according to your own law*, and do not trouble me with him.*"

4. They disown any authority as judges, and (since it must be so) are content to be prosecutors. They now grow less insolent and more submissive, and own, "*It is not lawful for us to put any man to death*, whatever less punishment we may inflict, and this is a malefactor whom we would have the blood of.*"

It was necessary that Christ should be put to death by the Romans, that, being *hanged upon a tree*, he might be *made a curse for us* (Gal. iii. 13), and *his hands and feet* might be *pierced.* As the Roman power had brought him to be born at Bethlehem, so now to die upon a cross, and both according to the scriptures.

II. Here is Pilate's conference with the prisoner, *v.* 33, &c., where we have,

1. The prisoner set to the bar. Pilate, after he had conferred with the chief priests at his door, entered into the hall, and called for Jesus to be brought in.

2. His examination. The other evangelists tell us that his accusers had laid it to his charge that *he perverted the nation, forbidding to give tribute to Cæsar*, and upon this he is examined.

(1) Here is a question put to him, with a design to ensnare him and to find out something upon which to ground an accusation: "*Art thou the king of the Jews?*" Some think Pilate asked this with an air of scorn and contempt: "What! *art thou a king*, who makest so mean a

figure?" Since it could not be proved he ever said it, he would constrain him to say it now, that he might proceed upon his own confession.

(2) Christ answers this question with another; not for evasion, but as an intimation to Pilate to consider what he did, and upon what grounds he went (*v.* 34): "*Sayest thou this thing of thyself*, from a suspicion arising in thy own breast, *or did others tell it thee of me*, and dost thou ask it only to oblige them?"

(3) Pilate resents Christ's answer, and takes it very ill, *v.* 35. This is a direct answer to Christ's question, *v.* 34. [1] Christ had asked him whether he spoke of himself. "No," says he; "*am I a Jew*, that thou suspectest me to be in the plot against thee?" [2] Christ had asked him whether others told him. "Yes," says he, "and those *thine own people*, who, one would think, should be biassed in favour of thee." [3] Christ had declined answering that question, *Art thou the king of the Jews?* And therefore Pilate puts another question to him more general, "*What hast thou done?*"

(4) Christ, in his next reply, gives a more full and direct answer to Pilate's former question, *Art thou a king?* explaining in what sense he was a king, but not such a king as was any ways dangerous to the Roman government, not a secular king, for his interest was not supported by secular methods, *v.* 36. Observe,

[1] An account of the nature and constitution of Christ's kingdom: It *is not of this world*. It is expressed negatively to rectify the present mistakes concerning it; but the positive is implied, it is *the kingdom of heaven*, and belongs to another world. Christ is a king, and has a kingdom, but *not of this world*.

[2] An evidence of the spiritual nature of Christ's kingdom produced. If he had designed an opposition to the government, he would have fought them at their own weapons, and would have repelled force with force of the same nature; but he did not take this course: *If my kingdom were of this world, then would my servants fight, that I should not be delivered to the Jews*, and my kingdom be ruined by them. But, *First*, His followers did not offer to fight; there was no uproar, no attempt to rescue him, though the town was now full of Galileans, his friends and countrymen, and they were generally armed; but the peaceable behaviour of his disciples on this occasion was enough *to put to silence the ignorance of foolish men*. *Secondly*, He did not order them to fight; nay, he forbade them, which was an evidence both that he did not depend upon worldly aids (for he could have summoned *legions of angels* into his service, which showed that his *kingdom was from above*), and also that he did not dread worldly opposition.

(5) In answer to Pilate's further query, he replies yet more directly, *v.* 37, where we have, [1] Pilate's plain question: "*Art thou a king then?*" [2] The good confession which our Lord Jesus witnessed before Pontius Pilate, in answer to this (1 Tim. vi. 13): *Thou sayest that I am a king*, that is, It is as thou

636

sayest, I am a king; for *I came to bear witness of the truth*. He explains himself, and shows how he is a king, as *he came to bear witness of the truth*; he rules in the minds of men by the power of truth. Christ's errand into the world, and his business in the world, were *to bear witness to the truth*. 1. To reveal it, to discover to the world that which otherwise could not have been known concerning God and his will and *good-will to men*, *ch*. i. 18; xvii. 26. 2. To confirm it, Rom. xv. 8. By his miracles *he bore witness to the truth* of religion, the truth of divine revelation, and of God's perfections and providence, and the truth of his promise and covenant, *that all men through him might believe*. Now by doing this he is a king, and sets up a kingdom.

(6) Pilate, hereupon, puts a good question to him, but does not stay for an answer, *v*. 38. He said, *What is truth?* and *immediately went out again*.

[1] It is certain that this was a good question, and could not be put to one that was better able to answer it.

[2] It is uncertain with what design Pilate asked this question. *First*, Perhaps he spoke it as a learner, as one that began to think well of Christ. *Secondly*, Some think he spoke it as a judge, enquiring further into the cause now brought before him: "Let me into this mystery, and tell me what the truth of it is, the true state of this matter." *Thirdly*, Others think he spoke it as a scoffer, in a jeering way: "Thou talkest of truth; canst thou tell what truth is, or give me a definition of it?" But, though

Christ would not tell Pilate what is truth, he has told his disciples, and by them has told us, *ch*. xiv. 6.

III. The result of both these conferences with the prosecutors and the prisoner (*vv*. 38–40), in two things:—

1. The judge appeared his friend, and favourable to him, for,

(1) He publicly declared him innocent, *v*. 38. This solemn declaration of Christ's innocency was, [1] For the justification and honour of the Lord Jesus. By this it appears that though he was treated as the worst of malefactors he had never merited such treatment. [2] For explaining the design and intention of his death, that he did not die for any sin of his own, even in the judgment of the judge himself, and therefore he died as a sacrifice for our sins, and that, even in the judgment of the prosecutors themselves, *one man should die for the people*, *ch*. xi. 50. [3] For aggravating the sin of the Jews that prosecuted him with so much violence.

(2) He proposed an expedient for his discharge (*v*. 39): *You have a custom, that I should release to you a prisoner at the passover*; shall it be this king of the Jews? He proposed this, not to the chief priests (he knew they would never agree to it), but to the multitude; it was an appeal to the people, as appears, Matt. xxvii. 15.

2. The people appeared his enemies, and implacable against him (*v*. 40): *They cried all again* and again, *Not this man*, let not him be released, *but Barabbas*. Observe, (1) How fierce and outrageous they were. (2) How foolish and absurd

they were, as is intimated in the short account here given of the other candidate: *Now Barabbas was a robber*, and therefore, [1] A breaker of the law of God; and yet he shall be spared, rather than one who reproved the pride, avarice, and tyranny of the priests and elders. [2] He was an enemy to the public safety and personal property. Thus those do who prefer their sins before Christ. Sin is a robber, every base lust is a robber, and yet foolishly chosen rather than Christ, who would truly enrich us.

CHAPTER NINETEEN

CHRIST EXAMINED
(vv. 1–15)

Here is a further account of the unfair trial which they gave to our Lord Jesus.

I. The judge abuses the prisoner, though he declares him innocent, and hopes therewith to pacify the prosecutors; wherein his intention, if indeed it was good, will by no means justify his proceedings, which were palpably unjust.

1. He ordered him to be whipped as a criminal, *v.* 1. (1) *That the scripture might be fulfilled*, which spoke of his being *stricken, smitten, and afflicted*, and *the chastisement of our peace* being *upon him* (Isa. liii. 5), of his giving his back to the smiters (Isa. l. 6), of the ploughers ploughing upon his back, Ps. cxxix. 3. He himself likewise had foretold it, Matt. xx. 19; Mark x. 34; Luke xviii. 33. (2) *That by his stripes we might be healed*, 1 Pet. ii. 4. (3) That stripes, for his sake, might be sanctified and made easy to his followers.

2. He turned him over to his soldiers, to be ridiculed and made sport with as a fool (*vv.* 2, 3).

See here the wonderful condescension of our Lord Jesus in his sufferings for us. Great and generous minds can bear anything better than ignominy, any toil, any pain, any loss, rather than reproach; yet this the great and holy Jesus submitted to for us.

II. Pilate, having thus abused the prisoner, presents him to the prosecutors, in hope that they would now be satisfied, and drop the prosecution, *vv.* 4, 5. Here he proposes two things to their consideration:—

1. That he had not found anything in him which made him obnoxious to the Roman government (*v.* 4).

2. That he had done that to him which would make him the less dangerous to them and to their government, *v.* 5. He brought him out to them, wearing the crown of thorns, his head and face all bloody, and said, "*Behold the man* whom you are so jealous of," intimating that though his having been so popular might have given them some cause to fear that his interest in the country would lessen theirs, yet he had taken an effectual course to prevent it, by treating him as a slave, and exposing him to contempt, after which he supposed the people would never look upon him with any respect, nor could he ever retrieve his reputation again. *Behold the man.* It is good for every one of us, with an eye of faith, to behold the man Christ Jesus in his sufferings. *Behold this king with the crown wherewith his mother*

crowned him, the crown of thorns, Cant. iii. 11. "Behold him, and be suitably affected with the sight. Behold him, and mourn because of him. Behold him, and love him; be still *looking unto Jesus*."

III. The prosecutors, instead of being pacified, were but the more exasperated, *vv.* 6, 7.

1. Observe here their clamour and outrage. It was violent and exceedingly resolute; they will have it their own way, and hazard the governor's favour, the peace of the city, and their own safety, rather than abate of the utmost of their demands.

2. The check Pilate gave to their fury, still insisting upon the prisoner's innocency: "*Take you him and crucify him*, if he must be crucified." This is spoken ironically; he knew they could not, they durst not, crucify him. But Pilate had not courage enough to act according to his conscience; and his cowardice betrayed him into a snare.

3. The further colour which the prosecutors gave to their demand (*v.* 7): *We have a law, and by our law*, if it were but in our power to execute it, *he ought to die, because he made himself the Son of God.* Now here observe, (1) They *made their boast of the law*, even when *through breaking the law they dishonoured God*, as is charged upon the Jews, Rom. ii. 23. (2) They discover a restless and inveterate malice against our Lord Jesus. (3) They pervert the law, and make that the instrument of their malice.

IV. The judge brings the prisoner again to his trial, upon this new suggestion. Observe,

1. The concern Pilate was in,

when he heard this alleged (*v.* 8): When he heard that his prisoner pretended not to royalty only, but to deity, he was *the more afraid*.

2. His further examination of our Lord Jesus thereupon, *v.* 9. That he might give the prosecutors all the fair play they could desire, he resumed the debate, went into the judgment-hall, and asked Christ, *Whence art thou?*

"Where wast thou, and in what world hadst thou a being, before thy coming into this world?"

3. The silence of our Lord Jesus when he was examined upon this head; but *Jesus gave him no answer*. This was not a sullen silence, in contempt of the court, nor was it because he knew not what to say; but, [1] It was a patient silence, that the scripture might be fulfilled, *as a sheep before the shearers is dumb, so he opened not his mouth*, Isa. liii. 7. [2] It was a prudent silence. When the chief priests asked him, *Art thou the Son of the Blessed?* he answered, *I am*, for he knew they went upon the scriptures of the Old Testament which spoke of the Messiah; but when Pilate asked him he knew he did not understand his own question, having no notion of the Messiah, and of his being the *Son of God*, and therefore to what purpose should he reply to him whose head was filled with the pagan theology, to which he would have turned his answer?

4. The haughty check which Pilate gave him for his silence (*v.* 10): "*Speakest thou not unto me?*"

5. Christ's pertinent answer to this check, *v.* 11, where,

[1] He boldly rebukes his arrogance, and rectifies his mistake.

God is the fountain of power; and the *powers that are*, as they are ordained by him and derived from him, so they are subject to him. They ought to go no further than his law directs them; they can go no further than his providence permits them. They are God's hand and his sword, Ps. xvii. 13, 14. Pilate never fancied himself to look so great as now, when he sat in judgment upon such a prisoner as this; who was looked upon by many as the *Son of God* and king of Israel, and had the fate of so great a man at his disposal; but Christ lets him know that he was herein but an instrument in God's hand, and could do nothing against him, but by the appointment of Heaven, Acts iv. 27, 28.

[2] He mildly excuses and extenuates his sin, in comparison with the sin of the ringleaders.

First, It is plainly intimated that what Pilate did was sin, a great sin, and that the force which the Jews put upon him, and which he put upon himself in it, would not justify him.

Secondly, Yet theirs that delivered him to Pilate was the greater sin. By this it appears that all sins are not equal, but some more heinous than others.

V. Pilate struggles with the Jews to deliver Jesus out of their hands, but in vain. We hear no more after this of any thing that passed between Pilate and the prisoner; what remains lay between him and the prosecutors.

1. Pilate seems more zealous than before to get Jesus discharged (*v.* 12): *Thenceforth*, from this time, and for this reason, because Christ

had given him that answer (*v.* 11), which, though it had a rebuke in it, yet he took kindly; and, though Christ found fault with him, he still continued to find no fault in Christ, but *sought to release him*, desired it, endeavoured it.

2. The Jews were more furious than ever, and more violent to get Jesus crucified. In this outcry they sought two things:—(1) To blacken the prisoner as an enemy to Cæsar. (2) To frighten the judge, as no friend to Cæsar. They intimate a threatening that they would inform against him, and get him displaced; and here they touched him in a sensitive and very tender part.

3. When other expedients had been tried in vain, Pilate slightly endeavoured to banter them out of their fury, and yet, in doing this, betrayed himself to them, and yielded to the rapid stream, *vv.* 13–15. After he had stood it out a great while, and seemed now as if he would have made a vigorous resistance upon this attack (*v.* 12), he basely surrendered.

It was the preparation of the passover, and *about the sixth hour*. Observe, 1. The day: It was the preparation of the passover, that is, for the passover-sabbath, and the solemnities of that and the rest of the days of the feast of unleavened bread. This is plain from Luke xxiii. 54, *It was the preparation, and the sabbath drew on.* So that this preparation was for the sabbath. 2. The hour: *It was about the sixth hour.* Some ancient Greek and Latin manuscripts read it about the third hour, which agrees with Mark xv. 25. And it appears by Matt. xxvii. 45 that he was upon the cross before the sixth hour. But it should seem to come in here, not as a precise determination of the time, but as an additional aggravation of the sin of his prosecutors, that they were pushing on the prosecution, not only on a solemn day, the *day of the preparation*, but, from the third to the sixth hour on that day, they were employed in this wickedness; so that for this day, though they were priests, they dropped the temple-service, for they did not leave Christ till the sixth hour, when the darkness began, which frightened them away. Some think that the sixth hour, with this evangelist, is, according to the Roman reckoning and ours, six of the clock in the morning, answering to the Jews' first hour of the day; this is very probable, that Christ's trial before Pilate was at the height about six in the morning, which was then a little after sun-rising.

4. The encounter Pilate had with the Jews, both priests and people, before he proceeded to give judgment, endeavouring in vain to stem the tide of their rage.

[1] He saith unto the Jews, *Behold your king*. This is a reproof to them for the absurdity and malice of their insinuating that this Jesus made himself a king. But Pilate, though he was far from meaning so, seems as if he were the voice of God to them.

[2] They cried out with the greatest indignation, *Away with him, away with him*, which speaks disdain as well as malice.

[3] Pilate, willing to have Jesus released, and yet that it should be their doing, asks them, *Shall I crucify your king?*

[4] The chief priests, that they might effectually renounce Christ, and engage Pilate to crucify him, but otherwise sorely against their will, cried out, *We have no king but Cæsar*. This they knew would please Pilate, and so they hoped to carry their point, though at the same time they hated Cæsar and his government.

GOLGOTHA (vv. 16–18)

We have here sentence of death passed upon our Lord Jesus, and execution done soon after.

I. *Pilate gave judgment* against Christ, and signed the warrant for his execution, *v.* 16.

II. Judgment was no sooner given than with all possible expedition the prosecutors, having gained their point, resolved to lose no time lest Pilate should change his mind, and order a reprieve.

1. They immediately hurried away the prisoner. The chief priests greedily flew upon the prey which they had been long waiting for; now it is drawn into their net.

2. To add to his misery, they obliged him, as long as he was able, to carry his cross (*v.* 17), according to the custom among the Romans; hence *Furcifer* was among them a name of reproach. Now Christ's carrying his cross may be considered, (1) As a part of his sufferings; he endured the cross literally. (2) As answering the type which went before him; Isaac, when he was to be offered, carried the wood on which he was to be bound and with which he was to be burned. (3) As very significant of his under-

taking, the Father having *laid upon him the iniquity of us all* (Isa. liii. 6), and he having to *take away sin* by *bearing it in his own body upon the tree*, 1 Pet. ii. 24. (4) As very instructive to us. Our Master hereby taught all his disciples to take up their cross, and follow him.

3. They brought him to the place of execution: He *went forth*, not dragged against his will, but voluntary in his sufferings. He went forth out of the city, for he was *crucified without the gate*, Heb. xiii. 12.

4. There they crucified him, and the other malefactors with him (*v.* 18): *There they crucified him.*

And now let us pause awhile, and with an eye of faith look upon Jesus. Was ever sorrow like unto his sorrow? See him who was clothed with glory stripped of it all, and clothed with shame—him who was the *praise of angels* made a *reproach of men*—him who had been with eternal delight and joy in the bosom of his Father now in the extremities of pain and agony. See him bleeding, see him struggling, see him dying, see him and love him, love him and live to him, and study what we shall render.

FINISHED (*vv.* 19–30)

Here are some remarkable circumstances of Christ's dying more fully related than before, which those will take special notice of who covet to know Christ and him crucified.

I. The title set up over his head. Observe,

1. The inscription itself which Pilate wrote, and ordered to be fixed to the top of the cross, declaring the cause for which he was crucified, *v.* 19. Pilate intended this for his reproach, but God overruled this matter, (1) That it might be a further testimony to the innocency of our Lord Jesus; for here was an accusation which, as it was worded, contained no crime. (2) That it might show forth his dignity and honour.

2. The notice taken of this inscription (*v.* 20): Here are two reasons why the title was so much read:—(1) Because the place where Jesus was crucified, though without the gate, was yet *nigh the city.* (2) Because it was written in Hebrew, and Greek, and Latin, which made it legible by all. God so ordering it that this should be written in the three then most known tongues, it was intimated thereby that Jesus Christ should be a Saviour to all nations, and not to the Jews only.

3. The offence which the prosecutors took at it, *v.* 21. They would not have it written, *the king of the Jews*; but that he said of himself, *I am the king of the Jews.*

4. The judge's resolution to adhere to it: "*What I have written I have written,* and will not alter it to humour them."

Hereby honour was done to the Lord Jesus. Pilate stuck to it with resolution, that he was the king of the Jews. What he had written was what God had first written, and therefore he could not alter it; for thus it was written, that Messiah the prince should be *cut off*, Dan. ix. 26. This therefore is the true cause of his death; he dies because the king of Israel must die, must thus die. When the Jews reject Christ, and will not have him for their king, Pilate, a Gentile, sticks to it that he is a king, which was an earnest of what came to pass soon after, when the Gentiles submitted to the kingdom of the Messiah, which the unbelieving Jews had rebelled against.

II. The dividing of his garments among the executioners, *vv.* 23, 24. Here observe, 1. The shame they put upon our Lord Jesus, in stripping him of his garments before they crucified him. 2. The wages with which these soldiers paid themselves for crucifying Christ. They were willing to do it for his old clothes. Nothing is to be done so bad, but there will be found men bad enough to do it for a trifle. 3. The sport they made about his seamless coat. We read not of any thing about him valuable or remarkable but this, and this not for the richness, but only the variety of it, for it was *woven from the top throughout*; there was no curiosity therefore in the shape, but a designed plainness. The soldiers thought it a pity to rend it, for then it would unravel, and a piece of it would be good for nothing; they would *therefore cast lots for it.* While Christ was in his dying agonies, they were merrily dividing his spoils. 4. The fulfilling of the scripture in this. David, in spirit, foretold this very circumstance of Christ's sufferings, in that passage, Ps. xxii. 18.

III. The care that he took of his poor mother.

1. His mother attends him to his death (*v.* 25): *There stood by the cross,* as near as they could get, *his mother,* and some of his relations and friends with her. (1) See here

the tender affection of these pious women to our Lord Jesus in his sufferings, When all his disciples except John, had forsaken him, they continued their attendance on him (2) We may easily suppose what an affliction it was to these poor women to see him thus abused, especially to the blessed virgin. Now was fulfilled Simeon's word, *A sword shall pierce through thy own soul,* Luke ii. 35. (3) We may justly admire the power of divine grace in supporting these women, especially the virgin Mary, under this heavy trial. We do not find his mother wringing her hands, or tearing her hair, or rending her clothes, or making an outcry; but, with a wonderful composure, *standing by the cross,* and her friends with her. Surely she and they were strengthened by a divine power to this degree of patience; and surely the virgin Mary had a fuller expectation of his resurrection than the rest had, which supported her thus.

2. He tenderly provides for his mother at his death. He saw her standing by, and knew her cares and griefs; and he saw John standing not far off, and so he settled a new relation between his beloved mother and his beloved disciple; for he said to her, "*Woman, behold thy son,* for whom henceforward thou must have a motherly affection"; and to him, "*Behold thy mother,* to whom thou must pay a filial duty." And so *from that hour,* that hour never to be forgotten, *that disciple took her to his own home.* See here,

(1) The care Christ took of his dear mother. He was not so much taken up with a sense of his suffer-

ings as to forget his friends, all whose concerns he bore upon his heart.

(2) The confidence he reposed in the beloved disciple. It is to him he says, *Behold thy mother*, that is, I recommend her to thy care, be thou as a son to her to guide her (Isa. li. 18); and *forsake her not when she is old*, Prov. xxiii. 22.

IV. The fulfilling of the scripture, in the giving of him vinegar to drink, *vv*. 28, 29. Observe,

1. How much respect Christ showed to the scripture (*v*. 28).

(1) It was not at all strange that he was thirsty.

(2) But the reason of his complaining of it is somewhat surprising; it is the only word he spoke that looked like complaint of his outward sufferings. But now he cried, *I thirst*. For, [1] He would thus express *the travail of his soul*, Isa. liii. 11. [2] He would thus take care to see the scripture fulfilled. Now, *First*, The scripture had foretold his thirst, and therefore he himself related it, because it could not otherwise be known, saying, *I thirst*; it was foretold that his tongue should cleave to his jaws, Ps. xxii. 15. *Secondly*, The scripture had foretold that in his thirst he should have vinegar given him to drink, Ps. lxix. 21.

2. See how little respect his persecutors showed to him (*v*. 29).

V. The dying word wherewith he breathed out his soul (*v*. 30): *When he had received the vinegar*, as much of it as he thought fit, *he said, It is finished*; and, with that, *bowed his head, and gave up the ghost*. Observe,

1. What he said, and we may

suppose him to say it with triumph and exultation—*It is finished*, a comprehensive word, and a comfortable one. (1) *It is finished*, that is, the malice and enmity of his persecutors had now done their worst. (2) *It is finished*, that is, the counsel and commandment of his Father concerning his sufferings were now fulfilled; it was a *determinate counsel*, and he took care to see every iota and tittle of it exactly answered, Acts ii. 23. (3) *It is finished*, that is, all the types and prophecies of the Old Testament, which pointed at the sufferings of the Messiah, were accomplished and answered. (4) *It is finished*, that is, the ceremonial law is abolished, and a period put to the obligation of it. (5) *It is finished*, that is, sin is finished, and an end made of transgression, by *the bringing in of an everlasting righteousness*. It seems to refer to Dan. ix. 24. (6) *It is finished*, that is, his sufferings were now finished, both those of his soul and those of his body. (7) *It is finished*, that is, his life was now finished, he was just ready to breathe his last, and *now he is no more in this world*, ch. xvii. 11. (8) *It is finished*, that is, the work of man's redemption and salvation is now completed, at least the hardest part of the undertaking is over; a full satisfaction is made to the justice of God, a fatal blow given to the power of Satan, a fountain of grace opened that shall ever flow, a foundation of peace and happiness laid that shall never fail. Christ had now gone through with his work, and *finished it*, ch. xvii. 4.

2. What he did: *He bowed his head, and gave up the ghost*. He was

voluntary in dying; for he was not only the sacrifice, but the priest and the offerer. His life was not forcibly extorted from him, but freely resigned.

THE PIERCED SIDE
(vv. 31–37)

This passage concerning the piercing of Christ's side after his death is recorded only by this evangelist.

I. Observe the superstition of the Jews, which occasioned it (v. 31). These Jews would be thought to bear a great regard for the sabbath, and yet had no regard to justice and righteousness; they made no conscience of bringing an innocent and excellent person to the cross, and yet scrupled letting a dead body hang upon the cross.

II. The dispatching of *the two thieves that were crucified with him*, v. 32.

III. The trial that was made whether Christ was dead or no, and the putting of it out of doubt.

1. They supposed him to be dead, and therefore *did not break his legs*, v. 33.

2. Because they would be sure he was dead they made such an experiment as would put it past dispute. *One of the soldiers with a spear pierced his side*, aiming at his heart, *and forthwith came thereout blood and water*, v. 34.

(1) The soldier hereby designed to decide the question whether he was dead or no, and by this honourable wound in his side to supersede the ignominious method of dispatch they took with the other two.

(2) But God had a further design herein, which was,

[1] To give an evidence of the truth of his death, in order to the proof of his resurrection. If he was only in a trance or swoon, his resurrection was a sham; but, by this experiment, he was certainly dead.

[2] To give an illustration of the design of his death. There was much of mystery in it, and its being so solemnly attested (v. 35) intimates there was something miraculous in it, that *the blood and water* should come out distinct and separate from the same wound; at least it was very significant; this same apostle refers to it as a very considerable thing, 1 John v. 6, 8.

1. They signified the two great benefits which all believers partake of through Christ—justification and sanctification; blood for remission, water for regeneration; blood for atonement, water for purification. 2. They signified the two great ordinances of baptism and the Lord's supper, by which those benefits are represented, sealed, and applied, to believers; they both owe their institution and efficacy to Christ. It is not the water in the font that will be to us *the washing of regeneration*, but the water out of the side of Christ; not the blood of the grape that will pacify the conscience and refresh the soul, but the blood out of the side of Christ.

IV. The attestation of the truth of this by an eye-witness (v. 35), the evangelist himself.

His record is undoubtedly *true*; for he wrote not only from his own personal knowledge and observation, but from the dictates of the Spirit of truth, that leads into all truth.

V. The accomplishment of the

scripture in all this (*v.* 36): *That the scripture might be fulfilled*, and so both the honour of the Old Testament preserved and the truth of the New Testament confirmed.

CHRIST'S BURIAL
(*vv.* 38–42)

We have here an account of the burial of the blessed body of our Lord Jesus. Here is,

I. The body begged, *v.* 38. This was done by the interest of *Joseph of Ramah*, or *Arimathea*, of whom no mention is made in all the New-Testament story, but only in the narrative which each of the evangelists gives us of Christ's burial, wherein he was chiefly concerned.

II. The embalming prepared, *v.* 39. This was done by Nicodemus, another person of quality, and in a public post. He brought a *mixture of myrrh and aloes*, which some think were bitter ingredients, to preserve the body, others fragrant ones, to perfume it. Here is,
1. The character of Nicodemus, which is much the same with that of Joseph; he was a secret friend to Christ, though not his constant follower. He at first *came to Jesus by night*, but now owned him publicly, as before, *ch.* vii. 50, 51.
2. The kindness of Nicodemus, which was considerable, though of a different nature. Joseph served Christ with his interest, Nicodemus with his purse.

III. The body got ready, *v.* 40. They *took it* into some house adjoining, and, having washed it from blood and dust, *wound it in linen clothes* very decently, with the spices melted down, it is likely, into an ointment, as *the manner of the Jews is to bury*, or to *embalm* (so Dr. Hammond).

IV. The grave pitched upon, in a garden which belonged to Joseph of Arimathea, very near the place where he was crucified. There was a sepulchre, or vault, prepared for the first occasion, but not yet used. Observe,

1. That Christ was buried without the city, for thus the manner of the Jews was to bury, not in their cities, much less in their synagogues.

2. That Christ was buried in a garden. In the garden of Eden death and the grave first received their power, and now in a garden they are conquered, disarmed, and triumphed over.

3. That he was buried in a new sepulchre. This was so ordered, (1) For the honour of Christ; he was not a common person, and therefore must not mix with common dust. (2) For the confirming of the truth of his resurrection, that it might not be suggested that it was not he, but some other that rose now, when many bodies of saints arose.

V. The funeral solemnized (*v.* 42): *There laid they Jesus*, that is, the dead body of Jesus.

Thus without pomp or solemnity is the body of Jesus laid in the cold and silent grave. Here lies our surety under arrest for our debts, so that if he be released his discharge will be ours. Here is the Sun of righteousness set for awhile, to rise again in greater glory, and set no more. Here lies a seeming captive to death, but a real conqueror over death; for here lies death itself slain, and the grave conquered. *Thanks be to God, who giveth us the victory.*

CHAPTER TWENTY

EASTER MORNING
(*vv.* 1–10)

In these verses we have the first step towards the proof of Christ's resurrection, which is, that the sepulchre was found empty. *He is not here*, and, if so, they must tell us where he is, or we conclude him risen.

I. Mary Magdalene, coming to the sepulchre, finds the *stone taken away*.

1. She *came to the sepulchre*, to wash the dead body with her tears, for she *went to the grave, to weep there*, and to *anoint it with the ointment* she had prepared.

2. She came as soon as she could, for she came, (1) Upon the *first day of the week*, as soon as ever the sabbath was gone. (2) She came *early, while it was yet dark*; so early did she set out.

3. She found the stone taken away, which she had seen *rolled to the door of the sepulchre.* Now this was, (1) A surprise to her, for she little expected it. (2) It was the beginning of a glorious discovery; the Lord was risen, though she did not at first apprehend it so.

II. Finding the stone taken away, she hastens back to Peter and John, who probably lodged together at that end of the town, not far off, and acquaints them with it: "*They have taken the Lord out of the sepulchre*, envying him the honour of such a decent burying-place, *and we know not where they have laid him*, nor where to find him, that we may pay him the remainder of our last respects."

III. Peter and John go with all speed to the sepulchre, to satisfy themselves of the truth of what was told them, and to see if they could make any further discoveries, *vv.* 3, 4. Some think that the other disciples were with Peter and John when the news came; for they *told these things to the eleven*, Luke xxiv. 9. (1) He that got foremost in this race was *the disciple whom Jesus loved* in a special manner, and who therefore in a special manner loved Jesus. (2) He that was cast behind was Peter, who had denied his Master, and was in sorrow and shame for it, and this clogged him as a weight; sense of guilt cramps us, and hinders our enlargement in the service of God. When conscience is offended we lose ground.

IV. Peter and John, having come to the sepulchre, prosecute the enquiry, yet improve little in the discovery.

1. John went no further than Mary Magdalene had done. (1) He had the curiosity to look into the sepulchre, and saw it was empty. He *stooped down*, and *looked in.* (2) Yet he had not courage to go into the sepulchre.

2. Peter, though he came last, went in first, and made a more exact discovery than John had done, *vv.* 6, 7.

(1) Observe here the boldness of Peter, and how God dispenses his gifts variously. John could out-run Peter, but Peter could out-dare John.

(2) Observe the posture in which he found things in the sepulchre. [1] Christ had left his grave-clothes

behind him there; what clothes he appeared in to his disciples we are not told, but he never appeared in his grave-clothes, as ghosts are supposed to do; no, he laid them aside. [2] The grave-clothes were found in very good order, which serves for an evidence that his body was not stolen away while men slept.

(3) See how Peter's boldness encouraged John; now he took heart and ventured in (*v.* 8), and *he saw and believed*; not barely believed what Mary said, that the body was gone (no thanks to him to believe what *he saw*), but he began to believe that Jesus was risen to life again, though his faith, as yet, was weak and wavering.

[1] John followed Peter in venturing. It should seem, he durst not have gone into the sepulchre if Peter had not gone in first.

[2] Yet, it should seem, John got the start of Peter in believing. Peter saw and wondered (Luke xxiv. 12), but John saw and believed. A mind disposed to contemplation may perhaps sooner receive the evidence of divine truth than a mind disposed to action. But what was the reason that they were so slow of heart to believe? The evangelist tells us (*v.* 9), as yet they *knew not the scripture*, that is, they did not consider, and apply, and duly improve, what they knew of the scripture, that he must *rise again from the dead*.

3. Peter and John pursued their enquiry no further, but desisted, hovering between faith and unbelief (*v.* 10). It is probable that the rest of the disciples were together; to them they return, to make report of what they had discovered, and to consult with them what was to be done; and, probably, now they appointed their meeting in the evening, when Christ came to them. It is observable that before Peter and John came to the sepulchre an angel had appeared there, rolled away the stone, frightened the guard, and comforted the women; as soon as they were gone from the sepulchre, Mary Magdalene here sees two angels in the sepulchre (*v.* 12), and yet Peter and John come to the sepulchre, and go into it, and see none. What shall we make of this? Where were the angels when Peter and John were at the sepulchre, who appeared there before and after? [1] Angels appear and disappear at pleasure, according to the orders and instructions given them. They may be, and are really, where they are not visibly; nay, it should seem, may be visible to one and not to another, at the same time, Num. xxii. 23; 2 Kings vi. 17. [2] This favour was shown to those who were early and constant in their enquiries after Christ, and was the reward of those that came first and stayed last, but denied to those that made a transient visit. [3] The apostles were not to receive their instructions from the angels, but from the Spirit of grace. See Heb. ii. 5.

CHRIST AND MARY
(*vv.* 11–18)

St. Mark tells us that Christ appeared first to Mary Magdalene (Mark xvi. 9); that appearance is here largely related; and we may observe,

    I. The constancy and fervency

of Mary Magdalene's affection to the Lord Jesus, *v.* 11.

1. She stayed at the sepulchre, when Peter and John were gone, because there her Master had lain, and there she was likeliest to hear some tidings of him.

2. She stayed there weeping, and these tears loudly bespoke her affection to her Master.

3. *As she wept, she looked into the sepulchre,* that her eye might affect her heart.

II. The vision she had of two angels in the sepulchre, *v.* 12. Observe here,

1. The description of the persons she saw. They were *two angels in white, sitting* (probably on some benches or ledges hewn out in the rock) one at *the head,* and the other at the *feet,* of the grave.

They sat, as it were, reposing themselves in Christ's grave; for angels, though they needed not a restoration, were obliged to Christ for their establishment.

2. Their compassionate enquiry into the cause of Mary Magdalene's grief (*v.* 13): *Woman, why weepest thou?*

3. The melancholy account she gives them of her present distress: *Because they have taken away* the blessed body I came to embalm, *and I know not where they have laid it.* The same story she had told, *v.* 2. In it we may see, (1) The weakness of her faith. (2) The strength of her love. Mary Magdalene is not diverted from her enquiries by the surprise of the vision, nor satisfied with the honour of it; but still she harps upon the same string: *They have taken away my Lord.*

III. Christ's appearing to her

while she was talking with the angels, and telling them her case. In this appearance of Christ to Mary observe,

(1) How he did at first conceal himself from her.

[1] He stood as a common person, and she looked upon him accordingly, *v.* 14. She *knew not that it was Jesus*; not that he appeared in any other likeness, but either it was a careless transient look she cast upon him, and, her eyes being full of care, she could not so well distinguish, or *they were holden, that she should not know him,* as those of the two disciples, Luke xxiv. 16.

[2] He asked her a common question, and she answered him accordingly, *v.* 15.

First, The question he asked her was natural enough, and what any one would have asked her: "*Woman, why weepest thou? Whom seekest thou?*"

Secondly, The reply she made him is natural enough; she does not give him a direct answer, but, *supposing him to be the gardener,* she said, *Sir, if thou hast carried him hence,* pray *tell me where thou hast laid him, and I will take him away.* See here, 1. The error of her understanding. She supposed our Lord Jesus to be the gardener, perhaps because he asked what authority she had to be there. 2. The truth of her affection. See how her heart was set upon finding Christ. She puts the question to every one she meets, like the careful spouse, *Saw you him whom my soul loveth?*

(2) How Christ at length made himself known to her, and, by a

pleasing surprise, gave her infallible assurances of his resurrection. Observe,

[1] How Christ discovered himself to this good woman that was seeking him in tears (*v.* 16): *Jesus saith unto her, Mary.* It was said with an emphasis, and that air of kindness and freedom with which he was wont to speak to her. Now he changed his voice, and spoke like himself, not like the gardener. Christ's way of making himself known to his people is by his word, his word applied to their souls, speaking to them in particular.

[2] How readily she received this discovery. Observe, *First*, The title of respect she gives him: *My Master—a teaching master.* The Jews called their doctors *Rabbies*, great men. Their critics tell us that *Rabbon* was with them a more honourable title than *Rabbi*; and therefore Mary chooses that, and adds a note of appropriation, *My great Master. Secondly*, With what liveliness of affection she gives this title to Christ. *She turned* from the angels, whom she had in her eye, to look unto Jesus. When *she thought it had been the gardener*, she looked another way while speaking to him; but now that she knew the voice of Christ *she turned herself.*

[3] The further instructions that Christ gave her (*v.* 17): "*Touch me not*, but go and carry the news to the disciples."

First, He diverts her from the expectation of familiar society and conversation with him at this time: *Touch me not, for I am not yet ascended.* 1. *Touch me not* thus at all, for I am to ascend to heaven. He bade the disciples touch him, for

the confirmation of their faith; he allowed the women to take hold of his feet, and worship him (Matt. xxviii. 9); but Mary, supposing that he was risen, as Lazarus was, to live among them constantly, and converse with them freely as he had done, upon that presumption was about to take hold of his hand with her usual freedom. This mistake Christ rectified; she must believe him, and adore him, as exalted, but must not expect to be familiar with him as formerly. See 2 Cor. v. 16. 2. "*Touch me not*, do not stay to touch me now, stay not now to make any further enquiries, or give any further expressions of joy, for *I am not yet ascended*, I shall not depart immediately, it may as well be done another time; the best service thou canst do now is to carry the tidings to the disciples; lose no time therefore, but go away with all speed."

Secondly, He directs her what message to carry to his disciples: *But go to my brethren, and tell them*, not only that I am risen (she could have told them that of herself, for she had seen him), but that *I ascend*. Observe,

Two full breasts of consolation are here in these words:—

(*a*) Our joint-relation to God, resulting from our union with Christ, is an unspeakable comfort. Speaking of that inexhaustible spring of light, life, and bliss, he says, He is *my Father, and your Father; my God, and your God.* It is the great condescension of Christ that he is pleased to own the believer's God for his God: *My God, and your God*; mine, that he may be yours; the God of the

Redeemer, to support him (Ps. lxxxix. 26), that he might be the God of the redeemed, to save them.

(*b*) Christ's ascension into heaven, in further prosecution of his undertaking for us, is likewise an unspeakable comfort: "Tell them I must shortly ascend; that is the next step I am to take." Now this was intended to be, [*a*] A word of caution to these disciples, not to expect the continuance of his bodily presence on earth, nor the setting up of his temporal kingdom among men, which they dreamed of. [*b*] A word of comfort to them, and to all *that shall believe in him through their word*; he was then ascending, he is now *ascended to his Father, and our Father*. This was his advancement; he ascended to receive those honours and powers which were to be the recompence of his humiliation; he says it with triumph, that those who love him may rejoice.

Some make those words, *I ascend to my God and your God*, to include a promise of our resurrection, in the virtue of Christ's resurrection; for Christ had proved the resurrection of the dead from these words, *I am the God of Abraham*, Matt. xxii. 32. So that Christ here insinuates, "As he is my God, and hath therefore raised me, so he is your God, and will therefore raise you, and be your God, Rev. xxi. 3. *Because I live, you shall live also*. I now ascend, to honour my God, and you shall ascend to him as your God.

IV. Here is Mary Magdalene's faithful report of what she had seen and heard to the disciples (*v*. 18): *She came and told the disciples*, whom she found together, *that she had seen the Lord*.

EVIDENCE OFFERED
(*vv*. 19–25)

The infallible proof of Christ's resurrection was his *showing himself alive*, Acts i. 3. In these verses, we have an account of his first appearance to the college of the disciples, on the day on which he rose. Now observe here,

I. When and where this appearance was, *v*. 19. It was *the same day* that he rose, *being the first day of the week*, the day after the Jewish sabbath, at a private meeting of the disciples, ten of them, and some more of their friends with them, Luke xxiv. 33.

II. What was said and done in this visit Christ made to his disciples, and his interview between them. We have five things in this appearance of Christ:—

(1) His kind and familiar salutation of his disciples: *He said, Peace be unto you*. This was not a word of course, though commonly used so at the meeting of friends, but a solemn, uncommon benediction, conferring upon them all the blessed fruits and effects of his death and resurrection. The phrase was common, but the sense was now peculiar. His speaking peace makes peace, *creates the fruit of the lips, peace*; peace with God, peace in your own consciences, peace with one another; all this peace be with you; not peace with the world, but peace in Christ.

(2) His clear and undeniable manifestation of himself to them, *v*. 20. And here observe,

[1] The method he took to convince them of the truth of his resurrection, They now saw him alive

whom multitudes had seen dead two or three days before. Now the only doubt was whether this that they saw alive was the same individual body that had been seen dead; and none could desire a further proof that it was so than the scars or marks of the wounds in the body. Now, *First*, The marks of the wounds, and very deep marks (though without any pain or soreness), remained in the body of the Lord Jesus even after his resurrection, that they might be demonstrations of the truth of it. Conquerors glory in the marks of their wounds. Christ's wounds were to speak on earth that it was he himself. *Secondly*, These marks he showed to his disciples, for their conviction. When Christ manifests his love to believers by the comforts of his Spirit, assures them that *because he lives they shall live also*, then *he shows them his hands and his side*.

[2] The impression it made upon them, and the good it did them. *First*, They were convinced that they saw the Lord; so was their faith confirmed. *Secondly*, *Then they were glad*; that which strengthened their faith raised their joy; *believing they rejoice*.

(3) The honourable and ample commission he gave them to be his agents in the planting of his church, *v.* 21. Here is,

[1] The preface to their commission, which was the solemn repetition of the salutation before: *Peace be unto you*.

[2] The commission itself, which sounds very great: *As my Father hath sent me, even so send I you*.

First, It is easy to understand how Christ sent them; he appointed them to go on with his work upon earth, and to lay out themselves for the spreading of his gospel, and the setting up of his kingdom, among men. He sent them authorized with a divine warrant, armed with a divine power,—sent them as ambassadors to treat of peace, and as heralds to proclaim it,—sent them as servants to bid to the marriage. Hence they were called *apostles— men sent*.

Secondly, But how Christ sent them as the Father sent him is not so easily understood; certainly their commissions and powers were infinitely inferior to his; but, 1. Their work was of the same kind with his, and they were to go on where he left off. 2. He had a power to send them equal to that which the Father had to send him. Here the force of the comparison seems to lie. By the same authority that the Father sent me do I send you.

(4) The qualifying of them for the discharge of the trust reposed in them by their commission (*v.* 22): *He breathed on them, and said, Receive ye the Holy Ghost*. Observe,

[1] The sign he used to assure them of, and affect them with, the gift he was now about to bestow upon them: *He breathed on them*; not only to show them, by this breath of life, that he himself was really alive, but to signify to them the spiritual life and power which they should receive from him for all the services that lay before them. Christ here seems to refer to the creation of man at first, by the breathing of the breath of life into him (Gen. ii. 7), and to intimate

that he himself was the author of that work, and that the spiritual life and strength of ministers and Christians are derived from him, and depend upon him, as much as the natural life of Adam and his seed. Now this intimates to us, *First*, That the Spirit is the breath of Christ, *proceeding from the Son*. *Secondly*, That the Spirit is the gift of Christ. The apostles communicated the Holy Ghost by the laying on of hands, those hands being first lifted up in prayer, for they could only beg this blessing, and carry it as messengers; but Christ conferred the Holy Ghost by breathing, for he is the author of the gift, and from him it comes originally.

[2] The solemn grant he made, signified by this sign, "*Receive ye the Holy Ghost*, in part now, as an earnest of what you shall further receive *not many days hence*." Let us see what is contained in this grant. *First*, Christ hereby gives them assurance of the Spirit's aid in their future work, in the execution of the commission now given them: "*I send you*, and you shall have the Spirit to go along with you." *Secondly*, He hereby gives them experience of the Spirit's influences in their present case. He had shown them his hands and his side, to convince them of the truth of his resurrection; but the plainest evidences will not of themselves work faith, witness the infidelity of the soldiers, who were the only eye-witnesses of the resurrection. "Therefore *receive ye the Holy Ghost*, to work faith in you, and to open your understandings."

(5) One particular branch of the power given them by their commission particularized (*v.* 23): "*Whosoever sins you remit*, in the due execution of the powers you are entrusted with, they are remitted to them, and they may take the comfort of it; *and whosoever sins you retain*, that is, pronounce unpardoned and the guilt of them bound on, *they are retained*, and the sinner may be sure of it, to his sorrow." Now this follows upon their receiving the Holy Ghost; for, if they had not had an extraordinary spirit of discerning, they had not been fit to be entrusted with such an authority; for, in the strictest sense, this is a special commission to the apostles themselves and the first preachers of the gospel, who could distinguish who were in the *gall of bitterness and bond of iniquity*, and who were not. By virtue of this power, Peter struck Ananias and Sapphira dead, and Paul struck Elymas blind. Yet it must be understood as a general charter to the church and her ministers, not securing an infallibility of judgment to any man or company of men in the world, but encouraging the faithful stewards of the mysteries of God to stand to the gospel they were sent to preach, for that God himself will stand to it. Two ways the apostles and ministers of Christ remit and retain sin, and both as having authority:— [1] By sound doctrine. They are commissioned to tell the world that salvation is to be had upon gospel terms, and no other, and they shall find God will say *Amen* to it; so shall their doom be. [2] By a strict discipline, applying the general rule of the gospel to particular persons. "Whom you admit into communion

with you, according to the rules of the gospel, God will admit into communion with himself; and whom you cast out of communion as impenitent, and obstinate in scandalous and infectious sins, shall be bound over to the righteous judgment of God."

III. The incredulity of Thomas, when the report of this was made to him, which introduced Christ's second appearance.

1. Here is Thomas's absence from this meeting, *v.* 24.

2. The account which the other disciples gave him of the visit their Master had made them, *v.* 25.

3. The objections Thomas raised against the evidence, to justify himself in his unwillingness to admit it. "Tell me not that you have seen the Lord alive; you are too credulous; somebody has made fools of you. For my part, *except I shall* not only *see in his hands the print of the nails*, but put my finger into it, *and thrust my hand* into the wound *in his side*, I am resolved *I will not believe*." Either he will be humoured, and have his fancy gratified, or he will not believe; see Matt. xvi. 1; xxvii. 42.

4. The open avowal of this in the presence of the disciples was an offence and discouragement to them It was not only a sin, but a scandal. As one coward makes many, so does one unbeliever, one sceptic, *making his brethren's heart to faint like his heart*, Deut. xx. 8. Had he only thought this evil, and then laid his hand upon his mouth, to suppress it, his error had remained with himself; but his proclaiming his infidelity, and that so peremptorily, might be of ill consequence to the rest, who were as yet but weak and wavering.

THOMAS CONVINCED
(*vv.* 26–31)

We have here an account of another appearance of Christ to his disciples, after his resurrection, when Thomas was now with them. And concerning this we may observe,

I. When it was that Christ repeated his visit to his disciples: *After eight days*, that day seven-night after he rose, which must therefore be, as that was, *the first day of the week*.

1. He deferred his next appearance for some time, to show his disciples that he was not risen to such a life as he had formerly lived, to converse constantly with them, but was as one that belonged to another world, and visited this only as angels do, now and then, when there was occasion.

2. He deferred it so long as seven days. And why so? (1) That he might put a rebuke upon Thomas for his incredulity. (2) That he might try the faith and patience of the rest of the disciples. (3) That he might put an honour upon the first day of the week, and give a plain intimation of his will, that it should be observed in his church as the Christian sabbath, the weekly day of holy rest and holy convocations.

II. Where, and how, Christ made them this visit. It was at Jerusalem, for the doors were shut now, as before, for fear of the Jews. Now observe, 1. That Thomas was with them; though he had withdrawn himself once, yet not a second time. 2. That Christ *came* in among them, and *stood in the midst*, and they all knew him, for he showed himself now, just as he had shown himself before (*v.* 19), still the same, and no changling. 3. He saluted them all in a friendly manner, as he had done before; he said, *Peace be unto you.*

III. What passed between Christ and Thomas at this meeting; and that only is recorded, though we may suppose he said a great deal to the rest of them. Here is,

1. Christ's gracious condescension to Thomas, *v.* 27. He singled him out from the rest, and applied himself particularly to him: "*Reach hither thy finger*, and, since thou wilt have it so, *behold my hands*, and satisfy thy curiosity to the utmost about the *print of the nails; reach hither thy hand*, and, if nothing less will convince thee, *thrust it into my side.*" Here we have, (1) An implicit rebuke of Thomas's incredulity, in the plain reference which is here had to what Thomas had said, answering it word for word, for he had heard it, though unseen; and one would think that his telling him of it should put him to the blush. (2) An express condescension to his weakness, which appears in two things:—[1] That he suffers his wisdom to be prescribed to. Great spirits will not be dictated to by their inferiors, especially in their acts of grace; yet Christ is pleased here to accommodate himself even to Thomas's fancy in a needless thing, rather than break with him, and leave him in his unbelief. [2] He suffers his wounds to be raked into, allows Thomas even to thrust his hand into his side, if then at last he would believe.

It is an affecting word with which Christ closes up what he had to say to Thomas: *Be not faithless but believing; do not thou become an unbeliever*; as if he would have been sealed up under unbelief, had he not yielded now.

2. Thomas's believing consent to Jesus Christ. He is now ashamed of his incredulity, and cries out, *My Lord and my God, v.* 28. We are not told whether he did put his finger into the print of the nails; it should seem, he did not, for Christ says (*v.* 29), *Thou hast seen, and believed*; seeing sufficed. And now faith comes off a conqueror, after a struggle with unbelief.

(1) Thomas is now fully satisfied of the truth of Christ's resurrection —that the same Jesus that was crucified is now alive, and this is he.

(2) He therefore believed him to be Lord and God, and we are to believe him so. [1] We must believe his deity—that he is God; not a man made God, but God made man, as this evangelist had laid down his thesis at first, *ch.* i. 1. [2] His mediation—that he is Lord, the one Lord, 1 Cor. viii. 6; 1 Tim. ii. 5. He is sufficiently authorized, as plenipotentiary, to settle the great concerns that lie between God and man, to take up the controversy which would inevitably have been our ruin, and to establish the correspondence that was necessary to our happiness; see Acts ii. 36; Rom. xiv. 9.

(3) He consented to him as his Lord and his God. In faith there must be the consent of the will to gospel terms, as well as the assent of the understanding to gospel truths. We must accept of Christ to

be that to us which the Father hath appointed him. This is the vital act of faith, He is mine, Cant. ii. 16.

(4) He made an open profession of this, before those that had been the witnesses of his unbelieving doubts. He says it to Christ, and, to complete the sense, we must read it, *Thou art* my Lord and my God; or, speaking to his brethren, *This is* my Lord and my God.

3. The judgment of Christ upon the whole (*v.* 29). Here,

(1) Christ owns Thomas a believer. Sound and sincere believers, though they be slow and weak, shall be graciously accepted of the Lord Jesus.

(2) He upbraids him with his former incredulity. If this must be the only method of proof, how must the world be converted to the faith of Christ? He is therefore justly blamed for laying so much stress upon this.

(3) He commends the faith of those who believe upon easier terms. Thomas, as a believer, was truly blessed; but rather *blessed are those that have not seen*. It is not meant of not seeing the objects of faith (for these are invisible, Heb. xi. 1; 2 Cor. iv. 18), but the motives of faith—Christ's miracles, and especially his resurrection; blessed are those that see not these, and yet believe in Christ.

IV. The remark which the evangelist makes upon his narrative, like an historian drawing towards a conclusion, *vv.* 30, 31. And here,

1. He assures us that many other things occurred, which were all worthy to be recorded, but are *not written in the book: many signs*. Some refer this to all the signs that

Jesus did during his whole life, all the wondrous words he spoke, and all the wondrous works he did. But it seems rather to be confined to the signs he did after his resurrection, for these were in the presence of the disciples only, who are here spoken of, Acts x. 41.

2. He instructs us in the design of recording what we do find here (*v.* 31): "These accounts are given in this and the following chapter, *that you might believe* upon these evidences; that you might believe that Jesus is the Christ, the Son of God, declared with power to be so by his resurrection."

CHAPTER TWENTY-ONE
THE SEA OF TIBERIAS
(*vv.* 1–14)

We have here an account of Christ's appearance to his disciples at the sea of Tiberias. As to the particulars of the story, we may observe,

I. Who they were to whom Christ now showed himself (*v.* 2): not to all the twelve, but to seven of them only.

II. How they were employed, *v.* 3. Observe,

1. Their agreement to go a fishing. Some think they did amiss in returning to their boats and nets, which they had left; but then Christ would not have countenanced them in it with a visit.

2. Their disappointment in their fishing. That night they caught nothing, though, it is probable, they *toiled all night*, as Luke v. 5. See the vanity of this world; the hand of the diligent often returns empty.

III. After what manner Christ made himself known to them. It is said (*v.* 1), *He showed himself.* His body, though a true and real body, was raised, as ours will be, a spiritual body, and so was visible only when he himself was pleased to make it so; or, rather, came and removed so quickly that it was here or there in an instant, *in a moment, in the twinkling of an eye.* Four things are observable in the appearance of Christ to them:—

1. He showed himself to them seasonably (*v.* 4): *When the morning was now come,* after a fruitless night's toil, Jesus *stood on the shore.* Christ's time of making himself known to his people is when they are most at a loss.

2. He showed himself to them gradually. The disciples, though they had been intimately acquainted with him, *knew not,* all at once, *that it was Jesus.* Little expecting to see him there, and not looking intently upon him, they took him for some common person waiting the arrival of their boat, to buy their fish.

3. He showed himself to them by an instance of his pity, *v.* 5. He called to them, *Children,*—"*Lads, have you any meat?* Have you caught any fish?" Here, (1) The compellation is very familiar; he speaks unto them as unto his sons, with the care and tenderness of a father: *Children.* (2) The question is very kind: *Have you any meat?*

4. He showed himself to them by an instance of his power; and this perfected the discovery (*v.* 6): he ordered them to *cast the net on the right side of the ship,* the contrary side to what they had been casting it on; and then they, who were going home empty-handed, were enriched with a great draught of fishes. Here we have, (1) The orders Christ gave them, and the promise annexed to those orders: *Cast the net* there in such a place, and *you shall find.* He from whom nothing is hid, no, not the *inhabitants under the waters* (Job xxvi. 5), knew on what side of the ship the shoal of fishes was, and to that side he directs them. (2) Their obedience of these orders, and the good success of it. As yet *they knew not that it was Jesus*; however, they were willing to be advised by any body, and did not bid this supposed stranger mind his own business and not meddle with theirs, but took his counsel; in being thus observant of strangers, they were obedient to their Master unawares. And it sped wonderfully well; now they had a draught that paid them for all their pains.

IV. How the disciples received this discovery which Christ made of himself, *vv.* 7, 8, where we find,

1. That John was the most intelligent and quick-sighted disciple. He whom Jesus loved was the first that said, *It is the Lord*; for those whom Christ loves he will in a special manner manifest himself to: his secret is with his favourites.

2. That Peter was the most zealous and warm-hearted disciple; for as soon as he heard it was the Lord (for which he took John's word) the ship could not hold him, nor could he stay till the bringing of it to shore, but into the sea he throws himself presently, that he might come first to Christ.

3. That the rest of the disciples were careful and honest hearted. Though they were not in such a

transport of zeal as to throw themselves into the sea, like Peter, yet they hastened in the boat to the shore, and made the best of their way (*v*. 8): *The other disciples*, and John with them, who had first discovered that it was Christ, came slowly, yet they came to Christ.

V. What entertainment the Lord Jesus gave them when they came ashore.

1. He had provision ready for them. When they came to land, wet and cold, weary and hungry, they found a good fire there to warm them and dry them, and fish and bread, competent provision for a good meal. (1) We need not be curious in enquiring whence this fire, and fish, and bread, came, any more than whence the meat came which the ravens brought to Elijah. (2) We may be comforted in this instance of Christ's care of his disciples; he has wherewith to supply all our wants, and *knows what things we have need of*.

2. He called for some of that which they had caught, and they produced it, *vv*. 10, 11. Observe here,

(1) The command Christ gave them to bring their draught of fish to shore: "Bring of the fish hither, which you have now caught, and let us have some of them."

(2) Their obedience to this command, *v*. 11. It was said (*v*. 6), *They were not able to draw the net to shore, for the multitude of fishes*. They had the curiosity to count them, and perhaps it was in order to the making of a dividend; they were in all a *hundred and fifty and three*, and all *great fishes*. These were many more than they needed for

their present supply, but they might sell them, and the money would serve to bear their charges back to Jerusalem, whither they were shortly to return.

3. He invited them to dinner. Observing them to keep their distance, and that *they were afraid to ask him, Who art thou?* because they *knew it was their Lord*, he called to them very familiarly, *Come, and dine*.

4. He carved for them, as the master of the feast, *v*. 13. Observing them to be still shy and timorous, *he comes, and takes bread himself*, and *gives them*, some to each of them, *and fish likewise*.

The evangelist leaves them at dinner, and makes this remark (*v*. 14): *This is now the third time that Jesus showed himself alive to his disciples*, or the greater part of them. *This is the third day*; so some. On the day he rose he appeared five times; the second day was that day seven-night; and this was the third. Or this was his third appearance to any considerable number of his disciples together; though he had appeared to Mary, to the women, to the two disciples, and to Cephas, yet he had but twice before this appeared to any company of them together.

PETER RE-COMMISSIONED
(*vv*. 15–19)

We have here Christ's discourse with Peter after dinner, so much of it as relates to himself, in which,

I. He examines his love to him, and gives him a charge concerning his flock, *vv*. 15–17. Observe,

1. Three times Christ asks Peter whether he loves him or no. The

first time the question is, *Simon, son of Jonas, lovest thou me more than these?* Observe,

[1] How he calls him: *Simon, son of Jonas.* He speaks to him by name, the more to affect him, as Luke xxii. 31. *Simon, Simon.* He does not call him *Cephas,* nor *Peter,* the name he had given him (for he had lost the credit of his strength and stability, which those names signified), but his original name, *Simon.*

[2] How he catechises him: *Lovest thou me more than these?*

First, Lovest thou me? If we would try whether we are Christ's disciples indeed, this must be the enquiry, Do we love him? But there was a special reason why Christ put it now to Peter. 1. His fall had given occasion to doubt of his love. 2. His function would give occasion for the exercise of his *love.* Before Christ would commit his *sheep* to his care, he asked him, *Lovest thou me?*

Secondly, Lovest thou me more than these? 1. "*Lovest thou me more than thou lovest these,* more than thou lovest these persons?" Or, "*more than thou lovest these things,* these boats and nets—more than all the pleasure of fishing, which some make a recreation of—more than the gain of fishing, which others make a calling of." Those only love Christ indeed that love him better than all the delights of sense and all the profits of this world. 2. "*Lovest thou me more than these love me,* more than any of the rest of the disciples love me? And then the question is intended to upbraid him with his vainglorious boast, *Though all men should deny thee, yet will not I.*

"Art thou still of the same mind?" Or, to intimate to him that he had now more reason to love him than any of them had, for more had been forgiven to him than to any of them, as much as his sin in denying Christ was greater than theirs in forsaking him. *Tell me therefore which of them will love him most?* Luke vii. 42.

Thirdly, The second and third time that Christ put this question, 1. He left out the comparison *more than these,* because Peter, in his answer, modestly left it out, not willing to compare himself with his brethren, much less to prefer himself before them. 2. In the last he altered the word, as it is in the original. In the first two enquiries, the original word conveys *Dost thou retain a kindness for me?* In answer to which Peter uses another word, more emphatic—*I love thee dearly.* In putting the question the last time, Christ uses that word: And dost thou indeed love me dearly?

2. Three times Peter returns the same answer to Christ: *Yea, Lord, thou knowest that I love thee.* Observe, [1] Peter does not pretend to love Christ more than the rest of the disciples did. [2] Yet he professes again and again that he loves Christ: *Yea, Lord,* surely *I love thee*; I were unworthy to live if I did not." He had a high esteem and value for him, a grateful sense of his kindness, and was entirely devoted to his honour and interest; his desire was towards him, as one he was undone without; and his delight in him, as one he should be unspeakably happy in. This amounts to a profession of repentance for his sin, for it grieves us to have affronted one we love; and to

a promise of adherence to him for the future: *Lord, I love thee, and will never leave thee.* Christ *prayed that his faith might not fail* (Luke xxii. 32), and, because his faith did not fail, his love did not; for faith will work by love. *He was grieved* when Christ asked him the *third time, Lovest thou me? v.* 17. *First,* Because it put him in mind of his threefold denial of Christ, and was plainly designed to do so; *and when he thought thereon he wept. Secondly,* Because it put him in fear lest his Master foresaw some further miscarriage of his, which would be as great a contradiction to his profession of love to him as the former was.

3. Three times Christ committed the care of his flock to Peter: *Feed my lambs; feed my sheep; feed my sheep.* [1] Those whom Christ committed to Peter's care were his lambs and his sheep. The church of Christ is his flock, *which he hath purchased with his own blood* (Acts xx. 28), and he is *the chief shepherd* of it. [2] The charge he gives him concerning them is to feed them. The word used in *vv.* 15, 17 strictly signifies to *give them food*; but the word used in *v.* 16 signifies more largely to do all the offices of a shepherd to them. The particular application to Peter here was designed, *First,* To restore him to his apostleship, now that he repented of his abjuration of it, and to renew his commission, both for his own satisfaction, and for the satisfaction of his brethren. *Secondly,* It was designed to quicken him to a diligent discharge of his office as an apostle. *Thirdly,* What Christ said to him he said to all his disciples;

he charged them all, not only to be fishers of men (though that was said to Peter, Luke v. 10), by the conversion of sinners, but feeders of the flock, by the edification of saints.

II. Christ, having thus appointed Peter his doing work, next appoints him his suffering work. Having confirmed to him the honour of an apostle, he now tells him of further preferment designed him—the honour of a martyr. Observe,

1. How his martyrdom is foretold (*v.* 18): *Thou shalt stretch forth thy hands,* being compelled to it, and *another shall gird thee* (as a prisoner that is pinioned) *and carry thee whither* naturally *thou wouldest not.*

2. The explication of this prediction (*v.* 19), *This spoke he* to Peter, *signifying by what death he should glorify God,* when he had finished his course.

3. The word of command he gives him hereupon: *When he had spoken thus,* observing Peter perhaps to look blank upon it, *he saith unto him, Follow me.* Probably he rose from the place where he had sat at dinner, walked off a little, and bade Peter attend him. This word, *Follow me,* was, (1) A further confirmation of his restoration to his Master's favour, and to his apostleship; for *Follow me* was the first call. (2) It was an explanation of the prediction of his sufferings, which perhaps Peter at first did not fully understand, till Christ gave him that key to it, *Follow me*: "Expect to be treated as I have been, and to tread the same bloody path that I have trodden before thee; *for the disciple is not greater than his Lord.*" (3) It was to excite him to, and

encourage him in, faithfulness and diligence in his work as an apostle.

EPILOGUE (*vv.* 20–25)

In these verses we have,

I. The conference Christ had with Peter concerning John, the beloved disciple, in which we have,

1. The eye Peter cast upon him (*v.* 20).

2. The enquiry Peter made concerning him (*v.* 21). John was younger than Peter, and, in the course of nature, likely to survive him: "Lord," says he, "what times shall he be reserved for?" Whereas, if God by his grace enable us to persevere to the end, and finish well, and get safely to heaven, we need not ask, "What shall be the lot of those that shall come after us?"

3. Christ's reply to this enquiry (*v.* 22), "*If I will that he tarry till I come*, and do not suffer as thou must, *what is that to thee*. Mind thou thy own duty, the present duty, *follow thou me.*"

(1) There seems to be here an intimation of Christ's purpose concerning John, in two things:— [1] That he should not die a violent death, like Peter, but should tarry till Christ himself came by a natural death to fetch him to himself. [2] That he should not die till after Christ's coming to destroy Jerusalem: so some understand his tarrying till Christ comes.

(2) Others think that it is only a rebuke to Peter's curiosity, and that his tarrying till Christ's second coming is only the supposition of an absurdity.

4. The mistake which arose from this saying of Christ, that *that disciple should not die*, but abide with the church to the end of time; together with the suppressing of this motion by a repetition of Christ's words, *v.* 23. Observe here,

(1) The easy rise of a mistake in the church by misconstruing the sayings of Christ, and turning a supposition to a position. Because John must not die a martyr, they conclude he must not die at all.

(2) The easy rectifying of such mistakes, by adhering to the word of Christ, and abiding by that. So the evangelist here corrects and controls that saying among the brethren, by repeating the very words of Christ. He did not say that that disciple should not die. Let us not say so then; but he said, *If I will that he tarry till I come, what is that to thee?* He said so, and no more. *Add thou not unto his words.* Let the words of Christ speak for themselves, and let no sense be put upon them but what is genuine and natural; and in that let us agree.

II. We have here the conclusion of this gospel, and with it of the evangelical story, *vv.* 24, 25. This evangelist ends not so abruptly as the other three did, but with a sort of cadency.

1. This gospel concludes with an account of the author or penman of it, connected by a decent transition to that which went before (*v.* 24): *This is the disciple which testifies of these things* to the present age, and wrote these things for the benefit of posterity, even this same that Peter and his Master had that conference about in the foregoing verses—John the apostle. Observe

here, (1) Those who wrote the history of Christ were not ashamed to put their names to it. John here does in effect subscribe his name. (2) Those who wrote the history of Christ wrote upon their own knowledge, not by hearsay, but what they themselves were eye and ear witnesses of. (3) Those who wrote the history of Christ, as they testified what they had seen, so they wrote what they had first testified. It was published by word of mouth, with the greatest assurance, before it was committed to writing. (4) It was graciously appointed, for the support and benefit of the church, that the history of Christ should be put into writing, that it might with the greater fullness and certainty spread to every place, and last through every age.

2. It concludes with an attestation of the truth of what had been here related: *We know that his testimony is true*. This may be taken either, (1) As expressing the common sense of mankind in matters of this nature, which is, that the testimony of one who is an eyewitness, is of unspotted reputation, solemnly deposes what he has seen, and puts it into writing for the greater certainty, is an unexceptionable evidence. Or, (2) As expressing the satisfaction of the churches *at that time* concerning the truth of what is here related.

Some take it for the subscription of the church of Ephesus, others of the angels or ministers of the churches of Asia to this narrative. Or, (3) As expressing the evangelist's own assurance of the truth of what he wrote, like that (*ch.* xix. 35), *He knows that he saith true*. He speaks of himself in the plural number, *We know*, not for majesty-sake, but for modesty-sake, as 1 John i. 1, *That which we have seen*; and 2 Pet. i. 16.

3. It concludes with an *et cetera*, with a reference to *many other things*; very memorable, said and done by our Lord Jesus, which were well known by many then living, but not thought fit to be recorded for posterity, *v.* 25. There were many things very remarkable and improvable, which, if they should be written at large, with the several circumstances of them, even the world itself, that is, all the libraries in it, could not contain the books that might be written. Thus he concludes like an orator, as Paul (Heb. xi. 32), *What shall I more say? For the time would fail me.*

The evangelist, concluding with *Amen*, thereby sets to his seal, and let us set to ours, an *Amen* of faith, subscribing to the gospel, that it is true, all true; and an *Amen* of satisfaction in what is written, as able to make us wise to salvation. *Amen*; so be it.